Max Planck Yearbook of United Nations Law, Volume 22 (2018)

# Max Planck Yearbook of United Nations Law

*Founding Editors*

Jochen A. Frowein
Rüdiger Wolfrum

VOLUME 22

The titles published in this series are listed at *brill.com/mpun*

# Max Planck Yearbook of United Nations Law

VOLUME 22 (2018)

*Edited by*

Frauke Lachenmann
Rüdiger Wolfrum

BRILL
NIJHOFF

LEIDEN | BOSTON

Typeface for the Latin, Greek, and Cyrillic scripts: "Brill". See and download: brill.com/brill-typeface.

ISSN 1389-4633
E-ISSN 1875-7413
ISBN 978-90-04-41090-9 (hardback)

Copyright 2019 by Koninklijke Brill NV, Leiden, The Netherlands.
Koninklijke Brill NV incorporates the imprints Brill, Brill Hes & De Graaf, Brill Nijhoff, Brill Rodopi, Brill Sense, Hotei Publishing, mentis Verlag, Verlag Ferdinand Schöningh and Wilhelm Fink Verlag.
All rights reserved. No part of this publication may be reproduced, translated, stored in a retrieval system, or transmitted in any form or by any means, electronic, mechanical, photocopying, recording or otherwise, without prior written permission from the publisher.
Authorization to photocopy items for internal or personal use is granted by Koninklijke Brill NV provided that the appropriate fees are paid directly to The Copyright Clearance Center, 222 Rosewood Drive, Suite 910, Danvers, MA 01923, USA. Fees are subject to change.

This book is printed on acid-free paper and produced in a sustainable manner.

PRINTED BY DRUKKERIJ WILCO B.V. - AMERSFOORT, THE NETHERLANDS

# Contents

List of Abbreviations    VII
List of Contributors    XII

### PART 1
### *The Law and Practice of the United Nations*

1  UN Security Council Reform—The Council Must Lead by Example    3
   *Hans Corell*

2  Lessons from the ILC's Work on 'Immunity of State Officials': Melland Schill Lecture, 21 November 2017    34
   *Michael Wood*

3  The United States and the Paris Agreement on Climate Change    70
   *Mohit Khubchandani*

4  On the Governance of International Judicial Institutions: The Development of Performance Indicators for the International Criminal Court    83
   *Andrea Carcano*

5  Protection and Use of Transboundary Groundwater Resources under Public International Law—An Analysis of the UN International Law Commission's Draft Articles on the Law of Transboundary Aquifers    114
   *Carolin Weber*

6  The Cross-Fertilization of UNCLOS, Custom and Principles Relating to Procedure in the Jurisprudence of UNCLOS Courts and Tribunals    142
   *Elena Ivanova*

7  Sustainable Development Goal 16 at a Cross-Roads    171
   *Frauke Lachenmann*

## PART 2
## *Legal Issues Related to the Goals of the United Nations*

8   Institutions of International Law: How International Law Secures
    Orderliness in International Affairs   189
    *Volker Roeben*

9   Case Comment: *Navtej Singh Johar v. Union of India*: The Indian
    Supreme Court's Decriminalization of Same-Sex Relations   218
    *Gautam Bhatia*

10  The Nomadic Sense of Law in an International
    Constitutionalism   234
    *William E. Conklin*

11  The Institutional and Constitutional Aspects of the Arab Maghreb
    Union and the Dispute on Western Sahara as an Obstacle: What
    Role does the European Union Play in Promoting Maghreb Regional
    Integration?   284
    *Mohamed Riyad M. Almosly*

12  The Control of Conventionality: Developments in the Case Law of the
    Inter-American Court of Human Rights and Its Potential Expanding
    Effects in International Human Rights Law   319
    *María Carmelina Londoño-Lázaro and Nicolás Carrillo-Santarelli*

13  Disaster Militarism? Military Humanitarian Assistance and Disaster
    Relief   347
    *Gabrielle Simm*

14  Social Movements and the Legal Field: Becoming-Constituent   376
    *Xenia Chiaramonte*

15  The International Regulation and Governance of Time   394
    *Andreas Witte*

## Book Review

Andrea Bianchi, Daniel Peat and Matthew Windsor (eds), *Interpretation in International Law*   427

# Abbreviations

| | |
|---|---|
| Art. | Article |
| Arts | Articles |
| ed. | editor |
| edn | edition |
| eds | editors |
| e.g. | exempli gratia |
| EJIL | European Journal of International Law |
| ELJ | European Law Journal |
| Env. | Policy & Law Environmental Policy and Law |
| Envtl L. Rep. | Environmental Law Reports |
| et al. | et alii |
| et seq. | et sequentes |
| etc. | et cetera |
| EuGRZ | Europäische Grundrechte-Zeitschrift |
| FAO | Food and Agriculture Organization |
| Fla. J. Int'l L. | Florida Journal of International Law |
| Fordham Int'l L. J. | Fordham International Law Journal |
| Fordham L. Rev. | Fordham Law Review |
| Foreign Aff. | Foreign Affairs |
| Foreign Pol'y | Foreign Policy |
| Ga. J. Int'l & Comp. L. | Georgia Journal of International and Comparative Law |
| Geo. Int'l Envt'l L. Rev. | Georgetown International Environmental Law Review |
| Geo. L. J. | Georgetown Law Journal |
| Geo. Wash. J. Int'l L. & Econ. | George Washington Journal of International Law and Economics |
| Geo. Wash. L. Rev. | George Washington Law Review |
| GYIL | German Yearbook of International Law |
| Harv. Int'l L. J. | Harvard International Law Journal |
| Harv. L. Rev. | Harvard Law Review |
| Hastings Int'l & Comp. L. | Hastings International and Comparative Law Review |
| HRLJ | Human Rights Law Journal |
| HRQ | Human Rights Quarterly |
| HuV-I | Humanitäres Völkerrecht – Informationsschriften |
| IAEA | International Atomic Energy Agency |
| ibid. | ibidem; in the same place |
| IBRD | International Bank for Reconstruction and Development |

| | |
|---|---|
| ICAO | International Civil Aviation Organization |
| ICC | International Criminal Court |
| ICJ | International Court of Justice |
| ICLQ | International and Comparative Law Quarterly |
| ICSID | International Centre for Settlement of Investment Disputes |
| id. | idem; the same |
| IDA | International Development Association |
| IDI | Institut de Droit international |
| i.e. | id est; that is to say |
| IFAD | International Fund for Agricultural Development |
| IJIL | Indian Journal of International Law |
| ILA | International Law Association |
| ILC | International Law Commission |
| ILCYB | Yearbook of the International Law Commission |
| ILM | International Legal Materials |
| ILO | International Labour Organization |
| ILR | International Law Reports |
| ILSA J. Int'l L. | ILSA Journal of International Law (International Law Students Association) |
| IMF | International Monetary Fund |
| IMO | International Maritime Organization |
| Indian J. Law & Tech. | Indian Journal of Law and Technology |
| Ind. Int'l & Comp. L. Rev. | Indiana International and Comparative Law Review |
| Ind. J. Global Legal Stud. | Indiana Journal of Global Legal Studies |
| Int'l Aff. | International Affairs |
| Int'l Law. | The International Lawyer |
| Int'l Rev. of the Red Cross | International Review of the Red Cross |
| Iowa L. Rev. | Iowa Law Review |
| IP | Die internationale Politik |
| Isr. L. R. | Israel Law Review |
| Isr. Y. B. Hum. Rts | Israel Yearbook on Human Rights |
| J. History Int'l L. | Journal of the History of International Law |
| J. Int'l Aff. | Journal of International Affairs |
| JA | Juristische Arbeitsblätter |
| JIEL | Journal of International Economic Law |
| JIR | Jahrbuch für internationales Recht |
| JPR | Journal of Peace Research |
| JWT | Journal of World Trade |
| Law & Contemp. Probs | Law and Contemporary Problems |

| | |
|---|---|
| LJIL | Leiden Journal of International Law |
| LNTS | League of Nations Treaty Series |
| Loy. L. A. Int'l Comp. L. Rev. | Loyola of Los Angeles International and Comparative Law Review |
| McGill L. J. | McGill Law Journal |
| Miami U. Int'l & Comp. L. Rev. | University of Miami International and Comparative Law Review |
| Mich. J. Int'l L. | Michigan Journal of International Law |
| Mich. L. Rev. | Michigan Law Review |
| Mil. L. Rev. | Military Law Review |
| Minn. J. Global Trade | Minnesota Journal of Global Trade |
| N. Y. U. J. Int'l L. & Pol. | New York University Journal of International Law and Politics |
| N. Y. U. L. Rev. | New York University Law Review |
| NAFTA | North American Free Trade Agreement |
| NATO | North Atlantic Treaty Organization |
| NILR | Netherlands International Law Review |
| NJCL | National Journal of Constitutional Law |
| NJW | Neue Juristische Wochenschrift |
| Nord. J. Int'l L. | Nordic Journal of International Law |
| NQHR | Netherlands Quarterly of Human Rights |
| NYIL | Netherlands Yearbook of International Law |
| Ocean & Coastal L. J. | Ocean and Coastal Law Journal |
| Ocean Dev. Int. Law | Ocean Development and International Law |
| OJEC | Official Journal of the European Communities |
| Pace Int'l Law Rev. | Pace International Law Review |
| para. | paragraph |
| paras | paragraphs |
| PCIJ | Permanent Court of International Justice |
| Pol. Sci. | Political Science |
| RADIC | Revue Africaine de Droit International et Comparé |
| RBDI | Revue Belge de Droit International |
| RdC | Recueil des Cours de l'Académie de Droit International |
| RDI | Revue de Droit International, de Sciences Diplomatiques et Politiques |
| RECIEL | Review of European Community and International Environmental Law |
| REDI | Revista Española de Derecho Internacional |
| Rev. Dr. Mil. Dr. Guerre | Revue de Droit Militaire et de Droit de la Guerre |
| RGDIP | Revue Générale de Droit International Public |

| | |
|---|---|
| RIAA | Reports of International Arbitral Awards |
| Riv. Dir. Int. | Rivista di Diritto Internazionale |
| RTDE | Revue Trimestrielle de Droit Européen |
| RUDH | Revue Universelle des Droits de L'homme |
| San Diego L. Rev. | San Diego Law Review |
| Santa Clara L. Rev. | Santa Clara Law Review |
| Stanford J. Int'l L. | Stanford Journal of International Law |
| Stanford L. Rev. | Stanford Law Review |
| SZIER/RSDIE | Schweizerische Zeitschrift für internationales und europäisches Recht / Revue Suisse de Droit International et de Droit Européen |
| Temp. Int'l & Comp. L. J. | Temple International and Comparative Law Journal |
| Tex. Int'l L. J. | Texas International Law Journal |
| Tex. L. Rev. | Texas Law Review |
| Transnat'l L. & Contemp. | Transnational Law and Contemporary Problems |
| Tul. Envtl L. J. | Tulane Environmental Law Journal |
| Tul. J. Int'l & Comp. L. | Tulane Journal of International and Comparative Law |
| U. Chi. L. R. | University of Chicago Law Review |
| UCDL Rev. | University of California Davis Law Review |
| UCLA J. Envtl L. & Pol'y | University of California Los Angeles Journal of Environmental Law and Policy |
| UCLA JILFA | University of California Los Angeles Journal of International Law and Foreign Affairs |
| UCLA Pac. Basin L. J. | University of California Los Angeles Pacific Basin Law Journal |
| UNCIO | United Nations Conference on International Organization |
| UNCITRAL | United Nations Commission on International Trade Law |
| UNCTAD | United Nations Conference on Trade and Development |
| UNDP | United Nations Development Programme |
| UNEP | United Nations Environment Programme |
| UNESCO | United Nations Educational, Scientific and Cultural Organization |
| UNFPA | United Nations Population Fund |
| UNHCR | United Nations High Commissioner for Refugees |
| UNICEF | United Nations Children's Fund |
| UNIDO | United Nations Industrial Development Organization |
| UNITAR | United Nations Institute for Training and Research |
| UNJYB | United Nations Juridical Yearbook |

| | |
|---|---|
| UNRWA | United Nations Relief and Works Agency for Palestine Refugees in the Near East |
| UNTS | United Nations Treaty Series |
| UNU | United Nations University |
| UNYB | Max Planck Yearbook of United Nations Law |
| UPU | Universal Postal Union |
| Va. J. Int'l L. | Virginia Journal of International Law |
| Va. L. Rev. | Virginia Law Review |
| Vand. J. Transnat'l L. | Vanderbilt Journal of Transnational Law |
| Vol. | Volume |
| VRÜ | Verfassung und Recht in Übersee |
| VVDStRL | Veröffentlichungen der Vereinigung der Deutschen Staatsrechtslehrer |
| Wash. L. Rev. | Washington Law Review |
| WFP | World Food Programme |
| WIPO | World Intellectual Property Organization |
| WMO | World Meteorological Organization |
| WTO | World Trade Organization |
| Yale J. Int'l L. | Yale Journal of International Law |
| Yale L. J. | Yale Law Journal |
| ZaöRV/ HJIL | Zeitschrift für ausländisches öffentliches Recht und Völkerrecht / Heidelberg Journal of International Law |

# Contributors

*Almosly, Mohamed Riyad M.*
Research Fellow at the Max Planck Foundation for International Peace and the Rule of Law, Heidelberg; Ph.D. Candidate at the Department of European, Public and International Law, Faculty of Law and Criminology, Ghent University

*Begoore, Yateesh*
Research Fellow at the Max Planck Foundation for International Peace and the Rule of Law, Heidelberg

*Bhatia, Gautam*
Advocate, New Delhi; BCL, M.Phil, D.Phil (Candidate), Oxford; LL.M., Yale Law School

*Carcano, Andrea*
Associate Professor of International Law; Senior Lecturer in International Law, Faculty of Law, University of Modena and Reggio Emilia

*Carrillo-Santarelli, Nicolás*
Associate Professor of International Law, Universidad de la Sabana, Colombia

*Chiaramonte, Xenia*
Postdoctoral Researcher, University of Bologna

*Conklin, William E.*
Professor of Law, University of Windsor, Canada

*Corell, Hans*
Ambassador (ret.); former Judge of Appeal; former Under-Secretary-General for Legal Affairs and the Legal Counsel of the United Nations (1994–2004)

*Ivanova, Elena*
Research Fellow at the Max Planck Institute Luxembourg for International, European and Regulatory Procedural Law; member of the International Max Planck Research School for Successful Dispute Resolution; Ph.D. candidate, University of Luxembourg

CONTRIBUTORS

*Khubchandani, Mohit*
Public International Lawyer, UN Office for the Coordination of Humanitarian Affairs, NY; Legal Trainee, New York State Supreme Court; Former Adviser, Permanent Mission of India to the United Nations; Former Associate, Office of the Attorney General for India; LL.M., Stanford Law School

*Lachenmann, Frauke*
Dr. phil; Senior Research Fellow at the Max Planck Foundation for International Peace and the Rule of Law, Heidelberg

*Londoño-Lázaro, María Carmelina*
Associate Professor of International Law; Director of the Master Program in International Law, Universidad de la Sabana, Colombia

*Röben, Volker*
Professor of Energy Law, International Law and Global Regulation at the University of Dundee; visiting Professor at the China University of Political Science and Law, Beijing; docent at the University of Turku; adjunct Professor at the University of Houston

*Simm, Gabrielle*
Senior Lecturer, Faculty of Law, University of Technology Sydney

*Weber, Carolin Mai*
Dr. iur., LL.M., Assessor iuris

*Witte, Andreas*
Principal Legal Counsel, European Central Bank, Frankfurt, Germany; Dr. iur.; MJur, MSc (Oxon)

*Wood, Michael*
Barrister, 20 Essex Street, London; Member of the UN International Law Commission

*The authors speak in their personal capacity only. Any views they express or information they provide cannot be attributed to the institutions with which they are or have been affiliated, or to the editors of the Max Planck Yearbook of United Nations Law.*

# PART 1

*The Law and Practice of the United Nations*

∴

CHAPTER 1

# UN Security Council Reform—The Council Must Lead by Example

*Hans Corell*

## Abstract

The point of departure in the present article is that the UN Security Council must be reformed. But this reform should not focus on extending the membership of the Council, which seems to be the main issue in the discussion at present. It is imperative that the Council is maintained as an executive organ since this is a precondition for its effective functioning. Too many members would destroy this requirement completely, in particular if additional members are granted veto power. Already 15 members may be past the limit for an executive organ. Additional members will endanger the Council's ability to fulfil its obligations under Art. 24 of the UN Charter: the primary responsibility for the maintenance of international peace and security.

Instead, the reform should focus on resolving the real problem with the Council, namely the manner in which the permanent members sometimes behave. The exercise of the veto power must be in conformity with the UN Charter, which now must be viewed against the background of the development of international law since the UN was established more than 70 years ago. The manner in which some permanent members exercise their veto power is simply not in conformity with the Charter.

Against this background it is absolutely necessary that the five permanent members engage in a profound discussion about their performance and the manner in which the veto power is exercised. Here, there is need for statesmanship. The members of the Security Council, and in particular the permanent members, must lead by example.

What the Council must focus on is conflict prevention. This requires determination and consequence. The focus must be on the challenges that humankind is facing and will face ever more in the future and the threats to international peace and security that these challenges are causing. The need for the rule of law and protection of human rights are obvious elements in this analysis. Furthermore, the growth of the world population in combination with climate change simply must be addressed in an effective manner. The Council must focus attentively on these 'conflict multipliers'.

The discussion must also focus on peacekeeping and responsibility to protect. With respect to responsibility to protect there is great need for improvement. We cannot accept in the 21st century that fundamental human rights are violated and that crimes against international humanitarian law are being committed on a large scale without consequences. Another important element in this context is empowerment of women. In addressing these questions there is need for close cooperation with regional organizations. This cooperation already exists, but the question is how it can be developed and what lessons can be learnt from the past.

Since the five permanent members are also recognized as nuclear-weapon States under the 1968 Non-Proliferation Treaty, they must confirm their obligations under this treaty and make serious their obligation to work for a nuclear-weapon free world.

A reform along the lines discussed in the present article can be made without amending the UN Charter.

**Keywords**

Climate – Executive – Human Rights – Nuclear – Population – Protect – Rule of Law – Statesmanship – Veto – Women

1       **Introduction**

The Max Planck Foundation for International Peace and the Rule of Law has invited me to contribute an article on proposals for the reform of the UN Security Council, specifically its composition and cooperation with regional organizations, adding that it would be open to other topics as well. Since I have focused on Security Council reform on many occasions after I left the UN in 2004, having served as the Organization's Under-Secretary-General for Legal Affairs and the Legal Counsel since 1994, I accepted this invitation. In so doing, I decided to focus on what I see as the main problem with the Security Council, namely the fact that the permanent five members do not always act in a manner than one would expect in today's world.

My reasoning should be viewed against the background of my years in the UN Secretariat, my activities thereafter and in particular as a member of the Council of the International Bar Association's Human Rights Institute (2005–2018),[1] as Legal Adviser to the Panel of Eminent African Personalities involved in the Kenya National Dialogue and Reconciliation (2008–2013), my focus on the polar regions in later years, and the present geopolitical situation.

In an article, published in 2017, I developed my thinking with respect to reforming the Security Council.[2] My conclusions were in brief:

---

1   See https://www.ibanet.org/IBAHRI.aspx (accessed 12 April 2019).
2   H. Corell, 'Reforming the United Nations Security Council' in J.C. Sainz-Borgo et al. (eds), *Liber Amicorum Gudmundur Eiriksson* (O.P. Jindal Global University 2017) 309.

- That the focus of a reform should not be on extending the membership of the Security Council but on a reform that could be executed almost immediately and without amendments to the UN Charter;
- That the reform should focus on the manner in which the members of the Security Council exercise their mandate and in particular the responsibility that rests with the five permanent members;
- That the guiding principle for this reform should be respect for the rule of law at the national and international levels and the demands on the Council that such a regime entails;
- That in a long-term perspective it would be preferable that any changes in the Council's composition are decided when the tendencies in the present geopolitical shift appear more clearly and when more members of the UN have chosen democracy;
- That the main responsibility rests with the permanent members of the Council and that, if they fail, there is a clear risk that the UN will lose authority and that the Organization will be undermined;
- That the lodestar for the reform must be to safeguard the system of collective security in the UN Charter; and
- That at present there is a clear risk that political expediency and an almost frantic focus on extending the membership of the Council may result in that it becomes inoperable with the consequence that the damage to the system of collective security will be irreparable.[3]

Against this background, the following presentation will focus on specific elements that the Security Council must take into consideration in today's world. Of particular importance here is that the use of the veto must be in conformity with the mandate of the Security Council and that the challenges we face in the following fields must be addressed to reduce the risk of conflict in the world: the need for the rule of law and human rights; the growth of the world population; climate change; responsibility to protect; empowerment of women; and nuclear disarmament.

## II    The Use of the Veto

Considering the reasons for the veto power it is obvious that the manner in which the use of the veto has developed over the years is not in conformity with the idea behind the inclusion of 'including the concurring votes of the permanent members' in Art. 27 (4) of the UN Charter. The fact that permanent members use the veto when there is no clear connection to their own security

---

3    Ibid., at 318–319.

undermines the authority of the Council and results in situations where people are exposed to suffering that is completely unacceptable.

I raised this matter in a letter to the members of the UN on 10 December 2008, suggesting that the permanent five members should make a solemn declaration that would be binding under international law along the lines of a draft attached to the letter. For ease of reference the draft declaration is annexed to the present article.

One of the four elements of the draft declaration is that the permanent members should use their veto power only if their most serious and direct national interests are affected and, in case they do use the veto power, explain their reasons for doing so.

I still believe that this is a path that the permanent five members should take. However, a more likely solution might be the one proposed by France and Mexico, namely a collective and voluntary agreement among the permanent members of the Security Council to the effect that the permanent members would refrain from using the veto in case of mass atrocities. As of 27 June 2017 this initiative was supported by 96 countries.[4]

The alternative is the Code of Conduct regarding Security Council Action against Genocide, Crimes against Humanity and War Crimes, proposed by the Accountability, Coherence and Transparency (ACT) Group in 2015. The Code 'calls upon all members of the Security Council (both permanent and elected) to not vote against any credible draft resolution intended to prevent or halt mass atrocities'.[5] As of January 2019, there were 119 States supporting the code, including two permanent members of the Security Council, namely France and the UK.[6] A prerequisite for a meaningful reform of the Security Council is that the three remaining permanent members join the Code. If not, we will unfortunately have to wait for the next Syria.

In this context, one should mention an interesting study by a campaign started by students at Uppsala University in Sweden, called 'Stop Illegitimate Vetoes'. As it appears from their website, they have analysed the 50 vetoes cast between 1991 (when the Soviet Union became the Russian Federation) and 10 March 2019: none by France and the UK, 11 by China, 23 by the Russian Federation,

---

4  Political Declaration on the Suspension of the Veto in Cases of Mass Atrocities, see https://perma.cc/QK6F-CTAM (accessed 12 April 2019).
5  Available at http://www.centerforunreform.org/?q=node/798 (accessed 12 April 2019).
6  See https://www.securitycouncilreport.org/un-security-council-working-methods/the-veto.php (accessed 12 April 2019).

and 16 by the US.[7] Their conclusion is that 48 of these vetoes are illegitimate since they do not concern the security of the members themselves.

## III    The Need for the Rule of Law and Human Rights

Looking at conflicts around the world, the root causes are basically the same: no democracy and no rule of law. A core ingredient in the rule of law is human rights. It is therefore necessary to strengthen the rule of law and protection of human rights.

One of the most disturbing elements in later years is that the rule of law and human rights are not respected in a manner that is absolutely necessary for achieving international peace and security. This is all the more regrettable as both the UN General Assembly and the Security Council have made clear statements relating to the importance of the rule of law and human rights. The General Assembly has also stressed the need for democracy.

Of particular importance in this context is that the members of the UN have come to an understanding that the rule of law is an indispensable prerequisite for international peace and security; see e.g. the Resolution adopted by the General Assembly on 24 September 2012 entitled 'Declaration of the high-level meeting of the General Assembly on the rule of law at the national and international levels'. The following two paragraphs of this Declaration are of particular relevance here:

> 1. We reaffirm our solemn commitment to the purposes and principles of the Charter of the United Nations, international law and justice, and to an international order based on the rule of law, which are indispensable foundations for a more peaceful, prosperous and just world.
> [...]
> 5. We reaffirm that human rights, the rule of law and democracy are interlinked and mutually reinforcing and that they belong to the universal and indivisible core values and principles of the United Nations.[8]

---

7   A Report is available at http://stopillegitimatevetoes.org/thereport/ and a Companion at http://stopillegitimatevetoes.org/wp-content/uploads/2018/06/Report-Companion-Revision-14.pdf (accessed 12 April 2019).
8   UNGA Res 67/1 'Declaration of the high-level meeting of the General Assembly on the rule of law at the national and international levels' (24 September 2012).

With respect to the definition of the rule of law, reference could be made to Secretary-General Kofi Annan's Report to the Security Council in 2004, entitled 'The Rule of Law and Transitional Justice in Conflict and Post-Conflict Societies':

> The rule of law [...] refers to a principle of governance in which all persons, institutions and entities, public and private, including the State itself, are accountable to laws that are publicly promulgated, equally enforced and independently adjudicated, and which are consistent with international human rights norms and standards. It requires, as well, measures to ensure adherence to the principles of supremacy of law, equality before the law, accountability to the law, fairness in the application of the law, separation of powers, participation in decision-making, legal certainty, avoidance of arbitrariness and procedural and legal transparency.[9]

For my part, I often use a very straightforward and brief definition, consisting of four elements: (1) democracy; (2) proper legislation respecting international human rights standards; (3) the institutions to administer this law, including independent and impartial courts; and (4) the individuals with the integrity and the knowledge to administer these institutions.

It should be noted that there is a special interdependence between the two first elements. This is because many countries are not yet democracies. It is, however, necessary to develop a legal order through legislation also in those countries. At the same time, to be fully legitimate, legislation has to be adopted by a national assembly that is elected in free and fair elections; and these can only be held in democratic societies. This means that there will be a fairly long transitional period in many countries before the two first conditions for the rule of law are met.

The third element, the institutions, including independent and impartial courts, is an obvious component.

The fourth element may be the most demanding challenge: the individuals with the integrity and the knowledge necessary to administer these institutions. This requires education—one could even say upbringing.

If we look at the need for the rule of law in a geopolitical perspective, it is imperative that a concerted effort is made to establish human rights, the rule of law and democracy in order to achieve proper world governance. It is crucial that the two paragraphs in the Declaration quoted above are taken seriously.

---

9   UNSC 'The Rule of Law and Transitional Justice in Conflict and Post-Conflict Societies: Report of the Secretary-General' (23 August 2004) UN Doc. S/2004/616.

Against this background the need for the rule of law, of which respect for human rights is a core element, and democracy in the world community is apparent. States that fall short in this respect deserve to be criticized; in present-day society this matter can no longer be considered internal within the meaning of Art. 2 (7) of the UN Charter. The rule of law is an indispensable prerequisite for proper global governance. In addition, and most importantly, the rule of law is not only a legal matter. It is much more comprehensive. It encompasses ethical elements that must be supported by all—also at the grassroots level.

Two further paragraphs from the 2012 Declaration could be quoted in this context:

> 12. We reaffirm the principle of good governance and commit to an effective, just, non-discriminatory and equitable delivery of public services pertaining to the rule of law, including criminal, civil and administrative justice, commercial dispute settlement and legal aid.
> 13. We are convinced that the independence of the judicial system, together with its impartiality and integrity, is an essential prerequisite for upholding the rule of law and ensuring that there is no discrimination in the administration of justice.

An initial challenge associated with establishing the rule of law is the requirement that the States themselves actually abide by the rule of law and that international organizations live up to their own proud declarations on the importance of the rule of law. Another challenge, as already mentioned, is the growing world population which can lead to tensions, in particular if aggravated by climate change that may have serious consequences for the human habitat.

Armed conflict is an issue, in particular conflicts generated by religious extremists. Yet another challenge is terrorism, which has to be vigorously combated, not through a 'war on terror'—a very dangerous misnomer—but through law enforcement.[10] A further major challenge is transnational organized crime, which has extremely serious effects on the proper governance of States. There is also an inherent risk that the territories of 'failed States' and States that do not have proper defence and police forces may become platforms for such criminal activity.[11]

---

10  Reference is made to the International Convention for the Suppression of the Financing of Terrorism (signed 9 December 1999, entered into force 10 April 2002) 2178 UNTS 197.
11  Reference is made to the United Nations Convention against Transnational Organized Crime (signed 15 November 2000, entered into force 29 September 2003) 2225 UNTS 209.

One of the most serious impediments to implementing the rule of law is corruption. States have to act with determination here and live up to their obligations. The 2012 Declaration states that:

> 25. We are convinced of the negative impact of corruption, which obstructs economic growth and development, erodes public confidence, legitimacy and transparency and hinders the making of fair and effective laws, as well as their administration, enforcement and adjudication, and therefore stress the importance of the rule of law as an essential element in addressing and preventing corruption, including by strengthening cooperation among States concerning criminal matters.

The Security Council in a Presidential Statement on 21 February 2014 recalled the 2012 Declaration, recognizing the need for universal adherence to and implementation of the rule of law, and the vital importance it attaches to promoting justice and the rule of law as an indispensable element for peaceful coexistence and the prevention of armed conflict. In the same Statement, the Security Council also reaffirmed its commitment to international law and the UN Charter and to an international order based on the rule of law and international law.[12]

The protection of human rights and criminal justice are likewise core elements in a rule of law system. Any governance system that cannot deliver in this respect is doomed to be defective. In the worst-case scenario, a State with a weak governance system risks becoming a 'failed State'. With increasing globalization and interconnection among States, those States that fall behind in establishing democratic governance under the rule of law will pose a threat to international peace and security, thus putting also other States, even fairly stable democracies, at risk.

It is important to note that, at present, there is no alternative to the existing system of world governance, which is through sovereign nation States interacting within the UN where almost all of them (193) are members. It is obvious that we should concentrate on how to improve the existing system. Members of the Security Council have an important role to play here through leading by example.

Governance has to be democratic, and the rule of law must be applied. And, as always, where power is exercised it must be scrutinized, in particular by

---

12  UNSC Statement by the President of the Security Council: The Promotion and Strengthening of the Rule of Law in the Maintenance of International Peace and Security' (21 February 2014) UN Doc. S/PRST/2014/5.

watchful and critical media. Furthermore, State sovereignty has to be exercised in the interest not of a sovereign but of the people, and relations to other States should be based on good neighbourliness.

The problem here is that States have a tendency to identify their national interests from a very narrow perspective, not to say on the basis of sheer self-interest. What is required in this analysis is more statesmanship and, in case of conflict, a preparedness to listen to others and, if possible, to adjust in a manner that may take their interests into consideration.

What all this boils down to is that people must gain knowledge and insight about what needs to be done and find the political will and the necessary techniques to achieve this. It is absolutely necessary that education about human rights and the rule of law is offered in schools as early as possible. Politicians and the general public must also be educated.

In a meeting of the InterAction Council of Former Heads of State and Government in 2008, former Chancellor Helmut Schmidt of Germany made a comment that inspired the elaboration of a paper called 'Rule of Law—A guide for politicians'. This guide is now available free of charge for downloading and printing from the web in 25 languages with more to come.[13]

During my ten years as UN Legal Counsel, I had the opportunity to follow the Council's work closely, not only formally but also in informal consultations and at the retreats that Kofi Annan arranged for the 15 UN Ambassadors and their spouses. At the beginning of this period, just after the Cold War, the Council actually began to work really well. But soon there were complications with serious consequences for the Council's ability to fulfil its core mission of preventing conflicts.

One grave issue is that the five permanent members often cannot agree when the need is the greatest. The latest serious instance is Syria.

Another serious problem is that permanent members themselves sometimes flagrantly violate the UN Charter. One example is the 2003 invasion by the US and the UK of Iraq which had disastrous consequences. This was followed by the Russian Federation's attack on Georgia in 2008 and on Ukraine in 2014.

These violations and the recent events in Syria demonstrate the disastrous consequences that occur when the Security Council does not respect its obligations under the UN Charter. The loadstar here must be the rule of law and

---

[13] 'Rule of Law—A guide for politicians', elaborated under the auspices of the Raoul Wallenberg Institute of Human Rights and Humanitarian Law at Lund University, Sweden, and the Hague Institute for the Internationalisation (now Innovation) of Law (HiiL), available at https://rwi.lu.se/2017/03/rule-law-guide-politicians/ (accessed 12 April 2019).

the obligations that it imposes on the Council. If the members of the Security Council show that they can join hands when a certain threshold is crossed in a conflict, it would send a very powerful signal around the world and help to prevent conflicts in the future.

## IV  The Growth of the World Population

When the UN was established in 1945, the world population was around 2 billion. According to the UN Population Division's 'World Population Prospects: The 2017 Revision', the current world population is 7.6 billion and is expected to reach 9.8 billion in 2050.[14] It is obvious that this enormous population growth will have extremely serious consequences for our human habitat. One serious effect will of course be rising $CO_2$ emissions unless science and business can develop methods for counteracting this development. For the Security Council, the population growth may constitute a serious 'threat multiplier', and needs to be observed with great attention by the members of the Council.

## V  Climate Change

As is commonly known, rising $CO_2$ levels have caused climate change that has to be addressed immediately. The 1992 UN Framework Convention on Climate Change (UNFCCC)[15] and the 2015 Paris Agreement[16] have been concluded to this end.

The central aim of the Paris Agreement is to strengthen the global response to the threat of climate change by keeping the global temperature rise this century well below 2 degrees Celsius above pre-industrial levels and to pursue efforts to limit the temperature increase even further to 1.5 degrees Celsius. There are presently 184 parties to this Agreement, including the permanent members of the Security Council, except the Russian Federation. Unfortunately, the US has recently decided to withdraw from this Agreement.

It goes without saying that a common effort simply has to be made to cope with the results of the climate change; there is a clear connection with international peace and security here. It may be that at the turn of the next century

---

14  UN DESA / Population Division 'World Population Prospects: The 2017 Revision' (21 June 2017).
15  United Nations Framework Convention on Climate Change (adopted 9 May 1992, entered into force 21 March 1994) 1771 UNTS 107.
16  Paris Agreement (adopted 12 December 2015, entered into force 4 November 2016), annexed to UN Doc. FCCC/CP/2015/10/Add.1.

there could be a one meter sea level rise. This would have disastrous effects on the globe and create millions of refugees. The refugees crossing the Mediterranean these days are but trickles in comparison to what will be the result of a sea level rise caused by melting graziers and sea ice.

I have often noted that many are not aware of the importance of the polar regions in this context. These regions are enormous areas. Around the North Pole we have the Arctic Ocean where the legal regime is the UN Convention on the Law of the Sea.[17] On the South Pole we have the Antarctic continent, where the legal regime is the 1959 Antarctic Treaty.[18] The size of the sea in the North, surrounded by continents, and the continent in the South, surrounded by sea, is basically the same: 14,000,000 km². This is almost one and a half times the size of the US.

The melting sea ice in the North may not affect the sea level all that much, but it reduces the albedo (reflection of solar radiation) effect of the white ice which causes the temperature to rise twice as fast in the Arctic as in the rest of the world. This also causes melting of the permafrost in large areas, entailing great problems. One effect is the release of methane, another important greenhouse gas which will increase global warming. And in Antarctica the glaziers on the continent contain 90 per cent of the freshwater resources of the globe. If that starts melting!

To this should be added the risk for further desertification in parts of the world, which will generate additional climate refugees. The impact of climate change on peace and security in Africa is increasing, particularly in the Lake Chad Basin, the Sahel region and the Horn of Africa region.

It is therefore important that the Security Council intensifies its focus on climate change as a 'threat multiplier'. The debate on 25 January 2019 is welcome, and it should definitely be reflected in the Council's work in the future, including possibly by the adoption of a resolution on the subject matter.[19]

## VI    Responsibility to Protect

The concept of responsibility to protect (R2P) was introduced in the UN system in September 2005 when the General Assembly, based on the proposal by

---

17    United Nations Convention on the Law of the Sea (concluded 10 December 1982, entered into force 16 November 1994) 1833 UNTS 3.
18    Antarctic Treaty (signed 1 December 1959, entered into force 23 June 1961) 402 UNTS 71.
19    See 'Climate Change Recognized as "Threat Multiplier", UN Security Council Debates its Impact on Peace' (25 January 2019) UN News, available at https://news.un.org/feed/view/en/story/2019/01/1031322 (accessed 12 April 2019).

the High-level Panel on Threats, Challenges and Change,[20] adopted the World Summit Outcome.[21] In this Resolution we find the two famous paragraphs 138 and 139:

> 138. Each individual State has the responsibility to protect its populations from genocide, war crimes, ethnic cleansing and crimes against humanity. This responsibility entails the prevention of such crimes, including their incitement, through appropriate and necessary means. We accept that responsibility and will act in accordance with it. The international community should, as appropriate, encourage and help States to exercise this responsibility and support the United Nations in establishing an early warning capability.
>
> 139. The international community, through the United Nations, also has the responsibility to use appropriate diplomatic, humanitarian and other peaceful means, in accordance with Chapters VI and VIII of the Charter, to help to protect populations from genocide, war crimes, ethnic cleansing and crimes against humanity. In this context, we are prepared to take collective action, in a timely and decisive manner, through the Security Council, in accordance with the Charter, including Chapter VII, on a case-by-case basis and in cooperation with relevant regional organizations as appropriate, should peaceful means be inadequate and national authorities are manifestly failing to protect their populations from genocide, war crimes, ethnic cleansing and crimes against humanity. We stress the need for the General Assembly to continue consideration of the responsibility to protect populations from genocide, war crimes, ethnic cleansing and crimes against humanity and its implications, bearing in mind the principles of the Charter and international law. We also intend to commit ourselves, as necessary and appropriate, to helping States build capacity to protect their populations from genocide, war crimes, ethnic cleansing and crimes against humanity and to assisting those which are under stress before crises and conflicts break out.

The Panel had also suggested that the Council, in considering whether to authorize or endorse the use of military force, should always address—whatever

---

20  UNGA 'A More Secure World: Our Shared Responsibility: Report of the High-Level Panel on Threats, Challenges and Change' (2 December 2004) UN Doc. A/59/565.
21  UNGA Res 60/1 '2005 World Summit Outcome' (16 September 2005).

other considerations it may take into account—at least the following five basic criteria of legitimacy:
(a) The seriousness of the threat,
(b) The question of proper purpose,
(c) The question whether the action is the last resort,
(d) The question whether the means are proportional, and
(e) The question whether there is a balance of consequences.[22]

The criterion last mentioned is in my view of particular interest. In the words of the Panel: Is there a reasonable chance of the military action being successful in meeting the threat in question, with the consequences of action not likely to be worse than the consequences of inaction?

It goes without saying that this criterion must be a determining factor when the Council considers whether any UN Member State would be prepared to contribute troops to the operation and when possible troop-contributing States make their own assessment. But above all, in case this assessment is made in a transparent manner, there is every reason to believe that a decision to use force or not to use force would be understood and respected by the world community.

In his Report of 12 January 2009 'Implementing the Responsibility to Protect', UN Secretary-General Ban Ki-moon referred to three pillars of the responsibility to protect:[23]
- The protection responsibilities of the State;
- International assistance and capacity-building;
- Timely and decisive response.

Reflecting on the development so far, he stated that it would be counterproductive, and possibly even destructive, to try to revisit the negotiations that led to the provisions of paragraphs 138 and 139 of the World Summit Outcome:

> Those provisions represent a remarkably good outcome, which will well serve the ultimate purpose of the responsibility to protect: to save lives by preventing the most egregious mass violations of human rights, while reinforcing the letter and spirit of the Charter and the abiding principles of responsible sovereignty.

---

22  See 'A More Secure World' UN Doc. A/59/565, at para. 207.
23  UNGA 'Implementing the Responsibility to Protect: Report of the Secretary-General' (12 January 2009) UN Doc. A/63/677.

The Security Council welcomed the adoption of the 2005 World Summit Outcome in October of the same year.[24] In April 2006, the Council went one step further and reaffirmed the provisions of paragraphs 138 and 139 regarding the responsibility to protect in a special Resolution.[25] The question is now how one should assess the performance of the Security Council since the adoption of the World Summit Outcome. Unfortunately, the result is not what many hoped for when the system was adopted.

Many views have been expressed about the system, both positive and critical. For my part, I am convinced that the Council simply must act in accordance with the provisions in the World Summit Outcome. Much has been written about this, and it is not possible to analyse all this material in a brief article. However, a very interesting review by Jared Genser of the Security Council's implementation of the responsibility to protect that was published in 2018 caught my attention.[26]

In the article the author has examined eleven situations against the background of the three pillars in the Secretary-General's report: Côte d'Ivoire, Libya, Mali, Central African Republic, Democratic Republic of the Congo, Sudan, South Sudan, Democratic People's Republic of Korea, Myanmar, Syria and Yemen. The three first situations are referred to under the heading 'More Successful Implementation', the following four are referred to under the heading 'Lack of Successful Implementation', while the four last situations are listed under 'Stalled Response'.

In the first category, government obstruction or cooperation have a decisive effect on the possibility of a successful implementation. They also demonstrate the vital importance of cooperation between regional organizations and the Security Council. The author finds that all three cases illustrate the importance of a rapid response capacity for the Security Council to act timely and decisively in the face of humanitarian crises.

With respect to the second category, the four case studies demonstrate that the Security Council's implementation of responsibility to protect is generally unsuccessful when the three conditions are not all met.

---

24   UNSC Res 1631 (2005).
25   UNSC Res 1674 (2006), at para. 4.
26   J. Genser, 'The UN Security Council's Implementation of the Responsibility to Protect: A Review of Past Interventions and Recommendations for Improvement' (Winter 2018) 18.2 Chicago J of Intl Law 419, available at http://bit.ly/r2pgenser (accessed 23 April 2019). The Global Centre on R2P has published a summary of the article which is available at http://www.globalr2p.org/media/files/un-security-council-application-of-r2p-jared-genser.pdf (accessed 23 April 2019).

With respect to the stalled responses, the author finds that a fourth condition has also prevented the Security Council from implementing its responsibility to protect mandate: the veto of the permanent five members.

The author concludes by making recommendations for improving the UN Security Council's implementation of responsibility to protect based on the following reasoning:

> The preceding historical analysis of the Security Council's country-specific implementation of R2P demonstrates the complexities and singularities that set each situation apart, but it also allows for the emergence of a set of factors that, when taken together, consistently have determined whether the Security Council will succeed or fail in its responsibility to implement R2P. What follows are recommendations for achieving better outcomes along those key factors, with the overarching goal of improving future Security Council implementation of R2P.[27]

I have a personal experience with respect to Syria in this context. When Kofi Annan was appointed Joint Special Envoy of the UN and the Arab League to Syria, he had been Chairman of the Panel of Eminent African Personalities on its mission in Kenya from January 2008 in the wake of the violence that was triggered by the 2007 disputed presidential elections. The elections had been followed by violence in which many people had lost their lives and hundreds of thousands had been internally displaced.

In Kenya, Kofi Annan and his colleagues on the Panel managed to bring the two competing sides together to negotiate and agree to form a coalition government. An agreement on the principles and partnership of a coalition government was signed on 28 February 2008. This was later confirmed in the 2008 Kenya National Accord and Reconciliation Act, which entered into force on 20 March 2008.[28] This act would govern the coalition government in the country for five years. During this period a new constitution was also adopted in August 2010.

In March 2012, Kofi Annan presented a six-point peace plan for Syria. In April 2012, we had a discussion on the situation in Syria. He wondered whether he could work in a similar manner in Syria as he had done in Kenya. During our discussion he fell silent for a while, then shook his head and said that he

---

27 Ibid., at 495.
28 I had the privilege of chairing the Legal Working Group on Governance that elaborated the draft of this legislation. The cooperation with its four Kenyan members was a very positive experience.

did not have the support of the Security Council which was a prerequisite for the mission to succeed, and that he would resign. This he did on 2 August 2012.

Against this background, paragraph 66 in Secretary-General Ban Ki-moon's report of 12 January 2009 should be kept in mind:

> In sum, as the United Nations community comes to articulate and implement a response strategy consistent with both the call in paragraph 139 of the Summit Outcome for 'timely and decisive' action and the provisions of the Charter, including its purposes and principles, this will make it more difficult for States or groups of States to claim that they need to act unilaterally or outside of United Nations channels, rules and procedures to respond to emergencies relating to the responsibility to protect. The more consistently, fairly and reliably such a United Nations-based response system operates, the more confidence there will be in the capacity of the United Nations to provide a credible multilateral alternative. This would also help to deter or dissuade potential perpetrators of such crimes and violations.[29]

The last sentence points to an important issue. Just as the criminal justice system is a necessary component of our societies at the national level, so it is necessary to develop a similar system at the international level.

This brings to the forefront the role of the international criminal justice system. According to Art. 13 (b) of the Rome Statute of the International Criminal Court (ICC),[30] the Court may exercise its jurisdiction with respect to a crime referred to in Art. 5 in accordance with the provisions of the Statute if a situation in which one or more of such crimes appears to have been committed is referred to the Prosecutor by the Security Council acting under Chapter VII of the Charter of the UN.

This means that the Council should always keep this option in mind. In this analysis it should be remembered that it is likely that the evidence might lead the Prosecutor to persons in very high positions at the national level, including the Head of State or Government. If the evidence leads in this direction, it is precisely persons at this level who should be brought to justice before the ICC. But then the process needs to be supported by the Security Council. This has not materialized in the cases of Libya and Sudan.

---

29   UNGA 'Implementing the Responsibility to Protect: Report of the Secretary-General' (12 January 2009) UN Doc. A/63/677, at para 66.
30   Rome Statute of the International Criminal Court (adopted 17 July 1998, entered into force 1 July 2002) 2187 UNTS 90.

As I have developed in an address concerning international prosecution of Heads of State for genocide, war crimes and crimes against humanity, the possibility of bringing officials at the level of Head of State or Government to justice at the international level is a necessary ingredient in a rules-based international society.[31] It is at this level that the principal standards applied in conflicts where international crimes may be committed are set, and it is at this level that the overriding orders are given.

If the officials who bear the greatest responsibility for international crimes committed in a particular situation are not brought to justice, this constitutes a clear risk not only for a continuation of the conflict at hand, but also for new conflicts in the future.

It is important that the Security Council lives up to its obligations with respect to responsibility to protect and to peacekeeping in general. In this context one should mention Secretary-General António Guterres' Action for Peacekeeping (A4P) initiative in September 2018.[32] Here, the Secretary-General called on Member States, the Security Council, host countries, troop- and police-contributing countries, regional partners and financial contributors to renew their collective engagement with UN peacekeeping and mutually commit to reach for excellence. The A4P is presently supported by 151 countries.

## VII  Empowerment of Women

Empowerment of women is one of the most central issues for the future. Although this continues to be a sensitive issue in some countries, the 1979 Convention on the Elimination of All Forms of Discrimination against Women now has 189 parties.[33] A comparison with the UN which currently has 193 Member States is telling.

It is obvious that in the modern world women must be allowed to participate in governance[34] as well as in family planning. This should be in the interest of all States. And since there is a direct correlation between the standing of

---

31  H. Corell, 'Challenges for the International Criminal Court' (Winter 2014) International Judicial Monitor, available at http://www.judicialmonitor.org/archive_winter2014/specialreport1.html (accessed 12 April 2019).

32  See https://peacekeeping.un.org/en/action-for-peacekeeping-a4p (accessed 12 April 2019).

33  Convention on the Elimination of All Forms of Discrimination against Women (adopted 18 December 1979, entered into force 3 September 1981) 1249 UNTS 13.

34  Note in this context Art. 21 of the Universal Declaration of Human Rights, UNGA Res 217 A (III) (10 December 1948).

the women in a society and the level of development in that society, States that are lagging behind in this respect will suffer in the long run. There is no doubt that countries that are lagging behind in this effort will also constitute 'threat multipliers' with respect to peace and security.

For the Security Council, the focus has been on women, peace and security since the Council started regular consideration of this agenda item in 2000, the same year that the Council adopted its famous Resolution 1325 (2000). The two main purposes of this Resolution is to protect women and children affected by armed conflict, and to ensure increased representation of women at all decision-making levels in national, regional and international institutions and mechanisms for the prevention, management, and resolution of conflict.

Over the years the Council has discussed many issues related to women: gender and sexual violence in armed conflict; human trafficking; forced marriage; reproductive rights; sexual slavery; kidnappings; and accountability for perpetrators.[35] The Council also holds yearly open debates to address the obstacles to the implementation of Resolution 1325 (2000), and the Council increasingly refers to women, peace and security-related issues under multiple items of its agenda.[36]

The latest open debate on that topic was held on 25 October 2018. The minutes from that meeting are alarming reading.[37] The UN head of the entity responsible for gender equality warned of 'systemic failure' to integrate women into such critical processes as peacekeeping, mediation and peace negotiations. According to UN Women, the entity dedicated to gender equality and the empowerment of women and a global champion for women and girls,[38] only 2 per cent of mediators, 8 per cent of negotiators and 5 per cent of witnesses and signatories to major peace processes between 1990 and 2017 were women.

Secretary-General António Guterres, in his remarks to the Security Council Open Debate on Women, Peace and Security of 25 October 2018, pointed out that the UN is placing the women, peace and security agenda at the heart of its partnerships with regional organizations. He noted that the participation of women in formal peace processes remains extremely limited and conflicts continue to have a devastating impact on women and girls around the globe.

---

35  See Repertoire of the Practice of the Security Council/Agenda Items/Thematic Items/ Women and Peace and Security, available at https://www.un.org/securitycouncil/content/repertoire/thematic-items (accessed 12 April 2019).
36  See e.g. Repertoire of the Practice of the Security Council, 20th Supplement (2016–2017).
37  See UNSC 8382nd Meeting (25 October 2018) UN Doc. S/PV.8382 and Press Release 'UN Gender Equality Chief Briefs Security Council' (25 October 2018) UN Doc. SC/13554.
38  See http://www.unwomen.org/en/about-us (accessed 12 April 2019).

Noting that recent data once again reveal the strong link between gender equality and peace, he emphasized: 'There is a significant gap between what we say in this chamber and what we do outside'.

In the UN Secretariat, special efforts are made to contribute to the protection of women. The Office on Genocide Prevention and the Responsibility to Protect with the two Special Advisers should be mentioned in this context. There is also the Office of the Special Representative of the Secretary-General for Children and Armed Conflict and the Office of the Special Representative of the Secretary-General on Sexual Violence in Conflict.[39]

The Informal Expert Group (IEG) on Women, Peace and Security, the first official Security Council Working Group on this topic should also be mentioned. It was created in 2016 pursuant to Security Council Resolution 2242 (2015).[40]

An interesting development after 2017 is the establishment of the African Women Leaders Network with its New York Group of Friends of the Network with the aim of mobilizing support for action from UN Member States. The group is co-chaired by Ghana and Germany and has approximately 40 members from Africa, Asia, Europe and Latin America.[41]

It goes without saying that these efforts to empower and protect women must continue with determination since this is of great importance to the mandate conferred on the Council by Art. 24 of the Charter: the primary responsibility for the maintenance of international peace and security.

## VIII  Nuclear Disarmament

### 1    *The Lack of Progress in Nuclear Disarmament*

Another very serious matter is the lack of progress in nuclear disarmament. I have addressed this question in the past.[42] It is true that we now have the Treaty

---

39   See under 'Special Advisers, Representatives and Envoys' at http://www.un.org/en/sections/about-un/secretariat/ (accessed 12 April 2019).

40   See UNSC 'Guidelines for the Informal Expert Group on Women and Peace and Security' (22 December 2016) UN Doc. S/2016/1106 Annex and PeaceWomen 'The 2242 Informal Expert Group on WPS', available at https://www.peacewomen.org/node/96169 (accessed 12 April 2019).

41   See UNSC 'Strengthening the Partnership between the United Nations and the African Union on Issues of Peace and Security in Africa, Including on the Work of the United Nations Office to the African Union: Report of the Secretary-General (6 July 2018) UN Doc. S/2018/678, at para. 9.

42   H. Corell, 'Is It Possible to Outlaw Nuclear Arms?' in Special Edition: Now Is the Time to Prohibit Nuclear Weapons! (February 2010) 120 Läkare mot Kärnvapen 6, available at

on the Prohibition of Nuclear Weapons,[43] adopted on 7 July 2017 by the UN conference to negotiate a legally binding instrument to prohibit nuclear weapons, leading towards their total elimination. The voting result was 122 States in favour, one vote against and one abstention. It was opened for signature by the Secretary-General on 20 September 2017, and it will enter into force 90 days after the fiftieth instrument of ratification, acceptance, approval or accession has been deposited. There are presently (12 April 2019) 70 signatories and 23 parties to the treaty.

As I argued in my 2010 article, there is certainly a need for this treaty, and its adoption is a very important development. There is no doubt about that.

However, there is a great problem of a legal nature here. None of the nuclear powers have endorsed the treaty, and no NATO country voted for it. In the preamble to the treaty, there are clear references to both the 1968 Treaty on the Non-Proliferation of Nuclear Weapons (NPT),[44] which is described as the cornerstone of the nuclear disarmament and non-proliferation regime, and which has a vital role to play in promoting international peace and security, and to the vital importance of the 1996 Comprehensive Nuclear-Test-Ban Treaty[45] and its verification regime as a core element of the nuclear disarmament and non-proliferation regime.

Even if it is a great success that there is now a treaty that prohibits nuclear weapons, a realistic assessment leads to the conclusion that it is extremely important that the nuclear powers fulfil their obligations under the NPT. Only when an elimination of the nuclear weapons according to this agreement is a reality will there be a general acceptance of the Treaty on the Prohibition of Nuclear Weapons.

The NPT recognizes five nuclear States: France, China, the Russian Federation, the UK and the US—in other words, the five permanent members of the Security Council. But as we know, there are more States that possess nuclear arms: India, Israel, Pakistan and now also North Korea. Here it should be noted that the next Review Conference of the NPT Treaty will be held in 2020. The Preparatory Committee for the Conference is scheduled to hold its third session from 29 April to 10 May 2019 at the UN Headquarters in New York. It is

---

http://slmk.org/wp-content/uploads/Lakare-mot-Karnvapen-120-ENG.pdf (accessed 12 April 2019).

43　Treaty on the Prohibition of Nuclear Weapons (adopted 7 July 2017, not yet entered into force) UN Doc. A/CONF.229/2017/8.

44　Treaty on the Non-Proliferation of Nuclear Weapons (adopted 1 July 1968, entered into force 5 March 1970) 729 UNTS 161.

45　Comprehensive Nuclear-Test-Ban Treaty (adopted 10 September 1996, not yet entered into force) GAOR 50th Session Supp 49, 14.

extremely important that this process can be led in a positive direction after the setbacks during later years.

One problem in this context is that most nuclear States believe that the Treaty on the Prohibition of Nuclear Weapons undermines the legal order based on the NPT. An additional great concern is that these States have begun to modernize their nuclear arsenals or claim that they intend to do so.

As is well known, on 8 July 1996, the International Court of Justice delivered an Advisory Opinion on the *Legality of the Threat or Use of Nuclear Weapons*.[46] The following clauses are of particular interest in the present situation:

> E. By seven votes to seven, by the President's casting vote,
> It follows from the above-mentioned requirements that the threat or use of nuclear weapons would generally be contrary to the rules of international law applicable in armed conflict, and in particular the principles and rules of humanitarian law;
>
> However, in view of the current state of international law, and of the elements of fact at its disposal, the Court cannot conclude definitively whether the threat or use of nuclear weapons would be lawful or unlawful in an extreme circumstance of self-defence, in which the very survival of a State would be at stake;
>
> F. Unanimously,
> There exists an obligation to pursue in good faith and bring to a conclusion negotiations leading to nuclear disarmament in all its aspects under strict and effective international control.[47]

In view of the fact that the nuclear-weapon States have not honoured this obligation and in view of what we now know of the effects of the use of nuclear weapons the question is if the proportionality principle that must be observed also under the law of self-defence can be respected. Is it under any circumstances possible to use nuclear arms without violating the principles and rules of humanitarian law? When using nuclear arms, is it at all possible to make a distinction between combatants and non-combatants? Is it legal to use weapons that are incapable of distinguishing between civilian and military targets?

Against this background maybe the General Assembly should request a second opinion from the International Court of Justice.

---

46   *Legality of the Threat or Use of Nuclear Weapons (Advisory Opinion)* [1996] ICJ Rep 226.
47   Ibid., at para. 105.

In conclusion it can be said that it is a success that there is now a treaty prohibiting nuclear weapons. But what is required now is that the nuclear-weapon States—the five permanent members of the Security Council—confirm their obligations under the NPT and make serious their obligation to work for a nuclear-weapon free world. It is obvious that all States that possess nuclear weapons must participate here.

## 2      *The Joint Comprehensive Plan of Action (JCPOA)*

Another problem related to the Security Council is the fact that the US has left the comprehensive, long-term solution to the Iranian nuclear issue, culminating in the Joint Comprehensive Plan of Action (JCPOA) concluded on 14 July 2015.[48] In this situation it is important to look at the JCPOA and Security Council Resolution 2231 (2015) and its Annexes A and B from the viewpoint of the UN Charter.

The Resolution is of course unique in many senses. An important point of departure is that the JCPOA was negotiated with the participation of the five permanent members of the Security Council. Furthermore, there are several references in the JCPOA that clearly indicate that an endorsement by the UN Security Council is a necessary requirement for the execution of the JCPOA.

Of utmost importance is the reference in the Resolution to Art. 25 of the UN Charter, which indicates that the purpose of the Resolution is to put an obligation on all UN members. The fact that the resolution is adopted under Chapter VII of the Charter should also be seen as an outflow of the obligations that fall upon the Security Council under Arts 24 and 39 of the Charter. The imperatives in the provisions must be noted in particular.

Against this background and considering the history behind the JCPOA, one must question whether the States that concluded the agreement can withdraw from it. However, even if a State that is a party to the JCPOA could withdraw from the agreement as such, this State would still be bound by the obligations on all States laid down in the Resolution. I refer in particular to operative paragraphs 2 and 26 of Resolution 2231, which read:

> 2. *Calls upon* all Members States, regional organizations and international organizations to take such actions as may be appropriate to support the implementation of the JCPOA, including by taking actions commensurate with the implementation plan set out in the JCPOA and this resolution

---

[48]   Joint Comprehensive Plan of Action (concluded on 14 July 2015) UN Doc. S/2015/544, as attached as Annex A to UNSC Res 2231 (2015).

and by refraining from actions that undermine implementation of commitments under the JCPOA;
[...]
26. *Urges* all States, relevant United Nations bodies and other interested parties, to cooperate fully with the Security Council in its exercise of the tasks related to this resolution, in particular by supplying any information at their disposal on the implementation of the measures in this resolution.

On 19 June 2018, the International Association Of Lawyers Against Nuclear Arms (IALANA) suggested that governments should consider requesting the International Court of Justice to render an Advisory Opinion on the legal consequences of Resolution 2231 and the JCPOA. In so doing, they made a reference to a 1971 Advisory Opinion in which the International Court of Justice:

> taking into account 'all circumstances', held legally binding a provision of a Security Council resolution which provision 'calls upon all States' to refrain from acts inconsistent with the Council's determination that 'the continued presence of the South African authorities in Namibia is illegal'. Similarly here, under all the circumstances, paras. 2 and 26 of Resolution 2231 are legally binding directives of the Security Council.[49]

It is also difficult to understand operative paragraph 27 of Resolution 2231. This provision is more or less a quote from paragraph xi in the Preamble of the JCPOA. One wonders what the analysis behind this provision is, since the effects of a conduct in accordance with the Resolution will have direct consequences for all States also to the extent that they are bound by the earlier Resolutions adopted by the Council.

Furthermore, the manner in which China, France, Germany, the Russian Federation, the UK, the US and the EU note in Resolution 2231 Annex B their understanding of the situation after the adoption of a resolution endorsing the JCPOA is significant. Their understanding is that the Security Council would make the practical arrangements to undertake directly the tasks specified in their statement,

---

[49] IALANA 'Nuclear Crossroads: The Urgent Need for Action to Prevent Catastrophe' (19 June 2018), referring to *Legal Consequences for States of the Continued Presence of South Africa in Namibia (South West Africa) notwithstanding Security Council Resolution 276 (1970) (Advisory Opinion)* [1971] ICJ Rep 16.

including to monitor and take action to support the implementation by Member States of these provisions, review proposals described in paragraph 2 of this statement, answer inquiries from Member States, provide guidance, and examine information regarding alleged actions inconsistent with the resolution.[50]

Taking all this into consideration, one can actually question whether the US withdrawal from the JCPOA is legal after the endorsement of the agreement by the Security Council. I refer here to paragraphs 28 and 29 in Annex A. Under all circumstances, the US is bound by the Resolution in the same manner as all UN Member States are bound by it. If they do not agree, maybe paragraphs 36 and 37 might offer an opportunity to find a solution of the problems generated by the behaviour of the US. Under all circumstances the question must be asked if this behaviour by a permanent member of the Security Council and a State under the rule of law is acceptable.

It is also interesting to note that the remaining parties to the JCPOA that are also members of the Joint Commission of the JCPOA, are of the opinion that preserving the nuclear deal is in the security interest of all, see the Statement from the Joint Commission of the Joint Comprehensive Plan of Action of 6 July 2018.[51]

## IX Cooperation between the Security Council and Regional Organizations

Cooperation between the Security Council and regional organizations is a matter that is given great attention within the UN. The focus is on cooperation between the UN and regional and sub-regional organizations in the prevention and resolution of conflicts. These organizations have an important role to play in conformity with Chapter VIII of the UN Charter.

Over the years there have been contacts, meetings and discussions with organizations like the African Union (AU), the Organization for Security and Cooperation in Europe (OSCE), the League of Arab States (LAS), the Organization of Islamic Cooperation (OIC), the European Union (EU), the Collective Security Treaty Organization (CSTO), the Shanghai Cooperation Organisation (SCO), and the Commonwealth of Independent States (CIS).

---

50   UNSC Res 2231 (2015) Annex B, at para. 7.
51   Available at https://eeas.europa.eu/headquarters/headquarters-homepage/48076/statement-joint-commission-joint-comprehensive-plan-action_en (accessed 23 April 2019).

Particular attention has been paid to Africa, where one of the UN local offices is the UN Office to the African Union (UNOAU). An important factor here is that half of the UN peacekeeping operations are currently deployed in Africa.

For many years there have been annual UN–African Union joint consultative meetings on the prevention and management of conflict. An important role is played here by the sub-regional organizations: the Intergovernmental Authority for Development (IGAD), the East African Community (EAC), the Southern African Development Community (SADC), the Economic Community of Central African States (ECCAS), and the Economic Community of West African States (ECOWAS).

One interesting area of this cooperation is in the field rule of law and security institutions and initiatives in this field. The UN Regional Centre for Peace and Disarmament in Africa and the African Union Master Road Map of Practical Steps for Silencing the Guns in Africa by 2020 could be mentioned in this context. The African Union–UN Framework for the Implementation of Agenda 2063 should also be mentioned here.[52] There is also work going on to establish regional standby forces in Africa.

The Secretary-General regularly issues reports on strengthening the partnership between the UN and the African Union on issues of peace and security in Africa. On 19 April 2017, a Joint UN–African Union Framework for Enhanced Partnership was signed. And on 18 September 2017, the UN and the African Union signed a Memorandum of Understanding on Peacebuilding to strengthen cooperation in support of efforts aimed at peacebuilding and sustaining peace in Africa, taking a concrete step towards the implementation of the Joint UN–African Union Framework for Enhanced Partnership in Peace and Security.

Of particular concern at present are the multifaceted challenges facing West Africa and the Sahel because of the various unresolved conflicts in these regions, the ongoing terrorist activities, trafficking and violent extremism, and the impact of climate change. These are matters on which the UN Office for West Africa (UNOWAS) has to focus. The same applies to the fight against Boko Haram in the Lake Chad Basin area and the humanitarian situation in the region.[53]

The regional cooperation in a more general perspective is organized in many different ways. There are biennial regional organizations meetings. The discussions focus on topics like local and national mediation, engaging non-State

---

52   See African Union Commission 'Agenda 2063: the Africa We Want' (April 2015).
53   See Repertoire of the Practice of the Security Council, 20th Supplement (2016–2017) Part 1, at 83–86 and 277–281.

armed groups, mediation of election-related violence, and natural resources mediation. In recent years more attention has been payed to mediation support, which has led to more mediation support capacities within intergovernmental organizations.

The five UN Economic Commissions should also be mentioned in this context. They focus on Europe (UNECE), Asia and the Pacific (UNESCAP), Latin America (ECLAC), Africa (ECA), and Western Asia (UNESCWA).

The Secretary-General has emphasized that regional economic communities and regional mechanisms are often the first to experience the early warning signs of impending conflict and have the most to gain from conflict prevention.[54] He has also stressed that they are important partners to the UN in promoting dialogue and reconciliation, exercising influence on parties to conflict to ensure the implementation of peace agreements, countering terrorism, preventing violent extremism and addressing migration issues.

But they could also cause problems. Reference is made to what is said under responsibility to protect above. Also the Secretary-General has said that that regional interests and proximity to the parties can complicate conflict prevention and resolution efforts.

With respect to the Security Council it is regularly reiterating its determination to take effective steps to further enhance the relationship between the UN and regional organizations, in particular the African Union, in accordance with Chapter VIII of the UN Charter.

Against this background it is easy to conclude that there is an obvious need for partnership in conflict prevention and peace-making. An important ingredient here is the need for the rule of law and protection of human rights. Another precondition is observance of international humanitarian law.

As a matter of fact, looking at the 17 Sustainable Development Goals there is one thing that must be understood. In order to reach all these goals, one of them must be attained, namely Goal 16:

> Promote peaceful and inclusive societies for sustainable development, provide access to justice for all and build effective, accountable and inclusive institutions at all levels

---

54  See UNSC 'Strengthening the Partnership between the United Nations and the African Union on Issues of Peace and Security in Africa, Including on the Work of the United Nations Office to the African Union: Report of the Secretary-General (6 July 2018) UN Doc. S/2018/678, at para 54.

Among the targets of this goal are 'promote the rule of law at the national and international levels', and 'substantially reduce corruption and bribery in all its forms'. These are absolutely crucial elements for creating the legal order that is a prerequisite for achieving all the other goals.

It is obvious that one-size-fits-all does not work in conflict prevention and peace-making. However, a common denominator must focus on the establishment of the rule of law and fighting corruption. It is interesting to see that the UN Secretariat has been reorganized in later years to focus on these matters, and also on fighting terrorism and transnational crime.

The question is also how to organize missions in the field. Depending on the situation—whether it is a peacekeeping operation, a peace enforcement operation, or an assistance mission of a different nature—the mission has to be tailored accordingly.

From my personal experience when the UN actually governed Kosovo and East Timor and was responsible for the legislation (through regulations issued by the Special Representative of the Secretary-General after vetting by the Department of Peacekeeping Operations and the UN Office of Legal Affairs) and the administration of justice I know how important it is to have a functioning police and defence force at the national level.

Here it turned out that it was very difficult to quickly establish well-functioning power and authority in these two provinces. Recruitment of police officers, prosecutors and judges is not made in an instant. The vacuum that came about was quickly filled by criminal elements. In such situations there is no other way but to turn to the military to avoid sheer anarchy.

As a matter of fact this has led me to the conclusion that within the State community there should be a common interest that every country has a reasonable armament so that other countries can be confident that order can be maintained there. Police must of course be present with the legal authority to use force to maintain law and order—that is a given. But if the situation becomes so serious that anarchy threatens, one must resort to other means, including assistance from the military. The point of departure must be that the main objective of the armed forces seen in this perspective shall be preventive—that criminals realize that there is no vacuum.

Another lesson in this field is that the personalities involved are able to perform their duties, be it at the national, regional or international level. This is also demonstrated by the analysis of the situations where the UN has exercised its responsibility to protect mentioned above.

At the same time, it is important to note that sometimes the solution can be a regional initiative, rather than that the UN gets involved. The Panel of Eminent

African Personalities in Kenya, appointed by the African Union, is an example. Kofi Annan, Benjamin Mkapa and Graça Machel managed to organize negotiations among two parties: the Government/PNU (President Kibaki) and ODM (Honourable Raila Odinga), which led to the conclusion of the agreement mentioned above and to the adoption of the legislation that was necessary for forming the grand coalition government.

## x    Concluding Observations

It is obvious that an effective Security Council is a precondition for establishing international peace and security in the future. The UN would be a formidable organization if all its members really followed the Charter. Of particular importance is that the permanent members of the Security Council bow to the law here. Security Council reform is necessary; but at the same time it is fundamental to preserve the Security Council as an executive organ. Too many members would destroy this requirement completely, in particular if additional members are granted veto power.

The hallmark of an executive organ is not that it is 'democratic' in the sense frequently expressed in the debate, but that it is representative.[55] The task of such an organ within an organization is to perform functions on behalf of all its members, applying rules laid down in the organization's constitution. In so doing, the members of the executive organ must observe those rules strictly and not act in self-interest. In the case of the UN, the rules that its executive organ must apply are laid down in the UN Charter. The Security Council must therefore faithfully apply those rules.

It has frequently been suggested that new members should be added to the Council. The figure eleven has been indicated by several States. If so many members are added, there is a clear risk that the Council becomes inoperable. The enlargement would also not solve the real problem with the Council, namely the conduct of the permanent members. In two of these members there are also major deficiencies with respect to democracy and the rule of law. And a third member has retreated from its leadership; the behaviour of its Head of State has severely affected the administration of an otherwise very competent foreign service.

Against this background and in the short-term perspective, Security Council reform should be limited to the elements suggested in the foregoing, which

---

55    The latest General Assembly debate on Security Council reform took place on 20 November 2018.

do not require changing even a comma in the UN Charter. However, for this reform to succeed the members of the Council must lead by example. What is needed is statesmanship—statesmen and stateswomen who can look to the horizon and understand that their responsibility extends not only to their own State but to the world community—not only to the present but also to coming generations. As it appears from the foregoing, we are far from this at present.

The permanent five members simply must engage in a profound discussion about their performance and the manner in which the veto power is exercised. Another requirement is that they can agree on how to set the example with respect to the rule of law and human rights. This may take time; but unless these improvements are realized, there is no way that we can create a world where human beings can live in dignity with their human rights preserved.

Furthermore, the members of the Council are fully aware of the risks that the growing world population and climate change entail. The question is whether they properly address these challenges. Spending money and other resources on peace operations that are generated by the inability of the Council to prevent conflict is not acceptable in today's world when we should be focussing on the challenges that will affect all humankind in the future.

With respect to empowerment of women, the matter is on the agenda of the Council, and it is clear that members are aware of the need for improvement in this area.

As regards nuclear disarmament, the obligations under the NPT must be honoured. Only if the permanent members make a serious effort to comply with their obligations will it be possible to bring the other States that possess nuclear arms into the circle.

Finally, with respect to responsibility to protect there is great need for improvement. The issue is clear: we cannot accept in the 21st century that fundamental human rights are violated and that crimes against international humanitarian law are being committed on a large scale without consequences.

Here the situation must be assessed in a broader perspective, including the fact that international criminal law has been developed and that international criminal tribunals have been established, in particular the International Criminal Court operating under the Rome Statute. The Council therefore has a very strong moral obligation to ensure accountability for perpetrators and to respond to the responsibility to protect.

This means that the necessary resources have to be mobilized so that the UN is in a position to act when this is required. It is, however, sad to note that these resources may not materialize in certain situations. The analysis that the Security Council must make will then lead to the sad but inevitable conclusion that the world community is unable to act. If the UN or a UN authorized arrangement cannot master enough resources to intervene in a credible and responsible manner we ultimately have to face the fact that no coercive action can be taken.

The members of the UN must therefore make a joint effort, including in particular through responsible, credible and even-handed action by the Security Council, to make certain that the system created by the Charter of the UN for the maintenance of international peace and security, including assuring human rights for all human beings, can be effectively upheld.

### Annex to a Letter of 10 December 2008 from Former Legal Counsel of the United Nations Hans Corell to the Governments of the Members of the United Nations

#### *Draft Declaration by the Permanent Members of the Security Council*[56]

We, the permanent members of the Security Council,

*Mindful* of the responsibility of the Security Council under the Charter of the United Nations for the maintenance of international peace and security;

*Realizing* that the ever present threats to international peace and security are now exacerbated by the effects of climate change in combination with a rapidly growing world population;

*Aware* of the fact that failure on the part of the Security Council to act in situations where action is obviously required may cause unnecessary human suffering and may tempt others to intervene, including by the use of force, without the required authorization of the of the Council;

*Realizing* that such actions by others will undermine the respect for the Charter of the United Nations and may in themselves pose a direct threat to international peace and security;

*Conscious* of the fact that a failure by the members of Security Council to set the example by scrupulously adhering to international law and the Charter of the United Nations will have devastating effects on the efforts to establish the rule of law at the national and international level,

---

[56] I would like to emphasize that the intention behind this proposal is to inspire a serious discussion of the issue and that the text should be regarded as food for thought rather than an attempt to propose the exact wording of such a declaration.

*Have agreed* to make the following solemn undertaking:

We pledge
- To scrupulously adhere to the obligations under international law that we have undertaken and in particular those laid down in the Charter of the United Nations;
- To make use of our veto power in the Security Council only if our most serious and direct national interests are affected and to explain, in case we do use this power, the reasons for doing so;
- To refrain in our international relations from the threat or use of force against the territorial integrity or political independence of any state unless in self-defence in accordance with Article 51 of the Charter of the United Nations or in accordance with a clear and unambiguous mandate by the Security Council under Chapter VII;
- To take forceful action to intervene in situations when international peace and security are threatened by governments that seriously violate human rights or fail to protect their populations from genocide, war crimes, ethnic cleansing and crimes against humanity or when otherwise the responsibility to protect is engaged. [end]

CHAPTER 2

# Lessons from the ILC's Work on 'Immunity of State Officials': Melland Schill Lecture, 21 November 2017

*Michael Wood*

## Abstract

The topic *Immunity of State officials from foreign criminal jurisdiction* has been on the programme of work of the International Law Commission since 2007. After ten reports from two Special Rapporteurs, by June 2019 it has yet to complete a first reading, not least because the topic has proved highly contentious both within the Commission and among States. The Commission could only adopt a central provision (on exceptions to immunity *ratione materiae*), exceptionally, having recourse to voting. There are several lessons to be learnt from the handling of the topic over the last twelve years, including for such crucial aspects of the Commission's working methods as the choice of topics; the need for a clear view of the Commission's aim in taking up a topic; the need for rigour in assessing the current state of international law; the importance of dialogue, within the Commission and between the Commission and States; and the utility or otherwise of voting.

## Keywords

International Law Commission – Immunity *ratione personae* – Immunity *ratione materiae* – State Officials – Official Acts

## 1   Introduction

It is a pleasure to return to the Manchester International Law Centre (MILC), and an honour to give the Melland Schill lecture this year. My particular thanks go to Iain Scobie and Jean d'Aspremont for their invitation. I congratulate them on reviving this important lecture series.[1]

---

1   See http://www.law.manchester.ac.uk/milc/about/melland-schill/ (accessed 27 March 2019). On 14 October 2015, Professor John Dugard delivered the first Melland Schill lecture since

My aim today is to shed some light on the way the UN International Law Commission (hereafter 'the Commission' or 'ILC') operates; and to do so by examining what has been described as 'one of the most controversial issues the Commission has ever dealt with',[2] *Immunity of State officials from foreign criminal jurisdiction*.[3]

---

1974, entitled 'Are Existing States Sacrosanct?'. On 5 May 2016, Judge Xue Hanqin of the International Court of Justice delivered the second lecture, entitled 'The Cultural Element in International Law', and on 14 September 2018 Professor Jan Klabbers lectured on 'Epistemic Universalism'. In conjunction with Manchester University Press, the University of Manchester Library has digitized the original series of Melland Schill Lectures (delivered between 1961 and 1974): https://www.escholar.manchester.ac.uk/search/?search=%22melland+schill%22&button_escholarsearch=Search (accessed 27 March 2019).

2  Germany, UN General Assembly's Sixth (Legal) Committee, 73rd session, 30th meeting (31 October 2018), available on the UN PaperSmart Portal at http://statements.unmeetings.org/media2/20305268/germany-82-cluster-3.pdf (accessed 27 March 2019).

3  H. Huang, 'On Immunity of State Officials from Foreign Criminal Jurisdiction' (2014) 13 Chinese Journal of International Law 1; 'Symposium on the Immunity of State Officials' (2015) 109 AJIL Unbound 153 (W.S. Dodge, 'Foreign Official Immunity in the International Law Commission: The Meanings of 'Official Capacity'' 156; C.I. Keitner, 'Horizontal Enforcement and the ILC's Proposed Draft Articles on the Immunity of State Officials from Foreign Criminal Jurisdiction' 161; R. O'Keefe, 'An "International Crime" Exception to the Immunity of State Officials from Foreign Criminal Jurisdiction: Not Currently, Not Likely' 167); S.D. Murphy, 'Protection of Persons in the Event of Disasters and Other Topics: The Sixty-Eighth Session of the International Law Commission' (2016) 110 American Journal of International Law 718, at 732–742; S.D. Murphy, 'Crimes Against Humanity and Other Topics: The Sixty-Ninth Session of the International Law Commission' (2017) 111 American Journal of International Law 970, at 981–988; G. Bernabei, 'Nobody's Land: Where All Step but No One Settles', available at http://ilawyerblog.com (accessed 27 March 2019); 'Symposium on the Present and Future of Foreign Official Immunity' (2018) 112 AJIL Unbound 1 (S.D. Murphy, 'Immunity *Ratione Materiae* of State Officials from Foreign Criminal Jurisdiction: Where is the State Practice in Support of the Exceptions?' 4; Q. Shen, 'Methodological Flaws in the ILC's Study on Exceptions to Immunity *Ratione Materiae* of State Officials from Foreign Criminal Jurisdiction' 9; P. Webb, 'How Far Does the Systemic Approach to Immunities take us?' 16; M. Forteau, 'Immunities and International Crimes before the ILC: Looking for Innovative Solutions' 22; R. van Alebeek, 'The "International Crime" Exception to the ILC Draft Articles on the Immunity of State Officials from Foreign Criminal Jurisdiction: Two Steps Back?' 27); C. Wickremasinghe, 'Immunities Enjoyed by Officials of States and International Organizations' in M. Evans (ed.), *International Law* (5th edn OUP 2018) 346; D. Tladi, 'The International Law Commission's Recent Work on Exceptions to Immunity: Charting the Course for a Brave New World in International Law?' (2019) 32 Leiden Journal of International Law 1; R. van Alebeek, 'Material Immunity of Foreign Officials from Criminal Jurisdiction for "Acts Committed in the Official Capacity" and Possible Exceptions Thereto' in T. Ruys, N. Angelet and L. Ferro (eds.), *Cambridge Handbook of Immunities and International Law* (CUP 2019) 496; H. Ascensio and B.I. Bonafe, 'L'Absence d'immunité des agents de l'état en cas de crime international: pourquoi en débattre encore?' (2018) 4 RGDIP.

I shall begin with a few words about the Commission, which has for its object 'the promotion of the progressive development of international law and its codification'.[4] It was established 70 years ago as a subsidiary organ of the UN General Assembly. It is composed of 34 individuals, 'persons of recognized competence in international law',[5] who act in their personal capacity, not on instructions from governments. The General Assembly elects the whole Commission every five years, with the seats distributed among the five UN regional groups in accordance with a formula laid down by the Assembly. As with all UN elections, political factors play a role.

Nowadays the Commission usually follows a standard procedure for dealing with topics. First, and crucially, a topic is normally chosen from amongst those proposed or taken up by members of the Commission,[6] and is placed first on the long-term programme of work. If it is decided to move forward with a topic it is put on the current programme of work, and a Special Rapporteur is usually appointed (often the member who proposed the topic). The choice of topics is not easy; and once on the current programme of work, they are not easily removed, even if it becomes clear that they are unlikely to lead to useful results.

The Special Rapporteur can be seen as the motor for the Commission in respect of his or her topic; without his or her efforts it would be difficult for the Commission to make progress. But it is the Commission as a whole which ultimately steers the topic and affixes its seal to the output. The Commission's work is a collective effort. Through careful negotiation and drafting, the Commission usually makes substantial improvements on proposals from the Special Rapporteur. At least, that was my experience with the topic for which I acted as Special Rapporteur, *Identification of customary international law*.

The Special Rapporteur (or, over time, Special Rapporteurs) produces a series of reports which are first debated in plenary. The Special Rapporteur's proposals may then be referred to the Drafting Committee, which is where the real negotiation usually takes place, against the background of the debate in plenary. The texts that emerge from the Drafting Committee, sometimes very significantly revised from those proposed by the Special Rapporteur, are adopted by the plenary, usually without significant amendment or debate. Commentaries are then prepared by the Special Rapporteur, and these are considered and adopted by the Commission in plenary, towards the end of the session, as part of

---

4  Statute of the International Law Commission, adopted by the General Assembly in resolution 174 (II) of 21 November 1947 (as amended), Art. 1.
5  Ibid., Art. 2 (1).
6  Topics have occasionally been proposed by the General Assembly, the Secretariat of the Commission, or other UN organs; and by States.

the process of adopting the Commission's Annual Report. This may be quite an unsatisfactory procedure, since it does not always allow adequate time for the careful consideration which the commentaries, an important element of the Commission's output, merit. Occasionally, where there is time and if the Special Rapporteur so wishes, a working group has reviewed a preliminary draft of the commentaries before the Special Rapporteur submits them for translation and discussion in plenary.[7]

After a first reading stage, there is normally a year off to enable sufficient time for States to submit written comments on the draft texts adopted by the Commission. Then a second (final) reading takes place, usually focused on considering the observations and comments of States. The final product is then submitted to the UN General Assembly, together with a recommendation as to future action (for example, to conclude a convention based on the Commission's text, or to bring the text to the attention of States and others).

States have many opportunities to comment in the course of the Commission's work on a topic, in particular in the debate in the Sixth Committee of the UN General Assembly on the Commission's Annual Report, which details the progress made with regard to each topic. Such input is important for the Commission's work, which is indeed intended to be useful to States, to whom the Commission reports and who are the ultimate law-makers in the international legal system.

The Commission is only part way through its work on the topic *Immunity of State officials from foreign criminal jurisdiction*. It has not yet completed a first reading, so any overall assessment would be premature. I nevertheless propose to draw on the work done so far in order to offer some thoughts on the Commission's role in today's world, a role that has sometimes been questioned. A key issue is the extent to which, for any particular topic on its programme of work, the Commission does or should engage in progressive development of international law as opposed to its codification, or indeed in proposing wholly new rules of law, especially as such distinctions have not always proven workable in practice.[8] More precisely, how far can the Commission's output on any

---

7  This was done with the second reading commentaries on *Responsibility of States for internationally wrongful acts* (2001); the first and second reading commentaries on *Identification of customary international law* (2016, 2018); some of the first reading commentaries on *Provisional application of treaties* (2017); and some of the commentaries on *Protection of the environment in relation to armed conflict* (2018).

8  See also M. Wood, 'The UN International Law Commission and Customary International Law', Morelli Lecture (27 May 2017) in E. Cannizzaro (ed.), *Methodologies of International Law* (forthcoming 2019).

particular topic be seen as setting out *lex lata* as opposed to *lex ferenda*? As I have said elsewhere,

> an important distinction needs to be made between the terms 'codification' and 'progressive development' on the one hand, and '*lex lata*' and '*lex ferenda*' on the other. At least as used in the Statute of the Commission, the former refers to the outcome of a process of reducing unwritten law to writing; it is inevitably a matter of degree. The latter is a clear-cut distinction: a rule is either existing law or it is not.[9]

The distinction between what the law is and what it might be is of great practical importance, if not for the Commission in its day-to-day work, then certainly for States and practitioners, and for judges, including those in national courts, who often need to know what the law is, or was, at any particular time.[10] The immunity of State officials is an area of international law that frequently comes before national courts and is often at issue in high-profile cases, so clarity on the part of the Commission is particularly important.[11]

A closely related question is whether the final output on a topic should be draft articles intended—in principle, at least—to form the basis of a multilateral convention, or whether it should be put forward as a restatement (in the case of codification), or as 'soft law' or something in the nature of a study.

It is worth recalling that, over the years, the Commission has made important contributions to the progressive development and codification of international law in the field of international immunities, including in the preparatory work of the Vienna Conventions on Diplomatic and Consular Relations of 1961 and 1963, and the United Nations Convention on Jurisdictional Immunities of States and Their Property of 2004.

There have also been less successful projects in the field, at least in the sense that they have not resulted in widely ratified conventions: the 1969 New York Convention on Special Missions, which as of June 2019 has only 39 States

---

9   Ibid., at para. 6.
10  See also M. Wood, 'What Is Public International Law? The Need for Clarity about Sources' (2011) 1 Asian Journal of International Law 205.
11  See also R. van Alebeek, 'The "International Crime" Exception to the ILC Draft Articles on the Immunity of State Officials from Foreign Criminal Jurisdiction: Two Steps Back?', supra note 3, at 32 ('Even if the ILC's general practice of declining to distinguish between progressive development and codification is sensible, such a distinction should have been drawn in the particular case of Draft Article 7. Whether, and how, the "international crimes" exception can be framed in terms of existing customary international law is the central question in the debate triggered almost two decades ago by the *Pinochet* case, and nearly all members who participated in the ILC debates articulated a position on this point').

Parties; the 1975 Vienna Convention on the Representation of States in their Relations with International Organizations of a Universal Character, not (yet) in force after more than 40 years, having achieved 34 of the 35 ratifications required; and the 1989 Draft Articles on the Status of the Diplomatic Courier and the Diplomatic Bag not Accompanied by Diplomatic Courier, which were given a 'decent burial' by the Sixth Committee in 1995.[12] A sub-topic on the immunities of international organizations was discontinued in 1992, and efforts to revive it in recent years have not been greeted with enthusiasm.[13] The reasons for the relative failure of these topics vary, but they were either seen as unnecessary or as conferring an undue scale of privileges and immunities. Most of these projects have, nevertheless, had some influence on the law. For example, the customary international law on the inviolability and immunity of persons on special missions was undoubtedly influenced by the adoption of the New York Convention in 1969.[14]

II    Work on the Topic *Immunity of State Officials From Foreign Criminal Jurisdiction* (up to 2018)

The topic *Immunity of State officials from foreign criminal jurisdiction* has been on the Commission's current programme of work since 2007.[15] There have been two Special Rapporteurs, Roman Anatolyevitch Kolodkin (Russian Federation) between 2007 and 2011, and Professor Concepción Escobar Hernández (Spain) from 2012 to the present.

Between 2008 and 2011, Kolodkin produced three reports,[16] but they contained no proposed draft articles. In addition, in 2008 the Commission's Secretariat

---

12  UNGA Decision 50/416 of 11 December 1995, by which the General Assembly brought consideration of the topic to a conclusion by bringing the Commission's final draft articles to the attention of Member States while reminding them of the possibility that this field of international law might be subject to codification at an appropriate future time.

13  See G. Gaja, 'Jurisdictional Immunity of International Organizations' Yearbook of the International Law Commission 2006, vol. II, Part 2, 201.

14  See A. Sanger and M. Wood, 'The Immunities of Members of Special Missions' in T. Ruys, N. Angelet and L. Ferro (eds.), *Cambridge Handbook of Immunities and International Law* (CUP 2019) 452; M. Wood, A. Sanger and Council of Europe (eds.), *The Immunities of Special Missions* (Brill 2019).

15  The topic was placed on the Commission's long-term programme of work in 2006, on the basis of a syllabus prepared by Mr Kolodkin: Yearbook of the International Law Commission 2006, vol. II, Part 2, at 191–196.

16  Preliminary Report (A/CN.4/601: Yearbook of the International Law Commission 2008, vol. II, Part 1, at 157–192); Second Report (A/CN.4/631: Yearbook of the International Law Commission 2010, vol. II, Part 1, at 395–426); Third Report (A/CN.4/646: Yearbook of the International Law Commission 2011, vol. II, Part 1, at 223–243).

published a detailed study on the topic.[17] Kolodkin's first report was debated in the Commission in 2008[18] and his second and third reports in 2011.[19]

Kolodkin's first report, while preliminary in nature, covered a range of important issues (not all of which have yet been dealt with by the Commission). The report clarified that the topic 'covers only immunity of officials of one State from national (and not international) criminal (and not civil) jurisdiction of another State (and not of the State served by the official)'.[20] It also observed that '[t]he basic source of the immunity of State officials from foreign criminal jurisdiction is international law, and particularly customary international law';[21] and that '[i]mmunity of State officials from foreign criminal jurisdiction is procedural and not substantive in nature'.[22] The first report explained that

> [a]ctions performed by an official in an official capacity are attributed to the State. The official is therefore protected from the criminal jurisdiction of a foreign State by immunity *ratione materiae*. However, this does not preclude attribution of these actions also to the person who performed them.[23]

With regard to immunity *ratione personae*, the first report suggested that

> [t]he high-ranking officials who enjoy personal immunity by virtue of their post include primarily Heads of State, Heads of Government and ministers for foreign affairs;

and that

> [a]n attempt may be made to determine which other high-ranking officials, in addition to the threesome mentioned, enjoy immunity *ratione personae*. It will be possible to single out such officials from among all

---

[17] Immunity of State Officials from Foreign Criminal Jurisdiction, Memorandum by the Secretariat (A/CN.4/596 and Corr.1).
[18] 2982nd–2987th meetings: Yearbook of the International Law Commission 2008, vol. I, at 175–234.
[19] 3086th–3088th, 3111th, and 3113th–3115th meetings: Yearbook of the International Law Commission 2011, vol. I, at 37–72, 249–251, 266–281, 282–290.
[20] Yearbook of the International Law Commission 2008, vol. II, Part 1, at 191, para. 130 (a).
[21] Ibid., at 184, para. 102 (a).
[22] Ibid., at 184, para. 102 (g) (adding that '[i]t is an obstacle to criminal liability but does not in principle preclude it').
[23] Ibid., at 184, para. 102 (h).

high-ranking officials, if the criterion or criteria justifying special status for this category of high-ranking officials can be defined.[24]

In the debate on Kolodkin's first report, members of the Commission were divided on the question of which holders of high-ranking office in a State should be recognized as entitled to immunity *ratione personae*, a question that appears to have been connected to the wider debate as to whether the Commission should approach the topic as a whole as an exercise in codification or as one of progressive development (or both).[25] The debate in the Sixth Committee in 2008 revealed differences among States as well, including on the question of exceptions to immunity and, more broadly, the approach that the Commission should adopt: while some delegations emphasized the usefulness of codification of existing law, others 'cautioned that the study of this topic by the Commission should take into account the balance of competing interests involved, namely, the prevention of impunity on the one hand and the stability of inter-State relations and the protection of the State's ability to perform its functions on the other'.[26]

---

24   Ibid., at 192, paras 130 (d) and (e).
25   In summarizing the debate, the Special Rapporteur noted that: 'With regard to immunity *ratione personae*, some members took the view that only Heads of State, Heads of Government and Ministers for Foreign Affairs enjoyed such immunity. Others, while admitting that other officials might also enjoy immunity *ratione personae*, cautioned the Commission against venturing beyond the limits of the "troika". At least two members held that, even if officials other than the troika enjoyed such immunity, the Commission should not mention them explicitly lest it prejudge the situation regarding other categories of persons who might enjoy personal immunity. At the same time, several members of the Commission—indeed perhaps the majority—considered that, in the light of current trends in the conduct of affairs of State, the Commission would have difficulty in confining its study to the troika. However, even those who were in favour of extending its scope felt that the Commission should exercise very great caution. State officials who might enjoy immunity *ratione personae* had been cited, for example, ministers of defence, ministers of foreign trade, Presidents of Parliaments, Vice-Presidents and judges. The question of immunity for officials representing the constituent units of federal States had also been raised. Many members had proposed, as an alternative to listing State officials who enjoyed immunity *ratione personae*, the definition of criteria that could be invoked to determine the categories of eligible persons. He [the Special Rapporteur] suggested that, in deciding on the approach to be adopted, a more thorough analysis of the judgment rendered by the ICJ in the *Certain Questions of Mutual Assistance in Criminal Matters* case should be undertaken': Yearbook of the International Law Commission 2008, vol. I, at 232, para. 29. See also Yearbook of the International Law Commission 2008, vol. II, Part 2 (Report of the Commission to the General Assembly on the Work of its 60th Session), at 138–139, para. 290.
26   For a summary of the 2008 debate, see A/CN.4/606: Report of the International Law Commission on the Work of its 60th Session (2008): Topical Summary of the Discussion Held

Kolodkin's second report was dedicated to 'the scope of immunity of a State official from foreign criminal jurisdiction'. Presenting the various considerations at play and drawing upon a wealth of materials it concluded, inter alia, that

> State officials enjoy immunity *ratione materiae* from foreign criminal jurisdiction, i.e. immunity in respect of acts performed in an official capacity, since these acts are acts of the State which they serve itself;
>
> Immunity *ratione materiae* extends to *ultra vires* acts of officials and to their illegal acts;
>
> Immunity *ratione materiae* does not extend to acts which were performed by an official prior to his taking up office; a former official is protected by immunity *ratione materiae* in respect of acts performed by him during his time as an official in his capacity as an official;
>
> Immunity *ratione personae*, which is enjoyed by a narrow circle of high-ranking State officials, extends to illegal acts performed by an official both in an official and in a private capacity, including prior to taking office. This is what is known as absolute immunity; and
>
> Immunity is valid both during the period of an officials stay abroad and during the period of an officials stay in the territory of the State which he serves or served. Criminal procedure measures imposing an obligation on a foreign official violate the immunity which he enjoys, irrespective of whether this person is abroad or in the territory of his own State.[27]

As regards exceptions to immunity, the report concluded, inter alia, that '[t]he various rationales for exceptions to the immunity of State officials from foreign criminal jurisdiction are not sufficiently convincing', and that it was 'difficult to talk of exceptions to immunity as a norm of international law that has developed, in the same way as it cannot definitively be asserted that a trend toward the establishment of such a norm exists'.[28] The report continued, however: 'That States are undoubtedly entitled to establish restrictions on the immunity of their officials from the criminal jurisdiction of one another by concluding an international treaty is another matter'; and it added that '[i]n this regard, the Commission could consider, alongside the codification of customary international law currently in force, the question of drawing up an

---

      in the Sixth Committee of the General Assembly during its 63rd Session, Prepared by the Secretariat, at 18–21, paras 89–110, especially paras 89–90, 106–110.

27    A/CN.4/631: Yearbook of the International Law Commission 2010, vol. II, Part 1, at 425–426, para. 94 (b), (f), (g), (i) and (m).

28    Ibid., at 426, para. 94 (n) and (o).

optional protocol or model clauses on restricting or precluding the immunity of State officials from foreign criminal jurisdiction'.[29]

Kolodkin's third report was dedicated mostly to 'procedural aspects of immunity', including the timing of consideration of immunity; invocation of immunity; and waiver thereof. Such procedural aspects are of much importance in the present context.

In the plenary debate in 2011, controversy persisted as to the approach that the Commission should take with respect to the topic, that is, the extent to which it should codify customary international law or engage instead in progressive development of the law. In summarizing the debate, the Special Rapporteur noted, *inter alia*, that

> [o]pinions had varied on who should enjoy personal immunity. Claims that ministers of foreign affairs or even the troika did not or should not enjoy immunity could not, in his view, be supported by objective political and legal analysis. The debate had revealed little support for such a position within the Commission. Several members had said that the group of officials who enjoyed personal immunity should be restricted to the troika. However, he had already drawn attention to a ruling of the International Court of Justice suggesting that, in addition to the troika, other high-level officials enjoyed personal immunity. Several rulings of national courts which recognized that personal immunity was enjoyed not only by the troika, but also by other high-level officials, such as ministers of defence and ministers of trade, were based on that ruling. The favourable disposition of governments had been taken into account by national courts in reaching such decisions, which were now facts of law. The logic behind those decisions resulted in part from global changes: important State functions, including representation of the State in international relations, were no longer the exclusive preserve of the troika. He was not aware of any legal rulings to the effect that absolutely no officials other than the troika enjoyed personal immunity. To what extent, then, was a restrictive approach grounded in law?
>
> Several members of the Commission had underscored the need for care and rigour in addressing the issue, and that was obviously the right approach. Indeed, he had applied it in formulating the proposals in his preliminary report on establishing the criteria that high-level officials other than the troika had to meet in order to enjoy personal immunity and in the suggestion in his third report that a distinction should be

---

29   Ibid., at 425, para. 93.

made between such individuals and the troika for procedural aspects of immunity, despite the fact that personal immunity was the same for both groups.[30]

Kolodkin did not stand for re-election in 2011, and so was no longer a member of the Commission in 2012.[31] That year the Commission appointed a new Special Rapporteur, Professor Concepción Escobar Hernández. She has so far produced seven reports (2012–2019).

The new Special Rapporteur's first (preliminary) report in 2012 recalled the work on the topic during the quinquennium 2007–2011 and presented a roadmap of the issues to be considered going forward (namely, immunity *ratione personae* and immunity *ratione materiae*; implications of the international responsibility of the State and the international responsibility of individuals; and procedural aspects of immunity).[32] The report recognized that 'the topic of the immunity of State officials from foreign criminal jurisdiction is not without controversy',[33] and that 'the points of contention [...] should [be addressed] in a systematic, ordered and structured manner'.[34] As to whether to approach the topic from the perspective of *lex lata* or *lex ferenda*, the Special Rapporteur stated her opinion that 'the topic of the immunity of State officials from foreign criminal jurisdiction cannot be addressed through only one of these approaches' and that 'both aspects must be taken into account in the future work of the Commission'.[35] At the same time, the Special Rapporteur indicated that 'she fully realizes the usefulness of beginning with *lex lata* considerations and including an analysis *de lege ferenda* of some topics, as needed, at a later date', in order to 'make it possible to address the topic in a balanced manner'.[36] She added that this was 'fully consistent with the Commission's mandate to pursue simultaneously the codification and progressive development of international

---

30   Yearbook of the International Law Commission 2011, vol. I, at 286–287, paras 22–23 (also noting at para. 24 that 'The most serious differences of opinion related to exceptions to immunity').
31   Kolodkin was re-elected by the Commission in a by-election in 2015, and again by the General Assembly in 2016. Upon returning to the Commission, although no longer Special Rapporteur, he took a full part in the consideration of the topic. In October 2017 he became a judge on the International Tribunal for the Law of the Sea, resigning from the Commission before its 2018 session.
32   A/CN.4/654: Yearbook of the International Law Commission 2012, vol. II, Part 1, at 41–51.
33   Ibid., at 47, para. 50.
34   Ibid., at 50, para. 72.
35   Ibid., at 51, para. 77.
36   Ibid.

law'.³⁷ Several members of the Commission expressed concern, however, at the Special Rapporteur's reference to '[all the] principles, values and interests of the international community as a whole' as a general normative framework.³⁸ For them, such a vague framework risked introducing a highly subjective element to the work.³⁹

The second report (2013) delineated the suggested scope of the topic, distinguished between the concepts of immunity and jurisdiction, and then focused on immunity *ratione personae* (and proposed six draft articles).⁴⁰ In the debate on the second report that year, concern was again expressed about a 'values-based' approach.

The Special Rapporteur's third report (2014) sought to mark the starting point for the consideration of the 'normative elements' of immunity *ratione materiae*.⁴¹ It discussed the concept of an 'official', and described terms employed to designate the persons to whom immunity *ratione materiae* would apply. In referring to the subjective scope of such immunity, the report proposed a draft article to the effect that 'State officials who exercise governmental authority benefit from immunity *ratione materiae* in regard to the exercise of foreign criminal jurisdiction'.⁴²

---

37   Ibid.
38   For example, ibid., at 48, para. 57.
39   See, for example, Yearbook of the International Law Commission 2012, vol. I, at 98, para. 15 (Mr. Nolte saying that 'the 'value' argument could not be so easily transposed to the rules and principles of international law. Rules of international law, such as the rules on immunity, also represented values. It was not sufficient simply to balance values against each other; such a balancing process must take place within the framework of general rules relating to the formation and evidence of customary international law. Needless to say, the Commission would also have to discuss in greater depth the more or less legal nature of the values to which the Special Rapporteur was referring'), at 11, para. 57 (Mr. Wisnumurti saying that 'it was necessary to be cautious about what was meant by that phrase [i.e. 'the principles and values of the international community']; a broad interpretation would be counterproductive'). But see at 116, para. 17 (Mr. McRae opining that 'in fact the Commission constantly referred to [values and principles of international law], because legal discourse was implicitly or explicitly all about values. The question at the heart of the topic under consideration, namely whether the value of relations between States took precedence over the value of combating impunity, was fundamentally a debate about the international community's values and principles. Legal language and methodology masked, but did not obliterate, the essential policy choices which were made individually and collectively in the course of a debate. The only current difference was that the Special Rapporteur admitted that state of affairs quite openly').
40   A/CN.4/661.
41   A/CN.4/673.
42   Ibid., at para. 151.

The fourth report (2015) sought to cover additional aspects of the material scope of immunity *ratione materiae*, namely, what constituted an 'act performed in an official capacity', and its temporal scope.[43] The Special Rapporteur emphasized that characterization of the subjective, material and temporal scope of immunity *ratione materiae* as 'the normative elements' of this type of immunity 'should not be read as a pronouncement on exceptions to immunity or as recognition that it is absolute or limitless in nature'.[44]

In her fifth report (2016), the Special Rapporteur sought to cover 'the limitations and exceptions to the immunity of State officials from foreign criminal jurisdiction'.[45] As we shall see, the fifth report (and draft Art. 7 proposed therein) gave rise to heated debate within the Commission and among States.

The Special Rapporteur's sixth report became available towards the end of the 2018 session.[46] While it began to discuss certain procedural issues, it did so in general terms; there were no proposals for draft articles. The debate within the Commission on the sixth report began at the end of the 2018 session and is to continue in 2019, together with the debate on her seventh report, which makes specific proposals on procedural matters (A/CN.4/729).

## III  Draft Articles 1–6

As of June 2019, the Commission has provisionally adopted, on first reading, seven draft articles with commentaries, one of which (on definitions) is still to be completed.[47]

---

43  A/CN.4/686.
44  Ibid., at para. 20.
45  A/CN.4/701.
46  A/CN.4/722.
47  See Commission's Annual Reports for 2013 (A/68/10), 2014 (A/69/10), 2016 (A/71/10), and 2017 (A/72/10):
Draft Art. 1: Scope of the present draft articles (Yearbook of the International Law Commission 2013, vol. II, Part 2, at 39–43);
Draft Art. 2 (e): State official (ILC Report 2014, at 231–236);
Draft Art. 2 (f): Act performed in an official capacity (ILC Report 2016, at 353–359);
Draft Art. 3: Persons enjoying immunity *ratione personae* (Yearbook of the International Law Commission 2013, vol. II, Part 2, at 43–47);
Draft Art. 4: Scope of immunity *ratione personae* (Yearbook of the International Law Commission 2013, vol. II, Part 2, at 47–50);
Draft Art. 5: Persons enjoying immunity *ratione materiae* (ILC Report 2014, at 236–237);
Draft Art. 6: Scope of immunity *ratione materiae* (ILC Report 2016, at 359–363);
Draft Art. 7: Crimes under international law in respect of which immunity *ratione materiae* shall not apply (ILC Report 2017, at 177–191).

The present section briefly describes draft Articles 1–6. The next two sections turn to draft Art. 7: Section IV describes the provisional adoption of the draft article; and Section V addresses some important issues to which its adoption gives rise. Section VI seeks to draw some lessons from the work on this topic to date.

*Draft Art. 1* addresses the scope of the draft articles. Para. 1 makes it clear that the draft articles cover immunity 'from the criminal jurisdiction of another State', that is, not from the jurisdiction of an international criminal court or tribunal; and para. 2 provides that the draft articles are without prejudice to the immunity enjoyed under special rules of international law. It gives a non-exhaustive list, referring to persons connected with diplomatic missions, consular posts, special missions, international organizations and military forces.[48] Such special rules include both treaty rules and rules of customary international law (for example, the immunity of persons on special missions both under the 1969 Convention on Special Missions and under customary international law).

*Draft Art. 2* so far only contains two definitions, of 'State official' and of 'act performed in an official capacity'. These are arguably unnecessary, but if retained they must of course be correct, and properly described in the commentary.

*Para. (e)* defines 'State official' to mean 'any individual who represents the State or who exercises State functions'. This is broad, covering both representation and the exercise of functions. The words 'any individual' imply that any person who exercises State functions is covered, even if he or she does not have the status of an official under national law.[49]

*Para. (f)* defines an 'act performed in an official capacity' to mean 'any act performed by a State official in the exercise of State authority'. Members of the

---

48   Draft Art. 1 reads:
     '1. The present draft articles apply to the immunity of State officials from the criminal jurisdiction of another State.
     2. The present draft articles are without prejudice to the immunity from criminal jurisdiction enjoyed under special rules of international law, in particular by persons connected with diplomatic missions, consular posts, special missions, international organizations and military forces of a State'.

49   Clarity is not, however, enhanced by the following remark in paragraph (9) of the commentary to draft Art. 2 (f): 'although the definition contained in draft article 2 (f) concerns an "act performed in an official capacity", the Commission considered it necessary to include in the definition an explicit reference to the author of the act, in other words, the State official. It thereby draws attention to the fact that only a State official can perform an act in an official capacity, thus reflecting the need for a link between the author of the act and the State' (A/71/10, at 356).

Commission, and States in the Sixth Committee, questioned the need for any such definition. The lengthy commentary to draft Art. 2 (f) raises some potentially difficult questions, which were picked up in the Sixth Committee:

> While support was expressed by some delegations for draft article 2 (f) [...] doubt was also expressed about the necessity of such a definition. The suggestion was made to broaden the scope to comprise all functions by State officials acting in their official capacity. Some delegations encouraged further analysis of various aspects of this definition, including: the legal regime concerning *de facto* officials acting under governmental direction and control; of the relationship between immunity and acts *iure gestionis*; of acts performed in an official capacity but for personal gain; and whether acts *ultra vires* could be considered official acts for purposes of immunity. Further clarification on the relationship between immunity *ratione materiae* and the attribution of conduct to a State under the law of State responsibility was also sought.[50]

One point is worth noting in particular. Unlike the previous Special Rapporteur, Professor Escobar Hernández had indicated that in her view *ultra vires* acts could not be official acts, and this was reflected in her draft commentary. Following discussion in plenary,[51] a revised draft commentary was adopted that concluded that '[t]he question whether or not acts *ultra vires* can be considered as official acts for the purpose of immunity from criminal jurisdiction will be addressed at a later stage, together with the limitations and exceptions to immunity'.[52]

Other definitions may be needed, including of 'immunity from criminal jurisdiction'. It is not yet entirely clear whether the expression includes inviolability.[53]

*Draft Art. 3*, entitled 'Persons enjoying immunity *ratione personae*', provides that 'Heads of State, Heads of Government and Ministers for Foreign Affairs enjoy immunity *ratione personae* from the exercise of foreign criminal jurisdiction'. There was significant disagreement within the Commission on this issue, both as to what the law is, and what it should be.

---

50  A/CN.4/703: Report of the International Law Commission on the Work of 68th Session (2016): Topical Summary of the Discussion Held in the Sixth Committee of the General Assembly during its 71st Session, Prepared by the Secretariat, at para. 53.
51  A/CN.4/SR.3345, at 15–16.
52  A/CN.4/SR.3346, at 6–7.
53  ILC Report 2017 (A/72/10), at para. 130.

In her second report in 2013, the Special Rapporteur recalled her suggested general analytical framework of 'all the norms, principles and values of international law that are relevant to the topic'.[54] She described both what she referred to as 'a strict interpretation that links and restricts immunity *ratione personae* to Heads of State, Heads of Government and ministers for foreign affairs' and 'a broader interpretation whereby immunity might also be enjoyed by other senior State officials, including, as often suggested, other members of the Government such as ministers of defence, ministers of trade and other ministers whose office requires them to play some role in international relations, either generally or in specific international forums, and who must therefore travel outside the borders of their own country in order to perform their functions'.[55] Then, based on a reading of the *Arrest Warrant* and *Certain Questions of Mutual Assistance in Criminal Matters* judgments of the International Court of Justice[56] and of State practice,[57] and because of 'the impossibility of drawing up an exhaustive list',[58] the Special Rapporteur 'consider[ed] that the subjective scope of immunity from foreign criminal jurisdiction *ratione personae should* be limited to Heads of State, Heads of Government and ministers for foreign affairs'.[59]

Within the Commission, different views were expressed as to which State officials enjoy immunity *ratione personae*. Several members expressed disagreement with the Special Rapporteur's 'restrictive approach', suggesting that the relevant international practice was not fully or accurately discussed in her report. In particular, attention was drawn to the International Court's pronouncement in the *Arrest Warrant* and *Certain Questions of Mutual Assistance in Criminal Matters* cases that 'in international law it is firmly established that, as also diplomatic and consular agents, certain holders of high-ranking office in a State, *such as* the Head of State, Head of Government and Minister for Foreign Affairs, enjoy immunities from jurisdiction in other States, both civil and criminal',[60] and to the significant endorsement of this view by States (including national courts). Against this background, the Special Rapporteur summarized the debate by stating her understanding that the Commission

---

54   A/CN.4/661, at para. 7 (c).
55   Ibid., at paras 57–62.
56   Ibid., at para. 62.
57   Ibid., at para. 63.
58   Ibid., at para. 64.
59   Ibid., at para. 67 (emphasis added).
60   *Arrest Warrant of 11 April 2000 (Democratic Republic of the Congo v. Belgium)* [2002] ICJ Rep 3, at 20–21, para. 51; *Certain Questions of Mutual Assistance in Criminal Matters (Djibouti v. France)* [2008] ICJ Rep 177, at 236–237, para. 170 (emphasis added).

should approach the matter 'from the dual perspective of *lex lata* and *lege ferenda*'.[61]

Eventually, the Commission provisionally adopted a draft article that specifies that Heads of State, Heads of Government and Ministers for Foreign Affairs enjoy immunity *ratione personae* from the exercise of foreign criminal jurisdiction, but does not refer to other holders of high-ranking office.

While the debates in the Commission's Drafting Committee are not public, the Statement of the Chairman of the Drafting Committee to the plenary indicates that the text provisionally adopted by the Drafting Committee (and eventually by the Commission on first reading) was the result of a compromise and did not reflect a consensus as to the content of existing law:

> Several members indicated that, contrary to the draft article proposed by the Special Rapporteur, immunity *ratione personae* now extends beyond the *troika* as there was practice to that effect. On the other hand, some other members disputed whether Ministers for Foreign Affairs enjoy immunity *ratione personae* under customary international law. This matter was raised in the Drafting Committee. The commentary will provide examples of State practice and case law in respect of the *troika*. In provisionally adopting the text of draft article 3 limited to the *troika*, it was recognized that other high-ranking officials of the State may benefit from immunity under rules of international law relating to special missions. The commentary to draft article 3 would clarify this point.
>
> A reservation was nevertheless expressed regarding draft article 3 as a whole. It was contended that the Drafting Committee, as well as the Commission in Plenary, had not given adequate consideration to whether the list of persons in draft article 3 precisely reflected the state of international law on this subject. Such a point of view was opposed by some members.[62]

*Draft Art. 4* concerns the scope of immunity *ratione personae*.[63] The Special Rapporteur's fifth report 'concluded that it had not been possible to determine the existence of a customary rule that allowed for the application of limitations or exceptions in respect of immunity *ratione personae*, or to identify a

---

61  Yearbook of the International Law Commission 2013, vol. I, at 41, para. 4 (3170th meeting).
62  Statement of the Chairman of the Drafting Committee, Mr. Dire Tladi (7 June 2013), at 11–13. See also the commentary to draft Art. 3: A/68/10, Yearbook of the International Law Commission 2013, vol. II, Part 2, at 45–46, para. (8).
63  Draft Art. 4 reads:
    '1. Heads of State, Heads of Government and Ministers for Foreign Affairs enjoy immunity *ratione personae* only during their term of office.

trend in favour of such a rule'.[64] Under the draft article, as under customary international law, immunity *ratione personae* during the term of office covers all acts, whether performed in a private or official capacity and whether carried out before or during office.

*Draft Art. 5*, entitled 'Persons enjoying immunity *ratione materiae*', is the first of the draft articles on immunity *ratione materiae* and is intended to define the persons who enjoy this category of immunity from foreign criminal jurisdiction. It provides that 'State officials acting as such enjoy immunity *ratione materiae* from the exercise of foreign criminal jurisdiction'.[65] This fairly straightforward formulation was adopted in 2014 without prejudice to possible exceptions to immunity *ratione materiae*, which were to be taken up later.[66]

In the following year (2015), discussion of the scope of immunity *ratione materiae* commenced, but could not be concluded. The Commission's report of that year does mention that, again,

> [t]he view was [...] expressed that it was necessary to strike a balance between fighting impunity and preserving stability in inter-State relations. In such circumstances, it was considered essential that there be transparency and an informed debate on whatever choices were to be made and on the direction to be taken.[67]

*Draft Art. 6*, adopted in 2016, was generally uncontroversial. Entitled 'Scope of immunity *ratione materiae*', it provides that:
1. State officials enjoy immunity *ratione materiae* only with respect to acts performed in an official capacity.
2. Immunity *ratione materiae* with respect to acts performed in an official capacity continues to subsist after the individuals concerned have ceased to be State officials.
3. Individuals who enjoyed immunity *ratione personae* in accordance with draft article 4, whose term of office has come to an end, continue to enjoy

---

2. Such immunity *ratione personae* covers all acts performed, whether in a private or official capacity, by Heads of State, Heads of Government and Ministers for Foreign Affairs during or prior to their term of office.
3. The cessation of immunity *ratione personae* is without prejudice to the application of the rules of international law concerning immunity *ratione materiae*'.

64  A/72/10, at 166, para. 83.
65  A/69/10, at 236.
66  Ibid., at 237, para. (5).
67  A/70/10, at 121, para. 194.

immunity with respect to acts performed in an official capacity during such term of office.[68]

## IV    Draft Art. 7: Provisional Adoption

*Draft Art. 7*, entitled 'Crimes under international law in respect of which immunity *ratione materiae* shall not apply', was highly controversial within the Commission and among States. The divisions go back to the debates on Kolodkin's reports in 2008 and 2011, but they were particularly acute in the debates in 2016/2017 and 2018, concerning the second Special Rapporteur's fifth report (2016) and her proposal for a draft Art. 7 on 'limitations and exceptions'[69] to immunity *ratione materiae*.[70]

---

68    A/71/10, at 359.
69    For an explanation of the terms 'limitations' and 'exceptions', see paragraphs (11)–(13) of the commentary to draft Art. 7: A/72/10, at 183–184. The Special Rapporteur's use of these terms was not entirely straightforward. She appeared to distinguish between cases where there is no immunity because the alleged offence was not an official act (or should be deemed not to be an official act), so no question of immunity *ratione materiae* could arise ('limitations'); and cases where specific crimes were to be excluded from immunity *ratione materiae* because, although they were official acts, they fell within one or more exceptions to immunity. In her view, draft Art. 7 was worded ('shall not apply') so that the listed crimes might be viewed in either way. See, for example, her explanation of this '[idea] central to the report': ibid., at 166, para. 80 ('she noted that the phrase "limitations and exceptions" echoed the different arguments put forward in practice for the non-application of immunity. The Special Rapporteur stressed that the distinction between limitations and exceptions, despite its theoretical and normative value for the systemic interpretation of the immunity regime, had no practical significance, as "limitations" or "exceptions" led to the same consequence, namely the non-application of the legal regime of the immunity of State officials from foreign criminal jurisdiction in a particular case'). See also ibid., at 174, para. 135 ('The Special Rapporteur reiterated her position that the distinction between limitations and exceptions, as set out in the report, helped to illuminate the concept of immunity of State officials and its role within the international legal system. In her view, that approach was not incompatible with the pragmatic formulation of draft article 7, which focused on the situation in which immunity "does not apply"; rather, that formulation avoided a number of controversies relating to the distinction between limitations and exceptions and found its basis in practice'); and at 167, 171, paras 86, 117–118 ('A number of members considered that the distinction between limitations and exceptions was useful and should be maintained. It helped to distinguish situations in which immunity was not at issue, because the relevant conduct could not be considered as an official act or as performed in official capacity, from cases in which immunity was excluded on the basis of exceptional circumstances […]. Some members noted that a distinction might provide theoretical clarity, but that it had no basis in the practice of States').
70    Draft Art. 7 as proposed by the Special Rapporteur in her fifth report (A/CN.4/701, at 95) read:

LESSONS FROM THE ILC'S WORK ON 'IMMUNITY OF STATE OFFICIALS' 53

In her fifth report, the Special Rapporteur acknowledged the limited and divergent State practice and referred to a 'trend', which suggested that her proposed draft Art. 7 was at most *lex ferenda*.[71] The Special Rapporteur indicated that, in her view,

> the Commission should approach the topic of immunity from foreign criminal jurisdiction, and in particular the question of limitations and exceptions, *from the perspectives of both codification and the progressive development of international law*. The challenge for the Commission was to decide whether to support a developing trend in the field of immunity, or whether to halt such development.[72]

Draft Art. 7 lies at the heart of the topic. In the debate in plenary, which for exceptional reasons stretched over two sessions (with a different membership), a good number of Commission members did not support reference of the Special Rapporteur's proposed draft Art. 7 to the Drafting Committee.[73] They and others did not accept the Special Rapporteur's assertion, from time to time, that her proposed draft article reflected existing customary international law; in their view, the various materials cited did not in fact support such a position.[74] The Special Rapporteur's alternative claim, that there was a 'trend' in the direction of her draft, was also strongly contested. These views

---

    'Crimes in respect of which immunity does not apply
    1. Immunity shall not apply in relation to the following crimes:
        i. Genocide, crimes against humanity, war crimes, torture and enforced disappearances;
       ii. Crime of corruption;
       iii. Crimes that cause harm to persons, including death and serious injury, or to property, when such crimes are committed in the territory of the forum State and the State official is present in said territory at the time that such crimes are committed.
    2. Paragraph 1 shall not apply to persons who enjoy immunity *ratione personae* during their term of office.
    3. Paragraphs 1 and 2 are without prejudice to:
       i. Any provision of a treaty that is binding on the forum State and the State of the official, under which immunity would not be applicable;
       ii. The obligation to cooperate with an international tribunal which, in each case, requires compliance by the forum State'.

71    Ibid., at 73, para. 179.
72    A/72/10, at 167, para. 84 (emphasis added).
73    Discussion on whether or not to refer draft Art. 7 to the Drafting Committee was cut short by a motion by one member to end the discussion, which was carried by a vote (see A/CN.4/SR.3365, at 18).
74    See summary of the debate in the Commission in 2016 (A/71/10, at 346–347, paras 214–220) and 2017 (A/72/10, at 168–169, paras 92–101); Tladi, 'The International Law Commission's

were repeated in the Drafting Committee, with some members urging that the draft article not be reported back to the plenary pending consideration of procedural safeguards that may prevent abuse of any exceptions to immunity.

The debate in the Sixth Committee in 2016 was necessarily preliminary since the Commission itself had only begun (but not completed) its own debate on the Special Rapporteur's fifth report; many delegations preferred to await the completion of the work on the fifth report within the Commission. Nevertheless, those who spoke 'observed that the topic involved fundamental principles of real practical significance for States, and urged the Commission to proceed cautiously and accurately'.[75] The Commission's Secretariat summarized the debate in 2016 as follows:

> Some delegations stressed the need to develop the topic focusing on the *lex lata*, while other delegations emphasized the need to also progressively develop this area of the law. Some delegations suggested that the Commission should consider the *lex lata* first prior to attempting to develop the topic *lex ferenda*; and some delegations observed that a clearer distinction between what was *lex lata* and *lex ferenda* within the draft articles was warranted. Several delegations emphasized that developments in international law must be taken into account when addressing the issue of exceptions, in particular international criminal law. However, a number of delegations were of the view that the customary international law rules on immunity of State officials did not recognize any exceptions to immunity and that no clear trend towards such a development had emerged.[76]

The revised draft Art. 7 that emerged from the Drafting Committee in 2017,[77] though somewhat more limited in substance, remained unacceptable to a significant number of Commission members. Nevertheless, after much debate, draft Art. 7 was provisionally adopted by the Commission by a recorded vote

---

Recent Work on Exceptions to Immunity: Charting the Course for a Brave New World in International Law?', supra note 3, at 8–11.

75   A/CN.4/703: Report of the International Law Commission on the Work of its 68th Session (2016): Topical Summary of the Discussion Held in the Sixth Committee of the General Assembly during its 71st Session, Prepared by the Secretariat, at para. 51.

76   Ibid., at para. 52. See also paras 55–56.

77   From the earliest days, the Commission's Drafting Committee has engaged in much more than drafting: see H.W. Briggs, *The International Law Commission* (Cornell University Press 1965), at 233–236. On the Drafting Committee generally, see the UN Secretariat's publication *The Work of the International Law Commission* (9th edn 2017), at 33–34.

(21 in favour, eight against, one abstention). This was striking: voting on core issues is nowadays very exceptional in the Commission. In the early years of its activity there was fairly frequent recourse to voting,[78] but over time voting as a method for adopting proposed texts had virtually died out.[79] Instead, efforts are made to reach a consensus and these are pursued as far as possible. But on this occasion, some members were not willing to postpone a decision until 2018, when the matter could have been considered together with procedural safeguards that may assist in preventing abuse of any exceptions that might be proposed.

Draft Art. 7, as provisionally adopted in 2017, lists six exceptions to immunity *ratione materiae*:

1. Immunity *ratione materiae* from the exercise of foreign criminal jurisdiction shall not apply in respect of the following crimes under international law:
   (a) crime of genocide;
   (b) crimes against humanity;
   (c) war crimes;
   (d) crime of apartheid;
   (e) torture;
   (f) enforced disappearance.

2. For the purposes of the present draft article, the crimes under international law mentioned above are to be understood according to their definition in the treaties enumerated in the annex to the present draft articles.[80]

The six exceptions are defined by reference to definitions in existing treaties. That is the purpose of para. 2 of the draft conclusion and the annex.[81] Whether definition by reference to existing instruments is a good technique may be debated: States that are not parties to the treaties to which reference is made may not wish to see them referred to in this way. But it is certainly convenient, and

---

78   I. Sinclair, *The International Law Commission* (Grotius Publications 1987), at 34.

79   See also L.T. Lee, 'The International Law Commission Re-Examined' (1965) 59 American Journal of International Law 545, at 550 ('The recent thawing of the Cold War has also produced an impact upon the Commission. Instead of settling an issue by majority vote, the Commission would devote lengthy sessions to resolve differences so that in the end a Quaker-like spirit for compromise and consensus could prevail. In this task, the Commission is well aided by its Drafting Committee—actually a misnomer, since its activities often concern substance instead of mere form').

80   See A/72/10, at 177–178. The annex lists certain multilateral treaties containing definitions of the listed crimes, which definitions are thus incorporated by reference into the draft articles.

81   See also ibid., at 189–191, paras (25) to (35).

avoids either the use of just the names of the crimes (as originally proposed by the Special Rapporteur) or a very lengthy set of definitions that might have dominated what is otherwise a relatively concise text.

Draft Art. 7 does not apply to persons while they enjoy immunity *ratione personae*. Nor does it apply to those subject to a special regime, such as persons connected with diplomatic missions, consular posts, special missions, and the military: this is clear from draft Art. 1.

Following the provisional adoption of draft Art. 7 by vote, the Commission proceeded to adopt a lengthy and contested commentary. The commentary, like the plenary debate and the votes, indicates clearly the differences within the Commission.[82] The divisions within the Commission are clear from the following:

- The Commission debate on Kolodkin's first report in 2008.[83]
- The Commission debate on Kolodkin's second report in 2011.[84]
- The partial debate within the Commission on Escobar Hernández's fifth report in 2016[85] and its completion in 2017.[86]
- The 20 July 2017 statement of the Chairperson of the Drafting Committee.[87]
- The adoption of draft Art. 7 by recorded vote on 20 July 2017, and the explanations of vote before and after the vote.[88]

---

82   The divisions within the Commission may perhaps best seen in paragraphs (5) to (8) of the commentary to draft Art. 7, with lengthy footnotes referring to and questioning the materials relied upon by the Special Rapporteur (A/72/10, at 178–183). Paragraphs (5) to (7) set out the views of those supporting the draft, though how far they really represent all their views is far from clear having regard to what was said in the plenary debate on the fifth report in 2016/2017; paragraph (8) sets out the views of those who opposed draft Art. 7.

83   See Yearbook of the International Law Commission 2008, vol. I, at 169–234; and the summary of the debate provided in Chapter X of the Commission's 2008 Annual Report (A/63/10).

84   See Yearbook of the International Law Commission 2011, vol. I, at 37–72, 249–251, 266–290; and the summary of the debate provided in Chapter VII of the Commission's 2011 Annual Report (A/66/10).

85   For the partial debate, see summary records of the Commission's meetings on 26 to 29 July 2016 (A/CN.4/SR.3328–3331); and the summary in Chapter XI of the Commission's 2016 Annual Report (A/71/10).

86   See summary records of the Commission's meetings on 18, 19, 23, 24, 26 and 30 May 2017 (A/CN.4/SR.3360–3365); and the summary in Chapter VII of the 2017 Annual Report (A/72/10).

87   See A/CN.4/SR.3378, at 3–9; for the verbatim text see http://legal.un.org/docs/?path=../ilc/documentation/english/statements/2017_dc_chairman_statement_iso.pdf&lang=EXXX (accessed 27 March 2019).

88   A/CN.4/SR.3378, at 9–16.

- The consideration of the Special Rapporteur's draft commentary on draft Art. 7 at plenary meetings on 3 and 4 August 2017.[89]
- The Commission's partial debate on the Special Rapporteur's sixth report in 2018.[90]

The two main views within the Commission were strongly put, and diametrically opposed. It is not obvious how they can be reconciled. The Special Rapporteur's seventh report in 2019, which proposes procedural provisions, will be important. Commission members who do not accept that draft Art. 7 is a statement of existing law might be ready to work on it as a proposal for new law, to be put to States for adoption (with or without amendment) or rejection as they see fit. This could be done by preparing draft articles explicitly intended to become a treaty. Some members did not wish to take the Special Rapporteur's proposed draft article further unless she made it clear that such should be the Commission's aim: their concern was that, otherwise, the draft article might be viewed by national courts as reflecting customary international law. Even then there would remain a risk that national courts might regards a proposal for a treaty as an indication of existing law or of a 'trend' upon which they might feel empowered to build.[91]

The Sixth Committee debate in 2017 revealed very divided views among States with regard to draft Art. 7. The following points emerged:[92]

---

89  A/CN.4/SR.3387 (3 August 2017); A/CN.4/SR.3388 (3 August 2017); A/CN.4/SR.3389 (4 August 2017). A comparison of the Special Rapporteur's draft commentary (in A/CN4/L.903/Add.2) and the commentary as adopted, as well as what was said in the debate on adoption of the commentary, is highly revealing.

90  See summary records of the Commission's meetings on 30 and 31 July (A/CN.4/SR.3438-3440); and A/73/10, Chapter XI.

91  Whether national courts should be at the forefront of the development of international law is questionable. The English courts have rejected any such role: see, for example, *Jones v Saudi Arabia* [2006] UKHL 26, para. 63 (Lord Hoffmann (with whom other Law Lords agreed) noting that international law 'is based upon the common consent of nations' and adding that '[i]t is not for a national court to "develop" international law by unilaterally adopting a version of that law which, however desirable, forward-looking and reflective of values it may be, is simply not accepted by other states').

92  See also A/CN.4/713: Report of the International Law Commission on the Work of its 69th Session (2017): Topical Summary of the Discussion Held in the Sixth Committee of the General Assembly during its 72nd Session, Prepared by the Secretariat, at 10–13, paras 29–44; J. Barkholdt and J. Kulaga, 'Analytical Presentation of the Comments and Observations by States on Draft Art. 7, Paragraph 1, of the ILC Draft Articles on Immunity of State Officials from Foreign Criminal Jurisdiction, United Nations General Assembly, Sixth Committee, 2017', KFG Working Paper Series, No. 14, Berlin Potsdam Research Group 'The International Rule of Law: Rise or Decline?' (April 2018).

- Very few States considered that draft Art. 7 reflected customary international law.
- Even if a slight majority seemed to support draft Art. 7 in some form or another, most of the supporters considered it was a proposal *de lege ferenda*.
- A considerable number of States asked the Commission to be clear about whether it considered draft Art. 7 to be *lex lata* or *lex ferenda*.
- A significant minority opposed draft Art. 7.
- The list of exceptions in draft Art. 7 was strongly criticized on various grounds.
- A very large majority considered that, if draft Art. 7 were to be adopted, there must be procedural safeguards to prevent the abuse of any exceptions that may be proposed.
- Some States urged the Commission to continue its efforts to seek to achieve a consensus.

Speakers in the Sixth Committee debate in 2018 continued to express deep concern about the topic in general and draft Art. 7 in particular.[93] For example, Algeria was of the view that '[o]wing to its complexity and political sensitivity, the topic "Immunity of State officials from foreign criminal jurisdiction" should be addressed with extreme caution'.[94] Australia 'remained unable to support that draft article [7], which had been provisionally adopted by a vote in the absence of a consensus, and continued to share concerns that, in its current form, the draft article did not reflect any real trend in State practice and, still less, existing customary international law'.[95] And the US representative said that

> [t]he Commission's categorical pronouncements in terms of immunity *ratione materiae* could not be said to rest upon customary international law. In particular, her delegation did not agree that draft article 7 of the draft articles provisionally adopted by the Commission at its sixty-ninth session was based on a clear trend in State practice.[96]

For Belarus, 'the only acceptable way of regulating immunity of State officials from foreign criminal jurisdiction was through the conclusion of an

---

93   A/CN.4/713: Report of the International Law Commission on the Work of its 70th Session (2018): Topical Summary of the Discussion Held in the Sixth Committee of the General Assembly during its 73rd Session, Prepared by the Secretariat, at paras 17, 30 et seq.
94   A/C.6/73/30, at para. 87 (Algeria).
95   A/C.6/73/30, at para. 36 (Australia).
96   A/C.6/73/29, at para. 38 (US).

international treaty'.[97] Indeed, the opposition by States to draft Art. 7 remained as strong as ever in 2018. It was summed up by the representative of Egypt:

> [H]is delegation did not concur with the Special Rapporteur's endeavour to formulate principles that would entail exceptions to the immunity granted to certain State officials. It therefore completely rejected draft article 7, which was not based on any existing international law or custom, or any tangible trend in State practice, or any international legal opinions. It amounted to a proposal for a completely new law, rather than the codification of existing international law or its progressive development. If the Commission wished to propose a new law, there was nothing to prevent it from formulating a model draft article which interested States could consider including in any treaty that they might conclude. Moreover, there were no clear legal criteria for the determination of the crimes listed in paragraph 1 of the draft article. The list clearly reflected political priorities and was largely based on the Rome Statute of the International Criminal Court, which had not been universally ratified. The Commission should therefore review draft article 7 in whole, and perhaps consider removing it entirely; it could not be accepted in its current form.[98]

## v    Draft Art. 7: Some Questions

Draft Art. 7 raises at least three important questions:
- Is it a codification of existing law (*lex lata*) or progressive development of the law/new law (*lex ferenda/lex nova*)? And linked to that, should the Commission make that explicit? Similarly, if draft Art. 7 were eventually to be adopted by the Commission, should the Commission recommend the adoption of a treaty?
- Should draft Art. 7 list less, more, or different exceptions?
- If exceptions are recommended by the Commission, what procedural safeguards should also be suggested?

### 1    *Is Draft Art. 7* lex lata *or* lex ferenda?

The weight to be given to the Commission's drafts as an aid to determining customary international law is not the same in all cases. Bearing in mind its dual object of codification and progressive development, a first question is whether

---

97    A/C.6/73/29, at para. 89 (Belarus).
98    A/C.6/73/30, at para. 66 (Egypt).

the Commission is claiming to state a rule of existing law (*lex lata*) or to make a proposal *de lege ferenda* or for new law (although it may well be silent about that). Even where it does claim to be stating existing law,

> [t]he weight to be given to the Commission's determinations [affirming the existence and content of a rule of customary international law or concluding that no such rule exists] depends [...] on various factors, including the sources relied upon by the Commission, the stage reached in its work, and above all upon States' reception of its output.[99]

The first Special Rapporteur's second report stated that there were no exceptions to immunity (*ratione personae* and *ratione materiae*) of State officials under the *lex lata* (except, possibly, a 'territorial crime' exception).[100]

The second Special Rapporteur's fifth report was less clear. In places, she suggested that there were 'limitations or exceptions' under the *lex lata* for certain core crimes (genocide, crimes against humanity, war crimes) and possibly also for the 'crime of corruption' and what she referred to as 'territorial tort' crimes. In other places, she suggested that there was merely a 'trend' in this direction. In introducing the report in 2017, the Special Rapporteur said that

> the report concluded that limitations and exceptions to the immunity of State officials from foreign criminal jurisdiction were extant in the context of immunity *ratione materiae* ['*se concluía que existían límites y excepciones a la inmunidad de jurisdicción penal extranjera de los funcionarios del Estado en relación con la inmunidad* ratione materiae'].

---

99  Para. (2) of the introductory commentary to Part Five of the Commission's 2018 conclusions on *Identification of customary international law*. The full passage reads: 'The output of the International Law Commission itself merits special consideration in the present context. As has been recognized by the International Court of Justice and other courts and tribunals, a determination by the Commission affirming the existence and content of a rule of customary international law may have particular value, as may a conclusion by it that no such rule exists. This flows from the Commission's unique mandate, as a subsidiary organ of the United Nations General Assembly, to promote the progressive development of international law and its codification; the thoroughness of its procedures (including the consideration of extensive surveys of State practice and *opinio juris*); and its close relationship with the General Assembly and States (including receiving oral and written comments from States as it proceeds with its work). The weight to be given to the Commission's determinations depends, however, on various factors, including the sources relied upon by the Commission, the stage reached in its work, and above all upon States' reception of its output': Report of the International Law Commission on the Work of its 70th Session (A/73/10), at 142–143, para. (2) (citations omitted)).

100  See supra note 28.

Although varied, the practice showed a clear trend towards considering the commission of international crimes as a bar to the application of immunity *ratione materiae* of State officials from foreign criminal jurisdiction, for the reason that such crimes did not constitute official acts, that the crimes concerned were grave or that they undermined the values and principles recognized by the international community as a whole.[101]

In summing up the plenary debate in 2017, while stressing the importance of national jurisprudence, the second Special Rapporteur admitted that 'it might have been limited and not sufficiently homogeneous'.[102]

As we have seen, the debates within the Commission in 2016/2017 and 2018 revealed very different views among members. Most speakers, even if supporting the inclusion of exceptions in the text to be developed by the Commission, did not consider that the second Special Rapporteur had made out a case for them to be considered as *lex lata*. The Special Rapporteur herself accepted that there was a general understanding that draft Art. 7 did not reflect customary international law.[103] She

> acknowledged the disagreement between members over a possible customary rule or emerging trend towards limitations and exceptions to immunity of State officials. She maintained that the Commission ought to focus on identifying the relevant rules *lex lata* and *lex ferenda* relating to immunity. [...] [T]he Special Rapporteur noted that the draft articles, like other projects of the Commission, contained elements of both codification and progressive development and that they should be assessed in that light.[104]

In any case, draft Art. 7 has so far been adopted on first reading only. As such, it does not represent the Commission's considered and final view, as to *lex lata* or otherwise. The commentary makes this abundantly clear.[105]

It is also noteworthy that the language of draft Art. 7 itself is essentially neutral on whether it is *lex lata* or new law. The wording 'shall not apply', however, sounds like treaty language, that is, like a proposed rule to be accepted or not by States. The first sentence of para. (1) of the commentary likewise suggests

---

101  A/72/10, at 166–167, para. 83.
102  Ibid., at 173, para. 132.
103  A/CN.4/SR.3388, at 4 (the Special Rapporteur suggesting that 'it had been generally agreed that a trend, rather than a norm of customary international law, could be identified').
104  A/72/10, at 174, para. 134.
105  See supra note 82.

that the exceptions are proposed for the purposes of the draft articles, not as a statement of general international law. It reads:

> Draft article 7 lists crimes under international law in respect of which immunity from foreign criminal jurisdiction *ratione materiae* shall not apply *under the present draft articles*[106] (emphasis added).

It was proposed that another sentence, based on the report of the Chairman of the Drafting Committee, be added at the end of para. (1) of the commentary, reading:

> The Commission proceeded in its work on the general understanding that the outcome of its work was without prejudice to, or taking a position on, the question whether the text of draft article 7, or any part thereof, codified existing law—reflecting *lex lata*—or whether the result constituted an exercise in progressive development, reflecting *lex ferenda*.[107]

Members of the Commission who opposed adding such a sentence did not do so because they disagreed with its substance.[108]

The lengthy commentary to draft Art. 7 reflects in unusual detail the different views within the Commission, including the view that the authorities cited (chiefly case-law and legislation) did not support the Special Rapporteur's views on the *lex lata* or the existence of a 'trend'.[109]

Writings on draft Art. 7 are similarly clear that it does not, and was not intended to, reflect existing customary international law.[110] Support within the

---

[106] A/72/10, at 168. The Special Rapporteur had proposed a different text: 'Draft article 7 refers to crimes under international law in respect of which immunity from foreign criminal jurisdiction *ratione materiae* does not apply'; for the extended debate over this change, see A/CN.4/SR.3387, at 10–13.

[107] A/CN.4/SR.3387, at 10 (Murphy).

[108] Ibid., at 13 ('Mr. Murphy said that his understanding of the views expressed was that those members who were opposed to his proposal for a third sentence objected to its placement rather than its content. He was prepared to withdraw the proposal in the interest of moving forward, even though it appeared to reflect the majority view of the Commission').

[109] See supra note 82.

[110] Murphy convincingly demonstrates, in respect of each of the six crimes listed in draft Art. 7, 'the lack of State practice—let alone widespread, representative, and consistent practice' ('Immunity Ratione Materiae of State Officials from Foreign Criminal Jurisdiction: Where is the State Practice in Support of the Exceptions?', supra note 3, at 4). His conclusion is as follows: 'All told, the State practice in support of the six exceptions listed in Draft Article 7 is not widespread, representative, or consistent. Rather than relying on existing practice, the Commission justifies Draft Article 7 on two grounds. First, it claims

Commission for the view that the exceptions reflect customary international law declined significantly between the 2011 debate and that in 2016/17:

> Whether, and how, the 'international crimes' exception can be framed in terms of existing customary international law is the central question in the debate triggered almost two decades ago by the *Pinochet* case, and nearly all members who participated in the ILC debates articulated a position on this point. The fact that almost 80 percent of members of the 2017 ILC were not prepared to adopt Draft Article 7 as existing law shows that the Rapporteur did not succeed in capitalizing on the majority consensus in the 2011 ILC in favor of a *lex lata* approach.[111]

## 2    Should Draft Art. 7 List Less, More, or Different Exceptions?

There was a widespread feeling in the Commission that the list of crimes in draft Art. 7 was drawn up without any well-developed criteria and simply reflected the personal preferences of some members.[112]

---

that there is a 'discernible trend' towards limiting such immunity, a claim that also is not borne out by the extremely limited practice cited. Second, the Commission claims that its draft articles must be shaped to fit 'an international legal order whose unity and systemic nature cannot be ignored'. That vague and cursory claim does not explain how the text of Draft Article 7 takes account of rules that seek to avoid interstate conflict, nor why some crimes are 'in' (apartheid) while other crimes are 'out' (slavery, trafficking in persons, aggression). What both claims do suggest, however, is that Draft Article 7 is not grounded in law, but in policymaking by the Commission. The divided views within the Sixth Committee appear to suggest the same. In that light, Draft Article 7 might be regarded as a proposal by the Commission for a new rule that could be embodied in a treaty, which states might choose to accept or reject. It cannot be regarded, however, as reflecting existing law' (at 8). See also Forteau, supra note 3: 'Does Draft Article 7 reflect customary law, or does it constitute progressive development of international law? For the Commission to consider that there is 'a discernible trend'—a view that many scholars agree with—is quite ambiguous in that regard. The reactions in the Commission and in the Sixth Committee tend to demonstrate the absence of a general *opinio juris* supporting Draft Article 7, which would then constitute progressive development, rather than codification, of international law' (at 24).

111   R. van Alebeek, 'The "International Crime" Exception to the ILC Draft Articles on the Immunity of State Officials from Foreign Criminal Jurisdiction: Two Steps Back?', supra note 3, at 32.

112   It does not help, indeed it confuses, to refer to this list as '*ius cogens* crimes': Tladi, 'The International Law Commission's Recent Work on Exceptions to Immunity: Charting the Course for a Brave New World in International Law?', supra note 3, at 3.

Some members suggested that the list of exceptions should be open-ended.[113] This approach, which would have introduced great uncertainty, was not accepted.

A minority within the Commission argued that the crime of *aggression* should be listed. Those opposed, including the Special Rapporteur, considered that attempts to prosecute State officials before national courts for the crime of aggression would contravene the sovereign equality of States, an issue that did not arise in the case of prosecution before an international court.[114]

Some Commission members suggested adding other crimes, including slavery, terrorism, and crimes against global cultural heritage.[115] In reply, 'the Special Rapporteur expressed her readiness to include the crime of *apartheid*, but continued to have reservations regarding the inclusion of other transnational crimes, as the latter were treaty based and did not derive from custom'.[116] The crime of *apartheid*, which the fifth report did not include in the list, was added by the Drafting Committee, but slavery, trafficking in persons, and other crimes identified in multilateral treaties, were not included. This is perhaps an example of what one member of the Commission referred to as 'arbitrary progressive development'.[117]

Although the fifth report proposed that the '*crime of corruption*' be listed as an exception, ultimately it was dropped.[118] A few members regretted this omission. The commentary asserts that the Commission's view is that the crime of corruption (understood as referring to 'grand corruption', which some regard as entailing a 'transnational' connection) involves an act that is not 'official' in nature, and therefore cannot attract immunity. But this seems hard to square with the 'limitations and exceptions' approach, unless 'limitations' refers only to acts that are in fact official acts but must for some reason be deemed not to be, a proposition for which there is no authority.

No member of the Commission argued for retention of what the fifth report termed the '*territorial tort exception*'.[119] According to the fifth report, the

---

113　See also A/72/10, at 172, para. 120.
114　Ibid., at para. 122; and 174, para. 137 ('the Special Rapporteur maintained her hesitancy regarding the inclusion of the crime of aggression, as it risked increased politicization of the entire project').
115　Ibid., at 172, para. 121.
116　Ibid., at 174, para. 137.
117　A/CN.4/SR.3387, at 12 (Petrič).
118　See also A/72/10, at 172, paras 123–125.
119　See the proposal in the fifth report, which read: *Crimes that cause harm to persons, including death and serious injury, or to property, when such crimes are committed in the territory of the forum State and the State official is present in said territory at the time that such*

exception 'was not restricted to the sphere of civil jurisdiction' and aimed at addressing major offences, such as sabotage and espionage.[120] While some took the view that 'immunity could exist in these circumstances and the exception should not be included in draft Art. 7 because there was insufficient practice to justify doing so', the commentary to draft Art. 7 asserts, without any real basis for doing so, that the Commission considered

> that certain crimes, such as murder [sc. assassination], espionage, sabotage or kidnapping, committed in the territory of a State in the aforementioned circumstances are subject to the principle of territorial sovereignty and do not give rise to immunity from jurisdiction *ratione materiae*, and therefore there is no need to include them in the list of crimes for which this type of immunity does not apply.[121]

## 3 *If There Were Exceptions, Should They be Accompanied by Procedural Safeguards, and if So What Should These be?*

There was general agreement that any exceptions would need to be accompanied by procedural safeguards, to guard against politically-motivated abuse. However, the Special Rapporteur did not submit a further report concerning this matter in 2017, nor did the sixth report in 2018 propose any draft provisions on the matter.[122] A seventh report with draft articles on certain procedural matters appeared in June 2019.

One proposed set of elements that might be considered for such safeguards includes the following. First, a forum State shall only deny immunity *ratione materiae* on the basis of an exception contained in draft Art. 7 when (a) the current or former State official is present in the forum State; (b) the alleged crime was committed in territory under the forum State's jurisdiction (or when its nationals were harmed by the crime); (c) the evidence that the official

---

*crimes are committed* (A/CN.4/701, at 95, draft Art. 7.1 (iii)). For the debate in 2016, see A/71/10, at 351, para. 244; and for the debate in 2017, see A/72/10, at 172–173, para. 126.

120    A/72/10, at 174, para. 138.
121    Ibid., at 188, para. (24) (adding that '[t]his is without prejudice to the immunity from criminal jurisdiction enjoyed under special rules of international law, as set forth in draft Art. 1, paragraph 2'). This paragraph (which is very different to the one proposed by the Special Rapporteur) was negotiated by a very small group, in the margins of the last plenary meeting of the session on 4 August 2017. On the 'territorial exception' more generally, see A. Sanger, 'Immunity of State Officials from the Criminal Jurisdiction of a Foreign State' (2013) 62 International and Comparative Law Quarterly 193; Webb, supra note 3, at 18–19.
122    A/72/10, at 170, para. 110.

committed the alleged offence is considered particularly strong; and (d) the decision to pursue a criminal proceeding against the official was taken at the highest level of government or prosecuting authorities that is appropriate under the forum State's national law. Second, if a decision is taken by the forum State to pursue a criminal proceeding, the forum State shall (a) notify the State of the official that it intends to pursue a criminal proceeding; and (b) if that other State is able and willing to submit the matter to prosecution in its own courts, then the proceeding shall be transferred to that other State.[123]

## VI   Lessons Learnt (or Not)

The handling of the topic *Immunity of State officials from foreign criminal jurisdiction* sheds light on several aspects of the Commission's work and working methods. It also invites reflection on how these may be improved going forward.

First, there is a need for the Commission to exercise great care in choosing topics. The Commission should not select topics on which diametrically opposed views are likely to be strongly held. This is likely to lead to failure—a 'train crash'. That cannot be helpful for the work and reputation of the Commission, certainly not if it happens often, and, more seriously, it is hardly likely to promote the Charter objective of the development or codification of international law.[124]

Second, it can be very helpful to have a good idea, as early as possible in the work on a topic (ideally at the outset, though this is often not done) what the Commission's aim is, and in particular what form the final output will have and what recommendation will be made to the UN General Assembly.[125] In the case of the present topic, the Commission's approach should have been determined by whether it was aiming to propose draft articles including as

---

123   See Murphy, 'Crimes Against Humanity and Other Topics: The Sixty-Ninth Session of the International Law Commission', supra note 3, at 988.

124   Having said that, even when a topic is unsuccessful, there may nevertheless be some useful side-effects. For example, the Commission made little progress on the topic *The obligation to extradite or prosecute* (aut dedere aut judicare), but one spin-off was an excellent Secretariat memorandum that was cited before the ICJ in the *Belgium v. Senegal* case: A/CN.4/630: Survey of Multilateral Instruments Which May Be of Relevance for the Work of the International Law Commission on the Topic 'The Obligation to Extradite or Prosecute (*aut dedere aut judicare*)' (2010).

125   Of course, the Commission's approach has at times changed in the course of working on a topic, as happened, for example, in relation to the law of treaties and State responsibility.

appropriate progressive development of the law with a view to proposing a treaty, to which States may or may not decide to become party. Failure to clarify this early on has greatly complicated debates within the Commission and among States.

Third, the role of the Special Rapporteur is crucial in keeping the Commission on track and united. Where there are significant differences of opinion within the Commission, it is usually possible to reconcile them through constructive debates and with the development of careful compromises either promoted by the Special Rapporteur or within a specially convened working group. Informal consultations among the most interested members, including between sessions, can be helpful in this regard.

Fourth, the Commission needs to listen carefully to the views of States, expressed in the Sixth Committee and elsewhere, and to take account of those views as far as possible.[126]

Fifth, the age-old debate over the Commission's dual object—progressive development of international law and its codification—is still very much with us, and can be central to work on a particular topic. In particular, should the Commission indicate whether its proposals are *lex lata* or not? This may sometimes be difficult, depending upon the subject-matter, if only because there may be different views on the question within the Commission. Yet there are certainly times when it may be particularly helpful and important that it does so, including when national courts are likely to be referred to the Commission's work.

Sixth, where the Commission is engaging in codification (at least 'strict' codification), and thus in identifying existing rules of customary international law and their content, it may be expected to set an example. It should follow its

---

[126] Concerns have long been expressed about the relationship between the Commission and the Sixth Committee. These were prominent once again in the Sixth Committee's 2018 debate on the Commission's Annual Report on its seventieth session, not expressly with reference to the present topic, but perhaps with it in mind. General Assembly resolution 73/265 of 22 December 2018 contains novel language concerning new topics: '8. *Encourages* the International Law Commission to take into account the capacity and views of Member States when including topics in its current programme of work', and, in relation to two new topics on the long-term programme of work, '9. [C]alls upon the Commission to take into consideration the comments, *concerns* and observations expressed by Governments during the debate in the Sixth Committee' (emphasis added). The resolution also included an important observation about the Commission's working methods: '15. *Recalls* the importance of an in-depth analysis of State practice and the consideration of the diversity of legal systems of Member States to the work of the International Law Commission'. The following seems to be addressed more to the Assembly itself: '22. *Underlines* in this regard the necessity to allow sufficient time for the consideration of the report of the International Law Commission in the Sixth Committee'.

own past practice[127] and the methodology which it itself has described in the topic *Identification of customary international law*.[128]

Seventh, should the Commission strive to reach consensus, or should it be ready to vote if necessary to move forward with a topic? A number of members have viewed consensus as a practice that does not allow the Commission to realize its full potential of developing the law. Some 20 years ago, a former member of the Commission opined that voting 'may not be as collegial as decision-making by consensus, [but] allows ILC to make progress when a small minority of recalcitrant members would thwart it, and tends to produce articles that are less mushy, thus giving clearer guidance to States'.[129] Yet it remains true that, in the words of a member of the Commission writing some 40 years earlier, 'the authority and effectiveness of drafts prepared by a codifying agency must be decisively impaired if formulated under the impact of the hazards and alignments of voting'.[130] Disagreement within the Commission inevitably reduces the chances that its product will be seen as promoting the development of international law (since it will be seen as controversial and give arguments to States who do not favour the topic), and will certainly reduce the likelihood of it being regarded as a reflection of customary international law. This is particularly the case when the disagreement is taken up by States in the Sixth Committee.

Finally, it has been suggested that the International Court of Justice is institutionally constrained from presenting 'morally desirable outcomes [...] as

---

127   See also the Secretariat Memorandum describing how the Commission itself had set about identifying rules of customary international law over the years: A/CN.4/659: Formation and Evidence of Customary International Law: Elements in the Previous Work of the International Law Commission that Could Be Particularly Relevant to the Topic (2013).

128   In 2018, the Commission adopted, on second and final reading, 16 draft conclusions with commentaries: A/73/10: Report of the International Law Commission on the Work of its 70th Session (30 April–1 June and 2 July–10 August 2018), at 119–156. On 20 December 2018, the General Assembly took note of the conclusions, the text of which was annexed to the resolution, with the commentaries thereto; brought them to the attention of States and all who may be called upon to identify rules of customary international law; and encouraged their widest distribution: UNGA Res 73/203 (20 December 2018).

129   S. McCaffrey, 'Is Codification in Decline?' (1997) 20 Hastings International & Comparative Law Review 639, at 658.

130   H. Lauterpacht, 'Codification and Development of International Law' (1955) 49 American Journal of International Law 16, at 37. On early exchanges in the Commission as to whether voting or consensus should be preferred as a procedure for decision-making see Briggs, supra note 77, at 236–239.

results of an objective application of legal methodology'.[131] The same may be said of the Commission when it is undertaking to codify the *lex lata* (as opposed to *lex ferenda*). Arguments about 'the soul of international law' and calls for a 'brave new world in international law' add nothing to legal argument.

## Acknowledgments

The text is based on the lecture as delivered, but some details have been added, and reference is made to later developments and writings. I am very grateful to Mr Omri Sender for his assistance.

---

[131] N. Petersen, 'The International Court of Justice and the Judicial Politics of Identifying Customary International Law' (2017) 28 *European Journal of International Law* 357, at 363.

CHAPTER 3

# The United States and the Paris Agreement on Climate Change

*Mohit Khubchandani**

### Abstract

In June 2017, US President Donald Trump announced that the US 'will withdraw from the Paris Accord'. This paper argues that the US is still a party to the Paris Agreement and that its current domestic policies, such as revocation of the Clean Power Plan and lifting the Coal Moratorium, constitute an internationally wrongful act.

### Keywords

Paris Agreement – Trump Administration – Climate Change

## 1      Introduction

The US is considered the emitter of 17.89% of the world's total emissions. Thus, its support of the Paris Agreement[1] was internationally applauded.

The Paris Agreement was adopted on 12 December 2015 at the 21st session of the Conference of the Parties (CoP) to the United Nations Framework Convention on Climate Change (UNFCCC). As of March 2019, it has 185 States Parties. The Paris Agreement contains a vow to restrict global warming to *less than 2°C above pre-industrial levels and to* pursue efforts to limit the temperature increase even further to 1.5°C[2] by cutting global emissions so as to minimize the effects of climate change.

---

\*   All views expressed in this research paper are those of the author.
1   Paris Agreement (adopted 12 December 2015, entered into force 4 November 2016) UN Doc. No FCCC/CP/2015/L.9 Annex.
2   Art. 2 (1) Paris Agreement.

The Paris Agreement requires all parties to put forward their best efforts through their nationally determined contributions (NDCs), and to keep strengthening these efforts in the years ahead. This calls upon parties to report regularly on their emissions and on their implementation efforts. According to Arts 9 (6) and 14, there will be a global stocktake every five years to assess the collective progress towards achieving the objectives of the Paris Agreement. In December 2018, at the Conference of Parties (CoP 24) held at Katowice, Poland, the countries agreed on a global stocktake every five years. The first global stocktake will take place in 2023.[3]

The US signed the Paris Agreement on 22 April 2016, the day it was opened for signature, and ratified it on 3 September 2016. The Paris Agreement entered into force for the US on 4 November 2016. As a part of its NDC, the US committed to reduce its greenhouse gas emissions (GHGs) by 26–28 percent below the 2005 level by 2025. This would include curbing carbon dioxide, methane, nitrous oxide, perfluorocarbons, sulphur hexafluoride and nitrogen trifluoride, all of which contribute to global warming.

If the US's current actions are juxtaposed with its commitments, it is safe to say that they should be subjected to international scrutiny. Since the Trump administration has taken over, a number of Presidential executive orders have been issued that negate the pro-climate efforts of the Obama administration. Just recently, the Environmental Protection Agency (EPA) announced its intention to repeal the Clean Power Plan (CPP), which is most likely to have a direct impact on the US's international climate commitments.

## II    The US Withdrawal from the Paris Agreement

### 1    *Did the US become a Party to the Paris Agreement?*

It has been argued that the Obama administration violated US law since, when it signed the Paris Agreement, it never sought Senate approval. This is because the Paris Agreement has always been considered a by-product of the UNFCCC. The Paris Agreement simply updates the UNFCCC, which was approved by the senate in 1992. The UNFCCC, in turn, authorizes the Conference of Parties (COP) to adopt 'amendments'[4] and 'protocols'.[5] Therefore, the Obama

---

3   D. Waskow et al., 'COP24 Climate Change Package Brings Paris Agreement to Life' (21 December 2018), available at https://www.wri.org/blog/2018/12/cop24-climate-change-package-brings-paris-agreement-life (20 March 2019).
4   Art. 15 UNFCCC.
5   Ibid., Art. 17.

administration's actions were in consonance with the mechanisms set forth in the convention. Arguably, what the States Parties did was to adopt new procedural requirements and mechanisms to encourage emission reductions and climate finance goals that were already adopted under the UNFCCC.[6]

At this juncture, it is helpful to recall the history of negotiations behind the Kyoto Protocol of 1997. It was also an agreement signed under the mandate of the UNFCCC.[7] The perambulatory clause of the Kyoto Protocol itself makes this position abundantly clear. As such, it would not have required the approval of the US Senate. However, on 25 July 1997, the US Senate passed the so-called Byrd–Hagel Resolution which stated that it was not the sense of the Senate that the US should be a signatory to the Kyoto Protocol. The Byrd–Hagel Resolution's negotiation parameters were followed scrupulously by the President and the US State Department during the negotiation of the Paris Agreement in 2015. A similar resolution that would have required the Paris Agreement to be submitted to the Senate was introduced in October 2015 but did not pass. Contrary to what many commentators have claimed, therefore, the Senate did have an opportunity to vote on the Paris Agreement, even though it was not required.[8]

However, the question of Senate approval is of purely political interest. The 1969 Vienna Convention on the Law of Treaties (VCLT) is the legal regime that determines how States enter into and leave treaties. While the US signed but never ratified the VCLT, its provisions are regarded as customary law and thus govern US treaty relations. Arts 27 and 46 VCLT are applicable:

> Art. 27 VCLT:
> A party may not invoke the provisions of its internal law as justification for its failure to perform a treaty. This rule is without prejudice to article 46.
>
> Art. 46 VCLT:
> (1) A State may not invoke the fact that its consent to be bound by a treaty has been expressed in violation of a provision of its internal law regarding competence to conclude treaties as invalidating its

---

6 M. Lewis, 'The Paris Climate Agreement is a Treaty Requiring Senate Review: Why and How Congress Should Fight President Obama's Power Grab' (24 February 2016) Competitive Enterprise Institute on Point No. 213.

7 Kyoto Protocol to the United Nations Framework Convention on Climate Change (adopted 10 December 1997, entered into force 16 February 2005) 2303 UNTS 148 ('Kyoto Protocol'). The preamble of the Kyoto Protocol reads '*The Parties to this Protocol, Being* Parties to the United Nations Framework Convention on Climate Change, hereinafter referred to as "the Convention"'.

8 Dobson, 'The Senate Story that Everyone is Missing'.

consent unless that violation was manifest and concerned a rule of its internal law of fundamental importance.
(2) A violation is manifest if it would be objectively evident to any State conducting itself in the matter in accordance with normal practice and in good faith.

In other words, the lack of Senate approval would only have invalidated the US's consent to the Paris Agreement if it had been evident to the other States Parties to the Paris Agreement that such approval was prescribed by US law. However, since this requirement is debated even within the US, this was clearly not the case. Thus, the approval of the US Senate or lack thereof are irrelevant to the case at hand.

## 2   Is the US still a Party to the Paris Agreement?
Art. 54 VCLT sets out that:

The termination of a treaty or the withdrawal of a party may take place:
(a) In conformity with the provisions of the treaty; or
(b) At any time by consent of all the parties after consultation with the other contracting States.

Art. 28 Paris Agreement, in turn, says that:

1. At any time after three years from the date on which this Agreement has entered into force for a Party, that Party may withdraw from this Agreement by giving written notification to the Depositary.
2. Any such withdrawal shall take effect upon expiry of one year from the date of receipt by the Depositary of the notification of withdrawal, or on such later date as may be specified in the notification of withdrawal.
3. Any Party that withdraws from the Convention shall be considered as also having withdrawn from this Agreement.

Art. 54 (a) VCLT does not apply to the case at hand since the Paris Agreement only entered into force for the US on 4 November 2016, less than three years ago. Art. 54 (b) VCLT is not applicable either since the other States Parties did not consent to the US's withdrawal—in fact, President Trump's decision has been widely criticized by the international community. Lastly, Art. 56 VCLT is not applicable since it only refers to treaties that do not contain a provision regarding termination, denunciation or withdrawal, and thus not to the Paris Agreement.

The US has likewise not offered any of the reasons for suspension of the operation or termination of the Paris Agreement according to Arts 57 ff. of the VCLT. Neither a supervening impossibility of performing its obligations under the Paris Agreement, Art. 61 VCLT, nor a fundamental change of circumstances, Art. 62 VCLT, have ever been claimed by the US.

Lastly, the US may have withdrawn from the Paris Agreement according to Art. 25 (1) UNFCCC. This provision states that: 'At any time after three years from the date on which the Convention has entered into force for a Party, that Party may withdraw from the Convention by giving written notification to the Depositary'.[9] Moreover, Art. 25 (3) prescribes that 'Any Party that withdraws from the Convention shall be considered as also having withdrawn from any protocol to which it is a Party'. The UNFCCC entered into force for the US on 15 October 1992, thus three-year period of Art. 25 (1) UNFCCC has passed; however, the US still remains a party to the UNFCCC and, consequently, also to the Paris Agreement.

As a result, the US's withdrawal from the Paris Agreement was not in accordance with the Law of Treaties. Hence, the US can only notify the Depositary of its withdrawal after 4 November 2019; the withdrawal would then take effect one year later, Art. 28 Paris Agreement.

## III  Do the US's Actions Constitute an 'Internationally Wrongful Act'?

Immediately upon threatening to withdraw from the treaty, the US has adopted governmental schemes to effectively negate its Paris Agreement commitments, whilst still being bound by it. It will be argued here that such actions constitute an internationally wrongful act under public international law. There is an internationally wrongful act of a State when conduct consisting of an act or omission 1. is attributable to the State under international law; and 2. constitutes a breach of an international obligation of the State. Art. 1 of the ILC Draft Articles on the Responsibility of States for Internationally Wrongful Acts (2001) says that 'every internationally wrongful act of a State entails the international responsibility of that State'.[10]

---

9   Emphasis added.
10  UN ILC 'Text of the Draft Articles with Commentaries Thereto: Responsibility of States for Internationally Wrongful Acts' (2001) GAOR 56th Session Supp 10, 59. For details of the Draft Articles see UN ILC Special Rapporteur J. Crawford 'First Report on State Responsibility' (24 April 1998) UN Doc. A/CN.4/490 and ADD.1–7; UN ILC Special Rapporteur J. Crawford 'Second Report on State Responsibility' (17 March 1999) UN Doc. A/CN.4/498 and ADD.1–4; UN ILC Special Rapporteur J. Crawford 'Third Report on State Responsibility'

The PCIJ as early as 1928 in the *Chorzow Factory Case* considered it a principle of international law that any breach of an agreement involves an obligation to make reparation. It held that 'it was an indispensable complement of a failure to apply a convention, and there is no necessity for this to be stated in the convention itself'.[11] This approach has also been affirmed in the environmental context by the ICJ in the *Case Concerning the Gabčíkovo-Nagymaros Project*.[12]

### 1   Breach of Environmental Obligations

Responsibility for environmental damage is a principle that has long been recognized in international environmental law. Principle 12 of the UNEP 'Draft Principles of Conduct in the Field of the Environment for the Guidance of States in the Conservation and Harmonious Utilization of Natural Resources Shared by Two or More States' (1978)[13] affirms that States are responsible for the fulfilment of their international environmental obligations relating to the utilization of shared natural resources, and that they 'are subject to liability in accordance with applicable international law for environmental damage resulting from violations of these obligations caused to areas beyond their jurisdiction'. Principle 2 of the 1972 Stockholm Declaration of the United Nations Conference on the Human Environment states that 'The natural resources of the earth, including the air, water, land, flora and fauna and especially representative samples of natural ecosystems, must be safeguarded for the benefit of present and future generations through careful planning or management, as appropriate', whereas Principle 21 says that

> States have, in accordance with the Charter of the United Nations and the principles of international law, the sovereign right to exploit their own resources pursuant to their own environmental policies, and the responsibility to ensure that activities within their jurisdiction or control do not cause damage to the environment of other States or of areas beyond the limits of national jurisdiction.

(15 March 2000) UN Doc. A/CN.4/507 and ADD.1–4; and UN ILC Special Rapporteur J. Crawford 'Fourth Report on State Responsibility' (2 April 2001) UN Doc. A/CN.4/517; see generally, J. Crawford, *The ILC's Articles on State Responsibility: Introduction, Text and Commentaries* (CUP 2002).

11   *Factory at Chorzow* (*Germany v Poland*) (*Claims for Indemnity*) (*Merits*) PCIJ Series A Nos 17, 19, at 47.
12   *Gabčíkovo-Nagymaros Project* (*Hungary/Slovakia*) [1997] ICJ Rep 7, at para. 149.
13   UNEP 'Draft Principles of Conduct in the Field of the Environment for the Guidance of States in the Conservation and Harmonious Utilization of Natural Resources Shared by Two or More States' (19 May 1978) (1978) 17 ILM 1097.

In the words of Sands and Peel, 'In the form presented by Principle 21 and Principle 2, the responsibility to prevent damage to the environments of other States or of areas beyond national jurisdiction has been accepted as an obligation by all States'.[14]

The obligations set out in the Paris Agreement are a concretization of their environmental duties, aimed at preventing climate change. It thus remains to be seen whether the US has implemented policies that violated its commitments under the Paris Agreement.

## 2   *Current US Policies in Violation of Its Obligations under the Paris Agreement*

We will now look at the various domestic policies adopted by the Trump administration that may violate the US's obligations under the Paris Agreement. The US's commitment under the Paris Agreement accounts for one fifth of the global emissions to be avoided by 2030. If US emissions continue at the present level, they could warm the world by an additional 0.3°C by 2100. This would raise the global temperatures well beyond the internationally agreed limit and may cause heatwaves, sea-level rise, displacement of people and loss of ecosystems.[15]

At present, US activities towards fulfilling its commitments under the Paris Agreement are critically insufficient.[16] Significant and highly adverse rollbacks of climate policy are now underway at the federal level. The Trump Administration is also considering a new import tariffs on solar panels, while the Secretary of Energy, Rick Perry has proposed a measure to prolong the life of coal plants scheduled for 'premature retirement' through a payment for their grid 'resiliency' attributes. Below we discuss some of the major executive actions that are setbacks to US's climate policy.

### a   Efforts to Revoke the Clean Power Plan

In October 2017, the Environment Protection Agency (EPA) officially proposed repealing the Clean Power Plan (CPP). The CPP, announced in August 2015, was former US President Barack Obama's flagship policy to combat climate change. In the wake of signing the Paris Agreement, under this international obligation, the US promised to lower the nation's GHG emissions to 26–28

---

14   Sand and Peel, *Principles of International Environmental Law* (2012), at 195 with further examples.
15   O. Milman, D. Smith and D. Carrington, 'Donald Trump Confirms US Will Quit Climate Agreement' (1 June 2017) The Guardian.
16   'Climate Action Tracker: USA' (last updated 29 November 2018) https://climateactiontracker.org/countries/usa/ (accessed 13 March 2019).

percent below 2005 levels by 2025. The CPP contained the first-ever national standards that addressed carbon pollution from power plants in the US. This happened against the backdrop of an 'endangerment finding' by the EPA in 2009, after the *Massachusetts v. Environmental Protection Agency* case in which the US Supreme Court held that greenhouse gases are air pollutants, and the federal states may sue the EPA if it fails to properly regulate these pollutants.[17]

Various multi-party litigations challenging the CPP are ongoing in the US Court of Appeals at the DC Circuit. All have been consolidated into one case, West Virginia v. EPA (pending). An interim mid-litigation application to the Supreme Court resulted in a stay of the rule, meaning that the rule does not have legal effect during the period of the litigation. Several rollback efforts by the government have already hurt the country's climate commitments, despite the plan still being merely formally in place, with the current administration trying to rescind it in the near future.

b       Revocation of the Climate Action Plan

President Trump's Executive Order on 'Promoting Energy Independence and Economic Growth' of March 2017[18] rescinded the Obama administration's Climate Action Plan of 2008 which was never fully implemented. The Executive Order established a national policy in favour of energy autonomy and economic growth; this was meant to facilitate the development of US's energy resources and to reduce unnecessary regulatory burdens associated with the development of those resources. In an interesting turn of events, that same day, EPA Administrator Scott Pruitt signed four federal register notices, including a formal announcement of review of the CPP. In his address, Scott Pruitt stated that the Obama administration had exceeded its legal authority while creating the CPP. He indicated that any regulation 'should be limited to modification of the existing plants'. He also mentioned that the federal states' concerns were disregarded.

c       Lifting the Coal Leasing Moratorium

In March 2017, then-Secretary of the Interior Ryan Zinke formally lifted the ban on new coal leasing on federal land; a policy shift that was central to US President Trump's Executive Order of 28 March 2017.[19] The Executive Order, while

---

17   *Massachusetts v EPA* (2007) 549 US 497 (US).
18   Executive Order 13783 (28 March 2017) 'Promoting Energy Independence and Economic Growth' 82 FR 16093.
19   The Secretary of the Interior Order No. 3354 'Supporting and Improving the Federal Onshore Oil and Gas Leasing Program and Federal Solid Mineral Leasing Program' (6 July 2017).

fulfilling a key campaign promise from Trump, generated opposition from environmentalists and public lands supporters who immediately challenged the Order in court. *The State of New Mexico et al. v. United States Department of the Interior* is presently being litigated at the District Court of Montana. The basic contentions raised are that new coal extraction would increase global warming and violate the Federal Government's statutory duty to use public lands 'in a manner that will protect the quality of scientific, scenic, historical, ecological, environmental, air and atmospheric, water resource, and archaeological values'.[20] New coal extraction would also burden State and local governments with expenses related to healthcare, flood control and other infrastructure needs related to potentially harmful effects of nearby mines.

It should be noted that the Executive Order provides no justification, besides asserting the 'lack of scientific certainty' standard, in permitting the coal leases. Back in 2016, then-Secretary of the Interior Sally Jewell, seeing that federally managed coal accounts for nearly 41 percent of the coal produced in the nation, and that the existing leasing regime (including royalty rates etc.) had not been modified since 1979, directed the Bureau of Land Management (BLM) to consider leasing and management reforms to the current federal coal program. Order No. 3338 'Discretionary Programmatic Environmental Impact Statement to Modernize the Federal Coal Program' prescribed a 'pause on leasing, with limited exceptions'. Section 4 of the Order recorded the reasons for conducting such an analysis.

Unfortunately, Secretary Zinke's Order did not address any of the concerns raised by Secretary Jewell, including 1. How, when and where to lease; 2. Fair return related concerns, including whether the decision to lease large amounts of relatively low-cost coal artificially drives down pricing in the US market and, if so, how the taxpayer may best be compensated for the reduced royalties; 3. Considerations on climate impacts, including the US's commitments under the UNFCCC; 4. How the federal coal program affects the job markets, and how the pricing and viability of energy sources is affected; 5. Outdatedness of existing reviews. This analysis was not reflected in the Zinke Order.

Further, the scientific uncertainty defence brought forward in Zinke's Order can be easily addressed by reference to the precautionary principle approach enshrined under the Rio and Stockholm declarations.[21] Various written

---

20    Bureau of Land Management 'H-1600-1 Land Use Planning Handbook' (2000), at I-1.
21    UNGA Res 48/190 'Dissemination of the Principles of the Rio Declaration on Environment and Development' GAOR 48th Session Supp 49 vol. I, at Principle 15 ('Rio Declaration'); UNGA Res 2581 (XXIV) 'United Nations Conference on the Human Environment' GAOR 24th Session Supp 30, 44, Principle 11 (Stockholm Declaration).

comments were invited and a Scoping Report was prepared. A perusal of the Report makes it abundantly clear that the public and stakeholders wish that a new Programmatic Environmental Impact Statement be conducted.[22]

d      Cap-and-Trade, Offsetting and Border Carbon Adjustment Policies
These are among the most preferred form of policies adopted by developed economies to meet their climate commitments. The US policies relating to these mechanisms are opaque and not uniform for all. Offsets are carbon reduction projects from reductions which are not covered by the cap. In most of the domestic cap-and-trade programs or proposals, entities included within the cap can meet their allowance requirements by paying for the reduction of greenhouse gas emissions from certified forestry or agricultural sources.[23]

The major congressional proposals allow offsets from both domestic and international sources.[24] Credible reductions from offsets are consistent with the overall market-based theory underlying cap-and-trade. As it does not matter geographically where a ton of carbon dioxide reduction comes from, in order to achieve maximum cost-effectiveness an emitter should be allowed to find the cheapest emissions reductions available regardless of industry sector or geographic location.[25]

However, the problem with the US market is that, under cap-and-trade, the supply of allowances is highly inelastic in the short term, changing only as a result of government policy decisions. With highly inelastic supply, shifts in demand can cause significant price changes, and irregular shifts in demand can produce price volatility.[26]

---

22    Department of the Interior Bureau of Land Management Washington Office, *Federal Coal Program: Programmatic Environmental Impact Statement—Scoping Report* vol. 1 (January 2017).
23    California Environmental Protection Agency Air Resources Board 'ARB Emissions Trading Program Overview' (21 October 2011).
24    House of Representatives H.R. 2454 'To Create Clean Energy Jobs, Achieve Energy Independence, Reduce Global Warming Pollution and Transition to a Clean Energy Economy', at para. 311 (adding a new Section 733 (a) (1) to the Clean Air Act that would require EPA's Administrator to establish a list of eligible offset projects); (adding a new Section 743 to the Clean Air Act that would create additional requirements for international offset credits); S. 1733 para. 101 (adding a new Section 732 to the Clean Air Act that would require the President to establish an offset program); ibid. (adding a new Section 744 to the Clean Air Act that would create additional requirements for international offset credits).
25    A.E. Carlson, 'Designing Effective Climate Policy: Cap-and-Trade and Complementary Policies' (2012) 49 Harvard Journal on Legislation 207, at 210.
26    L.H. Goulder, 'Markets for Pollution Allowances: What are the (New) Lessons?' (2013) 27.1 Journal of Economic Perspectives 87, at 92.

The price volatility comes from the selective approach in the combination of cap-and-trade, offsetting and border carbon adjustments (BCAs) both domestically and internationally. In order to alleviate carbon leakage and competitiveness concerns, it has been argued that emission pricing should be extended unilaterally to cover imported goods and services by applying BCAs. BCAs can also encourage emissions reductions abroad by motivating foreign producers outside the scheme to become more carbon efficient, or even to punish non-participation in abatement efforts.[27] In 2017, French President Emmanuel Macron called BCAs 'indispensable'. In Canada, Environment Minister Catherine McKenna has said they warrant a closer look. Mexico mentions them in their commitments under the Paris Agreement. Democratic lawmakers in the US added language calling for BCAs into a series of climate bills through the early 2000s. They almost succeeded when the Waxman-Markey cap-and-trade bill passed the House in 2009, but it died in the Senate.[28]

The US so far has failed to adopt uniform policies concerning BCAs, cap-and-trade and offsets on the federal level. This approach is being criticized internationally. In addition, some though not all US States have taken it upon themselves to undo the Trump effect. After Trump's announcement, 22 US States and Puerto Rico formed the US Climate Alliance with a commitment to meet the Paris Agreement goals.[29] They have pledged to achieve the US goal of reducing greenhouse gas emissions by 26–28 percent from 2005 levels by 2025 and meeting or even exceeding the targets of the federal Clean Power Plan. Also, the nine States currently participating in the Regional Greenhouse Gas Initiative (RGGI) have agreed to cut power plant carbon pollution by at least another 30 percent until 2030.[30]

Following the example of California, Virginia is moving forward with plans to develop a state cap-and-trade program, creating a path to joining RGGI. New York State has announced aggressive new energy efficiency[31] plans and a plan to tap into the offshore wind potential in the State.[32] California continues to

---

27 M. Sakai and J. Barrett, 'Border Carbon Adjustments: Addressing Emissions Embodied in Trade' (2016) 92 Energy Policy 102.
28 S. Shankman, 'Turning Trump's Trade War Into a Tool to Fight Climate Change' (16 July 2018), available at https://insideclimatenews.org (accessed 20 March 2019).
29 J. Schmidt, 'Action Marches on Despite Trump's Paris Agreement Decision' (1 July 2018), available at https://www.nrdc.org (accessed 20 March 2019).
30 B. Ho and J. Morris, 'RGGI Agrees to Cut Power Plant Pollution by Another 30%' (23 August 2017), available at https://www.nrdc.org (accessed 20 March 2019).
31 D. DeCostanzo and J. Morris, 'Cuomo Launches Ambitious Energy Efficiency Plan' (20 April 2018), available at https://www.nrdc.org (accessed 20 March 2019).
32 K. Kennedy, 'NY Releases Master Plan to Grow Offshore Wind Power' (30 January 2018), available at https://www.nrdc.org (accessed 20 March 2019).

lead the way by enacting an air quality and climate package that will extend its market-based cap-and-trade program to 2030.[33] However, these state-wide efforts are not sufficient to relieve the federal government from its international commitments discussed above.

### 3   Consequences of Committing an Internationally Wrongful Act and the Way Forward

States guilty of committing an internationally wrongfully act are not only under an obligation to cease those acts, but also in case of continuing acts to offer assurances of non-repetition if the circumstances require, Art. 30 Draft Articles. They also have to make full reparation for the injury caused, Art. 31 Draft Articles.

In the present case, damage to the climate caused by US actions (or inaction) is almost impossible to calculate, making successful recourse to legal means on behalf of States affected by climate change a Herculean task. Yet, from a political point of view, it is important to state the existence of such wrongdoing and to make full use of diplomatic means to urge the US to reverse their climate-damaging policies.

### Acknowledgments

An earlier version of this paper was submitted as a thesis for the purposes of meeting the partial requirements for the subject 'Environmental Law & Policy Colloquium: II' (LAW 8002) taught by Dr. Adam Abelkop at Stanford Law School. His contributions in honing and supervising the thesis have been extremely instrumental and merit due acknowledgement. The author would also like thank his program director Prof. Barton (Buzz) Thompson; Prof. Jonathan Greenberg, teaching fellow of the International Law LL.M program at Stanford Law School for their valuable suggestions. It will be out of place to not thank, Prof. Allen Weiner (former US agent at the Department of State) who taught him Public International Law; Prof. David J. Hayes (former US deputy secretary for the interior) who taught him Modern Crosscurrents in Energy & Environmental Law; Prof. Danny Cullenward, who taught him Climate Law & Policy and Professors Jeffrey D. Brown, Dan W. Reicher, David B. Rogers, and their teaching assistant Sudarshan Bhatija who taught him Clean Energy Project

---

33   K. Steinmetz, 'California Challenges President Trump with Cap-and-Trade Law: 'We Do Not Have to Wait for Washington" (25 July 2017), available at www.time.com (accessed 20 March 2019).

Development & Finance. The insights on US and International Environmental and Energy Regimes through these lectures helped him envision the roadmap for his thesis. Last but not the least, he would like to thank his parents Mrs. Neelam & Mr. Manoj Khubchandani, for their constant emotional and moral support while writing the thesis during his LL.M. year spent at Stanford Law School.

CHAPTER 4

# On the Governance of International Judicial Institutions: The Development of Performance Indicators for the International Criminal Court

*Andrea Carcano*

**Abstract**

This article reviews the recent effort of the Assembly of States Parties to the Rome Statute (ASP) to measure the performance of the International Criminal Court (ICC) through the identification of goals and performance indicators. Upon an analysis of the various performance indicators reports prepared by the ICC and pertinent scholarly contributions, it offers a critical review of the ASP's endeavour. While appreciating the usefulness of the large amount of information collected by the ICC in the said reports, it argues that the turn to managerialism brought about by the ASP's endeavour, while laudable in many respects, may constitute an encroachment on the exercise of the judicial function if not properly handled through a closer coordination with the goals set in the ICC Statute. It may, in fact, amount to 'micromanagement' with the consequence of diverting the ASP's attention from the more pressing task of developing—20 years after the signing of the Rome Statute—an innovative vision of the ICC's role for the next (20) years.

**Keywords**

Assembly of States Parties – Effectiveness – Goals – Governance – Indicators – International Criminal Court – Judicial Function – Performance – Rome Statute – Quality of Justice

## 1 Introduction

To a varying degree, international judicial institutions operate in a framework of constrained independence.[1] Externally, they are exposed to the political

---

[1] L.R. Helfer and A.M. Slaughter, 'Why States Create International Tribunals: A Response to Professors Posner and Yoo' (2005) 83 Cal. L. Rev. 899, at 955.

and volatile context of an international society of sovereign States.[2] States, either alone or via international organs such as the UN Security Council, can exert pressure on judicial institutions by denying or withdrawing support from those institutions in order to protect their interests and perceived prerogatives.[3] Internally, judicial institutions must comply with the mandate received and operate within the framework provided for by their constitutive instruments. Moreover, the relationship between creator–creation shapes their development. They are subject to a degree of authority exercised by the bodies or organizations statutorily exercising elements of governance over them.[4] Certainly, a degree of supervision is necessary,[5] for instance, to determine whether the financial resources allocated to a judicial body are managed efficiently and effectively, or that it implements reforms needed to improve its performance as judges may be proficient in law, but not in management. An excess of supervision, however, may be harmful. An independent exercise of the judicial function is a *conditio sine qua non* for the authority and credibility of an institution as a court of law.[6] True, international courts are not only legal, but also political, actors in the sense of exercising public authority and shaping public discourse.[7] Nonetheless, if they were political agents of the political actors establishing them, they would be exercising a political function, not a judicial one.

At the domestic level, the independence of the judiciary—when recognized—is normally encapsulated in constitutional documents adhering to the principle of the separation of powers. At the international level, where the model of separation of powers does not apply (although it is, at times, used by international scholars for analytical purposes), the relationship between political

---

2  K. Alter, L.R. Helfer and M. Madsen, 'How Context Shapes the Authority of International Courts' in K. Alter, L.R. Helfer and M. Madsen, *International Court Authority* (OUP 2018) 24, at 25–49.
3  See in this regard, D. Bosco, *Rough Justice* (OUP 2014), at 177–179, L. Vinjamuri, 'The International Criminal Court: the Paradox of its Authority' in K. Alter, L.R. Helfer and M. Madsen, *International Court Authority* (OUP 2018), at 340–341.
4  For a broader analysis see N.M. Blokker, 'The Judicialization of International Law' in A. Follesdal and G. Ulfstein (eds), *The Judicialization of International Law* (OUP 2018) 26.
5  On the relationship between law and politics as concerns the ICC see K.S. Gallant, 'The International Criminal Court in the System of States and International Organizations' (2003) 16 LJIL 553, at 559–560; S. Nouwen and W. Werner, 'Doing Justice to the Political. The International Criminal Court in Uganda and Sudan' (2010) 21 EJIL 941, at 961–965.
6  See in this regard R. Mackenzie and P. Sands, 'International Courts and Tribunals and the Independence of the International Judge' (2003) 44 Harvard J. Int'l L. 271; Y. Shany (ed.), *Assessing the Effectiveness of International Courts* (OUP 2014), at 97–105.
7  A. Bogdandy and I. Venzke, *In Whose Name? A Public Law Theory of International Adjudication* (OUP 2014), at 101–119.

and judicial actors is rather fluid and in need of appropriate systematization from both a theoretical and a practical perspective. This fluidity, with all the consequences stemming from it, owes not only to the difficulty of operating a proper division of labour within a horizontal international community of sovereign States, but also to the international courts' lack of financial independence. Unlike in the case of their domestic counterparts, which are 'self-funded' in the sense that public resources are allocated to them regularly on the basis of pre-determined needs, the budget of international courts, and in particular that of international criminal courts and tribunals, is the result of continuous creator–creation negotiations.[8] Budgetary needs of international criminal courts and tribunals, which generally are higher than those of domestic courts, have increased from one year to another depending on their workload[9]—something States could not determine *a priori* because of the difficulty and uncertainty of apprehending fugitives from international justice. The result is an inevitable tension between what a given court may consider adequate to exercise its function effectively and independently in respect of increasing workloads and what States are willing or able to contribute to the claimed need.[10] This makes it more difficult to rescind the umbilical cord between creator and creation and for courts to determine freely how the interests of justice can be best served. And when to these structural constraints also operational constrains are added, such as goals and performance indicators, the risk of encroachments on the independent exercise of the judicial function is, of course, at its zenith.

That being so, an interesting case-study of the relationship between creator–creation, and more broadly between politics and law, is that offered by the International Criminal Court (ICC). Although it claims to speak for the international

---

8   See generally C. Romano, 'International Courts and Tribunals: Price, Financing and Output' in S. Voigt, M. Albert and D. Schmidtchen (eds), *International Conflict Resolution. Conferences on New Political Economy* (Mohr Siebeck 2006) 189.

9   D. Mundis, 'The Judicial Effects of the "Completion Strategies" on the Ad Hoc International Criminal Tribunals' (2005) 99.1 AJIL 142; C. Romano, 'The *Price* of International Justice' (2005) 4 Law & Practice of *International Courts and Tribunals* 281; D. Wippman, 'The Costs of International Justice' (2006) 100.4 AJIL 861, M. Cherif-Bassiouni, 'Perspectives on International Criminal Justice' (2010) 50 *Va.* J. Int'l L. 270, at 308–311; S. Ford 'How Leadership in International Criminal Law is Shifting from the US To Europe and Asia: An Analysis of Spending on and Contributions to International Criminal Courts' (2010) 55 St. Louis Univ Law J. 953.

10  See among others, J. O'Donohue, 'Financing the International Criminal Court' (2013) 13 Int'L Crim. L. Rev. 269; S. Ford, 'How Much Money Does the ICC Need?' in C. Stahn (ed.), *The Law and Practice of the International Criminal Court a Critical Account of Challenges and Achievement'* (OUP 2014) 84, at 85–100.

community and aspires to universality,[11] the ICC is structurally and politically constrained by its nature as a treaty-based regime. It is the product not of the international community as a whole, but of the Assembly of States Parties to the ICC Statute (ASP) that, while representing many States, does not speak for the large majority of them, nor for the most populated. Internally, the ICC is constrained by a very detailed Statute and Rules of Procedure and Evidence, drafted directly by States.[12] The relationship between the ASP and the ICC is regulated by Art. 112 of the ICC Statute.[13] This article gives the ASP a number of supervisory functions over ICC bodies.[14] These functions include providing 'management oversight to the Presidency, the Prosecutor and the Registrar regarding the administration of the Court'[15] and the approval of the budget. Art. 112 does not include, however, an oversight of the judicial function, which remains independent and is not exercised in the name of the States Parties.

Despite the equilibrium reached in the ICC Statute, however, recent developments are a cause for concern. They raise questions about the proper relationship between the ASP and the ICC, and the path the ICC may have embarked on under the stewardship of the ASP. In light of these considerations, this paper aims at reviewing the recent effort by the ASP to create a mechanism for the evaluation of the performance of the ICC through the identification of Key Goals and the designing of appropriate performance indicators. The introduction of performance indicators is a new experiment at the ICC that is not provided for in its Statute. It could be perceived as a laudable innovation for better managing and evaluating the practice of the ICC and keeping costs under control, while enhancing transparency and accountability. However, upon review of the reports on performance indicators submitted by the ICC

11   This idea is expressed yearly in the omnibus ASP's Resolution; see most recently 'Strengthening the International Criminal Court and the Assembly of States Parties' (18 December 2019) ICC-ASP/17/Res.5, Preamble.
12   Rome Statute of the International Criminal Court (adopted 17 July 1998, entered into force 1 July 2002) 2187 UNTS 90; International Criminal Court Assembly of States Parties 'Rules of Procedure and Evidence' (3–10 September 2002) ICC-ASP/1/3; see also S.F. de Gurmendi, 'Enhancing the Court's Effectiveness' (2018) 16 JICJ 341, at 343.
13   See in this regard J. O'Donohue 'The ICC and the ASP' in C. Stahn (ed.), *The Law and Practice of the International Criminal Court* (OUP 2015), at 105; M. Du Plessis and C. Gevers, 'The Role of the Assembly of States Parties for the ICC' in R.H. Steinberg (ed.), *Contemporary Issues Facing the International Criminal Court* (2016 Brill/Nijhoff), at 159–172. See also A. Khan, 'What is the Proper Balance between Oversight and Independence?' (6 May 2011) ICC Forum.
14   R. Villacis, 'Working Methods of the Assembly of States Parties to the Rome Statute' (2018) 18 IntlCLR 563.
15   Ibid.

thus far, this paper offers a more critical reflection. This is not to downplay initiatives seeking efficiency and effectiveness in the exercise of the judicial function. Managerial insights are useful to a court of law, which, being a complex organization, requires being administered professionally and effectively. Rather, it is to generate a reflection on the content and nature of the efforts of the ASP—undertaken in conjunction with the ICC—and the priorities and objectives they foster, which bear on the future of the ICC in the long term.

This paper argues that the relationship between the identified Key Goals and the goals outlined in the ICC Statute may be unclear and pave the way to an impermissible 'switch in priorities' leading to an exclusively managerial approach to the judicial function. It suggests that the choice of performance indicators, while most helpful for appraising the productivity of the ICC, may be overly selective, leaving aside equally significant dimensions of the ICC's exercise of the judicial function. It also questions whether the ASP may not be involved in 'micro-management' that could divert the ASP's attention from the more pressing task of developing—20 years after the signing of the ICC Statute—an innovative strategy to ensure the ICC's success in the next two decades.

## II  The Development of Performance Indicators as a Response to Criticism

Approximately ten years after the entry into force of the ICC Statute, what Geoff Dancy calls the 'honeymoon period' between the ICC and States came to an end.[16] Strong criticism was levied against the ICC.[17] Critics drew attention to the selectivity of the situations and cases coming before the ICC,[18] the limited number of adjudicated cases since its opening in 2002, and the slowness of the proceedings, while the *ad hoc* tribunals fared better in comparison.[19] Criticism

---

16  G. Dancy, 'Evaluating ICC Performance: Design is Critical' (10 July 2017) ICC Forum.
17  M. deGuzman, 'Is the ICC Targeting Africa Inappropriately? A Moral, Legal, and Sociological Assessment' in R.H. Steinberg (ed.), *Contemporary Issues Facing the International Criminal Court* (2016 Brill/Nijhoff) 333, M. Ssenyonjo, 'State Withdrawal Notifications from the Rome Statute of the International Criminal Court: South Africa, Burundi and the Gambia' (2018) 29 CrimLF 63; G. Naldi and K.D. Magliver, 'The International Criminal Court and the African Union: a Problematic Relationship' in C.C. Jalloh and I. Bantekas, *The International Criminal Court and Africa* (OUP 2017) 111.
18  See generally R. Cole, 'Africa's Relationship with the International Criminal Court: More Political than Legal' (2014) 14.2 MJIL 1.
19  See in this regard S. Ford, 'Complexity and Efficiency at International Criminal Courts' (2014) 29 Emory Int'l L. Rev. 1.

also included claims of partiality raised by African States,[20] flawed prosecutorial strategies, and concerns about delays in the execution of arrest warrants.[21] Enthusiasm turned into disenchantment and scepticism.[22] This sentiment is still present today within the international community while it is understood that 'not all the tensions can be solved' in the case of an institution as complex as the ICC.[23] Not surprisingly, States Parties began to demand stronger efforts to render the ICC's proceedings more efficient and effective.[24]

In response to the above criticism, the ICC engaged in a process of review of its proceedings.[25] On 10 December 2010, the ASP established the Study Group on Governance 'with a view to strengthening the institutional framework of the Rome Statute system and enhancing the efficiency and effectiveness of the Court while fully preserving its judicial independence'.[26] On 23 October 2012, the Study Group produced a study identifying measures that could be used

---

[20] See, generally, A. Tejan-Cole, 'Is the ICC's Exclusively African Cases Docket a Legitimate and Appropriate Intervention or an Unfair Targeting of Africa?' in R.H. Steinberg (ed.), *Contemporary Issues Facing the International Criminal Court* (2016 Brill/Nijhoff) 366. See for instance the Decision of the African Union of October 2013, which in the Preamble reiterates 'AU's concern on the politicization and misuse of indictments against African leaders by ICC as well as at the unprecedented indictments of and proceedings against the sitting President and Deputy President of Kenya in light of the recent developments in that country'. Ext/Assembly/AU/Dec.1–2 (October 2013), at 1–3.

[21] For detailed analysis see: C.C. Jalloh, 'Introduction' in C.C. Jalloh and I. Bantekas (eds), *The International Criminal Court and Africa* (OUP 2017) 1; G. Naldi and K.D. Magliveras, 'The International Criminal Court and the African Union: A Problematic Relationship' in CC. Jalloh and I. Bantekas (eds), The International Criminal Court and Africa (OUP 2017) 111. See in this regard M. Swart, 'In the Eye of the Storm: The Kenyatta Case and the Dispute between the African Union and the International Criminal Court' (2014) African YB Int'l Humanitarian L. 133.

[22] M. Delmas-Marty, 'Ambiguities and Lacunae' (2013) 11 JICJ 553.

[23] C. Stahn, 'More than a Court, Less than a Court, Several Courts in One? The International Criminal Court in Perspective' in C. Stahn (ed.), *The Law and Practice of the International Criminal Court* (OUP 2015) lxxxix.

[24] For a detailed analysis of the concomitant normative efforts of the ICC and the States Parties to make ICC proceedings more efficient and expeditious via amendments to the Rules of Procedures and Evidence see H. Abtahi and S. Charania, 'Expediting the ICC Criminal Process: Striking the Right Balance between the ICC and States Parties' (2018) 18 IntlCLR 383.

[25] The OTP has developed performance indicators with a view to 'performing optimally from general administration to activities related to its core mandate'; S.S. Shoamanesh, 'Institution Building: Perspectives from within the Office of the Prosecutor of the International Criminal Court' (2018) 18 JICJ 496.

[26] ASP, 'Establishment of a Study Group on Governance' (10 December 2010) ICC-ASP/9/Res.2, at para. 1.

to expedite the criminal procedures.[27] It adopted a 'roadmap' with a view to 'reflect upon measures that could be envisaged in order to expedite the judicial proceedings and enhance their efficiency',[28] and identified 23 issues justifying amendments to the Rules of Procedure and Evidence.[29]

On 17 December 2014, the ASP adopted by consensus its yearly Resolution[30] in which the ASP tasked the ICC with a threefold request:

(a) [...] to intensify its efforts to enhance the efficiency and effectiveness of proceedings including by adopting further changes of practice; and

(b) [...] to intensify its efforts to develop qualitative and quantitative indicators that would allow the Court to demonstrate better its achievements and needs, as well as allowing States Parties to assess the Court's performance in a more strategic manner';

(c) [...] to include a specific item on the efficiency and effectiveness of Court proceedings on the agenda of the fourteenth session of the [ASP] with a view to strengthening the Rome Statute system.[31]

From 6 to 8 April 2016, the Federal Department of Foreign Affairs of Switzerland (FDFA), in cooperation with the ICC and the Open Society Justice Initiative (OSJI), organized a judicial retreat on indicators in Glion (Switzerland).[32] The objective for the retreat was to 'enable Court leadership and judges' to discuss the value and purpose of performance indicators, refine their scope and 'discuss next steps in indicator development'.[33]

## III  The ICC Reports on Performance Indicators

The introduction of a performance assessment mechanism for the ICC accords with a general and growing trend to seek ways to assess the public performance of international institutions in managerial rather than political terms. The UN has been at the forefront of this approach through the adoption of a results-based

---

27  ASP, 'Report of the Bureau on the Study Group on Governance' (23 October 2012) ICC-ASP/11/31, at paras 10–17 and Annex 1. See also ASP 'Report of the Bureau on Study Group on Governance' (15 October 2013) ICC-ASP/12/37, at paras 9–25.

28  ICC, 'Study Group on Governance: Lessons Learnt: First Report of the Court to the Assembly of States Parties' (22 November 2012) ICC-ASP/11/31/Add.1, at para. 1.

29  Ibid., Annex.

30  ASP, 'Strengthening the International Criminal Court and the Assembly of States Parties' (17 December 2014) ICC-ASP/13/Res.5.

31  Ibid., Annex I, at para. 7 (a)–(c).

32  See 'International Criminal Court Retreat on Indicators, 6–8 April Glion, Switzerland', Convenor's Summary (24 May 2016).

33  Ibid., at 1.

management approach at least for certain agencies.[34] As the three performance reports that will be reviewed show, the ICC has undertaken what is probably the most comprehensive effort thus far among international criminal jurisdictions. True, there were performance indicators at the ICTY and at the ICTR. The two experiences, however, ought not to be conflated. At the *ad hoc* tribunals, performance indicators were a late introduction brought about by a need for planning and complying with the so-called Completion Strategy. Under that strategy, the UN Security Council had required, in no uncertain terms, that the two *ad hoc* tribunals redoubled their efforts from a managerial perspective to expedite proceedings to ensure the completion of trial and appeal proceedings within the deadline it had set.[35] By contrast, in the case of the ICC, the introduction of an instrument of performance assessment may be seen as an attempt to inject new life into the ICC to strengthen it against criticism through the improvement of its daily performance.

At the time of writing, the ICC has submitted three reports on performance indicators to the ASP in 2015, 2016 and 2017. Thus far, no report has been issued concerning 2018. The next section reviews the reports in turn.

### 1 *First Performance Report*

On 12 November 2015, the ICC submitted to the ASP its Report of the Court on the Development of Performance Indicators for the International Criminal Court (hereinafter 'First Report'). Although noting that some performance indicators were included in its annual draft Programme Budget,[36] the First Report begins with the concession that the existing monitoring system 'does not provide a clear picture of the Court's performance over time in key areas that are seen as critical for its success'.[37] On this premise, it embraced the approach requested by the ASP.[38] The purpose of the new approach, says the First Report, is to 'allow both the Court and its stakeholders to assess the progress made by the institution over time in terms of the efficiency, effectiveness, productivity, and quality of its work'.[39]

---

34  See for instance UN Development Group, 'Results-Based Management Handbook: Harmonizing RBM Concepts and Approaches for Improved Development Results at Country Level' (October 2011).

35  See in this regard A. Carcano, 'Of Efficiency and Fairness in the Administration of International Justice: Can the Residual Mechanism Provide Adequately Reasoned Opinions?' (2017) 3 Questions of International Law 21.

36  See 'Report on Activities and Programme Performance of the International Criminal Court for the Year 2014' (4 May 2016) ICC-ASP/14/8.

37  First Report, at para. 2.

38  Ibid., at para. 7.

39  Ibid., at para. 4.

The First Report identified four Key Goals which concerned the 'major features of proceedings before the ICC'[40] that were 'critical for assessing the performance of the ICC':[41]

(a) The Courts proceedings are expeditious, fair and transparent at every stage;
(b) The ICCs leadership and management are effective;
(c) The ICC ensures adequate security for its work, including protection of those at risk from involvement with the Court; and
(d) Victims have adequate access to the Court.[42]

No explanation is provided as to why these goals and not others were chosen, but they reflect what the ASP had espoused in the above-mentioned Resolution. It is also possible to note that the first two Key Goals were already contained in the ICC's Strategic Plan for the years 2013–2017.[43] It is acknowledged that, in accordance with Art. 112, the ASP did not devise those goals itself. Had it done so, it would have been rather easy to label the endeavour as an encroachment on the exercise of the judicial function.[44] Nonetheless, the fact remains that the Key Goals were adopted in line with what the ASP has asked, and the ASP endorsed them subsequently.[45]

In addition to identifying the Key Goals, the First Report outlined the ICC's rationale in the selection of the performance indicators. Indicators were to be 'realistic' and not drawn 'in the abstract',[46] and limited to factors 'under the control of the institution itself'.[47] Showing a rather insular approach, the First Report chose not to borrow from the model of indicators in use in national jurisdictions because 'domestic methodologies are difficult to apply to the ICC, given its relatively limited number of cases and the diversity of underlying country situations'.[48] It also expressed caution with regard to the 'experience of other international courts and tribunals' since 'there may be institution-specific

---

40   Ibid.
41   Ibid., at para. 7.
42   Ibid.
43   The Strategic Plan was last updated in September of 2016; the update was presented to States Parties in the Hague Working Group on 16 September 2016. The Strategic Plan 2013–2017 is available online. At present, there is no publicly available version of the plan for the subsequent period.
44   See in this regard H. Woolaver and E. Palmer, 'Challenges to the Independence of the International Criminal Court from the Assembly of States Parties' (2017) 15 LJIL 641.
45   ICC-ASP/14/Res. 4 (26 November 2015), at para. 59.
46   First Report, at para. 8.
47   This excluded factors such as the number of referrals by States, number of arrests achieved; extent of judicial or other cooperation by external partners and stakeholders in judicial proceeding. See First Report, at para. 10.
48   Ibid.

factors which make direct comparisons difficult',[49] though it did not specify which these factors were.[50]

Lastly, it is in the First Report that the ICC took the decision to devise only 'mainly quantifiable indicators' as opposed to including quality indicators, which the 'stakeholder will recognize as reflecting key aspects of the Court's performance'.[51] Quantifiable indicators, in fact, could be 'measured over time' starting 'from the beginning of 2016 onwards' says the Report.[52] This focus, however, is a departure from what the ASP had asked, which included both quantifiable and quality indicators.[53] Moreover, the Report stated that the ICC did not try to develop 'specific indicators for external factors that can affect its performance'.[54] This owed to the understanding that because of the ICC's operating in eight different country situations, external factors such as 'security conditions' and the 'cooperation of local and international partners' could have a substantial impact on results-based performance and could vary significantly from one situation to another.[55]

## 2     Second Performance Report

On 11 November 2016, the ICC submitted the Second Court's Report on the Development of Performance Indicators for the International Criminal Court (hereinafter 'Second Report'). The Second Report recalled, and thus consolidated, the Key Goals and methodological choices made in the First Report. It clarified that the formulation of performance indicators remained 'a work in progress' being the 'first attempt at an international level to provide a holistic picture of judicial activities through performance indicators'.[56] The Report contains a brief explanation of the problematics connected with the formulation of adequate performance indicators in respect of the Key Goals. Interestingly, with respect to the first of the four Key Goals, the Second Report elaborates on the relationship between efficiency and fairness, labelling the two as 'inextricably linked concepts'.[57]

The Report remarks that expeditiousness and fairness are examples of potentially conflicting goals, which illustrates the difficulty of measuring a judicial

---

49    Ibid.
50    Ibid.
51    First Report, at para. 11.
52    Ibid.
53    Ibid.
54    Ibid., at para. 12.
55    Ibid., at para. 13.
56    Second Report, at para. 28.
57    Second Report, at para. 7.

institution's performance in qualitative terms.[58] While noting that 'expeditious proceedings' are a function of the Court's efficiency and effectiveness, it cautions that the speed of a trial is to be balanced by fairness as 'proceedings can only be as fast as the parties' rights allow'.[59] The Report does not, however, shed light on the implication of this statement. Instead, it stresses that the 'expeditiousness of proceedings is not only one of the central rights of an accused under letter c of Art. 67 (1), but also an obligation of a Chamber under Art. 64 (2) of the ICC Statute'. This statement calls for reflection.

First, Art. 64 (2), which is a norm placed under the rubric 'Functions and Powers of the Chamber', provides that the Trial Chamber 'shall ensure that a trial is fair and expeditious and is conducted with full respect for the rights of the accused'.[60] This means that a Chamber is required to conduct proceedings expeditiously, but not because this is a right of the accused. Quite to the contrary, that norm implies that proceedings may be slowed down if necessary in order to ensure the 'full protection of the rights of the accused', for instance, to grant extensions of time to an accused on account of preparing his defence adequately.

As to Art. 67 of the ICC Statute, it may be noted that the word 'central' appears nowhere in this provision. Art. 67 (1) does not state that proceedings must be expeditious, as one of the Key Goals requires. It only states that an individual should be tried 'without undue delay'.[61] This means that it is admissible that proceedings may be delayed for cogent reasons, but not if such reasons are absent. The expeditiousness of the proceedings may be fully justified by reasons of judicial economy, but not out of the need for protecting the rights of the accused alone. The latter's defence may certainly be better prepared if the span of time available is expanded.

In the Second Report, under each of the four Key Goals, the ICC identified items to be measured. For example, the first Key Goal (Fairness and Expeditiousness of Proceedings) was divided into the three areas of activity, namely:
- Duration of and activity during phases of cases;
- Registry services that contribute to the expeditiousness of proceedings irrespective of the phases;
- Transparency of proceedings.[62]

---

58    Ibid.
59    Second Report, at para. 15.
60    See text in W. Schabas, *An Introduction to the International Criminal Court* (CUP 2017), at 453–454.
61    Ibid., at 456–457.
62    Second Report, at 8–12.

Under each of these areas, the ICC devised 51, 4 and 9 performance indicators respectively, making a total of 64.[63]

Within the item 'Duration of and activity during phases of cases', the Second Report listed seven sub-phases of proceedings:
1. Confirmation of charges;
2. Trial preparation;
3. Trial hearing;
4. Judgment;
5. Sentencing;
6. Reparations;
7. Appeal.[64]

To give a sense to the reader of the nature of the effort performed by the Chamber, a recollection of the performance indicators at least for some of those phases is in order.

*Phase 1 (Confirmation of charges)* comprises ten indicators mainly of a quantifiable character. These are:
- Total duration of the phase;
- Number of suspects;
- Time lapse between transfer of suspect in ICC custody and assignment/appointment of permanent counsel;
- Number of charges confirmed;
- Number of motions of all parties and participants;
- Number of decisions and orders;
- Scheduled confirmation hearing date achieved;
- Amount of evidence submitted;
- Number of courtroom days;
- Number of languages supported in the courtroom.[65]

Under *Phase 2 (Trial preparation)*, the ICC identified nine indicators. These are:
- Total duration of the phase;
- Number of accused persons;
- Number of charges;
- Number of motions by the parties and participants;
- Number of decisions and orders (oral and in writing);
- Amount of disclosed material by the parties;
- Preparation time of the parties from the Trial Chambers initial scheduling order/decision until the start date of trial;

---

63   Ibid., at 9–12.
64   Ibid., at 9–11.
65   Ibid., at para. 39.

– Total amount of court days;
– Scheduled trial start date achieved.[66]

Under *Phase 5 (Sentencing)*, four indicators have been identified:
– Total duration of the phase;
– Number of pages of submissions;
– Number of courtroom days;
– Number of witnesses heard.[67]

Turning to the second of the Key Goals ('The ICC's leadership and management are effective'), the ICC stressed that 'effective management, communication and cooperation between the organs of the Court on topics of common concern are essential'.[68] The performance in these three areas by the ICC leadership and management, notes the Report, are normally evaluated in 'its reporting to external governance', such as reports presented to 'the ASP, the Committee on Budget and Finance, various audit bodies, or the New York and Hague Working Group facilitations of States Parties'.[69] The Report, however, elaborates on some internal indicators that could complement the external reporting obligations already in existence.[70]

As 'main aspects for measurement' of the second Key Goal, the Report identifies the following:
(a) Budget implementation rates per court organ;
(b) Average time of recruitment process;
(c) Percentage rate of staff appraisals conducted in a given time;
(d) Geography and gender balance of staff; and
(e) Relevant indicators regarding the Courts procurement process.[71]

This section of the Second Report closes with the interesting affirmation that it is a high-priority strategy objective for the Court to 'develop an effective performance management system, which recognizes staff performance and achievements'.[72]

### 3    *Third Performance Report*

In the Third Court's Report on the Development of Performance Indicators for the International Criminal Court of 15 November 2017 (hereinafter 'Third Report'), in order to prove the 'efficiency of the International Criminal Court',

---

66   Ibid., at 9–10.
67   Ibid., at 10.
68   Ibid., at para. 48.
69   Ibid.
70   Ibid., at 12.
71   Ibid., at para. 49.
72   Ibid., at para. 50.

the ICC presented to the ASP, for the first time, an 'analysis of its practice in light of the identified goals and performance indicators'.[73] This Report represents a follow-up to the First and Second Reports. The indicators contained therein remain essentially the same with a few technical adjustments, focusing on the mentioned four Key Goals.[74] The novelty lies in a very comprehensive submission of data. In this Report, the ICC reported data concerning five cases (*Ongwen*,[75] *Ntaganda*,[76] *Gbagbo and Blé Goudé*,[77] *Al Mahdi*[78] and *Bemba*[79]). These cases were pending before it at the time of writing the Report. In order to gauge the relevance and significance of the work performed by the ICC in the Third Report, it is apt to present here a good part of the collected data as indicated in the Report. For purposes of systematization and comparison, the information recalled here is divided in two groups. The first group contains the first three of the above cases; the second concerns the latter two.

a  *Ongwen, Ntaganda, Gbagbo and Blé Goudé*
The *Ongwen* and *Ntaganda* had one accused each, while the *Gbagbo and Blé Goudé* case had two.[80]

The number of confirmed charges was
– 70 in *Ongwen*;
– 18 in *Ntaganda*;
– 4 in *Gbagbo and Blé Goudé*.
The duration of the Confirmation phase was
– 14 months and 1 day in *Ongwen*;
– 14 months and 15 days in *Ntaganda*;

---

73  ICC 'Third Court's Report on the Development of Performance Indicators for the International Criminal Court' (15 November 2017), at para. 1. See also 'Report of the Bureau on the Study Group on Governance' (22 November 2017) ICC-ASP/16/19, at 2–5.
74  Third Report, at para. 15.
75  *The Prosecutor v. Dominic Ongwen*, ICC-02/04-01/15; trial opened on 6 December 2016 and resumed on 18 September 2018.
76  *The Prosecutor v. Bosco Ntaganda*, ICC-01/04-02/06; trial opened on 2 September 2015; closing statements took place on 28–30 August 2018.
77  *The Prosecutor v. Laurent Gbagbo and Charles Blé Goudé*, ICC-02/11-01/15. The *Blé Goudé* case and *Gbagbo* case were joined on 11 March 2015; trial opened on 28 January 2016; acquittal on 15 January 2019.
78  *The Prosecutor v. Ahmad Al Faqi Al Mahdi*, ICC-01/12-01/15; trial opened on 22 August 2016; verdict and sentence on 27 September 2016.
79  *The Prosecutor v. Jean-Pierre Bemba Gombo*, ICC-01/05-01/08; trial opened on 22 November 2010; verdict on 21 March 2016; upon appeal, acquittal on 8 June 2018.
80  For the following data, see the figures in Third Report, at 9–15.

- 30 months in *Gbagbo* and 8 months and 15 days in *Blé Goudé* respectively. These two latter cases were joined on 11 March 2015.

During the Confirmation phase, the parties filed
- 118 motions in *Ongwen* (80 Prosecution, 38 Defence, 4 Legal Representative for Victims (LRV) and 7 Office of Public Counsel for Victims (OPCV));
- 149 motions in *Ntaganda* (92 Prosecution and 42 Defence, 1 LRV and 14 OPCV);
- 465 motions in *Gbagbo and Blé Goudé* (223 Prosecution, 202 Defence and 40 LRV).

This led the Trial Chambers to issue
- 116 decisions and orders in *Ongwen*;
- 82 in *Ntaganda*;
- 169 in *Gbagbo and Blé Goudé*.

The number of victims authorized to participate was
- 2,026 in *Ongwen*;
- 1,119 in *Ntaganda*;
- 727 in *Gbagbo and Blé Goudé*.[81]

The duration of the Trial Preparation was
- 8 months and 11 days in *Ongwen*;
- 14 months and 25 days in *Ntaganda*;
- 19 months and 7 days in *Gbagbo*; and
- 13 months and 18 days in *Blé Goudé*.

During the Trial Preparation phase, the parties filed
- 94 motions in *Ongwen* (53 Prosecution, 30 Defence, 6 LRV and 5 OPCV);
- 334 motions in *Ntaganda* (200 Prosecution, 113 Defence, 5 LRV and 16 OPCV);
- 362 motions in *Gbagbo and Blé Goudé* (131 Prosecution, 209 Defence and 22 LRV).

The Trial Chambers issued
- 35 decisions and orders (3 oral and 32 in writing) in *Ongwen*;
- 111 decisions and orders (11 oral and 100 in writing) in *Ntaganda*.
- No number is provided in the Third Report for the corresponding decisions rendered in *Gbagbo and Blé Goudé*.

The scheduled trial start date was achieved in *Ongwen*, but neither in *Ntaganda* due to the defence request 'for adjournment in order to prepare for trial' nor in *Gbagbo and Blé Goudé* due to the joining of the two cases.

The Trial phase had

---

81 No information is provided concerning the number of authorized victims in *Gbagbo and Blé Goudé*. See however ICC, 'Case Information Sheet' (4 February 2019) ICC-PIDS-CIS-CIV-04-02/19.

- 55 witnesses in *Ongwen* (heard with differing modalities);
- 110 in *Ntaganda*;
- 91 in *Gbagbo and Blé Goudé*.

The number of participating victims was
- 4,100 in *Ongwen*;
- 2,291 in *Ntaganda*;
- 889 in *Gbagbo and Blé Goudé*.

During this phase, the motions filed totalled
- 418 in *Ongwen* (147 Prosecution, 51 Defence, 8 Victims and 212 Others);
- 813 in *Ntaganda* (436 Prosecution, 260 Defence, 60 Victims and 57 Others[82]);
- 503 in *Gbagbo and Blé Goudé* (331 Prosecution, 100 Defence, 22 Victims and 50 Others).

The Trial Chambers issued
- 186 decisions (35 oral, 40 in writing and 111 by email) in *Ongwen*;
- 491 (256 oral, 197 in writing and 38 by email) in *Ntaganda*;
- 367 (161 oral, 178 in writing and 28 by email) in *Gbagbo and Blé Goudé*.

The languages supported in the courtroom proceedings were
- 3 (English, Alcholi and French) in *Ongwen*;
- 4 (English, French, Kinyarwanda and Swahili) in *Ntaganda*;
- 3 (French, English and Dioula) in *Gbagbo and Blé Goudé*.

The Trial phase lasted for
- 9 months and 25 days in *Ongwen*;
- 24 months and 29 days in *Ntaganda*;
- 20 months and 3 days in *Gbagbo and Blé Goudé*.

None of these three cases had been completed as of 30 September 2017, which is the last date the Third Report takes into account.

b  *Al Madhi* and *Bemba*

Let us now examine the second group of cases, which comprises the case of *Al Madhi* and *Bemba*. In *Al Madhi*, the single accused responded to one confirmed charge. In *Bemba*, the five accused responded to a total of 42 confirmed charges.[83]

The Confirmation phase lasted
- 5 months and 25 days in *Al Madhi*;
- 11 months and 16 days in *Bemba*.

The parties filed
- 60 motions in *Al Mahdi* (56 Prosecution and 4 Defence);

---

82  'Others' includes submissions of and via the Registry such as, for example, Expert Reports.
83  For the following data, see the figures in Third Report, at 9–15.

- 354 motions in *Bemba* (105 Prosecution and 240 Defence).

The number of decisions issued, all of which were in writing, was
- 12 in *Al Mahdi*;
- 133 in *Bemba*.

The Confirmation phase lasted
- 5 months and 25 days in *Al Mahdi*;
- 11 months and 16 days in *Bemba*.

The Trial Preparation phase lasted
- 4 months and 30 days in *Al Mahdi*;
- 10 months and 19 days in *Bemba*.

During this phase, the parties filed
- 44 motions (34 Prosecution and 10 Defence) in *Al Mahdi*;
- 328 (113 Prosecutor and 215 Defence) in *Bemba*.

During the Trial phase, the parties filed
- 5 motions (one Prosecution, three Defence and one Victim) in *Al Mahdi* and
- 306 motions (63 Prosecution and 243 Defence) in *Bemba*.

In this phase, the Chamber issued
- 67 decisions (12 oral, 18 in writing and 37 by email) in *Al Mahdi* and
- 346 in *Bemba* (80 oral and 266 in writing).

The Trial phase lasted
- 3 days in *Al Mahdi*, and
- 8 months and 4 days in *Bemba*.

The subsequent Trial Deliberations phase lasted
- 1 month and 3 days in *Al Mahdi*, resulting in a 49 page judgment; and
- 4 months and 19 days in *Bemba*, resulting in a 458 page judgment.

The Sentencing phase lasted in *Bemba* 5 months and 3 days. The parties filed 85 motions (14 Prosecution and 71 Defence) and the Trial Chamber issued 22 decisions and orders. The number of pages of the sentencing decision was 100. As to the Appeals phase, the Third Report contains information only about the *Bemba* case as the other cases were still at the Trial phase at the moment of preparing the report. In the appeal of the *Bemba* case, which includes 5 appeals against conviction and 4 appeals against sentence, the Parties filed 207 motions (13 Prosecution, 189 Defence and 5 Others.[84] The Appeals Chamber issued 28 decisions and orders in a period of 11 months. The final judgment was 80 pages though it was accompanied by separate and dissenting opinions.[85]

---

84  Again, 'Others' includes submissions of and via the Registry such as, for example, Expert Reports.

85  *The Prosecutor v. Jean-Pierre Bemba Gombo (Judgment on the Appeal of Mr Jean-Pierre Bemba Gombo against Trial Chamber III's 'Judgment pursuant to Article 74 of the Statute')* Appeals Chamber (8 June 2018) ICC-01/05-01/08-3636-Red.

c        Reparations Phase in *Lubanga, Katanga, Al Mahdi* and *Bemba*

Finally, the Third Report provides a series of data concerning the Reparations phase in *Lubanga*,[86] *Katanga*,[87] *Al Mahdi* and *Bemba*.[88]

During this phase, the parties in the proceedings filed
- 548 motions in *Lubanga* (22 Victims, 19 Defence, 23 The Trust Fund for Victims (TFV) and 484 Others (including experts));
- 36 in *Katanga* (23 Victims, 11 TFV and 2 Other (including experts));
- 110 in *Bemba* (2 Prosecution, 6 Defence, 7 TFV and 95 Other (including experts)); and
- 379 in *Al Mahdi* (135 Victims, 4 Defence, 3 TFV and 237 Other (including experts)).

The Reparations order totalled
- 94 pages in *Lubanga* and
- 131 pages in *Katanga* with over 1000 pages of annex.

In 2015, 2016 and 2017, the Appeals Chamber handled 30 interlocutory appeals in total (17, 6 and 7 respectively). In 2015, the average duration between the completion of all submissions and the issuance of the appeal decision was 129 days; in both 2016 and 2017 the duration was 88 days.

## IV   The Debate over the Adoption of Key Goals and Performance Indicators

### 1   *The Rationale in Favour of Performance Indicators*

Several arguments can be, and have been, tendered in favour of the idea of appraising aspects of the work of the ICC through a system of goals and performance indicators. The underlying mind-set justifying the adoption of a managerial approach to the judicial function is relatively simple: 'in order to be able to achieve its goals', the ICC needs to be 'seen as effective and efficient'.[89] One can readily agree with this idea. There is no question that a court of law must be efficient in the sense of being productive and parsimonious in the use of the limited (and public) resources at its disposal and effective in the performance

---

86    *The Prosecutor v. Thomas Lubanga Dyilo*, ICC-01/04-01/06; trial opened on 26 January 2009; verdict on 14 March 2012; appeal judgment on 1 December 2014.
87    *The Prosecutor v. Germain Katanga*, ICC-01/04-01/07; trial opened on 24 November 2009; verdict on 7 March 2014; order on reparations 24 March 2017.
88    For this data, see the figures in Third Report, at 16–18.
89    C. Stahn, 'Remarks to the Assembly of States Parties in relation to Cluster I: Increasing the Efficiency of the Criminal Process', 14th Session of the Assembly of States Parties (18–26 November 2015).

of its duties. Nevertheless, as will be discussed in the next sections, pinpointing what the adjective 'effective' stands for and in respect to what goals can be used is not easy in the case of the ICC, a court vested with an 'overabundance' of goals and aspirations,[90] and burdened by the inevitable divergences among multiple constituencies and stakeholders.

A memorandum prepared by the convenor (Switzerland) for the ICC judicial retreat in Glion outlines the reasons for adopting a system of performance indicators.[91] First, indicators constitute 'a tool to better explain how the Court is performing and developing over time' so as to enhance 'the accountability of the institution vis-à-vis its stakeholders' because 'performance indicators can foster trust, show the Court's successes, challenges and needs'.[92] Second, they could 'contribute to a constructive relationship, in particular between the Court and the ASP' by 'directing the attention on factors adequately reflecting the performance of the institution'.[93] Moreover, they provide 'an incentive and a reference framework for the efficient management and functioning of the institution' and 'encourage self-reflection and simplify the diagnosis'.[94] Along these lines, Philip Ambach, has written that performance indicators serve the concern of stakeholders that 'money is well spent'; increase legitimacy towards stakeholders and 'the international community as a whole'; and may function as an 'internal compass' pointing to needed improvements.[95] Moreover, from a 'budgetary perspective, performance indicators may provide a compelling narrative for budgetary needs—or show where potential inefficiencies lie'.[96]

Finally, Geoff Dancy expresses support for appraising the performance of the ICC through appropriate criteria from a managerial perspective in order to increase efficiency and transparency.[97] He does so, however, with some hesitation towards the kind and quality of indicators chosen in the Second Report as some of the indicators may not be 'useful for evaluation'.[98] To sort the difficulty of finding appropriate indicators, Dancy argues that the ICC could hire 'trained

---

90   M. Damaška, 'What is the Point of International Criminal Justice?' (2008) 83 Chi.-Kent L. Rev. 329.
91   'International Criminal Court Retreat on Indicators, 6–8 April Glion, Switzerland', Convenor's Summary (24 May 2016).
92   Ibid., at 1.
93   Ibid.
94   Ibid.
95   P. Ambach, 'Performance Indicators for International(ised) Criminal Courts—Potential for Increase of an Institution's Legacy or "Just" a Means of Budgetary Control?' (2018) 3 International Criminal Law Review 426.
96   Ibid.
97   G. Dancy, 'Evaluating ICC Performance: Design Is Critical' (10 July 2017) ICC Forum.
98   Ibid.

impact assessors' with a view to 'use reliable indicators to establish whether effective or fair Court operations yields great impacts on the ground—and ultimately contribute to a better world'. He suggests in particular that the ICC could turn to 'high-level statisticians to conduct surveys and build, from the bottom up, indicators of complex concepts like trial fairness or transparency'. Supportive as he is of the ICC's effort, Dancy warns that 'we should resist the urge to be too critical at this stage', the reason being that the ICC 'is still assembling all of this raw data in one place and workshopping ideas about how to aggregate this data into more substantial indicators of performance'.

## 2   Perplexities

The perplexities of the choice of the Key Goals and performance indicators undertaken by the ICC that have emerged thus far revolve, in essence, around three main themes: first, the tension with the goals contained in the ICC Statute; second, the incompleteness of the information that the indicators provide; and third, the ICC's choice and preferences for quantifiable indicators over quality indicators instead of having both. These issues are discussed in turn.

### a   Lack of Coherence with ICC Statute's Goals

For Gabrielle McIntyre, 'the alignment of performance measures with the overall objectives of the Court is critical to identification of what performance matters for the success of the Court'.[99] According to Yuval Shany, the Key Goals are a 'hodgepodge of process and outcome goals', which impermissibly mix considerations of different sorts.[100] The problem, Shany says, is that the Key Goals are 'not sufficiently related to the core business of the ICC that is ending impunity and developing international criminal law'.[101] In another writing co-authored with Sigal Horowitz and Gilad Noam, Shany claims that the ICC has been entrusted with the following goals: (i) ending impunity; (ii) encouraging domestic proceedings against perpetrators; (iii) generating deterrence against future crimes; (iv) promoting peace and security; (v) internalization of international criminal law into domestic legal systems; (vi) development of international criminal law; (vii) satisfaction of victim needs; (viii) conveying a message of condemnation of international crimes; and (ix) projecting

---

99   G.L. McIntyre, 'Performance Assessment Cannot Take Place in a Vacuum' (10 July 2017) ICC Forum.
100  Y. Shany, 'An ICC Availability Bias?' (10 July 2017) ICC Forum.
101  Ibid.

an image of procedural fairness and legitimacy.[102] This list of goals, however, diverges from the four Key Goals and does not make clear what the prioritized goals are. According to Shany, it is striking that the ICC's most prominent goals relating to the fight against international crimes—arguably its *raison d'être*—are excluded.[103] Moreover, he stresses that the Key Goals pertain to judicial processes and not to judicial outcomes, and are thus of limited utility,[104] so it remains unclear how 'fewer or more prosecution motions' or 'number of court days' can affect the 'overall operational performance' of the ICC.[105]

Shany has hit the nail on the head. Clearly, effectiveness in the narrow sense of adherence to the Key Goals is of limited relevance if the pursuit of the ICC's mission would lag behind. Therefore, the overall assessment of the ICC must depend on whether it achieves the aspirations contained in its Statute. It is also not evident in respect of which objectives the Key Goals can be said to be 'key' and why they are so labelled.

On the other hand, the presence of goals in the ICC Statute is not necessarily an obstacle to the adoption of other (sub-)goals. There could be goals and performance indicators that fulfil a function different from and yet complementary to that of assessing the overall ability of the Court to reach the Statute's objectives. The ancillary function could be ensuring that the 'machine' works well, so that it has the necessary strength and resilience to be driven towards the chosen destination by its pilots, so to speak, notwithstanding the hardship of the journey. When considering the content of the Key Goals, however, one is left with the impression that they do not perform an ancillary function, but a principal one. They go as far as setting priorities for the direction of the 'machine' although the ICC Statute already does so. The Key Goals, at least the first two of them, impact on the exercise of the judicial function. They do so by directing the ICC Chambers towards the pursuit of an efficient, effective and expeditious exercise of the judicial function, without mentioning anything relating to the quality of justice that the ICC judges ought to achieve. In so doing, they steer the judicial function by privileging certain objectives over others. The word 'fair' is there in the first Key Goal. There is, however, no qualification as to whether it also includes the substantive dimension of fairness.

The second of the Key Goals shapes the way ICC leadership should be exercised in order to be regarded as effective, which, in a sense, significantly—and

---

102  S. Horovitz, G. Noam and Y. Shany, 'The International Criminal Court' in Y. Shany (ed.), *Assessing the Effectiveness of International Courts* (OUP 2016) 222.
103  Shany, 'An ICC Availability Bias?'
104  Ibid.
105  Ibid.

perhaps impermissibly as concerns the exercise of the judicial function—limits the choice of the ICC leaders in determining what is effective in order to execute the mandate entrusted to them. If the ICC were a corporation, it would most likely be up to its CEO to straighten things out by placing the various goals and expectations into a coherent framework. In so doing, he could distinguish between the goals of the ICC as an organization, the goals of each of the units constituting it, and the goals of the individuals working within them both at the levels of leadership and below. Because of the collegial structure of governance of the ICC and the direct involvement of the ASP, however, it is not possible to replicate the model of a private corporation with the ICC. The result is that, as things stand now, the lack of a coherent framework between the Key Goals and the goals contained in the ICC Statute leaves matters unclear and room for the prioritization of the former over the latter. Indeed, only for the Key Goals are performance indicators contemplated. This is logical part of the exercise undertaken. It also implies, however, an increased layer of attention for the achievement of the Key Goals over the ICC Statute's goals, which increases demands on the ICC judge to ensure compliance with the Key Goals. Perhaps, this approach fits the Members of the ASP concerned with saving financial resources and 'selling' the ICC as an efficient and effective institution. It has drawbacks, however, as shall be further clarified, from the perspective of an authoritative exercise of the international judicial function.

Furthermore, consider the target set in the first of the Keys Goals. Under this goal, ICC proceedings should be efficient, fair and expeditious. This aspiration is, formally speaking, irrebuttable. Nonetheless, it is easy to challenge it *in concreto* as incomplete and not coherent. To begin with, it would be reductive to qualify fairness as a mere procedural requirement guaranteeing to all the parties that they would be playing under the same set of rules. The substantive dimension of fairness needs to be factored in as well. It mandates that the submissions of the parties be taken as seriously as possible, and that proper reasoning be provided. Spending time reading through and mulling over the parties' arguments requires delaying the time within which a given decision or judgment is rendered. Hence, as observed by Alex Whiting, it is not necessarily true, and certainly not most of the time, that justice delayed is justice denied as the passage of time may, in some circumstances, represent an 'asset and result in a better pursuit of justice'.[106]

Moreover, crafting well-reasoned decisions is probably among the highest expressions of a sound exercise of the judicial function and is antithetical to the

---

106   A. Whiting, 'In International Criminal Prosecutions, Justice Delayed Can Be Justice Delivered' (2009) 50 Harv. Int'l L. J. 323.

idea of issuing non-routine decisions expeditiously. These kinds of decisions yield impact on the authority and credibility of a judicial institution within the communities of the accused, shape the development of international criminal law, and are commented on and discussed around the world. They could be a source of inspiration for future judges and legal officers. Issuing such decisions on often intricate and contested legal and factual issues may well require longer deliberations and debates among judges and more careful drafting and revising than average decisions. They may have little chance of being noticed within a system rewarding primarily efficiency and expeditiousness. Hence, a concern is that the implicit message resulting from the Key Goals set in the three Reports is that ICC judges would not need to bother with trying to issue high quality decisions, but only with producing procedurally fair decisions as fast as possible. A court of this kind may be more efficient in the eyes of the ASP. It may well, however, lack authority, and hence legitimacy and effectiveness for the greater community to which it speaks.

b  Under-Inclusiveness

As a unit of measurement that is used to consolidate complex data into a simple number or rank, performance indicators are a qualitative or quantitative way of measuring an output or an outcome. They are selective as they present the most important features relevant to informed decision-making about one issue or question.[107] They are objective in that they are data that show what their creators were concerned with learning, but are incomplete in that they do not show what others may have thought important to learn. Additionally, qualitative indicators concern, among other things, perception, opinion, reputation, degree of confidence in an institution, attitude surveys, and opinions of stakeholders and commentators.[108] Carsten Stahn cautions that performance indicators should not be used as an 'instrument to market ICC performance or to assert its superiority'.[109] Sarah Kendall seems to hit a similar note when observing that ICC States Parties may be concerned more with the *oikos*, that is, investments and efficiency that affects them directly than with the *polis*, namely, the idea of a public good worthy of being pursued no matter what.[110]

---

107  S.E. Merry, 'Measuring the World Indicators, Human Rights, and Global Governance' (2009) 103 Am.Soc'Y Int'l L. Proc 239.
108  Results-Based Management Handbook, at 19.
109  C. Stahn, 'Is ICC Justice Measurable? Re-Thinking Means and Methods of Assessing the Court's Practice' (10 July 2017) ICC Forum.
110  S. Kendall, 'Commodifying Global Justice: Economies of Accountability at the International Criminal Court' (2015) 13 JICJ 113, at 132.

As noted by Shany, the indicators identified by the ICC describe workloads or, in other words, outputs, rather than outcomes.[111] Therefore, while performance indicators provide a snapshot of what the ICC has been doing in a given year, it is difficult to gauge how well it is performing its mandate. From the Third Report discussed above, it is possible to learn how many interlocutory appeals have been disposed of in a given year, but not possible to measure whether that output is an improvement of efficiency in respect of previous years in the absence of quality indicators of the impact they had in terms of clarity and fairness on their addressees.

Under the second of the Key Goals, what is being measured, for instance, as it can be gauged by the content of the Third Report, is whether staff performance assessments are completed on time, staff recruitment is carried out as efficiently as possible, and whether gender requirements are respected.[112] Fundamental questions concerning the quality of the recruitment are not raised, however. An institution as complex, costly and far-reaching as to claim to have worldwide jurisdiction should be able to recruit the best possible candidates for the job, but there is no indicator evaluating the quality of the selected candidates. Neither are mentioned, as remarked by Gabrielle McIntyre, quality indicators measuring the behaviour and integrity of the ICC leadership.[113] These could include, for instance, the number of complaints resulting in litigation against the ICC by its employees and the measurement of staff morale and commitment through staff surveys.[114]

## v   The Weight of Litigation

According to the ICC, the introduction of Key Goals and performance indicators is a way for stakeholders 'to assess the progress made by the institution over time in terms of the efficiency, effectiveness, productivity, and quality of its work'.[115] Arguably, the effort undertaken by the ASP and the ICC, as it currently stands, succeeds only in part. Success and shortcomings need to be reflected upon. Certainly, the three Performance Reports are an invaluable source of information. Detailed and comprehensive information explaining what an international criminal court does in its daily activities has been made

---

111   Shany, 'An ICC Availability Bias?'.
112   Third Report, at 30–44.
113   McIntyre, 'Performance Assessment Cannot Take Place in a Vacuum', at 10.
114   Ibid.
115   First Report, at para. 4.

available to the public as opposed to being kept for internal records only. Because of this transparency, the idea that the introduction of performance indicators could serve to better communicate the ICC's achievements, needs, and shortcomings is validated. The significance of this will be further discussed in the course of this section.

What can instead be remarked on in terms of shortcomings is that the valiant effort undertaken by the ICC fails to keep track, not of the productivity of the various ICC units, but of the improvements in terms of efficiency, effectiveness and quality of justice or, in other words, of changes with the 'capacity and performance of the primary duty bearers'.[116] The absence of the distinction between outputs (indicators of productivity) and outcomes (indicators of results), and the absence of quality indicators, leaves one unsure about the significance of the data collected. It is difficult to put the data collected on a graded scale. There are also no ratings that could help reach conclusions on how efficient and how effective a given performance has really been in a given year. For instance, the fact that an ICC Chamber produces an average of 300 to 400 decisions per year in various forms (oral and written) is in and of itself an impressive number for it means an average of three to four decisions per week, or even more, depending on the case.

At the same time, performance indicators assessing only productivity do not shed light on whether a Chamber's performance is merely meeting expectations, considering the huge resources at its disposal—which include a team of legal officers and administrative support, or whether that Chamber is effectively performing beyond expectations, or something in between. Perhaps it should be for the ICC itself to draw its own conclusions, even by way of a summary, on its own performance. Moreover, what is absent in the three Performance Reports is the concept of quality of justice. The Key Goals do not place it as an objective and consequently it is not discussed as an item to be measured through performance indicators. Nonetheless, for a court that aspires to have potentially worldwide jurisdiction and serve as a point of reference for domestic courts, it is odd not to have a measurement of the 'quality of justice'. Admittedly, this is not an easy matter to measure. And yet, most importantly, it is not a responsibility of the ICC alone. As the ASP prompted and shaped the project of developing goals and performance indicators for the ICC and it is to this body that the ICC has reported annually, the ASP also bears responsibility for the consequences of its choices. Insofar as the ASP insists on developing a managerial mindset without calling for and stressing the importance of quality of justice, the perception that emerges is that of an ASP concerned more

---

116    Results-Based Management Handbook, at 13.

with the efficiency of justice rather than its quality. Because of this attitude, the ASP appears to be imposing upon the ICC its own priorities rather than allowing it to develop as an independent court of law focused on improving the quality of justice it delivers. Hence, from this perspective, the impression of an encroachment on the exercise of the judicial function arises.

That said, there may be truth in Victor Peskin's insight[117] that efficiency and effectiveness is in the eye of the beholder or, rather, the stakeholder, and thus determinations concerning their achievement rely to a great extent on how court officials, particularly their chief prosecutors, 'market' their progress toward achieving institutional goals. Where I see a problem with this approach, however, is that 'marketing'—albeit necessary—may not function when the product that is being sold does not have marketable features. In the case of the ICC, the existence of marketable outcomes could mean—amongst many possibilities—for instance, the prosecution of high-level officials as it was with the ICTY. The latter began receiving unprecedented attention and publicity from international media with the arrest of Slobodan Milošević. Moreover, Geoff Dancy's proposition to consider that we should not expect too much from the current effort and consider it more as a 'work in progress' that may bear more fruits in the future, holds reason. After all, measuring performance is a trait of many public and private organizations that should not be abandoned merely on the grounds of its difficulties.

All this duly noted, it occurs to me that it would be a lost opportunity if we were not to try to make a virtue of a necessity. We ought to try to learn from and reflect upon what the ICC has so meticulously done, rather than narrowing our outlook by pointing only to what the ICC should have done. In fact, the effort made by the ICC should not to be trivialized. The three Performance Reports constitute a radioscopy of the work of the ICC. What emerges from them is the complexity and magnitude of the work performed by the ICC. They show that the parties filed a large number of motions, often surpassing the hundreds filed in each case, and that the ICC is a deeply busy institution. It operates under the weight of considerable litigation originating from the numerous demands from the various parties, and is required to steer the navigation through numerous and complex procedural steps from the confirmation phase to the sentencing and reparations phase. For this reason, the ICC may be compared with a mass production factory concerned with making products (decisions)

---

117    V. Peskin, 'Assessing the Contemporary International Criminal Tribunals: Performance, Persuasion, and Politics' (2014) 108 Am. Soc'y Int'L Proc. 122, at 124.

for its clients (the parties, victims included) of the proceedings, which is busy with going through numerous production phases.

The weight of litigation is not, of course, a peculiarity of the ICC. Other international tribunals have also dealt with a heavy quantity of litigation before, during and after court proceedings. The form the proceedings have taken at the ICC is rather unique, however. The political choices that States made in Rome when drafting and adopting the ICC Statute shaped the structure of proceedings before the ICC in several ways. Firstly, for the first time in the history of international criminal law, victims—whose representatives may file numerous motions—participate in the ICC proceedings. Secondly, there are three complex, entirely new phases: a Preliminary Examination phase to decide on whether a case should be brought to trial, a Sentencing phase to determine the appropriate punishment, and a Reparations phase to determine how victims of crimes under the ICC should be compensated. These phases are motivated by noble aspirations. They add numerous steps and opportunities to ICC proceedings to make them fairer in the selection of cases and in the determination of their outcomes, and more inclusive and respectful of the traumas that entire communities have suffered. The drawback is that each of them attracts more litigation, hence rendering cases much longer, and requires the concerned Chamber to issue essentially three rulings, which are as long as judgments, per case.

Hence, the impression one is left with is that the parties, not the judges, are the ultimate controllers of the ICC proceedings, or at the very least that it is very difficult to streamline adequately the conduct of the parties. Litigation cannot be curbed by judges, particularly in adversarial proceedings such as those of the ICC. It is an inalienable right of the parties to voice their claims and a cornerstone feature to ensure the fairness of each phase of the ICC proceedings. Certainly, parties may well abuse their rights and engage in excessive or frivolous bickering, in which case the judges may exercise a controlling role, but this can only concern a smaller part of the litigation process.

Moreover, what surprises me to observe is that the difficulty of the journey and the related weight of litigation have not been made easier by the numerous signposts along the way. Never before has the concern for clarity, predictability and certainty of the applicable law been as vivid as in the case of the ICC. For several years, States met regularly to draft both the Statutes, and the Rules of Procedure and Evidence. Never before had an institution of international criminal justice been provided with such a detailed and comprehensive set of applicable law. Nonetheless, this gigantic contribution of clarification of the applicable law did not seem to have reduced the amount of litigation. In some instances, it may have favoured the latter because of the conflicting interpretations that abundant or convoluted legislation may create when applied to facts. In this regard, an additional concern that the ICC's applicable law failed in preventing was significant disagreement among judges, or at least in keeping it at arm's length. Certainly, this is not a new a phenomenon in the field of international criminal justice. The *ad hoc* tribunals (and in particular the ICTY) were not exempt from bickering among judges, particularly in the last years of their existence. In the case of the ICC today, however, the lack of collegiality, and disagreement about the content of the applicable law may have reached new heights and may be exacerbated by structural flows. Suffice to say that in 2018, the judges in the Appeals Chamber in *Bemba,* 20 years after the drafting of the ICC Statute, proved still incapable of agreeing on the content of the applicable standard of review, as documented in hundreds of pages of separate and dissenting opinions to a judgment of fewer than 100 pages.[118]

If these considerations stand scrutiny, they reveal that proceedings before the ICC are somewhat limping under the weight of a composite procedure, incessant litigation and unproductive disagreements among the judges. The result is a cacophony of sounds that silence the tune of justice. All this renders the ICC a court difficult to look at as the beacon of international justice worth following rather than departing from. What may thus be necessary is checking assumptions and reconsidering long-held views. Rather than assuming that proceedings can become more efficient and effective if the appropriate management tools are introduced, it may be asked whether the machine as currently structured is capable of performing significantly better or whether it may even do worse, should the number of cases increase.

This is not to suggest that the effort for better management of ICC proceedings ought to be abandoned. It is, instead, to realize the importance of checking whether the right questions are being asked when seeking to improve the functioning of the ICC. What may be hindering the ICC are not (or not only) operational difficulties, but structural ones. The traditional mindset whereby international criminal jurisdictions were 'too costly, slow and bureaucratic' may be somewhat misleading in the case of the ICC. This is because of the failure to pierce the surface of the appearance, and gauge the enormous structural constraints that weigh on the functioning of the ICC, and the unexpected difficulties that have emerged in the application of the ICC Statute.

That being so, the question of whether the ICC is in need of structural reforms as opposed to operational changes in order to become more efficient,

---

118   The 80 pages judgment was accompanied by a dissenting opinion of 269 pages, a separate opinion of 34 pages, and a concurring separate opinion of 176 pages. See *Bemba (Judgment on the Appeal).*

effective and just should not be kept aside. Now, 20 years after the adoption of the ICC Statute, that question is all the more pressing.

VI    Concluding Thoughts: Is the ICC International Enough?

This paper has reviewed the effort undertaken by the ASP and the ICC to improve the functioning of the Court in various areas through the adoption of the Key Goals and performance indicators. Although a work in progress, the effort is laudable. It provides a comprehensive picture of the work of the ICC that, being unfiltered, constitutes an objective way of knowing what the Court does on a daily basis. Nonetheless, the concern is that the ASP might be involved in micro-management rather than in much needed enlightened governance. The selectivity of the chosen goals and indicators bars us from having an 'overall performance of the ICC'. It does not put the Key Goals and performance indicators in sync with the objectives of the ICC Statute. In the absence of clarity about what is being prioritized, the likelihood of an encroachment on the judicial function on the part of the ASP is high. The desiderata of efficiency and effectiveness as set in the Key Goals may trump concerns for the quality of justice to be delivered by the ICC. However, as the ICC is an enterprise, but not a corporation, the quality of justice delivered remains the priority. While justice should not be above any cost, cost savings over justice would weaken the ICC's authority and credibility.

A review of the three Performance Reports suggests that the ICC operates under the weight of litigation and a complex procedure characterized by a number of phases higher than in other international tribunals. To the point of dismay, the abundance of the written law did not make ICC proceedings go more smoothly and more certain. The parties to the proceedings argue about the meaning of the applicable law and so do the judges, through overly lengthy separate and dissenting opinions. This reveals widespread uncertainty about the content of the applicable law, at least on certain issues, and a lack of collegiality, which is by definition a hindrance to the effective and proper exercise of the judicial function.

In view of the foregoing, it is submitted that not too much faith should be put in the remedial power of performance indicators as if the introduction of managerial tools within the ICC system, even when taken at their best, may add substantive, rather than peripheral, improvements. For more significant changes to occur, this paper argues that structural, not operational, changes are necessary. Thinking of, identifying and implementing structural changes requires among other things, modesty on the part of the ASP to accept that the ICC Statute, while a historical achievement, is not free from legal difficulties.[119] It should be amended in light of the experiences gained in the years after its adoption. Also with a view to increasing and improving efficiency and effectiveness, consideration could be given, for instance, to the possibility of amendments to the ICC Statute in the sense of joining the judgment phase with the sentencing phase, and to the simplification of a number of norms in the ICC Statute.

At the same time, for effecting structural change, a vision of what the ICC should become in the next 20 years is necessary. The ASP faces a choice between a cosmopolitan view of the ICC as a court of the international community of States as a whole and a more parochial view as the court of the States Parties. What may be gradually emerging is a reality where a court that is born from the desire to be universal in its quest for ending impunity turns out to be much less so. Perhaps thinking of an institution capable of exercising potentially worldwide jurisdiction is an act of hubris. Considering, however, an institution supported by a majority of States larger than the current one is not. Only by gaining wider support within the international community, it is submitted, can the ICC gain all the necessary resources and support for the functioning of such a large enterprise.

From this perspective, a question that should be asked then is whether the ICC is 'international' enough to attract wider support. Whether it is international enough depends, of course, on how its role and function is perceived and construed. It is not clear, in fact, in whose name the ICC is acting; whether the ICC is speaking in its own name as a court of and for the international community of States; or perhaps is just an agent of the States Parties; or something in between. To make the ICC more international, a more constructive relationship between the ASP and that part of the international community which is not party to the ICC, is necessary. The debate in this regard may include such questions as whether the ICC should, first, adhere more closely to customary international law (for all its flaws), being the language of the international community; second, have a closer relationship with the UN, to the point of becoming itself a UN court; third, be inclusive in both the selection of the Prosecutor, its judges and its staff as they should not necessarily be all citizens of a State Party, but should include the 'best and the brightest' from around the world; and lastly, whether jurisdictional triggers ought to be

---

[119] On the concept and function of modesty in international criminal justice see C. Stahn, *A Critical Introduction to International Criminal Law* (CUP 2019), at 412–413.

rethought in one way or another to increase States' support for and adherence to the ICC Statute.

All these issues and possibilities having been duly flagged for the purposes of prompting much needed debate and reflection on the future of the ICC; it may be apt and prudent, considering their complexity, to leave the analysis for another paper.

CHAPTER 5

# Protection and Use of Transboundary Groundwater Resources under Public International Law—An Analysis of the UN International Law Commission's Draft Articles on the Law of Transboundary Aquifers

*Carolin Mai Weber*

### Abstract

Groundwater is one of the world's most important water resources. Although it is highly susceptible for pollution and overexploitation, its extraction rate is predicted to increase over the next decades. Against this background, this article discusses the contribution of the UN International Law Commission's Draft Articles on the Law of Transboundary Aquifers to the protection of this precious resource. It first provides some information on the characteristics of groundwater and aquifers, then describes briefly the existing international legal regimes addressing transboundary groundwater and the evolution of the Draft Articles, and finally analyses the main criticisms and positive aspects of the Draft Articles.

### Keywords

Groundwater – Environmental Law – International Water Law – Transboundary Aquifers – UN International Law Commission – Draft Articles on the Law of Transboundary Aquifers

## 1 Introduction

In 2016, at its 71st Session, the UN General Assembly once again commended the International Law Commission's (ILC) Draft Articles on the Law of Transboundary Aquifers (hereinafter: Draft Articles), annexed to its Resolution 68/118 to the attention of States, as guidance for bilateral or regional agreements and arrangements for the proper management of transboundary aquifers.[1] This article analyses the contributions of the Draft Articles to the protection of one of the world's most precious water resource—groundwater.

It first provides background on the importance of groundwater and its special characteristics and then briefly outlines existing legal regimes addressing transboundary groundwater. After describing the drafting process, it finally discusses the main criticisms and positive aspects of the Draft Articles as the first official document codifying international legal rules for the management and protection of transboundary groundwater resources.

## II  Water Crisis: The Importance of Groundwater

In December 2017, the UN proclaimed the years 2018 through 2028 the International Decade for Action on Water for Sustainable Development in order to tackle the global water crisis and accelerate implementation of the 2030 Agenda.[2] The global water crisis is marked by formerly unknown pressure on water resources caused by increasing water demand. This is primarily due to the predicted population growth of 9.1 billion of people by 2050. Population growth leads to a higher global demand for food—which is expected to increase by 50% by the year 2030, as well as energy—predicted to rise by 60% by the year 2050.[3] Both industry sectors are highly water intense.[4] Furthermore, patterns of consumption are well known to shift towards demand for more water-intense products, such as meat and electronic devices.[5] Great challenges also accompany urbanization. Besides confronting an increasing demand for water, cities must also process more wastewater. Untreated wastewater influent poses high risks for water resources and ecosystems.[6] Climate change-induced

---

[1]  UNGA Res A/C.6/71/L.22 (4 November 2016). The UN General Assembly had already encouraged the governments to make those agreements and take into account the Draft Articles at its 63rd, 66th and 68th session. See 'The Law of Transboundary Aquifers'—UNGA Res 63/124 (11 December 2011), UNGA Res 66/104 (9 December 2011), UNGA Res 68/118 (16 December 2013).

[2]  UNGA Res 71/222 'Water for Sustainable Development' (21 December 2017).

[3]  UNESCO 'The United Nations World Water Development Report 4: Managing Water under Uncertainty and Risk' (2012), at 46.

[4]  Ibid.

[5]  UNESCO 'The United Nations World Water Development Report 2015: Water for a Sustainable World (2015), at 11.

[6]  UNESCO 'The United Nations World Water Development Report 4: Managing Water under Uncertainty and Risk' (2012), at 64.

natural disasters, including exacerbated risks of floods and droughts, accelerate challenges posed by human development.[7]

Freshwater is a finite resource. 97.5% of water on Earth is salt water found in oceans or seas. Freshwater accounts for only 2.5% of the global water resources.[8] Approximately two thirds of the Earth's fresh water is trapped in glaciers, ice caps, and snow in the polar regions. Groundwater constitutes 30% of the freshwater on Earth, whereas only 0.3% of all freshwater is contained in surface water bodies, such as rivers and lakes.[9] Although at present not all sources are fully accessible, groundwater is the biggest resource of freshwater on Earth. Due to use of modern technologies, groundwater is now a significant source of freshwater for human consumption, supplying nearly 50% of global drinking water and around 43% of all irrigation water.[10]

However, a large number of the world's groundwater resources—namely 273—are transboundary, in other words, they lie under the territory of more than one State.[11] Transboundary groundwater, as a shared natural resource, is at an even higher risk of overexploitation and mismanagement than domestic groundwater.[12]

## III   Characteristics of Groundwater Resources

Groundwater is part of the hydrologic cycle that describes the continuous movement of water between the atmosphere, the surface and the subsurface of the Earth.[13] Generally, the water in surface waters such as lakes, rivers or seas evaporates into the atmosphere and falls down on the Earth through precipitation. Precipitation either becomes part of surface waters or percolates into the ground. It can also be consumed by plants, which return water to the atmosphere through transpiration. If water infiltrates the ground, it becomes soil moisture or continues flowing downwards until it reaches the groundwater

---

7   Ibid., at 65.
8   UNESCO 'The United Nations World Water Development Report 2: Water—A Shared Responsibility' (2006), at 121.
9   Ibid., at 121, 125.
10  UNESCO 'The United Nations World Water Development Report 4: Managing Water under Uncertainty and Risk' (2012), at 85.
11  R.M. Stephan (ed.), *Transboundary Aquifers: Managing a Vital Resource* (UNESCO 2009), at 10.
12  S.C. McCaffrey, *The Law of International Watercourses* (OUP 2001), at 415.
13  C.W. Fetter, *Applied Hydrogeology* (4th edn Prentice-Hall 2001), at 4.

table.[14] Reaching the groundwater table,[15] the direction of flow changes and the now-called groundwater flows rather laterally. Surface water and groundwater are the same element, namely water flowing through the hydrologic cycle, although at different stages.[16]

Groundwater is found in aquifers.[17] An aquifer is a geologic formation porous enough to store water and permeable enough that the water is able to flow within it.[18] Every aquifer has an impermeable base layer that prevents the groundwater from seeping deeper into the ground. Hence, it creates an underground water reservoir.[19]

There are different types of aquifers. An unconfined aquifer is overlain by layers of permeable geologic material that allows water to seep into the aquifer. This can happen through an interrelation with a surface water resource, e.g. rivers or lakes.[20] There are also unconfined aquifers that are not linked to a water resource and fed for example by downward seeping rainwater.[21]

In contrast to unconfined aquifers, confined aquifers are bounded by two impermeable layers. However, unconfined aquifers do not necessarily lack a connection with surface water. In most cases, aquifers with confined parts also have unconfined parts. As a consequence, the confined part of the aquifer is fed by water flowing from the unconfined part.[22]

An important distinction is that between non-renewable and renewable aquifers. Non-renewable aquifers are detached from the hydrologic cycle. Thus, non-renewable aquifers are not recharged by influent water and do not

---

14 Ibid., at 5.
15 The groundwater table is the upper level of an underground surface in which the rock or soil is completely saturated with water, see M. Price, *Introducing Groundwater* (2nd edn Nelson Thornes 2002), at 6.
16 G. Eckstein and Y. Eckstein, 'A Hydrogeological Approach to Transboundary Groundwater Resources and International Law' (2003) 19 Am. U. Int'l L. Rev. 201, 208–209.
17 Groundwater is also found in *aquicludes* and *aquitards*. These geological formations do not or only at small amount transmit water and cannot be exploited. See J. Barberis, *International Groundwater Resources Law* (FAO 1986), at 4–6.
18 M. Price, *Introducing Groundwater* (Routledge 1996), at 9.
19 Eckstein and Eckstein, 'A Hydrogeological Approach to Transboundary Groundwater Resources and International Law', at 210.
20 Ibid., at 210–212; Barberis, *International Groundwater Resources Law*, at 4.
21 For example, the Mountain Aquifer underlying Israel and the West Bank, see Eckstein and Eckstein, 'A Hydrogeological Approach to Transboundary Groundwater Resources and International Law' at 210, 212.
22 For example the San Pedro Basin Aquifer underlying the US and Mexico, see Eckstein and Eckstein, 'A Hydrogeological Approach to Transboundary Groundwater Resources and International Law' at 210, 212.

discharge water. As a result, the amount of water in non-renewable aquifers is stagnant. Non-renewable groundwater is characterized by no or only little flow. Some non-renewable aquifers store water estimated to be thousands of years old. Those fossil aquifers are often to be found in arid climate due to inter alia its isolation from sources of recharge or paucity of recharge.[23]

Renewable aquifers are connected to the hydrologic cycle. They are hydraulically linked to surface water bodies, like rivers or lakes, which can be characterized as either influent or effluent. In the first case, the groundwater table is lower than the permeable layer of the surface water body. In the second case, the surface water body loses water, which percolates downwards into the aquifer and recharges it. In this case, the groundwater table is at a higher elevation than the surface water body and hence, the aquifer constitutes itself the recharging element. The differentiation between influent and effluent water bodies is important with regard to possible contamination. Through the process of recharge or discharge, the aquifer or the surface water resource can contribute to the pollution of the respective interrelated water body.[24]

Renewable groundwater, groundwater stored in a renewable aquifer, is not stagnant but rather in a stage of constant flow. It tends to flow towards natural discharge sites, more precisely surface water resources like rivers, lakes or the sea. It also does not flow in form of an underground water stream but seeps through the geologic formation.[25]

Despite their definitions, in practice, there is no clear-cut differentiation between non-renewable and renewable aquifers. For instance, non-renewable aquifers can also have connections to surface water bodies. The Nubian Sandstone Aquifer System is recharged by seeping Nile water. However, the amount of recharge is considered negligible.[26] Thus, this non-renewable aquifer is non-renewable because the current rate of renewal is very low relative to the aquifer's storage capacity. Hence, the exploitation of a non-renewable aquifer can only occur for a finite period of time.[27]

---

23   Ibid., at 215.
24   Ibid., at 214–215.
25   Ibid., at 217.
26   M. Alker, 'The Nubian Sandstone Aquifer System: A Case Study for the Research Project Transboundary Groundwater Management in Africa' in W. Scheumann and E. Herfeldt-Pähle (eds), *Conceptualizing Cooperation on Africa's Transboundary Groundwater Resource* (DIE 2008), at 240.
27   J. Margat, S. Foster and A. Droubi, 'Concept and Importance of Non-Renewable Resources' in S. Foster and D. Loucks (eds), *Non-Renewable Groundwater Resources* (UNESCO 2006), at 14.

As groundwater is part of the hydrologic cycle, it is also characterized by its *mobility*. Mobility entails two major consequences. The first is that groundwater flows, although at a slower rate than surface water, through the aquifer. In case of a transboundary aquifer, the groundwater thus crosses the border between States. Since the aquifer water is constantly moving, the portion of groundwater located in one State today may be found in the neighbouring State tomorrow. States thus cannot exercise the same territorial sovereignty over groundwater resources they can exercise over an immovable resource located entirely within their territory. Secondly, groundwater mobility concerns solely aquifers, which are part of the hydrologic cycle. Where the groundwater flows into surface water, e.g. a river or a lake, it is considered as surface water. Consequently, two different legal regimes apply to one identical resource.[28]

Groundwater resources are characteristically *highly vulnerable to pollution*. The slow flow rate of groundwater compared to surface water leads to low ability to decompose the once existing contamination. Furthermore, in the case of non-renewable groundwater, the absence of recharge and the stagnant character of those aquifers prevent any natural cleansing process. Once the aquifer is polluted, it is very expensive and time-consuming to clean, if possible at all, and the resource can be unusable for years or even decades.[29]

Non-renewable aquifers can be considered an *ending* resource because they lack natural recharge. In other words, the amount of water in a non-renewable aquifer is steady under normal conditions, or it can be diminished by human induced discharge. Sustainable use of non-renewable groundwater, by strict definition, remains problematic.[30]

## IV  Existing Legal Regimes Addressing Transboundary Groundwater

Groundwater was not high on the agenda of the international community until recent years. In the past, only very few international agreements exclusively

---

28  S.C. McCaffrey, 'International Water Cooperation in the 21st Century: Recent Developments in the Law of International Watercourses' (2009) 103 AJIL 272, 286.

29  G. Eckstein, 'A Hydrogeological Perspective of the Status of Groundwater Resources under the UN Watercourses Convention' (2005) 30 Colum. J. Envt'l L. 525, 560; Eckstein and Eckstein, 'A Hydrogeological Approach to Transboundary Groundwater Resources and International Law', at 210, 247.

30  C.M. Weber, *Grundwasser im Völkerrecht—Eine Untersuchung der Draft Articles der UN International Law Commission über das Recht grenzüberschreitender Aquifere im Kontext des internationalen Wasserrechts* (Duncker & Humblot 2019), at 33.

addressed groundwater in a local context.[31] In contrast, transboundary rivers or lakes were subject to hundreds of treaties by the second half of the 20th century.[32] Where treaties on surface water bodies include groundwater, they tend to treat the resource only as incidental. Hence, use and protection of groundwater is not adequately regulated.[33]

The reasons for this lack of interest in groundwater are numerous. One has to invoke the complex nature of aquifers, which differs from that of surface water. The special features of aquifers are, although not completely, only nowadays scientifically investigated.[34] However, although science gained a great insight into the resource of groundwater, factual uncertainties remain. For instance, the exact amount of water stored in an aquifer can in many cases only be roughly estimated.[35] Paucity of groundwater data compounds difficulties in precise prediction of the impacts of groundwater exploitation.[36]

---

31   For the Franco-Swiss Genevese Aquifer: Convention relative à la protection, à l'utilisation, à la réalimentation et au suivi de la nappe souterraine franco-suisse du Genevois [Convention on the Protection, Utilization, Recharge and Monitoring of the Franco-Swiss Genevese Aquifer] (signed 18 December 2017, entered into force 1 January 2008); for a discussion see G. de los Cobos, 'Transboundary Water Resources and International Law: the Example of the Aquifer Management of the Geneva Region' in L. Boisson de Chazournes, C. Leb and M. Tignino (eds), *International Law and Fresh Water* (Elgar 2013) 179. For the Nubian Sandstone Aquifer System: Technical Agreements on Monitoring and Data Sharing related to the Programme for the Development of a Regional Strategy for the Utilisation of the Nubian Sandstone Aquifer System, reprinted in S. Burchi and K. Mechlem, *Groundwater in International Law: Compilation of Treaties and Other Legal Instruments* (FAO/UNESCO 2005) 4. For the Northwestern Sahara Aquifer: Technical Agreement on the Establishment of a Consultation Mechanism for the Northwestern Sahara Aquifer System (done 2002), reprinted in S. Burchi and K. Mechlem, *Groundwater in International Law: Compilation of Treaties and Other Legal Instruments* (FAO/UNESCO 2005) 6. For the Iullemeden Aquifer System: Memorandum of Understanding relating to a Setting up of a Consultative Mechanism for the Management of the Iullemeden Aquifer System (signed 20 June 2009, not yet in force). For the Guaraní Aquifer System: Guaraní Aquifer Agreement (signed 2 August 2010, not yet in force); for a discussion, see F. Sindico, 'The Guaraní Aquifer System and the Law of Transboundary Aquifers' (2011) 13 ICLR 255.
32   K. Mechlem, 'Moving Ahead in Protecting Freshwater Resources: the International Law Commission's Draft Articles on Transboundary Aquifers' (2009) 22 LJIL 801, 803.
33   Ibid., at 804; A. Tanzi, 'Furthering International Water Law or Making a New Body of Law on Transboundary Aquifers? An Introduction' (2011) 13 ICLR 193.
34   See for instance, the case of offshore aquifers, R. Martin-Nagle, 'Transboundary Offshore Aquifers—a Search for a Governance Regime' (2016) 1 International Water Law 1.
35   For instance, the lifetime of the Nubian Sandstone Aquifer System ranges from 60–100 to 4,625 years, see Weber, *Grundwasser im Völkerrecht—Eine Untersuchung der Draft Articles der UN International Law Commission über das Recht grenzüberschreitender Aquifere im Kontext des internationalen Wasserrechts*, at 117.
36   G. Eckstein, 'Protecting a Hidden Resource: the UN International Law Commission and the International Law of Transboundary Groundwater Resources' (2004) Sustainable

Moreover, as groundwater is a hidden resource not visible as is surface water, limitations on sovereignty in cases of shared aquifers is less accepted than it is, for example, with respect to transboundary rivers or lakes.[37]

One of the first steps in the legal protection of transboundary groundwater resources was taken by the International Law Association (ILA). The scope of the 1966 Helsinki Rules on the Uses of Waters of International Rivers[38] covers the drainage basin, defined as 'a geographical area [...] determined by the watershed limits of the system of waters, including surface and underground water, flowing into a common terminus' (Art. II). The scope includes groundwater but only if it is connected with a surface water body through a common terminus. Moreover, none of the provisions set out specifically aquifer-related rules. In 1986, the ILA drafted the Seoul Rules on International Groundwaters.[39] The Seoul Rules constitute the first regulation exclusively dealing with transboundary groundwater resources. In particular, they regulate non-renewable transboundary groundwater resources, which were excluded by the Helsinki Rules. Art. I of the Seoul Rules states:

> The waters of an aquifer that is intersected by the boundary between two or more States are international groundwaters if such an aquifer with its waters forms an international basin or part thereof [...] whether or not the aquifer and its waters form with surface waters part of a hydraulic system flowing into a common terminus.

Furthermore, the Seoul Rules codify provisions relating to the protection and management of groundwater resources[40] and respect the relation between surface water and groundwater.[41] Although the Seoul Rules can be seen in this regard as a step forward in the protection of groundwater resources, they were not legally binding and in practice have little effect.[42]

The same is true for the most recent ILA work, the Berlin Rules on Water Resources[43] of 2004. The Berlin Rules include all aquifer types, including

---

Development Law & Policy 5; J. Barberis, 'The Development of International Law of Transboundary Groundwater' (1991) 31 Natural Resources Journal 167, at 168–169.

37 McCaffrey, *The Law of International Watercourses*, at 417.
38 ILA 'Helsinki Rules on the Uses of the Water of International Rivers' (August 1966) in ILA 'Report of the 52nd Conference, Helsinki', at 484.
39 ILA 'Rules on International Groundwaters' (August 1986) in ILA 'Report of the 62nd Conference, Seoul', at 251.
40 Arts III and IV Seoul Rules.
41 Art. II Seoul Rules.
42 E. Brown Weiss, *International Law for a Water-Scarce World* (Nijhoff 2013), at 117–119.
43 ILA 'Berlin Rules on Water Resources' (August 2004) in ILA 'Report of the 71st Conference, Berlin', at 337.

non-renewable ones and national groundwater resources.[44] They also set out detailed provisions regarding protection and management of groundwater resources and obligations of information and consultation.[45]

Another major effort to provide legal rules for the protection and management of international groundwater was undertaken by a group of experts who created a model treaty called the Bellagio Draft Treaty.[46] The Bellagio Draft Treaty was intended as practical guidance for further treaty-making and not as a mere restatement of rules on international water law.[47] However, the Bellagio Draft Treaty has not served as a model for a single agreement on groundwater resources.[48]

The UN Convention on the Law of the Non-Navigational Uses of International Watercourses (UN Watercourses Convention)[49] can be viewed as the milestone in the evolution of international water law, as it is the most comprehensive and authoritative framework in this area.[50] However, it suffers from gaps in the protection of groundwater resources. This is particularly obvious when considering the scope of the Convention. The Convention applies to international watercourses (Art. 1), defined as 'a system of surface and groundwaters constituting by virtue of their physical relationship a unitary whole and normally flowing into a common terminus'. This definition excludes various types of aquifers. The clause 'system of surface waters and groundwaters' excludes non-renewable aquifers,[51] as well as renewable ones without any connection to a surface water body,[52] from the scope of the Convention.[53] The requirement of a 'unitary whole [...] normally flowing into a common terminus' is also problematic as it does not adequately reflect hydrological realities. For

---

44  Arts 1, 42 (1) (b) Berlin Rules.
45  Arts 37–41 Berlin Rules.
46  R. Hayton and A. Utton, 'Transboundary Groundwaters: the Bellagio Draft Treaty' (1989) 19 Nat. Res. J. 663.
47  McCaffrey, *The Law of International Watercourses* 427.
48  K. Mechlem, 'Past, Present and Future of the International Law Transboundary Aquifers' (2011) 13 Int'l Comm. L. Rev. 209, at 213.
49  Convention on the Law of the Non-Navigational Uses of International Watercourses (adopted and opened for signature 21 May 1997, entered into force 17 August 2014) (1997) 36 ILM 700.
50  K. Mechlem, 'International Groundwater Law: Towards Closing the Gaps?' (2003) 14 Y. Int'l Env. L. 47, at 53.
51  For instance, the Nubian Sandstone Aquifer System, see Mechlem, 'International Groundwater Law: Towards Closing the Gaps?', at 53.
52  E.g. the Mountain Aquifer under Israel and the Gaza Bank which is solely recharged by rainwater. See Eckstein and Eckstein, 'A Hydrogeological Approach to Transboundary Groundwater Resources and International Law', at 213.
53  Mechlem, 'International Groundwater Law: Towards Closing the Gaps?', at 54–57.

instance, an aquifer can be hydraulically linked to various river basins. However, a river and an aquifer can also function as distinct water systems, although hydraulic linkages may exist. Moreover, surface water normally flows into a common terminus, for instance, into the sea. In contrast, aquifers can flow into several adjacent river basins. This phenomenon was illustrated in the 1927 case 'sinking of the Danube' or *Donauversinkungsfall* of the German *Staatsgerichtshof*.[54] Hence, in some cases the Convention's scope is difficult to determine. The exclusion of certain types of aquifers was in line with the ILC's original intention to cover groundwater only with regard to its interdependency and interrelation with surface water.[55]

There are also gaps in the normative content of the Convention with regard to groundwater resources. For instance, the no-harm principle in Art. 7 only covers harm resulting from the utilization of an international watercourse. In the case of aquifers, harm can also occur through use of adjacent land or a hydraulically linked resource. To give an example, pollution of a recharge zone is likely to affect the aquifer.[56]

A greater level of protection of groundwater resources has been achieved through the UN Economic Commission for Europe (UNECE) Convention on the Protection and Use of Transboundary Watercourses and International Lakes (UNECE Water Convention).[57] Initially developed as a regional instrument, the Convention has been open for ratification for non-UNECE members since 2013.[58] The UNECE Water Convention addresses 'transboundary waters' and is broader than the UN Watercourses Convention. According to Art. 1, 'transboundary waters' are 'any surface or ground waters which mark, cross or are located on the boundaries between two or more States'. Thus, the scope of the UNECE Water Convention includes every type of transboundary groundwater. Moreover, the Convention explicitly focuses on groundwater, by obligating prevention, control and reduction of transboundary impacts on water resources.[59]

---

54   *Staatsgerichtshof für das Deutsche Reich, Land Württemberg und Land Preußen gegen das Land Baden betreffend die Donauversinkung* (Judgment of 18 June 1927) RGZ 116.
55   UN ILC 'Report of the International Law Commission: 46th Session' (2 May–22 July 1994) UN Doc. A/49/10, at para. 216.
56   Mechlem, 'International Groundwater Law: Towards Closing the Gaps?', at 59–62.
57   Convention on the Protection and Use of Transboundary Watercourses and International Lakes (with Annexes) (done 17 March 1992, entered into force 6 October 1996) 1936 UNTS 269.
58   UN Doc. ECE/MP.WAT/13 (2 September 2003). The treaty modification entered into force on 6 February 2013.
59   Arts 2 and 3 UNECE Water Convention. For instance, Art. 3 (1) (k) lays down the obligation to adopt additional specific measures to prevent pollution of groundwaters.

Additionally, the 1999 Protocol on Water and Health,[60] which aims to improve water supply and sanitation, recognizes the importance of groundwater and addresses integrated management plans explicitly including groundwater.[61] Together with the Model Provisions on Transboundary Groundwaters of 2013,[62] the UNECE Water Convention provides a comprehensive basis for the protection and management of groundwater resources.[63]

## V  Evolving Regime of the ILC Draft Articles

The ILC Draft Articles on the Law of Transboundary Aquifers comprise nineteen articles that lay down a set of obligations and general principles, organized into four parts—Introduction (I), General Principles (II), Protection, Preservation and Management (III), and Miscellaneous Provisions (IV). Although the Draft Articles apply to groundwater resources, the ILC's work was clearly inspired by the UN Watercourses Convention, mainly due to the fact that it has its roots in the drafting process of the latter.

### 1  *Evolution of the ILC Draft Articles*

From an early stage, the ILC's work during the drafting of the UN Watercourses Convention primarily focused on surface water. Only in 1991, after 20 years of drafting and three years before the work was completed, the ILC decided to include groundwater in its agenda.[64] In 1992, Special Rapporteur Robert Rosenstock strongly recommended including all groundwater resources, especially non-renewable ones:

---

60   Protocol on Water and Health to the 1992 Convention on the Protection and Use of Transboundary Watercourses and International Lakes (adopted 17 June 1999, entered into force 4 August 2005) 2231 UNTS 202.
61   See Arts 2 (10), 6 (5) (b) Protocol on Water and Health.
62   UNECE 'Model Provisions on Transboundary Groundwaters' (2014) UN Doc. ECE/MP.WAT/40.
63   See also Mechlem, 'Past, Present and Future of the International Law Transboundary Aquifers' (2011), at 215. The UNECE recognized the importance of groundwater resources at an early stage, as shows the UNECE 'Charter on Groundwater Management' (1989) UN Doc. E/ECE/1197-ECE/ENVWA/12.
64   UN ILC 'Report of the International Law Commission: 46th Session' (2 May–22 July 1994) UN Doc. A/49/10, at 135.

If 'unrelated' confined groundwaters are excluded from the scope of the present draft articles, it would leave a lacuna or a vacuum in the management of transboundary water resources.[65]

However, the ILC rejected this proposal since it did not want to include a resource it had not considered while drafting its articles.[66] Considering the existing gap, which lead to a large number of aquifers not being covered by the Draft Articles, the ILC adopted a Resolution on Confined Transboundary Aquifers.[67] It recommended that in case of regulation of transboundary groundwater resources, the States should be guided by the principles of the Draft Articles.[68] Furthermore, it recognized 'the need for continuing efforts to elaborate rules pertaining to confined transboundary groundwater'.[69] In the following, the ILC integrated 'shared natural resources', i.e. confined transboundary groundwaters in the sense of non-renewable or fossil groundwaters, oil and gas, into its agenda.[70] Due to the continuous resistance of the States fearing that 'shared' could lead to a limitation of sovereignty rights, the ILC gave up this attribute.[71] The ILC assumed the law governing groundwater was more akin to that governing oil and gas than to that regulating surface water.[72] However, the newly appointed Special Rapporteur Chusei Yamada recommended in his first report of 2003 to begin with confined transboundary groundwater and considered it indispensable to gain deeper knowledge of this resource.[73] After examining transboundary groundwaters more thoroughly, the Special Rapporteur

---

65  UN ILC Special Rapporteur R. Rosenstock 'Second Report on the Law of the Non-Navigational Uses of International Watercourses' (1992) UN Doc. A/CN.4/462, at para. 39.
66  Mechlem, 'Moving Ahead in Protecting Freshwater Resources: the International Law Commission's Draft Articles on Transboundary Aquifers' 805; UN ILC 'Report of the International Law Commission: 46th Session' (2 May–22 July 1994) UN Doc. A/49/10, at 90.
67  UN ILC 'Report of the International Law Commission: 46th Session' (2 May–22 July 1994) UN Doc. A/49/10, 135.
68  Ibid.
69  Ibid.
70  UN ILC 'Report of the International Law Commission: 54th Session' (29 April–7 June and 22 July–16 August 2002), UN Doc. A/57/10, at para. 518.
71  For instance, States feared that 'shared' could be understood as 'shared ownership' or 'shared heritage of mankind', see UN ILC Special Rapporteur C Yamada 'Second Report on Shared Natural Resources: Transboundary Groundwaters' (9 March 2004) UN Doc. A/CN.4/539, at para. 3.
72  UN ILC 'Report of the International Law Commission: 55th Session' (5 May–6 June and 7 July–8 August 2003), UN Doc. A/58/10, at para. 376.
73  UN ILC Special Rapporteur C Yamada 'Shared Natural Resources: First Report on Outlines' (30 April 2003) UN Doc. A/CN.4/533, at para. 4.

suggested to remove the 'confined' and to replace 'groundwaters' by 'aquifers'. With the qualifier 'confined', the ILC intended to limit the scope to non-renewable groundwater resources.[74] From a hydrogeological point of view, however, non-renewable groundwater resources can be 'confined' or 'unconfined'.[75] In hydrogeological terms, groundwater should not be treated separately from the rock formation surrounding it, as it is contained in its pores.[76] Thus, the object of study should encompass both, the geologic formation and the water contained therein: the aquifer.[77]

The Special Rapporteur further recommended legally treating transboundary aquifers differently than oil and gas.[78] Although non-renewable groundwater and oil and gas resources have certain similarities, as they are both stored underground in a similar reservoir rock, they are substantively different. In contrast to oil and gas, water is crucial for human life, while fossil fuels are commercial commodities whose value is driven by market forces. Due to its high vulnerability to pollution, the exploitation of an aquifer poses a risk to water quality, whereas effluent groundwater does generally not cause any harm to the environment. Conversely, the exploitation of an oilfield can have substantive negative impacts on its surroundings.[79] The majority of the States followed this approach.[80]

Between 2003 and 2008, Special Rapporteur Yamada presented five reports. The third report included a draft of provisions on the law of transboundary aquifers without giving a recommendation on their future form.[81] The ILC

---

74  UN ILC 'Summary Record of the 2797th Meeting' (12 May 2004) UN Doc. A/CN.4/SR.2797, at para. 11.
75  UN ILC Special Rapporteur C Yamada 'Shared Natural Resources: First Report on Outlines' (30 April 2003) UN Doc. A/CN.4/533, at paras 19, 30. See also Mechlem, 'Moving Ahead in Protecting Freshwater Resources: the International Law Commission's Draft Articles on Transboundary Aquifers' 806–809; R.M. Stephan, 'The Draft Articles on the Law of Transboundary Aquifers: the Process at the UN ILC' (2011) 13 Int'l Comm. L. Rev. 223, at 224.
76  See also Stephan, 'The Draft Articles on the Law of Transboundary Aquifers: the Process at the UN ILC', at 226.
77  UN ILC Special Rapporteur C Yamada 'Second Report on Shared Natural Resources: Transboundary Groundwaters' (9 March 2004) UN Doc. A/CN.4/539, at para. 17.
78  UN ILC Special Rapporteur C Yamada 'Fourth Report on Shared Natural Resources: Transboundary Groundwaters' (6 March 2007) UN Doc. A/CN.4/580, at para. 14.
79  Ibid., at paras 12, 14.
80  UN ILC Special Rapporteur C Yamada 'Fifth Report on Shared Natural Resources: Transboundary Aquifers' (21 February 2008) UN Doc. A/CN.4/591, at para. 5.
81  UN ILC Special Rapporteur C Yamada 'Third Report on Shared Natural Resources: Transboundary Groundwaters' (11 February 2005) UN Doc. A./CN.4/551 and Add.1, at para. 4.

adopted the articles on their first reading.[82] The process within the ILC allows States to comment on the draft. The ILC received comments from 47 Member States and the Special Rapporteur presented the modified fifth report in 2008.[83] On the second reading, the ILC adopted the Draft Articles and submitted them to the UN General Assembly.[84] The UN General Assembly commended the Draft Articles to the attention of governments as guidance for bilateral or regional agreements and arrangements for the proper management of transboundary aquifers.[85]

## 2   Main Criticisms of the ILC Draft Articles

The ILC Draft Articles constitute a novelty in international water law as the first legal regime addressing solely groundwater resources. However, with the special features of groundwater and the importance of the resource for the global water supply in mind, shortcomings can be detected.

### a   Scope of Application

The first part of the Draft Articles 'Introduction' sets out the scope of application (Art. 1) and the relevant definitions (Art. 2). The Draft Articles apply to 'transboundary aquifers or aquifers systems'. According to Art. 2 (a), an aquifer is 'permeable water-bearing geological formation underlain by a less permeable layer and the water contained in the saturated zone of the formation'. Hence, an aquifer is the geologic formation and the water contained within it. Although the ILC does not use this term, 'the water contained in it' means from a hydrogeological perspective groundwater. In the ILC's view, this approach was scientifically most precise and leaves less ground for mistakes in application.[86] Including the rock formation in the scope acknowledges that many groundwater-related problems result from problems in the geologic formation. For example, degradation of groundwater quality can occur by pollutants washing out of the associated rock formation.[87] Since groundwater

---

[82]  UN ILC 'Report of the International Law Commission: 58th Session' (1 May–9 June and 3 July–11 August 2006), at para. 72.

[83]  UN ILC Special Rapporteur C Yamada 'Fifth Report on Shared Natural Resources: Transboundary Aquifers' (21 February 2008) UN Doc. A/CN.4/591, at para. 2.

[84]  UN ILC 'Report of the International Law Commission: 60th Session' (5 May–6 June and 7 July–8 August 2008), UN Doc. A/63/10, at paras 47–48.

[85]  UNGA Res 63/124 'The Law of Transboundary Aquifers' (11 December 2008).

[86]  UN ILC 'Report of the International Law Commission: 60th Session' (5 May–6 June and 7 July–8 August 2008) UN Doc. A/63/10, 32.

[87]  Mechlem, 'Moving Ahead in Protecting Freshwater Resources: the International Law Commission's Draft Articles on Transboundary Aquifers', at 808.

and the rock formation are interrelated, it is necessary to manage and monitor the groundwater and the rock formation jointly in order to properly protect the water.[88] However, leaving out the definition of 'groundwater' ignores the characteristics of the resource. Specifically, due to its mobility, only the groundwater, not the rock, crosses international borders.[89] This is even more problematic regarding the sovereignty clause in Art. 3. The definition focuses primarily on the rock and only secondarily on the groundwater as the 'water contained in the saturated zone of the formation'. Based on this definition, it appears the predominant concern of the ILC was with the geologic formation and not the water.[90] In contrast, the overriding focus of the ILA Seoul Rules is explicitly on groundwater.[91] This is even more true with regard to the attribute 'transboundary' that leaves out some types of aquifers as such situated entirely in the territory of one country but contributing water to a river that crosses a State boundary.[92]

The ILC Draft Articles' definition of an aquifer is also limited to those parts of the rock formation actually storing groundwater ('a permeable water-bearing geological formation [...] and the water contained in [it]'). Hence, potentially water-bearing zones, such as recharge and discharge zones, are excluded from the definition. In contrast, from the hydrogeological perspective, aquifers are classified according to potential for storing, transmitting, and producing water in usable quantities.[93] The ILC excluded those zones intentionally, arguing with the need for and difficulty in establishing geographic limitations for an aquifer. However, the recharge and discharge zones and the defined aquifer are interrelated. Protection of these zones is therefore crucial, since their contamination can lead to pollution of the geologic formation and water contained therein.[94] In this regard, Art. 11 provides for a certain level of

---

88   Mechlem, 'Past, Present and Future of the International Law Transboundary Aquifers', at 219.
89   Mechlem, 'Past, Present and Future of the International Law Transboundary Aquifers', at 219.
90   S.C. McCaffrey, 'The International Law Commission Adopts Articles on Transboundary Aquifers' (2017) 103 AJIL 272, at 283.
91   Ibid.; see Art. 1 Seoul Rules: 'the waters of international aquifers'.
92   See also Mechlem, 'Moving Ahead in Protecting Freshwater Resources: the International Law Commission's Draft Articles on Transboundary Aquifers', at 809; legal regulations that include all aquifer types are the ILA Berlin Rules and the UNECE Protocol on Water and Health.
93   Eckstein 'Protecting a Hidden Resource: the UN International Law Commission and the International Law of Transboundary Groundwater Resources', at 5, 7; Fetter, *Applied Hydrogeology*, at 95.
94   Eckstein 'Protecting a Hidden Resource: the UN International Law Commission and the International Law of Transboundary Groundwater Resources', at 5, 7.

protection. According to this provision, States shall 'take appropriate measures to prevent and minimize detrimental impacts on the recharge and discharge processes'. However, Art. 11 is located under the third part of the Draft Articles, namely 'Protection, Preservation and Management'. The General Principles set out in part two are therefore not applicable to recharge and discharge zones. With regard to the—from the hydrogeological perspective—artificial legal separation of the aquifer and the recharge and discharge zones, the ILC Draft Articles provide for a different legal treatment of the same resource: the groundwater.

Further legal problems arise from the water-bearing formation definition of aquifers. In the case of renewable aquifers, the share of the geologic formation actually storing groundwater is dependant on the recharge, and therefore constantly changing. In other words, if there is a drought, the share of rock bearing groundwater is smaller than during heavy rains. The definition can be regarded as 'dynamic'.[95] Eckstein describes it as a 'compromise between scientists and jurists'.[96] However, this means only the actual water-bearing geological formation is protected by the Draft Articles. Likewise as for the exclusion of the re- and discharge zones, only the protection of the potential water-bearing formation would prevent potential damage to the groundwater.

The ILC's decision to retain the attribute 'transboundary' and refrain from defining it as 'international' is also crucial to legal interpretations for groundwater protections.[97] 'Transboundary aquifers' are a subcategory of 'international aquifers'. An aquifer is only classified as transboundary if the aquifer itself crosses a border; thus, this definition excludes aquifers, which have an adjacent transboundary river. Both aquifers are international. From a hydrogeological point of view, there is no difference between those aquifers. Furthermore, since the UN Watercourses Convention covers all groundwater that is hydrologically linked to surface water, and thus also transboundary aquifers, there is an overlap between the two instruments. This overlap is problematic because the ILC Draft Articles are guided by the principle of sovereignty, which is inconsistent with the UN Watercourses Convention, as will be discussed below.[98]

---

95  G. Eckstein, 'Commentary on the UN International Law Commission's Draft Articles on the Law of Transboundary Aquifers' (2007) 18 Colo. J. Int'l L. & Pol'y 537, at 550.
96  Ibid., at 550.
97  UN ILC Special Rapporteur C Yamada 'Shared Natural Resources: First Report on Outlines' (30 April 2003) UN Doc. A/CN.4/533, at para. 38.
98  McCaffrey, 'The International Law Commission Adopts Articles on Transboundary Aquifers', at 284.

b	Principle of No Harm

The ILC Draft Articles include the principle of no harm. According to Art. 6 (1), aquifer States[99] are obliged 'to take all appropriate measures to prevent the causing of significant harm to other aquifer States or States in whose territory a discharge zone is located'. The relevant requirement is the significance of harm. The ILC did not provide for a definition of significant harm. The threshold was understood as more than detectable but not necessarily serious or substantial harm.[100] Hence, the ILC applied the interpretation of 'significant' it outlined in the previous drafting of the UN Watercourses Convention.[101] With regard to the high vulnerability of aquifers and their low ability to decompose contamination, during the drafting process, some States called for a lower threshold of significance compared to surface water.[102] Special Rapporteur Yamada, however, did not see the need for a lower threshold, arguing that the

> threshold of 'significant' harm is a flexible and relative concept. Factual considerations, rather than a legal determination, have to be taken into account in each specific case, [...] also bearing in mind the fragility of aquifers.[103]

This fragility cannot be underestimated, as there can be substantive delays between a harmful activity and the manifestation of this very harm, due to the slow flow rate of groundwater or the time needed for a contaminant to percolate through the soil.[104] It is very likely that harm to an aquifer would be detected considerably later than it would be in the case of surface water. Considering the challenge of cleaning of aquifers, there are convincing arguments for advocating for a lower threshold for significant damage, for instance, such as every negative impact on aquifers.[105]

---

99   An aquifer State is a 'State in whose territory any part of a transboundary aquifer or aquifer system is situated' (Art. 2 (d) Draft Articles).
100  UN ILC 'Report of the International Law Commission: 60th Session' (5 May–6 June and 7 July–8 August 2008) UN Doc. A/63/10, at 47.
101  Ibid.
102  UN ILC Special Rapporteur C Yamada 'Second Report on Shared Natural Resources: Transboundary Groundwaters' (9 March 2004) UN Doc. A/CN.4/539, at para. 25.
103  Ibid.
104  Mechlem, 'Moving Ahead in Protecting Freshwater Resources: the International Law Commission's Draft Articles on Transboundary Aquifers', at 814.
105  See also R. Wolfrum, 'Schutz und Management von Grundwasser aus der Sicht des Völkerrechts' (2018) 16 EurUP 109, at 111; for a discussion of a lower threshold in the general context of transfrontier pollution, see R. Wolfrum, 'Purposes and Principles of International Environmental Law' (1990) 33 GYIL 308, at 311.

The threshold of significance is of importance for the relation between the principle of no harm and the principle of equitable utilization (Art. 4). Art. 6 (3) addresses the case where significant harm is caused. In such scenario, the State causing the harm shall take 'all appropriate response measures to eliminate or mitigate such harm, having due regard for the provisions of draft articles 4 and 5'.[106] Unlike in the corresponding Art. 7 (2) of the UN Watercourses Convention, compensation is not addressed since the ILC saw the issue governed by rules of international law relating to State responsibility or international liability for acts not prohibited by international law.[107] By citing Arts 4 and 5, the ILC Draft Articles link the principle of no harm to the principle of equitable and reasonable utilization. However, the ILC gives no clear indication of priority between the two principles. Art. 12 could clarify the priority between the principles of no harm and equitable utilization, stating the obligation of States to prevent, reduce or control pollution of aquifers 'that may cause significant harm to other aquifer States'. 'Prevent' refers to new pollution, whereas 'control' and 'reduce' relate to already existing pollution.[108] Thus, Art. 12 only addresses impacts on the quality of water, and protects solely aquifer States. In contrast, Art. 6 is not limited to pollution and protects both aquifer States and States in whose territory a discharge zone is located. Art. 12 can be regarded as a preventive *lex specialis* to the general principle contained in Art. 6 (1) and (2), whereas Art. 6 (3) refers to the slightly different situation when harm has already occurred.[109] According to the ILC, Art. 12 also has priority over Art. 4.[110] Hence, an equitable utilization of an aquifer might lead to pollution causing significant harm to other aquifer States pursuant to Art. 12.[111] Besides the priority of the prevention of pollution, it cannot be inferred from the article's wording and commentary that the ILC wanted to introduce a general rule of primacy of the no harm principle over the principle of equitable utilization.[112]

---

106  Art. 6 (3) ILC Draft Articles.
107  UN ILC 'Report of the International Law Commission: 60th Session' (5 May–6 June and 7 July–8 August 2008) UN Doc. A/63/10, at 47.
108  Ibid., at 58.
109  Weber, *Grundwasser im Völkerrecht—Eine Untersuchung der Draft Articles der UN International Law Commission über das Recht grenzüberschreitender Aquifere im Kontext des internationalen Wasserrechts*, at 132.
110  UN ILC 'Report of the International Law Commission: 60th Session' (5 May–6 June and 7 July–8 August 2008) UN Doc. A/63/10, at 58.
111  Weber, *Grundwasser im Völkerrecht—Eine Untersuchung der Draft Articles der UN International Law Commission über das Recht grenzüberschreitender Aquifere im Kontext des internationalen Wasserrechts*, at132.
112  Ibid. at 133. In contrast, Mechlem argues that the principle of equitable utilization takes priority over the obligation not to cause significant harm, see Mechlem, 'Moving Ahead

Absolute priority for the principle of no harm is not completely desirable. In this case, aquifer States could continually be prevented from utilization with the argument of causing significant harm, especially if the aquifer has never been used. Considering the different levels of development of aquifer States,[113] the importance of groundwater for the water supply and fundamental human needs, such priority would have undesirable consequences. In case of primacy of the principle of equitable utilization, equitable and reasonable utilization of an aquifer that causes significant harm to the environment could nevertheless take place. This is particularly worrying regarding environmental protection, the high vulnerability of aquifers and also the mobility of groundwater—the latter might spread the harm. However, it would have been desirable to lay down a clear indication to which extent a principle prevails.[114]

c  Overlap with Other International Water Law Agreements

The ILC Draft Articles significantly overlap with other international water law agreements, especially the UN Watercourses Convention and the UNECE Water Convention.

The UN Watercourses Convention is applicable to all groundwater hydrologically linked to surface water.[115] The scope of the ILC Draft Articles covers 'transboundary aquifers'; thus, the majority of aquifers fall within the scope of both instruments.

There are three types of aquifers where no overlap occurs. The first type of aquifer not covered by the UN Watercourses Convention is a transboundary aquifer without any surface water connection, like fossil aquifers. These aquifers are covered by the ILC Draft Articles.[116] In contrast to the Convention, the ILC Draft Aricles are not applicable to an aquifer, which does not cross borders but is hydrologically linked with surface water flowing between two States.[117]

---

in Protecting Freshwater Resources: the International Law Commission's Draft Articles on Transboundary Aquifers', at 814–815.

113  For instance, the economically stronger aquifer States Egypt and Libya have used the Nubian Sandstone Aquifer System more intensively than the less developed aquifer State Chad. See Alker, 'The Nubian Sandstone Aquifer System', at 243–244.

114  For a solution to this conflict that differs between significant harm to water quality and to water quantity, see A.E. Utton, 'Which Rule Should Prevail in International Water Law Disputes: that of Reasonableness or that of No Harm?' (1996) 36 Natural Resources Journal 635.

115  Art. 2 (a) UN Watercourses Convention.
116  Art. 2 (a) Draft Articles.
117  Art. 2 (c) Draft Articles.

Both instruments are not applicable to mere domestic aquifers without any connection to surface water.[118]

However, the case of a non-transboundary aquifer flowing into a transboundary surface water resource is also problematic. From a hydrological point of view, there is no difference between this aquifer and a transboundary aquifer connected with surface water. The difference lies in the geopolitical borders that do not match hydrological realities. Both legal instruments, the ILC Draft Articles and the UN Watercourses Convention, are not perfectly congruent. As discussed above, the guiding principle of the ILC Draft Articles appears to be 'sovereignty', whereas that of the Convention is 'equitable utilization'.[119] Consequently, two hydrologically identical situations are treated under two different legal regimes, leading to an arbitrary splitting of the same resource.

The overlap concerning a transboundary aquifer hydrologically linked with surface water is also problematic. In the ILC Draft Articles, no provision refers to the Draft Articles' relationship with other water law instruments. The Special Rapporteur proposed the introduction of Art. 20 which states that the ILC Draft Articles would prevail over any inconsistent instrument, including the UN Watercourses Convention.[120] However, the article was removed due to sharp resistance of the States.[121] It is not surprising that the States were reluctant to introduce such norm, as the proposal contradicts the UN Watercourses Convention, which also declares prevalence over other inconsistent agreements.[122] The question of prevalence is not merely theoretical since both instruments are not entirely congruent, especially considering differing guiding principles of sovereignty and equitable utilization.

---

118   Art. 2 (b) UN Watercourses Convention; Art. 2 (c) Draft Articles.
119   McCaffrey, 'The International Law Commission Adopts Articles on Transboundary Aquifers', at 287.
120   See Art. 20: 1. The present Draft Articles shall not alter the rights and obligations of the States Parties which arise from other conventions and international agreements compatible with the present Draft Articles and which do not affect the enjoyment by other States Parties of their rights or the performance of their obligations under the present Draft Articles. 2. Notwithstanding the provisions of paragraph 1, when the States Parties to the present Draft Articles are parties also to the Convention on the Law of the Non-navigational Uses of International Watercourses, the provisions of the latter concerning transboundary aquifers or aquifer systems apply only to the extent that they are compatible with those of the present Draft Articles.
121   UN ILC 'Report of the International Law Commission: 60th Session' (5 May–6 June and 7 July–8 August 2008) UN Doc. A/63/10, at paras 39–42.
122   Art. 3 (1) UN Watercourses Convention: 'In the absence of an agreement to the contrary, nothing in the present Convention shall affect the rights or obligations of a watercourse State arising from agreements in force for it on the date on which it became a party to the present Convention'.

The conflict between the ILC Draft Articles and the UN Watercourses Convention could be resolved by applying the *lex specialis* rule. Consequently the ILC Draft Articles, as the regime exclusively applicable to aquifers, would prevail over the more general UN Watercourses Convention.[123] A point to remember in this regard is that of recharge and discharge zones: For instance, the watercourse of an aquifer can be considered as a discharge zone.[124] As already discussed above, those zones are not protected by the general principles (Arts 3 through 9), but only by the provisions on protection, preservation and management (Arts 10 through 15), which leads to arbitrarily splitting a hydrological unit. In case of an international watercourse, the discharge zones, as well as the hydrologically linked groundwater, fall under the scope of the UN Watercourses Convention. However, the general prevalence of the Convention is not preferable, since it is not exclusively designed for aquifers.

The same is true for the UNECE Water Convention. The Convention is applicable to 'transboundary waters', meaning 'ground waters which mark, cross or are located on boundaries between two or more States'.[125] Hence, groundwater falls under the scope of the UNECE Water Convention, but the rock formation does not. However, due to the linkage between rock and water, negative effects on the geological formation could be encompassed by 'transboundary impacts'[126] and 'measures for the prevention, control and reduction of water pollution'.[127] Consequently, the UNECE Water Convention protects the same aquifer types as the ILC Draft Articles. The need for groundwater protection is also considered in the UNECE Water Convention,[128] as it is in other UNECE instruments.[129] In particular, the UNECE Model Provisions on Transboundary Groundwaters of 2014 make reference to the ILC Draft Articles.[130] In contrast,

---

123 Also K. Mechlem, 'Moving Ahead in Protecting Freshwater Resources: the International Law Commission's Draft Articles on Transboundary Aquifers' (2009) 22 LJIL 801, at 809.
124 Art.2 (h) ILC Draft Articles. UN ILC 'Report of the International Law Commission: 60th Session' (5 May–6 June and 7 July–8 August 2008) UN Doc. A/63/10, at 38.
125 Art. 1 (1) UNECE Water Convention.
126 Art. 1 (2) UNECE Water Convention.
127 Art. 2 (3) UNECE Water Convention.
128 See for instance Art. 3 (1) (k) UNECE Water Convention.
129 Protocol on Water and Health to the 1992 Convention on the Protection and Use of Transboundary Watercourses and International Lakes (adopted 17 June 1999, entered into force 4 August 2005) 2231 UNTS 202. UNECE, Model Provisions on Transboundary Groundwaters, ECE/MP.WAT/40 (2014).
130 UNECE Model Provisions on Transboundary Groundwaters, at 4: 'The present exercise [the model provisions] builds on that instrument [the ILC Draft Articles] with a view to providing concrete guidance for implementing, with regard to groundwater, the 1992 Convention on the Protection and Use of Transboundary Watercourses and International

the UNECE Water Convention does not emphasize the principle of sovereignty; its focus is on prevention, control, and reduction of 'transboundary impact'.[131] In particular, the Convention highlights the great importance of environmental protection.[132] Emphasis on environmental protection can be attributed to context of the drafting and negotiating process of the UNECE Water Convention. The UNECE region, which is rich in water resources, at this time had to cope with water pollution and environmental protection; questions of equitable utilization or conflicts between sovereign States were of less concern.[133]

Comparable to the UN Watercourses Convention, the UNECE Water Convention is guided by a principle incongruent with that of sovereignty. The application of the principle of sovereignty as a *leitmotif* appears not to be preferable. On the other hand, the ILC Draft Articles as the aquifer-specific instrument should not be prevailed by more general instruments. This problematic outcome might have been ameliorated if the ILC had decided on the future form of the ILC Draft Articles. For instance, declaring the Draft Articles as a guide of practice could have prevented such conflicts.[134]

d    Sovereignty

A novelty compared to the UN Watercourses Convention is the emphasis put on sovereignty. According to Art. 3: 'Each aquifer State has sovereignty over the portion of a transboundary aquifer or aquifer system located in its territory. It shall exercise its sovereignty in accordance with international law and the present draft articles'. The provision is to be criticized in many ways.

First, the first sentence of Art. 3 clearly denies the mobility of groundwater. As the definition of an aquifer encompasses the geological formation and the water contained therein, the concept of sovereignty set out in Art. 3 also applies to both components. States can have sovereign rights over the portion

---

Lakes in the light of the lessons learnt and the experience gained from the implementation of the Convention'.

[131]    Arts 2 (1), 3 UNECE Water Convention. See also S.C. McCaffrey, 'International Water Cooperation in the 21st Century: Recent Developments in the Law of International Watercourses' (2014) 23 RECIEL 4, at 12.

[132]    See also Art.2 Abs.2 (a), (b), (c), (d) UNECE Water Convention.

[133]    McCaffrey 'International Water Cooperation in the 21st Century: Recent Developments in the Law of International Watercourses', at 12.

[134]    Ibid., at 284. For a discussion on the future form of the ILC Draft Articles, see Weber, *Grundwasser im Völkerrecht—Eine Untersuchung der Draft Articles der UN International Law Commission über das Recht grenzüberschreitender Aquifere im Kontext des internationalen Wasserrechts*, at 168–172; G. Eckstein and F. Sindico, 'The Law of Transboundary Aquifers: Many Ways of Going Forward but Only One Way of Standing Still' (2014) 23 RECIEL 32.

of the rock situated in their territory. The geological formation is immovable. Groundwater, on the other hand, flows through the aquifer and constantly moves from one State to another. From the hydrogeological perspective, it is impossible to exercise sovereignty over a movable resource. As McCaffrey says, the State 'has rights of use in it, but not sovereignty over, the water contained in that formation'.[135]

Second, it does not become clear from the wording of the provision which concept of sovereignty the ILC intended to introduce. The first sentence reminds of the doctrine of absolute sovereignty,[136] but it is moderated by the second sentence referring to 'international law and the present draft articles'. The first reference can be understood as addressing the concept of limited territorial sovereignty as the predominant concept in modern international law.[137] Also, the present Draft Articles—with the principles of equitable and reasonable utilization (Arts 4 and 5), cooperation (Art. 7) and no harm (Art. 6) do not promote absolute sovereign rights. However, as the States' obligation to exercise their sovereign rights 'in accordance with international law and the present draft articles' is only in the second sentence, the notion of sovereignty in the first sentence seems to be the guiding principle for interpretation.[138] Although far from identical with the outdated doctrine of absolute sovereignty, the focus on sovereignty differs from the previous evolution of international water law. Particularly, neither the UN Watercourses Convention as the major water law instrument, nor the International Court of Justice (ICJ) in its water-law related judgments in *Gabčíkovo-Nagymaros*[139] and *Pulp Mills*[140] emphasize the notion of sovereignty.[141]

---

135   Ibid., at 291.
136   See S.C. McCaffrey, 'The Harmon Doctrine One Hundred Years Later: Buried, Not Praised' (1996) 36 Natural Resources Journal 549.
137   See also R. Stephan and G. de los Cobos, 'State Sovereignty and Transboundary Aquifers' in T. Tvedt, O. McIntyre and T. Woldetsadik (eds), *A History of Water* vol. II *Sovereignty and International Water Law* (Tauris 2015) 297, at 299–300; Stephan, 'The Draft Articles on the Law of Transboundary Aquifers: the Process at the UN ILC', at 229; Mechlem, 'Moving Ahead in Protecting Freshwater Resources: the International Law Commission's Draft Articles on Transboundary Aquifers', at 811; Tanzi, 'Furthering International Water Law or Making a New Body of Law on Transboundary Aquifers? An Introduction', at 201; Brown Weiss, *International Law for a Water-Scarce World*, at 42.
138   See also McCaffrey, 'The International Law Commission Adopts Articles on Transboundary Aquifers', at 291.
139   *Gabčíkovo-Nagymaros Project (Hungary v. Slovakia)* [1997] ICJ Rep 7.
140   *Pulp Mills on the River Uruguay (Argentina v. Uruguay)* (*Judgment*) (20 April 2010) ICJ Doc. 2010 General List No. 135.
141   McCaffrey, 'The International Law Commission Adopts Articles on Transboundary Aquifers', at 291; S.C. McCaffrey, 'The Siren Song of Sovereignty in International Water Law

In its commentary, the ILC cites a number of international treaties and instruments allegedly supporting its concept of sovereignty.[142] None of these instruments explicitly cover groundwater resources and none of them address sovereignty over shared freshwater resources. The only two freshwater agreements, which refer to the sovereign right of the States refers to their right to exploit their own resources,[143] as set out in Principle 2 of the Rio Declaration: 'States have [...] the sovereign right to exploit their own resources'.[144] Principle 2 of the Rio Declaration, however, links the sovereign right to the responsibility of States to ensure that the exercise of this right does not cause harm to other States.[145] Although this responsibility could be compared with the exercise of sovereignty 'in accordance with international law and the present Draft Articles', the 'sovereign right' to exploit resources in the State's territory differs from the 'sovereignty over the portion of a transboundary aquifer'. The latter is not limited to the mere exploitation of the resource.

Third, the notion of limited sovereignty as a guiding principle of a water-law instrument is particularly worrying due to the importance of groundwater for the present and future global water supply. Bearing in mind the high value of the resource, the focus on sovereignty instead of balancing principles, such as the principles of reasonable and equitable utilization, no harm or cooperation, appears to put groundwater at a higher risk. It would therefore be desirable to put an emphasis on the latter principles or to restrict the sovereign right even more by advocating a concept which is not only limited by interests of other States but also by other interests, such as environmental protection or the needs of future generations.[146]

---

Relations' in T. Tvedt, O. McIntyre and T. Woldetsadik (eds), *A History of Water* vol. II *Sovereignty and International Water Law* (Tauris 2015), at 47.

142   UN ILC 'Report of the International Law Commission: 60th Session' (5 May–6 June and 7 July–8 August 2008) UN Doc. A/63/10, at 27.

143   Ibid. Two instruments of international water law are the Convention on the Sustainable Management of Lake Tanganyika (done 12 June 2003, entered into force 23 August 2005), reprinted in S. Burchi and K. Mechlem, *Groundwater in International Law—Compilation of Treaties and Other Legal Instruments* (FAO/UNESCO 2005) 178 and Protocol on Water and Health to the 1992 Convention on the Protection and Use of Transboundary Watercourses and International Lakes (adopted 17 June 1999, entered into force 4 August 2005) 2231 UNTS 202.

144   UN Conference on Environment and Development 'Rio Declaration on Environment and Development' (14 June 1992) UN Doc. A/CONF.151/26/Rev.1 (vol. I), at 3.

145   McCaffrey, 'The International Law Commission Adopts Articles on Transboundary Aquifers', at 286.

146   See Weber, *Grundwasser im Völkerrecht—Eine Untersuchung der Draft Articles der UN International Law Commission über das Recht grenzüberschreitender Aquifere im Kontext des internationalen Wasserrechts*, at 75–78.

Lastly, the focus on sovereignty could lead to a reduction in State practices and protections of transboundary resources. These concerns are not unfounded, as shows the 2010 Guaraní Aquifer Agreement. It refers in its preamble explicitly to the ILC Draft Articles and says that the aquifer States are 'the sole owners of this resource' and exercise 'sovereign territorial control over their respective portions of the Guaraní Aquifer System'.[147] The sovereignty provision can thus be regarded as a 'possible setback in the international water law process'.[148]

## 3 Positive Aspects of the ILC Draft Articles

There are also positive aspects of the ILC Draft Articles. The major achievements, which are briefly discussed in this article, are the principle of equitable utilization and the aspects of management.

### a Principle of Equitable Utilization

Art. 4 sets out the general principle of reasonable and equitable utilization, whereas Art. 5 identifies factors relevant to the application of the principle.

According to Art. 4 (a), States 'shall utilize transboundary aquifers or aquifer systems in a manner that is consistent with the equitable and reasonable accrual of benefits therefrom to the aquifer'. Remarkably, the ILC Draft Articles use the term 'benefit' and not 'allocation'. Thus, a greater variety of relevant factors can be considered in the application of the principle of equitable utilization. For instance, the role of the aquifer or aquifer system in the related ecosystem[149] can be taken into account. The focus on 'benefits' is also likely to lead to a more efficient use of the resource and optimization of human benefits.[150]

Moreover, focus on the role of the aquifer in the related ecosystem, pursuant to Art. 5 (1) (i), is important with regard to the protection of groundwater and the recognition of hydrological interdependencies. The role of the aquifer addresses the various purposive functions an aquifer has in a related ecosystem. The term 'related ecosystem' is to be read in conjunction with 'ecosystems' in Art. 10, which refers to an ecosystem dependent on aquifers or on groundwater stored in aquifers. The 'related ecosystem' exists within or outside aquifers and

---

147  Arts 1 and 2 Guaraní Aquifer Agreement.
148  Tanzi, 'Furthering International Water Law or Making a New Body of Law on Transboundary Aquifers? An Introduction', at 201.
149  Art.5 (1) (i) ILC Draft Articles.
150  O. McIntyre, 'International Water Resources Law and the International Law Commission Draft Articles on Transboundary Aquifers: A Missed Opportunity for Cross-Fertilisation?' (2011) 13 Int'l Comm. L. Rev. 237, at 244–245.

is dependent on the functioning of aquifers for survival. For instance, some lake ecosystems are dependent on aquifers for a certain volume or quality of groundwater.[151]

Art. 5 addresses balancing of the different factors. A great achievement is the introduction of Art. 5 (2) (3), which states that 'in weighing different kinds of utilization of a transboundary aquifer or aquifer system, special regard shall be given to vital human needs'. The ILC understood 'vital human needs' as the sufficient amount of water necessary to sustain human life, including for drinking and for food production in order to prevent starvation.[152] In contrast to the UN Watercourses Convention, which invoked 'vital human needs' only in the situation of a conflict between uses of an international watercourse,[153] the introduction of the factors relevant to the principle of equitable and reasonable utilization can be regarded as recognizing their high importance.[154] Moreover, it can be assumed from the wording of 'special regard' that there should be a prioritization of 'vital human needs' before any other utilization. This assumption is also supported by the reference to the 'population dependent on the aquifer or aquifer system in each aquifer State' in Art. 5 (1) (a) as first relevant factor. As 'vital human needs' are the only factor to which 'special regard' should be attributed, the ILC seems intent upon giving those needs an exceptional position.[155] Conversely, if an equal treatment of all factors would have been introduced, the States would be free to weigh industrial or touristic needs higher than vital human needs. Those cases can be seen in practice, as in Botswana, where the government evicted Bushmen and denied access to water in the Kalahari Reserve, whereas it granted access to the same water to a

---

151  UN ILC 'Report of the International Law Commission: 60th Session' (5 May–6 June and 7 July–8 August 2008) UN Doc. A/63/10, at 45.

152  UN ILC 'Report of the International Law Commission: 60th Session' (5 May–6 June and 7 July–8 August 2008) UN Doc. A/63/10, at 45.

153  Art.10 (2)—Relationship of different uses: 'In the event of a conflict between uses of an international watercourse, it shall be resolved with reference to articles 5 to 7, with special regard being given to the requirements of vital human needs'.

154  The ILC Draft Articles addresses 'vital human needs' also in Art.17 (3), which deals with emergency situations.

155  Weber, *Grundwasser im Völkerrecht—Eine Untersuchung der Draft Articles der UN International Law Commission über das Recht grenzüberschreitender Aquifere im Kontext des internationalen Wasserrechts*, at 121–122. See also R. Wolfrum, 'Schutz und Management von Grundwasser aus der Sicht des Völkerrechts', at 114. In contrast, according to Mechlem, the ILC failed to prioritize the role of vital human needs over other needs, see K. Mechlem, 'Moving Ahead in Protecting Freshwater Resources: the International Law Commission's Draft Articles on Transboundary Aquifers' (2009) 22 LJIL 801, at 813.

tourist agency, which used the water for a swimming pool.[156] The prioritization of vital human needs can help prevent such a situation.[157]

b      Management Aspects

The ILC recognized the need for a proper aquifer management by addressing management aspects in Arts 7 (2), 9 and 14. Art. 14 is the provision generally dealing with the management of aquifers. According to Art. 14, sentences 1 and 2, aquifer States shall establish and implement proper management plans for their transboundary aquifers or aquifer systems. Otherwise, aquifer States must enter, upon request, into consultation concerning aquifer management. The ILC clearly states that the general principles set out in part two of the ILC Draft Articles shall be applied to the management system. Management also encompasses protection, preservation, and the maximization of long-term benefits derived from the utilization of the aquifer.[158] According to Art. 14 (2), a 'joint management mechanism shall be established, wherever appropriate'. Although the ILC recognizes the great value in the joint management of aquifer States, it weakens the obligation by adding the qualification 'wherever appropriate' due to potential practical impossibilities.[159]

The mechanism for joint aquifer management is also addressed by Art. 7. Art. 7 (1) sets out the general obligation of aquifer States to cooperate, whereas Art. 7 (2) envisages the establishment of 'joint mechanisms for cooperation'. This term refers to a mutually agreeable means of decision-making among aquifer States as a commission, authority, or other institution. There are numerous possible types of cooperation. For example, cooperation could include the exchange of information and databases, monitoring and also management—as set out in Art. 14.[160] Joint management is also implicitly referred to in Art. 9. According to Art. 9, States are encouraged to enter into bilateral and regional

---

156   Survival International, 'The Bushmen', available at http://www.survivalinternational.org/tribes/bushmen (accessed 17 April 2019). Another example is the pollution of the Ogoniland in Nigeria, including groundwater contamination more than 4500 times Nigerian recommended levels. See 'Ogoni King: Shell Oil is Killing My People' (3 December 2016) The Guardian.

157   Weber, *Grundwasser im Völkerrecht—Eine Untersuchung der Draft Articles der UN International Law Commission über das Recht grenzüberschreitender Aquifere im Kontext des internationalen Wasserrechts*, at 121–122.

158   UN ILC 'Report of the International Law Commission: 60th Session' (5 May–6 June and 7 July–8 August 2008) UN Doc. A/63/10, at 63.

159   Ibid.

160   An example is the Franco–Swiss Genevese Aquifer Commission, UN ILC 'Report of the International Law Commission: 60th Session' (5 May–6 June and 7 July–8 August 2008) UN Doc. A/63/10, at 41.

agreements 'for the purpose of managing a particular transboundary aquifer or aquifer system'.

The management aspects in the ILC Draft Articles can be regarded as positive. The ILC acknowledges that management, in particular joint management outlined in several provisions, is crucial for the protection, preservation, and utilization of aquifers. One might argue that it would have been preferable to introduce a stricter obligation to establish joint management systems. Due to the shared nature of the resource, a transboundary aquifer can only be successfully managed jointly by the aquifer States.[161]

## VI   Conclusion

The ILC Draft Articles constitute an important contribution to the codification of rules applicable to international groundwater resources. Bearing in mind the increasing pressure on aquifers and the special characteristics of groundwater such as its high vulnerability to pollution, the attention of the ILC to this long-ignored resource is timely and reflects the need for adequate protection. The ILC Draft Articles take significant steps forward in the protection of this precious resource, as can be seen from the focus on vital human needs in the utilization of the aquifer. Nevertheless, shortcomings illustrate the disregard of fundamental features of the resource, such as the mobility of groundwater. An adequate and comprehensive protection of aquifers and groundwater is only possible on the basis of acknowledgement of hydrological realities. Moreover, if the ILC Draft Articles should become a legally binding regime, the overlap with important water law regimes might lead to confusion and potential conflicts. Since groundwater is irreplaceable for the current and future global water supply, these shortcomings should not be neglected in the further legal processes.

---

161   McCaffrey, 'International Water Cooperation in the 21st Century: Recent Developments in the Law of International Watercourses', at 279.

CHAPTER 6

# The Cross-Fertilization of UNCLOS, Custom and Principles Relating to Procedure in the Jurisprudence of UNCLOS Courts and Tribunals

*Elena Ivanova*

## Abstract

Cross-fertilization of international law entails interaction of norms in international law and can occur in the context of interaction between different sources of law; different branches of international law or different subject-matter areas; and interaction between a treaty norm belonging to a one area of international law and a customary norm arising from another area of international law. There are different avenues for cross-fertilization of international law: it can result from the application of Art. 31 (3) (c) of the Vienna Convention on the Law of Treaties (VCLT)[1] in the process of interpreting a particular treaty, from the application of other rules of international law together with a particular treaty or from reference to the jurisprudence of other international courts or tribunals by adhering to the approach adopted in this jurisprudence.

This article examines the question of cross-fertilization of international law in the context of the jurisprudence of the courts and tribunals operating within the dispute settlement system established under the UN Convention on the Law of the Sea (hereinafter 'UNCLOS' or 'Convention').[2] It will demonstrate how these adjudicatory bodies have employed Art. 31 (3) (c) VCLT, Art. 293 UNCLOS which explicitly enables them to apply other rules of international law not incompatible with the Convention, and the international jurisprudence in order to interpret and apply the UNCLOS while situating it the broader context of international law. Note will be taken of UNCLOS provisions incorporating or referring to other rules of international law which also contribute to the cross-fertilization of international law.

---

[1] Vienna Convention on the Law of Treaties (concluded 23 May 1969, entered into force 27 January 1980) 1155 UNTS 331.
[2] United Nations Convention on the Law of the Sea (concluded 10 December 1982, entered into force 16 November 1994) 1833 UNTS 3.

**Keywords**

Fragmentation of International Law – Interplay between Norms – Principle of Systemic Integration – Cross-Fertilization of International Law – ITLOS – UNCLOS – Proliferation of International Courts and Tribunals – Limited Jurisdiction

## 1    Introduction

The increasing number of treaties creating their own separate dispute settlement system with separate adjudicatory bodies vested with limited jurisdiction has raised concerns about the unity, respectively about the fragmentation of international law. Whereas fragmentation of international law is not necessarily a negative development, since the proliferation of treaties is rather an indication of the increased specialization of international law and adherence to the rule of law in international relations, the ensuing proliferation of specialized international courts and tribunals perceived as inclined to favour their own discipline[3] has raised concerns about conflicting interpretations of the law and/or conflicting adjudicatory results with their implications for legal certainty, the credibility of international adjudication and the international legal order.

The practice of relatively recently created international courts and tribunals demonstrates that international adjudicators tend to adopt common approaches to similar issues and accept a degree of cross-fertilization. In this paper, cross-fertilization is perceived as a positive development in international adjudication which counteracts the fragmentation of international law and indicates the willingness of international courts to examine the relations and the links between different sources of international law across different sectors, rather than adopting an isolationist and fragmented approach. The scope of this article is limited to the practice of UNCLOS courts and tribunal.[4]

Cross-fertilization is evident both in substantive and procedural law and results not only from reference to other rules of international law, but also from reference to the jurisprudence of the International Court of Justice (ICJ) and other adjudicatory bodies. It is indicative of an agreement among international courts on a range of issues from procedure to remedies. Common standards

---

[3]  Address by Judge G. Guillaume, President of the International Court of Justice, to the UN (26 October 2000).

[4]  See also *Digest of Jurisprudence of the International Tribunal for the Law of the Sea, 1996–2016* (ITLOS 2016) which has been taken into consideration in the preparation of this article.

and, in particular, common standards in procedure have theoretical implications, because the emergence of common rules in international adjudication finds resonance in the debate on the coherence of international law and the existence of a system of international law. Although international courts and tribunals do not exist and operate as part of a formal single dispute settlement system, given the absence of hierarchical and formal connections among them, the emergence of common approaches to procedure and the consistent reliance on international law for questions not regulated by a particular treaty permits the suggestion that they do not operate in self-contained regimes but rather perceive themselves as part of a common legal system. The emergence of common approaches to similar issues and the cross-fertilization of international law has positive implications for the unity, the clarification and the further development of international law; though it is to be noted that it should not be pursued overzealously because it can lead to resistance towards such development.

## II  Means for Cross-Fertilization

The UNCLOS has a very wide scope (it aims at settling all issues relating to the law of the sea) and is commonly regarded as an 'umbrella treaty'.[5] It has an impressive volume, but many of its provisions are framed in general terms and are both open to different interpretations and subject to further development and clarification through implementation agreements and/or adjudication. Its Preamble reaffirms that matters not regulated by the Convention continue to be governed by the rules and principles of general international law, thus silently acknowledging the inconclusiveness of the UNCLOS legal regime. Furthermore, Art. 293 expressly enables UNCLOS courts and tribunals to apply other rules of international law not incompatible with UNCLOS. Thus, customary international law, including the customary rules of interpretation, and principles relating to procedure have been pulled into the UNCLOS dispute settlement system and have 'enriched' or filled gaps in the Convention. Apart from Art. 293 UNCLOS, Art. 31 (3) (c) VCLT has been used as a route for referring to other rules of international law. In addition, when addressing issues not regulated by the UNCLOS and where uncertainty as to the precise content, source or legal status of the relevant rules of international law exists, UNCLOS tribunals have consistently consulted the jurisprudence of other international

---

5  The Convention establishes a comprehensive legal order for the world's seas and oceans. An integral part of the Convention is the system for dispute settlement set out in its Part XV.

courts and tribunals, including the ICJ. Finally, many UNCLOS provisions refer to or incorporate other rules of international law, thus serving to situate the Convention in the broader context of international law.

## 1   Art. 31 (3) (c) VCLT as an Operational Tool

Art. 31 (3) (c) VCLT directs international courts and tribunals to take account of other relevant rules of international law when interpreting and applying a particular treaty. It is regarded as reflecting a customary rule of interpretation and an expression of the principle of systemic integration (also referred to as the principle of harmonization). It emphasizes the unity of international law by prescribing that treaties should not be considered in isolation from other rules of international law, including general international law. As such it can be an operational tool for the cross-fertilization of international law.[6] Its actual meaning in practice is quite unclear though, given the general reluctance of international courts to refer to this principle expressly. Notably, both the International Tribunal for the Law of the Sea (ITLOS) and the WTO Dispute Settlement Body (DSB) have explicitly referred to Art. 31 (3) (c) VCLT, while confirming that it reflects customary international law. Yet none them has unequivocally determined the scope of this provision.

The principle of systemic integration and the wording of Art. 31 (3) (c) VCLT have attracted the attention of scholars and were extensively discussed in the 2006 Report on Fragmentation of International Law of the International Law Commission (ILC).[7] Until today, the uncertainty on the substantive scope of Art. 31 (3) (c) VCLT and the precise meaning of its terms persists.[8] Although Art. 31 (3) (c) VCLT appears to be rather straightforward insofar as it prescribes that in the interpretation of treaties account shall be taken of other relevant rules of international law, it does not specify how this should be done. Should this process be limited to interpreting the meaning of particular terms within

---

6  Judge Weeramantry has noted the potential of Art. 31 (3) (c) VCLT to address relations between custom and treaty: '[Art. 31 (3) (c) VCLT] scarcely covers this aspect with the degree of clarity requisite to so important a matter'. *Gabčíkovo-Nagymaros Project* (*Hungary/Slovakia*) (*Separate Opinion of Judge Weeramantry*) [1997] ICJ Rep 7, at 114.

7  UN ILC 'Fragmentation of International Law: Difficulties Arising from the Diversification and Expansion of International Law: Report of the Study Group' (17 July 2006) GAOR 61st Session Supp 10, at 403.

8  The uncertainty concerns the meaning of the terms 'rules' (the type of rules encompassed by that term), 'applicable' (whether these rules should be binding or no; whether they should be binding on all the parties to the treaty under interpretation or on the disputants only or they may not be binding on one or all the disputants), 'relevant'; the temporal scope of this provision (i.e., whether the relevant rules are those existing at the time of conclusion of the interpreted treaty or at the time of its application).

a treaty provision, or can it result in reading other rules into the provision, with the effect of adding content or substantive rules which are not otherwise present in the interpreted treaty? An overly intrusive interpretation may effectively result in the amendment or modification of a treaty without the necessary consent of the relevant parties which can hardly be the desired outcome of the judicial activity. So, the question to what extent one can utilize other rules of international law when interpreting a particular treaty remains open. Providing a conclusive answer to this question, however, is beyond the focus and the scope of the present study whose aims is to demonstrate that cross-fertilization of international law is actually taking place in practice despite its fragmented nature, and to highlight the means through which cross-fertilization has and could be achieved thus shedding some light on the potential and the limitations of these means with Art. 31 (3) (c) VCLT being among them.

Concerning the latter, however, two points merit attention. First, the rule-which-is-being-referred-to has to be 'taken into account' when interpreting the treaty rule, not applied instead of it as is the case with Art. 30 and successive treaties.[9] In other words, the rule-which-is-being-referred-to has a secondary role and there is no question of it displacing the interpreted rule.[10] This is so because Art. 31 (3) (c) VCLT aims to clarify the meaning and scope of an existing rule. In other words, it offers a route through which other rules of international law can be utilized by the law interpreter, but only for the purposes of interpretation. The process of interpretation governed by the principle of systemic integration, thus, is to be distinguished from the process of normative conflict resolution which on its part is addressed by other rules of international law[11] and logically follows the former. Art. 31 (3) (c) VCLT seeks a harmonious, i.e., balanced, interpretation of different relevant rules, but this end is not always achievable. Since in order for Art. 31 (3) (c) VCLT to be activated

---

9   P. Sands, 'Treaty, Custom and the Cross-fertilization of International Law' (1998) 1 Yale Human Rights & Development Law Journal 103.
10  Ibid., at 85; M. Villiger, *Commentary on the 1969 Vienna Convention on the Law of Treaties* (Nijhoff Leiden 2009), at 433. Villiger explains that in the case of customary rules, these may be even identical with and run parallel to the treaty rule. Non-identical customary rules on the same subject-matter may lead to a modification of the treaty term as a result of the subsequent practice running counter to the treaty provision. Furthermore, conflictive treaty norm can be regarded as an *inter se* modification of the applicable treaty. See also J. Pauwelyn, *Conflict of Norms in Public International Law. How WTO Law Relates to Other Rules of International Law* (CUP 2003).
11  The principles of *lex specialis* and *lex posterior*, among others, deal with conflicts of norms. Arguably, rules or principles of conflict resolution have a role to play in the interpretative process but only in the context of two conflicting interpretations based on the alleged relevance of two separate rules or sets of rules of international law and for the purposes of reaching a conclusion as to which interpretation should prevail.

the rule-which-is-being-referred-to must be 'relevant', i.e., it must concern the subject-matter of the interpreted treaty rule, it can potentially be in conflict with the latter. Under the principle of harmonization, the interpreted rule and the rule assisting the interpretation should, to the extent possible, be interpreted so as to give rise to a single set of compatible obligations.[12] Where no such result can be achieved, i.e., where there is a conflict of norms, other rules are to be applied to resolve that conflict. In this regard, a distinction has to be made between a *prima facie* conflict of norms and a genuine conflict of norms: the former can actually be resolved through the rule of interpretation reflected in Art. 31 (3) (c) VCLT, harmonizing the seemingly conflicting norms by interpreting them so as to render them compatible.

Art. 31 (3) (c) VCLT prescribes that other rules 'shall be taken into account'. The term 'shall' indicates that in interpreting a treaty, the adjudicatory body has no discretion as to whether to refer to other relevant rules of international law—it must do so. As far as the phrase 'take into account' is concerned, its ordinary usage or meaning suggests that this formulation is stronger than 'take into consideration' and weaker than 'apply'.[13] In any event, the rule of interpretation reflected in Art. 31 (3) (c) VCLT does not seem to permit the prevalence of another relevant rule over the interpreted one in case of conflict, nor could other rules be applied to the dispute solely by virtue of Art. 31 (3) (c) VCLT. Pursuant to Art. 31 (3) (c) VCLT, other relevant rules must be taken into account when interpreting the norm in question, but it is the latter norm that is applied and not the rule-which-is-being-referred-to.

Art. 31 (3) (c) VCLT is directly applicable to UNCLOS courts and tribunals pursuant to Art. 293 of the Convention.

## 2   Art. 293 UNCLOS

Art. 293 UNCLOS is concerned with the applicable law and prescribes that UNCLOS courts and tribunals shall apply other rules of international law not incompatible with the Convention. This provision appears to be rather straightforward to the extent that it clearly enables UNCLOS adjudicators to apply non-UNCLOS norms. Notably, it contains a limitation insofar as it requires these norms to be compatible with the Convention, i.e., with its object and purpose. Despite its clear-cut wording, the application of Art. 293 UNCLOS is not devoid of uncertainty due to the limited subject-matter jurisdiction of UNCLOS courts and tribunals. This is a general problem for specialized international courts regardless of whether or not their constitutive instruments contain a provision on applicable law enabling them to apply other rules of international law.

---

12    See 2006 Report on Fragmentation of International Law, Conclusions 4 and 21.
13    Sands, 'Treaty, Custom and the Cross-fertilization of International Law'.

While the limits of their jurisdiction *ratione materiae* do not necessarily attach to the applicable law, and in the case of UNCLOS courts and tribunals they certainly do not, it is still unclear to what extent such specialized courts and tribunals can refer to other rules of international law, especially other treaty rules, and what findings they can make in this regard.

Notably, the examined practice contains some references to other treaty rules, although they have been taken into account not by way of application of Art. 293 UNCLOS but through Art. 31 (3) (c) VCLT. Art. 293 has been operationalized for the purposes of applying general international law and custom.

## 3   Reference to International Jurisprudence

UNCLOS courts and tribunals have consistently leaned on the jurisprudence of other international courts and tribunals for the resolution of questions not regulated by the UNCLOS and where the content, legal status or source of relevant rules are debatable. Examples include issues both of procedure and substance. Notably, in cases of uncertainty as to whether particular rules have evolved into customary international law or constitute general principles of law, UNCLOS tribunals have adhered to the approach of other international tribunals, thus securing consistency in the international jurisprudence in the treatment of similar issues. This approach, on the one hand, contributes to the elucidation of concepts with unsettled legal status in international law, such as estoppel, while affirming the role of judicial decisions in the interpretative process; on the other hand, it adds legitimacy to and facilitates the acceptance of the judicial outcome.

## 4   Treaty Specific Provisions Referring to or Incorporating Other Rules of International Law

Certain provisions in the UNCLOS contain references to other rules of international law or incorporate such rules into the UNCLOS legal regime. Arts 295, 235 (1) UNCLOS constitute examples of incorporating international law by reference. Some of these provisions add additional layers to the incorporated law, thus either fine-tuning or introducing exceptions. These treaty-specific provisions are another means for cross-fertilization of international law. In the interpretation and application of such hybrid provisions, UNCLOS tribunals have consulted the international jurisprudence pertaining to the incorporated law where relevant. This approach contributes to the unified interpretation of international law.

The reference to 'other rules of international law' (or 'international law) occurs in many UNCLOS provision and serves to place the Convention in the wider context of public international law (Arts 138, 139 (2), 221 (1), 235 (1), 295,

303 (4), etc.). This allows 'international standards' (Arts 60 (3); 61 (3), 119 (1)) or 'the further development of international law' (Art. 235 (1)) to be integrated into the UNCLOS legal regime, thus confirming its nature of a 'living organism'. It also indicates the areas in which the UNCLOS deviates from (Art. 31) or develops international law. In addition, various UNCLOS provisions embody the phrase 'without prejudice [to other rules]' (Arts 70 (6), 139 (2), etc.).

## III   Cross-Fertilization in the Context of the Jurisprudence of UNCLOS Courts and Tribunals

UNCLOS tribunals faced with questions not regulated or not sufficiently or conclusively regulated by the Convention have frequently referred to other rules of international law—customary international law; principles relating to procedure; treaty rules, including rules belonging to other sectors of international law. Areas where cross-fertilization has happened include, but are not limited to, responsibility of States; law enforcement at sea; and procedure.

### 1   *Substantive Law*
#### a   Responsibility of States
##### (i)   *The Role of Arts 2, 5, 11, 31 and 33 of the ILC Draft Articles on State Responsibility in Determining Rights and Obligations under Art. 139 UNCLOS*

In its *Advisory Opinion Concerning Responsibilities and Obligations of States with Respect to Activities in the Area*,[14] the Seabed Disputes Chamber of the ITLOS was called upon to interpret and determine the meaning and scope of Art. 139 UNCLOS which prescribes that sponsoring States are responsible for ensuring that activities in the Area are carried out in conformity with Part XI of the Convention.

This exercise included an interpretation of the term 'damage' embodied in Art. 139. The Convention does not specify what constitutes compensable damage and who is entitled to compensation. In its introductory paragraphs, the Seabed Disputes Chamber stated that in interpreting the UNCLOS it was bound to apply the rules on interpretation of treaties in Arts 31–33 VCLT. While drawing support from the jurisprudence of the ICJ, arbitral tribunals and the WTO DSB, it acknowledged that these provisions reflected customary international

---

14   *Responsibilities and Obligations of States Sponsoring Persons and Entities with respect to Activities in the Area* (*Advisory Opinion*) ITLOS Case No. 17 (1 February 2011).

law.[15] Against this backdrop, the Seabed Disputes Chamber looked at Arts 2, 5, 11, 31 and 33 of the ILC Draft Articles on Responsibility of States for Internationally Wrongful Acts (hereinafter 'ILC Draft Articles') for guidance.[16] While referring to the international jurisprudence and Art. 2 of the ILC Draft Articles,[17] the Seabed Disputes Chamber highlighted that under the customary international law rule on liability, a State may be held liable even if no material damage has resulted from its failure to meet its international obligations. On this basis, it concluded that 'the damage in question would include damage to the Area and its resources constituting the common heritage of mankind, and damage to the marine environment'.[18]

Furthermore, while stating that Art. 139 (2) UNCLOS was in line with the rules of customary international law, it clarified that the liability of the sponsoring State under this provision is controlled by the rule of international law that the acts of private entities are not directly attributable to States except where the entity in question is empowered to act as a State organ (Art. 5 of the ILC Draft Articles) or where its conduct is acknowledged as adopted by a State as its own (Art. 11 of the ILC Draft Articles).[19]

Finally, it pointed out that the responsibilities and obligations of States with respect to activities in the Area include the obligation to provide for full compensation which is customary international law (reference was made to ICJ case law) reflected in Art. 31 (1) of the ILC Draft Articles.[20]

In sum, in addition to the purpose of defining the scope of particular terms within UNCLOS provisions, customary international law was referred to on the basis of Art. 31 (3) (c) VCLT in order to determine the substantive content of the obligations stemming from the UNCLOS. This exercise resulted in a harmonious interpretation of the UNCLOS and international law.

The same approach was adopted by the ITLOS Tribunal in the *Fisheries Advisory Opinion*[21] rendered in relation to the *Request for an Advisory Opinion submitted by the Sub-Regional Fisheries Commission (SRFC)*. The Tribunal

---

15   Ibid., at para. 57.
16   UN ILC 'Draft Articles on Responsibility of States for Internationally Wrongful Acts' (2001) GAOR 56th Session Supp 10, at 43.
17   Ibid., at para. 178, referring to *Rainbow Warrior (New Zealand v. France) (Award of 30 April 1990)* France–New Zealand Arbitration Tribunal (1990) 20 RIAA 215, and, notably, to the commentary to Art. 2 of the ILC Draft Articles.
18   *Responsibilities and Obligations of States with Respect to Activities in the Area (Request for Advisory Opinion Submitted to the Seabed Disputes Chamber)*, at para. 179.
19   Ibid., at para. 182.
20   Ibid., at para. 194.
21   *Request for an Advisory Opinion submitted by the Sub-Regional Fisheries Commission (SRFC) (Advisory Opinion)* ITLOS Case No. 21 (2 April 2015).

was called upon to determine, among other issues, to what extent a flag State can be held liable for illegal, unreported and unregulated (IUU) fishing activities conducted by vessels sailing under its flag. The Convention, as the ITLOS explicitly noted, provides no guidance in this regard.

Following the approach of the Seabed Disputes Chamber, the ITLOS referred to the ILC Draft Articles, in particular, Arts 1, 2, and 31 which address the international responsibility of States for internationally wrongful acts and the liability therefrom,[22] and stated that these are rules of international law which according to Art. 293 UNCLOS should guide its examination. While leaning on this law, and having initially established that the UNCLOS imposed on a flag State 'due diligence' obligations concerning IUU fishing activities conducted by vessels flying its flag in the exclusive economic zones (EEZ) of the SRFC Member States,[23] the ITLOS held that the flag State was liable for an internationally wrongful act, but the violation of a vessel of the laws and regulations of the SRFC Member States concerning IUU fishing activities in their EEZ was not *per se* attributable to the flag State. The ITLOS reached the conclusion that the flag State was not liable if it had taken all necessary and appropriate measures to meet its due diligence[24] obligations to ensure that vessels flying its flag

---

[22] Art. 1 of the ILC Draft Articles on State Responsibility states that every internationally wrongful act of a State entails the international responsibility of that State; Art. 2 of the ILC Draft Articles on State Responsibility prescribes that there is an internationally wrongful act of a State when conduct consisting of an action or omission (a) is attributable to the State under international law, and (b) constitutes a breach of an international obligation of the State; Art. 31 (1) of the ILC Draft Articles on State Responsibility states that the responsible State is under an obligation to make full reparation for the injury caused by the internationally wrongful act.

[23] The issue of flag State responsibility for IUU fishing activities is not directly addressed in the UNCLOS, but the latter contains general obligations which are to be met by the flag State in all maritime zones regulated by the Convention, including the EEZ of a coastal State (set out in Arts 91, 92, 94, 192, 193 UNCLOS) and specific obligations imposed on the flag State with regard to activities in the EEZ of a coastal State, in particular with regard to fishing activities conducted by national of the flag State (Art. 58 (3) and Art. 62 (4) UNCLOS). Drawing from the general obligation of all States, including the flag States, to protect and preserve the marine environment, and the specific obligation imposed on flag States to ensure that their nationals engaged in fishing activities within the EEZ of a coastal State comply with the conservation measures and other terms and conditions established in its laws and regulations, the ITLOS concluded that the flag State has an obligation stemming from the UNCLOS to take the necessary measures to ensure that its nationals and vessels flying its flags are not engaged in IUU fishing activities, including in the EEZ of the SRFC Member States. See *Fisheries Advisory Opinion*, at para. 124.

[24] The content of the 'due diligence' is addressed ibid, at paras 131–32, referring to the jurisprudence of the ICJ and the Advisory Opinion of the Seabed Disputes Chamber.

do not conduct IUU fishing activities in the exclusive economic zones of the SRFC Member States.[25]

(ii)  *The Role of the Precautionary Approach in Determining the Responsibility and Obligations of States Parties with Respect to Activities Conducted in the Area*

Although the UNCLOS makes no explicit or implicit mention of the precautionary approach, the *Advisory Opinion Concerning Responsibilities and Obligations of States with Respect to Activities in the Area* clarified that the precautionary approach is part of these obligations.

The Advisory Opinion explicitly stated that the precautionary approach is 'an integral part of the general obligation of due diligence of the sponsoring State, which is applicable even outside the scope of the Regulations'[26] and explained that this obligation requires them to take 'all appropriate measures to prevent damage that might result from the activities of contractors that they sponsor'; that this obligation applies in situations where scientific evidence concerning the scope and potential negative impact of the activity in question is insufficient but where there are plausible indications of potential risks, and that this obligation would not be met if those risks are disregarded.[27]

To support this proposition, the Seabed Dispute Chamber noted that the precautionary approach had been incorporated into a growing number of international agreements, many of which reflected Principle 15 of the Rio Declaration[28] which, in its view, had initiated a trend towards making this approach part of customary international law.[29]

---

25  Ibid., at para. 146.
26  Apart from the Convention and the Agreement relating to the Implementation of Part XI of the UNCLOS, the Seabed Disputes Chamber was also called upon to interpret the Regulations adopted by the Authority, namely, the Regulations on Prospecting and Exploration for Polymetallic Nodules in the Area of 2000, and the Regulations on Prospecting and Exploration for Polymetallic Sulphides in the Area of 2010. *Responsibilities and Obligations of States with Respect to Activities in the Area (Request for Advisory Opinion Submitted to the Seabed Disputes Chamber)*, at paras 58–59.
27  Ibid., at para. 131. Notably, in the preceding paragraphs the Seabed Disputes Chamber expressed the view that the 'due diligence' concept is a variable one and may change over time as measures considered sufficiently diligent at a certain moment may become not diligent enough in light of new scientific or technological knowledge, but, nonetheless, the standard of due diligence has to be more severe for the riskier activities. Ibid., at para. 117.
28  UN Conference on Environment and Development 'Rio Declaration on Environment and Development' (14 June 1992).
29  Ibid., at para. 135.

It drew further support from the ICJ jurisprudence, in particular, the statement in para. 164 of the ICJ judgment in *Pulp Mills on the River Uruguay*[30] that 'a precautionary approach may be relevant in the interpretation and application of the provisions of the Statute' (i.e., the environmental bilateral treaty whose interpretation was the main bone of contention between the parties).

Two points merit attention. First, the above interpretation was based on Art. 31 (3) (c) VCLT to which the Seabed Disputes Chamber referred in the introductory paragraphs.[31] It explicitly confirmed the customary nature of the rules in Arts 31–33 VCLT, noting that the ITLOS had never before stated this expressly but had done so implicitly, and that other international courts and tribunals, including the ICJ, arbitral tribunals and the WTO Appellate Body, had already confirmed this. This approach highlights the commonality in the rules of interpretation employed by the different international courts and tribunals despite their operation within different dispute settlement systems.

Second, if Art. 31 (3) (c) VCLT becomes operational when the 'relevant rule' has binding character,[32] any reference to the precautionary approach would necessitate its recognition as customary international law. While there has been no authoritative pronouncement in this regard, on a number of occasions the ITLOS, including through the Advisory Opinion of the Seabed Dispute Chamber, has taken significant steps in that direction[33] which have further bolstered the reputation of that tribunal as an environment-friendly dispute settlement forum.

The *Advisory Opinion Concerning Responsibilities and Obligations of States with Respect to Activities in the Area* is significant because it clarifies the content of the due diligence obligation and the notion of 'precautionary approach' and discusses the legal status of the latter. The Seabed Dispute Chamber explicitly recognized that the precautionary approach forms part of the due

---

30   *Pulp Mills on the River Uruguay (Argentina v. Uruguay) (Judgment)* [2010] ICJ Rep 14.
31   Ibid., at paras 57–58.
32   Villiger, *Commentary on the 1969 Vienna Convention on the Law of Treaties*, at 433.
33   For example, in the MOX Plant case the Tribunal, although abstaining from the articulation of the term precautionary approach, alluded to it by stating that 'prudence and caution' require cooperation in the exchange of information concerning risks for the Irish Sea from the operation of the MOX Plant and in devising measures to prevent the pollution of the marine environment. See *MOX Plant (Ireland v. United Kingdom) (Order)* ITLOS Case No. 10 (3 December 2001), at paras 84, 89. In the *Southern Bluefin Tuna Cases* the Tribunal stated that the parties should 'act with prudence and caution' to ensure that effective conservation measures are taken to prevent serious. See *Southern Bluefin Tuna Cases (New Zealand v. Japan; Australia v. Japan) (Provisional Measures)* ITLOS Cases Nos 3, 4 (27 August 1999), at para. 77.

diligence obligations. Although advisory opinions are not binding, they certainly have practical implications. On the one hand, they are likely to play a role in the decision-making of international tribunals dealing with similar legal issues in the future. As such they can have an impact across jurisdictions, given the inclination of international courts and tribunals to look into each other's jurisprudence. This feature of advisory opinions, on the other hand, indicates their potential to influence the future conduct of States.

The *Advisory Opinion Concerning Responsibilities and Obligations of States with Respect to Activities in the Area* also, touches upon the interaction between a treaty belonging to a particular area of international law and a custom arising in another area of international law, as well as on the interplay between treaty and custom more generally. It suggests that customary international law which has emerged after the conclusion of a treaty on the same subject-matter is to be read in the light of the obligations of the States Parties to that treaty and thus may qualify a conventional obligation; and this interaction can occur even across different sectors of international law.

In the subsequent *South China Sea Arbitration*,[34] the Arbitral Tribunal even went a step further by suggesting that a new rule of customary international law can modify the UNCLOS: '[A] new rule of customary international law may emerge to modify the provisions of a treaty. International law is not static'.[35]

(iii) *The Role of Art. 14 ILC Draft Articles on Diplomatic Protection in Clarifying Art. 295 UNCLOS*

Art. 295 UNCLOS prescribes that a dispute concerning the interpretation and application of the UNCLOS between the States Parties can be submitted to adjudication only after local remedies have been exhausted where this is required by international law. While this provision reflects the well-established principle of customary international law that exhaustion of local remedies is a prerequisite for the exercise of diplomatic protection, it does not specify the possible exceptions to this rule.

Notably, the principle is reflected in Art. 14 (1) of the Draft Articles on Diplomatic Protection adopted by the International Law Commission in 2006.[36] Art. 14 (1), in turn, refers to Art. 15 which introduces exceptions to the local remedies rule.

---

34   *South China Sea Arbitration (Philippines v. China) (Award)* Annex VII Tribunal (12 July 2016).
35   Ibid., at para. 274.
36   UN ILC 'Draft Articles on Diplomatic Protection' (2006) GAOR 61st Session Supp 10.

In the *M/V 'Virginia G'* case, the ITLOS was confronted with the application of Art. 295 UNCLOS and had to assess whether the exhaustion of local remedies principle applied in the case at hand. The ITLOS stated that:

> It is a well-established principle of customary international law that the exhaustion of local remedies is a prerequisite for the exercise of diplomatic protection. This principle is reflected in article 14, paragraph 1, of the Draft Articles on Diplomatic Protection adopted by the International Law Commission in 2006 [...]. It is also established in international law that the exhaustion of local remedies rule does not apply where the claimant State is directly injured by the wrongful act of another State.[37]

Thus, by reference to custom, the ITLOS complemented and clarified the content of the relevant UNCLOS provision. The ITLOS said that it was going to follow the approach adopted in its earlier case law,[38] thus providing consistency in its jurisprudence.

(iv)   *Reparation and Art. 304 UNCLOS: Customary International Law Complementing the UNCLOS Rules*

In *M/V 'SAIGA'* (*No. 2*), the ITLOS was seized of a claim for reparation which involved the invocation of Art. 304 UNCLOS and the responsibility of the defendant for an alleged internationally wrongful act. Art. 304 UNCLOS which deals with the responsibility and liability for damage provides that the UNCLOS provisions are without prejudice to the existing rules and the development of further rules regarding responsibility and liability under international law, thus effectively making these rule applicable within the UNCLOS dispute settlement system without, however, specifying the details.

In assessing the soundness of the legal claim, the ITLOS referred to international law and the jurisprudence of the ICJ to conclude that there is a well-established rule of international law that a State which suffers damage as a result of an internationally wrongful act by another State is entitled to obtain reparation; that under this rule the reparation must, as far as possible, wipe out all the consequences of the illegal act and reestablish the situation which would have existed if that act had not been committed; and that this rule was

---

37   *M/V 'Virginia G'* (*Panama v. Guinea-Bissau*) (*Judgment*) ITLOS Case No. 19 (14 April 2014), at para. 153.
38   Ibid., at para. 155.

applicable to the dispute at hand.[39] The rules on liability in international law were thus transferred into the UNCLOS through Art. 304 UNCLOS, complementing its regime on liability.[40] Notably, a claim for reparation under international law not related to an allegation of violation of obligations stemming from the UNCLOS cannot, in principle, trigger the jurisdiction of UNCLOS courts and tribunal.

b        Law Enforcement at Sea

Although the UNCLOS contains provisions dealing with law enforcement at sea, these provisions do not conclusively regulate all aspects of such law enforcement activities. For example, while Art. 73 UNCLOS enables the coastal State to arrest a ship in its EEZ for violating its fisheries laws and regulations, this norm does not specify whether such State can resort to use of force. Other provisions also provide for arrest of ships by coastal States (Arts 27, 105, 111 UNCLOS) without mentioning use of force. Under Art. 73 UNCLOS a littoral State can take *necessary* measures to ensure compliance with the laws and regulations adopted by it in conformity with the UNCLOS, but this provision does not clarify what the 'necessity' criterion entails. Questions relating to the use of force in the exercise of the rights under the UNCLOS and the state of necessity have indeed arisen before the ITLOS and have been resolved by resort to international law.

(i)      *Use of Force—No UNCLOS Rule*

In the *M/V 'SAIGA' (No. 2)* case, the ITLOS had to decide whether in arresting the *'Saiga'* (a ship flying the flag of Saint Vincent and the Grenadines which exercised bunkering activities in the EEZ of Guinea), Guinea had used excessive use of force. The Tribunal noted that the UNCLOS contains no express provision on the use of force. To resolve the matter, it referred to international law, applicable by virtue of Art. 293 UNCLOS, and clarified that this required that the use of force must be avoided as far as possible and, where force is unavoidable, it must not go beyond what is reasonable and necessary in the circumstances.[41] It then went on to establish whether the use of force by Guinean

---

39   *M/V 'SAIGA' (No. 2) (Saint Vincent and the Grenadines v. Guinea) (Merits)* ITLOS Case No. 2 (1 July 1999), at para. 170, referring to *Factory at Chorzów (Germany v. Poland) (Claim for Indemnity) (Merits)* PCIJ Series A No. 17, at 47.

40   Ibid., at para. 170.

41   'Although the Convention does not contain express provisions on the use of force in the arrest of ships, international law, which is applicable by virtue of Art. 293 of the Convention, requires that the use of force must be avoided as far as possible and, where force is unavoidable, it must not go beyond what is reasonable and necessary in the circumstances.

officers had met the requirements thus identified and concluded that Guinea had violated the rights of Saint Vincent and the Grenadines under international law.[42]

(ii)     *The Principle of Public Interest and Arts 56 and 58 (3) UNCLOS*
In the *M/V 'SAIGA' (No. 2)* case, the ITLOS was also faced with the question whether Guinea was justified in applying its customs laws in its EEZ within a customs radius extending to a distance of 250 kilometres from the coast, i.e., including parts of the EEZ, on the basis of other rules of international law (principle of public interest, among others) referred to in Art. 58 (3) UNCLOS.

Under the UNCLOS, the coastal State is *entitled to apply* its customs laws and regulations in its *territorial sea*; in the contiguous zone it is only *entitled to exercise the control necessary to prevent or punish* infringement of its customs laws and regulations *within its territory or territorial sea* (Art. 33); and in the EEZ, it has jurisdiction to apply its customs laws and regulation *only* in respect of islands, installations and structures (Art. 60 (2)). The UNCLOS does not entitle the littoral State to apply or exercise control to prevent infringement of its customs laws and regulations in any parts of the EEZ beyond the aforementioned ones.

Art. 58 states that in the EEZ, all States enjoy (subject to the relevant provisions of the UNCLOS) the freedoms referred to in Art. 87, including the freedom of navigation and the internationally lawful uses of the sea related to it. Art. 58 (3) further specifies that in the EEZ, all other States are under the obligation to comply with the laws and regulations adopted by the coastal State in accordance with the Convention and other rules of international law but *only in so far* as they are not incompatible with Part V UNCLOS.

In the case at hand, Guinea attempted to justify the application of its customs laws and regulations within its EEZ, i.e., to expand its jurisdiction in the EEZ, by reference to the principle of public interest,[43] which required an assessment of the interplay between the relevant UNCLOS provisions and international law.

The ITLOS clarified that Art. 58 (3) imposes on all other States an obligation to comply *only* with the legal measures covered by the scope of the coastal State's sovereign rights and jurisdiction in the EEZ[44] (excluding from the scope

---

Considerations of humanity must apply in the law of the sea, as they do in other areas of international law'. Ibid., at para. 155.
42   Ibid., at para. 159.
43   Ibid., at para. 129.
44   Ibid., at para. 131.

of this obligation compliance with legal measures not compatible with the UNCLOS), thus effectively setting the boundary between the rights stemming from the special legal regime established under the Convention, and rights and obligations stemming from international law.

It also stated that the principle of public interest would entitle Guinea to prohibit any activity in its EEZ which it decides to characterize as affecting its economic public interest, curtailing the rights of other States in the EEZ under the UNCLOS.[45] This reasoning alludes to the special balance between the interests of the littoral States and those of all other States achieved through the UNCLOS, including through the legal regime established under Part V.

(iii)    *Enforcement of Fisheries Law and Art. 73 UNCLOS*

As mentioned above, Art. 73 UNCLOS enables a coastal State to take the measures *necessary* to ensure compliance with the laws and regulations adopted by it in conformity with the UNCLOS, without specifying the meaning of the term 'necessary'. Art. 73 UNCLOS contains examples of such measures, but the list is not exhaustive.

In the *M/V 'Virginia G'* case, assessing the conformity of a disputed measure (the confiscation by Guinea-Bissau of the M/V 'Virginia G' and the gas oil on board) with Art. 73 UNCLOS, the ITLOS relied on international law and made reference to the principle of reasonableness which it regarded as applicable to enforcement measures adopted under the aforementioned UNCLOS rule.[46] Accordingly, the ITLOS found that the measure at hand was in violation of Art. 73 (1) UNCLOS. This was a case in which customary law elements were incorporated in a conventional right, thus restricting its application, independently of the limits set out in the Convention.

Art. 73 UNCLOS also does not specify the requirements to be complied with during enforcement operations. In clarifying the meaning of the provision, the ITLOS resorted to international law without, however, specifying the legal basis for this approach; arguably this was based on Art. 31 (3) (c) VCLT because the reference was made in the course of interpreting an UNCLOS provision. It held that international law sets out clear requirements (including the requirement that enforcement activities must be exercised by duly authorized identifiable officials of a coastal State and that their vessels must be clearly

---

45    Ibid.
46    '[T]he principle of reasonableness applies generally to enforcement measures under article 73 of the Convention. [...] [I]n applying enforcement measures due regard has to be paid to the particular circumstances of the case and the gravity of the violation'. *M/V 'Virginia G',* at para. 270.

marked as being on government service) that must be complied with by all States during enforcement operations, including operations under Art. 73.[47] Again, Art. 73 UNCLOS was read in the light of international law, effectuating their harmonious interpretation.

(iv)     *Immunity of Warships and Art. 32 UNCLOS*

An issue that intersects with law enforcement at sea is immunity of warships. Art. 32 UNCLOS prescribes that nothing in the UNCLOS affects the immunities of warships without, however, specifying the geographical scope of its application.

Art. 32 UNCLOS is a typical example of a treaty specific provision referring to other rules of international law. On the one hand, it clarifies the interaction between the UNCLOS rules pertaining to immunity of warships in Part II, subsections A and C (the latter includes Arts 30 and 31 UNCLOS) and the international law on immunity of warships, by specifying that the mentioned rules introduce exceptions to it. On the other hand, Art. 32 restates the immunity under international law of warships and other government ships operated for non-commercial purposes, and it is debatable whether it *regulates* immunity, i.e., incorporates the law to which it refers, or merely refers to an existing rule of international law. If the former, it can in principle be construed in light of international law as imposing an obligation to respect immunities of warships and other government ships operated for non-commercial purposes in internal waters.

These questions were at issue in the '*ARA Libertad*' case. The case concerned, among other things, a dispute between Ghana and Argentina as to whether the arrest and detention by Ghana of a warship belonging to the Argentinian Navy was in conflict with Art. 32 UNCLOS. The jurisdiction of the ITLOS was limited to prescribing provisional measures and it had to assess *prima facie* whether an Annex VII Arbitral Tribunal would have jurisdiction over the dispute at hand. The Tribunal held that Art. 32 UNCLOS afforded a basis on which *prima facie* jurisdiction might be founded, as Art. 32 does not specify the geographical scope of its application[48] and may thus include the immunity of warships in internal waters. Although the ITLOS did not have to decide conclusively on the precise scope of Art. 32 UNCLOS, its reasoning implies that it is possible to interpret Art. 32 UNCLOS as either regulating immunity, or as imposing an

---

47    Ibid., at para. 342.
48    '*ARA Libertad*' (*Argentina v. Ghana*) (*Provisional Measures*) (*Order*) ITLOS Case No. 20 (15 December 2012), at para. 63.

obligation corresponding to international law to respect immunity of warships in internal waters.

The Tribunal claimed in its Order that in accordance with international law, a warship enjoys immunity, including in internal waters.[49] In their Joint Separate Opinion, Judges Wolfrum and Cot strongly disagreed with the reasoning of the Tribunal, characterizing Art. 32 as a rule of reference, not as an incorporating rule.[50]

c     Authority to Conclude a Legally Binding Agreement (Art. 7 (2) VCLT) and Art. 15 UNCLOS

Art. 15 UNCLOS envisages the possibility that two States with opposite or adjacent coats conclude an agreement to the effect that one of the States concerned extends its territorial sea beyond the median line every point of which is equidistant from the nearest points from the baseline from which the breadth of the territorial sea of each of the two States is measured. The provision, however, does not specify who has the authority to conclude such an agreement. The question arose in *Delimitation of the Maritime Boundary in the Bay of Bengal (Bangladesh/Myanmar)*. The ITLOS took the position that this question is to be resolved by Art. 7 (2) VCLT.[51] The application of this provision was justified by reference to Art. 293 UNCLOS.

d     Maritime Delimitation and Arts 74 and 83 UNCLOS

Maritime delimitation is subject to certain judge-made rules which have emerged in the practice of international courts and tribunals. The ICJ in particular has identified some methods and principles for maritime delimitation which have been consistently followed, clarified and affirmed by UNCLOS courts and tribunals as well as by non-UNCLOS tribunals, such as the equidistance/relevant circumstances method as requiring a three-stage approach,[52]

---

49   Ibid., at para. 95.
50   '*ARA Libertad*' (*Argentina v. Ghana*) (*Provisional Measures*) (*Joint Separate Opinion of Judges Wolfrum and Cot*) ITLOS Case No. 20 (15 December 2012), at paras 38–51.
51   *Delimitation of the Maritime Boundary in the Bay of Bengal (Bangladesh v. Myanmar)* (*Judgment*) ITLOS Case No. 16 (14 March 2012), at para. 96. In the case at hand, controversy arose as to whether the Agreed Minutes could be regarded as an 'agreement' within the meaning of Art. 15 UNCLOS, respectively, whether the official who signed them could engage his country without having to produce full powers.
52   *Maritime Delimitation in the Black Sea* (*Judgment*) [2009] ICJ Rep 61, at paras 116, 120 and 122; *Delimitation of the Maritime Boundary in the Bay of Bengal (Bangladesh v. Myanmar)* (*Judgment*), at para. 240; *Delimitation of the Maritime Boundary between Ghana and Côte d'Ivoire* (*Ghana v. Côte d'Ivoire*) (*Judgment*) ITLOS Case No. 23 (23 September 2017), at para. 360.

the angle bisector method as a possible alternative, and the principle that the land dominates the sea through the projection of the coasts or the coastal fronts.

In *Delimitation of the Maritime Boundary in the Bay of Bengal (Bangladesh/ Myanmar)*, the ITLOS explicitly stated that decisions of international court and tribunals, referred to in Art. 38 (1) (d) ICJ Statute, are of particular importance in determining the content of the law applicable to maritime delimitation under Art. 74 and 83 UNCLOS.[53] Thus, it confirmed and applied the principle identified in the ICJ jurisprudence that the land dominates the sea through the projection of the coasts or the coastal fronts[54] and held that 'for a coast to be considered as relevant in maritime delimitation it must generate projections which overlap with those of the coast of another party',[55] although this principle has not been incorporated in the UNCLOS.

In the *Dispute Concerning Delimitation of the Maritime Boundary between Ghana and Côte d'Ivoire in the Atlantic Ocean*, the Special Chamber of the ITLOS was requested to determine a single maritime boundary dividing the maritime areas appertaining to Ghana and Côte d'Ivoire in the Atlantic Ocean and thus was concerned with claims arising, *inter alia*, under Arts 15, 74 and 83 UNCLOS. These provisions do not specify the precise methodology for the respective delimitation. Having noted that the international jurisprudence had developed in favour of the equidistance/relevant circumstances method, whereas the international decisions which adopted the angle bisector methodology were due to particular circumstances in each of the cases concerned,[56] the Special Chamber decided to apply the equidistance/relevant circumstances methodology, adopting the three-stage approach which it regarded as an 'internationally established approach' from which it chose not to deviate.[57]

---

[53] 'Decisions of international courts and tribunals, referred to in Art. 38 of the Statute of the ICJ, are also of particular importance in determining the content of the law applicable to maritime delimitation under Arts 74 and 83 of the Convention'. *Delimitation of the Maritime Boundary in the Bay of Bengal (Bangladesh v. Myanmar)* (*Judgment*), at para. 184.

[54] Ibid., at para. 185, referring to *Maritime Delimitation in the Black Sea* (*Judgment*) [2009] ICJ Rep 61, at para. 77.

[55] *Delimitation of the Maritime Boundary in the Bay of Bengal (Bangladesh v. Myanmar)* (*Judgment*), at para. 198.

[56] *Dispute Concerning the Delimitation of the Maritime Boundary between Ghana and Côte d'Ivoire in the Atlantic Ocean (Ghana v. Côte d'Ivoire)* (*Judgment*) ITLOS Case No. 23 (23 September 2017), at para. 289.

[57] Ibid., at para. 360.

e    Arts 192 and 194 UNCLOS in the Context of the Provisions of the CBD and the CITES and International Environmental Law

The Arbitral Tribunal in the *South China Sea Arbitration (Philippines v. China)* was called upon to interpret Arts 192 and 194 UNCLOS, while taking account of the relevant provisions of the Convention on Biological Diversity (CBD)[58] and the Convention on International Trade in Endangered Species of Wild Fauna and Flora (CITES).[59] It operationalized Art. 31 (3) (c) VCLT (through Art. 293 UNCLOS), and stated that it enabled it to determine the content of Arts 192 and 194 UNCLOS[60] by reference to other rules of international law. The approach of the Arbitral Tribunal is interesting for several reasons: first, the interpretation took account of other *treaty* rules suggesting that the term 'rules' in Art. 31 (3) (c) VCLT includes treaty rules; second, reference was made to rules belonging to others sectors of international law; third, the interpretation was not limited to the scope of the terms of the interpreted rules but went into the substance of these rules, qualifying the level of protection due under these rules.

Thus, in interpreting the term 'ecosystem' and the phrase 'rare or fragile ecosystem' in Art. 194 UNCLOS, the Arbitral Tribunal referred to Art. 2 CBD which defines ecosystem to mean 'a dynamic complex of plant, animal and micro-organism communities and their non-living environment interacting as a functional unit' and concluded that the marine environments in question constituted 'rare or fragile ecosystems'.[61]

It should be noted that not all States Parties to the UNCLOS were parties to the CBD, whereas both disputants were parties to it. The Arbitral Tribunal did not actually make any mention of participation in the CBD, nor did it examine the question whether identity of parties is required for a treaty to inform the interpretation of another treaty under Art. 31 (3) (c) VCLT. However, CBD rules were taken into account, even though it has been argued that only rules which are binding on all the parties to the treaty in question meet the threshold of Art. 31 (3) (c) VCLT.[62]

In the interpretation of Art. 192, the Arbitral Tribunal also considered the CITES. It noted that this convention is the subject of almost universal

---

58  Convention on Biological Diversity (concluded 5 June 1992, entered into force 29 December 1993) 1760 UNTS 79.
59  Convention on International Trade in Endangered Species of Wild Fauna and Flora (opened for signature 3 March 1973, entered into force 1 July 1975) 993 UNTS 243.
60  *South China Sea Arbitration (Philippines v. China) (Award on Jurisdiction and Admissibility)* Annex VII Tribunal (29 October 2015), at para. 176.
61  *South China Sea Arbitration (Philippines v. China) (Award)* Annex VII Tribunal (12 July 2016), at para. 945.
62  Villiger, *Commentary on the 1969 Vienna Convention on the Law of Treaties*, at 433.

adherence and forms part of the general corpus of international law that informs the content of Arts 192 and 194 UNCLOS.⁶³ In particular, by reference to the CITES appendixes listing species threatened with extinction or species which may become so, the Arbitral Tribunal identified sea turtles (*Cheloniidae*), giant clams (*Tridacnidae*) and many of the coral species affected by China's harvesting activities in the disputed marine areas as threatened or endangered species whose conservation as well as the protection and preservation of whose habitat fall within the scope of the obligation stemming from Art. 192 UNCLOS.⁶⁴

In addition to discussing the scope of the terms of Art. 192 UNCLOS, the Arbitral Tribunal delved into the substance of the provision which imposes a general obligation to 'protect and preserve the marine environment' but says nothing about the required level of protection. The Arbitral Tribunal stated that the content of this obligation is informed by the provisions of Part XII and the corpus of international law relating to the environment:

> The corpus of *international law relating to the environment*, which informs the content of the general obligation in Art. 192, requires that States 'ensure that activities within their jurisdiction and control respect the environment of other States or of areas beyond national control'. Thus, States have a positive 'duty to prevent, or at least mitigate' significant harm to the environment when pursuing large-scale construction activities.⁶⁵

---

63   *South China Sea Arbitration (Philippines v. China) (Award)*, at para. 956.
64   The responsibility of China under Art. 192 UNCLOS was invoked with respect to its widespread harvesting of giant clams through the coral substrate accompanied with harvesting of coral species and sea turtles (*Cheloniidae*). While noting that Appendix I to the CITES enlists sea turtles (*Cheloniidae*) as species threatened with extinction, the Arbitral Tribunal held that the conservation of such species as living resources is part of the general obligation stemming from Art. 192 UNCLOS to protect and preserve the marine environment. In addition, the Arbitral Tribunal stated that giant clams (*Tridacnidae*) and many of the corals species affected by China's harvesting activities are listed in Appendix II to CITES and are unequivocally threatened, even if they are not subject to the same level of international controls as Appendix I species and are therefore subject to the duty to prevent the harvest of endangered species following from Art. 192 UNCLOS. See *South China Sea Arbitration (Philippines v. China) (Award)*, at paras 956–57.
65   Ibid., at para. 941, referring to *Legality of the Threat or Use of Nuclear Weapons (Advisory Opinion)* [1996] ICJ Rep 226, at para. 29; *Indus Waters Kishenganga Arbitration (Pakistan v. India) (Partial Award)* Permanent Court of Arbitration (18 February 2013) 31 RIAA 55, at para. 451, quoting *Arbitration Regarding the Iron Rhine (Ijzeren Rijn) Railway between the Kingdom of Belgium and the Kingdom of the Netherlands (Award)* Permanent Court of Arbitration (24 May 2005) 27 RIAA 35, at para. 59.

The Tribunal then went on to determine the content of the relevant international law relating to the environment, referring to the international jurisprudence.[66]

Notably, the content of the relevant rules of international environmental law was not established by reference to a particular source of law but rather on the basis of the understanding of the ICJ on what environmental obligations entail. Whereas the harmonizing of the approaches of international courts is desirable, some discussion of the respective sources of law and their interaction with the UNCLOS would have been helpful.

However, drawing on the jurisprudence of UNCLOS courts and tribunals and decisions of the ICJ, the Arbitral Tribunal affirmed that the content of the obligation under Art. 192 is given shape in Art. 194 (5) UNCLOS and entails a due diligence obligation to adopt certain measures necessary to protect and preserve rare or fragile ecosystems. According to the Arbitral Tribunal, due diligence means that the obligation goes beyond the mere adoption of rules and measures and necessitates vigilance in their enforcement and in the exercise of administrative control. Art. 192 UNCLOS thus enshrines a due diligence obligation to prevent the harvesting of species that are recognized internationally as being at risk of extinction and requiring international protection,[67] as well as the obligation to prevent the harmful activities that would affect depleted, threatened, or endangered species indirectly through the destruction of their habitat.[68]

The significance of the reasoning of the Arbitral Tribunal lies in the clarification of highly sensitive issues such as the content of the general obligation to protect and preserve the environment, the concept of 'due diligence' and 'obligation of conduct' and the link between the them,[69] as well as in the identification and endorsement of views shared among international adjudicatory bodies, including the ICJ.

## 2  *Procedure*

The UNCLOS embodies a comprehensive dispute settlement regime which envisages the establishment of arbitral tribunals and a permanent tribunal and includes their statutes. The ITLOS Statute, being the most detailed among them, to a significant degree reflect the content of the ICJ Statute. However,

---

66  Ibid.
67  *South China Sea Arbitration (Philippines v. China) (Award)*, at para. 956.
68  Ibid., at para. 959.
69  Ibid., at para. 941, referring to the *Fisheries Advisory Opinion*, paras 118–136, and *Pulp Mills on the River Uruguay (Argentina v. Uruguay)*.

the UNCLOS and some of the aforementioned statutes fail to address various procedural issues, for example, *proprio motu* decisions, non-appearance, and the meaning of the terms 'dispute' and 'legal question' for the purpose of establishing jurisdiction. When faced with questions of this kind, UNCLOS tribunals have frequently resorted to international law and/or sought guidance from the jurisprudence of the ICJ and other international courts.

a       *Proprio motu* Decision

The ITLOS Statute does not say whether the ITLOS has the power to examine *proprio motu* the basis of its jurisdiction. This question arose in the *'Grand Prince' (Prompt Release)* case.[70] To resolve the matter, the ITLOS referred to the 'settled jurisprudence in international adjudication', including its own practice, and affirmed that a tribunal must at all times be satisfied that it has jurisdiction to entertain the case submitted to it. Thus, it had the power to examine *proprio motu* the basis of its jurisdiction and to deal with such questions regardless of whether or not they had been raised by the parties.[71] On this basis, it went on to examine whether the Application had been 'made on behalf of the flag State of the vessel', even though this particular objection to jurisdiction had not been put forward by the respondent.[72]

b       Non-Appearance

Art. 28 ITLOS Statute addresses very briefly the question of non-appearance, but otherwise many of its aspects remain unresolved in the UNCLOS and its annexes. One of them is the effect of non-appearance on the prescription of provisional measures. This issue arose in the *'Arctic Sunrise'* case where the ITLOS was confronted with a request for the prescription of provisional measures submitted by the Kingdom of the Netherlands and the non-participation of the Russian Federation in the proceedings.

The ITLOS relied on the established jurisprudence of the ICJ and distilled from it the following:

> [T]he absence of a party or failure of a party to defend its case does not constitute a bar to the proceedings and does not preclude the Tribunal from prescribing provisional measures, provided that the parties have been given an opportunity of presenting their observations on the

---

[70]   *'Grand Prince' (Belize v. France) (Prompt Release) (Judgment)* ITLOS Case No. 8 (20 April 2001), at para. 77.

[71]   Ibid., at paras 77–79.

[72]   Ibid., at paras 80 et seq.

subject [...]; the non-appearing State is nevertheless a party to the proceedings [...]; as stated by the International Court of Justice, '[a] State which decides not to appear must accept the consequences of its decision, the first of which is that the case will continue without its participation; the State which has chosen not to appear remains a party to the case, and is bound by the eventual judgment [...]'.[73]

Regrettably, the Tribunal did not refer to Art. 28 of the ITLOS Statute, missing an occasion to contribute to the interpretation of that provision. Instead, it tacitly followed the practice of the ICJ[74] without engaging in a comprehensive discussion on non-appearance and its overall impact on judicial proceedings, including the disadvantages non-participation may bring to the non-appearing party, for example, weakening of that party's position due to the fact that the court will have to rely on the facts and arguments that are presented by the participating side or that are publicly available.[75]

Nonetheless, while endorsing the practice of the ICJ, the ITLOS outlined what can be regarded as an international procedural rule on non-appearance. This rule was subsequently affirmed in the awards on jurisdiction and on the merits in the *'Arctic Sunrise'* case[76] as well as in the *South China Sea Arbitration* in relation to China's non-participation in the proceedings.[77]

---

[73] *'Arctic Sunrise' (Kingdom of the Netherlands v. Russian Federation) (Provisional Measures) (Order)* ITLOS Case No. 22 (22 November 2013), at paras 48–52, referring to *Military and Paramilitary Activities in and against Nicaragua (Nicaragua v. United States of America) (Merits)* [1986] ICJ Rep 14, at para. 28.

[74] The same observation was made by Judges Wolfrum and Kelly in their Separate Opinion in the *'Arctic Sunrise'* case. See *'Arctic Sunrise' (Kingdom of the Netherlands v. Russian Federation) (Provisional Measures) (Joint Separate Opinion of Judge Wolfrum and Judge Kelly)* ITLOS Case No. 22 (22 November 2013). Notably, Judge Wolfrum and Judge Kelly are critical of the Tribunal's approach to the question of non-appearance.

[75] This is not the only possible effect of non-participation. See the Joint Separate Opinion of Judge Wolfrum and Judge Kelly in *'Arctic Sunrise'*, at para. 5. Non-appearance of a State Party in the proceedings may, of course, be part of a domestic political strategy, especially if that State had only slim chances of winning the case. A declaration that a tribunal lacks jurisdiction over a dispute, coupled with non-appearance in the proceedings, may help to shift the public blame from the government to the court if the case is lost. Obviously, such a result is not in the interests of justice and hinders the effective execution of a judgment.

[76] *'Arctic Sunrise' (Kingdom of the Netherlands v. Russian Federation) (Jurisdiction) (Award)* Annex VII Tribunal (26 November 2014), at para. 60; *'Arctic Sunrise' (Kingdom of the Netherlands v. Russian Federation) (Merits) (Award)* Annex VII Tribunal (14 August 2015), at para. 10.

[77] The Arbitral Tribunal made explicit reference to the *'Arctic Sunrise'* Case as well as to the ICJ jurisprudence referred to in that case. *South China Sea Arbitration (Philippines v. China) (Award on Jurisdiction and Admissibility)*, at para. 114.

Concerning the *South China Sea Arbitration*, the reference to the practice of the ICJ and the ITLOS was made in the course of interpreting Art. 9 UNCLOS Annex VII (default of appearance) which reproduces verbatim Art. 28 ITLOS Statute. Thus, the reference to the international jurisprudence in that arbitration has a twofold effect: it elucidates the content of Art. 9 UNCLOS Annex VII and also contributes to a unified approach among international adjudicatory bodies on the issue of non-participation.

c      Dispute under Art. 288 UNCLOS

The existence of a 'dispute', Art. 288 UNCLOS, constitutes a threshold requirement for the exercise of an UNCLOS court's or tribunal's jurisdiction. UNCLOS contains no definition of the term, but UNCLOS courts and tribunals have consistently held that the concept of a dispute is well-established in international law, referring to the ICJ jurisprudence. Thus, the Annex VII Arbitral Tribunal in the *South China Sea Arbitration* reiterated that a dispute is a disagreement on a point of law or fact, a conflict of legal views or of interests between two persons; whether such a disagreement exists is a matter for objective determination; a mere assertion by one party that a dispute exists is not sufficient to prove the existence of a dispute any more than a mere denial of the existence of the dispute proves its nonexistence; it is not adequate to show that the interests of the two parties to such a case are in conflict, it must be shown that the claim of one party is positively opposed by the other; and the dispute must have existed at the time the proceedings were commenced.[78]

This is not random enumeration of the various findings of the ICJ on the concept of a dispute. Rather, the Arbitral Tribunal proceeds in a systematic manner, distilling from the case law the essential components of a dispute. The jurisprudence of UNCLOS courts and tribunals may thus contribute to ascertaining all the elements that must be present in order a dispute to exist. The same approach was already adopted in its earlier case law.[79]

d      Legal Question under Art. 191 UNCLOS

Art. 191 UNCLOS enables the Seabed Disputes Chamber to give advisory opinions at the request of the Assembly or the Council on legal questions arising within the scope of their activities. The existence of a 'legal question' appears to constitute a threshold requirement but the term is not defined. The Seabed Disputes Chamber has referred to the ICJ jurisprudence to ascertain the

---

78   Ibid., at para. 149, referring to the ICJ jurisprudence mentioned therein.
79   *Southern Bluefin Tuna Cases (New Zealand v. Japan; Australia v. Japan) Southern Bluefin Tuna Cases (New Zealand v. Japan; Australia v. Japan) (Provisional Measures)*, at para. 44.

criteria, namely, 'questions "framed in terms of law and rais[ing] problems of international law [...] are by their very nature susceptible of a reply based on law."'[80]

### e   Estoppel

In the *Dispute Concerning Delimitation of the Maritime Boundary between Ghana and Côte d'Ivoire in the Atlantic Ocean*, the Special Chamber of the ITLOS was faced with an estoppel argument.[81] Ghana maintained that Côte d'Ivoire had recognized a customary equidistance maritime boundary and was therefore estopped from objecting to a boundary based on equidistance,[82] whereas Côte d'Ivoire raised doubts about the notion of estoppel and its applicability to maritime delimitation.[83] UNCLOS contains no rule on estoppel. The status of estoppel in international law is also undefined.[84] Without engaging in a discussion on the source of this rule or rejecting its applicability to the dispute, the Special Chamber simply followed the approach of the ICJ which the ITLOS had already referred to in its earlier case law, thus indicating the emergence of a common approach to estoppel. It affirmed that

> in international law, a situation of estoppel exists when a State, by its conduct, has created the appearance of a particular situation and another State, relying on such conduct in good faith, has acted or abstained from an action to its detriment. The effect of the notion of estoppel is that a State is precluded, by its conduct, from asserting that it did not agree to, or recognize, a certain situation.[85]

---

80   *Responsibilities and Obligations of States with Respect to Activities in the Area (Request for Advisory Opinion submitted to the Seabed Disputes Chamber)*, para. 39, referring to *Accordance with International Law of the Unilateral Declaration of Independence in Respect of Kosovo (Advisory Opinion)* (22 July 2010) ICJ Doc 2010 General List No. 141, at para. 25, and *Western Sahara (Advisory Opinion)* [1975] ICJ Rep 12, at para. 15.
81   *Delimitation of the Maritime Boundary between Ghana and Côte d'Ivoire (Ghana v. Côte d'Ivoire)* (*Judgment*), at para. 229.
82   Ibid., at para. 230.
83   Ibid., at para. 235.
84   T. Cottier and J.P. Müller, 'Estoppel' (last updated 2011) in R. Wolfrum (ed.) *Max Planck Encyclopedia of Public International Law* (OUP Oxford 2008–), available at http://www.mpepil.com/ (27 February 2019).
85   *Delimitation of the Maritime Boundary between Ghana and Côte d'Ivoire (Ghana v. Côte d'Ivoire)* (*Judgment*), at para. 242, referring to *Delimitation of the Maritime Boundary in the Bay of Bengal (Bangladesh v. Myanmar)* (*Judgment*), which on its part refers to the ICJ case law, at para. 124.

It found that the first condition for estoppel was not met in the case at hand and rejected Ghana's claim that Côte d'Ivoire was estopped from objecting to the customary equidistance boundary.[86]

Apart from contributing to the emergence of a common understanding among international courts on the issue of estoppel, the reasoning of the Special Chamber also demonstrates that the lack of clarity as to the legal status of a rule of international law may be irrelevant as long as it can be established that the notion is widely accepted by international courts and what its content is.

## IV   Conclusion

The above review of the jurisprudence of UNCLOS courts and tribunals demonstrates a certain degree of cross-fertilization among UNCLOS, custom, principles relating to procedure and even international environmental law, both in procedural and substantive issues. Its direct effect is filling gaps in UNCLOS or clarifying its provisions without impairing its legal regime or affecting the achievement of its purposes. The legitimacy of this result is secured through reference to rules binding on all States Parties to the UNCLOS which have gained universal acceptance, or through reference to the settled international jurisprudence and the authoritative pronouncements of the ICJ.

The indirect effect of this cross-fertilization is the settlement of disputes in accordance with the rule of law, without allowing the lack of an explicit rule in the interpreted treaty to impede the process of judicial dispute resolution or the effective function of the courts and tribunals established under the UNCLOS. Yet this cross-fertilization also contributes to the clarification and development of international law, elucidating the links and relationships between different sources of law and between different sectors of international law. As a result, cross-fertilization ultimately facilitates the coherence and unity of international law.

The paper has also demonstrated how Art. 31 (3) (c) VCLT, along with other provisions, could be operationalized in order for UNCLOS to be integrated in the system of international law. Obligations under a particular treaty are not to be seen in isolation from other relevant rules of international law, and Art. 31 (3) (c) VCLT provides the tool for this kind of assessment, albeit with its inherent limitations. The consistent examination of the links and interrelationships among the different sources of international law, coupled with a harmonized

---

86   *Delimitation of the Maritime Boundary between Ghana and Côte d'Ivoire (Ghana v. Côte d'Ivoire)* (*Judgment*), at paras 245–46.

approach to related issues, contributes to legal certainty and predictability in international adjudication, bolsters the trust in adjudication, enhances the credibility of the treaty regimes involved, and helps us view treaties and international tribunals as interconnected elements of a single international legal order.

CHAPTER 7

# Sustainable Development Goal 16 at a Cross-Roads

*Frauke Lachenmann*

**Abstract**

The negotiation process of the Sustainable Development Goals (SDGs) process was extremely ambitious. It sought to remedy all the shortcomings of the Millennium Development Goals (MDGs) by ensuring transparency, ownership of the countries of the Global South, strong involvement of civil society groups and stakeholders, and creating a truly transformative set of sustainable development goals. Yet, it did not manage to avoid all the mistakes that were characteristic of the formulation of the MDGs. In addition, it struggled with its very own problems.

The article traces the developments and debates that led to the formulation of Goal 16 on the rule of law. It shows that the success of this ambitious goal largely depends on the refinement of the indicator framework and the review mechanism.

**Keywords**

Rule of Law – Sustainable Development Goals – SDG 16 – Indicators

## 1    Introduction

The Sustainable Development Goals have now been around for a little more than three years, and they are due to be achieved by 2030. In the summer of 2019, the High-Level Political Forum on Sustainable Development (HLPF) will convene once more, and this time it will discuss Goal 16. While the overarching theme of rule of law runs throughout all of the SDGs, it is most explicit in SDG 16, titled 'Promote peaceful and inclusive societies for sustainable development, provide access to justice for all and build effective, accountable and inclusive institutions at all levels'. This article will look at the developments that have brought us to this place, starting with the debate about the concept of 'rule of law' at the United Nations over the last decades, the SDG negotiations, and where we stand today.

There are as many definitions of the rule of law as scholars writing about it. For the purpose of this article, a few remarks may suffice: The rule of law on the national level is understood as comprising a number of principles of a formal and procedural character. The formal principles concern the generality, clarity, publicity, stability, and prospectivity of the norms that govern a society. The procedural principles concern the processes by which these norms are administered, and institutions—like courts and an independent judiciary.

On some accounts however (this is called the 'thick' or substantive model), the rule of law also comprises certain substantive ideals like human rights, democracy, even some elements of the welfare state (equality and equity). So there is a convergence with political concepts and values.

In addition to national rule of law, increasingly, it is also discussed to what extent the rule of law exists or should exist on the international plane, specifically, how the rule of law manages relations between States on the one hand, and States and international organizations on the other, as well as the extent to which the United Nations and other international organizations are bound by it in their work.

## II  Rule of Law at the UN

While rule of law as a *term* has a relatively recent history at the UN, some scholars and Member States argue that the *concept* is already enshrined in the Preamble of the UN Charter. The Preamble claims that the Members States are determined 'to establish conditions under which justice and respect for the obligations arising from treaties and other sources of international law can be maintained'. Whether this is really the normative foundation of the rule of law in the UN framework remains contested among the members.

Although UN development policy has included certain governance principles since the 1940s, most observers refer to the Earth Summit in 1992 as the moment when a rule of law concept entered into the UN development policy. The Rio Declaration[1] set out 27 principles on environment and development, with Principle 10 of the Rio Declaration calling for the participation of citizens. Many scholars have referred to the emphasis on participation as a first step towards the formulation of a democracy goal.

In September 2000, world leaders adopted the Millennium Declaration[2] on which the eight Millennium Development Goals are based. The Millennium

---

1   UNGA 'Report of the United Nations Conference on Environment and Development, Rio de Janeiro, 3–14 June 1992, Annex I: Rio Declaration on Environment and Development' UN Doc A/CONF.151/26 (vol. I).
2   UNGA Res 55/2 'Millennium Declaration' (8 September 2000).

Declaration went beyond Rio in that it did not just formulate environmental objectives, but also social and economic goals. It sought to create a global partnership to reduce poverty, improve health, and promote peace, human rights, gender equality, and environmental sustainability by 2015. This time, the importance of the rule of law was explicitly mentioned:

> [W]e resolve […] to strengthen respect for the rule of law in international as in national affairs [and] we will spare no effort to promote democracy and strengthen the rule of law, as well as respect for all internationally recognized human rights and fundamental freedoms, including the right to development.

Within the MDGs themselves, rule of law is only implicitly referenced. The first seven goals do not address elements of the rule of law directly, but they do reference inclusive and representative societies and equality. Only MDG 8, on developing a global partnership for development includes a target on 'developing further an open, rule-based, predictable, non-discriminatory trading and financial system' which is part of the rule of law at the international level. The MDGs did not formulate a rule of law concept on the domestic level, however.

In 2004, the Secretary-General in a report on transitional justice and the rule of law in conflict and post-conflict societies, argued that it is the purpose of United Nations peace operations to 'build […] the rule of law and foster […] democracy'. He acknowledged that there are multiple understandings of the term 'rule of law' and then went on to define it for the purposes of the UN and its work:

> [The rule of law] refers to a principle of governance in which all persons, institutions and entities, public and private, *including the State itself*, are *accountable* to laws that are publicly promulgated, equally enforced and independently adjudicated and which are consistent with international *human rights* norms and standards. It requires, as well, measures to ensure adherence to principles of *supremacy* of law, *equality* before the law, *fairness* in the application of law, *separation of powers*, *participation* in decision-making, legal certainty, avoidance of arbitrariness and procedural and legal transparency.

This was the most comprehensive and 'thick' definition put forward on the UN level until that date, and it came to be frequently quoted in later documents.

The 2005 World Summit, which was a follow-up summit to the Millennium Summit, in its outcome document argued that both good governance and the rule of law are essential for sustained economic growth, sustainable development and the eradication of poverty and hunger.

Shortly after, the topic was taken up by the Sixth Committee of the General Assembly, which has included the rule of law in its agenda annually since its sixty-first session in 2006. But it was here, in the Sixth Committee, that the first cracks started to show, and the polarization of the Member States over the rule of law became apparent.

It was the 2012 Rio+20 outcome document, 'The Future We Want'[3] that eventually kicked off the SDG process. 'The Future We Want' endorsed a very substantial notion of the rule of law and emphasized the causal connection between rule of law and development: 'We acknowledge that democracy, good governance and the rule of law, at the national and international levels, as well as an enabling environment, are essential for sustainable development'.

This was followed by the 2012 High-Level Declaration on the Rule of Law[4] where the Member States unanimously reaffirmed their 'solemn commitment to the purposes and principles of the Charter of the United Nations, international law and justice, and to an international order based on the rule of law'.

They went on to 'reaffirm that human rights, the rule of law and democracy are interlinked and mutually reinforcing and that they belong to the universal and indivisible core values and principles of the United Nations'. The Declaration endorsed human rights and fundamental freedoms for all, independence of the judicial system, equal access to justice, and claimed that the rule of law and development are strongly interrelated and mutually reinforcing.

One would think that, following this Declaration, which was passed unanimously, it should have been easy to achieve consensus on a comprehensive definition of the rule of law and ways of measurement. But the post-2015 process would come to show that the underlying differences persisted.

### III    MDGS

So how did we get to the SDGs?

The Sustainable Development Goals were largely an attempt to build on the MDGs but also remedy their shortcomings.

---

3   UNGA Res 66/288 'The Future We Want' (27 July 2012).
4   UNGA Res 67/1 'Declaration of the High-level Meeting of the General Assembly on the Rule of Law at the National and International Levels' (24 September 2012).

The MDGs have produced mixed results.[5] On the one hand, there has been tremendous progress in some countries, and on some metrics. Extreme poverty has fallen below 11% of the world population. The proportion of families living on less than $1.90 per person a day has fallen from almost 27% in 2000 to 9.2% in 2017, with much of this progress achieved in Asia. Mortality in children under five years old has been halved.[6]

But the creation of the MDG framework was very much driven by the United States, Europe and Japan, with the support of the World Bank, the IMF and the OECD. By one account, only 22% of the world's national parliaments formally discussed the MDGs. Generally, there was very little involvement of developing countries and civil society constituencies in the drafting process which has led to a lack of national ownership for the goals.

The MDGs were still guided by a top-down vision of development aid, based on a 'compact' in which richer nations commit themselves to meeting aid obligations, while poorer countries provide the 'appropriate policy context for development'. The prevailing view at the time was that poverty and other development issues were largely a result of adverse geographical and economic circumstances, whereas today consensus is that sounds institutions are central to development.[7] Many authors from the Global South have criticized that the MDG targets are presented not as political but as technical problems, where the solution appears as simply increasing financial resources. The developed countries, on the other hand, were hardly taken to task:

> [O]ne of the most persistent accountability deficits in the current MDG framework has been the difficulty of holding industrialized countries to account for the commitments they made to the global partnership for development, and for the transitional human rights impact of their development aid, trade, and investment policies.[8]

---

5   For an overview of critiques of the MDGs see M. Fehling, B.D. Nelson and S. Venkatapuram, 'Limitations of the Millennium Development Goals: a Literature Review' (2013) 8.10 Global Public Health 1109; I.T. Winkler and C. Williams, 'The Sustainable Development Goals and Human Rights: a Critical Early Review' (2017) 21 The International Journal of Human Rights 1023.
6   See e.g. UN High Commissioner for Human Rights Michelle Bachelet (Opening Statement, 16 January 2019).
7   E.g. D. Rodrik, 'Goodbye Washington Consensus, Hello Washington Confusion?' A Review of the World Bank's "Economic Growth in the 1990s: Learning from a Decade of Reform"' (2006) 44.4 Journal of Economic Literature 973.
8   UN DESA CDP Background Paper No. 25 'Transitioning from the MDGs to the SDGs: Accountability for the Post-2015 Era' (June 2015) ST/ESA/2015/CDP/25.

The MDGs were also criticized for looking at averages, rather than at the progress of vulnerable groups of society. In the words of the Sustainable Development Solutions Network (SDSN):

> Our poor ability to understand how people of different ages, capabilities or income levels have been faring under the MDGs has hampered the design and implementation of strategies to tackle discrimination and ensure achievement of the goals. A number of studies have now demonstrated that progress has often been made amongst those groups that are easiest to reach or whose situations are the easiest to ameliorate, leaving many of the poorest and most vulnerable behind. Others have pinpointed cases of perverse incentives where only the poorest benefitted most. For this reason, it is very important that the indicators for Sustainable Development Goals and Targets can be disaggregated.[9]

## IV    SDGS

By 2010, the deadline for achieving the MDGs was drawing closer and the Secretary-General was mandated with initiating activities towards the post-2015 agenda. One stream was the High-Level Panel of Eminent Persons, installed in 2012, co-chaired by UK Prime Minister David Cameron, a multi-stakeholder initiative consisting of representatives from civil society, the private sector, academia and local governments, alongside State representatives. In May 2013 the High-Level Panel delivered a report containing recommendations on the content of the post-2015 development agenda.

At the same time, the Rio+20 Conference on Sustainable Development proposed that a new set of goals, the so called Sustainable Development Goals (SDGs), should be prepared by an Open Working Group (OWG) led by governments. The OWG had 30 seats that were allocated according to a constituency-based system of representation; most were shared by several countries to ensure maximum representation. The OWG did allow for representations from civil society but was at heart a vehicle for States. In September 2013 it was decided that the UN Secretary-General's process and the Rio+20 process should be coordinated.

The negotiations towards the SDGs were more complex than any other drafting process the UN has ever seen; yet by the end of the day, the outcome

---

9    SDSN 'Indicators and a Monitoring Framework for the Sustainable Development Goals: Launching a Data Revolution for the SDGs' (15 May 2015).

was largely a result of debates in the OWG, the forum for States. The OWG met 13 times between March 2013 and July 2014. At its final meeting in New York, the OWG (co-chaired by Kenya and Hungary) completed its work by adopting a final compilation of 17 proposed goals and 169 targets on sustainable development for the post-2015 development agenda.[10]

Situating the SDGs in international law, they can be seen as a set of norms 'at the softest end of the "hard-to-soft" continuum' as one paper put it.[11] The degree of legalization—as defined by the level of obligation, precision and delegation, respectively—is low. There are no rules or commitments that are binding under international or domestic law. Many targets are reformulations of existing obligations drawn from treaties and other formal and informal instruments.

On 4 December 2014, the UN Secretary-General presented his Synthesis Report on the post-2015 agenda which included the SDGs as formulated by the OWG, and the 2030 Agenda for Sustainable Development was adopted by the UN General Assembly on 25 September 2015.[12]

At the beginning of the process, the willingness and the consensus necessary for an inclusion of the rule of law had appeared to be present. The 2013 report of the High-Level Panel of Eminent Persons proposed to give the rule of law a prominent place in the post-2015 agenda.[13] Civil society groups considered the rule of law as one of the most important issues to address in the post-2015 development process; in fact, the MyWorld Survey, a global citizen survey led by the United Nations and partners about the Sustainable Development Goals,

---

10   For the SDG process see A. Wiik and F. Lachenmann, 'Rule of Law and the Sustainable Development Goals' in F. Lachenmann, T.J. Röder and R. Wolfrum (eds), *Max Planck Yearbook of United Nations Law* vol. 18 (Brill Leiden 2015) 286; N. Arajärvi, 'The Rule of Law in the 2030 Agenda' (June 2017) KFG Working Paper Series No. 9; J. Beqiraj and L. McNamara, 'The Rule of Law and Access to Justice in the Post-2015 Development Agenda: Moving Forward but Stepping Back' (August 2014) Bingham Centre Working Paper 2014/04.

11   A. Persson, N. Weitz and M. Nilsson, 'Follow-up and Review of the Sustainable Development Goals: Alignment vs. Internalization' (2016) 25.1 RECIEL 59–68, at 60.

12   UNGA Res 70/1 'Transforming Our World: the 2030 Agenda for Sustainable Development' (25 September 2015).

13   High-Level Panel of Eminent Persons on the Post-2015 Development Agenda 'A New Global Partnership: Eradicate Poverty and Transform Economies through Sustainable Development' (2013): '[P]eople the world over expect their governments to be honest, accountable, and responsive to their needs. We are calling for a fundamental shift—to recognize peace and good governance as core elements of wellbeing, not optional extras. This is a universal agenda, for all countries. Responsive and legitimate institutions should encourage the rule of law, property rights, freedom of speech and the media, open political choice, access to justice, and accountable government and public institutions. We need a transparency revolution, so citizens can see exactly where and how taxes, aid and revenues from extractive industries are spent. These are ends as well as means.'

lists 'an honest and responsive government' as the top-four priority of citizens around the world.

The OWG itself at the beginning of its work seemed open to a strong rule of law goal. It noted that the Rio conference had concluded that 'democracy, good governance and the rule of law, at the national and international levels, as well as an enabling environment are essential for sustainable development'. Accordingly, the different versions of the proposed SDGs adopted by the OWG up to the so-called 'Zero Draft Version' of 2 June 2014 contained a stand-alone goal on the rule of law. Ahead of the 12th Session from 16–20 June 2014, the Co-Chairs finally circulated the first draft for the 'official' SDGs. Rule of law was included as Goal 16, which read: 'Achieve peaceful and inclusive societies, rule of law, effective and capable institutions'.

What is striking is the change of procedure in Session 12. While earlier sessions had been documented very thoroughly, only one State statement was made public from Session 12: Russia strongly opposed Goal 16, in particular rule of law, coining it as 'one of the most dubious elements'.[14] At the same time, the OWG sessions themselves were unexpectedly closed to the public by the Co-Chairs, drawing strong criticism from the Major Groups and other civil society representatives.

After Session 12, on 30 June 2014, the Co-Chairs disseminated the Revised Zero Draft. This contained a Goal 16 that has little in common with the first draft. What was omitted was anything that would have mandated political changes: Accountability of the executive, especially in financial matters; the formal criteria of legality as formulated by Fuller (publicized, accessible laws); civil and political rights (due process, legal aid, right to information, free speech).

Access to information and freedom of speech were merged, with less strong language. Freedom of the media, however, was deleted, as were references to legal aid and due process in respect of access to justice. Most remarkable is the substitution of 'the rule of law' with 'access to justice' in Goal 16, with the rule of law being relegated to a target. Given the lack of documentation, it is not clear who and what prompted these sudden changes.

It had been announced from the start that the choice of the goals to be included in the post-2015 development agenda should be a result of State negotiations with input from civil society organizations and stakeholders. However, when the Kenyan Co-Chair stated in the final OWG meeting that civil society

---

14  Points by the Russian delegation on proposed Goal 16 'Achieve peaceful and inclusive societies, rule of law, effective and capable institutions' (Open Working Group on Sustainable Development Goals, 19 June 2014).

must 'respect the sanctity of this room', meaning the General Assembly, and effectively shut out all non-State Parties, it became clear that the involvement of non-State actors was largely symbolic. While the closing of the sessions to the public and the interest groups at the eleventh hour may have made sense to the Chairs of the Open Working Group in light of the difficulties of reaching a consensus on the wording of Goal 16, it was a slap in the face of the civil society groups that were attending the process, and also a blunt admission of the limitations of the procedural model that had been chosen.

## v  RoL Debate in the OWG and the Sixth Committee

To understand the course of the debate on the rule of law in the OWG, it is helpful to also look at the discussions going on in the Sixth Committee at the same time.[15] The conflict that culminated in the OWG had been a long time in coming. It is a conflict that largely runs along the Global North–Global South divide on the one hand, and between autocratic and democratic States on the other hand.

The first point of contention is the international legal basis of the rule of law. Russia has long argued that the rule of law is not an inalienable part of the Charter, stating that the Charter does not mention 'rule of law' at all. Russia also has objected to the Secretary-General's 2004 definition of the term.

Related to this is the argument that any domestic rule of law goal would conflict with Article 2, paragraph 7 of the UN Charter, which says the UN cannot intervene in matters that are essentially within the domestic jurisdiction of any State. Any shortcomings in social, economic and environmental fields, so the argument goes, could be used as an excuse for interference in domestic affairs. This position was supported by the Non-Aligned Movement, chaired by Iran. They highlighted the need to respect national sovereignty and national circumstances, and expressed their concern about unilateral and extraterritorial measures based on political considerations.

In the Sixth Committee's 70th meeting (2015), Iran on behalf of the NAM made this clear by saying:

> The international community must not replace the national authorities in the task of establishing or strengthening the rule of law at the national level, but only to provide them with the necessary support at their

---

15   See also N. Arajärvi, 'The Rule of Law in the 2030 Agenda' (June 2017) KFG Working Paper Series No. 9, at 6 et seq.

> request. [...] It is also necessary to take into account the customs and the national political and socioeconomic realities to prevent imposition of pre-established models upon Member States that would hinder the resolution of existing problems in each country.[16]

And Russia added:

> Provision of assistance to the States upon their request in questions of construction of constitutional order and improvement of the legislation is an important task. At the same time, making the 'legitimacy' of national constitutions and State organs dependent on some abstract conceptions is unacceptable.[17]

National sovereignty was a concern not just for autocratic States, but also for recipients of foreign and international aid, who feared a return to the days of aid conditionality. If rule of law reforms are included as 'conditionalities' for eligibility for structural and large-scale support, developing countries argue that purely domestic issues would suddenly be at the discretion of a host of foreign or international actors.

The second point of contention is the balance between rule of law on the domestic level against rule of law on the international level. Developed countries continue to emphasize the promotion of the rule of law at the national level, through strong institutions, inclusive decision-making, promotion of human rights and non-discrimination, and good governance. The BRICS and many developing countries, on the other hand call for more emphasis on the rule of law at the international level, including the promotion of sovereign equality, ending foreign occupation, more equal representation at international financial institutions, and strengthening the rule of law within the UN itself, specifically the reform of the Security Council. At the 2015 meeting of the Sixth Committee, Belarus said that 'It would also like to see information in the next report of the Secretary-General on how basic criteria of the rule of law were

---

16   Statement of 14 October 2015, at 3.
17   Statement of 14 October 2015 (the author would like to thank Victor Yurkov and Mindia Vashkmadze for their translation from the Russian). On Russia's stance see also Points by the Russian delegation on proposed Goal 16 'Achieve peaceful and inclusive societies, rule of law, effective and capable institutions' (Open Working Group on Sustainable Development Goals, 19 June 2014): 'There is also a possibility that the task of ranking States will be seconded to NGOs currently active in this domain (e.g. to the World Justice Project—the organization invited to a series of the UN rule of law events with one single purpose—to demonstrate that the rule of law can and must be measured on a national level)'.

upheld within the Organization, including predictability and transparency in decision-making, fulfilment by officials of their mandates and mechanisms for challenging decisions taken by the Secretariat'.[18]

A third argument, pushed by Brazil, Russia, Bolivia, Ecuador, India, Pakistan and Sri Lanka, concerned the inclusion of conflict prevention and post-conflict peace-building in the rule of law goal. This was seen as an attempt to bring a so-called 'fourth dimension' into sustainable development that is alien to the agreed three-dimensional concept. They argued that the OWG had no mandate in this matter and that questions of peace and security should be left to the responsible UN fora, specifically, the Security Council and the Peacekeeping Commission.[19]

The fourth point of contention is the development paradigm. Some States in the past have challenged the causal connection between rule of law and development; after all, a number of the most successful developing countries, particularly the East Asian 'tiger' economies, Rwanda and Ethiopia have been thriving under autocratic, even though the majority opinion today is that there is a link between robust institutions and development. The Special Rapporteur on the Promotion of Truth, Justice, Reparation and Guarantees of Non-Recurrence, on the other hand, presented a report in August 2013 in which he highlighted that recent experience demonstrated that narrow developmental efforts that exclude justice and rights considerations fail to achieve sustainable human development (A/68/345, para. 64). The report clarifies that justice, security and development cannot be promoted one at the expense of the other, either through reductionism or strict sequencing. It argues that serious human rights violations leave in their wake conditions that hamper development, including a weak sense of entitlement and deep social mistrust.

Fifth, some governments also argued on conceptual grounds. Egypt and other countries maintained that more work needs to be done by the General Assembly to elaborate a common understanding of rule of law, including its parameters and elements, and that it is therefore premature to mainstream the notion of rule of law in the context of the SDGs.

At the same time, many States reject the idea that there *should* be a uniform definition of the rule of law. As the NAM said at the Sixth Committee's 70th meeting: 'There is no single agreed definition of the rule of law. [...] The data

---

18   UN Sixth Committee 'Summary Record of the 6th Meeting' (15 October 2015) UN Doc A/C.6/70/SR.6.
19   Cf. the Statement of Brazil at IDLO's Partnership Forum (11 January 2017), available at https://www.idlo.int/news/highlights/idlos-partnership-forum-origins-goal-16 (accessed 28 February 2019).

gathering activities of UN bodies must not lead to a unilateral formulation of rule of law indicators and ranking of countries in any manner.'[20] China, likewise, contested the existence of a uniform rule of law and used the phrase 'socialist rule of law' in a statement to the Sixth Committee.

To some in the OWG, however, the language of Goal 16 did not go far enough. They called for language on ending colonial occupation and foreign occupation, addressing root causes of terrorism to achieve sustainable development, and an end to unilateral economic sanctions and other coercive economic measures.

## VI  Goals, Targets, Indicators

The SDG 16 that resulted from this conflicted process is extremely reduced and came as a disappointment to many: international lawyers and human rights advocates everywhere, especially in the Global South.

In spite of this criticism, the SDG process moved forward. In 2015, the UN Statistical Commission endorsed the formation of the Inter-agency and Expert Group on SDG Indicators (IAEG-SDGs), consisting of national statistical offices and, as observers, regional and international organizations and agencies. The IAEG-SDGs was tasked with developing a global indicator framework for the SDGs, with the possibility of future refinements.

Currently, the SDGs comprise 17 goals, 169 targets and 303 indicators.[21] Proposed Goals 1–6 build on the core agenda of the MDGs, while Goals 7–17 break new ground. Democracy, good governance and the rule of law still appear in the 2030 agenda, probably as a concession to the High-Level Panel of Eminent Experts and other stakeholders, but they have been relegated to the Introduction. Except for target 16.3, they are no longer to be found in of the 'operative' part of the agenda. What the targets and indicators currently do measure is: violence; the effectiveness of criminal justice institutions; illicit financial and arms flows; corruption; public services; access to information; and the role of developing countries in international organizations.

Structurally, one striking flaw is the inconsistent treatment of goals and targets in the formulation of Goal 16. At some point, the rule of law was relegated from an actual goal to target 16.3.

---

20   Statement of 14 October 2015, at 4.
21   Cf. Global Indicator Framework for the Sustainable Development Goals and Targets of the 2030 Agenda for Sustainable Development, annexed to UNGA Res 71/313 'Work of the Statistical Commission pertaining to the 2030 Agenda for Sustainable Development' (6 July 2017).

Then there is the issue of measurement: the rule of law is notoriously difficult to measure.[22] Six SDG 16 indicators are currently categorized as 'Tier III' in the UN DESA Statistics Division Metadata repository; meaning that 'no internationally established methodology or standards are yet available for the indicator, but methodology/standards are being (or will be) developed or tested'. Worse yet, the SDG rule of law indicators do not seem to follow a coherent methodology. Some indicators measure formal institutions, others measure behaviour, while yet others measure beliefs, leaving unanswered what the relative importance of these measures is.[23]

Still, most remarkable is the limited ground that these indicators cover. Compare this with the World Justice Project Rule of Law Index which is the most comprehensive index of its kind and the only to rely solely on primary data: it uses 44 indicators across eight primary rule of law factors, each of which is scored and ranked globally and against regional and income peers: Constraints on Government Powers, Absence of Corruption, Open Government, Fundamental Rights, Order and Security, Regulatory Enforcement, Civil Justice, and Criminal Justice. Overall, there are now more than 150 indicators being used by various global indices purporting to capture 'governance' and related aspects of institutional quality, including the rule of law.

A recent article in Quartz Africa says:

> Conveniently missing from the menu of high-level discussion topics [in the SDGs] are the very causes of the world's most persistent social ills: lack of respect for democratic values and basic human rights. [...] Critically important terms like 'anti-corruption', 'civil liberties', 'free expression', 'press freedom', 'independent judiciary', 'separation of powers', 'free and fair elections', and 'civil society' are also absent. In other words, the basic freedoms that underpin and advance human development are missing from the SDG equation. Despite their feel-good vibe the SDGs are [...] assisting a status quo in which 93 countries, and an estimated four billion people, are ruled by authoritarian regimes, according to Human Rights Foundation. And despite the perceived success of the SDGs, there

---

22   Generally M. Versteeg and T. Ginsburg, 'Measuring the Rule of Law: A Comparison of Indicators' (2017) 42.1 Law & Social Inquiry 100.

23   For the challenges in drafting the indicator framework, and possible solutions, see e.g. DFG and UNU, 'Measuring Sustainable Development: How Can Science Contribute to Realizing the SDGs? Background Paper (2 April 2015) with Results from the Conference (20 May 2015)'. For concrete suggestions concerning Goal 16, see M. Loewe and N. Rippin (eds), 'The Sustainable Development Goals of the Post-2015 Agenda: Comments on the OWG and SDSN Proposal' (DIE-GDI 2015), at 81 et seq.

has been twelve consecutive years of decline in global freedom, according to a recent report by Freedom House.[24]

On the upside, there was a recognizable effort to mainstream the rule of law in the SDGS. Goal 1 says: 'By 2030, ensure that all men and women, in particular the poor and the vulnerable, have equal rights to economic resources, as well as access to basic services, ownership and control over land and other forms of property [...]'; Goal 5 seeks to 'End all forms of discrimination against all women and girls everywhere' and assesses pertinent legal frameworks; and Goal 10 wants to 'Reduce inequality within and among countries [...] including by eliminating discriminatory laws [...] and promoting appropriate legislation in this regard'. This cross-cutting reinforcement of equality and property rights is to be welcomed.

As far as the international rule of law is concerned, much remains to be done. SDG 17 largely equates global partnership with the provision of means of implementation, and does not go much further than MDG 8. Global governance still suffers from a deficit of both accountability and legitimacy. There are severe asymmetries in the various decision-making processes where developing countries have limited influence on shaping the rules and regulations they must abide by.

## VII  Conclusion

The SDG process was extremely ambitious. It sought to remedy all the shortcomings of the MDGs by ensuring transparency, ownership of the countries of the Global South, strong involvement of civil society groups and stakeholders, and creating a truly transformative set of sustainable development goals. Yet, the OWG did not manage to avoid all the mistakes that were characteristic of the formulation of the MDGs. In addition, it struggled with its very own problems.

Indeed, the marginalization of rule of law in the agenda, and the endorsement of the shrunken SDGs by, among others, the leaders of Syria, Eritrea or China is hardly encouraging. But as UNDP Administrator Helen Clark has said: 'Progress on SDG 16 will not be fast, and in some countries, we see regression, but in others, from The Gambia to Malaysia, we see the power of the ballot box

---

24    J. Smith, 'How the UN's Sustainable Development Goals Undermine Democracy' (7 June 2018), available at https://qz.com/africa/1299149/how-the-uns-sustainable-development-goals-undermine-democracy/ (accessed 18 April 2019).

to bring about change'.[25] SDG 16, defective as it may be, can potentially be utilized as political leverage. As one paper put it: 'Goal 16, without doubt, places a foot in the door for at least one aspect of the rule of law.'[26]

The SDGs also deserve credit for the fact that today's global goals are no longer about donors and recipients but about national ownership and partnership. Agenda 2030 states:

> Cohesive nationally owned sustainable development strategies, supported by integrated national financing frameworks, will be at the heart of our efforts. We reiterate that each country has primary responsibility for its own economic and social development and that the role of national policies and development strategies cannot be overemphasized.[27]

In addition, the SDGs are predicated on the idea of 'leaving no one behind', while the MDGs by contrast focused on averages. Vulnerable groups are finally given the needed attention in the new framework.

Much depends now on the refinement of the indicator framework and the review mechanism. Initially, there was widespread resistance to a proposed global 'peer-review' mechanism for the SDGs: Developing countries, in particular, feared that a peer-review mechanism would simply provide new avenues of conditionality and 'paternalistic finger-wagging from rich countries'[28] as Kate Donald and Sally-Anne Way put it. Still, by now 102 Member States have presented their Voluntary National Reviews (VNRs) to the High-level Political Forum on Sustainable Development with another 41 countries to present their first reviews in 2019 and ten countries presenting for the second time. As the name says, this mechanism is not mandatory—each country is free to decide on the scope and format of its review.

In the past, the UN has had almost no means at its disposal to effectively motivate Member States to implement sustainable development measures. The Annual Ministerial Review (AMR), introduced in 2005, was celebrated as

---

25 J. Smith, 'How the UN's Sustainable Development Goals Undermine Democracy' (7 June 2018), available at https://qz.com/africa/1299149/how-the-uns-sustainable-development-goals-undermine-democracy/ (accessed 18 April 2019).
26 J. Beqiraj and L- McNamara, 'The Rule of Law and Access to Justice in the Post-2015 Development Agenda: Moving Forward but Stepping Back' (August 2014) Bingham Centre Working Paper 2014/04.
27 UNGA Res 70/1 'Transforming Our World: the 2030 Agenda for Sustainable Development' (25 September 2015), at para. 63.
28 K. Donald and S.-A. Way, 'Accountability for the Sustainable Development Goals: A Lost Opportunity?' (10 June 2016) Ethics & International Affairs.

an important achievement at the time, but proved to be insufficient as only a small number of countries could be induced to present their progress reports, review was undertaken by the States of their choice, and there was no follow-up procedure.[29]

In 2016, the AMR mechanism was replaced by the VNR. The VNR process builds on and goes beyond monitoring and data collection. In this framework, the governments are asked critical, analytical questions to determine the reasons for their successes and failures and to recommend measures needed to improve goal attainment in the future. This new approach is country-led and takes into account national realities, recognizing that country ownership is central to the implementation of the agenda. The process is intended to facilitate learning from national experiences and to promote accountability to citizens. The jury is still out on the success of this process, but the first few years have seen an increasing acceptance by States.

Lastly, civil society will play a central role in the success or failure of the SDGs. Citizens and stakeholders need to try and remedy the shortcomings of the process by getting involved in the SDG discourse. Peer review; naming and shaming on the State level; and the force of the ballot will be key to any future development. It is likely that the data revolution will heavily impact the implementation and measurement of the goals. The justice sector; the legal profession; human rights institutions and NGOs; corporations, agencies, and conferences all have their place and role in the process if we want it to be ongoing.

### Acknowledgments

This article is based on a keynote speech given at the Conference on Rule of Law in the 2030 Sustainable Development Agenda, Loyola University Rome Campus, 1–2 February 2019. I would like to thank the organizers, in particular Thomas McInerney, and the participants of the conference for inspiring discussions and valuable comments on this paper.

---

29   Cf. M. Beisheim, 'Reviewing the Post-2015 Sustainable Development Goals and Partnerships: A Proposal for a Multi-level Review at the High-level Political Forum' (January 2015) SWP Research Paper.

## PART 2

## *Legal Issues Related to the Goals of the United Nations*

∴

CHAPTER 8

# Institutions of International Law: How International Law Secures Orderliness in International Affairs

*Volker Roeben*

## Abstract

This article is a plea for adopting a reinvigorated, analytic perspective on contemporary international law, building on MacCormick's powerful insights into law's essential structure. The article proposes that international law as whole forms an institutional normative order. The idea of institutional normative order has certain conditions. These link a normative conception of international law with the means of achieving it. The article makes three arguments on these conditions. It first argues that the function of international law is to create order in the sense of orderliness for its principal users, States and international organizations. It then claims that international law establishes normative order through international rules that are binding from the viewpoint of States and international organizations. An international process of rule-making embedded in State practice turns norms into such rules. The process is being held as a bindingness-creating mechanism because it formalizes rules through recognized means and organizes collective consent to authorize them. States and international organizations then apply these rules by exercising international legal powers under a defeasible presumption of legality. Third, the article argues that this normative order becomes institutionalized. The institutions of international law are grounded in ideas about agencies, arrangements, and master-norms that integrate the mass of international rules and principles. The article exemplifies these arguments for UN-driven international law with the relating recent jurisprudence of the International Court of Justice (ICJ), the International Tribunal for the Law of the Sea (ITLOS) and Annex VII tribunals, and the Court of Justice of the European Union. The upshot of this idea of international law as institutional normative order is unity, or indeed a system. No part of international law can be seen outside of this context and hence the burden of argumentation is on those wishing to make the case for divergence.

Keywords

Theory of International Law – UN Law – International Courts and Tribunals

1    Introduction

Contemporary public international law has quantitatively and qualitatively much evolved over past periods.[1] It is also increasingly specialized. The purpose of this article is to offer a fresh analytic perspective to help international lawyers make sense of their subject as a whole in this rapidly changing picture.[2]

The article thus positions itself within a rich, recent literature. Much debated in that literature is the normative proposal that international law ought to be understood through the prism of constitutional principles.[3] It been also been proposed to extend the positivist conception that law is based on a *Grundnorm* to international law.[4] The suggestion that international law forms a system is legal-reconstructive.[5] Critical approaches see international law as constructive of a particular political economy,[6] or as argumentation.[7] It could furthermore be seen as modes of making assertions about compelled conduct by States.[8] Law and economics and rational choice explain international law through the utility of States.[9] Pluralism places international law's position

---

1   Cf J.H.H. Weiler, 'The Geology of International Law—Governance, Democracy and Legitimacy' (2004) 64 ZaöRV 547 (distinguishing 'layers' in the evolution of international law, the current layer being regulatory).
2   The terms public international law and international law will be used interchangeably.
3   J. Klabbers, A. Peters and G. Ulfstein, *The Constitutionalization of International Law* (OUP 2009).
4   J. von Bernstorff, *The Public International Law Theory of Hans Kelsen* (CUP 2010).
5   J. Crawford, *Principles of Public International Law* (8th edn OUP 2012).
6   Cf TWAIL authors, A. Anghie and B.S. Chimni, 'Third World Approaches to International Law and Individual Responsibility in Internal Conflicts' (2003) Chinese J. Int'l L. 77.
7   M. Koskenniemi, *From Apology to Utopia* (2nd edn CUP 2006) (hereafter referred to as *From Apology*) and *The Politics of International Law* (Hart 2011). In *The Gentle Civiliser of Nations, The Rise and Fall of International Law 1870–1960* (CUP 2001), he advocates for a 'culture of formalism', further J. Klabbers, 'Towards a Culture of Formalism? Martti Koskenniemi and the Virtues' (2013) 27.3 Temple Int'l & Comp. L. J. 417.
8   D. Patterson, 'Postmodernism' in D. Patterson (ed.), *Companion to the Philosophy of Law and Legal Theory* (2nd edn Blackwell 2012) 375.
9   From this common starting point, scholars have arrived at divergent conclusions. Compare, for instance, J. Trachtman, *The Future of International Law* (CUP 2011) with A.O. Sykes, 'When is International Law Useful?' (2013) 45.3 NYU J. of Int'l L. & Politics 723, and J. Goldsmith and R. Posner, *The Limits of International Law* (OUP 2007).

within the growing 'disorder of normative orders' above the State.[10] Finally, there are several process-based conceptions of international law such as the New Haven School, although these arguably are not very interested in the normativity of international law. Professors Thorpe and Brunnée have recently proposed to see international law as social interaction of States and non-State actors.[11] They argue that international law as all law can only arise in the context of social norms based on shared understandings. International law is built, maintained, and sometimes destroyed through a continuing practice. Internal features, the so-called criteria of legality, are crucial to international law's ability to inspire 'fidelity'. This article accepts the point of Thorpe and Brunnée that international law ought to be conceptualized from the perspective of its users. In practical terms, these users at least predominantly remain States and international organizations.[12] As Professor Klabbers has noted, international law references the internal viewpoint of States as *opinio iuris*.[13] The internal viewpoint is commonly the starting point of positivist conceptions of law.

The internal viewpoint is also the starting point of an institutional approach to law, originally formulated by the late Professor Neil MacCormick.[14] In distinction from Hart's rule of recognition positivism, he emphasized that law creates orderliness as a peculiar normative order that turns spontaneous norms into binding rules through certain formal processes. These rules then can be applied and become institutionalized. While MacCormick's own work has focused on the law of the constitutional State, it can inspire the idea to see international law institutional normative order.[15] This idea then has

---

10  P. Schiff Berman, *Global Legal Pluralism: A Jurisprudence of Law beyond Borders* (CUP 2014); critical A. Galán and D. Patterson, 'The Limits of Normative Legal Pluralism: Review of Paul Schiff Berman, *Global Legal Pluralism: A Jurisprudence of Law beyond Borders*' (2013) 11.3 International Journal of Constitutional Law 783.
11  J. Brunnée and S.J. Toope, *Legitimacy and Legality in International Law* (CUP 2010).
12  The article uses these terms in the sense of aggregates. It hence does not need to take a position on the realist or critical argument that behind States and international organizations there are lawyers at work and that they generate a multiplicity of uses and agendas that cannot be reduced to a single use or agenda through the fiction of States or IOs. It is also true that TWAIL scholars have powerfully argued that in the Global South populations are at the 'receiving end' of international law—e.g. of the policies of international financial institutions and also international investment law. But the purpose of this article is analytic rather than normative.
13  J. Klabbers, *International Institutional Law* (CUP 2011).
14  N. MacCormick, *Institutions of Law* (CUP 2007). See also F. Schauer, 'Institutions and the Concept of Law: A Reply to Ronald Dworkin (with Some Help from Neil MacCormick)' (2009) University of Virginia Law School, Public Law and Legal Theory Working Paper Series No. 129.
15  Ibid., at 35, 39.

certain conditions that need to be met cumulatively. The first such condition is to make a normative argument about international law. The argument is to establish the point or function of international law.[16] It is submitted that the point of international law is to secure international order in the sense of orderliness.[17] It serves to secure the orderly conduct of States in international matters. The two further conditions concern how international law secures such orderliness: it does so by providing a specific normative rather than factual order and then by institutionalizing this normative order.

First, international law provides normative order directing States in the conduct of international affairs. This requires distinguishing norms from international rules.[18] Norms regularize the international conduct of States. But international rules are distinct because they ought to be complied with, they are binding. International rules are recognizable for States because of their formal, conditional structure. An international process of rule-making produces such rules. This process serves to formalize and authorize international rules. Prominent means of formalizing international rules are treaties, but alternatives for formalizing norms into rules exist, such as resolutions of international organizations, texts issued by expert bodies, and judicial decisions. In the international process of legalization, formalization and authorization of norms into rules may occur at different points in time. Authorization itself indeed presents a paradox. It results primarily from collective consensuality, for instance by a treaty attracting the determined quorum of ratifying States for its entry into force. The individual consent authorizes the rule for this State, but it is neither sufficient nor necessary for the rule to become binding international law. This single international rule-making process produces international rules on several tiers. The substantive international rules are located on the primary tier. Further rules for application and enforcement fall on a secondary and tertiary tier. This indicates a shift in the application of international rules, away from relational obligations and rights and towards international legal powers that States hold and whose exercise is covered by a defeasible presumption of lawfulness.

Second, this normative order is institutional. International rules become fully intelligible only when seen in their institutional context. This institutional context is formed by ideas about international law. The institutions of international law coalesce on the foundations, the agencies, arrangements for

---

16   The descriptive definition becomes circular where it means that international law is the law of its subjects, see Crawford, *Principles*, at 115.
17   MacCormick, *Institutions*, at 1–2, 281–285.
18   The concept of rules features prominently in J. D'Aspremont, 'The Idea of 'Rules' in the Sources of International Law' (2014) 84 British Yb of Int'l L. 103. This article focuses on the institutional process of making rules rather than ascertaining them.

making international law, and master-norms that give impetus and direction to the rule-making process. Sustainable development, international security and human dignity have emerged as such master-norms. When these master-norms are underpinned by machinery, then international law becomes fully institutionalized.

The article's ambition is to present a conceptual proposal about international law. Yet it also aims to test this proposal against the reality of UN-driven international law and relating recent jurisprudence, comprising the International Court of Justice (ICJ), the International Tribunal for the Law of the Sea (ITLOS), UNCLOS Annex VII tribunals, and the Court of Justice of the European Union (CJEU).

The remainder of the article develops the idea that international law is an institutional normative order in three parts. It deals with the condition that international law forms a normative order in two steps. Part I demonstrates that international rules that steer States' conduct are formalized and authorized through a single rule-making process. Part II demonstrates that international rules are applied in a structured manner, by States and international organizations exercising legal powers under a defeasible presumption of lawfulness. Part III then turns to the institutions of international law. It argues that international law generates institutional normative order because it is able to formulate ideas about its own foundations and the common interest, ultimately of humanity. The conclusions point out that this institutional normative order conception comprises all UN driven rules and principles of international law. It also points out some methodological implications.

## II  International Law as Normative Order: Formalizing and Authorizing International Rules

This part takes up the condition that international law forms a normative order. Central to this normative order is the concept of international rules. Art. 38 (1) of the ICJ Statute refers to international 'rules' in the context of setting out the sources of international.[19] So what characterizes a rule of international law? Taking a cue from MacCormick, the broader category of norm should be

---

19   Art. 38 (1) (a) Statute of the International Court of Justice (adopted 26 June 1945, entered into force 24 October 1945) 145 BSP 832 (ICJ Statute): 'international conventions, [...] establishing *rules*'; and Art. 21 (1) (b) ICC Statute: '*rules* of international law' (emphases added).

the starting point in answering this query.[20] The convergent conduct of States on an international matter over time will result in the formation of a norm, which will attract compliant conduct in turn. International rules are distinct from norms, however, because they *compel* conduct; they ought to be complied with. In the eyes of States and international organizations, international law is immediately recognizable as part of the broad human endeavour of law because it follows the conditional format of a rule: a set of criteria is connected with certain consequences. Of course, international law is decentralized and lacks central organs for producing such rules, with the limited exception of the UN Security Council. It does have, however, a rule-making process. This process is embedded in State practice and affirmed every time that States make use of it. It comprises the two distinct elements of formalizing and of authorizing an international rule. These two elements may coincide. But it is also possible that a norm is first formalized as rule and receives authorization only at a later stage.

The following separately discusses formalization (1) and authorization by States (2) and also by international organizations (3) and by the international community of States (4). Such formalization and authorization produce binding international rules, principles and standards (5).

## 1 *Formalizing the Rules of International Law*

Formalization of international rules is a process, not an occurrence.[21] The starting point is a social norm. Where such a norm has attracted compliant behaviour by States, it reaches a tipping point at which it can be formalized as a rule. The uptake is often initiated by the UN General Assembly.[22] Through a resolution, it formalizes the norm and launches the further steps in the process of turning it into a formal rule.[23]

---

20  Under Art. 38 (1) (b) ICJ Statute, States must be convinced that a general practice is legally motivated. This conviction (*opinio iuris*) is empirical.

21  See M. Finnemore and K. Sikkink, 'International Norm Dynamics and Political Change' (1998) 52.4 Int'l Org 887, at 896, 901 (norm-affirming events).

22  For instance, Written Statement of the EU, *Request for an Advisory Opinion submitted by the Sub-Regional Fisheries Commission* (23 November 2013) ITLOS Case No. 21 (flag State control over IUU fishing starting with UNGA resolution).

23  Examples abound. The norm against the use of chemical weapons finds a formal embodiment in rules of the Convention on the Prohibition of the Development, Production, Stockpiling and Use of Chemical Weapons and on their Destruction (opened for signature 13 January 1993, entered into force 29 April 1997) 1974 UNTS 45, and again by UNSC Res 2118 (27 September 2013) on the removal of chemical weapons from Syria. The norm against commercial whaling is formalized in the International Convention for the Regulation of Whaling (signed 2 December 1946, entered into force 10 November 1948)

The catalogue of Art. 38 (1) (a)–(d) of the ICJ Statute does not just name sources for the ascertainment of existing law. It defines preferred means for giving the norm the form of a rule.[24] These means shape the rule to a specific degree of explicitness. Treaties usually produce fully explicit rules laid down in writing.[25]

Yet there is no *numerus clausus* of means for formalizing rules. Alternatives to treaty exist.[26] Resolutions adopted by international organizations may serve as such alternative. Expertise-based texts are another.[27] Courts and tribunals developing an *acquis judiciaire* can formalize an international rule.[28] The 2014 *M/V 'Virginia G'* case uses a synthesis of domestic legislation to formalize an international rule. The ITLOS there referenced the practice of coastal States to formulate a rule filling the gap in Art. 73 of the UNCLOS on bunkering in the exclusive economic zone.[29]

A synopsis of consistent State practice also formalizes rules. To compensate for the lack of a textual basis, custom relies on judicial or expert verification.[30] The rule then determines what counts as practice,[31] while actual negative practice can be disregarded where it is overlain by argumentative adherence to the rule.[32] State practice also has rule-making capacity in the dynamic

---

 161 UNTS 72, *Whaling in the Antarctic (Australia v. Japan, New Zealand Intervening)* (*Judgment*) [2014] ICJ Rep 226, at paras 42–48, and *Whaling in the Antarctic (Australia v. Japan, New Zealand Intervening)* (*Declaration of Judge Keith*) [2014] ICJ Rep 336.

24  See J. D'Aspremont, *Formalism and the Sources of International Law. A Theory of the Ascertainment of Legal Rules* (OUP 2011) (sources as means for the ascertainment of rules).

25  Art. 38 (1) (a) ICJ Statute: 'establishing rules *expressly* recognized' (emphasis added).

26  Further, R. Wolfrum and V. Röben (eds), *Developments of International Law in Treaty Making* (Springer 2005).

27  The WTO Appellate Body has effectively made the Codex Alimentarius the standard for presumed compliance with the Agreement on Technical Barriers to Trade, WTO *EC-Trade Description of Sardines—Report of the Appellate Body* (26 September 2002) WT/DS231/AB/R, DSR 2002:VIII, 3451.

28  *The People's Republic of Bangladesh v. The Republic of India* (*Award*) (7 July 2014), at para. 339 (Art. 38 (1) (d) ICJ Statute) (hereinafter *Bay of Bengal Arbitration*).

29  *M/V 'Virginia G' (Panama v. Guinea-Bissau)* (*Judgment*) (16 April 2014) ITLOS Case No. 19, at para. 253.

30  D. Regan, 'International Adjudication' in S. Besson and J. Tasioulas (eds), *The Philosophy of International Law* (OUP 2010) 225, at 228.

31  For instance, relevant practice for State immunity is primarily formed by the decisions of national courts and for acquisition of territory by certain effective exercises of State power (*effectivités*). *Frontier Dispute (Burkina Faso v. Niger)* (*Judgment*) [2013] ICJ Rep 44, at para. 78.

32  *Military and Paramilitary Activities in and against Nicaragua (Nicaragua v. United States of America)* (*Merits*) [1986] ICJ Rep 14.

development of treaties.[33] General principles produce international rules from the converging national legal orders, and they also need to be verified.

## 2  Authorization

Formalization is necessary but not sufficient for a binding international rule. This requires authorization. International law does not carry its authority in itself, but it is authorized by a political community that controls its content.[34] The power to authorize international law rests, primarily, with States. States form political communities that authorize international law.[35] Such a community can be two States, it can also be a multitude of States or the 'international community of States' (as a whole). International law is hence inevitably authorized collectively, through at least two States.

Professor Brunnée has pointed out that treaties present a paradox.[36] Treaties require consensuality, that is, independent approval of States to become binding international law. But each approval on its own does not suffice to bring the treaty into existence. There must be matching decision(s), in the case of a bilateral treaty that of another sovereign or in the case of a multilateral treaty of several other sovereigns. This paradox is key to conceiving of authorization of international rules. Authorization of international law lies in the hands of *several* States.[37]

The authorization of treaties is collective in the sense that the support of several States is indispensable for the rule to become binding at all. Collective consent provides primary authority in the sense that it brings the international rule into existence. The collective authorization can be provided by groupings of States. A representative group of States may authorize a rule for the entire international community of States.[38] That is evidently so for

---

[33]  Art. 31 (3) (a) and (b) Vienna Convention on the Law of Treaties (concluded 23 May 1969, entered into force 27 January 1980) 1155 UNTS 331 (VCLT).

[34]  MacCormick, *Institutions*, 39–61.

[35]  The article here considers States and international organization as political entities. In Part IV it will show that international law, in turn, is capable of institutionalizing both States and international organizations as its agencies.

[36]  J. Brunnée, 'Treaties' in R. Wolfrum (ed.), *Max Planck Encyclopedia of Public International Law* (OUP Oxford 2008–) http://www.mpepil.com/ (accessed 15 April 2019).

[37]  International law recognizes unilateral acts as binding, see *Obligation to Negotiate Access to the Pacific Ocean (Bolivia v. Chile)* (*Judgment*) (1 October 2018) General List No. 153, at para. 146. But the bindingness of unilateral acts in turn is grounded in an international rule.

[38]  *North Sea Continental Shelf (Federal Republic of Germany/Denmark, Federal Republic of Germany/Netherlands)* [1969] ICJ Rep 4 (there applied to rules of international customary law).

multilateral treaties. Multilateral treaties determine the quorum of accessions for their entry into force. This quorum is the abstractly determined critical mass of States for the matter at hand, but not any concrete individual State. The individual consent of each State supplies secondary authority that determines the geographical scope of the rule. Even this role of individual reciprocal consent has been diminishing, as treaties may compel conduct by a party also towards non-treaty third States. Collective authorization also pertains to customary international law, with only the persistent objector rules providing for individual (non-)consent.

## 3   *International Organizations*

In addition to States, international organizations and, increasingly, the organized meetings of the parties to a treaty have authority, even beyond the express or implied authorization through the constitutive treaty—functionalism—.[39] Thus, resolutions and decisions of international organizations have the legal effect that the members have provided for through the constitutive treaty, expressly or impliedly.[40] That includes making rules binding for States without their (explicit) consent.[41] The so-called tacit-consent procedure substitutes collective decision-making for consent of all members in this manner.[42] Beyond this functionalism of conferred competences, there is a shift towards own institutional authority. The ILC Reports on Art. 31 (3) (a) and (b) of the VCLT recognize the role of meetings of parties for the dynamic development of the underlying treaties.[43] Decisions of such meetings, which institutionalize collective membership, have authority. They enrich the normative content of the treaty.

This shift towards institutional authorization is reflected in the recent international jurisprudence. Prominently, in *Whaling in the Antarctic*,[44] the

---

39   UNGA Res 60/1 '2005 World Summit Outcome (16 September 2005), paras 138–149, launched the ongoing process of legalizing the Responsibility to Protect that comprises mandatory measures of the UN Security Council and State practice.

40   Art. 25 and Chapter VII of the UN Charter (adopted 26 June 1945, entered into force 24 October 1945) 1 UNTS 16; Art. III International Convention for the Regulation of Whaling (signed 2 December 1946, entered into force 10 November 1948) 161 UNTS 72.

41   J. Brunnee, 'Legislation' in R. Wolfrum (ed.), *Max Planck Encyclopedia of Public International Law* (OUP Oxford 2008–) http://www.mpepil.com/ (accessed 15 April 2019).

42   N. Krisch, 'The Decay of Consent: International Law in an Age of Global Public Goods' (2014) 108 AJIL 1.

43   UN ILC 'First Report on Subsequent Agreements and Subsequent Practice in Relation to Treaty Interpretation by Georg Nolte, Special Rapporteur' (19 March 2013) UN Doc. A/CN.4/660.

44   *Whaling in the Antarctic (Australia v. Japan: New Zealand Intervening)* (*Judgment*).

ICJ accepted that recommendatory resolutions adopted by an international organization at unanimity gain legal significance as aid in interpretation of the constitutive treaty.[45] But even non-unanimous resolutions carry authority. They will have a legal effect of a taking-into-account-type because of the general duty of all members to cooperate with the international organization.[46] In *Pulp Mills*, the ICJ has furthermore indicated that international bodies may issue texts under an own institutional authority.[47] The text at issue was UNEP's 1987 Goals and Principles for Environmental Impact Assessments. The principles not only formalize a rule-book that can be applied. The Court accords legal weight to them because UNEP was the body entrusted by the international community of States with safeguarding the shared value of environmental protection. The Court then referred to the principles to concretize the customary international law rule that States carry out an EIA for projects with a significant transboundary impact. The Advisory Opinion in *Chagos* is the culmination of this jurisprudence. There the Court found the UN Charter to entrust the UN General Assembly with broad oversight over the implementation of the principle of self-determination.[48] In the exercise of this oversight function, the UN General Assembly could then pass resolutions for the binding rule that former colonies must gain their independence in full territorial integrity. The Court hence recognizes that the authority of an international body that rests on its functions for global governance, rather than narrower and specific competences, underpins its resolutions with binding force.[49]

## 4   The International Community of States

This 'international community of States' is, among other things, a concept for thinking about the collective authorization of international rules. The

---

[45]   The technical basis advanced by the Court is the VCLT, Art. 31 (3) (a) or (b), on subsequent agreement to an interpretation or subsequent practice establishing an agreement of the parties regarding the interpretation of the treaty. *Whaling in the Antarctic*, at para. 83.
[46]   *Whaling in the Antarctic*, at para. 83: 'The Court however observes that the States parties to the ICRW have a duty to co-operate with the IWC and the Scientific Committee and thus should give due regard to recommendations calling for an assessment of the feasibility of non-lethal alternatives'.
[47]   *Pulp Mills on the River Uruguay (Argentina v. Uruguay) (Judgment)* [2010] ICJ Rep 14, at para. 205.
[48]   *Legal Consequences of the Separation of the Chagos Archipelago from Mauritius in 1965 (Advisory Opinion)* (25 February 2019) General List No. 169.
[49]   Para. 139: '[T]he Court, in determining the obligations reflected in these resolutions, will have to examine the functions of the General Assembly in conducting the process of decolonization'.

literature offers a range of definitions.[50] A systems theory guided approach, favoured here, would locate the concept in the international political system. It then describes the central organization of that system. This organization is the aggregate of States and each State is included *eo ipso*.[51] Non-State actors are not but can be admitted.[52] The point of this organization is to enable iterative cooperation on matters of common interest.[53] That cooperation is aided by shared values, even though these may be thinner than within each State.[54] The collaboration between States to respond to their political priorities may then lead to international rule-making.[55] The international community of States has unlimited access to international law, on the basis of the principle that most international law is dispositive and hence can be changed where priorities change. It starts the above described rule-making process, for instance through a UN General Assembly resolution.[56] The resulting international rules then evidence the values of that community.

Cooperation is generally an expectation that leaves the choice of means to States.[57] There is no general duty for States to cooperate, although area-specific cooperation duties exist.[58] States may enshrine in international law a specific obligation to cooperate, or to negotiate and even to negotiate towards a certain objective.[59] However, general international rules enable cooperation.[60]

---

[50] These cannot be discussed in detail here. Influential is T. Franck, *Fairness in International Law and Institutions* (OUP 1995), at 12 ('a community is defined by having a corpus of rules that it deems legitimate and by having agreed on a process that legitimizes the exercise of authority').

[51] B. Simma, 'From Bilateralism to Community Interest' (1997) 250 Recueil des Cours 229, at 233 ('international community of States').

[52] Crawford, *Principles*, at 126.

[53] A. Hurrell, *On Global Order* (OUP 2007), at 95–117 ('complex global governance' to refer to managerial element of the present international political system).

[54] Further M. Hakimi, 'Constructing an International Community' (2017) 111 AJIL 317.

[55] For the institutional economics of international cooperation see Trachtman, *Future*, at 24–31.

[56] *Questions relating to the Obligation to Prosecute or Extradite (Belgium v. Senegal) (Judgment)* [2012] ICJ Rep 422, at para. 99.

[57] UNGA Res 2625 (XXV) 'Declaration on Principles of International Law concerning Friendly Relations and Cooperation among States in Accordance with the Charter of the United Nations' (24 October 1970) emphasizes international cooperation, yet does not define it.

[58] *Access to the Pacific*, at para. 163 (discussing Art. 2 (3) UN Charter).

[59] See *Obligations concerning Negotiations relating to Cessation of the Nuclear Arms Race and to Nuclear Disarmament (Marshall Islands v. United Kingdom) (Preliminary Objections) (Judgment)*, concerning applications brought by the Marshall Islands against nine States for alleged failure to fulfil their obligation to negotiate under the treaty to end the nuclear arms race at an early date.

[60] Trachtman, *Future*, at 255 (distinguishing enabling, constraining and supplemental constitutional functions of international law).

The Vienna Conventions enable safe communication and hence cooperation between States.[61] Their protection is therefore a priority of the international community.[62] These cooperation-enabling rules are complemented by the foundational principles of the UN Charter constraining States acting unilaterally to advance their interests. The categorical prohibition of the use of force by Art. 2 (4) UN Charter precludes States from pursuing change through military pressure.[63] Sovereign equality, Art. 2 (1) UN Charter, precludes unilateral action undermining cooperative approaches.[64] Sovereign immunity prevents States from pursuing change interests though domestic law pressures.[65] The ICJ judgment in *Jurisdictional Immunities* reflects this role of sovereign immunity in stabilizing cooperative approaches and outcomes, in this case the final agreement reached on war reparations when challenged by unilateral action based on human rights. Essentially, treaty-based normative hierarchies serve the same purpose of stabilizing collective cooperation, by constraining individual States or groups of States from setting rules that deviate from the multilateral treaty. Art. 103 UN Charter is a well-known instantiation. The arbitral tribunal in the *South China Sea* case has powerfully reinforced this function of treaty-internal normative hierarchy for Art. 311 UNCLOS, setting aside all rules on the law of the sea that might empower States unilaterally to claim ocean resources and conflict with the concepts by which the UNCLOS allocates those resources.[66]

The international community of States has been consolidating its position within the international rule-making process. This consolidation translates into exclusive competence over certain matters. *Ius cogens* is such a matter.

---

61  Namely the Vienna Conventions on Diplomatic Relations (done 18 April 1961, entered into force 24 April 1961) 500 UNTS 95, and on Consular Relations (concluded 24 April 1963, entered into force 19 March 1967) 596 UNTS 261, and the customary law on the immunity of States and certain State organs.

62  *US Diplomatic and Consular Staff in Tehran (US v. Iran) (Request for the Indication of Provisional Measures)* [1979] ICJ Rep 7, at 19 (priority of the international community).

63  By denying a right to unlimited warfare for any belligerent party, humanitarian law contains armed conflicts with a view to reinstating the political process. D. Kennedy, *Of Law and War* (Princeton University Press 2006), for critical assessment of international law's constraints on warfare.

64  *Questions relating to the Seizure and Detention of Certain Documents and Data (Timor-Leste v. Australia) (Provisional Measures) (Order)* (3 March 2014) (hereinafter *Documents Seized*).

65  *Jurisdictional Immunities of the State (Germany v. Italy: Greece Intervening) (Judgment)* [2012] ICJ Rep 99, paras 94, 104, where the Court places the respect sovereign immunity within the context of the negotiated settlement of the consequences of war.

66  See *South China Sea Arbitration (Philippines v. China) (Award)* (12 June 2018) PCA Case No. 2013–19, at para. 89.

The international community exclusively may confer peremptory status on an international rule.[67] As such, it becomes a conflict rule determining the validity of any, bilateral or multilateral treaty-based rule.[68] The peremptory rule thus precludes any contracting out by States. The international community is also exclusively competent to regulate spaces beyond national jurisdiction, the deep seabed, the high seas, and outer space. Other global public goods fall under the proviso that the matter is of common concern. That is namely the case for the global climate. The competence of the international community is not exclusive but rather concurrent: the collectively agreed rules permit bilateral treaties, but preclude any deviation.

## 5     Rules, Principles and Standards

There is thus a single rule-making process for international rules. The resulting rules fall on several tiers, though. There are substantive rules to steer conduct on a primary tier, rules on application on a secondary tier and rules on enforcement on a third tier. Standards are open rules that serve to incorporate external events.[69]

This process produces international rules that are general and abstract. They are general in the sense that that they have the same content for all States and abstract in the sense that they apply to indeterminate instances. Reservations to treaties break this generality, by creating exceptions for one State party in relation to all others. Multilateral treaties often seek to ensure generality of their rules for all parties by prohibiting reservations. The geographical scope of application of each rule then of course varies.[70] It can be bilateral, regional or universal. Multilateral treaties aspire to establish quasi-universality. Customary international rules are universal by default.[71]

International rules are supplemented by principles. Principles are also binding and hence distinct from norms. They are distinct from rules in that they are imbued with unlimited application while the scope of application of a rule

---

67    VCLT, Art. 53.
68    *Territorial and Maritime Dispute (Nicaragua v. Colombia) (Preliminary Objections) (Judgment)* [2007] ICJ Rep 832, at paras 79–81 (Nicaragua barred from defeating a treaty for invalidity on other grounds because it had complied with it before).
69    In this sense, 'standards' for the prevention of pollution from vessels are referred to alongside rules in Art. 211 UNCLOS. Like rules and principles, standards steer conduct *ex ante* although they are sometimes said to be applicable *ex post*, D. Bodansky, *The Art and Craft of International Environmental Law* (Harvard University Press 2010).
70    In instances of contention, this is a treaty's scope of application *ratione personae, temporae* and *materiae*; A. Aust, *Modern Treaty Law and Practice* (3rd edn CUP 2013).
71    See A. Cassese, *International Law* (2nd edn OUP 2005), at 162; nuanced Crawford, *Principles*, at 28, also on the persistent objector.

is limited.[72] International law uses the term 'principle' in three senses.[73] The principle may establish a broad synthesizing conception;[74] it may indicate a larger idea of as yet incomplete realization;[75] or, the principle may be a rationale from which rules can be deduced.[76] The UN Charter, in Art. 2, enshrines principles in the sense of rationales. In *Jurisdictional Immunities,* the ICJ qualified these principles as 'constitutive' for international law.[77] It there referred to the principle of sovereign equality (Art. 2 (1) UN Charter) as the rationale of the customary law of State immunity. In *Documents Seized,* the Court used the principles of peaceful settlement of disputes and equality of States to protect the integrity of legal proceedings between States against interference by either party, overcoming the lack of extant procedural rules for inter-State disputes.[78]

## III   Applying and Enforcing International Rules

As international rules are general and abstract, they must be applied in any given instance. McCormick has shown that normative order comprises rules, but also a structured process of applying these rules. This part hence moves from international rules to analysis of their application of international law. It first clarifies that the rules of international law are of either discretionary or

---

72   Cf Art. 38 (1) (c) ICJ Statute: 'the general principles of law' and in Art. 21 (1) (b) ICC Statute: 'principles [...] of international law'.
73   On this distinction generally, A. Halpin, *Definition in the Criminal Law* (Hart 2006).
74   For instance market access in WTO law.
75   The Rio Principles are legally incomplete, and hence in need of continuing legal realization and concretization. In *Pulp Mills*, the ICJ has recognized that the EIA principle has now been realized in customary international law. *Mox Plant (Ireland/UK) (Provisional Measures) (Order)* (3 December 2001) ITLOS Case No. 10, at 95, qualifies cooperative protection of the marine environment as a 'fundamental principle' of the law of the sea, suggesting as yet incomplete realization in the United Convention on the Law of the Sea (concluded 10 December 1982, entered into force 16 November 1994) 1833 UNTS 3 (UNCLOS).
76   *Accordance with International Law of the Unilateral Declaration of Independence in respect of Kosovo (Advisory Opinion)* [2010] ICJ Rep 403, at para. 70, implies that extending the rationale of self-determination to non-colonial context was for the international political process, rather than adjudication. The ICJ settled the exclusively State–State rationale of self-defence different from legislative tendencies in *Armed Activities in the Congo (DR Congo v. Uganda) (Judgment)* [2005] ICJ Rep 168, at para. 147.
77   *Jurisdictional Immunities*, at para. 57.
78   In *Documents Seized*, the Court deduces from Art. 2 (3) UN Charter the rule that communications between a State and counsel must not be interfered with by the other State party to the legal dispute.

strict application. It then explores that the obligation is a vehicle for applying a rule, to which legal power is an alternative. Finally, the part demonstrates that international courts are making increasing use of the concept of international legal powers that States hold and exercise under a defeasible presumption of lawfulness.

### 1      Strict and Discretionary Application

A fundamental distinction, then, is between strict and discretionary application of international rules. An international rule is for strict application if States must apply the rule in all instances and have no choice. Application is discretionary where a State is free to make the initial decision to apply the rule. This distinction corresponds to the categories of law-making treaties and contract-making multilateral treaties. That categorization primarily relates to the content of treaties, with the former comprising treaties on a public interest of the international community of States and the latter referring to treaties to establish reciprocal exchanges.

But those treaty categories also reflect critical differences in application. Law-making treaties contain strictly applicable rules, while a contract-making treaty presupposes the exercise of discretion. The UN Charter, the UN Law of the Sea Convention, UN human rights treaties, and also WTO-based world trade law are law-making treaties laying down strictly applicable rules. Of the contract-making type are the Vienna Conventions on diplomatic and consular relations, which leave it to each party to decide whether and with whom it wants to enter into a relation governed by the Convention. However, that initial discretionary decision then triggers further rules that are to be applied strictly, for instance on diplomatic immunity etc.[79]

### 2      From Rights and Obligations to Defeasible Powers

Whether strict or discretionary, application of a rule is different from the rule itself. Application is about individualizing the general and abstract international rule for a specific actor in a situation. This requires a constructive unit through which his individualizing function can be performed. The obligation in international law is such a unit. In *Access to the Pacific*, the ICJ has confirmed that obligation in international law only arises under an extant rule of international law.[80] The obligation defines a concrete legal relationship: the obligated State owes a specific conduct to another State, to several States in the case of

---

79    Arts 2 and 9 of the Vienna Convention on Diplomatic Relations.
80    *Access to the Pacific*, at para. 91.

*erga omnes (partes)* obligations,[81] or to the international community. To the international obligation can correspond the right of another State to demand that the obligation be performed.

International rules are traditionally applied through this relational unit, expressed in the obligation of one State and the right of another. This is conventional for bilateral treaties. But there is no reason to deny that multilateral treaties also create *obligations* and the right for each party to demand of any other that it perform its obligations. Sovereignty under the UN Charta and customary international law can also be construed as the right of each State to demand that all others meet their obligation to respect its jurisdiction.[82] This relational structure of obligation and right is continued into the reaction to the 'primary' obligation going unfulfilled. In such case, a 'secondary' obligation becomes incumbent on that State to cease the violation and to make reparation.[83] To such secondary obligation corresponds the right of the injured State to invoke those obligations for itself, and a right of non-injured other States to invoke those obligations for the benefit of a collective interest a law-making treaty protects.[84]

This relational unit of obligation and rights gives international law a subjective, quasi-contractual and static appearance. Yet, obligation and right is merely one of several possible units for applying international rules. In thinking about alternatives, the international rule remains the principal reference. International rules enable States, as much as they constrain them. They confer international legal powers where such power is the capability of a State of altering the legal situation of other actors. States hold such international power towards other States. They may also hold it towards a private party.

A State in exercising such power produces decisions covered by a presumption of lawfulness. This presumption of lawfulness is defeasible, however. The principal ground of defeasibility remains that the decision does not conform to the power-conferring rule. This is not new. In *Certain German Interests in Polish Silesia*, the Permanent Court of International Justice had already affirmed that it could review national legislation for its conformity with a State's

---

81    *Obligation to Prosecute*, at para. 69.
82    *East Timor (Portugal v. Australia) (Judgment)* [1995] ICJ Rep 90, at para. 29 (self-determination as an obligation on every State owed to all others—*erga omnes*).
83    Art. 42 (b) and Art. 48 (1) (a) of the UN ILC 'Draft Articles on the Responsibility of States for Unlawful Acts' (2001), annexed to UNGA Res 56/83 (12 December 2001) (ARSIWA).
84    See also J. Crawford, 'Responsibility to the International Community as a Whole' (2001) 8 Indiana Journal of Global Legal Studies 303, at 313–314.

international obligations.[85] Yet, contemporary international law now recognizes supplementary grounds of defeasibility. Such grounds results from the constraints that the international rule of law and human rights place generally on States when exercising any of their powers.[86] These constraints entail the duty to disregard facts established unlawfully through their violation.[87]

The presumption of lawfulness can be defeated in several fora. The default forum remains each State, under the rule that it is for the sovereign to auto-apply international law including through its domestic courts. This forum is increasingly overlain by international fora with jurisdiction to settle disputes through decisions capable of becoming *res iudicata*. The ICJ remains the only international court with general jurisdiction. But it is complemented by a range of courts and tribunals with jurisdiction over particular international law. These courts and tribunals have begun to fulfil an international judicial function.[88] The international judicial function is organizationally specialist, but procedure and remedies are converging.[89] The conceptual problems of adjudication arising are not substantially different from those on the national plane, including the judicial review of State decisions potentially resulting in a declaration of invalidity.[90] Incidental review of decisions by State officials against the fundamental prohibitions on waging wars on aggression and committing genocide and crimes against humanity takes place through international criminal courts.[91] The international judicial function remains based on

---

85   *Certain German Interests in Polish Upper Silesia* (*Germany v. Poland*) (*Merits*) PCIJ Series A No. 7.

86   *Certain Questions of Mutual Assistance in Criminal Matters* (*Djibouti v. France*) (*Separate Opinion of Judge Keith*) [2008] ICJ Rep 177, at paras 127–28 (rule of law); Arctic Sunrise Case (Kingdom of the Netherlands/Russian Federation) (Provisional Measures) (Order) (*Joint Separate Opinion of Judges Wolfrum and Kelly*) (22 November 2013) ITLOS Case No. 22, at para. 13 (human rights as constraints on the exercise of a State's powers in its exclusive economic zone).

87   *Kosovo*, at para. 81; G.I. Hernandez, 'A Reluctant Guardian: The International Court of Justice and the Concept of International Community' (2012) 83 British Yb Int'l L. 13.

88   *Frontier Dispute* (*Burkina Faso v. Niger*) (*Judgment*) [2013] ICJ Rep 44, paras 45–46.

89   The *Namibia Opinion*, [1971] ICJ Rep 16, had stressed the invalidity of legal acts that South Africa had taken in relation to Namibia after the revocation of its mandate by the Security Council. *Mutual Assistance*, at para. 203, implies that the declaratory relief of illegality of a decision would be available.

90   See L. Boisson de Chazournes, 'Plurality in the Fabric of International Courts and Tribunals: The Threads of a Managerial Approach' (2017) 28 EJIL 13 (international courts and tribunals are adopting a managerial approach to coordinating the exercise of their respective jurisdiction).

91   The International Criminal Court and the UN Security Council established international criminal tribunals.

consent.[92] The constitutive role of consent for adjudication has been diminishing marginally, though. For instance, advisory proceedings do not require consent, not even of directly concerned States,[93] while increasingly settling important legal questions. The presumption of a lawful decision can also be defeated in non-judicial fora, such as the UN. Such executive control is distinguished from judicial control by the fact that it does not generate *res iudicata*.[94]

The concept of rule-application through international legal powers can be transferred to international organizations. These, under their constitutive treaty, hold limited powers over their Member States and sometimes also over individuals.[95] Decisions taken in the exercise of such powers may be defeasible before the organization's own court.[96] Or they may be defeasible, as an incidental question, before an external court or tribunal.[97]

## 3  Defeasible Legal Power and International Judicial Review

The defeasible international legal power is not just a theoretical construct. As will be demonstrated, international courts and tribunals are making use of the concept to structure the judicial review of whether a certain State conduct has been internationally lawful.

Prominently in *Whaling in the Antarctic*, the ICJ reviewed the power that Art. VIII of the International Convention for the Regulation of Whaling confers on States to permit the taking whales for scientific purposes for its proportionate exercise by Japan.[98] In *Obligation to Prosecute*, the Court clarified the

---

92   *Mutual Assistance*, at para. 48.
93   *Interpretation of Peace Treaties with Bulgaria, Hungary and Romania (Advisory Opinion)* [1950] ICJ Rep 221.
94   UNGA 'Territorial Integrity of Ukraine. Canada, Costa Rica, Germany, Lithuania, Poland and Ukraine: Draft Resolution' (24 March 2014) UN Doc. A/68/L.39.
95   *Responsibilities and Obligations of States Sponsoring Persons and Entities with respect to Activities in the Area (Advisory Opinion)* (1 February 2011) ITLOS Case No. 17 (for the International Seabed Authority).
96   Crawford, *Principles*, at 196–199. On internal judicial review of staff matters see *Judgment No. 2867 of the Administrative Tribunal of the International Labour Organization upon a Complaint Filed against the International Fund for Agricultural Development (Advisory Opinion)* [2012] ICJ Rep 10. Judicial control of UNSC action may occur in contentious and in advisory proceedings both direct and incidentally, see *Kosovo*, at paras 94–100.
97   The CJEU has pointed out (Case C-584/10 P—*Commission and Others v. Kadi* (2013) ECLI:EU:C:2013:518, at para. 131) that such diffuse defeasibility of the decisions of international organizations rests of the convergence of human rights on the universal level and regional levels.
98   *Whaling in the Antarctic*, at paras 59–61, 62–69; *Pulp Mills*, at paras 80 and 169 (power to authorize the operation of a factory under a bilateral treaty with constraining procedural and substantive obligations).

powers of a State under the UN Convention against Torture regarding private parties. It then reviewed the (non-)exercise of that power.[99] In *Navigational and Related Rights,* the Court reviewed the power of a State party under a bilateral treaty to regulate private commerce on a navigable river, interpreting it in the light of subsequent multilateral law development.[100] And in *Mutual Assistance,* the Court reviewed a State's exercise of an international legal power regarding another State under a bilateral extradition treaty.[101]

The ITLOS, adjudicating under the 1982 UN Law of the Sea Convention, also refers to defeasible powers. For instance, the 2014 *M/V 'Virginia G'* case involved the regulation of offshore bunkering for fishing vessels. The Tribunal first determined that the Convention conferred such power on the coastal State.[102] It then reviewed the coastal State's exercise of that power, including the proportionality of any enforcement action.[103] In its *SRFC Advisory Opinion,* ITLOS indicates that Parties' exercise of their powers under UNCLOS will be subject, generally, to their responsibility for the achieving the broader and evolving objectives of the Convention.

## 4   Enforcing International Law

In addition to rules and application, normative order is concerned with enforcement. The bindingness of international rules would be called into question were there to be no reaction to non-compliance. Enforcement is such a reaction, to bring about compliant behaviour through the exercise of an international legal power. Enforcement powers for States do not inhere in the substantive international rules, not even those of *ius cogens* quality.[104] They must be conferred by separate rules.

---

99   *Obligation to Prosecute,* at paras 98–95, identifies parties' power under the Convention against Torture and Other Cruel, Inhuman or Degrading Treatment or Punishment (adopted 10 December 1984, entered into force 26 June 1987) 1465 UNTS 112 (CAT) to prosecute for torture, as well as the need to exercise that power. *Legal Consequences of the Construction of a Wall in Occupied Palestinian Territory (Advisory Opinion)* [2004] ICJ Rep 136, at para. 159, identifies the power of States to prosecute under the Fourth Geneva Convention and then the need to do so.

100  *Case Concerning Navigational and Related Rights (Costa Rica v. Nicaragua) (Judgment)* [2009] ICJ Rep 213, at paras 85–133.

101  *Mutual Assistance,* at para. 145 (power to refuse to carry out extradition request); also *Application of the Interim Accord of 13 September 1995 (the former Yugoslav Republic of Macedonia v. Greece) (Judgment)* [2011] ICJ Rep 644, at para. 70 (power to object to membership of another State in an international organization).

102  *M/V 'Virginia G',* at para. 220.

103  Ibid., at para. 225.

104  *Jurisdictional Immunities,* at para. 93.

Such enforcement powers are conferred by the customary law of State responsibility, under which non-compliance by a State creates powers for other States to bring about compliance by the offender. This is the function of countermeasures another State may take.[105] The law of treaties empowers one State Party to terminate a treaty in cases of material breach by another.[106] Such reciprocal enforcement works well for rules that provide for the exchange between States of concessions or other advantages. These rules are self-enforcing in the sense that non-compliance can be addressed effectively by the reaction of another State Party. Much of international trade law is in that sense self-enforcing, although it makes suspending compliance subject to quasi-judicial authorization.[107]

By contrast, treaty-specific enforcement mechanisms are needed for non-reciprocal international rules. These mechanisms range from incentives for compliance to sanctions for non-compliance.[108]

But enforcement may also recombine rules from different subject-matters of international law. For instance, human rights law provides enforcement for international environmental law that is deficient in its own enforcement. This turns private parties into enforcers of international law.[109]

## IV Institutions of International Law

International rules constitute international law as a normative order. This normative order then becomes institutionalized. The term 'institution' requires some clarification. There is a more technical use of legal institution that international lawyers will often have in mind when they refer to institutions.[110] This contrasts with broader understandings of the term in the literature.[111]

---

105  Art. 49 ILC Draft Articles on State Responsibility.
106  Art. 60 (1) VCLT.
107  Further A.O. Sykes, 'When Is International Law Useful?' (2013) 45.3 NYU J. Int'l L. & Politics 787.
108  There is centralized, administrative enforcement of the international law of the ozone layer and to an extent for international human rights law. Further M.E. O'Connell, *The Power and Purpose of International Law* (OUP 2011).
109  The judgment of the Netherlands Appeals Court in *Urgenda Foundation v. The State of the Netherlands* (9 October 2018) ECLI:NI:GHDHA:2018:2610 provides enforcement of the international law of climate change, through the channel of the European Convention of Human Rights and the fundamental rights to life and a private and family life thereunder.
110  S. Talmon, *Recognition of Governments in International Law: With Particular Reference to Governments in Exile* (OUP 1998).
111  A. Buchanan, 'Legitimacy of International Law' in S. Besson and J. Tasioulas (eds), *The Philosophy of International Law* (OUP 2010) 79, at 80 (institution is 'a persisting pattern

This article adopts such a broader understanding. As understood here, institutions articulate ideas about international law.[112] Institutions, then, are schemes of international law's own making. They ensure the autonomy of international law. This autonomy extends to the very subjects of international law. International law is hence able to institutionalize both States and international law. It can institutionalize the foundations of its own functioning.

Yet institutions do not generate law by themselves. Rather, the institutional idea must be turned into law to be operational through the usual rule-making process. The following discussion of the institutions of international law is hence predicated on the international rule-making process that has been explained above. There cannot be institutionalization without a generally available rule-making process. There is, however, a template that guides the requisite rule-making. That template foresees rules on starting and ending the institution, and what the legal consequences are. These may be labelled the institutive, the terminative, and the consequential rules of the institution. Full institutionalization happens where rules are underpinned by machinery for judicial or quasi-judicial interpretation and application.

Extant institutions of contemporary international law revolve around agencies (1), law-making arrangements (2), and master-norms to direct the development of international law (3).

## 1   *Institution-Agencies*

International law institutionalizes organizations whose purpose it is to act on the international plane. These organizations may be labelled institution-agencies.[113]

The sovereign State is the primary agency of international law. It is the residual holder of competences. The international law of the State follows the template of institutive, terminative and consequential rules, laid down in customary law. The institutive rule for statehood pertains to the three elements of effective government over a people on a territory. This rule is underpinned by

---

of organized, rule-governed, coordinated behaviour', such as treaty-making, customary law, and global governance institutions); S. Oeter, 'Theorising the Global Legal Order—An Institutionalist Perspective' in A. Halpin and V. Roeben (eds), *Theorising the Global Legal Order* (Hart 2009) 61 (institutionalism depicting rational-choice based self-coordination of States); V. Lowe, 'The Politics of Law-Making: Are the Method and Character of Norm Creation Changing?' in M. Byers (ed.), *The Role of Law in International Politics: Essays in International Relations and International Law* (OUP 2000) 207; R. Keohane, *Power and Governance in a Partially Globalized World* (2002), at 13 (discussing the broader sense of belief and expectation necessary for the maintenance of institutions).

112   MacCormick, *Institutions*, at 36.
113   Ibid., at 35.

the principle of self-determination of peoples. The principle normatively anticipates lacking effective control in decolonization contexts. In a non-colonial context, self-determination may come to underpin the claim of a people to statehood.[114] It then needs to be balanced with the countervailing principle of the territorial integrity of the extant State. Conflicts between two countervailing principles are reconciled through political or judicial channels.[115] Statehood may be terminated, by the people, triggering State succession rules. The consequences of statehood are international legal subjectivity and sovereignty. Sovereignty denotes the bundle of competences that each State holds. Comprised is the competence to engage in international rule-making and jurisdiction to apply and enforce international law with effect to the territory. The *domaine réservé* competence over internal matters is dispositive.[116] These are complemented by functionally delimited competences over portions of the oceans, of the flag in areas beyond national jurisdiction, and also over disputed land territory.[117] States generally hold these competences for autonomously determined priorities, yet increasingly they must exercise them for internationally determined priorities.[118] These competences are then protected against interference by other States. International rules prohibit transboundary physical harm, intervention, the use of force and any other interference with its political independence or territorial integrity.

Intergovernmental international organizations are secondary agencies. Their point is to organize cooperation of States on common interests. Under the institutive rules for all international organizations, States must agree to set them up and confer on them competences for achieving specific objectives. States remain free to terminate any international organization. The principal legal consequence is that the international organization enjoys autonomy in rule-making, application and enforcement. It is placed above the members in the sense that these have to carry out the law of the organization in good faith. This hierarchy is reversed where States direct the organization through

---

114　*Kosovo*, at para. 82 (the principle's realization for non-colonial contexts requires rule-development).

115　The Separate Opinion of Judge Keith in *Jurisdictional Immunities* explains State immunity as the result of the reconciliation through State practice of the principle of territorial integrity of the forum State on the one hand and the sovereign equality on the other.

116　Crawford, *Principles*, at 455.

117　*S.S. Lotus (France v. Turkey)* (1927) PCIJ Series A No. 10, implies that sovereignty confers territorial and extraterritorial prescriptive jurisdiction.

118　In *Certain Activities Carried out by Nicaragua in the Border Area (Costa Rica v. Nicaragua)* *(Provisional Measures) (Order)* [2011] ICJ Rep 6, at paras 79–80, the Court recognizes that the Ramsar Convention confers the competence on Costa Rica to protect aspects of the global environment in the disputed territory.

treaty change or other means. The point of organizing international cooperation can, however, also be realized in the alternative formation of the meeting of the parties to multilateral treaties, with the consequence that these fulfil substantial quasi-legislative functions in developing and implementing the treaty beyond the traditional confines of an international organization: The less autonomous formation ends up holding more authority.

## 2  Institution-Arrangements: The Role of the Law of Treaties

Institution-arrangements share the point that they are not agencies in themselves, but result from their acts.[119] From the acts of States and international organizations result treaties. As codified in the VCLT, the law of treaties becomes the principal institution-arrangement of the contemporary, treatified international law.

The VCLT defines the template for the life-cycle of treaty. It determines how to institute and terminate treaty. The Convention's rules apply to the substantive treaty by default, unless that treaty specifically derogates from them. The VCLT overarches all treaties.[120] It ensures the autonomy of treatified international law.[121]

It also prescribes the consequence of treaty, and hence the four characteristics of treaty-based international law: *pacta sunt servanda*, systemic unity, *effet utile* and dynamic development, and rights of individuals. Art. 26 of the VCLT enshrines the bindingness of a treaty, with supremacy over domestic law (Art. 27) and regional law.[122] Art. 42 shores this up, mandating that a treaty can be impeached only under certain conditions. In Art. 31 (3) (c), the VCLT secures the systemic unity of all treaty-based international law. It is the lever to internalize rules from separate and independent treaties, within the limit of the wording. The prioritization of object and purpose of the treaty among the means of interpretation injects dynamism, again within the terms used.[123] Parties can also change the treaty through subsequent agreement, explicitly or

---

119  N. MacCormick, 'Institutions, Arrangements, and Practical Information' (1988) 1 Ratio Juris 73.
120  In its *Wightman* judgment of 10 December 2018, the European Court of Justice (Full Court) accepted that the Vienna Convention applies to the founding treaties of the European Union (Case C-621/18—*Wightman and Others* (2018) ECLI:EU:C:2018:999, at paras 70 and 71).
121  UNILC 'Fragmentation of International Law: Difficulties Arising from the Diversification and Expansion of International Law. Report of the Study Group of the International Law Commission Finalized by Martti Koskenniemi' (13 April 2006) UN Doc. A/CN.4/L.682.
122  *Obligation to Prosecute*.
123  Art. 31 (1) VCLT.

through concordant practice.[124] Finally, all treaties are susceptible of conferring rights and obligations on individuals. Those are normally justiciable before international courts, such as the ICJ. The point of *LaGrand* is precisely this: the State may bring an action to enforce rights of the individual created by a treaty that traditionally had been considered as creating rights only between the parties.[125]

Effective, *effet utile* orientated approaches to treaty are grounded in Art. 31 (1) of the VCLT, which makes 'object and purpose' of the substantive treaty the paramount reference of the entire interpretative exercise. One has to focus on the legislative programme of the treaty, rather than the object and purpose of its individual provisions. This focus goes beyond the established interpretive principle of effectiveness, understood as the technique that the interpreter of a treaty must normally seek to give the terms of each treaty provision a meaning which leads them to have practical effect.[126] That legislative programme is to be ascertained from the treaty preamble, which otherwise only has the contextual weight that Art. 31 (2) of the VCLT accords it. The recent jurisprudence has driven forward the paramountcy of the legislative programmes. In the case of UNCLOS, the 2012 *Territorial and Maritime Dispute* case has powerfully effectuated the legislative programme of the Convention. There, the ICJ referenced the preamble that UNCLOS is to establish the legal order of the oceans. It concluded that meant that Nicaragua as a State party had to apply the Convention rules regarding the outer continental shelf and to submit its claim to the Continental Shelf Commission in the instance, even though Colombia was not a party.[127] This interpretation affects the role that the consent of each party to a treaty has. Any such consent has been thought to be limited, *ratione personae*, *temporae*, and *materiae*.[128] But effective and uniform application requires that a party apply the treaty beyond these limits. Thus, it must apply the treaty irrespective of whether the contesting other State is also bound to do so. In that case, the Court also effectuated UNCLOS, Art. 121 on islands, which as

---

124  Art. 31 (3) (a) (b) VCLT.
125  *LaGrand Case (Germany v. United States of America)* (*Judgment*) [2001] ICJ Rep 466.
126  *Application of the International Convention on the Elimination of All Forms of Racial Discrimination (Georgia v. Russian Federation)* (*Preliminary Objections*) (*Judgment*) [2011] ICJ Rep 70, at para. 133. A broader principle of effectiveness has been propagated by Judge Lauterpacht in *Admissibility of Hearings of Petitioners by the Committee on South Africa* (*Advisory Opinion*) [1956] ICJ Rep 23, at 48–49; *Norwegian Loans (France v. Norway)* [1957] ICJ Rep 9, at 94–95; and *Interhandel (Switzerland v. USA)* (*Judgment*) [1957] ICJ Rep 6, at 65–66.
127  *Territorial and Maritime Dispute (Nicaragua v. Colombia)* (*Judgment*) [2012] ICJ Rep 624, at paras 125–127.
128  Arts 11 and 34, and 54 VCLT.

indissociable regime crystallized into custom, including its third paragraph on the own continental shelf of each island, regardless of whether that rule actually was supported by State practice.[129] In the 2012 *Maritime Dispute* case between Peru and Chile, the Court effectuated a UNCLOS legislative programme of universal rules. The Court prioritized the Convention's general rules of equidistance, special circumstances and proportionality for overwhelming maritime zone at issue. By contrast, the specific bilateral delimitation agreement between the parties was interpreted restrictively.[130] The evolutive interpretation ensures that the treaty programme itself can adapt to subsequent broader developments in international law unforeseeable at the time of adoption can still be covered. In *Navigational Rights* the Court expressly favours the evolutive interpretation of a bilateral treaty on commercial river navigation so that it covers the progressive development of international economics and law since its inception.[131]

The judgment in *Obligation to Prosecute* effectuates the legislative programme of the UN Convention against Torture (CAT). The case concerned the requested extradition of former dictator Habré from Senegal to Belgium under the CAT. The Court referred to the preamble to opine that the Convention's objective was to render the fight against torture more effective. This finding then informed both procedure and substance. Procedurally, it meant that each State Party can invoke instances of non-compliance by any other so that Belgium had standing to invoke the CAT *qua* being a party even though no national was concerned.[132] Substantively, the Court read preamble and key provisions together to conclude that the Convention establishes a mechanism for effectively combating torture, with the concrete consequence that Senegal had to prosecute the alleged torture case and could not simply choose extradition.[133] The Court then also ensured that the thus determined programme was uniformly applied over time. The Court stressed that States Parties could not prosecute acts committed before the entry into force of the convention for them.[134] But it made clear that the torture prohibition was enshrined in customary law so that

---

129  *Territorial and Maritime Dispute,* at para. 139.
130  *Maritime Dispute (Peru v. Chile) (Judgment)* [2014] ICJ Rep 3, at paras 103–51.
131  *Navigational Rights,* at paras 57–70.
132  *Obligation to Prosecute,* at para. 70. In *Application of the International Convention on the Elimination of All Forms of Racial Discrimination (Georgia v. Russian Federation) (Order for Interim Protection)* [2008] ICJ Rep 353, Georgia had standing in a dispute concerning ethnic Georgians.
133  *Obligation to Prosecute,* at paras 94–5.
134  Ibid., at para. 100.

each State could prosecute.[135] The Court has also effectuated the programme of the Genocide Convention. In the *Bosnia* case, it read into it a prohibition for States Parties to commit genocide, in addition to their expressly stipulated obligation to criminalize the individual commitment of genocide.[136] This renders the Genocide Convention effective in protecting human dignity.[137]

## 3  Institution-Norms

In addition to institutionalizing agencies and arrangements, international law also institutionalizes its meta-norms. Meta-norm is a value-bound, evaluative concept. Such master-norms are situated at a level of abstraction above international rules and principles. A master-norm then embodies a value applicable horizontally to the whole or most of international law. As such master-norms currently arguably qualify sustainable development,[138] international security,[139] and human dignity.[140]

A master-norm is not rule-producing by itself, though. Rather, it is operationalized pursuant to a general template. The template calls for the master-norm to be articulated through an agenda-setting UN conference and then to be formalized in a central multilateral treaty aspiring to universal membership, either as a stand-alone convention or as a framework convention-cum-implementing treaty.[141] Thus, global security is centred on the UN Charter, sustainable development of the oceans on UNCLOS and that of the climate

---

135  Ibid., at paras 99 and 102.
136  *Application of the Convention on the Prevention and Punishment of the Crime of Genocide (Bosnia and Herzegovina v. Serbia and Montenegro) (Judgment)* [2007] ICJ Rep 43, at paras 155–179.
137  See *Application of the Convention on the Prevention and Punishment of the Crime of Genocide (Croatia v. Serbia) (Additional Pleadings of the Republic of Croatia) (J. Crawford)*.
138  UNGA Res 66/288 'The Future We Want' (27 July 2012).
139  The UN Security Council interprets the term international security widely. It has declared international terrorism and the proliferation of weapons of mass destruction as such to be a threat, requiring action on a 'global level', UNSC Res 2129 (2013) (17 December 2013). Further J. Brunnée and S.J. Toope, 'The Use of Force: International Law after Iraq' (2004) 53 International and Comparative Law Quarterly 785.
140  Reaffirming the Universal Declaration of Human Rights and the two UN Covenants, the Vienna Declaration and Programme of Action, adopted by the World Conference on Human Rights in Vienna on 25 June 1993 (UN Doc. A/CONF.157/23), recalls in its preamble the faith of the Charter in the dignity and worth of the human person restates the organizing principles for international human rights law in I. 1.: 'All human rights are universal, indivisible and interdependent and interrelated'.
141  An alternative technique are treaty networks or 'serial bilateral treaties'. E. Benvenisti and G.W. Downs, 'The Empire's New Clothes: Political Economy and the Fragmentation of International Law' (2007) 60.2 Stanford L. Rev 595, at 610, 611.

on the UNFCCC,[142] and human dignity in the UN Covenants and supplementary human rights treaties. These multilateral treaties institute general rules, removing the power to make reservations that States by default hold under the VCLT.[143] They substitute uniform rules for the particular-plural ordering of international matters.[144] They establish machinery for centralized rule-making on harmonization, coordination or mutual recognition of domestic law, and for centralized application and enforcement.[145] They also allocate to parties international legal powers to apply these rules. The multilateral treaty may then be further implemented by parties entering into bilateral and regional treaties.

As a consequence, the master-norm becomes the institutional context for all treaties within its ambit. This calls for the foundational multilateral treaty to be integrated with all other applicable treaties. The following discussion highlights how the recent international jurisprudence reflects this approach, selectively for the master-norms of international security and human dignity.

The master norm of international security is founded in the UN Charter. The Charter sets forth the supporting principles in Art. 2, on sovereign equality, pacific settlement of disputes, the prohibition to use force, and the self-determination of peoples. The ICJ has integrated those principles with other treaties external to the Charter. This is well illustrated by two cases concerning the 1955 Treaty of Amity between Iran and the US. There, the UN Charter bears on the interpretation of that treaty' exemption clause for national security measures. In the 2003 case *Oil Platform*, the Court construed this clause narrowly to comply with Art. 51 UN Charter on self-defence and Art. 2 (4) on non-use of force.[146] In the 2018 provisional measures of *Iran v. US*, the Court has construed the clause equally narrowly to comply with the demand for humanitarian relief.[147]

---

142   UN Framework Convention on Climate Change (adopted 9 May 1992, entered into force 21 March 1994) 1771 UNTS 107.

143   Arts 28, 30 VCLT; UN ILC 'Guide to Practice on Reservations to Treaties' in 'Report of the International Law Commission on Its Sixty-Third Session (26 April–3 June and 4 July–12 August 2011)' UN Doc. A/66/10, 19.

144   *South China Sea* (UNCLOS concept of the EEZ displaces any pre-existing customary rights to marine resources).

145   See S. Krasner (ed.), *International Regimes* (Cornell University Press 1983) ('regime' deemed to be present where a treaty also provides the organization for its implementation).

146   *Oil Platforms (Iran v. United States)* (*Judgment*) [2003] ICJ Rep 161, at para. 43.

147   *Alleged Violations of the 1955 Treaty of Amity, Economic Relations, and Consular Rights (Islamic Republic of Iran v. United States of America)* (*Provisional Measures*) (*Order*) (3 October 2018) General List No. 173.

A similar approach of integrating the Charter with external treaties has been adopted by other international courts. In *Polisario*, the European Court of Justice gave effect to the principle of self-determination for a treaty on trade and development concluded by the European Union with Morocco.[148] Referring to the ICJ jurisprudence, the ECJ classified self-determination as an *erga omnes* principle of international law. It deduced the presumption that States and international organizations such as the EU intend to act consistently with this principle. The Court then turned the VCLT into an instrument to effectuate this presumption. Thus, the Convention's third-party rule means here that the parties cannot have intended to extend the treaty to the territory belonging to the people of West Sahara. And the Convention's later-in-time rule means here that the parties cannot have intended for the earlier treaty that was consistent with self-determination to have been modified by later agreements.

The *Sadio Diallo* judgments demonstrate how the International Court of Justice pursues this integrating approach to the master norm of human dignity and the supporting human right law. The Court found that the human right to liberty of Mr Diallo could be enforced through diplomatic protection by his State of nationality against a host State.[149] In ruling on the merits, the Court then shaped a single standard of unlawful detention from a synopsis of the universal UN Covenant on Civil and Political Rights with regional human rights treaties, integrating these instruments.[150]

## V  Conclusions

This article has cast a particular light on how international lawyers ought to think about their subject, without aiming to revisit all theoretical work where international lawyers discuss the project of international law. It has spelled out an analytic perspective building on MacCormick's insights, making visible that international law forms an institutional normative order directing States in the conduct of international affairs.

If this idea of institutional normative order describes the essence of international law convincingly, then it is indeed a system contrary to Hart's criticism,

---

148   Case C-104-16 P—*Council of the European Union v. Front Populaire pour la liberation de la saguia—el-harmra et du rio de oro (Front Polisario)* (21 December 2016) ECLI:EU:C:2016:973.

149   *Ahmadou Sadio Diallo (Republic of Guinea v. Democratic Republic of the Congo) (Preliminary Objections) (Judgment)* [2010] ICJ Rep 639.

150   *Ahmadou Sadio Diallo (Republic of Guinea v. Democratic Republic of the Congo) (Judgment)* [2010] ICJ Rep 639; *Compensation owed by the Democratic Republic of the Congo to the Republic of Guinea (Guinea v. DRC) (Judgment)* [2012] ICJ Rep 324, at paras 13 and 39.

unifying its increasingly specialized subject-matters. Order becomes the overarching function for all international law. An international rule-making process embedded in practice serves to turns norms into binding international rules. This process formalizes the rules through treaties and alternatives such as resolutions, institutional decisions and expert texts. It also organizes their authorization through collective consent of States while individual consent authorizes the rule for that State. The produced international rules in all areas are applied through international legal powers, with the exercise of a power by a State being contestable and increasingly subject to judicial control as to lawfulness. And international law has institutionalized the agencies—the State and international organizations—; the legal arrangements—treaty—; and the master-norms of sustainable development, international security and human dignity that integrate all international rules.

This unity entails obvious methodological consequences. International lawyers cannot see any part of international law in isolation of the whole, but rather each part must be seen as operating in this institutional order. The burden of argumentation is on those wishing to dispute that in any specific field the defining features do not apply. The rule-making process formalizes rules increasingly through alternatives to treaty, collective authorization, and these rules confer a power on States that they apply under a defeasible presumption of legality and generally applicable constraints. This burden is also on those wishing to argue that the institutions of international law and its master norms and foundations in multilateral treaties do not extend to a given matter.

### Acknowledgments

The author wishes to thank Prof. Jean d'Aspremont, Dr. Luca Siliquini-Cinelli, Prof. Isabel Feichtner, Prof. Stefan Oeter and Prof. Andrew Halpin for conversation, comments and suggestions.

CHAPTER 9

# Case Comment: *Navtej Singh Johar v. Union of India*: The Indian Supreme Court's Decriminalization of Same-Sex Relations

*Gautam Bhatia*

### Abstract

The Indian Supreme Court's judgment in *Navtej Singh Johar*, delivered in September 2018, decriminalizing same-sex relations in India, generated a storm of discussion and debate, in both India and in the world beyond. Apart from its clear and sharp verdict that held that the Indian Constitution protected the rights of the LGBTQ+ community, the decision was also noteworthy because it reversed the Court's own prior judgment, delivered a mere five years before (in 2013), that had upheld the constitutional validity of the law that penalized same-sex relations.

In this case comment, we set out the chronology of judicial decisions that led to the final judgment in *Navtej Singh Johar*: the judgment of the High Court of Delhi in 2009, which first decriminalized same-sex relations, the 2013 judgment of the Indian Supreme Court that reversed it, and the various judicial proceedings that continued to rumble on in the Court—an additional round known as the 'curative hearing', and separate litigation on the constitutional status of the right to privacy. Within this context, the paper then discusses the multiple opinions that were delivered by the Bench in *Navtej Singh Johar*, and examines the reasons on the basis of which the Court held that Section 377 of the Indian Penal Code—insofar as it criminalized same-sex relations between consenting adults—violated the fundamental rights to equality, non-discrimination, freedom of expression, and life and personal liberty, guaranteed by the Constitution of India. The article will conclude by setting out some possibilities for the way forward, in light of the judgment.

### Keywords

LGBTQ+ Rights – Judicial Review – Non-Discrimination – Privacy – Supreme Court of India

## I   Introduction

On 6 September 2018, a five-judge bench of the Supreme Court of India handed down its judgment in *Navtej Singh Johar v. Union of India*.[1] *Navtej Johar* decriminalized same-sex relations between consenting adults. It did so by reading down Section 377 of the Indian Penal Code of 1860, which penalized 'carnal intercourse against the order of nature', to exclude the above category of relationships.

*Navtej Johar* marked the culmination of a long and topsy-turvy legal battle. As early as 1995, the Indian courts had been approached with petitions asking for the decriminalization of homosexuality (note that the Indian Constitution authorizes the Supreme Court and the High Courts of each federal unit, the State, to review laws for compliance with the Constitution, and invalidate them in case of breach).[2] In 2001, Naz Foundation, a non-governmental organization that works on HIV/AIDS and sexual health, initiated public interest litigation[3] before the High Court of Delhi, asking that Section 377 be struck down as unconstitutional. After being initially rebuffed for raising an 'academic dispute', Naz Foundation—along with a host of other parties—finally got their day in court, and in 2009, a two-judge bench of the Delhi High Court held that Section 377 was unconstitutional to the extent that it criminalized same-sex relations between consenting adults, in private (*Naz Foundation v. NCT of Delhi*).[4] The LGBTQ+ community's victory, however, was short-lived. Four years later, on appeal, the Supreme Court reversed the judgment of the High Court and reinstated Section 377 (*Suresh Kumar Koushal v. Naz Foundation*).[5]

This was not the end of the story. The Indian Supreme Court has evolved a judicial mechanism that allows its own final judgments to be challenged, and—in exceedingly rare circumstances—reconsidered ('curative petition').[6] In 2016, the Supreme Court took the unusual step of agreeing to hear curative

---

1   *Navtej Singh Johar v. Union of India* [2018] 10 SCC 1.
2   Art. 32 of the Constitution of India (1949).
3   Public Interest Litigation is a special form of litigation in India, where an individual or a body approaches the Court not in their personal capacity as an affected party, but in order to agitate a cause in the 'public interest'. Often (as in the case of Naz Foundation) but not always, this will be *on behalf* of affected parties, who are either too destitute—or too diffuse—to approach the courts in their own right.
4   *Naz Foundation v. Govt. of NCT of Delhi* (High Court of Delhi) (2009) 160 DLT 277.
5   *Suresh Kumar Koushal and another v. Naz Foundation and others* [2014] 1 SCC 1.
6   *Rupa Ashok Hurra v. Ashok Hurra* [2002] 4 SCC 388.

petitions challenging its 2013 *Koushal v. Naz Foundation* judgment 'in open court', by a bench of five judges[7] (an overwhelming number of such petitions are considered and dismissed by judges in their chambers).

While the curative petitions were pending, however, on 24 August 2017, a nine-judge bench of the Supreme Court handed down its judgment in *Justice K.S. Puttaswamy v. Union of India*,[8] affirming that privacy was a guaranteed fundamental right under the Indian Constitution. In its judgment, the Court took the even more unusual step of singling out *Koushal v. Naz Foundation* as having been wrongly decided. Since the issue was not directly before it, the nine-judge bench in *Puttaswamy* could not expressly overrule it. The observations that it made, however, left no doubt that the reconsideration and overruling of *Koushal v. Naz Foundation* was little more than a formality. This duly happened a few months later, in *Navtej Johar v. Union of India*.

This chronology is essential to understand the context in which *Navtej Johar* was heard by the Court and the long history of litigation and argumentation that the Court drew upon when finally handing down its judgment decriminalizing same-sex relations. With this as the backdrop, the article will be structured in the following manner: It will examine Section 377 of the Indian Penal Code—the subject of *Navtej Johar*—and its inconsistent application by courts over the years (II); next, the 2008 judgment of the Delhi High Court, and its reversal by the Supreme Court in 2013 (III); the privacy judgment that set the scene for *Navtej Johar* (IV); the judgment in *Navtej Johar* itself (V); and it will conclude by discussing some of the potential future developments which have now been opened up because of the reasoning and conclusions set out in the judgment (VI).

## II  Section 377 of the Indian Penal Code

Section 377 of the Indian Penal Code penalizes 'carnal intercourse against the order of nature'.[9] These terms, of course, are neither self-defining nor self-interpreting. The Indian Penal Code was drafted in 1861, by the colonial British regime, and—imbued by Victorian morality—its framers refused to provide any guidance on how to understand the section, on the basis that the subject matter was too disgusting to allow for any discussion.[10]

---

7   *Naz Foundation v. Suresh Kumar Koushal* [2016] 7 SCC 485.
8   *Justice K.S. Puttaswamy v. Union of India* [2017] 10 SCC 1.
9   Section 377 of the Indian Penal Code (1860).
10  A. Gupta, 'Section 377 and the Dignity of Indian Homosexuals' (18 November 2006) 41 Economic and Political Weekly 4815.

In the absence of interpretive guidance, judicial authorities tasked with applying the law to specific situations (perhaps expectedly) came to different conclusions. One set of cases insisted that 'natural' carnal intercourse necessarily had to (at least theoretically) carry the possibility of procreation. Consequently, sexual relations that were not penile-vaginal—or not leading up to penile-vaginal intercourse—were prohibited by the section.[11] Another set of cases focused on 'sexual perversions', noting, for example, that the 'orifice of the mouth was not meant [...] by nature [...] for sexual intercourse'.[12] The issue was further clouded by the fact that a number of cases involved sexual relations between adults and minors, and adults and animals, where the phrase 'unnatural' did not refer so much as to the method of intercourse, as it did to the relations between the parties.[13]

In all the cases before the courts, however, the issue was always whether a particular sexual *act* contravened Section 377 of the Indian Penal Code. And through the mesh of the conflicting decisions that emerged, at least a few things could be seen clearly: first, that heterosexual, penile-vaginal sexual intercourse was deemed 'natural'; and secondly, non-penile-vaginal intercourse, to the extent that it was not *preparatory* to the former, was at least potentially illegal. For this reason, while heterosexual individuals may or may not have been in violation of the law, homosexual individuals were always potentially in breach—or, to use a term that would become famous later on—living 'in the shadow of criminality'.

## III   *Naz Foundation* and *Koushal v. Naz*

Before the Delhi High Court, it was argued that Section 377, as it stood, violated Arts 14, 15 (1), 19 (1) (a), and 21 of the Indian Constitution.

Art. 14 guarantees to all person equality before law, and the equal protection of laws.[14] The Petitioners argued that Section 377 singled out homosexuals as a class, and treated them unfairly, without any basis or justification. Art. 15 (1) prohibits the State from discriminating on grounds of—*inter alia*—sex.[15] The Petitioners argued that discrimination on the grounds of sexual orientation arose out of the same set of stereotypes and presumptions that underlay sex discrimination—or, at the very least, sexual orientation was a ground

---

11   *Khandu v. Emperor* AIR 1925 Sind 286; *Nowshirwan Irani v. Emperor* AIR 1934 Sind 206.
12   *Lohana Vasantlal Devchand v. The State* [1968] 9 CLR 1052.
13   *Khandu v. Emperor* AIR 1934 Lah 261 (oral sex with a bullock); *Childline India Foundation v. Allan John Waters* [2011] 2 SCC (Cri) 900 (child sexual abuse).
14   Art. 14 of the Constitution of India.
15   Art. 15 (1) of the Constitution of India.

'analogous' to that of sex. Art. 19 (1) (a) enshrines the right to freedom of speech and expression.[16] The Petitioners argued that this also contained the freedom of sexual expression, which was being chilled and stifled by the operation of the law. And lastly, Art. 21 protects the right to life and personal liberty.[17] The Petitioners argued that privacy—as a facet of liberty—was also within the scope of Art. 21, and the criminalization of sexual choice evidently violated that right.

The response of the State was straightforward and rested on two prongs: public health and public morality. On the first count, the State argued that prohibiting same-sex relations was necessary to check the spread of AIDS. On the second count, it argued that public morals in India disapproved of homosexuality and that Parliament was entitled to give effect to public morality in framing its laws.[18]

In *Naz Foundation*, the High Court of Delhi rejected the State's arguments, and in doing so, crafted some innovative rights-jurisprudence. First, the Court noted that because Section 377 targeted individual identities and personal characteristics, in examining its constitutionality, it would not apply the traditional standards of deference (that were applicable, for example, to testing economic legislation) when it came to assessing the State's arguments.[19] Rather, it would apply the stricter standard of 'proportionality'—familiar from comparative constitutional jurisdictions—which was still at a nascent stage in Indian constitutional law. On this basis, instead of accepting the State's public health justification, the Court examined its tenability in detail and found it to be at odds with existing, credible scientific literature.[20] In fact, the weight of scientific consensus suggested that the LGBTQ+ population was *more* at risk of AIDS if same-sex relations were criminalized, as it drove them underground, and discouraged safe-sex practices.[21]

What of the State's second defence—that of public morality? The petitioners contested the very existence of an anti-LGBTQ+ public morality in India, but the Court did not need to go that far. It swiftly held that the public morality that was being invoked by the State—a morality based on exclusion and subordination of a particular group of individuals—was directly in conflict with *constitutional morality*, i.e., the set of values that underpinned the Constitution's

---

16  Art. 19 (1) (a) of the Constitution of India.
17  Art. 21 of the Constitution of India.
18  *Naz Foundation v. Govt. of NCT of Delhi* (High Court of Delhi) (2009) 160 DLT 277; Written Submissions of the Union of India, at 81–96 (on file with the author).
19  Ibid., at para. 92.
20  Ibid., at paras 62–71.
21  Ibid.

fundamental rights chapter.[22] Indian constitutional morality, the Court held, counted inclusiveness, pluralism, and respect for diverse ways of life, as fundamental, structuring values. And no law that violated a constitutional provision, and was at odds with constitutional morality, could be defended on the *bare* ground that it was giving effect to public morals.

With the State's justifications out of the way, the rest of the analysis was relatively straightforward. On an application of the proportionality standard, with the public health and public morality justifications no longer in play, the High Court found that, in singling out sexual orientation for disadvantageous treatment, Section 377 denied to the LGBTQ+ community the equal protection of laws; that discrimination on the grounds of sexual orientation was akin to sex discrimination; and that Section 377 amounted to a clear breach of the fundamental right to privacy.

Notably, the High Court of Delhi buttressed its judgment by copious references to international and comparative law, all of which demonstrated a worldwide judicial trend towards decriminalizing same-sex relations, on some—or a combination of—the rights to equality, non-discrimination, privacy, and dignity. *Lawrence v. Texas*[23] (US), *National Coalition for Gay and Lesbian Equality v. Minister of Justice*[24] (South Africa), *Dudgeon v. the United Kingdom*[25] (European Court of Human Rights), *Toonen v. Australia*[26] (UN Human Rights Committee), and *Dhirendra Nadan v. State*[27] (Nepal) were all referred to by the High Court in a separate section titled 'Global Trends in Protecting the Privacy and Dignity Rights of Homosexuals', to illustrate the point.

While, four years later, the Delhi High Court's judgment was overturned by the Supreme Court in *Koushal v. Naz Foundation*, curiously, the Supreme Court failed to engage with most of the issues that were considered and analysed in *Naz Foundation*. The Supreme Court's only substantive engagement was with the distinction between *acts* and *identities*: the Court held that because Section 377—by virtue of its own language—only criminalized a set of *acts* (constituting 'carnal intercourse against the order of nature'), Arts 14 and 15 (1) of the Constitution—which protected *persons* from unequal or discriminatory treatment—could not even apply in the first place.[28] This (effective) sleight

---

22  Ibid., at para. 79.
23  *Lawrence v Texas* 539 US 558 (2003).
24  *National Coalition for Gay and Lesbian Equality v Minister of Justice* (1998) 12 BCLR 1517 (CC).
25  *Dudgeon v The United Kingdom* (1981) ECtHR Ser. A No.45.
26  *Toonen v Australia* CCPR/C/50/D488/1992.
27  *Dhirendra Nadan v State* (26 August 2005) Criminal Appeal No. HAA 85 & 86 of 2005.
28  *Suresh Kumar Koushal v. Naz Foundation* [2014] 1 SCC 1, at para. 65.

of hand spared the Court from undertaking any substantive analysis at all on the questions pertaining to the constitutional violations, the character of the judicial standards to be applied, and the engagement with the justifications provided in defence of the provision. The Court concluded by observing that it was the Parliament's job—if it so desired—to amend or modify Section 377, in order to decriminalize same-sex relations.[29]

## IV    The Privacy Judgment (*Puttaswamy*)

The judgment in *Koushal*—which effectively *re-criminalized* an entire community of people—caused great furore, and the case was kept alive through the process of the curative petition (described above). In the meantime, however, another constitutional controversy was brewing. During the course of hearings regarding a challenge to India's national biometric identification system, the State contended that the Indian Constitution did not guarantee a fundamental right to privacy. It was argued that this position—flowing from a literal reading of the constitutional text—had been affirmed by two benches of the Supreme Court of eight and six judges in the 1950s and 60s respectively, and all subsequent judgments that *had* held that there existed a fundamental right to privacy, had been delivered by benches of smaller judges. Under the Indian system of judicial precedent, a smaller bench was bound by a larger bench.

The Court found enough force in this argument to refer the question to an even larger bench of nine judges so that the issue of whether or not there existed a fundamental right to privacy under the Indian Constitution could be considered afresh.[30] The nine-judge bench handed down its judgment in August 2017, unanimously affirming that privacy was, indeed, a fundamental right under the Indian Constitution (*Puttaswamy v. Union of India*). The *Puttaswamy* judgment was significant in that it contained six separate opinions, each of which not only affirmed the existence of the right to privacy but spent some time fleshing out its nature and its contours. All judges agreed that privacy had multiple dimensions, one of which was the right to decisional privacy, i.e., the right to make private, intimate, and personal choices, free of State interference.[31]

---

29    For a more detailed examination of these judgments, see G. Bhatia, *The Transformative Constitution* (Harper 2019), at Ch. 2.
30    *Justice K.S. Puttaswamy v. Union of India* [2015] 8 SCC 735.
31    *Justice K.S. Puttaswamy v. Union of India* [2017] 10 SCC 1.

This was already a resounding rebuke to the *Koushal v. Naz Foundation* judgment, which had failed to even return a substantive finding on the privacy challenge, let alone engage with the issue in any meaningful way. However, the Court went even further. Five out of nine judges—constituting a majority—categorically singled out the *Koushal* judgment, and expressly stated that it had been wrongly decided. Writing the plurality opinion on behalf of four judges, Justice Chandrachud labelled *Koushal* as a 'discordant note' in Indian constitutional history, and emphasized that the rights of the LGBTQ+ community 'inhere in the right to life. They dwell in privacy and dignity. They constitute the essence of liberty and freedom. Sexual orientation is an essential component of identity. Equal protection demands protection of the identity of every individual without discrimination'.[32] In his concurring opinion, Justice Kaul noted that 'one's sexual orientation is undoubtedly an attribute of privacy'.[33] Both judges went on to state that they were expressing no definitive opinion about *Koushal*, as that case was not before them, but the import of these observations could not have been more explicit.

## V    *Navtej Johar v. Union of India*

By the time *Navtej Johar* came up for hearing before the Supreme Court, almost one year after *Puttaswamy*, the writing was evidently on the wall. This was made particularly clear midway through the hearing, when the Additional Solicitor-General, on instructions from the State, informed the bench that the State would not defend Section 377, but rather, leave the question of its constitutionality 'to the wisdom of the Court'. Section 377 was defended, ultimately, by a set of Christian religious groups.

Arguments before the Supreme Court were now made in the shadow of the *Puttaswamy* judgment, and the stronger foundations that it offered. At their heart, however, they took the same form as the arguments that had been made before the Delhi High Court a decade ago: that criminalizing same-sex relations fundamentally violated the constitutional guarantees of equality before the law, non-discrimination, the freedom of expression, and the rights to life and personal liberty. The Supreme Court delivered its judgment on 6 September 2018, overruling *Koushal v. Naz Foundation*, substantially restoring the

---

32    Ibid., at para. 127 (Plurality Opinion of Chancrachud J.).
33    Ibid., at para. 80 (Concurring Opinion of Kaul J.).

judgment of the Delhi High Court in *Naz Foundation v. NCT of Delhi*, and decriminalizing same-sex relations in India, once and for all.[34]

*Navtej Johar* was decided by a bench of five judges, four of whom wrote separate opinions. While all four judges agreed that Section 377 violated Arts 14, 15 (1), 19 (1) (a), and 21 of the Indian Constitution, their analyses centred on different issues. To understand the full breadth of the judgment, we must examine each in turn.

### 1   Choice

Chief Justice Dipak Misra—who wrote for himself and on behalf of Justice Khanwilkar—located 'personal choice' at the heart of his judgment. The Chief Justice demonstrated awareness of the fraught debate between people who argue that sexual orientation is an immutable personal characteristic, that individuals are born with and cannot change; and those that argue that it is a question of an intimate and personal choice. Noting the existing debate, he observed that:

> When we talk about identity from the constitutional spectrum, it cannot be pigeon-holed singularly to one's orientation that may be associated with his/her birth and the feelings he/she develops when he/she grows up. Such a narrow perception may initially sound to subserve the purpose of justice but on a studied scrutiny, it is soon realized that the limited recognition keeps the individual choice at bay.[35]

While the Chief Justice did go on to refer to 'innate characteristics', it was nevertheless the focus on choice that was his basis for rejecting *Koushal*'s facile distinction between 'acts' and 'identities'. He noted that the 'individuality of a person and the acceptance of identity invite advertence to some necessary concepts which eventually recognize the constitutional status of an individual that resultantly brushes aside the act and respects the dignity and choice of the individual'.[36] In other words, even though Section 377 *on its terms* merely singled out a set of acts for proscription and punishment ('carnal intercourse against the order of nature'), in its *effect*, it affected individual status—the status that was grounded in the sense of personal dignity, and the exercise of personal choice.

This conceptual framework then allowed the Chief Justice to undertake his substantive analysis of the constitutional claims. Because it denied the exercise of personal choice without any defensible reason, Section 377 was both

---

34   *Navtej Singh Johar v. Union of India* [2018] 10 SCC 1.
35   Ibid., at para. 11 (Plurality Opinion of the Chief Justice).
36   Ibid., at para. 92 (Plurality Opinion of the Chief Justice).

'irrational' and 'arbitrary', and therefore failed the standard tests for constitutionality under Art. 14;[37] it also failed Art. 21, which was to be understood to guarantee 'intimacy in privacy [as] a matter of choice'.[38]

The distinction between legal form and practical effect, as a matter of constitutional equality and non-discrimination, was important not just for the Chief Justice's holding, but more broadly, in the overall framework of Indian fundamental rights jurisprudence. However, its full development would take place in the concurring opinions, which we shall turn to shortly.

## 2   Arbitrariness

Justice Nariman's concurring opinion shared much of the conceptual analysis undertaken by the Chief Justice, especially on the issue of choice and dignity. Furthermore, like the Chief Justice, Justice Nariman also found that Section 377 was 'arbitrary', and therefore, violated Art. 14's guarantee of the equal protection of laws. He arrived at this conclusion, however, by a slightly different route. One of the tests under Art. 14 of the Indian Constitution is whether a law—or an executive act—is 'arbitrary'. While there had been dispute in the past over what, precisely, constituted 'arbitrariness', and whether 'arbitrariness' could be judicially invoked to strike down a law (or only executive action), by the time of *Navtej Johar*, the law was fairly well-settled that primarily legislation could be struck down if it was 'manifestly arbitrary'.

Within this constitutional framework, Justice Nariman correctly observed that under the Mental Healthcare Act of 2017, discrimination on grounds of sexual orientation was expressly prohibited in the domain of mental health.[39] This suggested that Parliament itself no longer subscribed to the natural/unnatural distinction between heterosexuality and homosexuality, which was at the heart of Section 377. When combined with the contemporary scientific consensus, Justice Nariman was therefore easily able to hold that between 'carnal intercourse against the order of nature' and 'carnal intercourse in accordance with the order of nature', there was now only a distinction without a difference. This meant that the text of Section 377, in basing itself upon the natural/unnatural dichotomy, had no rational basis anymore, and was nothing more than arbitrary.[40]

Justice Nariman also made the additional, interesting point—that had been canvassed before the Delhi High Court in 2009, and had been accepted by it,

---

37   Ibid., at para. 268.14 (Plurality Opinion of the Chief Justice).
38   Ibid., at para. 268.10 (Plurality Opinion of the Chief Justice).
39   S. 18 (2) of the Mental Healthcare Act (2017).
40   *Navtej Singh Johar v. Union of India* (Concurring Opinion of Nariman J.) [2018] 10 SCC 1, at para. 353.

but had since fallen by the wayside somewhat—that *pre*-Constitutional laws did not possess the element of the 'presumption of constitutionality'. The presumption of constitutionality refers to the doctrine that when a statute is challenged, the burden of justifying that there has been a constitutional violation lies upon the challenger. Thus, all other things being equal, a Court will uphold a legal provision, rather than strike it down. The rationale for this is that an elected legislature is deemed to know the needs of its people, and also to possess the legitimacy to make laws, vested in it through the process of elections. Consequently, a Court will—at least initially—defer to Parliamentary wisdom, and only invalidate a statute if it has an affirmative reason to do so.

As Justice Nariman noted, however, the very basis of the presumption of constitutionality does not exist for a law that dates back to colonial times:

> The presumption of constitutionality of a statute is premised on the fact that Parliament understands the needs of the people, and that, as per the separation of powers doctrine, Parliament is aware of its limitations in enacting laws—it can only enact laws which do not fall within List II of Schedule VII of the Constitution of India, and cannot transgress the fundamental rights of the citizens and other constitutional provisions in doing so. Parliament is therefore deemed to be aware of the aforesaid constitutional limitations. Where, however, a pre-constitution law is made by either a foreign legislature or body, none of these parameters obtain. It is therefore clear that no such presumption attaches to a pre-constitutional statute like the Indian Penal Code.[41]

Missing in Justice Nariman's analysis, however, was an adequate response to a well-known objection: if the post-colonial Parliament has seen fit *not* to repeal colonial legislation, then does that not imply that the democratic legislature has, at least impliedly, *acquiesced* to the continuation of that legislation? And if so, why would the presumption of constitutionality not apply with equal force to such a situation? While Justice Nariman did not answer the question, we might argue that, at least in the case of rights-infringing statutes, this would amount to an unfair double-burden on the individuals at the receiving end: not only had their rights been taken away by a process in which they had no effective participation (i.e., legislation by a colonial regime), but they were now expected to be the ones to take the affirmative political steps in order to regain their rights.[42] It would—at least intuitively—appear much fairer to remove

---

41    Ibid. (Concurring Opinion of Nariman J.), at para. 361.
42    A version of this argument was initially made by Akhil Amar, in the context of abortion statutes in the US, which were legislated before women had the right to vote. See A. Amar,

the presumption of constitutionality, at least in cases where constitutional rights were at stake.

## 3   Indirect Discrimination

It was in the concurring judgments of Justices Chandrachud and Malhotra, however, that certain important conceptual advances were made. Justice Chandrachud, for example, tackled the vexing act/identity distinction by focusing on the concept of indirect discrimination, which had hitherto remained unexplored in the equality and discrimination jurisprudence of the Indian Supreme Court.[43] He began his analysis by noting the inadequacy of understanding equality and non-discrimination simply as a matter of fair classification:

> Equating the content of equality with the reasonableness of a classification on which a law is based advances the cause of legal formalism. The problem with the classification test is that what constitutes a reasonable classification is reduced to a mere formula: the quest for an intelligible differentia and the rational nexus to the object sought to be achieved. In doing so, the test of classification risks elevating form over substance. The danger inherent in legal formalism lies in its inability to lay threadbare the values which guide the process of judging constitutional rights'.[44]

Rather, he held that 'Art. 14 has a substantive content on which, together with liberty and dignity, the edifice of the Constitution is built. Simply put, in that avatar, it reflects the quest for ensuring fair treatment of the individual in every aspect of human endeavour and in every facet of human existence'.[45]

This substantive content, in turn, was to be determined by examining the *effect* of a legal provision upon the lived realities of people, in the fullest sociopolitical and economic context, rather than simply looking at the *form* of the

---

*America's Unwritten Constitution: The Precedents and Principles We Live by* (Basic Books 2012), at Ch. 9.

43  A few months before the judgment in *Koushal*—in January 2018—the a two-judge bench of the Delhi High Court had applied the concept of indirect discrimination to a case involving a spouse's right to medical services. See *Madhu v. Northern Railway* (High Court of Delhi) (1 January 2018) LPA 640/2017. Apart from that, however, the Indian Courts were yet to decisively highlight the distinctions between direct and indirect discrimination, and affirm that both were prohibited by the Constitution; indeed, indirect discrimination had, historically, been failed to be recognized as discrimination at all, by a majority of judicial decisions.

44  *Navtej Singh Johar v. Union of India* (Concurring Opinion of Chandrachud J.) [2018] 10 SCC 1, at para. 409.

45  Ibid.

provision. In the case of Section 377, this played out in the following way: there was documented evidence to show that homosexual individuals lived their lives 'in the shadow of criminality'. This was because:

> *Section 377 criminalizes behaviour that does not conform to the heterosexual expectations of society. In doing so it perpetuates a symbiotic relationship between anti-homosexual legislation and traditional gender roles.* [...]
> If individuals as well as society hold strong beliefs about gender roles—that men (to be characteristically reductive) are unemotional, socially dominant, breadwinners that are attracted to women and women are emotional, socially submissive, caretakers that are attracted to men—it is unlikely that such persons or society at large will accept that the idea that two men or two women could maintain a relationship.[46]

A complete examination of the context revealed, therefore, that not only was Section 377 subjecting a class of people to persecution and stigma, it was doing so on the basis of gender stereotypes and gender roles, which was precisely what the equality and non-discrimination clauses of the Constitution were designed to prohibit. As Justice Chandrachud noted, therefore:

> Statutes like Section 377 give people ammunition to say 'this is what a man is' by giving them a law which says 'this is what a man is not'. Thus, laws that affect non-heterosexuals rest upon a normative stereotype: 'the bald conviction that certain behaviour—for example, sex with women—is appropriate for members of one sex, but not for members of the other sex'.[47]

This analysis, therefore, neatly located itself within an evolved discrimination law framework, one that is found in multiple jurisdictions such as Canada, South Africa, Germany, and the European Court of Human Rights. Justice Chandrachud began by noting that Section 377 had discriminatory effect, regardless of its form. This effect was felt by a group of people who were identified and isolated through their sexual orientation; and the basis of this effect was a set of prejudices and stereotypes that were explicitly excluded by the Constitution as justificatory reasons. In other words, Section 377 was the prototype of an indirectly discriminatory law: neutral in form, but discriminatory in effect, and unconstitutional when that discriminatory effect was placed within the broader social context. As pointed out above, this represented a significant breakthrough, as it was the first time that an Indian Supreme Court judgment

---

46   Ibid., at para. 448 (Concurring Opinion of Chandrachud J.).
47   Ibid., at para. 451 (Concurring Opinion of Chandrachud J.).

seriously engaged with the concept of indirect discrimination—a concept that is, by now, well-known to constitutional courts the world over.

As an aside, it is interesting to note that Justice Chandrachud consciously resisted perhaps the only trap that the Delhi High Court had allowed itself to fall into: to construct a public/private binary, and restrict the right of sexual expression to 'private spaces'. Justice Chandrachud, on the other hand, was acutely alive to the problems that this might cause, and therefore, he took care to note that 'the right to sexual privacy, founded on the right to autonomy of a free individual, must capture the right of persons of the community to navigate public places on their own terms, free from State interference'.[48]

## 4   Illegitimate Purpose

Historically, the classification test under Art. 14 of the Indian Constitution has focused on whether a law intelligibly differentiates between those it burdens and those it does not, and whether this intelligible differentia bears a rational nexus with a State goal. This two-pronged test to determine whether a law passes muster under the equal protection guarantee has been dominant in Indian constitutional jurisprudence; it also, however, has a third element that is not often discussed—that the purpose must be legitimate. The reason why this remains somewhat in the background is because there is a thin line between a court deeming a purpose to be 'illegitimate', and simply 'undesirable public policy in the opinion of the court'. In the absence of a principle to determine which purposes count as legitimate and which do not, the Supreme Court has—understandably—hesitated to go into this area.

That approach changed, however, with the last of the concurring opinions. Justice Malhotra noted that Section 377 violated Art. 14 because '[it] creates an artificial dichotomy. The natural or innate sexual orientation of a person *cannot be a ground* for discrimination. Where a legislation discriminates on the basis of an intrinsic and core trait of an individual, it *cannot* form a reasonable classification based on an intelligible differentia'.[49]

In other words, therefore, selecting an 'intrinsic and core' individual trait for discriminatory treatment was *ipso facto* ruled out by Art. 14's guarantee of equal protection of laws, and equal treatment before the law. The State may do so in the most intelligible fashion, and in a manner that has a rational nexus with the goal of treating certain groups or classes in a hostile fashion; however, it is the very purpose itself that is ruled out by the Constitution.

This takes us back to the judgment of the High Court: the reason for this— that Justice Malhotra did not go into—was that there were certain legislative

---

48   Ibid., at para. 471 (Concurring Opinion of Chandrachud J.).
49   Ibid., at para. 637.3 (Concurring Opinion of Malhotra J.; emphasis added).

purposes that were directly contrary to constitutional values themselves—or, in the words of the High Court, to 'constitutional morality'. Values of pluralism and tolerance of diverse forms of life were at the core of the Constitution; and therefore, laws that violated equal protection and equal treatment, and which could *only* be justified by invoking reasons that were directly at variance with these values, could not stand scrutiny.

Lastly, following the approach of the High Court in *Naz* Foundation—and contrary to *Kaushal*—all the judges in *Navtej Johar* referred to comparative jurisprudence on the subject. In the nine years since the judgment of the Delhi High Court, the trend had shifted further towards decriminalisation, as was pointed out by counsel arguing for the petitioners. The Supreme Court was now able to draw upon judgments from the Philippines[50] and Trinidad and Tobago,[51] in addition to all the judgments that the High Court of Delhi had relied upon.

VI  Conclusion: The Way Forward

The judgment of the Indian Supreme Court in *Navtej Johar v. Union of India* is significant for many reasons. First, and most importantly, of course, is its outcome: the judgment ensured that India joined the list of countries where same-sex relations were no longer criminal and that it did so through the judgment of a constitutional court that affirmed the fundamental rights of the LGBTQ+ community.

Secondly, there is the reasoning employed by the four judges. In their focus on dignity, personal choice, privacy, equality, and non-discrimination, the judges engaged in a dialogue with other constitutional courts that have come to similar conclusions, in similar cases, in recent years. The analysis in *Navtej Johar* would sound immediately familiar to someone who has engaged, for example, with the judgment of the US Supreme Court in *Lawrence v. Texas*,[52] the judgment of the South African Constitutional Court in *National Coalition for Gay and Lesbian Equality*,[53] or the judgment of the UN Human Rights Committee in *Toonen v. Australia*.[54] The Indian Supreme Court, therefore, joined a

---

50  *Ang Ladlad LGBT Party v Commission of Elections*, G.R. No. 190582, Supreme Court of the Philippines (2010).
51  *Jason Jones v Attorney-General*, Claim No. (CV) 2017-00720 (2018).
52  *Lawrence v. Texas* (US Supreme Court) [2003] 539 US 558.
53  *National Coalition for Gay and Lesbian Equality v. Minister of Justice* (Constitutional Court of South Africa) 1998 (12) BCLR 1517.
54  UN HRC 'Communication No. 488/1992, *Toonen v. Australia*' (25 December 1991).

growing, global consensus among constitutional courts about the importance of using constitutional instruments to protect core values of personhood, autonomy and dignity, especially in the context of sexual orientation.

At the same time, however, the judgment made significant conceptual advances *within* the context of Indian constitutional jurisprudence. Justice Chandrachud provided a rigorous theoretical framework for assessing indirect discrimination, which was sensitive to effect, context, and the interface between legal texts and the lived realities of people. And Justice Malhotra provided a constitutional principle that could be invoked to rule out certain types of laws—motivated by bare hostility towards individuals or groups of individuals, on the basis of their personal characteristics—at the threshold, without engaging in any further constitutional enquiry.

And thirdly, *Navtej Johar* is important for the further possibilities that it throws up. During oral arguments, counsel for the Petitioners argued that the Court should go a step further than decriminalization, and positively affirm that the LGBTQ+ community was entitled to equal civil rights, both in the public and the private sphere, including with respect to access to housing and private employment. Other counsel urged the Court to go even further, and consider some manner of affirmative action for a community that had been heavily disadvantaged for many decades. These moves were resisted by the State, whose counsel insisted that its concession was limited only to the issue of criminalization and that it would contest the point if the Court intended to go any further.

The Court's judgment, finally, was limited to decriminalization. Its reasoning, however—as we have seen above—was broad and wide-ranging. With the principles laid down in *Navtej Johar*—and the depth and the breadth with which they have been articulated—there is no reason why the judgment cannot become a springboard for other, more ambitious litigation: the basic framework set out by *Navtej Johar* now allows for plausible claims to be made in the domain of equal civil rights, affirmative action, and—ultimately—equal marriage. When and how that happens, of course, remains to be seen.

### Acknowlegments

The author was professionally involved in *Navtej Singh Johar v. Union of India*, as one of the counsel appearing on behalf of 'Voices Against 377', an organization of LGBTQ+ groups petitioning the court for decriminalizing same-sex relations.

CHAPTER 10

# The Nomadic Sense of Law in an International Constitutionalism

*William E. Conklin*

## Abstract

This article examines the place of Nomadic peoples in an international constitutionalism. The article claims that an important element of a Nomadic culture is its sense of law. Such a sense of law differs from a constitutionalism which has privileged fundamental principles aimed to constrain acts of the executive arm of the State. Such a constitutionalism is shared by many contemporary domestic legal orders. Public international law also takes such a constitutionalism for granted. In the focus upon rules to constrain the executive arm of the State, the sense of law in Nomadic communities has slipped through arguments which the jurist might consider inclusive of the protection of such communities. This problem is nested in a legacy which has weighted down the history of European legal thought.

The article initially identifies three forms of nomadism. The social phenomenon of nomadism has been the object of juristic commentary since the Greeks and Romans. The image of Nomadic peoples in such a legacy has imagined Nomadic peoples as lawless although the article argues that a sense of law has existed in such communities. Such a sense of law contradicts a State-centric international legal order. Public international law has reserved a special legal space relating to Nomadic peoples. The article identifies four arguments which might be rendered to protect Nomadic peoples in such a State-centric international community. Problems are raised with each such argument.

## Keywords

Nomadic People – Constitutionalism – Culture – Minority – Human Rights – Indigenous

## 1   Introduction

Nomadic peoples are understood in terms of their frequent movement from place to place. Their social relationships are markedly dependent upon climate, water, land, municipal by-laws, access to food, resources, spiritualism, and the relation of the group with the regulatory State. Nomadic communities are important social and political entities in territories of some countries (such as Mongolia, Afghanistan, Kyrgyzstan, Romania, West African States, Norway, Sweden, Denmark (Greenland), India and Brazil, for example). There are several millions of Nomadic individuals on the globe.

Though some Nomadic groups have experienced a deep cultural and historical association with land, they have also been considered politically invisible in the past (Tibet, Western Russia, North Africa, the Middle East, and particular geographical areas of Canada, for example). The political invisibility of Nomadic peoples arguably reached its high mark in international law canons during the 19th century. By the 20th century, such States have claimed absolute or radical title to all land. In addition, the international community assigned a reserved domain which 'by international law is solely within domestic jurisdiction' (Art. 15 (8) of the Covenant of the League of Nations) or 'essentially within the domestic jurisdiction of any State' (Art. 2 (7) of the UN Charter). Such a 'sole' or 'essential' reserved space for the State member included the State's legal authority to confer, withdraw, or condition an individual as a legal person (that is a national) recognized as having rights in the international community. Such a domain reserved for the State in the international community has often left Nomadic peoples *de iure*, diplomatically and effectively stateless.

Nomadic communities, however, have retained their cultural practices and beliefs despite the efforts of a State-centric administrative structure to regulate, assimilate, deny, and restrict the flourishing of such communities. The dependence of Nomadic communities upon a mixed economy as a supplement or primary source to livelihood has added to the difficulty of Nomadic groups to be sustained. This has especially been so, for example, for the Roma of Europe and the Bedouin of the Middle East and North Africa.

Aside from climate, other external factors have worked against the sustenance of Nomadic cultures. One has involved the introduction of territorial State borders and the requirement, beginning in the 1830s, of passports or other documentation verifying a person's nationality. A second factor has been the introduction of a mixed economy, mechanization, industrialization and the internet. Such factors have required that members of one form of a Nomadic community supplement their livelihood with temporary or permanent employment, business and trade. The third external constraint has involved the administration of refugee law by State officials as well as the practices of local residents and policies of municipal officials towards members of Nomadic groups. Nomadic communities have depended upon local inhabitants and governments in two ways. The first has concerned the State's ultimate claim to own all land, water and resources inside its territorial borders. Secondly and perhaps related to such a claim, the State has imposed laws and an institutional governmental structure with the effect, if not the intent, of regulating the cultures of the Nomadic peoples.

State authority, traditionally recognized as confined to a reserved domain, by the international community, has been accepted as transcendent over Nomadic peoples. Such a freedom of the State has remained in the background of constitutionalism. Such a domestic constitutionalism has had an international character because constitutionalism emerged as part and parcel in a State-centric internationalism.[1] For this reason, I describe my effort as the placing of Nomadic communities in international constitutionalism. In particular, constitutionalism emerged in response to the English, French and American Revolutions. The objective of constitutionalism was to constrain the acts of political leaders of the State. A Nomadic sense of law, however, has been independent of such a genesis by constitutionalism. Arguments in favour of the protection of Nomadic communities have faced problems when contextualized in constitutionalism's objective. I address such problems in a moment.

## II   Three Forms of Nomadic Peoples

Nomadism has had three forms. The first two forms have generally been identified as a traditional (or 'tribal') community. One form has been identified with hunting, fishing and gathering; the second has shifted to pastoralism and herding. These two forms of Nomadism have been the object of discussion over the centuries from the Greeks to the Romans to the early modern juristic writings to the present-day adjudication and commentary. The third form of Nomadism, contemporary with a mixed economy and regulatory State, has been characterized as peripatetic.

---

1   This nexus of domestic constitutionalism with an international community has been the focus of W.E. Conklin, 'Territorial Knowledge, Sociality and the Congruence of International and Constitutional Law' in M. Novaković (ed.), *The Common Law and the Civil Law Today—Convergence and Divergence* (Vernon Press, forthcoming 2019); W.E. Conklin, *Statelessness: the Enigma of an International Community* (Hart 2014/2015); W.E. Conklin, 'The Exclusionary Character of the Early Modern International Community' (2012) 81 Nordic J. Int'l L. 133; W.E. Conklin, 'The Peremptory Norms of the International Community' (2012) 23 EJIL 837 and 869; W.E. Conklin, 'The Myth of Primordialism in Cicero's Theory of *ius gentium*' (2010) 23.3 Leiden Journal of International Law 479.

## 1  Hunting, Fishing and Gathering

First, there are traditional (more commonly described as 'tribal') communities whose Nomadism is characterized by the dependence upon hunting, fishing and gathering.

Much as the modern State-centric legal order has taken hold of the dominant inhabitants of a territory, the identity of the State and of the individual has been associated with a State's claim of radical title to a fixed bounded territory. As I shall explain, jurists have mapped a sense of territory into how legal concepts are understood. Each legal concept has a boundary which defines the identity and scope of the space of the concept. Property, contract, sovereignty and a right exemplify such a bounded concept. Such concepts manifest territorial-like bounded spaces in one's consciousness. Such a sense of law as 'territorial' knowledge is alien to the sense of law in a Nomadic community.

The clash between a State-centric legal structure and the sense of Nomadic law as social practices is exemplified by a close study of several Nomadic groups. For the Sámi of present-day Greenland (Denmark), Norway, Sweden and the western peninsula of Russia, for example, hunting, fishing and gathering have been essential to livelihood. During the 19th century, this form of Nomadism shifted to the herding of reindeer in the forests.[2] In centuries past, the Inuit territory, presently claimed by the State of Canada, similarly shared collective memories of a Nomadic way of life. Their livelihood especially relied upon hunting and fishing until more recently when climate change increasingly impacted their way of life. As European military and administrative arrangements were established in North America during the 18th and 19th centuries, the inhabitants of formerly settled villages in present-day north-eastern US and the St. Lawrence area of present-day Canada migrated westward, reaching the prairies where they led a Nomadic life primarily dependent upon hunting and fishing.[3] Such continual movement in search of nourishment lacked the fixity on land needed for an exclusive claim, let alone title, to land as property.

---

2   M. Ahrén, 'Indigenous Peoples' Culture, Customs, and Traditions and Customary Law—The Saami People's Perspective' (2006) 21.2 Ariz J. Int'l & Comp L. 63; R.P. Wheelerburg and N. Gutsol, 'Traditional Sami Reindeer Herding Village Resource Territories on the Western Kola Peninsula, Russia' (2010) 46.3 Polar Record 222.

3   P.C. Albers, 'Changing Patterns of Ethnicity in the Northeastern Plains' in J.D. Hill (ed.), *History, Power and Identity: Ethnogenesis in the Americas, 1492–1992* (Iowa University Press 1996) 90, at 116; D.R. Snow, 'The First Americans and the Differentiation of Hunter-Gatherer Cultures' in B.G. Trigger and W.E. Washburn (eds), *The Cambridge History of the Native Peoples of the Americas* vol. 1 *North America, Part l* (CUP 1996) 125, at 161–163, 193–194.

## 2  Pastoralism and Herding

A second Nomadic group has depended upon pastoralism and herding. This form of Nomadism, in turn, has again depended upon changing climatic conditions. The etymology of the very word, 'Nomad', draws from the Greek word, *nemein* or 'to pasture'. Land and water have taken on an important need to maintain pastoralism and, through the Nomadic group's experience of time, to protect spiritual relations with water and land. Whether the latter spiritual relation has been constitutionally protected varies from country to country and from court to court.[4]

As will be noted, pastoralism and herding have been associated with the emergence of a 'civilized people'.[5] Since Greek and Roman times, leading juristic commentaries and later Anglo-American court judgments have considered pastoralism and herding a social 'advance' over the hunting, fishing and gathering of the first form of Nomadism.[6] Many States have enacted laws and instituted administrative policies which have had the effect, if not the objective, of encouraging hunters and gatherers to change their culture to one of pastoralism and herding. Common law courts, for example, have advocated such a cultural change.[7]

To take an example of this second form of Nomadism, the Sámi of Scandinavia, during the 19th century, shifted their source of livelihood and culture from hunting and fishing (the first form of Nomadism) to the herding of reindeer in the forests. They migrated from the mountains in the winter to the coastal areas in the summer. As another example, for centuries, groups living along the Hudson Bay in Canada regularly moved from the Bay inland during the winter months. The Sámi in Scandinavia and Inuit in Canada have depended upon the livelihood of hunting and fishing until pastures have dried up, seals or other objects of prey have become scarce, or other environmental factors have discouraged animals and fish from a livelihood resource. With such environmental changes, so too pastoralists and herders have found it necessary to migrate. As further examples, pastoralism and herding in central Asia and the Sahel area of West Africa has depended upon fresh pastures and water.

---

4   *Sawhoyamaxa Indigenous Community v. Paraguay* IACtHR Series C No. 146 (29 March 2006), at para. 131.
5   *US v. New Mexico*, 438 US 696 (1978), 717 fn 4 per Rehnquist; *US v. Southern Ute Tribe or Band of Indians*, 402 US 159, 91 S Ct 1336 (1971).
6   *Mabo v. Queensland (No. 2)* (1992) 175 CLR 1 (3 June 1992), at para. 34 per Brennan. See also W. Blackstone, *Commentaries on the Laws of England in Four Books* (1753; Lippincott 1893), vol. 1, bk. l, Ch. 4, at 106–108.
7   See e.g., *Montana v. US*, 450 US 544, 101 S Ct 1245 (1981).

This, in turn, has led Nomadic groups to follow livestock (camels, sheep, goats, cattle, reindeer) and to direct livestock to fresh locations. Better known are the traditional Bedouin communities which inhabited and still inhabit the Sahara, Sinai and Arabian deserts.

3     *Peripatetic Nomads*

A third form of Nomadism has emerged with industrialization, mercantilism, mechanization, an exchange economy, the internet, and the municipal and regulatory State. In this more recent social phenomenon, the values, practices, rituals and assumptions of the culture of a Nomadic group have been retained although members of the group have sought temporary employment or other activity in the mixed economy of urban areas. Such Nomadic groups are described as peripatetic.

In particular, both hunters and fishers (the first form of Nomadism) as well as pastoralists and herders (the second form) have been influenced by the advance of the 19th and 20th century mixed economies. The State has especially regulated the use of water and land. As a consequence, the first two forms of Nomadic communities have been modified. Members of Nomadic communities in a traditional (or 'tribal') form have increasingly become traders, service providers, commercial Nomads or itinerant agricultural workers. Some peripatetic Nomadic groups have been entirely assimilated into the State-centric legal culture. Others, however, have retained elements of their past Nomadic culture with a hybrid assimilation involving the exchange economy and formal deference to State regulations. The collective memories and social practices of such Nomadic groups have been assimilated into the group's dependence upon outside monetary support to supplement livelihood. Many Bedouin groups have dispersed into urban areas of Israel and the Palestinian Occupied Territory, for example. With the Soviet collectivist and mechanized regulation during the second decade of the 20th century, the Sámi traditional dependence upon reindeer herding in Western Russia has been modified by the introduction of large reindeer herds, mixed economies and itinerant labour.[8] In like vein, the Inuit dependence in Canada upon a livelihood of seals and other mammals has risked decline with the melting of the ice caps in the Arctic. The market economy has also set the stage for a dependence of Nomadic groups upon full- and part-time employment outside Indigenous reservations as well as upon government support.

---

8   R.P. Wheelerburg and N. Gutsol, 'Traditional Sami Reindeer Herding Village Resource Territories on the Western Kola Peninsula, Russia' (2010) 46.3 Polar Record 222.

Although peripatetic groups usually possess traditions, rituals and collective memories of an identifiable culture from decades and centuries past, another peripatetic group—travellers—has emerged in more recent times. Travellers provide such economic functions as bargee families, employees of circuses, fairgrounds and carnivals. One can locate travellers throughout the globe. Examples of travellers in Europe are the Roma, Sinti, Irish Travellers, the 'Indian gypsies' of India, and the Sámi of Scandinavia. Other examples are clans which, continually moving from the threat of war, physical violence, ethnic and religious discrimination and death, are internally displaced. The Rohingya of Myanmar recently exemplify the latter. A more recent example of travellers is 'peoples of the street' who sometimes seem to move as a group with the climate, opportunities and arguably unintended State-sponsored harm.

## III Are Nomadic Peoples Protected by International Indigenous Law?

It is tempting to associate Nomadic peoples with the international protection of Indigenous peoples. This is not necessarily clear-cut. Indeed, I shall argue in a moment that Nomadic peoples slip through the gaps intended for the protection of Indigenous peoples.

First, treaties and declarations, retrieved in my final section, have especially focussed upon Indigenous peoples who have been the object of colonialization. Such protection rules out Nomadic peoples who find themselves in a non-colonized State or arguably a colonizing State of other territories.

Second, the sense of law shared by members of Nomadic groups may well lack the deference to the centralized State despite the incorporation of such deference for Indigenous inhabitants. This deference is recognized and codified, for example, in various Reports of the Organization of American States (OAS).[9] The 15th meeting in the drafting of a Declaration on the Rights of Indigenous Peoples similarly provides that one has to be 'mindful' that Nomadic-Indigenous inhabitants 'play a special role in strengthening State institutions

---

9  OAS Permanent Council 'Nineteenth Meeting of Negotiations in the Quest for Points of Consensus: Draft American Declaration on the Rights of Indigenous Peoples' (17–19 May 2016) OEA/Ser.K/XVI GT/DADIN/doc.334/08 rev. 12. OAS Permanent Council 'Fifteenth Meeting of Negotiations in the Quest for Points of Consensus: Record of the Current Status of the Draft American Declaration on the Rights of Indigenous Peoples' (9–11 February 2015) OEA/Ser.K/XVl GT/DADIN/doc.334/08 rev.8, at para. 1. See also OAS Permanent Council 'Thirteenth Meeting of Negotiations in the Quest for Points of Consensus: Record of the Current Status of the Draft American Declaration on the Rights of Indigenous Peoples' (20 January 2011) OEA/Ser.K/XVI GT/DADIN/doc.334/08 rev. 6.

and in attaining unity based on democratic principles'.[10] By virtue of Art. IV of the draft American Declaration on the Rights of Indigenous Peoples,

> [n]othing in this Declaration may be interpreted as implying [...] any right to engage in any activity or to perform any act to the Charter [...] or construed as authorizing or encouraging any action which would dismember or impair, totally or in part, the territorial integrity or political unity of sovereign and independent States.[11]

The various Understandings by State officials, attached to the draft Declaration, reiterate the subjection of any Indigenous community to the sovereignty of the State. The statement of Colombia, for example, reminds one that the Declaration is not a legally binding norm for the State and the statement of Canada infers that the Declaration is subject to Canada's Constitution as if the latter lacks any deference to an international undertaking.[12]

Third, unlike the self-identity of Indigenous communities with fixed territorial spaces, Nomadic peoples frequently move because of factors external to their control. Climate is one such factor. Climate, for example, impacts the accessibility and availability to pasture and water, fish and animals, for example. A Nomadic community's movement also responds to the scarcity and movement itself of objects of dependence: goats, cattle, reindeer, seals, fish, and other objects of nature. Groups inhabiting places with extreme differences in climate may inhabit the shores of lakes and rivers during the summer and move inland during winter months in order to find protection from weather conditions. Climate and the scarcity of food impact a Nomadic community's traditions and self-identity.

Finally, I shall highlight in Section v.1 how the international treaty and declaratory law relating to the protection of Indigenous peoples possess gaps that

---

10   OAS Permanent Council 'Fifteenth Meeting of Negotiations in the Quest for Points of Consensus: Record of the Current Status of the Draft American Declaration on the Rights of Indigenous Peoples' (9–11 February 2015) OEA/Ser.K/XVl GT/DADIN/doc.334/08 rev.8, at para. 1.

11   OAS Permanent Council 'Nineteenth Meeting of Negotiations in the Quest for Points of Consensus: Draft American Declaration on the Rights of Indigenous Peoples' (17–19 May 2016) OEA/Ser.K/XVI GT/DADIN/doc.334/08 rev. 12, Art. IV.

12   See esp. the Statement of Canada to the effect that the relevant international undertakings are subject to the State's 'Constitution'. This is ironic in that the Canadian constitutional law incorporates international customary law except as regards criminal law. *R. v. Hape* [2007] 2 SCR 292, at paras 34–39, 53–56; *Ezokola v. Canada (Citizenship and Immigration)* 2 SCR 678, at paras 42–49, 51.

exclude the second (pastoralism and herding), the third (peripatetic) and even the first (hunting and fishing, in some circumstances) forms of Nomadism.

## IV   A Sense of Law in a Nomadic Community

The sense of law in a Nomadic community has slipped through the usual protections of international constitutionalism. How does the sense of law in a Nomadic community compete with a sense of law in international constitutionalism?

### 1  *Experienced Events*

Unlike the intellectually transcendent standards of international law and domestic constitutionalism, Nomadic law emanates from an experiential knowledge.[13] Such an experiential knowledge emanates from social relationships in contrast with the traditional analytic quest for intellectually transcendent sources, the sources being situated in a hierarchy of institutions such as judicial tribunals and a hierarchy of concepts with the concepts of constitutionalism at the pinnacle. One common feature of the sense of law shared by members of a Nomadic community, then, is the absence of a sharing of such sources.[14] At best, a Nomadic leader, drawing upon rituals, traditions, customs, the personal memories, and collective memories of the group, may gesture or articulate a pre-intellectual act that emanates from events experienced by members. Unwritten and unspoken events have inculcated ambiguous territorial borders of the group's pastures or familiar hunting grounds, for example. No institutional source, such as a legislature, court or an administrative agency, posits a rule as to whom may direct the sheep to graze here rather than there. The shepherd or herder follows the sheep or the reindeer. The shepherd directs sheep along this rather than that path. And yet, the moisture, temperate climate and rich vegetation needed and desired by the herd may well constrain where the herd goes.

---

13   I have elaborated the gist of experiential legal knowledge in 'Legal Time' in (2018) 31 Canadian J. of Jurisprudence and Law 281; *Statelessness: the Enigma of an International Community* (Hart 2014/2015), at Chs 6–9; 'Human Rights and the Forgotten Acts of Meaning in the Social Conventions of Conceptual Jurisprudence' (2014) 2 Metodo: International Studies in Phenomenology and Philosophy 169; 'The Ghosts of Cemetery Road: Two Forgotten Indigenous Women and the Crisis of Analytical Jurisprudence' (2011) 35 Australian Feminist L. Journal 3.

14   C. Bailey, *Bedouin Law from Sinai and the Negev: Justice Without Government* (Yale University Press 2009).

## 2  Immanent Law

This takes one to a second feature of the sense of law in Nomadic communities. Here, a sense of law emanates *from* the members independent of the laws of a sovereign State.

In particular, a practice, custom, ritual, story or symbol of the first two forms of Nomadism is personally experienced in the day-to-day life of a Nomadic member. Collective memories especially embody how a Nomadic community, including of the third form, responds to an external constraint. Evidence suggests that the member of the community may act without the deference expected in constitutionalism.[15] As documented of the Bedouin community, the personally experienced events, as manifesting a sense of law of a Nomadic group, exist only if activated by the community, not by the State's institutions.[16] Similarly, the Roma of Rumania, it has been documented, lack the sense of rulership characterizing non-Roma laws; the politics of a Roma community are independent of the centralized State politics.[17] The point is that Nomadic laws emanate from events experienced as a personal or collective memory.

To take another example of the immanent character of a Nomadic community's sense of law, such an immanence is recognized by the Constitution of Norway. By Art. 110 (a) of the Constitution, '[i]t is the responsibility of the authorities of the State to create conditions enabling the Sami people to preserve and develop its language, culture and way of life'. The Sámi Parliament possesses the jurisdiction to enact laws concerning the historical rights, use of ancestral land, and an understanding of what the Sámi consider obligatory. In effect, the Constitution incorporates the Sámi into the State-centric legal order. It is now State-constituting people with its own Parliament.[18] That said, most Norwegian constitutional texts are silent regarding any State jurisdictional authority over law-making, law-applying and law-enforcement in the autonomous governmental structures of Nomadic communities. In addition,

---

15  *Guerin v. R* [1984] 2 SCR 335, at 381; *St. Catharine's Milling and Lumber Co. v. The Queen* (1888) 14 App. Cas. 46, at 54, per Lord Watson; C. Bailey, *Bedouin Law from Sinai and the Negev: Justice Without Government* (Yale University Press 2009); D. Chatty (ed.), *Nomadic Societies in the Middle East and North Africa: Entering the 1st Century* (Brill 2006), at 242; *Calder v. Attorney-General of British Columbia* [1973] SCR 313, at 328.

16  C. Bailey, *Bedouin Law from Sinai and the Negev: Justice Without Government* (Yale University Press 2009), at 12–22.

17  See esp. Peter Berda with Forew by Fred R. Myers, *Materializing Difference: Consumer Culture, Politics, and Ethnicity among Romanian Roma* (Toronto: University of Toronto Press, 2019), 23–34.

18  A. Sandberg, 'Collective Rights in a Modernizing North—on Institutionalizing Sámi and Local Rights to Land and Water in Northern Norway' (2008) 2.2 Int'l J. of the Commons 269.

a deep sense of law, independent of the State, remains with the Sámi peoples. This immanent sense of law has embodied the acts of the Sámi through the centuries.[19] Immanently induced customs, social practices, rituals, spiritual beliefs and other social phenomena contrast with the acts of intellectualism associated with such concepts as a right or property or jurisdiction.

Added to the above, social events may have demarcated a parcel of land over which herds graze or over which the community travels from place to place. Similarly, customs may pertain to where one group may fish or which fields of fruit may be the object of gathering for this or that group. Events demarcate the use of land by a Nomadic group and others who may possess title to the same land or to adjoining land. Mountains, rivers, fish or animals may be the object of spiritual beliefs for one group and not another. Such beliefs emanate from the members' experienced events through experiential time in contrast with a structured measurable time on a clock or calendar. The immanent sense of such an experienced time is induced from personal and collective memories of the members.

This immanent character to a Nomadic sense of law also contrasts with the market justice system that lies in the background of the contemporary concept of constitutionalism. This especially so of Peripatetic Nomads. To take the example of the Sámi peoples, land, water and resources are not valued with reference to land title, exchange value, markets, rights or interest group politics as manifested in the State's institutional structure. Rather, land, water or other resources, such as reindeer, are valued for their opportunity for food, temporal security and their symbolic role in the spiritual well-being of the Sámi. More generally, nature, as represented by land, sacred mountains or a lake, may possess a soul.[20] Events are experienced through such an animistic understanding of the world. Collective memories play into the sense of law shared by members of a Nomadic group. The most important feature of such collective memories with respect to the Sámi peoples, for example, is the interdependent relation of the group's context-specific meanings with the environment in which a particular Sámi group has found itself. A recent study of the Roma in Rumania has described how the sense of politics in the Roma community is independent of the rulership sense of law as a centralized pyramidal institutional structure.[21]

---

19  M. Ahrén, 'Indigenous Peoples' Culture, Customs, and Traditions and Customary Law—The Sami People's Perspective' (2006) 21.1 Ariz J. Int'l & Comp L. 63.
20  L. Waters, 'Indigenous Peoples and the Environment: Convergence from a Nordic Perspective' (2001/2002) 20.2 UCLA J. Envtl L. & Pol'y 237, at 252.
21  See Peter Berda with Forew by Fred R. Myers, *Materializing Difference: Consumer Culture, Politics, and Ethnicity among Romanian Roma* (Toronto: University of Toronto Press, 2019), 23–34.

## 3  In an Environment Not of One's Own Choosing

The member finds her- or himself *in* an environment. The member of a Nomadic group does not necessarily choose this or that legal avenue nor does the member choose to live here or there. The member of a Nomadic group is thrown into an external context. The resource where the group has been living may have been replete. Climate may have caused a draught, blizzard, or the melting of the Arctic. A municipality may be intentionally or effectively requiring or enforcing a travelling group to leave the area, or to lack health facilities or otherwise constitutionally protected social security, a housing standard or access to public schooling. The Nomadic group may well find itself in mercantile practices or conventions, taken for granted by other communities, about right and wrong. The everyday practices of members of the group may well differ and contradict such expectations. Their laws are constituted from an ethos that remains independent of the sense of law in and by a State.

With such external constraints, the Nomadic group must respond *to* the environment in which it finds itself. The Sámi, for example, must negotiate with the weather, climate, topography, scarcity of a source for food, and movement of the reindeer.[22] Such an environment is not necessarily the product of nature, however. As noted, the gatherer, hunter or shepherd in a traditional community of Nomadic people may be presented with two diverging trails. A stampede of animals or a virus may also present an external coping constraint.

## 4  One's Environing World (*Umwelt*)

Such an action or performative character of a Nomadic group's pre-intellectual legal culture contrasts with the contemporary basis of legitimacy of an adjudicative decision—the intentional justification of the decision with universally applicable norms. But the environment is not of a Nomadic group's own choosing. Further, the Nomadic group's environment does not enter into constitutionalism until *after* the *a priori* universal norms of the constitutionalism are applied onto the juridical representation of the group's experienced world. In effect, the application of a constitutional right withdraws members of a Nomadic group from their context-specific social practices. Their practices are reduced to general categories already elements of the centralized legal order. At best, if recognized as legal persons (that is, as nationals), Nomadic members are categorized as a 'minority'. As such, they are supposedly to be treated equally with other 'minorities' as if all minorities share the same sense of legal obligation towards a State-centric legal order. Their rituals, practices, spiritual

---

[22]  M. Ahrén, 'Indigenous Peoples' Culture, Customs, and Traditions and Customary Law—The Saami People's Perspective' (2006) 21.2 Ariz J. Int'l & Comp L. 63, at 69–70.

beliefs and experiential world are thereby non-legal phenomena of a subjectivity alien to the intellectually transcendent concepts of constitutionalism.

Returning to the first and second forms of nomadism, the communities are constrained by a scarcity of resources, such as prey, fish, reindeer, goats, seals, or cattle. In addition, unusual and rapid climate conditions have impacted the traditional reliance upon vegetation for grazing. Such has recently been experienced by the Mongolian Nomads, the Bedouin, the Sámi of Russia and Scandanavia, and the nomadic groups in West Africa as examples only as examples. The social and economic conditions of the 120,000 in Kuwait are of concern.[23] With regard to peripatetic nomadic peoples, such as the traveller groups, the partial dependence upon the mixed economy has sometimes been impacted by the interpretation or application of a municipal housing by-law. For example, the by-laws in France, Italy, Portugal and Spain have placed constraints upon the length of time that the Roma may camp at a location.[24] Documentation is offered elsewhere concerning the impact of local State laws for access of children to public education. As an example, parents not infrequently change the names of their children in order that they gain access to the territory of another State. Upon the latter's deportation of the children, the children's name differs from that of the parents, thereby disqualifying the children from access to schooling. The administration of refugee laws has functioned to obstruct Roma entry and then, when the names of children have been changed, to render problematic their return to the territory of recent origin. The frequent movement of peripatetic nomads has impacted a difficulty of accessing social security as well as public education for children.[25]

In particular, a Nomadic group lacks the conscious and voluntary decision-making which is taken for granted in a modern State-centric legal culture. The latter role of intentionality, of course, is part and parcel of both criminal and civil laws of a modern State. Instead, a member of a Nomadic group acts because 'that is the way members have always acted'. If a leader of a Nomadic group renders a decision, the boundary of what counts as a legitimate decision is not consciously posited by a council, assembly or judicial tribunal. The boundary of a Nomadic group's constraint is not necessarily authored by the group. Nomadic groups have to cope with a situation not of their own choosing.

---

23   For documentation, see W.E. Conklin, *Statelessness: the Enigma of an International Community* (Hart 2014/2015), 123.

24   For this and other legal constraints upon Traveller communities, see W.E. Conklin, *Statelessness: the Enigma of an International Community* (Hart 2014/2015), 124.

25   See Ecorys (formerly ECOTEC Research and Consulting) 'Study on the School Education of Children pf Occupational Travellers in the EU: A Final Report to the Directorate eu/education/more-information/doc/travel_en.pdf, 11–34.

The place of a Nomadic group thrown into external constraints contrasts with the presumed sense of individual freedom and of rationally informed legal constraints.

## 5   Collective Memories

From the standpoint of members of a Nomadic group, in contrast with the adjudicative act in constitutionalism, a physical object or a land mass may function as a symbol in the group's collective memory.[26] A collective memory about a land mass, such as a mountain, a rock, a river with plentiful fish, a forest protecting reindeer from blizzards, or other natural objects may symbolize (as opposed to signify) a spiritual as well as the source of life for a Nomadic community. A collective memory is a memory of the group. It pre-exists the member's entry into the group. Such phenomena are not the product of justifying intellectual reflection, deliberation or conscious decisions characterizing international constitutionalism. Nor does a Nomadic group recognize a State border as the controlling factor in the need for the group to move its herd, to seek an alternate source of fish, to seek employment or the like, or to possess a legal bond with each other. Nor does a Nomadic group necessarily possess loyalty to any government as the dominating factor in the group's social structure. Nor does membership in a Nomadic group depend upon a decision of the State concerning legal membership or nationality in the State. Nor is the Nomadic group's immanently experienced sense of law the consequence of a conscious decision of the group.

A collective memory, membership in a Nomadic group, or a sense of obligation as to the grazing or fishing grounds or habitat of the group is immanent in the way of life of the group. As with the externality of climate, local inhabitants, the regulatory role of the State and the like, such an immanent character to a Nomadic collective memory radically differs in nature from the centralized governmentality and conscious decision-making of a State bureaucracy. Aside from such externally experienced factors, what is more important to the nature of law in a Nomadic group is the immanent character of a law in a Nomadic group. Such an immanent character to collective memory concerns the habitual grazing parcels, the paths to cross from one parcel to another, the climate and scarcity of animal and fishing resources, the marriage partner of a prospective member, the participation in the group's rituals, and the fair-dealing of the prospective member with other members or the Nomadic group.

---

26   S. Karstedt, *Legal Institutions and Collective Memories* (Hart 2009); A. Assmann, *Cultural Memory and Western Civilization: Functions, Media, Archives* (CUP 2011); W.E. Conklin, *Statelessness: the Enigma of an International Community* (Hart 2014/2015), at 205–206.

## 6  The Strangeness of Constitutionalism's Structure of Concepts

Because of the role of an immanently experienced sense of law and because of the need to cope with external natural and human constraints that threaten the existential world of the Nomadic group, international and constitutional standards are brought *to* the Nomadic group. That is, jurisdiction, rights, property, separation of powers, independence of courts and the like are brought *to* the Nomadic member as a possible legal person. What are brought to the member of a Nomadic group—what jurists have traditionally considered as 'laws'—are rules, principles and other intellectual standards-concepts, not events that the member has experienced.

From the standpoint of constitutionalism, such concepts apply to an individual if the State's judiciary recognize or fail to recognize the member as a legally defined person. Such a person is an intellectual construction as opposed to an experiential being. The legal personhood is imposed upon the individual member of a Nomadic group and the member's experienced events. Constitutionalism is thereby presumed to exist analytically prior to the experienced events of the Nomadic group. Indeed, the priority in time, space and analysis of intelligible standards of international constitutionalism are arguably the key to the 'rule of law'. In sum, law is presumed to exist analytically and temporally prior to the experiential world of the Nomadic group.

In contrast, however, the sense of law from memories—personal and collective—of events emanates *from* the experienced events of members of the Nomadic group. Even if a State institution or official recognizes a member of a Nomadic group as a national (that is, as a legal member of the State and therefore of the international community) by virtue of the reserved domain of the international community, the sense of law experienced by a member of the Nomadic group is submerged inside the State-centric legal discourse. The member of a Nomadic community thereby becomes alien or strange to that discourse. From the standpoint of the Nomadic members, the international institutions and norms as well as the domestic constitutionalism risk being perceived and understood as strange. In this schism between how a member understands law and how a jurist understands law, one must not forget that international constitutionalism and domestic constitutionalism, again, aims at constraining the executive arm of a State-centric legal order. The immanent character of a Nomadic law is personal in the sense of having been experienced in context-specific events.

## 7  *Higher Laws?*

In addition, a sense of law in a Nomadic culture combines with social relationships to such an extent that, unlike modern constitutionalism, it is difficult to understand what one might call Nomadic social-laws as if posited consistent with a constitutionalism is an autonomous and intellectually 'higher' than day-to-day context-specific experienced events. Complex social relationships, often nuanced, complex and subtle social assumptions and expectations, guide action inside and between Nomadic groups as if the action is law-creative.[27] The Nomadic laws are often induced from oral communications manifesting a sense of law.[28] Events may be so repeated—or what seems to members as a repetition—by the Bedouin, for example, that the memories of the events have identified a boundary to each community's grazing territory.[29] The clan conveys permission for the clan member to act.[30] The clan itself possesses authority to exclude an individual from membership in the clan although the clan member may choose to leave the clan.[31] The customs are transmitted orally and by gestures.[32]

## 8   The Left-over

The immanent sense of law experienced by a Nomadic community is a left-over to constitutionalism's directed constraint and resistance to the power of political rulers and the executive arm of a State's governmentality. The 'left-over' has been reinforced by several features of constitutionalism working to exclude Nomadic peoples from constitutional protection. Aside from the assumed image of Nomadic peoples as lawless and situated at the low end of the ladder of social hierarchy, Nomadic groups are frequently on the move. Without a fixity on a territory, the inhabitants could hardly be said to possess a legal claim to own a parcel of land as property, let alone as private property.

---

27   C. Bailey, *Bedouin Law* at 16–18, 60–100.
28   *Guerin v. R* [1984] 2 SCR 335, at 388; W.O. Weyrauch, 'Oral Legal Tradition of Gypsies and Some American Equivalents' in W.O. Weyrauch (ed.), *Gypsy Law: Romani Legal Traditions and Culture* (University of California Press 2001), at 243–275, 272–273; F.H. Stewart, 'Customary Law among the Bedouin of the Middle East and North Africa' in D. Chatty (ed.), *Nomadic Societies in the Middle East and North Africa: Entering the 1st Century* (Brill 2006) 239, at 252; C. Bailey, *Bedouin Law from Sinai and the Negev: Justice Without Government* (Yale University Press 2009), at 209.
29   N. Kram, 'The Naqab Bedouins: Legal Struggles for Land Ownership Rights in Israel' in A. Amara, I. Abu-Saad and O. Yiftachel (eds), *Indigenous (In)justice: Human Rights Law and Bedouin Arabs in the Naqab/Negev* (Harvard University Press 2012) 126, at 139–141.
30   C. Bailey, *Bedouin Law from Sinai and the Negev: Justice Without Government* (Yale University Press 2009), at 60–100.
31   F.H. Stewart, 'Customary Law among the Bedouin of the Middle East and North Africa' in Chatty (ed.), *Nomadic Societies in the Middle East and North Africa* (Leiden: Brill, 2006), 239–279, at 252.
32   W.O. Weyrauch, 'Oral Legal Tradition of Gypsies and Some American Equivalents' in W.O. Weyrauch (ed.), *Gypsy Law: Romani Legal Traditions and Culture* (University of California Press 2001), at 243–275.

## 9 The Legal Bond as a Social Bond

One needs to return to the early modern theory of constitutionalism in order to appreciate the critical issues about how constitutionalism submerges the sense of law experienced in a Nomadic community. Rousseau explained that 'the essence of the body politic consists in the union of obedience and liberty, and these words, *subject* and *sovereign*, are correlatives, the notion underlying them being expressed in the one word, 'citizen'.[33] A Nomadic group, for example, would only become a 'subject' by the State's conferral of citizenship onto the individual member of the Nomadic community. According to Rousseau's contemporary, Vattel, a State's decision whether an individual should be recognized as a national (that is, as a legal person) depended upon the individual's allegiance to the State. If lacking in allegiance to the State, the individual could be expelled from the State's territory.[34] The State could thereby claim its own constitutional authority over any inhabitant on its territory. Such a universalist claim incorporated members of Nomadic groups.[35] Although they struggled with the idea, both David Hume and Adam Smith again left it to the State to decide whether an individual possessed allegiance to the State.[36] But the frequent movement of Nomadic communities leaves their allegiance to the State's authority suspect. An individual's use or ownership of a fixed territorial space is pivotal to the perception of allegiance by State officials. The legal bond as a bond between individual inhabitant and the State is thereby suspect.

In sum, a legal bond of the individual–State relation has been manifested by a one-way direction from the State *to* the individual.[37] As the majority of the Court has stated in *Nottebohm*, a leading judgment of the International Court of Justice, '[i]t is for every sovereign State, to settle by its own legislation the rules relating to the acquisition of its nationality, and to confer that nationality by naturalization granted by its own organs in accordance with that legislation'.[38] As a Canadian judge has also asserted, 'the status of statelessness is not one that is optional for an applicant. The condition of not having a country of nationality must be one that is beyond the authority of the applicant to

---

33  J.-J. Rousseau, *The Social Contract* (1762), at bk. III, ch. 13[5], 111.
34  E. Vattel, *The Law of Nations* (1797; Liberty Fund 2008), at bk. 1 C 19, bk. 1, C 19, at para. 223 (3).
35  Ibid., at bk. 1, C 3, at paras 26, 36–37, 69.
36  D. Hume, *A Treatise of Human Nature* (1738; OUP 1978), at 549; A. Smith, *Lectures on Jurisprudence* (1762–62; Liberty Press 1978), at 403, para. 18.
37  Though an alternative sense of a legal bond can also be drawn from 19th and 20th century international law (see W.E. Conklin, *Statelessness: the Enigma of an International Community* (Hart 2014/2015), at 196–199).
38  *Nottebohm (Liechtenstein v. Guatemala) (Second Phase)* [1955] ICJ Rep 4, at 20.

control. Otherwise, a person could claim statelessness merely by renouncing his or her former citizenship'.[39] Even when the ICJ and PCA have recognized 'certain ties of a legal character' for a Nomadic people, the group has had to possess allegiance to the State.[40] Without a fixed settlement on a State's territory, the risk is that a Nomadic community can hardly be perceived as exhibiting allegiance *to* the State. Universalist constitutional rights have thereby lacked a social basis in a Nomadic community. The freedom of the State to deny constitutional recognition to Nomadic peoples is especially pronounced in a 'state of emergency'.[41] The consequence is that members of Nomadic groups may remain unrecognized as legal persons on a State's territory.

## v  Four Arguments to Protect Nomadic Peoples

Against the background of the incongruity of international constitutionalism and Nomadic legal cultures, the issue arises 'what constitutional principle is harmed by virtue of a State's action or inaction towards Nomadic communities?' The response to such an issue is complex and nuanced. However, four very different approaches to such an issue can be gleaned from international and constitutional adjudication.

### 1  *The Problematic of Decolonization as the Structured Basis for a Nomadic Right*

There is a risk that the international law recognition and protection of Nomadic peoples living in a formerly or present colonized State is under-inclusive of Nomadic peoples. To be sure, there is much textual support that one is 'Indigenous' if one is left to self-declare oneself as Indigenous. If the individual member of a Nomadic group finds her- or himself on the territory of a State without a colonial past, then the individual is excluded from treaties and international customary norms addressing Indigenous peoples.

The problem is that most Nomadic groups find themselves in 'independent' States where they were not Indigenous to the territory. Putting such a possibility

---

39  *Bouianova v. Canada (Minister of Employment and Immigration)* (1993) 67 FTR 74, at para. 12.
40  *Western Sahara (Advisory Opinion)* [1975] ICJ Rep 12, at para. 152; *Territorial Dispute (Libyan Arab Jamahiriya/Chad)* [1994] ICJ Rep 6, especially the Dissenting Opinion of Judge Sette-Camara; *Eritrea v. Yemen (Phase One: Territorial Sovereignty and Scope of the Dispute)* (1998) 114 ILR 1, at para. 123 (PCA).
41  C. Schmitt, *Political Theology: Four Chapters on the Concept of Sovereignty* (1922; University of Chicago Press 2005); G. Agamben, *State of Exception* (University of Chicago Press 2005).

to the side for the moment, the terms of the UNDRIP have often been said to be 'aspirational' and therefore of no legally obligatory character.[42] Even if such an opinion were not considered, the proclamation may well provide *indicia* of a customary international legal obligation. The central focus of UNDRIP, however, concerns the decolonization of the Indigenous Nomadic communities. Nor are the latter protected by ILO Convention No. 169 concerning Indigenous and Tribal Peoples in Independent Countries (1989) and ILO Convention No. 107 concerning the Protection and Integration of Indigenous and other Tribal and Semi-Tribal Populations in Independent Countries (1957).[43] That is, the Declaration and the two treaties do not extend legal recognition to Nomadic groups that were not colonized or to States that exist independent of colonialism.[44] Their habitual residence varies through time. As to the scope of the Declaration and the two treaties, the objective is set out in a way which only possibly addresses some Nomadic groups of the first of the three forms identified above and then only if the groups were Indigenous to a territory where they were colonized. This is especially so of the peripatetic Nomadic peoples who move from place to place in the quest of employment, non-discriminatory host residents and by-laws, and congenial climate. Further, they had to be Nomadic and continuously Nomadic to the present day.

The two multilateral treaties have explicitly addressed the form of Nomadic community as traditional (that is tribal). ILO Convention No. 107 aimed to protect and 'integrate' Indigenous 'and other tribal and semi-tribal populations' into 'independent' or sovereign States. This treaty may be outdated shortly after my effort is in print in that States may denounce the treaty's obligations between 2 June 2019 and 2 June 2020. The provisions of the treaty, however, remain indicative of the exclusionary legacy of an international constitutionalism.

The preamble of ILO Convention No. 107, as an example, sets out the objective of protecting and integrating Indigenous 'and other tribal and semi-tribal populations in independent countries'. The preamble continues that such populations must be 'not yet integrated into the national community'. In such

---

42  UNGA Res 61/178 'United Nations Declaration on the Rights of Indigenous Peoples' (13 September 2007).
43  ILO 'Convention No. 169 concerning Indigenous and Tribal Peoples in Independent Countries' (adopted 27 June 1989, entered into force 5 September 1991) 1650 UNTS 383; ILO 'Convention No. 107 concerning the Protection and Integration of Indigenous and other Tribal and Semi-Tribal Populations in Independent Countries' (adopted 26 June 1957, entered into force 2 June 1959) 328 UNTS 247.
44  See also UNGA Res 1541 (XV) 'Principles Which Should Guide Members in Determining Whether or Not an Obligation Exists to Transmit the Information Called for under Art. 73 e of the Charter' (15 December 1960).

a situation, the social, economic or cultural 'situation hinders' such populations from 'benefiting fully from the rights and advantages' enjoyed in a State. Consistent with the legacy of Nomadic peoples in European legal thought, the treaty takes a hierarchy of societies for granted. If a Nomadic group is 'tribal' or 'semi-tribal', to use the terms of the treaty, the community finds itself at the bottom of a hierarchy of societies. They have been 'prevented [...] from sharing fully in the *progress* of the national community *of which they form part*'.[45] Against the background of such an assumption, Art. 1 (1) (a) provides that social and economic conditions of such a community are at a 'less advanced stage' than the stage reached by the other social groups of the national community. Art. 1 (1) (b) adds that a member of a tribal or semi-tribal population is considered Indigenous if, first, he/she is a member by virtue of 'descent' (that is, blood-relation) of ancestry at conquest or colonialization. One study authorized by the UN Economic and Social Council states that 'descent' includes a 'caste or tribe-based' community.[46] In sum, any Nomadic community said to be 'Indigenous' is differentiated from a State-centric legal order. By Art. 1 (2), a 'semi-tribal' community is 'in the process of losing their tribal characteristics' though its members 'are not yet integrated into the national community'. By Art. 2, a government has the duty to protect 'populations' and to integrate them 'progressive[ly] into the life of their respective countries'. 'At that time' members of a Nomadic community are considered 'belong[ing]' to their own community rather than to the State.

The second treaty, ILO Convention No. 169, is an attempt to overcome an assimilationist presumption. Despite such an objective, both treaties share the objective of only addressing a traditional (or 'tribal') community that finds itself in a territory that was colonized. Aside from the requirement that a contemporary Nomadic community is only considered 'Indigenous' if it finds itself on the territory of an independent State that has been earlier colonized, the two treaties only extend to traditional communities, thereby excluding two of the forms of Nomadism (agricultural and peripatetic) identified above.

In particular, ILO Convention No. 169 only applies to two categories of individuals: first, 'tribal peoples in independent countries' distinguished from other peoples in the State. Such tribal peoples must possess a legal status 'wholly or partially regulated by their own customs or traditions' or by the State's special

---

45   Emphasis mine.
46   UN Commission on Human Rights 'Prevention of Discrimination and Protection of Indigenous Peoples and Minorities: Working Paper by R. Kalidas Wimala Goonesekere on the Topic of Discrimination Based on Work and Descent, Submitted pursuant to Sub-Commission Resolution 2000/4' (14 June 2001) UN Doc. E/CN.4/Sub.2/2001/16, at para. 7.

laws and regulations. By virtue of its preamble, the State must recognize the 'aspirations' of the peoples to control their own institutions, ways of life and economic development as well as to develop 'their identities, languages and religions'. This duty is subject to the recognition of such autonomy 'within the framework of the States in which they live'.

The second category includes peoples from independent States. Here, they must be regarded Indigenous to a territory by their 'descent' (blood relation) from the critical date of conquest, colonization or the establishment of State borders and retain some or all of their institutions. Art. 1 (1) (2) expressly defers to the self-identification of a person as Indigenous. This might suggest that any member of a Nomadic group might be entitled to declare her/himself as Indigenous. Pushed to its limits, such a possibility would nullify the very objective of the treaty to privilege the rights of persons Indigenous in the communities identified in Art. 1, however. The second and third form of Nomadism would certainly be excluded from the intended scope of the treaty. So, too, the first form would be excluded if the Nomadic group inhabited the territory of a State that emerged independent of colonialism. Although Arts 14–16 recognize strong duties on the part of the State, such duties only relate to traditional communities that were objects of colonialism, conquest or State control of the territory on which the Nomadic group pursues its livelihood. Nomadic individuals and groups which exist independent of a colonial State are excluded from protection.

## 2 The Constitutional Obligation to Protect a Nomadic Group as a 'Minority'

### a  Protection of a 'Minority' from Standpoint of an International Customary Norm

There is another argument to the international and domestic recognition and protection of Nomadic groups. This draws from the second international law source for possible protection: namely, international human rights law. One critical feature of international human rights law and the basic texts of constitutionalism concerns the protection of a Nomadic group as a minority. A minority is generally considered an ethnic group which possesses an ethnic homeland. A 'homeland' represents a territorial space where the members of the minority can be territorially identified. Human rights treaties protect minorities on the basis of race, gender, religion and the like.[47]

---

47  Art. 2 (1) International Covenant on Civil and Political Rights (adopted 16 December 1966, entered into force 23 March 1976) 999 UNTS 171; Art. 5 (d) (iii) International Convention on the Elimination of all Forms of Racial Discrimination (opened for signature 7 March

As an example, Art. 26 of the ICCPR provides that '[i]n those States in which ethnic, religious or linguistic minorities exist, persons belonging to such minorities shall not be denied the right, in community with other members of their group, to enjoy their own culture, to profess and practise their own religion, or to use their own language'.[48] In like vein, Art. 8 of ILO Convention No. 169 incorporates 'fundamental rights defined by the national legal system and with internationally recognized human rights'. Art. 9 states that offences committed by members of an Indigenous group may be subject to the customary methods of the group as long as compatible with 'internationally recognized human rights'. By Art. 30 of the Rights of the Child Convention,

> [i]n those States in which ethnic, religious or linguistic minorities or persons of Indigenous origin exist, a child belonging to such a minority or who is Indigenous shall not be denied the right, in community with other members of his or her group, to enjoy his or her own culture, to profess and practise his or her own religion, or to use his or her own language.[49]

The UNDRIP follows up in Art. 46 (2) with the State duty to ensure that the rights of any Indigenous group (which, again, includes the first form of Nomadism that exists by virtue of existing in a colonized State) may be subject to the posited laws of the State or international human rights obligations. Such obligations 'shall be non-discriminatory and strictly necessary solely for the purpose of securing due recognition and respect for the rights and freedoms of others' as posited by the State institutions. The interpretation of the Declaration must be maintained with the principles of respect for human rights and non-discrimination aside from other well-known principles.

Several points suggest that the protection of a Nomadic group, as a 'minority', is suspect. For one thing, any Nomadic group's claim of possessing a sense of law separate from a sovereign State is questionable since the 'minority' is of the State. By Art. 29 (c) of the Convention on the Rights of the Child, for example, the 'minority' is subject to 'the national values of the country in which the child is living, the country from which he or she may originate, and for civilizations different from his or her own'.

---

1966, entered into force 4 January 1969) 660 UNTS 195. For domestic basic constitutional texts protective of a 'minority', see Art. 33 Slovak Constitution; Art. 18, 19, 20 (3) Romanian Constitution.

48   Arts 1 (1), 1 (2), 27 ICCPR; UN HRC 'General Comment No. 23: The Rights of Minorities (Art. 27)' (8 April 1994) GAOR 49th Session Supp 40 vol. 1, 106.

49   Convention on the Rights of the Child (adopted 20 November 1989, entered into force 2 September 1990) 1577 UNTS 3.

In addition, colonization has not always been completed in the territory which the Nomadic group presently inhabits.

Further, the proscribed categories of discrimination concerning a Nomadic group suggest grounds of social construction rather than biological grounds such as 'race' or 'ethnicity'. To take the Convention on the Rights of the Child as an example, a State has a duty of non-discrimination against all forms of discrimination and punishment on the basis of the *beliefs* of the child's parents, legal guardians and family members.[50] Art. 2 (2) of the Convention continues that the State has a duty to protect the child. Art. 30 similarly recognizes a State duty to protect a member of an *ethnic, religious or linguistic* 'minority' 'to enjoy his or her own *culture*, to profess and practice his or her own *religion*, or to use his or her *own language*'.[51] Such grounds of discrimination against a Nomadic group member are non-biological in contrast with such criteria as race, ethnicity and the like. This point is reaffirmed by Art. 29 (c) of the Convention on the Rights of the Child. Art. 29 (c) recognizes a State duty pertaining to the education of a child with 'respect for the child's parents, his or her own cultural identity, language and values'. 'National origin' is certainly unlikely to be a category addressing such a Nomadic group since the group frequently moves from one State's territory to another's even when one is an infant or child. Many Nomadic group members are members by virtue of culture rather than descent or ethnic origin, race or colour. More importantly, perhaps, it is difficult to consider a Nomadic community as a 'minority' like any other ethnic or racial 'minority' in a modern State. Some Nomadic communities represent the majority or substantial number of the population in a State. The grounds of discrimination against members of a Nomadic group may well be manifested by the tradition of caste such as one finds in Bangladesh, India, Nepal, Pakistan and Sri Lanka. It is difficult to understand caste as an ethnic or national origin, or a race. Perhaps 'descent' or blood-relation could be used to categorize members of a caste.

Finally, the early focus upon an individual right as if a bounded territorial space protecting an individual has also expanded into the concept of collective or 'communal' rights.[52] Some collective rights also miss the nature of the legal cultures of Nomadic groups, however. As an example, most constitutional bills of rights entrench individual rights and, by doing so, the nature of the legal cultures of communal bonding into a Nomadic group is undervalued if not legally unrecognizable. The assimilation of Nomadic cultures into a State-centric

---

50   Ibid. Emphasis mine.
51   Emphasis mine.
52   *R v. Powley* [2003] 2 SCR 207, at para. 24.

constitutional regime has been aided by constitutions inscribed in a code. This assimilation has been the case, for example, in Norway with an amendment to the written constitution whereby the Sámi have been recognized for their historical rights, their ancient use of lands and their perceptions of rights.[53]

b     Are Nomadic Peoples a 'Minority'?

The UN General Assembly has resolved that States have an obligation to protect 'persons belonging to national or ethnic, religious or linguistic minorities'.[54] Any one group is distinguished from others on the basis of social, cultural and economic conditions. Art. 1 (1) ILO Convention No. 169 analogically extends to Nomadic peoples in understanding the identity of a minority as including 'their own customs or traditions' that 'retain some or all of their own social, economic, cultural and political institutions'.[55] The issue remains, however, whether international and domestic tribunals possess the enforcement mechanisms to protect and to establish the social, economic and political conditions to recognize and protect the Nomadic group as a minority.[56]

c     The Strangeness of 'Collective Rights' in a Nomadic Legal Culture

The deeper issue, independent of 'what is a minority', concerns whether the domestic and global constitutional protection of minorities reduces and abstracts from the immanent and experiential character of the sense of law shared by members of a Nomadic community. There are two elements of the higher-ordered international constitutionalism that contradict and arguably undermine the sense of law shared by members of a Nomadic community. First, the constitutionalism and internationalism have generally held out that a sense of law and of remedies protects an individual rather than a community. It is difficult to isolate an individual member from a Nomadic community, however. Such a communal sense of a right continues temporally after

---

53   A. Sandberg, 'Collective Rights in a Modernizing North—on Institutionalizing Sámi and Local Rights to Land and Water in Northern Norway' (2008) 2.2 Int'l J. of the Commons 269, at 279.

54   UNGA Res 47/135 'Declaration on the Rights of Persons Belonging to National or Ethnic, Religious and Linguistic Minorities' (18 December 1992).

55   Art. 1 (1) ILO Convention No. 169.

56   J. Gilbert, *Nomadic Peoples and Human Rights* (Routledge 2014); J.P. Liégeois, The Council of Europe and Roma: 40 Years of Action (Council of Europe 2012), at 111–125; A.K. Meijknecht, *Minority Protection, Standards and Reality: Implementation of Council of Europe Standards in Slovakia, Romania and Bulgaria* (Asser Press 2004), at 51–90.

constitutionalism has taken hold of State-centric adjudication.[57] The second is that a minority right abstracts from and reduces the multiplicity of experienced events of a Nomadic group, let alone the multiplicity of differently experienced events by a Nomadic group as a 'minority'. The effect is that the sense of law shared by members of any Nomadic community is submerged in the official (that is, legal) intellectually transcendental language.

With respect to the first element of constitutional protection, the common law has highlighted a right as an individual, not a collective, possession. A Nomadic right has been described as *sui generis* ('unique', 'peculiar') by virtue of the incongruity of such an individualism with a communal right.[58] The consequence is that the dominant cultural view has considered the law as an aggregate of individual rights. The ICCPR Optional Protocol[59] only permits individual Nomadic persons and individual Nomadic victims at that, for example, to access the Human Rights Committee. In addition, although collective rights are often entrenched in coded constitutions, such 'collective' rights are attributed to groups as if the group is an individual with an exclusionary boundary. Property is attributed to the individual, such as an individual person or the sovereign State as bounded individual. The State's exclusionary sense of title to land has also coloured the constitutional protection of Nomadic peoples as a minority.[60] The 'common interest' of a community is held out as an aggregate of individual interests rather than of the ethos of a community.

The second element of the transcendentalism of international constitutionalism concerns how the multiplicity of diverse Nomadic groups is abstracted into a general category as if the experienced events being categorized are invariably the same from one Nomadic community to the next and from one member of a Nomadic community to the next member. I have retrieved above, however, that a Nomadic minority possesses a radically different sense of law than that of a State-centric administrative structure. The latter enforces rules and other intellectualized standards. What is important to appreciate is that this very sense of a 'minority' is encapsulated with reference to such a State-centric legal discourse.

---

57   *Guerin v. R* [1984] 2 SCR 335, at 376–379 per Dickson; *Roberts v. Canada* [1989] 1 SCR 322, at 340; *Delgamuukw v. British Columbia* [1997] 3 SCR 1010, at 1082.
58   *Delgamuukw v. British Columbia* [1997] 3 SCR 1010, at 1014, 1082–1083 per Lamer C.J.C.; *Calder v. Attorney-General of British Columbia* [1973] SCR 313, at 328.
59   Optional Protocol to the International Covenant on Civil and Political Rights (adopted 16 December 1966, entered into force 23 March 1976) 999 UNTS 302.
60   UN HRC 'General Comment No. 23: The Rights of Minorities (Art. 27)' (8 April 1994) GAOR 49th Session Supp 40 vol. 1, 106, at 158; UN HRC 'Communication No. 760/1997, *Diergaardt et al v. Namibia*' (7 July 1998) UN Doc. CCPR/C/63/D/760/1997, at para. 10.6.

The reductive character of the transcendental international constitutionalism is exemplified by the experienced events of very different complex Indigenous communities, some of which remain Nomadic to this day. Despite the fact that Canada's Indigenous inhabitants find themselves in five very different language groups, each with its own dialect, and despite their very different immanently experienced sense of law amongst Nomadic communities prior to the political conquest, contact and sovereignty, the Canadian Supreme Court has reduced constitutional rights of Indigenous inhabitants as if there is an essence to 'Indianness', to use the term of the Court. One is hard pressed to access the 'essence' or 'core' of such an 'Indianness' that is said to lie at 'the heart' of the constitutional recognition of an 'Aboriginal' person.[61] It is as if the legal person associated with an 'Aboriginal right' hinges upon the fact of one's 'Indianness'. The Court leaves it to governmental officials to decide who exhibits such 'Indianness' in context-specific events. Once a member of a Nomadic community is so reduced to the category 'Indianness', the member may become entitled to State support concerning welfare, public education, health benefits, legal employment, entertainment and spiritual regulations. The sense of law in a particular context-specific Nomadic community risks being either assimilated into or quashed by the dominant, State-centric legal culture.

## 3   The Use of Land

Aside from the claim that Nomadic peoples are protected as Indigenous and aside from the claim that Nomadic peoples are a 'minority', there is a third argument that addresses the protection of Nomadic peoples. This concerns the dependence of the first two forms of Nomadism upon the Nomadic community's use of land. Because peripatetic Nomadic groups are frequently moving and dependent upon temporary employment and other external factors such as municipal by-laws, land use is of lesser importance than to a claim of habitual residence, however transient. Once again, however, the approach is problematic.

### a   The Argument

I have highlighted how a State is legally obligated to protect a Nomadic people if the community finds itself on a territory whose State has emerged sovereign from a formerly colonized context. The argument draws particularly from ILO Convention No. 169 which addresses Indigenous and tribal peoples of an independent, formerly colonized State. In such a context, according to Art. 13 (2),

---

61   *Delgamuukw v. British Columbia* [1997] 3 SCR 1010, at paras 270, 271 per Lamer C.J.C.; *Dick v. The Queen* [1985] 2 SCR 309, at 326–328; *R v. Coté* [1996] 3 SCR 139, at 191.

the individual or group is entitled to 'the total environment of the areas which the peoples concerned occupy or otherwise use'. By Art. 14, such a Nomadic community may use a parcel of land if the land is 'not exclusively occupied by them, but to which they have traditionally had access for their subsistence and traditional activities'. Art. 14 (1) then explicitly addresses that 'particular attention shall be paid to the situation of Nomadic peoples and shifting cultivators [the second form of Nomadism] in this respect'. Art. 14 (2) provides a State duty to identify the lands which have been traditionally occupied and to guarantee 'an effective protection of their rights of ownership and possession'. By Art. 14 (3), land disputes with Nomadic residents, however, must be established 'within the national legal system'. By Arts 16 (1) and (2), one may not be removed from such lands unless 'relocation' is considered necessary. In that case, the consent of the Nomadic group is required. If consent cannot be obtained, 'national laws and regulations' as to the relocation procedure must be followed. By Art. 16 (3), such relocated traditional Nomadic groups possess 'the right to return to their traditional lands'. If the State removes such a Nomadic people from the traditional use of land, such an act shall be an 'exceptional measure' with their 'free and informed consent' with due process and with full compensation 'in money or kind'. By Art. 4 (2), a government possesses the duty to 'guarantee effective protection of their rights of ownership and possession'.

When this treaty is linked with the UNDRIP, a case might be made that the State owes a customary international duty to recognize, respect and protect a Nomadic community that has taken form on a territory claimed by a colonial or decolonized State. By Art. 11 of the UNDRIP, Nomadic peoples Indigenous to a colonized State 'shall not be forcibly removed from their lands or territories'. Again, 'the free, prior and informed consent' must be given by the Nomadic-Indigenous group with a 'fair and just compensation' with the option of return. Art. 16 explicitly addresses Nomadic peoples. For one thing, States possess a duty to ensure that Nomadic groups that are Indigenous possess

> (d) access to water resources on their ancestral lands is protected from encroachment and unlawful pollution. States should provide resources for Indigenous peoples to design, deliver and control their access to water.

By Art. 26 (1), such a Nomadic people has 'the right to the lands, territories and resources which they have traditionally owned, occupied or otherwise used or acquired. By Art. 26 (2), the Nomadic group has 'the right to own, use, develop and control the lands, territories and resources that they possess by reason of traditional ownership or other traditional occupation or use, as well as those which they have otherwise acquired'. By Art. 26 (3) the colonial or de-colonized

State has an international duty to recognize and protect 'these lands, territories and resources'. The State has a duty to 'give legal recognition and protection to these lands'. By Art. 32 (1), the Nomadic peoples in formerly colonized States are said to possess 'the right' to determine and posit priorities and strategies to develop and use their lands. By Art. 32 (2) a State has a duty to 'consult and co-operate in good faith' for any State-authorized project affecting the Indigenous lands. By Art. 36, any territorial border may not be used to prevent a member of a Nomadic group in a formerly colonized State from 'the right to maintain and develop contacts, relations and co-operation' with others across the border.

If one turns to a specific right, such as the right to water (this being of concern for the persons in the first form of Nomadism), General Comment No. 15 of the Committee on Economic, Social and Cultural Rights again excludes Nomadic groups that find themselves on a territory claimed by a non-colonial State or a State that is independent of a legacy of colonialism. A Nomadic community's use of land is only protected if it finds itself in a colonized or colonizing context and if the community has 'traditionally faced difficulties in exercising this right, including women, children, minority groups, Indigenous peoples, refugees, asylum-seekers, internally displaced persons, migrant workers, prisoners and detainees'.[62]

As it stands, ILO Convention No. 107 also provides in Arts 13 (1) and (2) that the use or occupation of land by a Nomadic group, described as Indigenous, is subject to 'the framework of national laws and regulations [...] in so far as they [...] do not hinder their economic and social development'. By Art. 12 (2), if removal of these populations is necessary as an exceptional measure, the group must be provided 'with lands of quality at least equal to that of the lands previously occupied by them, suitable to provide for their present needs and future development'. In cases where chances of alternative employment exist and where the members of the Nomadic group prefer to have compensation in money or in kind, the State has a duty to compensate them with appropriate guarantees. By Art. 12 (3), persons thus removed shall be fully compensated for any resulting loss or injury. National agrarian programmes shall secure to the populations concerned treatment equivalent to that accorded to other sections of the national community with regard to

> (a) the provision of more land for these populations when they have not the area necessary for providing the essentials of a normal existence, or for any possible increase in their numbers;

---

62   UN Committee on Economic, Social and Cultural Rights 'General Comment No. 15: The Right to Water' (26 November 2002) ESCOR [2003] Supp 2, 120, at para. 16.

(b) the provision of the means required to promote the development of the lands which these populations already possess.

In a first reading of the above documents, it would seem apparent that a Nomadic community that has used land for the purposes of hunting, fishing and gathering, as in the first form of Nomadism, or of pastoralism and herding, as in the second form, possesses an international right, as a community, to its use of traditional resources.

There are several reasons, however, why an international customary norm that recognizes and protects the use and possession of land by a Nomadic community is suspect. It is difficult to claim that any such norm recognizes and protects the Nomadic group's sense of law examined above, in juxtaposition with the State-centric authority to enact, administer, adjudicate, regulate and enforce laws.

More specifically, the State has a duty to consult regarding the relocation of a Nomadic community and a duty to offer due respect to the customs, traditions and land tenure systems of the Nomadic group concerned. Such a procedural duty does not represent a recognition of the constitutional authority of the Nomadic group independent of the State. Art. 43 of the UNDRIP recognizes the right of a Nomadic group (in a colonized or de-colonized State) to receive 'the minimum standards for the survival, dignity and well-being of the Indigenous peoples of the world'. The 'minimum standard' is not compared with that of non-Nomadic peoples but of other Nomadic peoples. The standard must be that of survival and subsistence.[63]

Is such a State duty an obligation or a mere aspirational 'duty'? What is 'unlawful pollution' if international law reserves the regulatory authority of the State to legislate and regulate pollution? And what is 'pollution' if State authorities claim that there is no perceptible climate change? In addition, States 'should take steps to ensure that (e) Nomadic and traveller communities have access to adequate water at traditional and designated halting sites'. It is apparent that a Nomadic-Indigenous group is not guaranteed access to water to which the group has traditionally had access. It is just that the State 'should take adequate steps'. What is 'adequate' would appear to be left to the State governmental authority.

---

[63] This is the criteria noted in ILO 'Convention No. 169 concerning Indigenous and Tribal Peoples in Independent Countries' (adopted 27 June 1989, entered into force 5 September 1991) 1650 UNTS 383, Art. 14.

b        The Constraint on the Nomadic Use of Territory by the State's Radical Title to Land

The State, as a legal person, is defined by the 1933 Montevideo Convention,[64] as requiring a territoriality in four ways: a permanent population, a defined territory, a government and a capacity to enter into relations with other States. Each criterion of statehood pertains to the association of the State with the exclusive bordered possession and title to such a parcel of land. A Nomadic community lacks such requisites of statehood by virtue of the group's continual movement. Lacking a territorial border, let alone exclusive ownership to the territory inside the border, a Nomadic group still experiences an identity with a territory. Such an experiential attachment to land or water induces an identity with an experienced 'place' rather than a territorial 'space'.[65] The Nomadic sense of land, as an experienced place, is embodied with collective memories of the experiences of the group in the past. But legal space, as territorial (as opposed to experiential space), is produced and productive of objects independent and intellectually transcendent of the experiential embodiment of place by Nomadic groups.

More particularly, the State possesses a 'final', 'absolute', 'pure legal estate' or 'radical' title to all land within it territorial borders.[66] Once a State makes a claim to own a territory, the government representing the State can take possession over the claimed land.[67] The claim of ownership over all land within a territorial border provides the legal backdrop to the absolutism of European monarchs historically prior to the constitutionalism introduced by the English, French and American Revolutions of the 17th and 18th centuries. The constitutionalism of the common law adjudication has consistently presumed that the State possesses radical, absolute title to all land over which it possesses intellectual possession.[68] This presumption is expressly incorporated into the basic texts of the American and Canadian Constitutions, for example. The method of acquiring radical title is considered juridically non-justiciable.[69]

---

64   Convention on Rights and Duties of States (signed 26 December 1933, entered into force 26 December 1934) 165 LNTS 19 (Montevideo Convention).
65   E.S. Casey, *Getting Back into a Place* (Indiana University Press 2009).
66   E. Vattel, *The Law of Nations* (1797; Liberty Fund 2008), at bk. 2, ch. 7, paras 82, 81, 86, 88; *Johnson and Graham's Lease v. M'Intosh* (1823) 8 Wheaton 543, at 588, per Marshall C.J.; *Worcester v. Georgia* (1832) 31 US (6 Peters) 515; *St. Catharine's Milling and Lumber Co. v. The Queen* (1888) 14 App. Cas. 46; *Amodu Tijani v. Secretary, Southern Nigeria* [1921] 2 AC 399, at 402–403; *Island of Palmas* (*Netherlands v. United States of America*) (1928) 2 RIAA 829; *Guerin v. R* [1984] 2 SCR 335, at 379.
67   *Johnson and Graham's Lease v. M'Intosh* (1823) 8 Wheaton 543, at 573.
68   See the references, note 135.
69   *Mabo v. Queensland* (*No. 2*) (1992) 175 CLR 1 (3 June 1992), at para. 28, per Toohey.

As a consequence, the sense of law experienced by members of a Nomadic group can hardly remain independent of the State's totality of legal authority. That sense of law, again, concerns an immanently experienced event or events independent and temporally prior to the intellectualism of constitutionalism. The continual movement of the Nomadic community undermines or, at least, renders problematic its experiential attachment to land as evidentiary *indicia* of the community's title or even use of the land, however transient. Rather, the group's constitutional interest is held to be *inchoate* ('lacking a legal category' or lacking a 'complete category'). At best, any Nomadic group can only possess a *usufructory* right to land.[70] By this, the inhabitant can use the land but not own it, sell it, or exchange it for some other object. Except upon surrender to the State, the 'non-economic' use of land is situated into a 'legal straitjacket'.[71] Interestingly, *usufructory* was a term used in Roman law to denote the interest of an owner 'in slaves, beasts, and other things, as well as land and buildings'.[72] Since the traditional cultures of Nomadic groups do not and cannot possess title to their lands of habitation (due to their lack of fixity of habitation on a territory), their land and water could be 'discovered' by European settlers and military officials.[73] In such circumstances, the use of land is considered *terra nullius* ('land belonging to no-one').

c  The Argument from the Standpoint of International Constitutionalism

This argument concerning the Nomadic use of land rests in the historical identity of a Nomadic community with a territory. Both the Australian and Canadian Supreme Courts have recognized the continuous physical occupation of a tract of land as the basis of a constitutional title to land.[74] This continuous physical occupation, however, must have existed before the colony of Australia was authorized by the British Government to enact laws or before the Canadian State became sovereign, the latter being an issue which remains unclear and variable for different territorial parts of Canada.[75] The colonial charter by the British State is the cut-off date because of the presumption that

---

70   *Guerin v. R* [1984] 2 SCR 335, at 380–382.
71   *Delgamuukw v. British Columbia* [1997] 3 SCR 1010, at paras 131–132.
72   *Justinian's Institutes* (Duckworth 1987), at 2.4; A. Borkowski and P. du Plessis, *Textbook on Roman Law* (OUP 2005), at 157–158.
73   *Campbell v. Hall* (1774) 98 ER 1045.
74   *Delgamuukw v. British Columbia* [1997] 3 SCR 1010, at para. 149; *Mabo v. Queensland (No. 2)* (1992) 175 CLR 1 (3 June 1992), at paras 28, 83, 94.
75   *Delgamuukw v. British Columbia* [1997] 3 SCR 1010, at paras 150–51; *Mabo v. Queensland (No. 2)* (1992) 175 CLR 1 (3 June 1992), at para. 45.

an absence of centralized governmentality of Nomadic-Indigenous communities opened the door for a State to export a colony to the territory inhabited by Nomadic-Indigenous communities.[76] The date of sovereignty is the cut-off date in Canada because the State is recognized in international law as claiming radical title to all land it claims to own on that date.[77] Given such a State claim, individual members of a Nomadic community do not possess a 'right' to property, such as fee simple. Instead, their right is a *sui generis* interest in land.[78] This is so despite the 'special bond' which a parcel of land may hold in the collective memory of the Nomadic community.[79] The individual's right is a right to the land, not to property.[80]

### d   Hard and Soft Property Rights

The property rights of Nomadic peoples are of two types: soft and hard. The soft rights join with the cultural ethos of a community with the dependence of the members of the group upon the use of or spiritual association land. So, for example, soft rights to land fulfil their cultural expectations and livelihood as exemplified by the implied water rights of inhabitants of a reservation.[81] Such water rights have preserved the cultural identity of the inhabitants. The water rights have effectively trumped the State's claim to own water as a natural resource.[82] I shall examine this soft sense of Nomadic property in the fourth approach to constitutional protection.

The hard sense of a property right has been highlighted by the Australian High Court.[83] In *Mabo*, a people had inhabited a small island with limited contact with Australians. As such, the people were held to possess title to the island land prior to and independent of Australia's claim to radical title under its control. Here, the grounding of the property right of the Indigenous group (that is also Nomadic) has been said to be nested in custom.

Because Nomadic groups continually move, however, the hard sense of a constitutional right to land, as property, is problematic. The right rests upon compelling anthropological evidence about any Nomadic group and, further,

---

76   *Mabo v. Queensland (No. 2)* (1992) 175 CLR 1 (3 June 1992), at paras 51, 67, 68, 69 per Brennan.
77   *Delgamuukw v. British Columbia* [1997] 3 SCR 1010, at paras 111, 143–45.
78   Ibid., at paras 111, 124, 125, 128.
79   Ibid., at para. 128.
80   Ibid., at para. 140.
81   *Winters v. United States*, 207 US 564 (1908).
82   A.D. Tarlock, 'Tribal Justice and Property Rights: The Evolution of Winters *v.* United States' (2010) 50 Natural Resources 471, at 481.
83   *Mabo v. Queensland (No. 2)* (1992) 175 CLR 1 (3 June 1992), at para. 33 per Brennan.

evidence about the Nomadic culture continuous to the present. In addition, it is unclear whether the property right of a Nomadic group exists by virtue of the spiritual identity of the group with a territorial place.[84] In sum, the Nomadic character of a group makes it difficult for the group to make a claim of title to land. It appears that the claim must historically trace the dependence of the Nomadic community upon the particular parcel of land historically prior to European contact (as in the case of *Mabo*) or prior to the sovereignty of the State (as in Canada).[85] If constitutionalism only protects groups which possess title to land in a hard sense, Nomadic peoples would be denied constitutional protection if they were Nomadic prior to any such cut-off (or cut-in) date.[86] This is aside from the fact that some tracts of land in North America, for example, were sparsely inhabited and that the cut-in date of the constitutionalism has varied over many decades due to the fact that the date of effective control and the State's claim to ownership of land has varied from one territorial region to another.

### 4  The Protection of the Distinct Culture of a Nomadic Group

Independent of the possible protection of a Nomadic community as Indigenous, as a 'minority' and as its use of land, a final argument has emerged in international constitutionalism. This has concerned the constitutional protection of the culture of such a community.

### a  Indicia of an International Customary Norm concerning Protection of a Nomadic Culture

Various human rights treaties recognize the protection of the 'way of life' of distinct minorities of a State.[87] In particular, the ICCPR provides that '[a]ll peoples have the right to self-determination', '[i]n no case may a people be deprived of its own means of subsistence' and '[i]n those States in which ethnic, religious or linguistic minorities exist, persons belonging to such minorities shall not be denied the right, in community with other members of their group, to enjoy their own culture, to profess and practise their own religion, or

---

84   *Western Australia v. Ward (Miriuwung-Gajerrong Case)* (2002) 213 CLR 1, at para. 14.
85   *Delgamuukw v. British Columbia* [1997] 3 SCR 1010, at para. 139.
86   *R v. Adams* [1995] 4 SCR 707, at para. 27, affirmed in *R v. Marshall; R v. Bernard* [2005] 2 SCR 220, at para. 66. I have examined the issues in more detail in 'Legal Time' (2018) 31 Canadian J. of Jurisprudence and Law 281.
87   Art. 27 International Covenant on Civil and Political Rights (adopted 16 December 1966, entered into force 23 March 1976) 999 UNTS 171; UN HRC 'General Comment No. 23: The Rights of Minorities (Art. 27)' (8 April 1994) GAOR 49th Session Supp 40 vol. 1, 106, at para. 7.

to use their own language'.[88] Art. 2 of the Inter-American Declaration on the Rights of Indigenous Peoples requires that 'States recognize and respect the multicultural and multilingual character of Indigenous peoples, who are an integral part of their societies'.[89] By Art. 3, Indigenous peoples have the right to self-determination. By virtue of that right they 'freely determine their political status and freely pursue their economic, social and cultural development'. By Art. 2 (1) of the Convention on the Protection and Promotion on the Diversity of Cultural Expressions, 2005, a guiding principle of such a protection and promotion is respect for human rights and fundamental freedoms.[90] Such a treaty retains the principle of sovereignty.[91] The treaty provides that a 'cultural content' refers to the symbolic meaning, artistic dimension and cultural values that originate from or express cultural identities'.[92] If one turns to General Comment 23 of the Committee on the Elimination of Racial Discrimination, a State possesses a duty to 'recognize and respect Indigenous distinct culture, history, language and way of life'. However, such a duty defers to how such a distinct culture, history, language and way of life function 'as an enrichment of the State's cultural identity and to promote its [the State's] preservation'.[93]

Implicit in this constitutional argument is the claim that Nomadic peoples, who are also Indigenous and who find themselves in a territory that has been the object of colonization, ought to be assimilated into the legal order. For one thing, as noted above, ILO Convention No. 107 has taken for granted that Nomadic peoples from a colonial State or formerly colonizing State are located at a less advanced stage than the colonizers.[94] The more recent ILO Convention

---

88  Arts 1 (1), 1 (2), 27 ICCPR; UN HRC 'General Comment No. 23: The Rights of Minorities (Art. 27)' (8 April 1994) GAOR 49th Session Supp 40 vol. 1, 106.

89  OAS Permanent Council 'Thirteenth Meeting of Negotiations in the Quest for Points of Consensus: Record of the Current Status of the Draft American Declaration on the Rights of Indigenous Peoples' (20 January 2011) OEA/Ser.K/XVI GT/DADIN/doc.334/08 rev. 6.

90  Convention on the Protection and Promotion of the Diversity of Cultural Expressions (opened for signature 20 October 2005, entered into force 18 March 2007) 2440 UNTS 311.

91  Art. 2 (2) Convention on the Protection and Promotion of the Diversity of Cultural Expressions.

92  Art. 4 (2) Convention on the Protection and Promotion of the Diversity of Cultural Expressions.

93  UN Committee on the Elimination of Racial Discrimination 'General Recommendation XXIII on the Rights of Indigenous Peoples' (18 August 1997) GAOR 52nd Session Supp 18, 122.

94  By Art. 2, a government has the duty to develop 'co-ordinated and systematic action 'for the protection and 'progressive integration of the group into the life of their respective countries'. To this end, by Art. 2 (b), the State has a duty to promote 'the social, economic and cultural development' of a Nomadic group in a colonial or formerly colonized State; and, by Art. 2 (c), to create the possibility of national integration' independent of

No. 169 has also stressed the importance of a State duty to protect the autonomy of a Nomadic culture in a colonized or colonizing State. As with ILO Convention No. 107, the cultural rights of such a group are to be protected. By Art. 32, this includes any effort by members of such a Nomadic group which desire to cross a State's territorial border.

Art. 29 of the Convention on the Rights of the Child identifies the importance of a child's cultural identity in her or his education. By Art. 30, the child of a 'minority' or of an 'Indigenous origin' 'shall not be denied the right, in community with other members of his or her group, to enjoy his or her own culture'. However, Art. 31 intends that the child may not be prevented from playing and participating in recreational activity of the national community. When one turns to the UN General Assembly Declaration on the Rights of Indigenous Peoples, the theme of the State's duty to protect a Nomadic culture of a colonized or colonizing State is constant. The right to self-determination, as protected in Art. 3, includes the freedom of the Nomadic group to pursue its political, economic, social and cultural development. This is stated to be a matter of choice of the Nomadic-Indigenous community, not that of the State regulations. By Art. 4, the right to self-determination includes 'the autonomy or self-government in matters relating to their internal and local affairs, as well as ways and means for financing their autonomous functions'. By Art. 8 (1), the State has a duty to prevent 'forced assimilation or destruction' of a Nomadic culture in a colonized or colonizing State. Art. 8 (2) specifies institutional means which proscribe the assimilation or destruction of a Nomadic culture. Art. 31 specifies a diversity of elements of a Nomadic culture subject to the Declaration's identity of an Indigenous person.

My point is that a sense of law constitutes a critical element of the culture of the Nomadic community. ILO Convention No. 169 frames the sense of law in a Nomadic community as involving customs, institutional activities of the community, how land is used or possessed by members of the Nomadic community, the cultivation of land, and culture. ILO Convention No. 107 acknowledges such a Nomadic sense of law by highlighting 'customary laws' of the group by the State officials. By Art. 2 (2) (b) of ILO Convention No. 107, the customs and traditions of the group are to be protected by State authorities. By Art. 8, the State officials have a duty to consider the Nomadic customs in regard to penal

---

measures that exclude the group by an 'artificial assimilation' into the national community. By Art. 2 (4) the use of State force is excluded. Art. 4 (a) continues the State duty to integrate a Nomadic community into the traditional or first form of the colonial, colonized or colonizing State, it must take account 'of the cultural and religious values and of the forms of social control' in the community. Any disruption of the values and institutions of the group must be the concern of a State government unless the group consents to the replacing cultural form.

matters. Cultures, traditions, histories, aspirations and the use of land or resources, identified in the UN Declaration on the Rights of Indigenous Peoples, might well be considered elements of a Nomadic sense of law.

Further, however the sense of law in a particular Nomadic community is understood, customary international norms open into a State-centric legal order. Such a State-centric sense of law trumps the sense of law in a Nomadic community. First, there are specific treaty references to the existing State-centric legal order as the ultimate referent of the autonomy of a Nomadic group's legal order. As Art. 7 (2) of ILO Convention No. 107 provides, for example, Nomadic customs and institutions must not be incompatible with the State-centric legal order or its 'integration programmes'. Art. 13 (1) holds out the freedom of a Nomadic group in a colonial or colonizing State to own or use land as in the past but this 'past' must remain 'within the framework of national laws and regulations'. By Art. 13 (1), the paternalism of the State's authority is manifested by State intervention if the Nomadic culture 'hinder[s] the social and economic development of the Nomadic community'. A recent meeting of the Permanent Council of the Organization of American States provides that a Nomadic community, if Indigenous to a colonial, colonized or colonizing State, 'play[s] a special role in strengthening State institutions and in attaining national unity'.[95] Even if texts are interpreted as indicative of an international customary obligation to protect Nomadic peoples, such a customary international legal norm may be inconsistent with a deference to the protection of a Nomadic group.[96]

---

95    OAS Permanent Council, 'Nineteenth Meeting of Negotiations in the Quest for Points of Consensus: Draft American Declaration on the Rights of Indigenous Peoples' (17–19 May 2016) OEA/Ser.K/XVI GT/DADIN/doc.334/08 rev. 12, Art. IV.

96    See e.g., OAS 'American Declaration on the Rights of Indigenous Peoples' (15 June 2016) AG/RES.2888 (XLVI-O/16). By Art 4, no 'State, people or person' shall act in a manner that is 'construed as authorizing or encouraging any action which would dismember or impair, totally or in part, the territorial integrity or political unity of sovereign and independent States'. However, see Arts 13, 14, 16, 28. See also UN Sub-Commission on Prevention of Discrimination and Protection of Minorities 'Draft UN Declaration on the Rights of Indigenous Peoples' (26 August 1994) UN Doc. E/CN.4/Sub.2/1994/45, Arts 16, 26; Proposed American Declaration on the Rights of Indigenous Peoples, approved by the Inter-American Commission on Human Rights on 26 February 1997, at its 1333rd session, OEA/Ser/ LV/II.90, Doc. 9, rev. 2 (1997), Art. 18, at 654–676. The Permanent Council of the OAS provides in the 2015 15th meeting that the Indigenous Peoples of the Americas 'play a special role in strengthening State institutions and in attaining national unity'. By Art. 10, however, the Indigenous group is free from an 'external attempt at assimilation'. By Art. 10 (2), a State 'shall not carry out, adopt, support, or favor any policy to assimilate the Indigenous Peoples or to destroy their cultures'. By Art. 12 (11), Indigenous peoples have a right to cultural identity and integrity and to their cultural heritage, both tangible and intangible, including historic and ancestral heritage.

b      Indicia of Constitutional Protection of Nomadic Cultures

This final argument in support of the relation of international constitutionalism with a Nomadic community pertains to the 'way of life' in the Nomadic culture. The notion of a distinct culture of a traditional (tribal) Nomadic community has been held to offer constitutional protection in Sweden.[97] A Nomadic or quasi-Nomadic legal culture has also been the object of adjudication in Canada.[98] International constitutionalism holds out the protection of 'a practice, custom or tradition integral to the distinctive culture of the aboriginal group claiming the right'.[99] The important feature of the cultural approach to the constitutional protection of Nomadic groups is that 'the prior social organization and distinctive cultures' of Nomadic peoples be distinguished from the historic territorial occupation of land.[100]

The key to a Nomadic culture, as explained above, is the sense of law experienced and immanent in social events. A collective memory manifested such events. The consequence is that Nomadic law is immanent from the sociality of the Nomadic group. The sociality and immanence of a Nomadic law, in turn, is embodied from personally experienced events and from the collective memory of the members of the Nomadic community. A Nomadic culture can be directly connected with the experiential attachment of members to land, for example. Referring to a series of judgments of the Canadian Supreme Court, the claim of title is linked to such a culture if a group's connection with land is 'of a central significance to their distinctive culture'.[101] The 'central and distinctive' element of a culture is said to have 'made the society what it was'.[102] This doctrine has been extended in South America to situations where modernization has impacted the resources upon which Nomadic groups have been dependent for livelihood.[103] The principle is also accepted in other jurisdictions.[104]

---

97   *Nordmaling* Case T 4028–07 (27 April 2011), at 12; see A. Savari and H. Beach, 'The 2011 Swedish Supreme Court Ruling: A Turning Point for Sami Rights' in (2011) 15.2 Nomadic Peoples 130, at 131.
98   *R v. Adams* [1995] 4 SCR 707, at paras 26–30; *Delgamuukw v. British Columbia* [1997] 3 SCR 1010, at para. 39 per Lamer; *R v. Marshall; R v. Bernard* [2005] 2 SCR 220, at para. 66; *R v. Van der Peet* [1996] 2 SCR 507, at paras 46, 74.
99   *R v. Van der Peet* [1996] 2 SCR 507, at para. 46.
100  *R v. Van der Peet* [1996] 2 SCR 507, at para. 74, cited approvingly in *R v. Adams* [1995] 4 SCR 707, at para. 29.
101  *R v. Adams* [1995] 4 SCR 707, at para. 26; *R v. Van der Peet* [1996] 2 SCR 507, at para. 55.
102  *R v. Van der Peet* [1996] 2 SCR 507, at para. 55.
103  *Saramaka People v. Suriname* (*Judgment*) IACtHR Series C No. 172 (28 November 2007); *Xákmok Kásek Indigenous Community v. Paraguay* (*Judgment*) IACtHR Series C No. 214 (24 August 2010); *Sawhoyamaxa Indigenous Community v. Paraguay* (*Judgment*) IACtHR Series C No. 146 (29 March 2006), at para. 18.
104  *Jalang ak Paran & Kampong anak Amih v. Govt of State of Sarawak & Borneo and Pulp and Paper sdn, bhd* Civil Appeal No. Q-01–133–06 (2011) 419; *Mabo v. Queensland* (*No. 2*) (1992) 175 CLR 1 (3 June 1992), at para. 41 per Brennan.

THE NOMADIC SENSE OF LAW IN INTERNATIONAL CONSTITUTIONALISM        271

The constitutional focus upon the context-specific culture of pastoral and hunting groups (the second sense of Nomadism) has, during recent years, been extended to peripatetic Nomads such as the Roma in the UK.[105] Constitutional recognition and protection is left problematic if a State institution undermines the legality of a Nomadic custom. The withdrawal of the legality to a Nomadic custom by an institutional State source does not satisfy constitutional protection. Nor is the constitutional protection met if a member or members of the peripatetic group refrain from travelling for some time due to illness, old age or the educational needs of children.[106] The critical test is that the member of the group provides evidence that he/she has intentionally given up the Nomadic 'habit of life'.[107] Such is described as a 'functionalist' test.[108] The hunting and breeding of reindeer in Scandinavian forests has been held to constitute such a Nomadic 'habit of life'.[109]

What a Nomadic group considers a 'culture' may well differ seriously from the commonplace intuition of the jurist of constitutionalism.[110] What is common is that a culture is sometimes taken as a shared environing world. One's environing world manifests the experienced phenomena which filter perceived objects. The genesis of the Nomadic community's self-identity with a territorial place, drawn from such experiential knowledge, has been said to be an important element of a Nomadic culture.[111] Another view is that the culture manifests an organic element of a society or community. The experiential identity with a Nomadic culture has been protected despite the modification of the culture by technology, economy and other factors of globalization.[112]

---

105    *Wrexham Co Borough Council v. (1) The Nat'l Assembly of Wakes (2) Michael Berry (3) Florence Berry* (Civ Div) [2003] EWCA Civ 835 (19 June 2003); *Hearne v. Secretary of State for Wales and Camarthenshire Co Council* [1999] EWHC Admin 494 (25 May 1999).
106    *Wrexham* ibid., at 66.
107    *Hearne* ibid.
108    *Wrexham* ibid., at para. 57; *Mills v. Cooper* [1967] 2 QB 459, per Diplock; UN HRC 'Communication No. 197/1985, *Kitok v. Sweden*' (27 July 1988) UN Doc. CCPR/C/33/D/197/1985; UN HRC 'Communication No. 431/1990, *Sara v. Finland*' (23 March 1994) UN Doc. CCPR/C/50/D/431/1990.
109    *Kitok* ibid.; *Sara* ibid.
110    *R v. Sappier; R v. Gray* [2006] 2 SCR 686, at para. 44. See also, M.T. Loveland and D. Popescu, 'The Gypsey Threat Narrative: Explaining Anti-Roma Attitudes in the European Union' (2016) 40.3 Humanity & Society 329. For various theories of a sense of culture see R. Cotterrell, 'Law in Culture' (2004) 17.1 Ratio Juris 1; S. Engle Merry, *Human Rights and Gender Violence* (University of Chicago Press 2006) ch. 1.
111    UN HRC 'General Comment No. 23: The Rights of Minorities (Art. 27)' (8 April 1994) GAOR 49th Session Supp 40 vol. 1, at 158; UN HRC 'Communication No. 760/1997, *Diergaardt et al v. Namibia*' (7 July 1998) UN Doc. CCPR/C/63/D/760/1997, at para. 10.6.
112    UN HRC 'Communication No. 431/1990, *Sara v. Finland*' (23 March 1994) UN Doc. CCPR/C/50/D/431/1990, at para. 7.4; UN HRC 'Communication No. 511/1992, *Länsman v. Finland*' (26 October 1994) UN Doc. CCPC/C/52/D/511/1992; UN HRC 'Communication No.

c     Attachment to Land

In particular, in contrast with the three constitutional arguments concerning Indigenous Nomadic personhood, the community's minority status and its claim to use territory, the basis of State protection now concerns 'a particular practice, custom or tradition taking place on the land [which] was integral to the distinctive culture of that group, *even if they have not shown that their occupation and use of the land was sufficient to support a claim of title to the land*'.[113] The doctrine requires that such a practice be 'protect[ed]' even if that group has not provided evidence of 'their connection with the piece of land on which the activity was taking place was of a central significance to their distinctive culture'.[114] It helps that the Nomadic culture is 'site-specific' to the social practice integral to the group's culture and that the practice has a 'substantial connection' to the land.[115] 'Occupation' of land does not necessarily involve the construction of dwellings or the enclosure of fields. Rather, what 'occupation' signifies is 'the use of definite tracts of land for hunting, fishing or otherwise'.[116] Interestingly, such a sense of 'occupation' of territory involves a shared experiential attachment to land. A Nomadic culture need not be characterized as synonymous with the exclusive control over a territory.[117]

d     What is a Distinctive Nomadic Culture?

What is signified by a 'culture', of course, is not entirely clear. This is especially so with regard to a Nomadic culture. What is important concerning the identity of a Nomadic culture are several issues raised in Canadian adjudication. First, a Nomadic culture manifests a continual movement. However, what is a Nomadic culture if it is considered frozen at some distinct point in time such as the critical date of the ratification of a basic text, conquest, sovereignty or settler contact?[118] Second, as noted above, common law courts generally require that such a frozen sense of a Nomadic culture remains continuous from a critical date in the past to its present.[119] Such a constitutional requirement undermines the very nature of a Nomadic community which, after all,

---

197/1985, *Kitok v. Sweden*' (27 July 1988) UN Doc. CCPR/C/33/D/197/1985; UN HRC 'Communication No. 167/1984, *Ominayak, Chief of the Lubicon Lake Band v. Canada*' (26 March 1990) *UN* Doc. CCPR/C/38/D/167/1984.

113   *R v. Adams* [1995] 4 SCR 707, at para. 26, emphasis the Court's.
114   Ibid., at para. 26.
115   Ibid., at para. 30; *R v. Marshall; R v. Bernard* [2005] 2 SCR 220, at para. 67.
116   *R v. Marshall; R v. Bernard* [2005] 2 SCR 220, at para. 56.
117   Ibid., at para. 64.
118   *R v. Van der Peet* [1996] 2 SCR 507, at paras 56, 60–61.
119   Ibid., at para. 60.

is continuously moving. Third, what is 'integral' cannot be 'incidental' to the 'integral practices, customs and traditions'.[120] What is 'integral', the Canadian Supreme Court continues, concerns 'whether, without the concrete practice, custom or tradition, the culture in question would be fundamentally altered or other than it is'.[121]

It is unclear as to whether it is left to State institutions to identify what groups are Nomadic. Anthropology experts are necessary to aid in any such endeavour. Indeed, the culture of a Nomadic group may be filled with intellectual contradictions. The culture may well change through time as the group copes with different external environments, climates, municipal laws, languages, commercial practices and the like. It may be that a Nomadic group does not even recognize itself as a distinct 'culture' or even as possessing a name until constitutionalists 'observe' the social conventions of the group. In such a context, the judiciary passively observes the Nomadic customs as 'out there' fixed in time and place. Indeed, it is difficult to gather a sense of a Nomadic 'culture' from the terms of the recently ratified Convention on the Protection and Promotion of the Diversity of Cultural Expressions. Interestingly, it is only after the fact and from an external standpoint that a group be conferred a name. To take an example, during his several years in Gaul and Germania, Caesar posited over 120 names for diverse Nomadic groups despite their distinct existence without such names before Caesar's sojourn.

The issue that has arisen concerns 'what is the nature of what is 'integral' to a distinct culture'? What is considered 'integral' has not been such at the present day but of the 'pre-existing distinctive societies [...] prior to contact with the Europeans'.[122] Evidence of a trade practice prior to contact, for example, may not represent 'the defining feature of the Nomadic culture nor might it be vital to the 'collective identity' to the group.[123] The same may be said, for example, of the practice of gambling in a group's culture centuries ago.[124]

More generally, 'a sensitive and generous approach to the evidence' is required in assessing the nature of the distinct culture of a Nomadic group. This requires a close and rigorous study of the relation of a context-specific social practice of the Nomadic group to the culture of the group as a whole.[125] Oral evidence may be introduced to establish 'what would a certain practice or

---

120 Ibid., at para. 55, 7.
121 Ibid., at paras 59, 55–58.
122 Ibid., at para. 44.
123 *Mitchell v. MNR* [2001] 1 SCR 911, 199 DLR (4th) 385, at para. 66 per Binnie.
124 *R v. Pamajewon* [1996] 2 SCR 821, at para. 28.
125 *R v. Marshall; R v. Bernard* [2005] 2 SCR 220, at para. 68.

event have signified in their world and value system'.[126] This requires a sociological and anthropological study of 'the *traditional way of life*', including 'the group's size, manner of life, material resources, and technological abilities, and the character of the lands claimed' and 'the manner in which the society used the land *to live*, namely to establish villages, to work, to get to work, to hunt, to travel to hunting grounds, to fish, to get to fishing pools, to conduct religious rites, etc'.[127] Added to such evidence is the need to study 'the means of survival, their socialization methods, their legal systems, and, potentially, their trading habits'.[128] It is difficult not to conclude that extensive anthropological and social historical resource material are needed in order to access a knowledge of a distinct Nomadic culture.[129] The critical feature is not that a social practice is essential to the survival of the Nomadic group. Rather, what is crucial, according to the Inter-American Court of Human Rights, is that the practice forms 'part of their worldview, of their religiousness, and consequently, of their cultural identity'.[130] Such factors constitute the life-world of members of a Nomadic group.

Although extensive evidence has sometimes gone some distance pertaining to the life-world of the Nomadic group, the issue as to 'what is the nature of a culture?' is moot according to judgments involving some South American Nomadic communities.[131] The Canadian Courts have cautioned that one must resist 'facile assumptions based on Eurocentric traditions of gathering and passing on historical facts'.[132] As an example, private property, emergent from feudal seignority, privileges exclusivity in contrast with the communal and spiritual sense of how land is 'used' amongst Nomadic groups.[133] The same

126  *R v. Marshall; R v. Bernard* [2005] 2 SCR 220, at paras 68–69; *Guerin v. R* [1984] 2 SCR 335, at 388.
127  *Delgamuukw v. British Columbia* [1997] 3 SCR 1010, at paras 149, 193, cited approvingly in *R v. Marshall; R v. Bernard* [2005] 2 SCR 220, at para. 49.Emphasis mine.
128  *R v. Sappier; R v. Gray* [2006] 2 SCR 686, at para. 45.
129  *Sawhoyamaxa Indigenous Community v. Paraguay* IACtHR Series C No. 146 (29 March 2006), at para. 118; *Comunidad Indígena Yakye Axa v. Paraguay (Judgment)* IACtHR Series C No. 125 (17 June 2005); *A v. Agawa* (1988) 53 DLR (4th) 101, at 215–216.
130  *Comunidad Indígena Yakye Axa v. Paraguay (Judgment)* IACtHR Series C No. 125 (17 June 2005), at para. 135.
131  *Sawhoyamaxa Indigenous Community v. Paraguay* IACtHR Series C No. 146 (29 March 2006), at para. 34; *Xákmok Kásek Indigenous Community v. Paraguay (Judgment)* IACtHR Series C No. 214 (24 August 2010), at paras 16–17; *Comunidad Indígena Yakye Axa v. Paraguay (Judgment)* IACtHR Series C No. 125 (17 June 2005), at para. 34–39.
132  *R v. Marshall; R v. Bernard* [2005] 2 SCR 220, at paras 61, 68.
133  *Delgamuukw v. British Columbia* [1997] 3 SCR 1010, at para. 155–158 per Lamer; *Sawhoyamaxa Indigenous Community v. Paraguay* IACtHR Series C No. 146 (29 March 2006), at

concerns constitutionalism's sense of 'collective space'.[134] In sum, what one means by 'culture' is 'inherently cultural' in that what contemporary members of a legal profession consider 'culture' hardly matches with what a Nomadic group considers 'culture'.[135]

e      The Unwritten Character of the Constitutional Protection of a Nomadic Culture

More generally, to take the common law example, the constitutional principle of the protection of a minority culture, such as arguably a Nomadic community, is not understood with reference to a basic text. Instead, the constitutional obligation on the part of State institutions to protect a minority culture is an implicit 'independent principle underlying our constitutional order', as the Supreme Court of Canada has put it.[136] Such an implicit principle has been held to be a 'broader principle' than any basic text signifies. In particular, the principle of the protection of a minority (amongst other principles) is 'not explicitly made part of the Constitution by any written provision other than in some respects by the oblique reference to the preamble of a statute named the Constitution Act, 1867'.[137] Such a principle, according to the unanimous *Secession Reference*, involves 'the vital unstated assumptions' that 'inform and sustain the constitutional text'.[138] Accordingly, a constitution would be 'impossible' to imagine without an implicit constitutional obligation of the State authorities to protect minorities.[139] Such a constitutional obligation possesses the character of 'a fundamental postulate', a 'predicate', a 'belief' and 'the content of the assumptions' of 'an orderly framework' 'which form[s] the very foundation of the Constitution'.[140]

Now, the key is not the observable practice as an object of empirical observation. The unwritten character of the constitutional protection of a distinct Nomadic culture must possess an action or law-creative character. That

---

        para. 120l; *Xákmok Kásek Indigenous Community v. Paraguay* (*Judgment*) IACtHR Series C No. 214 (24 August 2010), at para. 97–99.

134    *Mayagna (Sumo) Awas Tingni Community v. Nicaragua* IACtHR Series C No. 79 (31 August 2001); Arts 5, 89, 180, 181 of the Constitution of Nicaragua; P. Garnsey, *Thinking about Property: From Antiquity to the Age of Revolution* (CUP 2007), at 114–115.

135    *R v. Sappier; R v. Gray* [2006] 2 SCR 686, at para. 44 per Bastarche.

136    See, eg, *Secession Reference* [1998] 2 SCR 217, at paras 49–54, 79–82. See also *Lalonde v. Ontario (Commission de restructuration des services de santé)* (2001), 56 OR (3d) 505 (Ontario Court of Appeals).

137    Ibid., at para. 51.

138    Ibid., at para. 49.

139    Ibid., at para. 51.

140    Ibid., at paras 54, 70 (quoting from *Roncarelli v. Duplessis* [1959] SCR 121, at 142), 76–78.

is, an unwritten assumption is not the object of empirical observation. Rather, an action- or ascriptive character must be attributed to what 'give[s] rise to substantive legal obligations' or 'full legal effect'.[141] The constitutional assumptions/principles, the Court continues, are 'not merely descriptive, but are also invested with a powerful normative force, and are binding upon both Courts and Governments'.[142] In this light, the constitutional obligation to protect a Nomadic Indigenous group has been extended to the recognition and protection of the Métis (the offspring of Indigenous inhabitants and European settlers), thereby providing support for the constitutional protection of Nomadic groups that did not exist at the time of European contact.[143]

Because of the interpretive principle that every constitutional provision signifies an object, the entrenchment of respect for dignity and inviolability of the person provides a background to the constitutional duty of a State to protect a Nomadic culture.[144] The constitutions of the former Eastern Europe explicitly entrench the protection of a 'home' and, by inference, the culture of a Nomadic group.[145] The explicitly protected right to life implies the right to a livelihood and, by inference, the duty of the State not to render decisions which undermine the livelihood of a Nomadic group.[146]

More specific implied rights reinforce the general unwritten character of a constitutional duty of a State to protect a Nomadic culture. Of particular importance in this regard is the right to move freely without interference by the State.[147] The general rights of equal protection and non-discrimination provide further implied support for the protection of a Nomadic culture.[148] By not

---

141   *Secession Reference* [1998] 2 SCR 217, at para. 54.
142   Ibid., at para. 54.
143   *R v. Powley* [2003] 2 SCR 207.
144   See eg. Arts 2 (1), 5 (2) Greek Constitution; Greece Law No. 927/1979 as amended by Law No. 1419/1984 and Law No. 2910/2001; Arts 12 (1), 19 (1) Slovak Constitution.
145   See eg. Arts 21, 33 Slovak Constitution; Arts 33, 35 Bulgaria Constitution.
146   UN HRC 'Communication No. 167/1984, *Ominayak, Chief of the Lubicon Lake Band v. Canada*' (26 March 1990) UN Doc. CCPR/C/38/D/167/1984; UN HRC 'Communication No. 197/1985, *Kitok v. Sweden*' (27 July 1988) UN Doc. CCPR/C/33/D/197/1985; UN HRC 'Communication No. 431/1990, *Sara v. Finland*' (23 March 1994) UN Doc. CCPR/C/50/D/431/1990; UN HRC 'Communication No. 511/1992, *Länsman v. Finland*' (26 October 1994) UN Doc. CCPC/C/52/D/511/1992; *Adong bin Kawau & Ors v. Kerajaan Negeri Johore* [1997] 1 MLJ 418, at para. 164.
147   *Adong bin Kawau* ibid., at 430.
148   *Sejdić v. Bosnia and Herzegovina* (*Judgment*) ECtHR App 27996/06, 34836/06 (22 December 2009), at para. 43; J.S. Gehring, 'Roma and the Limits of Free Movement in the European Union' in W. Maas (ed.), *Democratic Citizenship and the Free Movement of People: Immigration and Asylum Policy in Europe* (Brill 2013), at 145–147; W.K. Barth, *On Cultural Rights: The Equality of Nations and the Minority Legal Tradition* (Nijhoff 2008), at 194–197;

recognizing and protecting a Nomadic culture, a social hierarchy favouring the non-Nomadic inhabitants is institutionalized by negative implication.[149] The freedom of religious practice attaches to the spiritual identity with land and with the mythic origin of the Nomadic people.[150] The State is obligated to investigate racial motives of actions against a peripatetic Nomadic group.[151] The failure to have a required registration for a marriage in a group has been found adequate for a survivor to receive a pension.[152]

f     The Nomadic Culture from the Perspective of the Nomadic Group
The critical feature of the constitutional protection of a Nomadic culture is held to be the standpoint of the Nomadic group, not that of the State. Words are easier to utter than is effective protection of the object of the words, however.

The Canadian Courts caution that the study of the Nomadic perspective must shy from 'a formalistic or narrowing way' as well as from 'anthropological curiosities and, potentially, racialized aboriginal stereotypes'.[153] Judge L'Heureux-Dubé, dissenting in *Van der Peet*, clarified this principle by emphasizing that the context-specific culture must be understood 'through the eyes of aboriginal people, not through those of the non-native majority or the distorting lens of existing regulations'.[154] Even with title to land as the clue to the Nomadic culture, for example, the jurist must examine 'the equivalent [of title] in the aboriginal culture at issue' rather than in 'deeds or Euro-centric assertions of ownership'.[155] If Nomadic attachment to the use of territory were coloured by exclusivity and control of land, 'any aboriginal rights to Nomadic peoples' would be difficult to ascertain.[156] This would be so because most Nomadic-Indigenous inhabitants in Western Canada east of the Rockies had been at contact or had remained Nomadic some years after European

---

J.P. Liégeois, *The Council of Europe and Roma: 40 Years of Action* (Council of Europe 2012), at 129–133.

149    *Proposed Amendments to the Naturalization Provisions of the Constitution of Costa Rica (Advisory Opinion)* IACtHR Series A No. 4 (19 January 1984), at para. 55.

150    *Sawhoyamaxa Indigenous Community v. Paraguay* IACtHR Series C No. 146 (29 March 2006), at para. 131.

151    *Bekos and Koutropoulos v. Greece (Judgment)* ECtHR App 15250/02 (13 December 2005), at para. 69.

152    *Muños Díaz v. Spain (Judgment)* ECtHR App 49151/07 (8 December 2009).

153    *R v. Marshall; R v. Bernard* [2005] 2 SCR 220, at para. 48; *R v. Sappier; R v. Gray* [2006] 2 SCR 686, at para. 46; *R v. Sparrow* [1990] 1 SCR 1075, at 1099.

154    *R v. Van der Peet* [1996] 2 SCR 507, at para. 162.

155    *R v. Marshall; R v. Bernard* [2005] 2 SCR 220, at para. 61.

156    *R v. Adams* [1995] 4 SCR 707, at para. 27, cited approvingly in *R v. Marshall; R v. Bernard* [2005] 2 SCR 220, at para. 66.

contact.[157] In sum, Nomadic peoples do not need to establish a connection with land to establish a fixed constitutional right of a 'distinctive culture'.[158]

In sum, the requisite of the perspective of the Nomadic groups is more difficult than it might seem. What is a Nomadic community as a 'pre-existing distinctive society' prior to European contact? What is the 'central and significant part of a Nomadic community's distinctive culture today'? Is it realistic for jurists to take for granted that a culture remains unchanged through experienced time? How integral is a particular ritual, use of land, social practice and the like to a contemporary Nomadic community? How does one distinguish a 'central' as opposed to an 'incidental' feature of a pre-existing culture? How is such a culture understood and protected if it is subject to limits imposed by the State justification of the limits?

g      Two Forms of the Principle of Protection of a Nomadic Culture

Two versions have been offered of the constitutional protection of a distinctive Nomadic culture.

(i)      *A Culture Frozen in Time*

The first version freezes the Nomadic culture in a historical moment and then resituates the frozen culture into today's official language.[159] The culture that constitutionalism protects today must be traceable backwards in history to a period prior to European contact.[160]

If Nomadism is taken as the social fact of the pre-contact life of Indigenous peoples, however, there rests little possible constitutional right of property for a Nomadic community that was prior to contact. The Australian High Court has explicitly held out the basic structure of constitutionalism as 'a skeletal principle of our legal system' that cannot be brought into question.[161] So too has the Canadian Supreme Court.[162] The basic doctrines of the common law have been considered essential features of such a skeleton. The constitutional requisite of a Nomadic-Indigenous community's historical continuous control

---

157  P.C. Albers, 'Changing Patterns of Ethnicity in the Northeastern Plains' in J.D. Hill (ed.), *History, Power and Identity: Ethnogenesis in the Americas, 1492–1992* (Iowa University Press 1996) 90; *R v. Van der Peet* [1996] 2 SCR 507, at para. 26.
158  *R v. Adams* [1995] 4 SCR 707, at para. 26.
159  *R v. Van der Peet* [1996] 2 SCR 507, at paras 46, 60–67; *R v. Adams* [1995] 4 SCR 707, at paras 37–46; *R v. Côté* [1997] 3 SCR 139, at paras 58–68; *Mitchell v. MNR* [2001] 1 SCR 911, 199 DLR (4th) 385, at para. 143 per Binnie.
160  *R v. Van der Peet* [1996] 2 SCR 507, at para. 44.
161  *Mabo v. Queensland (No. 2)* (1992) 175 CLR 1 (3 June 1992), at paras 43, 46.
162  *Secession Reference* [1998] 2 SCR 217, at paras 49–54.

THE NOMADIC SENSE OF LAW IN INTERNATIONAL CONSTITUTIONALISM    279

over land has been considered one such basic doctrine of common law constitutionalism. Such a continuous control, however, has the effect of excluding Nomadic communities from the constitutional protection of their use of land because of the very continuity of a Nomadic community alleged to characterize pre-contact inhabitants.[163] In addition, even if a Nomadic group possessed a fixed location at pre-contact, the group's identity with the land might well have been 'washed away' with 'the tide of history', this being likely with the continual movement of Nomadic groups. Continual movement also contradicts the general requirement that territory be occupied by a group with 'sufficient precision'.[164] The occupation of the land must have existed before the arrival of settlers and continued to the present-day.[165] The territorial principle represents land occupation over pastoral and hunting Nomadism.[166]

Canadian Courts have taken for granted that Nomadism was common when European military and governmental officials made contact with Indigenous inhabitants in North America. Such was not invariably the case. When the European officials met the Pacific Coast Indigenous inhabitants, they found settlements that had survived along the coast for four thousand years. The northern area east of the Mississippi had also had established villages. The Iroquoian Indigenous peoples were farming land with established settlements north of the lakes presently named Ontario and Erie. The Nomadic form of a traditional community, continually on the move, does appear to be primarily characteristic of the Indigenous peoples of the prairies. The Mackenzie and Yukon River peoples characterized the second form of Nomadism—hunting and fishing. In sum, the image of pre-contact peoples as Nomadic—seeped as is the image in the legacy of European legal thought—does not fit the pre-contact life of Indigenous inhabitants.[167] To take one example, such an image of the Nomadic community is generalized by the Canadian Supreme Court to include pre-contact Nomadic Indigenous peoples who 'varied the location of

---

163   *Amodu Tijani v. Secretary, Southern Nigeria* [1921] 2 AC 399, at 402–403; Special Rapporteur of the Sub-Commission on Prevention of Discrimination and Protection of Minorities J.R. Martinez Cobo, 'Study of the Problem of Discrimination against Indigenous Populations' (1987) UN Doc. E/CN.4/Sub.2/1986/7/Add.4, at para. 379.

164   *The Wik Peoples v. Queensland* (1996) 141 ALR 129, HCA, at para. 213 per Kirby, affirming *Mabo v. Queensland (No. 2)* (1992) 175 CLR 1 (3 June 1992), para. 59, 69, 71 A per Brennan.

165   *Amodu Tijani v. Secretary, Southern Nigeria* [1921] 2 AC 399, at 402–403; *Guerin v. R* [1984] 2 SCR 335, at 381.

166   *Mabo v. Queensland (No. 2)* (1992) 175 CLR 1 (3 June 1992), at paras 3, 12, 16, 33, 34, 46 per Brennan.

167   See esp. P.C. Albers, 'Changing Patterns of Ethnicity in the Northeastern Plains' in J.D. Hill (ed.), *History, Power and Identity: Ethnogenesis in the Americas, 1492–1992* (Iowa University Press 1996) 90.

their settlements both before and after contact'.[168] As another example, pre-contact inhabitants on the West Coast and interior British Columbia thereof of present-day Canada were traders.[169] A reductive image of pre-contact, non-Nomadic inhabitants has been the consequence.

(ii) *The Transcription of the Traditional Nomadic Culture into Requisites of the Present*

Although the frozen meaning has dominated the constitutional protection of a Nomadic culture, another version of the cultural approach to Nomadic peoples has also been offered. Here, there is a recognition that a Nomadic culture changes through calendar time and that the judiciary are under a constitutional duty, for example, to take cognizance of the contemporary equivalent of sustenance in comparison with the pre-contact Nomadic culture. The constitutional duty, despite being an 'unwritten' or 'uncoded' postulate of the contemporary legal order, pertains to the basics of food, clothing and housing, supplemented by a few amenities. Such basics must be the modern equivalent of what the Nomadic people in question formerly took from the land or water. This, requirement, in turn, is said to possess 'a high standard of honourable dealing which the Constitution and the law imposed'.[170]

That said, the transcription of a traditional culture into contemporary needs and values does not support 'excess or accumulated wealth' today, one is advised. This is so because the traditional Nomadic culture is limited by what the contemporary State posits as a minimum standard.[171] Such a minimal social security would still leave the (former and present) Nomadic peoples at the low-end of the contemporary social hierarchy in a modern State.

In addition, the State's objectives have been held out to be sufficiently wide to trump any constitutional claim by a group that retains a traditional style of life. The objectives 'consistent' with the purpose of reconciliation of a State-centric legal structure with a Nomadic legal culture includes 'the development of agriculture, forestry, mining, and hydroelectric power, the general economic development of the interior of British Columbia, protection of the environment or endangered species, the building of infrastructure and the settlement of

---

168  *R v. Adams* [1995] 4 SCR 707, at para. 27; *R v. Marshall; R v. Bernard* [2005] 2 SCR 220, at para. 58.

169  R. Fisher, 'The Northwest from the Beginning of Trade with Europeans to the 1880s' in B.G. Trigger and W.E. Washburn (eds), *The Cambridge History of the Native Peoples of the Americas* vol. 1 *North America, Part 2* (CUP 1996) 117–182, 122–123.

170  *R v. Gladstone* [1996] 2 SCR 723, at para. 165; *R v. Van der Peet* [1996] 2 SCR 507, at para. 261 per McLachlin.

171  *R v. Van der Peet* [1996] 2 SCR 507, at para. 312.

foreign populations to support those aims'.[172] Further, when presented with a treaty between a traditional community and the State, the enactment of a treaty right does not exist independent of any State authority.[173] For example, the treaty passage protecting a Nomadic group's 'gathering of berries' in pre-contact times must not 'evolve' into the right to 'gather' natural gas today.[174] In addition, trade amongst Nomadic groups existing in a traditional way of life cannot interfere with the contemporary State-centric market economy except for a right to trade for necessaries of life.[175]

## VI    Conclusion

In sum, the classical view of international constitutionalism as a State-centric governmentality, emergent from the English, French and American Revolutions, has been modified and challenged as of late. A network of treaties, peremptory norms and emergent global associations and corporations modifies the State-centric governmentality. Experts about the jurisdiction of transnational governmental structures, rules about the relations of the organizations and a symbolism about regional units such as 'Europe', 'NAFTA' and the like coordinate the transnational units. In addition to State-centric governmental structures, pyramidal structures have accompanied the global organizations. The question is whether a higher-ordered transcendental structure of institutions and rights—the institutions represented by the transnational network and the rights represented by peremptory norms—is displacing or has displaced the State-centric constitutionalism. The disclosure of the forgotten Nomadic peoples in classical constitutionalism remains problematic with any revised transcendental global constitutionalism. This is so because the external foundation to constitutionalism rested in an intellectually higher source in comparison with the statutes and precedents representing ordinary laws.

Three forms of Nomadic peoples exist. The first concerns hunters, fishers and gatherers. The second addresses pastoralists. Third, peripatetic communities are dependent upon a mixed economy despite their continual movement from

---

172   *Tsilhqu'in Nation v. British Columbia* [2014] 2 SCR 257, at para. 83; *Lax Kw'alaams Indian Band v. Canada (Attorney General)* [2011] 3 SCR 535, at para. 46; *Delgamuukw v. British Columbia* [1997] 3 SCR 1010, at para. 165; *R v. Gladstone* [1996] 2 SCR 723, at para. 75.
173   *R v. Marshall* [1999] 3 SCR 456, 177 DLR (4th) 513 (*Marshall No. 1*), at para. 42; *R v. Marshall* [1999] 3 SCR 533, 179 DLR (4th) 193 (*Marshall No. 2*), at para. 38; *Lax Kw'alaams Indian Band v. Canada (Attorney General)* [2011] 3 SCR 535, at para. 44.
174   *Lax Kw'alaams Indian Band v. Canada (Attorney General)* [2011] 3 SCR 535, at para. 51.
175   *R v. Marshall* [1999] 3 SCR 456, 177 DLR (4th) 513 (*Marshall No. 1*), at para. 58.

place to place. The specific contexts where Nomadism is practised are complex and diverse throughout the globe. Amongst other factors, the sense of law of a Nomadic group radically differs from the sense of law taken for granted in international constitutionalism.

In particular, constitutionalism, emergent after the English, French and American Revolutions of the 17th and 18th centuries, entertained an intellectually transcendent law. Such a transcendent law rendered ordinary laws of the State inoperative and void. The sense of law of a Nomadic community has emerged immanently from the events experienced in the past by the group as a whole. The sense of a law, as immanent from events experienced by a Nomadic community, differs from the analytic method and the characterization of constitutionalism as a matter of rights, property, contract, jurisdiction, the State and possessive individualism. The sense of an imminent law also differs from the legal consciousness of a higher structure of intellectually constructed standards. The transcendent structure of concepts is the product of acts of intellectualism drawn from reflection, deliberation and a decision. The latter structure characterizes a State-centric sense of law. Instead, though their laws draw immanently from experienced events, Nomadic peoples often do not consciously choose this or that law as if a law is a concept. This is so because they find themselves trying to cope with external environmental and the State regulatory constraints. They find their constraints *in* their world, not in some inaccessible concept representing the higher-ordered international constitutionalism. The Nomadic group responds to external phenomena that leave them with little choice.

The legacy of the international constitutionalism about Nomadic peoples has juxtaposed with a State-centric, official language against the customs of traditional (or tribal) Nomadic communities, scattered pastoralists, hunters and fishers and, thirdly, peripatetic Nomadic groups. Such Nomadic communities lack a centralized pyramidal institutional structure with a shared rights-consciousness amongst expert knowers in the Nomadic community. This profound schism between State-centric and an immanent experiential sense of law characterized early Greek and Roman juristic writings. Such an early acceptance of a radical schism between 'law' and the 'lawlessness' of Nomadic communities continued into Augustan legal thought, early modern legal thought and has continued into the constitutionalism of 19th and 20th century Europe and North American adjudication.

The problematic of the gulf in a sense of law manifested by constitutionalism on the one hand and the sense of law experienced by members of a Nomadic community on the other has therefore concerned this issue: 'what is the basis of harm caused to Nomadic groups and, in particular, the legal cultures of

Nomadic groups if their sense of law radically differs from constitutionalism?' This is especially problematic when one addresses the general problems emergent from the State-centric international constitutional effort to recognize and protect a Nomadic legal order: the emergence of a misdirected constitutionalism, the social bond as a State-posited legal bond in a Nomadic community, the reserved domain in the international community, the Nomadic use of territory if one is not a national, the paramountcy of State law over a Nomadic law, and the absence of governmentality in a Nomadic group.

Four contemporary constitutional arguments have been retrieved in order to raise the prospect of a general constitutional right to protect Nomadic peoples. The first concerns the protection of a Nomadic group in an independent State whose emergence was characterized by colonialism. The second has concerned the minority status of Nomadic peoples. The reductive and generalized character of such a constitutional protection of a 'minority' contradicts the diversity and immanent character of Nomadic legal cultures, however. The third, grounded in an experiential attachment to land, has required a fixed and continuous possession and control of land. Such a legal requirement has been at odds with the continuous movement of Nomadic peoples. The fourth argument, drawn from unwritten conventions of a State-centric legal order independent of a basic text, has focused upon the protection of Nomadic cultures. The latter approach finds support with judicial remedies. Whether international constitutionalism is reconcilable with the complexities and nuances of a context-specific Nomadic culture remains moot. This is especially so in that the constitutionalism trumps the sense of law immanent in a Nomadic community. Such a sense of law radically differs from constitutionalism. And yet, such a sense of law remains integral to a context-specific Nomadic culture.

### Acknowledgments

I am grateful for Dr. Frauke Lachenmann's and the Reviewers' feedback, and for the research aid of our librarian, Annette Demers. I have also benefited from Vida Shahriar Bahram and Nathan Prendergast.

CHAPTER 11

# The Institutional and Constitutional Aspects of the Arab Maghreb Union and the Dispute on Western Sahara as an Obstacle: What Role does the European Union Play in Promoting Maghreb Regional Integration?

*Mohamed Riyad M. Almosly*

## Abstract

The current era is witnessing a proliferation of challenges of a transnational character that do not recognize the geographical limits of sovereign States, such as human traficking and pollution. Therefore, States have to establish new regional cooperative methods to find effective solutions for these challenges. Although the Maghreb States (i.e. Algeria, Libya, Mauritania, Morocco and Tunisia) have been suffering from the negative impacts of such challenges over the last few decades, they have not yet created an effective regional cooperative framework. In this respect, since its establishment in 1989 among the Maghreb States, the Arab Maghreb Union (AMU, Union) has not been successful in stimulating Maghreb regional integration. The current study addresses a topic that has not yet been fully exploited by legal studies in the English language. It examines, first, the genesis and institutional structure of the AMU as well as the constitutional aspects of the 1989 AMU Treaty; second, the role of the EU's multilateral and bilateral instruments in promoting Maghreb regional integration; and third, the dispute on Western Sahara between Morocco and the Polisario Front and its effect on Maghreb regional integration. The article concludes that Maghreb regional integration has so far failed due to the institutional and constitutional limits of the AMU Treaty and the political division among the Maghreb States resulting from the Western Sahara conflict. In addition, the EU so far has not followed a consistent and single approach in promoting the Maghreb integration nor did it play any role in solving the dispute on Western Sahara.

## Keywords

Arab Maghreb Union – EU Multilateral Frameworks towards the Maghreb States – Relative Effect of International Agreements – Euro – Mediterranean Association Agreement – Western Sahara – *Council v. Front Polisario Case* – *Western Sahara Campaign UK v. Commissioners for Her Majesty's Revenue and Customs*

## 1    Introduction

The establishment of the Arab Maghreb Union (AMU) in February 1989 among Algeria, Libya, Mauritania, Morocco and Tunisia (AMUMS or Maghreb States) was a major breakthrough towards creating regional integration in the Maghreb.[1] Unfortunately, soon after its foundation, the AMU failed to achieve its main objectives due to several reasons, the most detrimental of which has been the conflict between Morocco and the Polisario Front (supported by Algeria) on Western Sahara.[2] The AMU failure led to a lack of regional cooperation among the Maghreb States, which has negatively impacted the economy of the Maghreb and the security of its neighbours. According to the European Commission and the High Representative of the Union for Foreign Affairs and Security Policy / Vice President of the European Commission (HRVP), 'the real cost of non-integration [of the Maghreb] goes beyond economic growth to include security, and wider human development in the region'.[3] Therefore, considering the current rise of transnational challenges, such as terrorism and human trafficking, the reinvigoration of the AMU project and the creation of a functional cooperative channel between the Maghreb States and the EU have now become necessary not only for economic reasons but also for consolidating the security of both sides.[4] To assess the obstacles of the

---

1    For the purpose of this article, Maghreb regional integration refers to all forms of integration that could generate a comprehensive cooperation among the Maghreb States in, for instance, the political, economic and social sectors.
2    E. Lannon, 'The EU's Strategic Partnership with the Mediterranean and the Middle East: A New Geopolitical Dimension of the EU's Proximity Strategies' in A. Dashwood and M. Maresceau (eds), *Law and Practice of EU External Relations: Salient Features of a Changing Landscape* (CUP 2008) 360, at 364.
3    Commission of the European Union and HRVP 'Joint Communication to the European Parliament, the Council, the European Economic and Social Committee and the Committee of the Regions: Supporting Closer Cooperation and Regional Integration in the Maghreb: Algeria, Libya, Mauritania, Morocco and Tunisia' JOIN(2012)36 final (17 December 2012), at para. 9.
4    S. Wolf, *The Mediterranean Dimension of the European Union's Internal Security* (Palgrave Macmillan 2012), at 169.

Maghreb regional cooperation, Section II of this article examines the institutional and constitutional aspects of the AMU. Section III scrutinizes the role of the EU's multilateral and bilateral instruments in promoting Maghreb regional integration. Section IV studies the dispute on Western Sahara and analyses the two cases brought before the Court of Justice of the EU (CJEU) challenging the territorial application of specific agreements[5] concluded between the EU (and its Member States) and Morocco to Western Sahara.

## II    The Arab Maghreb Union (AMU)

### 1    *The AMU Genesis*

The successful establishment of the Gulf Cooperation Council (GCC) on 25 May 1981 among Bahrain, Kuwait, Oman, Qatar, Saudi Arabia and the United Arab Emirates stimulated the Maghreb States to create their own regional organization. The first fundamental step towards strengthening Maghreb regional integration was taken on 10 June 1988 when the heads of the AMUMS met in Algeria and announced the Ziralde Declaration. In that Declaration, the heads of the AMUMS decided to establish a joint committee, which was later named as the Maghreb Committee, to study the possibilities of creating a union among the Maghreb States. Following the Ziralde meeting, another summit was held on 17 February 1989 in Morocco in which the AMUMS took two important decisions: first, they adopted the Marrakesh Declaration that announced the conclusion of the Treaty instituting the AMU among the AMUMS (AMU Treaty),[6] which consists of 19 articles and describes, *inter alia*, the principles and objectives of the AMU as well as the main functions of its institutions. Second, they approved the proposals that were submitted by the Maghreb Committee and considered them as a 'Work Program' to be implemented by the AMU institutions in the future.[7]

---

5   The dispute brought before the CJEU mainly related to the territorial scope of the Euro–Mediterranean Agreement Establishing an Association between the European Communities and their Member States, of the One Part, and the Kingdom of Morocco, of the Other Part (signed 26 February 1996, entered into force 1 March 2000) [2000] OJ L70/2 (EU–Morocco EMAA), and of the sectoral protocols concluded on the basis of this agreement between the EU (then EC) and its Member States and Morocco.

6   Treaty instituting the Arab Maghreb Union (with Declaration) (signed 17 February 1989, entered into force 1 July 1989) 1546 UNTS 161 (AMU Treaty). The articles of the AMU Treaty, the official documents related to the AMU and the Rules of Procedure of the AMU institutions included in this research were translated by the author from the Arabic version.

7   Presidency Council 'Decision on the Approval of the Recommendations and Proposals of the Maghreb Committee and its Sub-Committees' (17 February 1989).

In addition to being a regional cooperative framework, the AMU was also conceived as an embodiment of the sense of the AMUMS's affiliation to several commonalities such as religion, culture and identity.[8] The AMUMS's constitutions explicitly point towards this meaning and reiterate the aspirations of those States to create a regional bloc under the emblem of unity and mutual interests.[9]

## 2   The AMU Objectives

Art. 2 AMU Treaty stipulates five main objectives of the AMU: (1) To consolidate the brotherhood ties among the Member States and their people; (2) To achieve the prosperity of the Member States' societies; (3) To contribute to the maintenance of peace that is based on justice and fairness; (4) To implement common policies in various sectors;[10] (5) To work towards the gradual achievement of free movement of persons, services, goods and capital among the Member States.

What is clear from the text of Art. 2 AMU Treaty, is that the AMU objectives are rather ambitious as they aim at gradually creating a common market that guarantees the freedom of movement of 'persons, services, goods and capital' among the AMUMS. It is interesting to note here that the four freedoms the

---

8   Art. 17 AMU Treaty allows the AMUMS to admit other States belonging to the Arab and/or African group.
9   See, for instance, (1) Chapter (5) of the 2014 Tunisian Constitution which states that 'Tunisia is part of the Arab Maghreb and works towards the achievement of its unity'. (2) The Preamble of the 2011 Moroccan Constitution says that '[Morocco] emphasizes and commits itself to work on building the Maghreb Union as a strategic choice'. (3) The Preamble of the 1991 Mauritanian Constitution 'declare[s] its determination to work towards the achievement of the unity of the Grand Arab Maghreb, Arab Nation and Africa'. (4) The Preamble of the 1996 Algerian Constitution and the 2016 Draft Constitution provides that Algeria is an 'unalienable part of the Grand Arab Maghreb'. The provisions of the above-mentioned constitutions were translated by the author from the Arabic versions.
10  Art. 3 AMU Treaty further clarifies that the objectives of the common policies referred to in Art. 2 AMU Treaty are: (1) At the international level, reaching harmonization and establishing diplomatic cooperation among the AMUMS on the basis of dialogue. (2) In the defence sector, maintaining the independence of all the AMUMS. (3) In the economic sector, achieving industrial, agricultural, trade and social development in the AMUMS, especially by launching common projects and preparing general and qualitative programs. (4) In the cultural sector, initiating cooperation that aims at devolving education at all its levels, maintaining the moral and spiritual values derived from the magnanimous Islamic principles, and preserving the national identity. The Member States shall take the necessary means to achieve these objectives, specifically by establishing common academic, cultural, and specialized research institutions among them.

AMU aims at achieving are identical to those established by the EU Single Market.[11] Theoretically, the ambitious approach of the AMU Treaty made the integration road among the AMUMS shorter than it would normally be, i.e. by first concluding a free trade agreement, secondly a customs union and then a common market. However, despite such theoretical advantage, the problem remains that the AMU Treaty does not specify the procedures through which the common market among the AMUMS can be achieved. Moreover, the Maghreb was lacking the infrastructural, institutional and planning capacities as well as qualified human resources that are required to implement such ambitious project. Hence, it would have been better if the AMUMS had followed a 'step-by-step' approach similar to that the EU has been following since 1952.[12] The EU started with sectoral integration in the coal and steel sectors, on the basis of the Treaty Establishing the European Coal and Steel Community (ECSC) of 1952.[13] Then, the EU Member States gradually widened and deepened the scope of their integration through the adoption of several treaties.[14] During their third summit on 10–11 March 1991, the AMUMS attempted to follow the gradual approach to integration by adopting a timeline to establish a free-trade area by 1992; a customs union by 1995; a common market by 2000; and an economic and monetary union at a later date.[15] But, as will be shown below, the

---

11   Art. 26 (2) of the Treaty on the Functioning of the European Union (signed 13 December 2007, entered into force 1 December 2009) [2008] OJ C115/47 (TFEU).

12   E. Lannon, 'Extending the Geographical Scope of the ENP: The Neighbours of the EU's Neighbours' in S. Florensa (ed.), *European Neighbourhood Policy Review* (IEMed 2016) 26, at 30.

13   Treaty instituting the European Coal and Steel Community (signed 18 April 1951, entered into force 23 July 1952) 261 UNTS 140.

14   Treaty establishing the European Economic Community (signed 25 March 1957, entered into force 1 January 1958) 294 UNTS 17 (Treaty of Rome); Treaty establishing the European Atomic Energy Community (Euratom) (signed 25 March 1957, entered into force 1 January 1958) 294 UNTS 260; Single European Act (signed 17 February 1986, entered into force 1 July 1987) 1754 UNTS 3; Treaty on European Union (signed 7 February 1992, entered into force 1 November 1993) [1992] OJ C191/1 (TEU); Treaty of Amsterdam Amending the Treaty on European Union, the Treaties establishing the European Communities and Certain Related Acts (signed 2 October 1997, entered into force 1 May 1999) [1997] OJ C340/308; Treaty of Nice Amending the Treaty on European Union, the Treaties establishing the European Communities and Certain Related Acts (signed 26 February 2001, entered into force 1 February 2003) [2001] OJ C80/1; Treaty of Lisbon Amending the Treaty on European Union (TEU) and the Treaty establishing the European Community (signed 13 December 2007, entered into force 1 December 2009) [2007] OJ C306 (TFEU).

15   A. Aghrout, *From Preferential Status to Partnership: The Euro–Maghreb Relationship* (Ashgate 2000), at 19.

political controversies among the AMUMS hampered the implementation of those steps.[16]

### 3   The AMU Institutional Structure[17]

a   The Presidency Council, the Prime Ministers Meeting, and the Council of Ministers of Foreign Affairs

The Presidency Council of the AMU consists of the heads of the AMUMS. Each Member State of the AMU chairs the Presidency Council for one year on a rotating basis and has one vote.[18] The competences of the Presidency Council vis-à-vis the AMU institutions will be examined in the following sections but suffice to note here that this institution is the only body among the AMU institutions empowered to issue, on the basis of unanimity, binding decisions on the Maghreb States.[19] The Presidency Council meets on an annual basis and may hold extraordinary summits.[20] Six Presidency Council summits have been held since the establishment of the AMU.[21] The seventh summit was supposed to be held in Algeria in 1995 but this did not take place due the following reasons: first, the controversies between Algeria and Morocco were deepened because of the position of both sides regarding the dispute on Western Sahara, see below. These disagreements were further aggravated as a result of the Atlas Asni Hotel incident, which led to the closure of borders between Algeria and Morocco.[22] Secondly, Libya declined to receive the AMU presidency from Algeria on 30 January 1995[23] and did not attend the fifth and sixth summits because it was not satisfied with some of the AMUMS that implemented the sanctions imposed against it by the UN Security Council.[24]

---

16   Aghrout also mentions that the implementation of different economic policies by the AMUMS was one of the obstacles to achieve the steps agreed upon during the third AMU summit (at 20).
17   See Figure 11.1.
18   Art. 4 AMU Treaty.
19   Art. 7 AMU Treaty.
20   Arts 4–5 AMU Treaty.
21   The place and date of the six summits are: (1) Tunisia, 21–23 January 1990; (2) Algeria, 21–23 July 1990; (3) Ras Lanuf/Libya, 10–11 March 1991; (4) Casablanca/Morocco, 15–16 September 1991; (5) Nouakchott/Mauritania 10–11 November 1992; (6) Tunisia 2–3 April 1994.
22   On 24 August 1994, a terrorist attack occurred in the Atlas Asni Hotel in Marrakesh, Morocco. Morocco accused Algeria of having committed the attack and imposed a visa requirement on Algerians entering the Moroccan territory. Algeria retaliated by closing its borders with Morocco. See A. Ben Antar, 'The Arab Maghreb Union between Assumption and Reality' (3 October 2004) Al Jazeera TV.
23   Aghrout, *From Preferential Status to Partnership: The Euro–Maghreb Relationship*, at 19.
24   The UNSC imposed sanctions against Libya through two resolutions: UNSC Res 748 (1992) 'Libyan Arab Jamahiriya', and UNSC Res 883 (1993) 'Libyan Arab Jamahiriya'. These sanctions were imposed due to the involvement of several Libyan officials in the bombing

Besides the summits of the Presidency Council, Art. 7 AMU Treaty also provided the possibility for the Prime Ministers of the AMUMS to meet, but it did not provide further details on the competences, objectives and institutional structure of such a meeting.

The AMU Treaty also established the Council of Ministers of Foreign Affairs to supervise the work of the Secretary General, the Follow-up Committee and the four Specialized Ministerial Committees of the AMU and to report on the progress achieved to the Presidency Council.[25] It also prepares the Presidency Council summits[26] and was instructed to 'take the necessary measures to preserve the identity and interests of the Maghreb citizens living in the EU and to report on this matter'.[27] The Council of Ministers of Foreign Affairs has so far held 34 meetings, the last of which was in Tunisia on 5 May 2016.

b       The Follow-Up Committee, the Specialized Ministerial Committees and the Secretariat

The Follow-up Committee is composed of one member from the Ministerial Cabinet or the General People's Committee of each AMUMS.[28] In addition to the Follow-up Committee, four thematic Ministerial Committees were established pursuant to Art. 10 AMU Treaty: a Food Security Committee; an Economic and Financial Committee; an Infrastructure Committee; and a Human Resources Committee.[29] Each Committee adopts its own Rules of Procedures (RoP) and is composed of the ministries (or other institutions) of the AMUMS,

---

of an American and a French aircraft. The American aircraft 'Pan Am Flight 103' was destroyed on 21 December 1988 over Lockerbie City in Scotland while the French aircraft 'Union de Transports Aériens Flight 772' was exploded on 19 September 1989 over the Niger. The UNSC sanctions on Libya were lifted by UNSC Res 1506 (2003) 'Lockerbie Case' on the basis of the '[Libyan Government's] acceptance of responsibility for the actions of Libyan officials, payment of appropriate compensation [to the affected families], renunciation of terrorism, and a commitment to cooperating with any further requests for information in connection with the investigation'. See A.M. Ameen Laajal, 'The Obstacles of Maghreb Regional Integration and the Ways to Overcome them' (2010) 5 Almophaker Journal 23.

25    Arts 8–9 AMU Treaty; Arts 7–8 Rules of Procedures of the Secretariat of the AMU (23 July 1990), annexed to the Presidency Council 'Decision of the Second Summit' (21–23 July 1990) (Secretariat RoP).
26    Art. 8 AMU Treaty.
27    Presidency Council of the AMU 'Minutes of the First Summit in Tunisia' (21–23 January 1990).
28    Art. 9 AMU Treaty.
29    Presidency Council 'Decision on the Creation of Specialized Ministerial Committees' (23 January 1990), annexed to the Presidency Council 'Decision of the First Summit' (21–23 January 1990).

# THE EU ROLE IN PROMOTING MAGHREB REGIONAL INTEGRATION 291

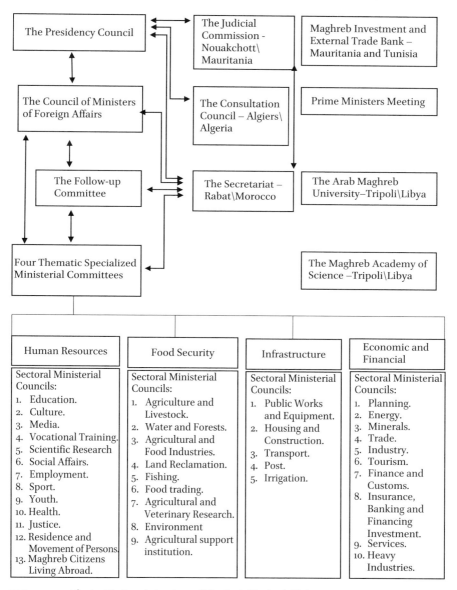

FIGURE 11.1  The institutional structure of the Arab Maghreb Union
SOURCE: AUTHOR'S COMPILATION ON THE BASIS OF THE AMU CONSTITUTING DOCUMENTS AND THE AMU (ARABIC) WEBSITE, AVAILABLE AT HTTP://WWW.MAGHREBARABE.ORG/AR/ORG.CFM (ACCESSED 4 MARCH 2019).

whose field of speciality is similar to that of the Committee in question.[30] The four Committees comprise Sectoral Ministerial Councils and Work Teams that work on the achievement of further sectoral integration among the AMUMS (see Figure 11.1).[31] The functions of the Follow-up Committee and the four Committees are interrelated. Both sides report the progress achieved in their work to the AMU Council of Foreign Affairs Ministers and cooperate with the Secretariat to, first, ensure coherency in the work of the AMU institutions and, second, implement the Work Program prepared by the Maghreb Committee in 1989.[32]

Another institution of the AMU whose work is intertwined with the abovementioned Committees of the AMU is the Secretariat. It is located in Rabat and has a legal personality and financial independence.[33] The Secretariat's staff is delegated by its Secretary General who shall be designated by the AMU Presidency Council for a term of three years, which can only be renewed once.[34] On the basis of Art. 5 Secretariat RoP, the most important functions of this institution are (1) implementing the Presidency Council decisions in coordination with the AMU institutions and (2) conducting administrative tasks related to the AMU institutions such as archiving and storing documents; preparing reports on the AMU development progress; and performing secretary tasks.[35]

c     The Consultation Council

The Consultation Council is the parliamentary body of the AMU and was established on the basis of Art. 12 AMU Treaty. It is composed of 150[36] members that enjoy parliamentary immunity and 'must be chosen from the parliamentary organs of the Member States or in accordance with the internal system of each Member State' for five year terms.[37] It holds ordinary sessions on an

---

30    Ibid., Arts 4 and 7.
31    Ibid., Art. 5.
32    Ibid., Arts 3 and 6; Art. 9 AMU Treaty.
33    Art. 2 Secretariat RoP; Art. 11 AMU Treaty.
34    Art. 6 Secretariat RoP.
35    The Secretariat of the AMU can also conclude agreements with other institutions. In this respect, see for instance, the Cooperation Agreement between the AMU Secretariat and the Arabic Institute for Human Rights (21 September 2016) and the Cooperation Agreement between the AMU Secretariat and the Arab League Educational, Cultural and Scientific Research Organisation (ALECSO) (25 June 2007).
36    30 members from each AMUMS. The number was raised from 100 to 150 in accordance with Presidency Council 'Decision of the Sixth Summit' (2–3 April 1994).
37    Arts 2, 3 and 8 Rules of Procedures of the Consultation Council of the AMU annexed to Presidency Council 'Decision of the Second Summit' (21–23 July 1990) (Consultation Council RoP); Art. 12 AMU Treaty.

annual basis and may hold extraordinary sessions on the basis of a Presidency Council request.[38] It has so far held seven ordinary sessions, the last of which was in Algeria from 9–10 June 2010. The Consultation Council has the capacity to issue opinions on the draft decisions submitted to it by the Presidency Council and may submit recommendations to the latter on what it considers appropriate to achieve the AMU's objectives.[39] Although the Consultation Council creates parliamentary cooperation among the AMUMS, it suffers from certain obstacles that may impede its effectiveness. First, it is only a consultative body that has no powers to issue binding decisions. Second, it is not a fully independent institution, as its budget is approved by the Presidency Council.[40] Third, Art. 12 AMU Treaty allows the AMUMS to appoint, in accordance with their 'internal system', members in the Consultation Council that are not necessarily parliamentarians. As a result, the parliamentary character of this institution can be undermined. It would have been more democratic if the AMU Treaty had mentioned that the members of the Consultation Council should be elected by a direct universal suffrage of the Maghreb citizens, as is the case with the members of the European Parliament who are elected by the EU's citizens.[41] However, this is not expected at this stage because even the EU had its first elected parliament in 1979, i.e. after more than two decades from the entry into force of the ECSC Treaty in 1952. As a fourth obstacle, the Consultation Council cannot amend its RoP without getting the amendment proposal signed by all its members, accepted by two quarters of them and approved by the Presidency Council.[42] Such a rigid procedure might affect the work dynamism of this institution.

d    The Judicial Commission

The Judicial Commission is based in Nouakchott, Mauritania and was established on the basis of Art. 13 AMU Treaty by the Presidency Council of the AMU during its third summit on 10–11 March 1991. It is composed of ten judges, two of whom are designated by each of the AMUMS and serves in office for a term of six years.[43] The Judicial Commission has jurisdiction over (1) disputes referred to it by the AMU Presidency Council or the AMUMS and related to the

---

38  Art. 24 Consultation Council RoP; Art. 12 AMU Treaty.
39  Arts 1 and 32 Consultation Council RoP; Art. 12 AMU Treaty.
40  Art. 39 Consultation Council RoP.
41  Art. 14 (3) TEU.
42  Art. 44 Consultation Council RoP.
43  Arts 4 and 5 Rules of Procedures of the Judicial Commission of the AMU annexed to Presidency Council 'Decision of the Third Summit' (10–11 March 1991) (Judicial Commission RoP).

interpretation and implementation of the AMU Treaty and/or the agreements that were concluded within the AMU framework;[44] (2) disputes between the AMU institutions and their staff;[45] and (3) disputes regarding the interpretation and implementation of the 1991 Maghreb Bank Agreement.[46] The decisions of the Judicial Commission are final and binding, but it can also give consultative opinions on issues referred to it by the Presidency Council.[47]

e       The Maghreb Investment and External Trade Bank (Maghreb Bank)

The AMUMS signed the Agreement Establishing the Maghreb Investment and External Trade Bank (Maghreb Bank Agreement) on 9–10 March 1991. The creation of the Maghreb Bank was one of the measures towards the implementation of Art. 3 (3) of the AMU Treaty in which the AMUMS committed themselves to cooperate in the economic field. Although the Maghreb Bank Agreement was already signed in 1991, the Bank has only recently started its work when the highest body of the Bank,[48] the General Assembly, held its first meeting in Tunisia on 21 December 2015. The meeting in question was attended by the finance ministers of the AMUMS and the Libyan Minister of Foreign Affairs and has several important outcomes: first, all the AMUMS paid their share in the US$500 million that were required by Art. 5 (B) of the Maghreb Bank Agreement as the start-up capital of the Bank. Second, the Administration Council Members of the Bank were appointed. Third, it was decided that the Bank's seat would be in Tunisia and its first branch will be opened in Nouakchott, Mauritania. Fourth, the Bank's RoP was approved. Hence, the above-mentioned meeting of the General Assembly has taken the first main steps towards the practical and official start of the Bank's work. This would definitely boost the regional cooperation among the AMUMS and might generate positive impact from the projects that will be financed by the Maghreb Bank. However, one should not exaggerate the expected results, as the Bank's capital is extremely low in comparison with the challenges facing the Maghreb region.

---

44    Art. 24 Judicial Commission RoP.
45    Art. 25 Judicial Commission RoP.
46    The disputes related to the interpretation and implementation of the Maghreb Bank Agreement may also be settled amicably or through a provisional arbitration committee to be appointed by the disputed parties. See Art. 18 (A) Maghreb Bank Agreement; Art. 20 Investment Guarantee and Encouragement Agreement among the Maghreb Union Member States (23 July 1990).
47    Arts 42 and 49 Judicial Commission RoP.
48    Arts 9 and 10 (A) Maghreb Bank Agreement.

f       The Arab Maghreb University and the Maghreb Academy of
        Science

These two institutions are located in Tripoli, Libya and were established by the Presidency Council during its second summit on 21–23 July 1990 to achieve interrelated tasks. The University aims at facilitating research activities within the AMUMS and providing the AMU with researchers specialized in the key priority areas of the Union. Similarly, the Maghreb Academy was established to promote scientific research programs in the Maghreb and to organize scientific conferences.[49]

## 4   *The Constitutional Aspects of the AMU Treaty*

The AMU Treaty was concluded for an unlimited period, which reflects the AMUMS' intention to create a permanent cooperative framework. Furthermore, although the scope of the AMU Treaty is very limited, as it comprises only 19 articles, it is a *traité cadre* or framework treaty, i.e. its content can be widened and deepened by the AMUMS without the need to negotiate a new agreement.[50] The other important merit of the AMU Treaty is that it established a comprehensive institutional structure that aims at strengthening cooperation between the executive and parliamentary institutions of the AMUMS. It also created a dispute settlement mechanism that has the capacity to issue binding decisions, namely the Judicial Commission.

However, the short, general and basic nature of the provisions of the AMU Treaty reflect the absence of a strategic vision of the constituting Member States and leaves the AMU with a constitutional vacuum in many aspects. The AMU Treaty lacks certain aspects necessary for any regional organization such as, for instance, an explicit reference to the Union's legal personality, the Union's capacity to conclude international agreements, and a clear mandate for the Union institutions and their competences vis-à-vis the national authorities of each Member State. Also, the AMU does not create cooperation between the regional governments or municipalities of its Member States, as is the case with the EU Committee of the Regions. In addition, the AMU suffers from a democratic deficit for at least two reasons. First, the Consultation Council of the AMU was not given strong parliamentary competences such as the power to issue binding decisions. Second, the AMU does not involve civil society organizations in the cooperative process.

---

49    Maghreb University Journal, *Documents from the Arab Maghreb Union* vol. 2 (2006), at 9.
50    E. Lannon, 'Lectures on the Constitutional Aspects of the European Union's Integration' (given at Ghent University February–June 2016); A. Aust, *Modern Treaty Law and Practice* (2nd edn CUP 2007), at 122.

Another obstacle to the AMU success is that the AMU follows an intergovernmental cooperative method, namely, its Presidency Council cannot take binding decisions without achieving unanimity among its Member States.[51] Likewise, any amendment to the AMU Treaty enters into force only after receiving a unanimous ratification from the AMUMS.[52] Consequently, considering the political disharmony among the Maghreb States, this working method has been one of the major reasons behind the AMU failure. Hence, the difficulty to achieve consensus among the AMUMS has negatively impacted the work dynamism of the AMU institutions. Compared to the AMU Treaty, the GCC Charter of 25 May 1981 does not require unanimity among its Member States in all cases. Art. 9 GCC Charter provides that:[53]

> Resolutions of the Supreme Council in substantive matters shall be carried by unanimous approval of the Member States participating in the voting, while resolutions on procedural matters shall be carried by majority vote.

Although the GCC decision-making mechanism is not an exemplary model for regional cooperation, it is definitely more flexible than that of the AMU. However, it can be argued that the intergovernmental method followed by the AMU and the limited scope of the AMU Treaty are not the only obstacles for this regional organization, as the AMU Treaty was only a first step that had to be gradually developed. Instead, the main impediment to the AMU lies in the dispute between Morocco and the Polisario Front (supported by Algeria) on Western Sahara. Section IV examines this issue but before that the following section studies the EU role in encouraging regional integration in the Maghreb.

## III   The EU Role in Promoting Maghreb Regional Integration

Beyond any doubt, creating effective cooperative frameworks between the EU and its immediate Southern Mediterranean neighbours has become a matter of necessity to tackle the current transnational challenges such as human trafficking and terrorism.[54] The Global Strategy for the EU's Foreign and Security

---

51   Art. 7 AMU Treaty.
52   Art. 18 AMU Treaty.
53   Charter of the Co-operation Council for the Arab States of the Gulf (signed 25 May 1981, entered into force 25 May 1981) 1288 UNTS 131.
54   G. De Búrca, 'Europe's *raison d'être*' in D. Kochenov and F. Amtenbrink (eds), *The European Union's Shaping of the International Legal Order* (CUP 2014) 37; N. Ghazaryan, *The*

Policy (EUGS) stressed that the EU shall not only build strong relationships with its Mediterranean neighbours but shall also encourage regional cooperation among the Mediterranean States and their neighbours, which in practice means establishing cooperative frameworks between the EU, the Maghreb, the Mashreq, the Horn of Africa, the Sahel, and the Arab Gulf.[55] The political objective to strengthen regional cooperation among the Mediterranean States emphasized in the EUGS is also accompanied with a legal obligation on the EU to promote the integration of these States into the world economy. In this respect, Art. 21 (2) TEU emphasizes that:

> The [EU] shall define and pursue common policies and actions, and shall work for a high degree of cooperation in all fields of international relations in order to: ... [e] encourage the integration of all countries into the world economy, including through the progressive abolition of restrictions on international trade.

Building on that, the EU engagement with the Mediterranean currently has two dimensions: first, the north–south cooperation that seeks to integrate the market of some of the Mediterranean States with the EU Internal Market. Second, the south–south dimension that theoretically endeavours to promote regional integration among the Mediterranean partners. As will be explained below, although achieving these two dimensions is already stipulated as one of the main objectives of many multilateral and bilateral frameworks and agreements concluded between the EU and the Maghreb States, the EU still follows fragmented approaches to achieve these objectives (see Table 11.1).

### 1  Regional Integration among the AMUMS as an Objective of EU Multilateral Policies

The EU has created three multilateral frameworks regulating the relations with its Mediterranean partners,[56] the first of which was the Euro–Mediterranean

---

*European Neighbourhood Policy and the Democratic Values of the EU: A Legal Analysis* (Hart 2014), at 4.

55  HRVP, 'Shared Vision, Common Action: A Stronger Europe: A Global Strategy for the European Union's Foreign And Security Policy' (June 2016), at 34; E. Lannon, 'Introduction: The "Neighbours of the EU's Neighbours", the "EU's Broader Neighbourhood" and the "Arc of Crisis and Strategic Challenges" from the Sahel to Central Asia' in S. Gstöhl and E. Lannon (eds), *The Neighbours of the European Union's Neighbours: Diplomatic and Geopolitical Dimensions beyond the European Neighbourhood Policy* (Routledge 2014) 2.

56  In addition to these policies, other cooperative frameworks have been established such as the '5+5 Dialogue' between the AMUMS and France, Italy, Malta, Portugal and Spain.

TABLE 11.1  The bilateral and multilateral frameworks linking the EU (and its Member States) and the AMU Member States[a]

| Country | Multilateral frameworks with the EU ||||||  Bilateral or regional legal agreements with the EU ||
|---|---|---|---|---|---|---|---|---|
| | EMP | ENP | UfM | SPMME | JEAS | Cotonou Agreement | EMAA | EPA |
| Algeria | * | * | * | * | * | | * | |
| Morocco | * | * | * | * | | | * | |
| Tunisia | * | * | * | * | * | | * | |
| Mauritania | | | * | | * | * | | * |
| Libya | | | | | * | | | |

a   SOURCE: AUTHOR'S COMPILATION BASED ON TABLES IN E. LANNON 'INTRODUCTION', AT 14–17.

Partnership (EMP). The EMP was established by the 1995 Barcelona Declaration adopted by the EU (and its Member States) and twelve Mediterranean States.[57] It aimed at creating cooperation between the participant States in three chapters concerning political and security issues; economic and financial matters; and social, cultural and human affairs.[58] As a means to strengthen cooperation in the second chapter, the EMP partners agreed to consider the 'regional cooperation and integration' among them as one of the 'long-term objectives' of the Partnership.[59] The EMP partners further planned to create a Euro–Mediterranean free trade area by the end of 2010.[60] Also, the financial

  Such frameworks were excluded from this research because they do not involve all the EU Member States.
57  Barcelona Declaration, adopted at the Euro–Mediterranean Conference (27–28 November 1995). The States participating in the EMP were Algeria, Cyprus, Egypt, Israel, Jordan, Lebanon, Malta, Morocco, Syria, Tunisia, Turkey, and Palestine. As Cyprus and Malta only became EU Member States in 2004, they joined the EMP in 1995 as Mediterranean States.
58  E. Lannon et al., 'EU's Promotion of Regional and Sub-regional Economic Integration and Cooperation: Transitional Processes and other Experiments of Regional Economic Integration in Europe, the Mediterranean and Asia Compared' in S. Florensa (ed.), *The Arab Spring in Comparative Perspective: SSN-EuromescoJoint Policy Study* (IEMed 2015) 102.
59  Barcelona Declaration.
60  Ibid. Unfortunately, this objective was not achieved by 2010 due to political and technical obstacles that are beyond the scope of this study. To accelerate the process towards the achievement of a Euro–Mediterranean free-trade area, the Agadir Agreement came into force on 6 July 2006 to gradually establish a free-trade area among the Arab

regulations of the EMP, MEDA (1996–1999) and MEDA II (2000–2006),[61] set the encouragement of regional cooperation as one of their main objectives.[62] In this regard, para. III of Annex II to MEDA II stated that:

> Regional, subregional and cross-border cooperation shall be supported in particular by: (a) establishing and developing structures for regional cooperation between the Mediterranean partners, and between them and the European Union and its Member States.[63]

Whereas the EMP approach focused on promoting regionalism between its States participants, in 2007 the European Neighbourhood Policy (ENP) was created with more emphasis on strengthening the bilateral relationships between the EU and its neighbours.[64] Since its establishment, the ENP has suffered from a lack of homogeneity of some of its objectives and principles. On the one hand, the ENP emphasized that one of its long-term goals is to promote regionalism between the EU and its neighbours through the establishment of a Neighbourhood Economic Community.[65] In addition, both of the ENP's financial instruments, the European Neighbourhood and Partnership Instrument (ENPI) and its successor, the European Neighbourhood Instrument (ENI), stressed that the EU financial assistance shall focus on consolidating

---

Mediterranean States (Egypt, Jordan, Morocco and Tunisia so far) and between them and the EU. The Agadir Agreement was intended to be compatible with other agreements that aim at liberalizing trade among the Arab States such as the Greater Arab Free-Trade Area (GAFTA) (in force since 1 January 1998 among 17 States) which intends to create a free-trade area among the League of Arab States.

61  MEDA is short for 'mésures d'accompagnement financières et techniques'.

62  Council Regulation (EC) No. 1488/96 of 23 July 1996 on Financial and Technical Measures to Accompany (MEDA) the Reform of Economic and Social Structures in the Framework of the Euro–Mediterranean Partnership [1996] OJ L189/1; Council Regulation (EC) No. 2698/2000 of 27 November 2000 amending Regulation (EC) No. 1488/96 on Financial and Technical Measures to Accompany (MEDA) the Reform of Economic and Social Structures in the Framework of the Euro–Mediterranean Partnership [2000] OJ L 311/1.

63  Council Regulation (EC) No. 2698/2000 of 27 November 2000; see also Annex II to Council Regulation No. 1488/96 of 23 July 1996.

64  Regarding this point see Commission of the European Communities 'Communication from the Commission to the European Parliament and the Council: A Strong European Neighbourhood Policy' COM(2007) 774 final (5 December 2007), at 3; Commission of the European Communities 'Communication from the Commission to the Council and the European Parliament: On Strengthening the European Neighbourhood Policy' COM(2006) 726 final (4 December 2006), at 11.

65  Commission of the European Communities COM(2006) 726 final (4 December 2006), at 4–5.

regional cooperation.⁶⁶ On the other hand, the EU in the ENP has been following the principles of conditionality and differentiation. The EU evaluates the partners' commitment in achieving certain objectives, and based on the result of such evaluation, the EU either grants its State partner more technical and financial assistance or sanctions the partner in question.⁶⁷ An example of such evaluation criteria can be found in Art. 4 ENI, which stresses that the deepness of the EU relationship with its partners shall go hand in hand with the partners' commitment to fulfil certain requirements, such as undertaking reforms and promoting democracy.⁶⁸ The principles of conditionality and differentiation followed under the ENP shifted the EU focus from promoting regionalism into establishing different levels of bilateral relationships with its neighbours. Consequently, unlike the EMP that was built to bring all the State participants under one multilateral initiative, the ENP resulted in establishing privileged bilateral relationships between the EU and a few Mediterranean States, namely Jordan and Morocco that were granted 'advanced status' and Tunisia that was given a 'privileged partnership'.⁶⁹

---

66   Art. 2 (z) of Regulation (EC) 1638/2006 of the European Parliament and of the Council of 24 October 2006 Laying down General Provisions establishing a European Neighbourhood and Partnership Instrument [2006] OJ L 310/1. Para. 2 of Annex II to Regulation (EU) 232/2014 of the European Parliament and of the Council of 11 March 2014 establishing a European Neighbourhood Instrument [2014] OJ L 77/27.

67   Commission of the European Communities 'Communication from the Commission to the Council and the European Parliament: Wider Europe—Neighbourhood: A New Framework for Relations with our Eastern and Southern Neighbours' COM(2003) 104 Final, Brussels (11 March 2003), at 15–17; European Commission and HRVP 'Joint Communication to the European Council, the European Parliament, the Council, the European Economic and Social Committee and the Committee of the Regions: A Partnership for Democracy and Shared Prosperity with the Southern Mediterranean' COM(2011) 200 final (8 March 2011), at 5; European Commission and HRVP 'Joint Report to the European Parliament, the Council, the European Economic and Social Committee and the Committee of the Regions: Report on the Implementation of the European Neighbourhood Policy Review' JOIN(2017) 18 final (18 May 2017), at 11. See also E. Lannon, 'More for More or Less for Less: from the Rhetoric to the Implementation of European Neighbourhood Instrument in the Context of the 2015 ENP Review' in *IEMed. Mediterranean Yearbook 2015* (IEMed 2015) 220.

68   Regulation (EU) No. 232/2014 of 11 March 2014 (15 March 2014) OJ L 77/27.

69   European Commission and HRVP 'Joint Communication to the European Parliament, the Council, the European Economic and Social Committee and the Committee of the Regions: A New Response to a Changing Neighbourhood' COM(2011) 303 final (25 May 2011), at 17; 'The EU–Tunisia Relations: Privileged Partnership Action Plan 2013–2017', available in French at https://eeas.europa.eu/sites/eeas/files/plan_action_tunisie_ue_2013_2017_fr.pdf (accessed 5 March 2019).

In addition to the EMP and the ENP, the EU and 15 of its neighbours[70] established another regional cooperative framework during the 2008 Paris summit, namely the Barcelona Process: Union for the Mediterranean, which was later renamed as Union for the Mediterranean (UfM).[71] Similar to the ENP, the UfM theoretically aims at strengthening regional integration among its States participants.[72] However, the UfM has failed in achieving its objectives due to several methodological and technical obstacles such as operating under a low budget[73] and depending on intergovernmental methods that require unanimity among its States participants in every aspect.[74]

What is problematic is that the EU and particularly the European Commission have never substantially justified the added value of the UfM to the already established EMP and ENP. Furthermore, as the EMP was practically frozen with the establishment of the UfM in 2008, it is unclear whether the latter replaced the former or whether these policies overlap. Another similar point can be raised regarding the relationship between the UfM and the ENP, as the European Commission has not yet issued a single document to explain how these two frameworks function together.

Hence, fragmentation is a common characteristic of the EU multilateral frameworks and consequently of the EU approach in promoting regional cooperation between its Mediterranean neighbours. This is particularly true regarding the EU approach towards the AMUMS because, first, only Algeria, Morocco and Tunisia were covered by the EMP, the ENP and the UfM (see Table 11.1). Second, as previously mentioned, due to the ENP conditionality and differentiation principles, the EU treats the AMUMS unequally and thus has granted only Morocco and Tunisia privileged bilateral relationships. Third, whereas Libya is still not part of any multilateral framework of the EU with its

---

70  Albania, Algeria, Bosnia and Herzegovina, Egypt, Jordan, Israel, Lebanon, Mauritania, Monaco, Montenegro, Morocco, Palestine, Syria (suspended), Tunisia and Turkey.
71  Council of the European Union 'Barcelona Process: Union for the Mediterranean Ministerial Conference: Marseille, 3–4 November 2008: Final Declaration' 15187/08 (Presse 314) (4 November 2008), at 3.
72  Council of the European Union 'Joint Declaration of the Paris summit for the Mediterranean, Paris, 13 July 2008' 11887/08 (Presse 213) (15 July 2008), at 8.
73  The budget of the current projects of the UfM that covers 42 States is around €5 billion according to UfM Co-Presidency 'UfM Roadmap for Action: The Union for the Mediterranean an Action-Driven Organisation with a Common Ambition (adopted by the Ministers of Foreign Affairs, on 23 January 2017)' Doc. de Séance No. 2/17 (23 January 2017), at 3.
74  Council of the European Union 'Joint Declaration of the Paris Summit for the Mediterranean, Paris, 13 July 2008' at 11, para. 10. See also, for instance, R. Gillespie, 'The Union for the Mediterranean: An Intergovernmentalist Challenge for the European Union?' (2011) 49.6 Journal of Common Market Studies 1208.

neighbours,[75] Mauritania has only participated in the UfM.[76] Also, the EU has treated Mauritania differently by including it in the EU–African, Caribbean and Pacific States (ACP) framework.

In this respect, it might be argued that the differences between the national priorities of each EU Member State have attributed to the EU failure in forming a single external approach towards the Maghreb. An example of such differences is the disagreement between on the one hand the Northern[77] and Eastern EU Member States and on the other hand the EU Mediterranean Member States[78] on whether the EU should grant financial aid to the Maghreb States or whether the EU should give the agricultural and textile products of the Maghreb States a free access to the EU Internal Market. Because the latter group has similar export patterns to those of the Maghreb States, it has favoured the option of aid to protect their national products.[79] In fact, the divergence in the views between the Southern and Northern EU Member States has not only influenced the current EU Mediterranean policies but also its previous ones, i.e. the 1972–1989 Global Mediterranean Policy (GMP) and the 1992–1995 Renewed Mediterranean Policy (RMP).[80]

---

75   Libya's participation in the EMP was always conditioned on its acceptance of the Barcelona *acquis* and the lifting of the UNSC sanctions. See 'Third Euro–Mediterranean Conference of Foreign Affairs Ministers of the EMP States Participants, Chairman's Formal Conclusions' (15–16 April 1999), at para. 37. See also Commission of the European Communities COM(2003) 104 final (11 March 2003), at 17.

76   It should be mentioned here that Mauritania has officially applied to participate in the EMP in 2005 (Council of the European Union 'Agreed Conclusions for the 7th Euro–Mediterranean Conference of Ministers of Foreign Affairs, Luxembourg, 30–31 May 2005' C/05/134 9598/05 (Presse 134) (31 May 2005), at 8), but its application was accepted by EMP States participants in 2007, i.e. shortly before the end of the EMP activities (Council of the European Union 'Agreed Conclusions of the 9th Euro–Mediterranean Meeting of Ministers of Foreign Affairs, Lisbon, 5–6 November 2007' C/07/255 14743/07 (Presse 255) (6 November 2007), at 4).

77   This is particularly true for Germany and the United Kingdom.

78   These States are France, Greece, Italy, Portugal and Spain.

79   Aghrout, *From Preferential Status to Partnership: The Euro–Maghreb Relationship* 36; K. Pieters, 'The Mediterranean Countries (Morocco, Algeria, Tunisia, Libya, Egypt, Jordan, Syria and Lebanon)' in S. Blockmans and A. Lazowski (eds), *The European Union and Its Neighbours—A Legal Appraisal of the EU's Policies of Stabilisation, Partnership and Integration* (TMC Asser Press 2006) 393, at 396; K. Knio, *The European Union's Mediterranean Policy: Model or Muddle? A New Institutionalist Perspective* (Palgrave Macmillan 2013), at 54.

80   A. Tovias, 'The EU's Mediterranean Policies under Pressure' in R. Gillespie (ed.), *Mediterranean Politics* vol. 2 (Pinter 1996) 10, at 12.

## 2 Regional Integration among the AMUMS as an Objective of the EU–AMUMS Bilateral and Regional Agreements

The legal nature, scope and objectives of the bilateral and/or regional agreements between the EU (and its Member States) and each of the AMUMS are different. Three layers of relationships can be identified in this respect: first, the EU–Libya relationship that has not yet been covered by a bilateral agreement. Second, the Euro–Mediterranean Association Agreements (EMAAs) concluded with Algeria,[81] Morocco[82] and Tunisia,[83] Art. 1 (2) of which emphasizes the importance of developing regional integration in the Maghreb as one of their main objectives. The third layer refers to the regional Economic Partnership Agreement (EPA) between the EU (and its Member States) and Mauritania plus other West African States.[84] The Agreement was initialled between the negotiating parties on 30 June 2014 and was signed by Mauritania on 21 September 2018 but has not yet entered into force.[85] One of the main objectives of the EPA, pursuant to Art. 1 (b), is 'to promote regional integration, economic cooperation and good economic governance in the West African region'. In addition to EPA, Mauritania was included in the Cotonou Agreement between the EU and the ACP States, which also seeks to encourage regional cooperation among the ACP States.[86] The Cotonou Agreement stressed, in Art.

---

81   Euro–Mediterranean Agreement establishing an Association between the European Community and its Member States, of the One Part, and the People's Democratic Republic of Algeria, of the Other Part (signed 22 April 2002, entered into force 1 September 2005) [2005] OJ L 265/2.

82   Euro–Mediterranean Agreement establishing an Association between the European Communities and their Member States, of the One Part, and the Kingdom of Morocco, of the Other Part (signed 26 February 1996, entered into force 1 March 2000) [2000] OJ L 70/2.

83   Euro–Mediterranean Agreement establishing an Association between the European Communities and their Member States, of the One Part, and the Republic of Tunisia, of the Other Part (signed 17 July 1995, entered into force 1 March 1998) [1998] OJ L 97/2 (EU–Tunisia EMAA).

84   Those States are members of the Economic Community of West Africa (ECOWAS) and the West African Economic and Monetary Union (UEMOA). The text of this agreement can be found in Council of the European Union 'Economic Partnership Agreement between the West African States, the Economic Community of West African States (ECOWAS) and the West African Economic and Monetary Union (UEMOA), of the One Part, and the European Union and its Member States, of the Other Part' interinstitutional file: 2014/0265 (NLE) (3 December 2014) (Or. fr) 13370/14.

85   For a brief overview regarding the entry into force process of EPAs, see European Commission 'Overview of Economic Partnership Agreements' (October 2018), available at http://trade.ec.europa.eu/doclib/docs/2009/september/tradoc_144912.pdf (accessed 5 March 2019).

86   Partnership Agreement between the Members of the African, Caribbean and Pacific Group of States of the One Part, and the European Community and its Member States,

2 of its 2010 revised version, that 'regionalization' is one of the 'fundamental principles' of the agreement and stipulated that 'Particular emphasis shall be put on regional integration, including at continental level'. The inclusion of Mauritania in the EPA despite the fact that it is not a member of ECOWAS and UEMOA refers to the fact that the EU has followed a different bilateral path with respect to this country than the one pursued with other Maghreb States.

Although the EMAAs and EPA emphasize regional integration as one of their main objectives, such instruments promote integration on the basis of the EU vision rather than on the interests of the AMUMS, which was expressed in the formation of the AMU. The EMAAs and the EPA pursue inconsistent objectives regarding integration, as, while the former stipulates the consolidation of Maghreb integration as one of their objectives, the latter promotes the regional integration of Mauritania with the West African countries instead of including it with the rest of the Maghreb States. The same can be noted regarding the EU multilateral policies where Mauritania was only included in the UfM. In addition to Mauritania's peculiar position, Libya has its own special situation as it has no bilateral ties with the EU, nor is it included in the EU multilateral policies vis-à-vis the Mediterranean States. Hence, the EU approach in promoting Maghreb regional integration is inconsistent because it has not yet formulated a single bilateral or regional approach towards the AMUMS. Thus, although the EU recognized that 'the Maghreb remains one of the least integrated regions in the world',[87] its real intention to encourage such integration can be questioned.

In addition to its inconsistent approach, the EU is still keen not to take any role in settling the longstanding dispute between Morocco and the Polisario Front. The EU has often announced that the people of Western Sahara shall exercise their right to self-determination, but at the same time it has not pursued further action with respect to encouraging the implementation of this right. The next section briefly examines the dispute on Western Sahara as well as the main aspects and impact of the recent judgments of the General Court (GC) of the Court of Justice of the EU (CJEU) in *Council v. Front Polisario*[88] and the judgment of the European Court of Juctice (ECJ) of the CJEU in *Western Sahara Campaign UK v. Commissioners for Her Majesty's Revenue and Customs*.[89]

---

of the Other Part (signed 23 June 2000, entered into force 1 April 2003) [2000] OJ L317/3 (amended 4 November 2010) [2010] OJ L 287/3 (Cotonou Agreement).

87  European Commission and HRVP (17 December 2012) JOIN(2012) 36 final, at para. 9.

88  Case C–104/16 P *Council of the European Union v. Front populaire pour la libération de la saguia-el-hamra et du rio de oro (Front Polisario)* (Judgment of 21 December 2016).

89  Case C–266/16 *Western Sahara Campaign UK v. Commissioners for Her Majesty's Revenue and Customs and Secretary of State for Environment, Food and Rural Affairs* (Judgment of 27 February 2018).

## IV  Western Sahara: An Obstacle to Maghreb Regional Integration

### 1  *Western Sahara: Non-Self-Governing Territory*

Western Sahara is a territory that is surrounded by Algeria in the east, the Atlantic Ocean in the west, Morocco in the north and Mauritania from the east to the south.[90] It was under Spanish colonial rule between 1884[91] and 1976. Since 1963, it was classified by the UN as a non-self-governing territory 'whose peoples have not yet attained a full measure of self-government'[92] within the meaning of Chapter XI of the UN Charter.[93] On the basis of this classification, the UN General Assembly called upon Spain to give effect to Resolution 1514 (XV), i.e. to enable the people of Western Sahara to exercise the right to self-determination through a referendum.[94] It shall be mentioned here that Resolution 1514 (XV) was issued by the UN General Assembly on 14 December 1960 to emphasize 'the necessity of bringing to a speedy and unconditional end colonialism in all its forms and manifestations'.[95] The Resolution also stressed that the people of the colonized territories should be allowed to exercise their right to self-determination, 'by the virtue of [which] they freely determine their political status and freely pursue their economic, social and cultural development'.[96]

However, because Morocco and Mauritania had claimed that Western Sahara was part of their territories before it was colonized by Spain, the UN General Assembly issued Resolution 3292 (XXIX) on 13 December 1974 in which it asked the International Court of Justice (ICJ) to deliver an advisory opinion on the question:

---

90  The word 'Sahara' means desert in Arabic.
91  As noted by *Western Sahara (Advisory Opinion)* [1975] ICJ Rep 12, at 38, para. 77.
92  Art. 73 Charter of the United Nations (adopted 26 June 1945, entered into force 24 October 1945) 1 UNTS 16.
93  S. Koury, 'Legal Strategies at the United Nations: A Comparative Look at Namibia, Western Sahara, and Palestine' in S.M. Akram et al. (eds), *International Law and the Israeli-Palestinian Conflict: A Rights-Based Approach to Middle East Peace* (Routledge 2011) 151. The UN still considers Western Sahara as a non-self-governing territory in addition to 16 other territories, see http://www.un.org/en/decolonization/nonselfgovterritories.shtml (accessed 5 March 2019).
94  UNGA Res 2229 (XXI) 'Question of Ifni and Spanish Sahara' (20 December 1966). D.-E. Simma Khan, G. Nolte, A. Paulus and N. Wessendorf (eds), *The Charter of the United Nations. A Commentary* vol. II (3rd edn OUP 2012) 1835.
95  UNGA Res 1514 (XV) 'Declaration on the Granting of Independence to Colonial Countries and Peoples' (14 December 1960).
96  Ibid.

Was Western Sahara (Rio de Oro and Sakiet El Hamra) at the time of colonization by Spain a territory belonging to no one (*terra nullius*)? If the answer to the first question is in the negative, what were the legal ties between this territory and the Kingdom of Morocco and the Mauritanian entity?[97]

In addition, the UN General Assembly called upon Spain not to conduct any referendum until the UN General Assembly determines the appropriate means to decolonize Western Sahara.[98]

The ICJ's advisory opinion, delivered on 16 October 1975, stated that Western Sahara was not a *terra nullius* territory during the Spanish colonization. The Court concluded that although 'legal ties' were found between on the one hand Mauritania and Morocco and on the other hand Western Sahara, none of these ties sufficed to grant sovereign rights to one of the former over the latter.[99] Thus, the ICJ added that the ties cannot 'affect the application of Resolution 1514 (XV) in the decolonization of Western Sahara'.[100]

Consequently, Morocco interpreted the ICJ advisory opinion in its favour and announced on 6 November 1975 the 'Green March' in the course of which around 350,000 Moroccan marchers crossed the border from Morocco to Western Sahara.[101] After a few days of the Green March, Spain, instead of organizing a referendum in Western Sahara, met with Mauritania and Morocco in Madrid to determine the fate of Western Sahara. The outcome of the meeting, which is also known as 'Madrid Accords', was that Spain shall withdraw its forces from Western Sahara and that the administration of this territory shall be transferred to Mauritania and Morocco.[102] Hence, on the basis of the Madrid Accords, Spain withdrew its forces on 26 February 1976[103] and Western Sahara

---

97    UNGA Res 3292 (XXIX) 'Question of Spanish Sahara' (13 December 1974).
98    Ibid.
99    *Western Sahara (Advisory Opinion)* [1975] ICJ Rep 12, at 68, para. 162.
100   Ibid.
101   A. Theofilopoulou, 'United Nations Mission for the Referendum in Western Sahara (Minurso)' in J.A. Koops, N. Macqueen, T. Tardy and P.D. Williams (eds), *The Oxford Handbook of United Nations Peacekeeping Operations* (OUP 2015) 327.
102   This agreement is also often referred to as the 'Tripartite Agreement'. See Declaration of Principles on Western Sahara by Spain, Morocco and Mauritania (signed 14 November 1975, entered into force 19 November 1975) 988 UNTS 259.
103   Regarding the legal responsibility of Spain vis-à-vis Western Sahara, see the Opinion of the Advocate General of the CJEU (Case C–104/16 P *Council of the European Union v. Front populaire pour la libération de la saguia-el-hamra et du rio de oro (Front Polisario)* (13 September 2016), at para. 188) in which he pointed out that, although Spain has considered itself to be exempted from any international responsibility arising with respect to

was annexed by Morocco from the North and by Mauritania from the South. Some argued that Spain left Western Sahara because the Moroccan stance at that time was supported by the US and France,[104] while others attributed the withdrawal to the benefits Spain received in return by signing a 'fishing agreement with [Morocco] and [getting] a profitable stake in the exploitation of the Western Sahara's Bu-Craa phosphate deposits'.[105]

The UN did not recognize the Madrid Accords and thus upheld its position in favour of organizing a referendum for the people of Western Sahara to freely determine their future. Also, as a reaction to the Madrid Accords, the Popular Front for the Liberation of Saguia el Hamra and Rio de Oro (Polisario Front), supported by Algeria, established the Saharawi Arab Democratic Republic (SADR) on 27 February 1976 as the sole representative of the people of Western Sahara.[106] As a result to that, an armed conflict started between Morocco and Mauritania on the one side and SADR on the other side.

In 1979, Mauritania concluded a peace agreement with the Polisario Front and withdrew its forces, but Morocco took control over the part of the territory that was under the authority of Mauritania. The war continued between Morocco and the Polisario Front until a ceasefire in 1991. The ceasefire came as a result to the agreement reached between the two sides on Settlement

---

Western Sahara since its withdrawal, it remains in accordance with international law 'the only entity to have the capacity, or indeed the obligation, to protect, including legally, the rights of the people of Western Sahara, in particular its right to self-determination and its sovereignty over the natural resources of the territory'.

104 Theofilopoulou, 'United Nations Mission for the Referendum in Western Sahara (Minurso)', at 327; M. Munene, 'History of Western Sahara and Spanish Colonisation' in N. Botha, M. Olivier and D. Van Tonder (eds), *Conference on Multilateralism and International Law with Western Sahara as a Case Study* (VerLoren van Themaat Centre, University of South Africa 2010) 94.

105 R. Gillespie, *Spain and the Mediterranean: Developing a European Policy towards the South* (Palgrave Macmillan 2000) 43. According to the same source, the fishing agreement was not ratified by Morocco and the phosphate exploitation did not take place due to the armed conflict in Western Sahara.

106 The Polisario Front is a liberation movement established on 10 May 1973 to resist the Spanish colonialism in Western Sahara. Its General Secretary, currently Mr. Ibrahim Ghali, serves as the President for the SADR. SADR operates from Tindouf, Algeria and was admitted as a Member State to the African Union (AU) on 22 February 1982. Due to this admission, Morocco withdrew from the AU in 1984 until it was readmitted during the 28th summit of the AU held in Addis Ababa, Ethiopia on 31 January 2017 (AU Directorate of Information and Communication '28th African Union Summit Concludes with Swearing in of New Commission and Readmission of Morocco' (31 January 2017) Press Release N°17/28AU Summit).

Proposals on 30 August 1988.[107] To implement the Settlement Proposals and mainly to facilitate the organization of a referendum in Western Sahara, the UN Security Council established the UN Mission for the Referendum in Western Sahara (MINURSO).[108] The MINURSO has failed to deliver on its main promises so far due to several reasons, such as the controversy between Morocco and the Polisario Front over who should participate in the referendum.[109] The parties in question accept that the dispute should be solved by the exercise of the right to self-determination, but they disagree regarding the meaning of such right and the methods to implement it. In this respect, while Morocco believes that the right to self-determination would only extend to autonomy for Western Sahara, the Polisario Front claims that it includes the right to achieve full independence.[110] However, despite the failure of MINURSO, the UN Security Council has extended its mandate until 30 April 2019.[111]

Currently, Morocco controls the biggest part of Western Sahara. Although several decades have passed since the UN has assumed the responsibility to facilitate the negotiations on Western Sahara, it has not been able to settle this issue. Similar to its failure in solving the conflict in Palestine, the UN is once again unable to deliver peace in Western Sahara. Thus, there is a need for new methods and new international players to politically resolve the dispute between Morocco on the one hand and the Polisario Front supported by Algeria on the other. It can be argued in this respect that there is no entity in the world more in need of playing the role of peace negotiator in Western Sahara than the EU. This need stems from the fact that the conflict about Western Sahara has been for the last five decades one of the main obstacles to achieving permanent peace in North Africa and normal relations between Morocco and Algeria. The conflict in question has not only led to the failure of the AMU but also has a persistent negative impact on the stability of the Maghreb, which also threatens the stability of the Maghreb's neighbours including the EU. Unfortunately, although the EU recognizes that its internal security directly depends

---

107   The 'settlement proposals' agreed between Morocco and the Polisario Front were suggested by the UN Secretary General in cooperation with the Chairman of the Assembly of Heads of State and Government of the African Union (AU). See UNSC Res 690 (1991) 'Western Sahara'.
108   UNSC Res 690 (1991) 'Western Sahara'.
109   Theofilopoulou, 'United Nations Mission for the Referendum in Western Sahara (Minurso)', at 335.
110   See the Moroccan Initiative for Negotiating an Autonomy Statute for the Sahara Region, available at https://www.diplomatie.ma/en/Aidememoire/tabid/2958/language/en-US/Default.aspx (accessed 6 March 2019).
111   UNSC Res 2440 (2018) 'The Situation concerning Western Sahara' (31 October 2018).

on the stability of its Mediterranean borders,[112] it has not yet played any role in resolving the dispute about Western Sahara that has always been one of the main threats to peace in the region. Recently, the EU position regarding Western Sahara has attracted attention due to the CJEU rulings on whether some of the agreements concluded between the EU and Morocco also apply to products originating from Western Sahara.

2    *The Dispute Regarding the Territorial Application of the EU–Morocco EMAA and Its Subsequent Agreements*

Similar to its relationship with many other Mediterranean countries, the EU bilateral relationship with Morocco is based on a Euro–Mediterranean Association Agreement (EMAA). The EU and Morocco consider the EMAA in question and its seven annexes and five protocols as a framework agreement that sets the main objectives of the partners and the scope of bilateral cooperation.[113] On the basis of this framework agreement, many sectoral agreements and protocols were concluded between the EU and Morocco to deepen the scope of cooperation between the two sides in various fields such as trade and aviation (see Table 11.2). Recently, the question whether the agreements concluded between the EU and Morocco apply to Western Sahara has attracted the attention of the international community. Two cases were brought before the CJEU challenging the territorial application of the EU–Morocco EMAA and the following agreements concluded on its basis: first, the Agreement in the Form of an Exchange of Letters between the European Union and the Kingdom of Morocco Concerning Reciprocal Liberalization Measures on Agricultural Products, Processed Agricultural Products, Fish and Fishery Products, the Replacement of Protocols 1, 2 and 3 and their Annexes and Amendments to the [EMAA] between the European Communities and their Member States, of the one part, and the Kingdom of Morocco, of the other part' (hereafter referred to as the Liberalization Agreement);[114] second, the Fisheries Partnership Agreement between the European Communities and the Kingdom of Morocco (Fisheries Agreement).[115] The following sections briefly examine the above two cases brought before the CJEU.

---

112   HRVP, 'Shared Vision, Common Action: A Stronger Europe: A Global Strategy for the European Union's Foreign And Security Policy' (June 2016), at 7.
113   Preamble EU–Morocco EMAA (18 March 2000), at 2.
114   Signed 13 December 2010, entered into force 1 September 2013 [2012] OJ L 241/4.
115   Signed 26 July 2006, entered into force 28 February 2007 [2006] OJ L 141/4.

a      The Territorial Application of the EMAA and the Liberalization Agreement Concluded between the EU and Morocco

To further liberalize trade between the EU and Morocco under the framework of the EMAA, both sides concluded the Liberalization Agreement.[116] However, the Polisario Front considered that the EU importation of products originating from Western Sahara on the basis of the Liberalization Agreement without the consent of the people of that territory infringes their fundamental rights under international law. Therefore, it requested the General Court (GC) of the CJEU in *Front Polisario v. Council*[117] to annul the Decision of the Council of the EU on the Conclusion of the Liberalization Agreement.[118] At the outset, the GC found that the EMAA and consequently the Liberalization Agreement are applicable to Western Sahara on the grounds that

> the conclusion of an agreement between the [EU] and a non-Member State which may be applied on a dispute[d] territory [i.e. Western Sahara in this case] is not, in all cases, contrary to EU law or international law.[119]

However, the GC noted that although such prohibition is not clearly established under international and EU law, certain restrictions are nevertheless applicable on the discretion of the EU institutions to conclude such agreements. Such restrictions include the obligation of the EU institutions to assess before the conclusion of such agreements whether the application of these agreements would violate the rights of the citizens of the territories in question and whether by virtue of these agreements the exploitation of the resources of those territories would be undertaken to the detriment of their population.[120]

---

116   Art. 16 EU–Morocco EMAA (18 March 2000). Paras 1–7 Liberalization Agreement introduced the following changes to the EU–Morocco EMAA: deleted Art. 10 EMAA; amended (replaced) Arts 7, 15, 17 and 18 (1) EMAA; changed the heading of Chapter II of Title II of the EMAA from 'Agricultural and Fishery Products' to 'Agricultural Products, Processed Agricultural Products, Fish and Fishery Products'; and replaced Protocols 1, 2 and 3 EMAA with new provisions and two Annexes.
117   Case T–512/12 *Front populaire pour la libération de la saguia-el-hamra et du rio de oro (Front Polisario) v. Council of the European Union* (Judgment of 27 February 2018).
118   Council Decision 2012/497/EU of 8 March 2012 on the Conclusion of an Agreement in the Form of an Exchange of Letters between the European Union and the Kingdom of Morocco concerning Reciprocal Liberalisation Measures on Agricultural Products, Processed Agricultural Products, Fish and Fishery Products, the Replacement of Protocols 1, 2 and 3 and their Annexes and Amendments to the Euro–Mediterranean Agreement establishing an Association between the European Communities and their Member States, of the One Part, and the Kingdom of Morocco, of the Other Part [2012] OJ L 241/2.
119   Case T–512/12 *Front populaire pour la libération de la saguia-el-hamra et du rio de oro (Front Polisario) v. Council of the European Union* (Judgment of 10 December 2015), at para. 220.
120   Ibid., at paras 223–228.

TABLE 11.2  The main agreements linking the EU (and its Member States) to Morocco[a]

| | |
|---|---|
| Euro–Mediterranean Association Agreement | OJ L 70/2 (18 March 2000, in force 1 March 2000) |
| Agreements on Scientific and Technical Cooperation | OJ L 37/9 (10 February 2004, in force 14 March 2005) |
| Agreement on Morocco Participation in EU Operation Althea | OJ L 34/47 (8 February 2005, not yet in force) |
| Fisheries Agreement | OJ L 141/4 (29 May 2006, in force 28 February 2007) and its three Protocols OJ L141/9 (29 May 2006), OJ L202/3 (5 August 2011) and OJ L 328/2 (7 December 2013, in force 15 July 2014) |
| Agreements on Aviation | OJ L 386/57 (29 December 2006, in force 19 March 2018) |
| Agreements on Certain Aspects of Air Services | OJ L 386/18 (29 December 2006, in force 1 April 2010) |
| Protocols on Dispute Settlement | OJ L176/2 (5 July 2011, in force 1 November 2012) |
| Protocols on the General Principles for Participation in Union Programmes | OJ L 90/2 (28 March 2012, in force 1 October 2012) |
| Liberalization Agreement on Agricultural Products, Processed Agricultural Products, Fish and Fishery products | OJ L 241/4 (7 September 2012, in force 1 September 2013) |
| Regional Convention on pan-Euro–Mediterranean Preferential Rules of Origin | OJ L 54/4 (26 February 2013, not yet in force) |
| Agreement on a Civil Global Navigation Satellite System (GNSS) | OJ L 76/3 (23 March 2016, in force 1 March 2015) |

a  SOURCE: AUTHOR'S COMPILATION ON THE BASIS OF THE DATABASE OF TREATIES AND AGREEMENTS OF THE COUNCIL OF THE EU, AVAILABLE AT HTTP://WWW.CONSILIUM.EUROPA.EU/EN/DOCUMENTS-PUBLICATIONS/TREATIES-AGREEMENTS/ (ACCESSED 6 MARCH 2019).

That being said, and because the Council failed to prove to the GC that it had undertaken the required assessment, the GC annulled the Decision of the Council of the EU on the Conclusion of the Liberalization Agreement as far as it is applicable to Western Sahara.[121]

Later, due to the appeal submitted by the Council of the EU against the judgment of the GC, the case was brought again before the European Court of Justice (ECJ) in *Council v. Front Polisario*.[122] The ECJ had a different understanding of the case in question. It ruled that the GC erred in law by concluding that the EMAA and the Liberalization Agreement apply to Western Sahara because this conclusion contradicts the right to self-determination granted to Western Sahara under international law, which prevents the application of any international agreement to that territory without acquiring the consent of its people.[123] Furthermore, the ECJ found that the GC judgment is in conflict with the customary international rule on the territorial scope of treaties[124] since neither of the two agreements in question explicitly stipulated that it applies to Western Sahara,[125] nor did the Council of the EU and the European Commission intend such application.[126] The ECJ also pointed out that the GC judgment is in disagreement with the customary principle of the relative effect of international agreements that is codified in Art. 34 of Vienna Convention on the Law of Treaties (VCLT),[127] which provides that 'A treaty does not create either obligations or rights for a third State without its consent'. The ECJ noted that the status of 'non-self-governing territory' attached to Western Sahara renders that territory a 'third party' within the meaning of the principle of the

---

121 Ibid., at para. 247.
122 Case C–104/16 P *Council of the European Union v. Front populaire pour la libération de la saguia-el-hamra et du rio de oro (Front Polisario)* (Judgment of 21 December 2016).
123 Ibid., at paras 92 and 123.
124 The principle of the territorial scope of treaties is stipulated in Art. 29 Vienna Convention on the Law of Treaties (concluded 23 May 1969, entered into force 27 January 1980) 1155 UNTS 331 (VCLT), which provides that 'Unless a different intention appears from the treaty or is otherwise established, a treaty is binding upon each party in respect of its entire territory'.
125 In this regard, Art. 94 EU–Morocco EMAA (18 March 2000) provides that: 'This Agreement shall apply, on the one hand, to the territories in which the Treaties establishing the European Community and the European Coal And Steel Community are applied and under the conditions laid down in those Treaties and, on the other hand to the territory of the Kingdom of Morocco'.
126 Case C–104/16 P *Council of the European Union v. Front populaire pour la libération de la saguia-el-hamra et du rio de oro (Front Polisario)* (Judgment of 21 December 2016), at paras 94–99.
127 Ibid., at para. 107. For more information on the principle of the relative effect of international agreements, see E. David, 'Article 34 (1969)' in O. Corten and P. Klein (eds), *The Vienna Conventions on the Law of Treaties: A Commentary* vol. I (OUP 2011) 887.

relative effect of international agreements, and thus neither the EMAA nor the Liberalization Agreement applied to Western Sahara.[128] Therefore, the ECJ annulled the GC judgment.[129] It also maintained the Council of the EU Decision on the Conclusion of the Liberalization Agreement. In addition, because the Liberalization Agreement is not applicable to Western Sahara, the ECJ concluded that the Polisario Front was not directly and individually concerned by the application of that agreement, within the meaning of Art. 263 TFEU, and thus considered its claims as inadmissible.[130]

It might be argued that both the GC and the ECJ judgments have in practice similar effect because both judgments annulled the application of the EMAA and the Liberalization Agreement to Western Sahara. This argument cannot be upheld because these judgments were concluded on the basis of distinct grounds and thus entail different consequences. On the one hand, the GC noted that, on the basis of international and European law, there is no clear legal basis that forbids the application of the EMAA and the Liberalization Agreement to Western Sahara. However, despite the absence of such legal basis, the GC annulled the Council of the EU Decision on the Conclusion of the Liberalization Agreement on the grounds that the Council of the EU failed to fulfil its obligation to assess whether the fundamental rights of the people of Western Sahara would be violated by the application of the Liberalization Agreement. Hence, according to the GC ruling, if such rights would be respected, the EMAA and the Liberalization Agreement could be applicable to Western Sahara. On the other hand, the ECJ judgment contends that, on the basis of international law, Western Sahara is *ab initio* out of the territorial scope of the EMAA and the Liberalization Agreement and therefore the agreements cannot be applied to that territory without the consent of its people. However, what the judgments of the GC and the ECJ have in common is that both courts followed the least politically sensitive approach by concentrating on the question whether the EU–Morocco EMAA and Liberalization Agreement apply to Western Sahara

---

128   Case C–104/16 P *Council of the European Union v. Front populaire pour la libération de la saguia-el-hamra et du rio de oro (Front Polisario)* (Judgment of 21 December 2016), at paras 88–93 and 103–107. Similar views were expressed by the CJEU Advocate General in Case C–104/16 P *Council of the European Union v. Front populaire pour la libération de la saguia-el-hamra et du rio de oro (Front Polisario)* (Opinion on 13 September 2016), at para. 105.

129   Case C–104/16 P *Council of the European Union v. Front populaire pour la libération de la saguia-el-hamra et du rio de oro (Front Polisario)* (Judgment of 21 December 2016), at para. 127.

130   Ibid., at paras 130–134; Art. 263 (4) TFEU provides that 'Any natural or legal person may, under the conditions laid down in the first and second paragraphs [of Art. 263], institute proceedings against an act *addressed* to that person or which is of *direct* and *individual* concern to them, and against a *regulatory act* which is of *direct* concern to them and does not entail implementing measures' (emphasis added).

pursuant to international law instead of examining whether the EU has in practice violated the rights of the people of Western Sahara through the importation of products originating from that territory.

b   The Territorial Application of the EMAA and the Fisheries Agreement and Its Subsequent Protocols Concluded between the EU and Morocco

The main purpose of the Fisheries Agreement is to allow the vessels of the EU to fish in the Moroccan waters on the condition that the former pays financial compensation to the latter. The terms regulating the fishing operations and indicating the EU financial contributions were stipulated in three successive Protocols annexed to the Fisheries Agreement, the last of which entered into force in 2014 for a period of four years.[131] Similar to the grounds on which the Front Polisario based its argument against the Council of the EU in *Front Polisario v. Council*,[132] Western Sahara Campaign UK brought a case before the High Court of Justice (England and Wales) (HCJ) against the Commissioners for Her Majesty's Revenue and Customs, Secretary of State for Environment, Food and Rural Affairs.[133] In this case, Western Sahara Campaign UK sought the invalidation of both the EU–Morocco EMAA as well as the Fisheries Agreement and its last Protocol on the grounds that the application of these agreements to products originating from Western Sahara without the Sahrawis' consent infringes the rights of those people under international law.[134] Thus, according to the plaintiff, the EU violated its obligation under Art. 3 (5) TEU to respect international law by accepting the application of the agreements in question to Western Sahara.[135] Consequently, the HCJ referred the case to

---

[131] The three protocols that replaced each other are: Protocol Setting out the Fishing Opportunities and Financial Contribution Provided for in the Fisheries Partnership Agreement between the European Community and the Kingdom of Morocco (entered into force 28 February 2007) [2006] OJ L 141/9; Protocol between the European Union and the Kingdom of Morocco Setting out the Fishing Opportunities and Financial Compensation Provided for in the Fisheries Partnership Agreement between the European Community and the Kingdom of Morocco (signed 13 July 2011) [2011] OJ L 202/3; Protocol between the European Union and the Kingdom of Morocco Setting out the Fishing Opportunities and Financial Contribution Provided for in the Fisheries Partnership Agreement between the European Union and the Kingdom of Morocco (signed 18 November 2013, entered into force 15 July 2014) [2013] OJ L 328/2.

[132] Case T–512/12 *Front populaire pour la libération de la saguia-el-hamra et du rio de oro (Front Polisario) v. Council of the European Union* (Judgment of 10 December 2015).

[133] Case C–266/16 *Western Sahara Campaign UK v. Commissioners for Her Majesty's Revenue and Customs and Secretary of State for Environment, Food and Rural Affairs* (Judgment of 27 February 2018).

[134] Ibid., at para. 32.

[135] Ibid.

the ECJ for a preliminary ruling on whether the EMAA as well as the Fisheries Agreement and its last Protocol are applicable to Western Sahara and its adjacent sea.[136] By drawing an analogy between this case and its judgment in *Council v. Front Polisario*, the ECJ ruled that neither the EMAA nor the Fisheries Agreement and its Protocol apply to Western Sahara.[137] Again, the ECJ based its judgment mainly on the grounds that the application of these agreements to Western Sahara would contradict the right to self-determination granted to the people of Western Sahara and the principle of the relative of international agreements, which the EU is bound to respect pursuant to Art. 3 (5) TEU.[138]

It should be noted here that the ECJ applied the principle of the relative effect of international treaties in both the case brought by Western Sahara Campaign and in *Council v. Front Polisario* by relying on the customary nature of that principle, which also makes it applicable to non-State actors. Otherwise, Art. 34 VCLT in which the principle of the relative effect of international treaties is codified refers to the non-applicability of an international agreement to a 'third State' not a 'third party'. The same approach was followed by the ECJ in *Firma Brita GmbH v. Hauptzollamt Hamburg-Hafen* in which the ECJ ruled out the applicability of the EU–Israel EMAA[139] to the Palestinian Territories (West Bank) by considering the Palestine Liberation Organization (PLO) as a 'third party' within the meaning of the principle of the relative effect.[140]

## 3  The Impact of Council v. Front Polisario *on the Bilateral Relationship between the EU and Morocco*

The political disharmony between Algeria and Morocco increased following the delivery of the judgment of the GC of the CJEU in *Front Polisario v. Council*. While Algeria announced that it was 'satisfied' with the GC judgment,[141] Morocco expressed its frustration. However, the Moroccan position was

---

136  See Ibid., at paras 34–38 for a detailed description of the questions referred from the HCJ to the CJEU.
137  Ibid., at paras 39, 73 and 83.
138  Ibid., at para. 63.
139  Euro–Mediterranean Agreement establishing an Association between the European Communities and their Member States, of the One Part, and the State of Israel, of the Other Part (signed 20 November 1995, entered into force 1 June 2000) [2000] OJ L 147/3.
140  Case C-386/08 *Firma Brita GmbH v. Hauptzollamt Hamburg-Hafen* (Judgment of 25 February 2010), at paras 42–53. See A. Proelss, 'The Personal Dimension: Challenges to the *pacta tertiis* Rule' in C.J. Tams et al. (eds), *Research Handbook on the Law of Treaties* (Elgar 2014) 235.
141  See Ministry of Foreign Affairs of the Republic of Algeria, 'Western Sahara: Algeria "Satisfied" with Cancellation of EU–Morocco Agreement by the EU Court of Justice' (10 December 2015), available at http://www.mae.gov.dz/news_article/3600.aspx (accessed 6 March 2019).

changed after the delivery of the ECJ judgment in *Council v. Front Polisario*, which annulled the abovementioned GC judgment. In reaction to the statement of the Polisario Front that considered the ECJ judgment as a 'strong victory' for the people of Western Sahara,[142] the Moroccan Ministry of Foreign Affairs and Cooperation declared that it 'took note of the ECJ judgment that corrected the legal deviations, changed the wrong political assessments and annulled the unfounded conclusions given by the GC'.[143] Surprisingly, even though the ECJ judgment was very clear in considering Western Sahara as a 'third party' vis-à-vis Morocco and the EU, the statement of the Moroccan Ministry of Foreign Affairs and Cooperation added that

> Morocco took note that the ECJ conclusions do not doubt the legality and legitimacy of the Moroccan discretion to conclude agreements that can be applied to the Moroccan Sahara.[144]

It is not yet clear towards what the EU relationship with Morocco is heading. The EU has direct sea and land borders (Spain's two autonomous cities, Ceuta and Melilla) with Morocco. The EU is interested in maintaining strong relations with Morocco for obvious reasons, the most important of which relate to tackling the security and migration challenges. In this regard, there are concerns that the EU's efforts to stop the migrant flows from North Africa might outweigh its commitment to promote its values.[145] The EU should promote a

---

142  Amohamed Khudad (Member of the National Secretariat of the Polisario Front and the Saharawi Coordinator with MINURSO), 'The Polisario Front Considers the CJEU Judgment a Strong Victory for the People of Western Sahara and its Struggles' (21 December 2016), author's translation; available in Arabic at http://www.spsrasd.info/news/ar/articles/2016/12/21/6068.html (accessed 6 March 2019).

143  Moroccan Ministry of Foreign Affairs and Cooperation 'Morocco Took Note of the CJEU Judgment that Rejected the Front Polisario's Appeal Due to its Inadmissibility' (21 December 2016), author's translation; available in Arabic at https://www.diplomatie.ma/arab/Politique%C3%A9trang%C3%A8re/Europe/tabid/1606/vw/1/ItemID/14286/language/en-US/Default.aspx (accessed 6 March 2019).

144  Ibid. (author's translation). See also the EEAS 'Déclaration conjointe par Federica Mogherini et le Ministre des Affaires étrangères et de la coopération du royaume du Maroc Salahddine Mezouar' (21 December 2016), available at https://eeas.europa.eu/headquarters/headquarters-homepage/18042/declaration-conjointe-par-federica-mogherini-et-le-ministre-des-affaires-etrangeres-et-de-la_en (accessed 6 March 2019).

145  The EU values are set out in Art. 2 TEU: 'The Union is founded on the values of respect for human dignity, freedom, democracy, equality, the rule of law and respect for human rights, including the rights of persons belonging to minorities. These values are common to the Member States in a society in which pluralism, non-discrimination, tolerance, justice, solidarity and equality between women and men prevail'.

consistent approach with respect to its values, otherwise its credibility may be undermined.[146]

## V  Conclusion

Despite its ambitious founding treaty that aimed at creating a common market in 1989, the AMU has so far failed to achieve political and economic integration among its Member States. The institutional and constitutional limits of the AMU Treaty are part of the reason for this failure. The AMU Treaty is composed of only nineteen articles and lacks many elements that are essential for the constituent treaty of any successful regional organization, such as provisions describing the competences of the AMU institutions vis-à-vis the national authorities of the AMUMS. A more comprehensive treaty is needed to fill the gaps and to detail how integration can be strengthened in the Maghreb. In this respect, the AMUMS should be realistic when formulating their objectives and should follow a gradual approach to integration, for instance, starting with a free-trade area and then gradually deepening the cooperation.[147] Creating a common market right away without providing the required human, infrastructural and financial resources will not help in establishing an effective regional cooperative framework. The AMU decision-making process was also a major obstacle as it is based on an intergovernmental method that requires unanimity among the AMUMS for any decision or amendment to the AMU Treaty. Furthermore, the AMU institutional structure suffers from a democratic deficit for at least two reasons; first, the Consultation Council that is supposed to be the AMU's parliamentary body cannot issue binding decisions. Second, civil society organizations were not given the opportunity to participate in the institutional framework of the AMU and thus to contribute to developing the AMU project.

However, although the above-mentioned points impeded the AMU from achieving its goals, the analysis in this article showed that the main reason behind the AMU failure has been the conflict about Western Sahara which has destabilized the region for many decades and negatively impacted the relationship between Algeria and Morocco. Without solving this dispute, neither a permanent peace in the region nor a regional integration of the Maghreb can be conceived. Unfortunately, in addition to the UN's inability to settle this

---

146   E. Lannon, 'The 2015 Review of the European Neighbourhood Policy and the Future of Euro–Mediterranean Relationships' (2015) 42.2 Dis Politika—Foreign Policy—A Biannual Journal of the European Foreign Policy Institute 82.
147   Lannon, 'Lectures on the Constitutional Aspects of the European Union's Integration'.

issue, the EU has not yet played any role in this respect. In its recent Global Strategy,[148] the EU did not even refer to the necessity of settling the Western Sahara dispute despite the negative impact this issue has had on the stability of the EU's Mediterranean neighbourhood for the last five decades. Thus, the EU should play a greater role in finding a solution to the Western Sahara conflict in order to secure the EU borders and to create the appropriate political atmosphere to reinvigorate Maghreb regional integration.

The EU has not yet followed a consistent and single bilateral and multilateral approach in promoting integration in the Maghreb. The EU approach is based on its own vision of the Maghreb rather than on the aim to build on the progress achieved by the AMUMS, which is reflected in the creation of the AMU. This becomes clear from the different bilateral agreements the EU concluded with the AMUMS and the distinct multilateral frameworks the EU established for these States. As far as legal agreements are concerned, while the EU and its Member States concluded bilateral EMAAs with Algeria, Morocco and Tunisia, they distinctly dealt with Mauritania by including it in the ACP–EU Cotonou Agreement and in the ECOWAS–EU Economic Partnership Agreement. At the multilateral level, whereas Mauritania was included only in the UfM, Algeria, Morocco and Tunisia were covered by both the ENP and the UfM. In addition, Libya remains outside any multilateral policy and has no bilateral agreement with the EU. Instead of its current differentiated approach that is based on the ENP, the EU should have dealt with the AMUMS as one regional block through, for instance, the conclusion of an EU–Maghreb Association Agreement. However, if such an agreement cannot be realized due to practical and political reasons, the EU may conclude a framework agreement with the AMUMS on the basis of which all the bilateral EMAAs shall be revised. In addition to the advantages of bringing the AMUMS under a single agreement and harmonizing the EU's bilateral agreements with the Maghreb States, the framework agreement would also be a great opportunity to create a legal framework for the EU's relationship with Libya.

## Acknowledgments

The author would like to thank Prof. Dr. Erwan Lannon at the Faculty of Law and Criminology of Ghent University and the Editorial Committee of the Max Planck Yearbook on United Nations Law for their valuable comments on the draft of this article.

---

148 HRVP, 'Shared Vision, Common Action: A Stronger Europe: A Global Strategy for the European Union's Foreign And Security Policy' (June 2016).

CHAPTER 12

# The Control of Conventionality: Developments in the Case Law of the Inter-American Court of Human Rights and Its Potential Expanding Effects in International Human Rights Law

*María Carmelina Londoño-Lázaro and Nicolás Carrillo-Santarelli*

### Abstract

The control of conventionality is a doctrine, developed by the Inter-American Court of Human Rights in its case law, according to which State agents are required to strive to make sure that domestic norms and practices are consistent with what Inter-American and other human rights law standards require. The doctrine as it has been developed posits that not only judges, but also any other State authorities must take these standards into account. The Court has made clear that its own pronouncements are to be considered too, not only in contentious cases but also in advisory opinions. Some argue that the Court has gone too far; others contend that the doctrine simply reaffirms the States' obligation to adjust domestic practices and norms to international obligations and make internationally recognized human rights effective. Moreover, as long as a multi-level dialogue is permitted and some risks of fragmentation or unreasonable impositions are avoided, the doctrine may help to achieve the objectives of preventing both the congestion of the regional system and repetitive violations, and the legitimacy of the Court may be further strengthened if it admits some latitude in State decisions. Finally, the doctrine requires State authorities to consider extra-American developments, UN developments included; and can help actors from other human rights systems identify developments and principles positively applied throughout the Americas, which may serve as examples.

### Keywords

Control of Conventionality – Inter-American Court of Human Rights – Multi-Level Dialogue – Principle of Effectiveness – Inter-American Human Rights System

# I  Introduction

The Inter-American Court of Human Rights (hereinafter 'Inter-American Court' or 'Court') has developed in its case law a doctrine on the control of 'conformity' with Inter-American standards, best known as the control of conventionality. Despite its apparent novelty, the doctrine is based on the principle of effectiveness[1] and well-established elements of international law such as (i) the obligation to adjust domestic norms and practices to international obligations; (ii) the fact that responsibility may attach to the actions and omissions of all State agents regardless of their functions and hierarchy, including legislators; and (iii) the impossibility of invoking domestic law to excuse the non-observance of international commitments.

That being said, while it is based on those solid foundations, the doctrine is novel in the sense that it seeks to make all State agents aware of their role and responsibility in ensuring that their State lives up to the Inter-American standards that are so dear in a region as the Americas, which has had and still has endemic and systematic human rights problems.

Furthermore, as is explained below, the doctrine (if accepted) might address two major problems, namely scarcity of resources and backlog, of the Inter-American human rights system. This system is composed of two main bodies, the Court as its judicial body, and the Commission, which is tasked with promoting human rights, and is the only entity allowed to present applications before the Court.

Additionally, beyond the regional scope, the control of conventionality may have a future in international human rights law, provided some essential conditions of legitimacy are satisfied, including use of the doctrine in a manner perceived to be fair and consistent with international law. This implies meeting aspects of 'publicness' that permit to review the pronouncements of the Court.[2]

This article will, first, clarify what the doctrine means. The second section will describe the evolution of the concept in Inter-American contentious cases and advisory opinions, followed by a third section presenting some controversies. The fourth section critically analyses the control of conventionality in light of the theory of sources of international law, a framework that allows

---

1  Recognized for the Inter-American Court as the *effet utile* principle established in Art. 2 of the American Convention on Human Rights (signed 22 November 1969, entered into force 18 July 1978) 1144 UNTS 123 (Pact of San José).
2  B. Kingsbury, 'The Concept of "Law" in Global Administrative Law' (2009) 20.1 EJIL 23, at 32–33.

to examine the conditions for the doctrine to operate legitimately within the regional system and, eventually, beyond its frontiers. A fifth section provides insights on the lessons that the past, the present and the potential future of the control of conventionality provide, and also examines how their identification can help to evaluate the strengths, risks and possibilities of ensuring a consistent and convenient use of the doctrine, which among others can increase the effective enjoyment of human rights in local contexts. Likewise, the fourth and fifth sections show that the doctrine, which besides Inter-American standards can look at universal ones, may be useful in other human rights systems.

## II  Overview and Meaning of the Doctrine

The doctrine of the 'control of conventionality'—also referred to as control of conformity with Inter-American standards—was formally endorsed by the Inter-American Court of Human Rights in 2006. From its creation, it has been the object of much debate and analysis. In sum, the doctrine requires *all* State agents to strive to make the conduct of their State consistent with Inter-American and other international human rights standards as far as their powers permit. Initially it was only applied to the judiciary, later to a wider spectrum of other agents; and in addition to treaty provisions, case law and other instruments different from the 1969 American Convention on Human Rights (hereinafter 'the Convention', 'the American Convention' or 'ACHR') were included.

The idea of a—diffuse—control of conventionality that ought to be carried out by national judges was first discussed in the *Almonacid Arellano v. Chile*[3] case in 2006, and the then-President of the Court, Sergio García-Ramírez, had also employed such an expression to explain the reach of the powers of the Court itself.[4] Shortly afterwards, there was an intense activity of the Court, evinced in the large number of judgments delineating the contours of the—then new—doctrine.

Judge García-Ramírez has described the control of conventionality that is to take place on the domestic level in the following manner:

---

3  *Almonacid Arellano v. Chile* (Judgment) IACtHR Series C No. 154 (26 September 2006).
4  *Myrna Mack Chang v. Guatemala* (Judgment) IACtHR Series C No. 101 (25 November 2003), at para. 30; *Vargas Areco v. Paraguay* (Judgment) IACtHR Series C No. 155 (26 September 2006), at paras 6–7; *Dismissed Congressional Employees (Aguado Alfaro et al.) v. Peru* (Judgment) IACtHR Series C No. 158 (24 November 2006), at para. 5; E. Ferrer Mac-Gregor, 'El control difuso de convencionalidad en el Estado Constitucional' in H. Fix-Zamudio and D. Valdés (eds), *Formación y perspectivas del Estado en Mexico* (UNAM 2010), at 173.

[P]ower granted or recognized on behalf of certain jurisdictional bodies—or all jurisdictional bodies [...] to verify the consistency between domestic acts—basically domestic provisions with a general reach, such as Constitution, laws, regulations, etc.—and provisions of international law [...]. As a result of this verification, which obviously entails carrying out an interpretation, there will be legal consequences: basically, the confirmation or voiding (obtained by different means and with different nomenclatures) of the domestic legal act that is consistent with, or contrary to, the international legal system.[5]

From 2006 afterwards, the control of conventionality doctrine has been considered to imply two things: first, an inherent power of the Court to verify the compatibility of State conduct with the provisions of the American Convention, making the international stage an independent and autonomous level of control of legality that neither operates as a 'fourth instance' after domestic justice nor replaces the latter.[6] In the same vein, authors such as André de Carvalho Ramos have argued that the control of conventionality is different and independent from domestic law controls such as constitutionality controls, and that both must be satisfied for a domestic actor to operate properly.[7]

Second, the Court considers the control of conventionality to be a true legal obligation that binds 'judges and bodies linked to the administration of justice'.[8] In an effort to establish the doctrine in the Inter-American system, the Court reaffirmed it in several cases, although with different wordings. These different formulations may be deemed by some as having diverging scopes.[9] Questions have arisen with regard to (i) the extent of the control on the national

---

[5] S. García, 'El control judicial interno de convencionalidad' (2011) 5 IUS—Revista del Instituto de Ciencias Jurídicas de Puebla 123, at 126 (translation by the authors).

[6] The Court has held that it does not replace the functions or role of domestic judges. Among others, *Heliodoro Portugal v. Panamá* (Judgment) IACtHR (12 August 2008), at para. 203; *Ríos et al. v. Venezuela* (Judgment) IACtHR No. 194 (28 January 2009), at para. 303; *Perozo et al. v. Venezuela* (Judgment) IACtHR Series C No. 195 (28 January 2009), at para. 317.

[7] A. Carvalho Ramos, 'Control of Conventionality and the Struggle to Achieve a Definitive Interpretation of Human Rights: The Brazilian Experience' (2016) 64 Revista IIDH 11.

[8] Among others, concurring opinion of Judge *ad hoc* Eduardo Ferrer Mac-Gregor Poisot to *Cabrera García and Montiel Flores v. Mexico* (Judgment) IACtHR Series C No. 220 (26 November 2010), at para. 44.

[9] M. Londoño, 'El principio de legalidad y el control de convencionalidad de las leyes: confluencias y perspectivas en el pensamiento de la Corte Interamericana de Derechos Humanos' (2010) 128 Boletín Mexicano de Derecho Comparado 761; I. Suárez, *Control de convencionalidad y auto-precedente interamericano* (Universidad de La Sabana—Grupo Editorial Ibáñez 2015); C. Laplacette, *Teoría y práctica del Control de Constitucionalidad* (Editorial BDF 2016).

level, (ii) the subjects bound by it, and (iii) the standard of conventionality that is required.

That being said, nowadays, the corpus of the Inter-American case law on the matter permits to identify five features of the doctrine, namely:

(a) It calls for the verification of the compatibility of domestic norms and practices with the Convention, other Inter-American treaties the respective State is bound by, and the Court's case law;
(b) It is an obligation of every public authority in the exercise of its functions;
(c) In order to ascertain compatibility with the Convention, in addition to the treaty as such, the Court's case law and other Inter-American treaties the State is party to must be taken into account;
(d) It is a control that must be carried out by every public authority *ex officio*; and
(e) Its implementation may entail the suppression of norms that are contrary to the Convention and other pertinent treaties, or interpreting norms in a manner that is consistent with those treaties, depending on the powers that a given public authority has.[10]

Those features were affirmed by the Court's case law, although there have been struggles. We will briefly explore some of the most important cases to elucidate the main benefits and challenges of the doctrine.

## III  Consolidation of the Doctrine in the Inter-American Case Law

In 2006, considering the amnesty law in Chile that bolstered impunity of crimes against humanity, the Inter-American Court in *Almonacid Arellano v. Chile* held that:

> [D]omestic judges and courts are bound to respect the rule of law, and therefore, they are bound to apply the provisions in force within the legal system. But when a State has ratified an international treaty such as the American Convention, its judges, as part of the State, are also bound by such Convention. This forces them to see that all the effects of the provisions embodied in the Convention are not adversely affected by the enforcement of laws which are contrary to its purpose and that have not had any legal effects since their inception. In other words, the Judiciary must exercise a sort of 'conventionality control' between the domestic

---

10  IACtHR, 'Cuadernillo de jurisprudencia de la Corte Interamericana de Derechos Humanos N° 7: control de convencionalidad' (2017).

legal provisions which are applied to specific cases and the American Convention on Human Rights. *To perform this task, the Judiciary has to take into account not only the treaty, but also the interpretation thereof made by the Inter-American Court, which is the ultimate interpreter of the American Convention*[11] (emphasis added).

Thus, the Inter-American Court identified an obligation arising from the principle of effectiveness (Art. 2 ACHR) and from the duty to ensure everybody's free and full exercise of rights and freedoms (Art. 1 (1) ACHR), which, considered in conjunction, require any judge and every other State agent that performs jurisdictional powers or has any role in the administration of justice to control domestic laws and conduct with the aim of ensuring their compatibility and consistency with the American Convention.

In the 2007 *Boyce v. Barbados* case, the Court even held that constitutional provisions are also subject to the control of conventionality, which is consistent with the idea that a contradiction between the Constitution of a State and its international human rights commitments engages State responsibility, as already indicated in the case *The Last Temptation of Christ*.[12]

In *Boyce v. Barbados*, the Court found that a statutory norm and a constitutional provision in Barbados conflicted with the American Convention.[13] The former enshrined the mandatory death penalty for murder, and the second one was a 'saving clause' that precluded the judicial scrutiny of norms enacted prior to the 1966 Constitution, even if they were challenged as being contrary to fundamental rights and freedoms.[14]

The law that required the mandatory death penalty for murder cases, having been enacted prior to 1966, was shielded against scrutiny for alleged inconsistency with fundamental rights, as had been concluded by high Barbados courts. Their decisions, however, were rejected by the Court:

> The analysis of the [*Judicial Committee of the Privy Council*] should not have been limited to the issue of whether the [Offences against the Person Act] was unconstitutional. Rather, the question should have also been whether it was 'conventional'. That is, Barbadian courts, including

---

11   *Almonacid Arellano v. Chile* (Judgment) IACtHR Series C No. 154 (26 September 2006), at para. 124.
12   *The Last Temptation of Christ (Olmedo Bustos et al. v. Chile)* (Judgment) IACtHR Series C No. 73 (5 February 2001), at paras 87–90.
13   *Boyce et al. v. Barbados* (Judgment) IACtHR Series C No. 169 (20 November 2007), at paras 80, 123, 241.
14   Ibid., at paras 65, 75, 241.

the JCPC, and now the Caribbean Court of Justice, must also address whether the law in Barbados restricts or violates the rights recognized in the Convention.[15]

The Court insisted that States cannot justify failure to observe their obligations under the American Convention on the basis of domestic law, even when constitutional provisions are invoked.[16]

In 2008, in its *Heliodoro Portugal v. Panama* decision, the Court stressed the importance of the control of conventionality for the sake of ensuring that the content of provisions of the American Convention is not annulled or negatively affected in practice by domestic norms or institutional practices contrary to them.[17] All of the judiciary is required to carry out the control of conventionality. Furthermore, as has been well pointed out by Eduardo Ferrer Mac-Gregor, the development of the doctrine in the Court's case law has led to the conclusion that its scope has increased 'to cover not just judges and judicial entities, but also authorities more generally, including the legislature'.[18] We agree with this consideration, insofar as all of them may face situations in which their *ex officio* efforts 'within the framework of their respective competences'[19] to make sure that their States observe their international human rights obligations are called for.

Furthermore, the doctrine was now said to require checking the consistency of norms and internal practices with the American Convention, the case law of the Inter-American Court *and* other Inter-American treaties the State is a party to. In the case against Panama, the Court considered that the absence of a crime of forced disappearance in Panama's law amounted to a violation of its obligations under the American Convention on Forced Disappearance

---

15   Ibid., at para. 78.
16   Ibid., at para. 77, wherein it was said that 'aforementioned conclusion of the JCPC was arrived at by a purely constitutional analysis that did not take into account the State's obligations under the American Convention as interpreted by this Court's jurisprudence. In accordance with the Vienna Convention on the Law of Treaties, Barbados is bound to comply with its obligations under the American Convention in good faith, and it may not invoke the provisions of its internal law as justification for its failure to comply with its treaty obligations. In the present case, the State is precisely invoking provisions of its internal law for such purposes'.
17   *Heliodoro Portugal v Panama* (Judgment) IACtHR Series C No. 186 (12 August 2008), at para. 180.
18   E. Ferrer Mac-Gregor, 'The Constitutionalization of International Law in Latin America: Conventionality Control, the New Doctrine of the Inter-American Court of Human Rights' (2017) 109 AJIL Unbound 93, at 95.
19   Ibid., at 93.

of Persons, and accordingly judges in Panama were called upon to carry out a control of conventionality and prevent impunity.[20]

The expansion of the control standard as including other human rights treaties would be confirmed in other cases, and the Court later indicated that the standard included its own interpretation of the treaties.[21]

The doctrine was affirmed in several cases brought against Mexico, which had a great impact on the Inter-American case law. The judgments in *Radilla Pacheco* (2009), *Fernández Ortega* (2010), *Rosendo Cantú* (2010), and *Cabrera García and Montiel Flores* (2010) established that the legal criteria for material and personal competence of military courts in Mexico have to be interpreted in accordance with the principles of Inter-American case law, which apply to all human rights violations that have been allegedly perpetrated by members of the armed forces.[22]

Those four cases address the inconsistency between Mexican norms and practices concerning the competence of the military jurisdiction to examine alleged human rights violations, and Inter-American standards; and the decisions in those cases strongly influenced the 2011 amendment of the Mexican Constitution.[23] On the basis of what the Court said, national judges should refer cases on human rights violations by members of the armed forces to the ordinary criminal jurisdiction,[24] in line with Inter-American case law. Also, an interpretation that is consistent with the Inter-American standards may sometimes be sufficient in terms of control of conventionality. In this vein, a reform of Art. 13 of the Mexican Constitution was found to be unnecessary, as it was sufficient to interpret the article in a manner consistent with Inter-American standards.[25]

---

20  *Heliodoro Portugal v Panama* (Judgment) IACtHR Series C No. 186 (12 August 2008), at para. 185, where it is said that 'the specific obligation to define the offense of forced disappearance of persons arose for the State on March 28, 1996, when the Inter-American Convention on Forced Disappearances of Persons entered into force in Panama'.

21  *The Rio Negro Massacres v. Guatemala* (Judgment) IACtHR Series C No. 250 (4 September 2012), at para. 262; *Gudiel Álvarez et al. ('Diario Militar') v. Guatemala* (Judgment) IACtHR Series C No. 253 (20 November 2012).

22  *Cabrera García and Montiel Flores v. Mexico* (Judgment) IACtHR Series C No. 220 (26 November 2010), at para. 233.

23  On the constitutional reform, see H. Fix-Zamunio, 'Las reformas constitucionales mexicanas de junio de 2011 y sus efectos en el Sistema Interamericano de Derechos Humanos' (2011) 11 Revista Iberoamericana de derecho público y administrativo 232; J. Morales, 'Reforma constitucional de derechos humanos: hacia un nuevo derecho en México' (September 2014) 19 Revista PERSEO.

24  *Fernández Ortega v. Mexico* (Judgment) IACtHR Series C No. 215 (30 August 2010), at para. 237.

25  *Rosendo Cantú et al. v. Mexico* (Judgment) IACtHR Series C No. 216 (31 August 2010), at paras 219–221.

The concept established in *Radilla Pacheco* requires not only adjusting domestic legislation, but also State practice. According to the Court:

> [N]ot only the suppression or issuing of the regulations within the domestic legislation guarantee the rights enshrined in the American Convention, pursuant with the obligation included in Article 2 of that instrument. The development of State practices leading to the effective observance of the rights and liberties enshrined in the same is also required. Therefore, the existence of a regulation does not guarantee in itself that its application will be adequate. It is necessary that the application of the regulations or their interpretation, as jurisdictional practices and a manifestation of the State's public order, be adjusted to the same purpose sought by Article 2 of the Convention.[26]

*Cabrera García and Montiel Flores* is noteworthy for having been the first time when a State claimed that a control of conventionality had been effectively performed, arguing that the Inter-American Court lacked competence to hear the merits of the case because the Court cannot serve as a court of 'fourth instance.'[27] The Court responded by saying that the State's arguments actually pertained to the merits of the case, and that the Court would later identify 'whether the presumed conventionality control allegedly exercised by the State involved observance of the State's international obligations in accordance with this Court's case law and with the applicable international law'.[28] With this pronouncement, the Court noted that it has the power to review the control of conventionality carried out by State authorities. Judge *ad hoc* Eduardo Ferrer Mac-Gregor explored this aspect in his concurring opinion.[29]

---

[26] *Radilla-Pacheco v. Mexico* (Judgment) IACtHR Series C No. 209 (23 November 2009), at para. 338.

[27] *Cabrera García and Montiel Flores v. Mexico* (Judgment) IACtHR Series C No. 220 (26 November 2010), at para. 13. An argument on the control of conventionality had already been raised in the defence of a State (Peru) before, although not in a way as strong and based on facts as the one presented by Mexico. On this other case, see: *Dismissed Congressional Employees (Aguado-Alfaro et al.) v. Peru* (Judgment) IACtHR Series C No. 158 (24 November 2006).

[28] *Cabrera García and Montiel Flores v. Mexico* (Judgment) IACtHR Series C No. 220 (26 November 2010), at para. 21.

[29] For the judge, the supranational review does not turn 'the Inter-American Court into a "court of appeals" or court of "fourth instance," because its actions are limited to the analysis of certain violations of the international commitments made by the respondent State in each particular case, and not of each and every one of the actions of domestic judicial bodies, which obviously in this latter case would mean substituting the domestic jurisdiction, violating the very essence of the reinforcing and complementary nature of the international courts'. See the concurring opinion of Judge Eduardo Ferrer Mac-Gregor

The judgment is also remarkable because the Court analysed which agents and public servants have to carry out a control of conventionality *ex officio*, namely judges and bodies linked to the administration of justice at all levels. While the Court confirmed that the control of conventionality must be carried out in light of the provisions of the American Convention and the Court's interpretation of it, the Court did not determine whether advisory opinions should also be taken into account—that would be clarified later, with the Court indicating that they have to be considered. Nevertheless, the Court insisted that the control must be performed by judicial servants in the exercise of their functions and within the framework of pertinent procedural regulations.[30]

In the *Gomes Lund v. Brazil* decision of 2010, the Court elaborated on the question which State agents are called to perform a control of conventionality. By interpreting general obligations (Arts 1 (1) and 2 ACHR, and Arts 8 and 15 ACHR jointly), the Court declared the incompatibility of a Brazilian amnesty law with the American Convention, reiterated its case law on the matter by insisting that legislation of that kind lacks legal effect, and specified that the judicial branch is not the only one subject to the control of conventionality. Rather,

> when a State is a Party to an international treaty such as the American Convention, all of its organs, including its judges, are also subject to it, wherein they are obligated to ensure that the effects of the provisions of the Convention are not reduced by the application of norms that are contrary to the purpose and end goal and that from the onset lack legal effect.[31]

On this basis, the Court dismissed a defence raised by the respondent State concerning its domestic laws as being indispensable for the transition towards democracy and national reconciliation. According to Brazil, the regulation at issue had been enacted in accordance with democratic rules and had been declared to be in conformity with the Brazilian Constitution by the Federal Supreme Tribunal of Brazil in 2010. Nevertheless, for the Inter-American Court, '[t]he conventional obligations of States Parties bind all the powers and organs of the State, those of which must guarantee compliance with conventional obligations and its effects (*effet utile*) in the design of its domestic law'.[32]

---

to *Cabrera García and Montiel Flores v. Mexico* (Judgment) IACtHR Series C No. 220, at para. 11 (26 November 2010).

30 As explained in *Radilla Pacheco v. Mexico* (Judgment) IACtHR Series C No. 209 (23 November 2009), at para. 339.

31 *Gomes Lund et al. ('Guerrilha do Araguaia') v. Brazil* (Judgment) IACtHR Series C No. 219 (24 November 2010), at para. 176.

32 Ibid., at para. 177.

Accordingly, neither necessity nor democracy arguments could be accepted. In the case of *Gelman v. Uruguay*, the Court argued that:

> The bare existence of a democratic regime does not guarantee, *per se*, the permanent respect of International Law [...]. The democratic legitimacy of specific facts in a society is limited by the norms of protection of human rights recognized in international treaties [...] in such a form that the existence of one true democratic regime is determined by both its formal and substantial characteristics, and therefore, particularly in cases of serious violations of nonrevocable norms of International Law, the protection of human rights constitutes [an] impassable limit to the rule of the majority, that is, to the forum of the 'possible to be decided' by the majorities in the democratic instance, those who should also prioritize 'control of conformity with the Convention' [...] which is a function and task of any public authority and not only the Judicial Branch.[33]

This doctrine, according to which the control of conventionality is an obligation of every public authority, power and organ, was also confirmed in *Massacres of El Mozote and Nearby Places v. El Salvador* in 2012.[34]

Apart from the question of who must carry out a control of conformity with the Inter-American standards at the national level, it must be noted that the concept of 'domestic norms' is not limited to legislation enacted by the legislative branch. As can be gleaned from the 2010 judgment in the *Xákmok Kásek Indigenous Community vs. Paraguay* case, every type and category of norm, including presidential decrees,[35] must follow the logic of the Inter-American standards and be adjusted to them.

The early stage of the formation of the doctrine may be considered to conclude with the 2012 *Santo Domingo Massacre v. Colombia* decision. While the judgment does not introduce meaningful changes to the doctrine, it does perceive the control as a dynamic task jointly carried out by domestic and international authorities,[36] thus highlighting the principle of subsidiarity in the Inter-American system of human rights. According to the Court, 'a dynamic and complementary control of the States' treaty-based obligations to respect

---

33   *Gelman v. Uruguay* (Judgment) IACtHR Series C No. 221 (24 February 2011), at para. 239.
34   *Massacres of El Mozote and Nearby Places v. El Salvador* (Judgment) IACtHR Series C No. 252 (25 October 2012), at para. 318.
35   *Xákmok Kásek Indigenous Community v. Paraguay* (Judgment) IACtHR Series C No. 214 (24 August 2010), at para. 161.
36   *Santo Domingo Massacre v. Colombia* (Judgment) IACtHR Series No. 259 (29 November 2012), at para. 143.

and ensure human rights has been established between the domestic authorities (who have the primary obligation) and the international instance (complementarily), so that their decision criteria can be established and harmonized'.[37]

An overall analysis of the case law during the period that has been just examined shows that the doctrine mainly seeks to ensure the adjustment of the national legal system—and associated policies and practices—to the Inter-American standards. It is a means to realize the principle of effectiveness enshrined in Art. 2 ACHR, which is a basis of the 'new' obligation the doctrine refers to. It may require different types of conduct of State agents, be it the non-application or elimination of a norm or practice contrary to the Convention, be it changing norms, be it interpreting domestic legislation in conformity with the Inter-American case law, or be it the creation of new norms or practices.

## IV  Difficulties

Nevertheless, even if it were possible to summarize all the good faith efforts the Court desires the States to make, it cannot be ignored that the doctrine of the Court has some theoretical and practical difficulties.

In its recent Advisory Opinion OC-24/17, the Court argued that control of conformity with Convention standards also has to consider its advisory opinions and not just its decisions in contentious cases, because both serve the goal of protecting human rights.[38] Furthermore, the Court argued that if domestic bodies strive to ensure consistency with what the Court says in its advisory opinions, this will help to prevent abuses, the engagement of State responsibility and applications or decisions against it.[39] Still, there does not seem to be complete consensus among the Inter-American judges on the binding effect of advisory opinions and the duty to consider them as part of a control of conventionality. Indeed, Judge Vio Grossi, though concurring with the idea that the control of conventionality may fulfil preventive functions, affirmed that there

---

37   Ibid.
38   *Gender Identity, and Equality and Non-Discrimination with regard to Same-Sex Couples. State Obligations in relation to Change of Name, Gender Identity, and Rights Deriving from a Relationship between Same-Sex Couples (Interpretation and Scope of Articles 1 (1), 3, 7, 11 (2), 13, 17, 18 and 24, in relation to Article 1, of the American Convention on Human Rights)* (Advisory Opinion OC-24/17) IACtHR Series A No. 24 (24 November 2017), at para. 26.
39   Ibid., at paras 61, 71.

is no direct and formal binding effect of advisory opinions.[40] Still, beginning with Advisory Opinion OC-21/14, the Court has been arguing (verbatim) that

> the different organs of the State must carry out the corresponding control of conformity with the Convention, based also on the considerations of the Court in exercise of its non-contentious or advisory jurisdiction, *which undeniably shares with its contentious jurisdiction the goal of the inter-American human rights system, which is 'the protection of the fundamental rights of the human being'*. Furthermore, the interpretation given to a provision of the Convention through an advisory opinion provides all the organs of the Member States of the OAS, including those that are not parties to the Convention but that have undertaken to respect human rights under the Charter of the OAS [...] with a source that, by its very nature, also contributes, *especially in a preventive manner, to achieving the effective respect and guarantee of human rights. In particular, it can provide guidance when deciding matters relating to children in the context of migration and to avoid possible human rights violations*.[41]

Similar ideas were later expressed in Advisory Opinions OC-23/17,[42] OC-24/17 (as shown above) and OC-25/18.[43]

## V  Local Controversies and Reactions to the Doctrine in the Region

Problems appear whenever the case law of the Court is seen as being too distant from the text and spirit of the Convention, for example, when there are accusations of judicial activism, leading to problems in the acceptance and

---

40   Advisory Opinion OC-24/17, Separate Opinion of Judge Eduardo Vio Grossi, at paras 121, 131, 133.

41   *Rights and Guarantees of Children in the Context of Migration and/or in Need of International Protection* (Advisory Opinion OC-21/14) IACtHR Series A No. 21 (19 August 2014), at para. 31 (emphasis added).

42   *The Environment and Human Rights (State Obligations in relation to the Environment in the Context of the Protection and Guarantee of the Rights to Life and to Personal Integrity—Interpretation and Scope of Articles 4 (1) and 5 (1) of the American Convention on Human Rights)* (Advisory Opinion OC-23/17) IACtHR Series A No. 23 (15 November 2017), at para. 28.

43   *The Institution of Asylum, and its Recognition as a Human Right under the Inter-American System of Protection (Interpretation and Scope of Articles 5, 22 (7) and 22 (8) in relation to Art. 1 (1) of the American Convention on Human Rights)* (Advisory Opinion OC-25/18) IACtHR Series A No. 25 (30 May 2018), at para. 58.

application of the doctrine. Problems also arise due the lack of consistency in the findings of the Court and the ensuing lack of clarity as to what the Inter-American standards are. Some claim that certain decisions of the Court demonstrate a misunderstanding or ignorance of national realities or may have unforeseeable effects with regard to socially sensitive issues.

Hence, even though the control of conventionality is expected to harmonize basic mandatory standards in the region of the Americas in the field of human rights—this being, for some, an effect of the so-called *ius constitutionale commune*—, an aspiration with multiple benefits,[44] it cannot be ignored that there are controversies and questions surrounding the doctrine. Scholars have reacted to the doctrine in different ways. For example, Alfonso Santiago refers to it in a formal and descriptive way, regarding it as the verification of the adjustment of domestic norms or acts to the norms, principles and standards of the 'new' international human rights law. However, he cautions about possible abuses if the margin of appreciation of States is ignored by the regional Court.[45] On the other hand, for Andrea Bianchi the doctrine represents 'the control of the supremacy of the American Convention on Human Rights over domestic law norms and, depending on the interpretation and reach we give to it, it can amount to a simple and innocent wordplay or a risky abandonment of sovereignty in the judicial sphere'.[46]

We will turn now to a brief examination of how some States Parties to the American Convention have adopted the doctrine.

## 1    *Argentina*

The Supreme Court of Argentina welcomed the doctrine of the control of conventionality in the *Mazzeo* case,[47] even including an excerpt of the *Almonacid Arellano* decision referred to above. Some years later, in the *Rodríguez Pereyra* case, the Argentinian Court held that:

> [J]udicial bodies of the countries that have ratified the American Convention on Human Rights are required to carry out, *ex officio*, the control of conventionality, setting aside domestic norms contrary to that treaty. Thus, it would be illogic to accept that the National Constitution—which

---

44  A. Bogdandy, 'Ius Constitutionale Commune en América Latina: una mirada a un constitucionalismo transformador' (2015) 34 Revista Derecho del Estado 3; E. Ferrer Mac-Gregor, op. cit., at 99.
45  S. Alfonso, *En las fronteras entre el Derecho Constitucional y la Filosofía del Derecho* (Marcial Pons 2010), at 196.
46  A. Bianchi, 'Una reflexión sobre el llamado "control de convencionalidad"' (23 September 2010) LL 2010-E1090.
47  *Mazzeo, Julio Lilo et al.* (*Judgment*) Supreme Court of Argentina (13 July 2007) 330:3248.

grants constitutional status to the aforementioned Convention (art. 75.22)—, on the one hand, introduces its provisions in the domestic law and hence permits the implementation of the interpretive rule—formulated by its authentic interpreter, that is to say the Inter-American Court of Human Rights—obliging national courts to carry out a control of conventionality *ex officio* and, on the other hand, prevents the same Courts from resorting to a similar examination with the aim of ensuring its supremacy in relation to local norms with a lower hierarchy.[48]

Nevertheless, in a more recent decision, *Ministerio de Relaciones Exteriores y Culto*, the same Argentinian Supreme Court refused to render a 2011 judgment ineffective in spite of the fact that the Inter-American Court had ordered this.[49] To justify its decision, the Supreme Court held that:

> From the point of view of the international obligations accepted by our country, the structural principles of the Inter-American system of human rights, self-defined as subsidiary, must be taken into account [...]. This subsidiarity is manifested, among others, in the treaty requirement of exhausting domestic remedies before accessing the regional system [...] and in the principle according to which the Inter-American Court does not act as just another instance in cases examined by national Courts. The Inter-American Court is, therefore, not a 'fourth instance' that reviews or annuls State judicial decisions. Rather, in accordance to said structural principles, it is subsidiary, supportive and complementary.[50]

By saying this, the Supreme Court made it clear that in the face of apparently unavoidable conflicts between the text of its national constitution and treaty norms, in the Argentinian system judges must give priority to constitutional norms before treaty rules.

### 2    *Costa Rica*

Another landmark case is *Artavia Murillo et al. (in Vitro Fertilization)*. The case revealed a conflict between the Inter-American Court of Human Rights and the Constitutional Chamber of the Supreme Court of Costa Rica in relation to

---

48   R. Pereyra, J. Luis y otra c. Ejército Argentino s/daños y perjuicios (*Judgments*) Supreme Court of Argentina (27 November 2012) 335:2333.

49   See A. Santiago, '¿Desobediencia debida? ¿Quién tiene la última palabra?' (23 February 2017) Edición. Especial LL.

50   J. Hitters, 'Control de Convencionalidad: ¿Puede la Corte Interamericana de Derechos Humanos dejar sin efecto fallos de los Tribunales Superiores?' (2017) LL 2.

*in vitro* fertilization. Decree 24029-S of 1995, adopted by the executive of Costa Rica, regulated such treatments.[51] This being a subject over which the legislative branch had competence, and considering the right to life of the unborn, the Constitutional Chamber declared it unconstitutional on 15 March 2000.[52]

As a reaction to that decision, the applicants went before the Inter-American system, and the Court decided against the State of Costa Rica:

> [T]he pertinent State authorities must take the appropriate measures to ensure that the prohibition of the practice of IVF is annulled as rapidly as possible so that those who wish to use this assisted reproduction technique may do so without encountering any impediments [...]. [T]he State must, as soon as possible, regulate those aspects it considers necessary for the implementation of IVF, taking into account the principles established in this Judgment.[53]

Nevertheless, the legislative of Costa Rica declined to enact the regulations the Inter-American Court had demanded of the State, on the understanding that the order was contrary to its Constitution which protects the rights of the unborn. Eventually, the executive itself adopted Decree 39210-MP-S which permitted IVF treatments in order to fulfil what the Inter-American Court had ordered the State to do.[54]

On 3 February 2016, that Decree was declared unconstitutional by the Supreme Court of Costa Rica[55] on the basis of a 'violation of the principle of legal reservation and because the modification of the legal system, on the basis of constitutional procedures enshrined in article 2 of the American Convention on Human Rights, must be made by means of a formal law'.

Confronted with this scenario, Costa Rica made three presentations (4, 11 and 16 of February 2016) before the Inter-American Court in which it requested the temporary validity of the executive Decree until a superior norm was enacted. In response to that request, on 26 February 2016 the Court passed a

---

51   Costa Rica, Decree 24029-S of 1995.
52   *Acción de inconstitucionalidad promovida por Hermes Navarro Del Valle* Constitutional Chamber of the Supreme Court of Justice of Costa Rica (15 March 2000) File 95-001734-0007-CO, Res: 2000-02306.
53   *Artavia Murillo et al. ('In Vitro Fertilization') v. Costa Rica* (Judgment) IACtHR Series C No. 257 (28 November 2012), at paras 336–337.
54   See D. Arguedas Ortiz, 'Finalmente, Costa Rica vuelve a permitir fecundación in vitro' (12 September 2015) Inter Press Service.
55   Constitutional Chamber of the Supreme Court Justice of Costa Rica (15 March 2000) Decision No. 2016–001692.

decision on the monitoring of compliance with its judgment in which it indicated that on the basis of the American Convention and the reparations it had ordered, IVF had to be understood as being 'authorized in Costa Rica' and that the use of that technique had to be 'immediately allowed', both in the public and private realm, without the necessity of a legal act that recognized or regulated the possibility of using the technique.[56]

### 3  Dominican Republic

In 2013, the Constitutional Court of the Dominican Republic adopted Judgment TC/0168/13 in what was known as the *Juliana Deguis Pierre* case,[57] declaring that children born to foreigners in transit over Dominican territory were not Dominican nationals.

After the publication of the judgment, the Inter-American Commission on Human Rights claimed that the State was in breach of the American Convention which sets forth in Art. 20 that '[e]very person has the right to the nationality of the State in whose territory he was born if he does not have the right to any other nationality', and that '[n]o one shall be arbitrarily deprived of his nationality or of the right to change it'. The Commission also argued that the decision of the Constitutional Court was contrary to the judgment of the Inter-American Court in the case of *Girls Yean and Bosico v. the Dominican Republic*[58] which indicated that the migratory status of a person is not transmitted to their children, and that the condition of having been born in the territory of the State is the only one that had to be demonstrated in order to acquire nationality when it comes to individuals who would not have any nationality if the one of the State in which they were born is not granted to them.

The *Juliana Deguis Pierre* case came before the Inter-American Court which issued a judgment on 28 August 2014 in the case of *Expelled Dominicans and Haitians v. Dominican Republic*, saying that

> the State must adopt, within a reasonable time, the necessary measures to annul any type of norm, whether administrative, regulatory, legal or constitutional, as well as any practice, decision or interpretation that establishes or has the effect that the irregular status of parents who are aliens constitutes grounds for denying Dominican nationality to those born on

---

56  *Artavia Murillo et al. ('In Vitro Fertilization') v. Costa Rica (Monitoring Compliance with Judgments)* IACtHR (*26 February 2016*), at para. 26.
57  *Juliana Deguis Pierre*, Judgment TC/0168/13 (*23 September 2013*).
58  *Girls Yean and Bosico v. Dominican Republic* (Judgment) IACtHR *Series C No. 130 (8 September 2005)*.

the territory of the Dominican Republic, because such norms, practices, decisions or interpretations are contrary to the American Convention.[59]

On 23 October 2014, the Dominican government issued a statement rejecting the judgment.[60] Shortly after, on 4 November 2014, the Constitutional Court of the Dominical Republic in Judgment TC/0256/14 declared the 'unconstitutionality of the instrument of acceptance of the competence of the IACHR signed by the President of the Dominican Republic on nineteen (19) February nineteen ninety nine (1999)'. According to the Constitutional Court, that acceptance had not been approved by the legislative branch in accordance with the Constitution of the Dominican Republic, but only by the President. With this argument, the decision of the Inter-American Court on *Haitian Immigrants* was rejected and ignored. Needless to say, Inter-American Commission went on to reject the judgment of the Constitutional Court,[61] claiming that:

> There is also no basis in international law by which the judgment of the Constitutional Court may be understood to have effect in the future. The American Convention does not establish the possibility that a State that continues to be a party to the treaty can release itself from the jurisdiction of the Inter-American Court. […] [A]bsent an express provision, interpreting the American Convention as limiting the scope of the Court's jurisdiction would run contrary to the object and purpose of international human rights protections.[62]

## 4   Chile

A Chilean case in which censorship was debated proved to be less controversial. The Constitution of Chile permitted prior censorship with regard to films. Specifically, Art. 19 (12) indicated that 'the law will establish a system of censorship for the exhibition and publicity of cinematographic productions'. In *The Last Temptation of Christ (Olmedo Bustos et al.)*,[63] the Inter-American Court found Chile to be in breach of Art. 13 ACHR which protects freedom of thought and expression.

---

59   *Expelled Dominicans and Haitians v. Dominican Republic* (Judgment) IACtHR Series C No. 282 (28 August 2014), at para. 469.
60   'Gobierno rechaza fallo de Corte contra el país' (24 October 2014) El Día.
61   OAS Press Release 'IACHR Condemns Judgment of the Constitutional Court of the Dominican Republic' (6 November 2014).
62   Ibid.
63   *The Last Temptation of Christ (Olmedo Bustos et al.) v. Chile* (Judgment) IACtHR Series C No. 73 (5 February 2001).

## 5   Mexico

In the course of its 2011 constitutional reform,[64] Mexico incorporated into its Constitution the protection of human rights recognized in international treaties. Art. 1 now says: 'norms on human rights will be interpreted in conformity with this Constitution and international treaties on the subject, always favouring the broadest possible protection of persons'. After the amendment, the Supreme Court of Mexico held that the only permissible limitations to human rights recognized in international treaties are those having a direct foundation in the constitutional text.[65] As has been pointed out in doctrine, (our translation) 'in this way [the Mexican Court] asserted via implication the final supremacy of the Constitution in relation to international treaties on human rights when the Constitution itself does not permit a limitation to a right recognized in a greater way in an international treaty'.[66]

These cases show that the controversies surrounding the notion of the control of conventionality are substantial and not few in number. However, those critiques might be met by increasing the legitimacy of the doctrine. The following is an attempt towards this aim, based on the general theory of sources of international law.

## VI   A Critical Appraisal of the Doctrine of the Control of Conventionality in Light of the Theory of Sources of International Law

While the control of conventionality seems to be entrenched in the mindset of the Inter-American Court of Human Rights at the moment, it is worth considering if that doctrine respects the competences and obligations of States under international law, and if it is consistent with the sources that create such obligations. In other words, while the doctrine of the control of conventionality seems to be useful, it is important to demonstrate that it does not contradict the current international legal structure—and to ask if an alternative approach might be preferable.

At first glance, the doctrine seems to run counter to the fact that international law lacks a *stare decisis* rule, as has been well explained by John Jackson.[67] However, further analysis may show the doctrine—if understood in

---

64   Decree published in the Official Gazette of the Federation on 10 June 2011.
65   Supreme Court of Mexico, 'Contradicción de tesis 293/2011', Intervention of Minister José Ramón Cossío Díaz in the 29 August 2013 plenary session.
66   A. Santiago, op. cit.
67   J.H. Jackson, *Sovereignty, the WTO and Changing Fundamentals of International Law* (CUP 2009), at 175.

certain ways—to be in accordance with international law and permitting to achieve important objectives.

Scarcity of institutional resources and the work backlog of international bodies may be arguments in favour of persuading State authorities to heed the *obiter dicta* and *ratio decidendi* of the Court even in cases they were not parties to, thus saving time and resources that would have to be spent by the replication of very similar cases being brought before the Inter-American system. Interestingly, in Advisory Opinion OC-22/16 the Court said that advisory opinions serve to achieve a certain preventive function akin to the ones achieved by the control of conventionality.[68]

Apart from that, the doctrine may generate multi-level dialogue[69] between domestic and international authorities discussing the same norms and issues, thus facilitating the change of precedents of the Inter-American Court itself—which has, in the past, changed its position and practice on aspects such as when there may be *ad hoc* judges, and has also corrected orders on the identification of victims that proved to be false.[70]

While States may not be directly bound by an advisory opinion or a decision issued in proceedings on a contentious case (insofar as the former are not formally binding and the latter are only mandatory for the parties),[71] this does not allow States to completely ignore the *content* of the standards established by an international judicial body. After all, the Inter-American Court itself has stated that its rulings have 'legal relevance for all the OAS Member States that have adopted the American Declaration [...] as well as for the organs of the OAS whose sphere of competence relates to the matter that is the subject of

---

[68] *Entitlement of Legal Entities to Hold Rights under the Inter-American Human Rights System (Interpretation and Scope of Art. 1 (2), in relation to Arts 1 (2), 8, 11 (2), 13, 16, 21, 24, 25, 29, 30, 44, 46 and 62 (3) of the American Convention on Human Rights, as Well as of Art. 8 (1) (A) and (B) of the Protocol of San Salvador)* (Advisory Opinion OC-22/16) IACtHR Series A No. 22 (26 February 2016), at para. 26.

[69] M. Attard, 'Repensando los diálogos interjurisdiccionales desde el Abya Yala: La construcción plural de los derechos en un contexto multinivel' in J. Acosta et al, *De anacronismos y vaticinios: Diagnóstico sobre las relaciones entre el derecho internacional y el derecho interno en Latinoamérica* (Universidad de La Sabana, SLADI and Universidad Externado de Colombia 2017), at 294 et seq.

[70] *Article 55 of the American Convention on Human Rights* (Advisory Opinion OC-20/09) IACtHR Series A No. 20 (29 September 2009), at paras 51–52: '[U]ntil now the Court had not found reasons [...] for modifying the interpretation observed until now [...]. [W]hen there is reason to do so, the review of a previously created interpretation is not only possible but necessary'; *Massacre of Mapiripán v. Colombia (Monitoring Compliance with Judgment)* IACtHR (23 November 2012), at paras 3, 6–7, 11–12, 18, 24, 30, 34, 38, 44.

[71] This is expressly indicated in Art. 68 (1) of the American Convention on Human Rights, which indicates that '[t]he States Parties to the Convention undertake to comply with the judgment of the Court in any case to which they are parties' (emphasis added).

the request',[72] on the understanding that if they are concerned with human rights or related issues, the interpretation of the main regional body must be taken into account.

How? In our opinion, States are required to *consider in good faith* pronouncements of the Inter-American Court, even those that do not directly and formally bind them, under certain conditions. This logic is similar to that expressed by the Inter-American Court in the sense that recommendations issued by the Inter-American Commission are not legally binding, and thus ignoring them does not engage international responsibility, but still States must consider implementing them by virtue of the principle of good faith. According to the Court,

> a recommendation does not have the character of an obligatory judicial decision for which the failure to comply would generate State responsibility, [yet] in accordance with the principle of good faith, [...] if a State signs and ratifies an international treaty, especially one concerning human rights, [...] it has the obligation to make every effort to apply with the recommendations of a protection organ [...] whose function is *'to promote the observance and defence of human rights'* in the hemisphere'.[73]

Judge Vio Grossi himself argued that, despite the fact that States are not directly and formally bound by advisory opinions, the control of conventionality carried out in light of what the Inter-American Court rules, serves to prevent abuses and the engagement of State responsibility.[74]

In other words, advisory opinions or decisions against other States are not formally and directly binding for third parties *as such*, but their content may be if it is correctly founded upon Inter-American standards—this logic is similar to the idea that custom may be applicable to a State in a given case even if a treaty with the same or a very similar content is not.[75] Likewise, Eduardo Ferrer Mac-Gregor has argued that one of the three functions that may be accomplished by the doctrine is related to preventing 'the implementation of national laws which are manifestly incompatible with the Inter- American Convention

---

72 *Rights and Guarantees of Children in the Context of Migration and/or in Need of International Protection* (Advisory Opinion OC-21/14) IACtHR Series A No. 21 (19 August 2014), at para. 32.
73 *Baena Ricardo et al. v. Panama* (Judgment) IACtHR Series C No. 72 (2 February 2001), at paras 191–192.
74 Advisory Opinion OC-24/17, Separate Opinion of Judge Eduardo Vio Grossi, at para. 61.
75 *Military and Paramilitary Activities in and against Nicaragua (Nicaragua v. United States of America) (Merits)* [1986] ICJ Rep 14, at paras 173–182.

and which are null and void ab initio'.[76] This preventive aim, in turn, not only seeks to avoid violations but also to ensure that States 'satisfactorily meet their obligations'.[77]

Concerning the preventive aim of advisory opinions, if States heed what the Court has said about States in similar situations, then abuses and the engagement of their responsibility may be prevented. This is especially so considering that not only judges but all State agents, to the extent of their powers, are called upon to make their States comply with their international obligations (or, at the very least, refer a situation to the competent authority).[78] It should be added that dissemination and education on Inter-American human rights standards can be a factor potentially increasing compliance with these standards.[79]

To sum up, the doctrine of the control of conventionality may be said to be neither new nor revolutionary, but merely reiterates that States are required to adjust their norms and practices to commitments they have accepted with a deductive method[80] that looks at certain international treaty norms and case law, especially considering that there is no single 'model' on how to perform said control,[81] which is a reason why domestic competences are not imperilled by the doctrine. In fact, the doctrine seeks to prevent abuses; however, in our opinion, more extreme interpretations that would make advisory opinions binding, or judgments binding on third parties, would be contrary to the logic of international law. Rather, those pronouncements are to be considered in good faith, and States must be aware that failing to heed what the Court says risk eventually violating human rights. Furthermore, as argued elsewhere in this article, States can engage in a multi-level dialogue with the Court.

---

76  E. Ferrer Mac-Gregor, 'The Constitutionalization of International Law in Latin America: Conventionality Control, the New Doctrine of the Inter-American Court of Human Rights' (2017) 109 AJIL Unbound 93, at 98.
77  Ibid.
78  This argument is analogous to the consideration that agents whose subordinates perpetrate serious abuses but lack the power to prevent or punish them must, at the very least, 'submit the matter to the competent authorities', as indicated in Art. 28 of the Rome Statute of the International Criminal Court.
79  This has also been argued in relation to international humanitarian law, see F. Kalshoven and L. Zegveld, *Constraints on the Waging of War: An Introduction to International Humanitarian Law* (ICRC 2001), at 139–140.
80  T. Lundmark and H. Waller, 'Using Statutes and Cases in Common and Civil Law' (2016) 7 Transnational Legal Theory 429.
81  IACtHR, *Cuadernillo de jurisprudencia de la Corte Interamericana de Derechos Humanos N° 7: control de convencionalidad*, at 11.

Considering how influential case law is in practice and how often the Court refers to its own precedents, States wishing to avoid international condemnation would do well to take into account what the regional Court has said in other cases, since such assertions are likely to be confirmed. On the other hand, if there is to be a dialogue, it is important for the Court to fully explain its position, disagreements that exist with it, and to make sure that the different stakeholders and perspectives are heard in its decision-making processes.

This may enhance and preserve its *auctoritas* and the procedural fairness of its proceedings.[82] Altogether, the doctrine is based on and consistent with considerations about the duty to adjust domestic norms and practices to international ones, and about the obligation of State agents to make international standards and rights effective. The doctrine can become a valuable example for other human rights systems if care is taken to avoid some risks, identified in the next section.

## VII Reflections on the Past, Present and Future of the Doctrine of Conventionality Control in the International Human Rights Law *corpus iuris*

The doctrine of conventionality control is a legal analytical and jurisprudential tool based on the—customary and treaty—State duty to adapt practices and norms to international legal requirements that seek to promote and protect human rights,[83] and also on the necessity of preventing the impunity of serious human rights violations. It seeks, among other things, to counter the passivity of judges and other State authorities when they are called upon to evaluate the content of national law and its conformity with regional or universal human rights standards.

The doctrine is also instrumental insofar as it is a means to ensure the domestic effectiveness of the American Convention—or other human rights instruments, for that matter—and identify norms or practices contrary to it that ought to be removed from the legal system.

The doctrine serves to consolidate the Latin American *ius commune*—that is to say, harmonized or even unified standards on the protection of human

---

82   T.M. Franck, *Fairness in International Law and Institutions* (Clarendon Press 1995), at 7.
83   *The Last Temptation of Christ (Olmedo Bustos et al. v. Chile)* (Judgment) IACtHR Series C No. 73 (5 February 2001), at paras 87–90; Art. 2 of the American Convention on Human Rights.

rights in the Americas. This is an aspiration of the human rights system itself—one that other systems share.

The control of conventionality is also consistent with the principle of subsidiarity.[84] This is so because it is neither necessary nor convenient to clog a supranational regime with repetitive cases—especially one which has faced resource-related problems, such as the Inter-American one. This function is achieved through erecting the judicial supervisory body of the Inter-American system as a quasi-constitutional actor.[85] As to the rationale behind this, indeed, it is preferable for domestic authorities to address like cases in light of what supranational bodies have said, provided their interpretations are sound. This requires the openness of regional and international bodies to reconsider decisions or assess whether there are relevant distinctions between cases. While the Inter-American system's main bodies are reluctant to endorse margin of appreciation-like doctrines, their legitimacy will nonetheless be enhanced if they take into account local or other considerations.

Lastly, the doctrine also seeks to bring about consistency in the conduct of different addressees of international human rights standards. After all, the control of conventionality is a doctrine based on the idea that the Inter-American case law is coherent. It would not be logical to require domestic authorities to observe treaty standards that were not consistently interpreted by the Court.

As the previous considerations show, the doctrine has potential benefits and is based on a positive understanding of supranational action. However, and in spite of the good faith with which the Court—overall a positive actor in the Americas—has promoted and defended the doctrine, theory and practice have also shown that there are some difficulties and controversies as to the implementation of the doctrine, some of which have been explored thus far. Some aspects merit further analysis.

First, there is a variety of constitutional models in the region as a comparative study of Latin American legal systems shows. This has led to discussions about limits on the Court and the self-restraint it should demonstrate, and the leeway addressees have in their consideration of local aspects and how to meet their own obligations. There is a certain fear of excessive and unwarranted influence of international authorities when deciding on sensitive local issues,

---

84  P.G. Carozza, 'Subsidiarity as a Structural Principle of International Human Rights Law' (2003) 97 AJIL 38.
85  E. Ferrer Mac-Gregor, 'The Constitutionalization of International Law in Latin America: Conventionality Control, the New Doctrine of the Inter-American Court of Human Rights' (2017) 109 AJIL Unbound 93, at 99.

leading to debates on how to combine universalist and pluralist normative aspirations.

Second, as indicated, criticisms as to the legitimacy of the Inter-American Court may be raised when it decides on 'culture wars' or issues that are socially or politically sensitive. There may be accusations that the Court fails to consider alternative interpretations, that it endorses contested options, or that it simply imposes its own ideological preferences.[86] This might result in resistance to its *auctoritas*, to the doctrine of the control of conventionality, and States might withdraw from the American Convention. It must be kept in mind that the doctrine, after all, has the potential to—and often seeks to—bring about not only legal but also social and cultural transformations.

Third, if certain pronouncements of the Court are vague or ambiguous, or even if not, domestic authorities of different States—or even the same State—may come up with contradictory and disparate interpretations and 'implementations' running contrary to the harmonization the doctrine purports to defend.

Fourth, and related to the previous concern, there is the uncertainty about the future consistency of Inter-American case law. A State agent may conscientiously follow what the Court has said, only to find that conduct rejected by the Court in a later decision. The dynamism of the evolutionary interpretation the Court relies so much upon detracts from the fact that State agents seek foreseeability and stability in the rules that guide their conduct, and it sometimes attaches great importance to soft law or selectively chosen domestic precedents.

Lastly, there is the judicial activism that the Court has sometimes been accused of. In light of the importance of a system with checks and balances, some question whether there is a possibility of controlling the regional Court's actions. The control of conventionality seems to give even greater power to the Court, which would require it to truly listen to different opinions.

The previous concerns merit further reflection but in no way lead to the conclusion that the control of conventionality is a doctrine that is necessarily 'dangerous' or contrary to international law. Indeed, that doctrine has many potential benefits and can fill gaps in the region of the Americas and elsewhere, and generate or strengthen a culture of observance of human rights law thanks to the internalization it can produce.[87] Furthermore, States are required to strive to meet their international legal requirements in good faith,

---

86    A.P. Díaz, 'Corte dicta sentencia en caso de Fecundación in Vitro' (14 January 2013) Corte IDH Blog, available at http://corteidhblog.blogspot.com/2013/01/corte-dicta-sentencia-en-caso-de.html (accessed 27 March 2019).

87    H.H. Koh, 'Why Do Nations Obey International Law?' (1997) 106 Yale L.J. 2599.

and this seems to include taking into account what supranational bodies have said in pronouncements they are not directly and formally bound by—which applies not only to the Inter-American system. The following remarks identify possible courses of action.

On the one hand, in order to respect the differences that may exist between legal or social models and traditions, the Court ought to accept a certain margin of appreciation with regard to complex issues and the means of implementing regional or international standards. This implies not always imposing a single model requiring, for instance, that all authorities of all States subject to the Court's jurisdiction have the very same position or implement a given standard in exactly the same way.

On the other hand, in order to avoid a possible fragmentation in the domestic implementation of the doctrine, all national authorities competent to do so should consistently refuse to apply domestic norms that are clearly contrary to Inter-American standards. This condition of an evident contradiction may be more palatable to States, whose authorities could still engage in interpretations that complement those of the Court. The Court, in turn, may accept some of those as valid throughout the region; others as confined to a given situation or society; and still others as based on interpretations the Court rejects. This might lead to an exchange of opinions and a true dialogue, with domestic authorities later commenting on the Court's position. Likewise, the domestic judicial authorities must respect due process and access to justice when it comes to issues pertaining to Inter-American standards.

The debate about the doctrine is indicative of the increasing interaction between international human rights and domestic law, in which judges have a crucial role. For State agents to live up to what is expected of them, they should, on the one hand, act with consistency and in a reasonable manner when considering Inter-American case law. The Court, in turn, is expected to consider both fidelity to the Convention and other applicable standards, and an evolutionary dynamic of the *corpus iuris* it is entrusted with. Any excessive activism in order to promote ideological or political positions may expose a judicial body to criticism and erode the trust in the system.

Furthermore, domestic and regional or other authorities should be open to the idea of an integrated law, e.g. regional law, seeking to protect individuals, who should be considered the protagonists of human rights law. Better education of judges and other authorities in international law, more independence and professionality, and the strengthening of national judicial systems could also place judges in a better position to engage in a meaningful dialogue with Inter-American bodies, and could thus reduce the risk of domestic judges rebelling against the Court when they do not understand the commitments of their States or simply fail to grasp the role and importance of supranational bodies—which have had a remarkably positive impact in the Americas and elsewhere.

Altogether, when carried out in good faith[88] by both international and domestic authorities, the control of conventionality can help to achieve efficiency, non-duplication of proceedings, domestic and direct applicability of harmonized Inter-American standards, and a regional dialogue. Other universal and regional human rights systems may find the doctrine equally useful.


## VIII  Conclusions

In a region with so many human rights problems and a regional system struggling with scarcity of resources, the doctrine of the control of conventionality has the potential to advance socialization and acculturation. If the idea of the control of conventionality ends up being fully internalized in States in the region—or at least in some States—, then the Court may *de facto* become some sort of regional 'constitutional' supranational body. Whether this is desirable or not has to be the subject of a different study.

Yet, controversy about certain pronouncements of the Inter-American Court are unavoidable, especially when it decides on issues that are socially sensitive, be it because they are part of the so-called 'culture wars' or because they question ingrained traditions or social habits. Furthermore, academics and others may legitimately question the correctness of the Court's interpretations. Yet if the Court refuses to engage in a meaningful multi-level dialogue, it risks alienating influential actors in the region or making States withdraw from the Convention as Venezuela has already done.

Needless to say, the Court needs to strike a balance, and it may not be driven to endorse positions that are contrary to human dignity (an elusive term in legal debates[89]), considering that States may be all too eager to criticize a regional Court because of its condemnation of State abuses, either to avoid further scrutiny or to gain popularity at home with people holding extreme positions. Matters are further complicated because of the Court's reluctance, even in complex and controversial cases, to adopt a margin of appreciation or

---

88    M. Kotzur, 'Good Faith (Bona Fide)' in R. Wolfrum (ed.), *Max Planck Encyclopedia of Public International Law* (OUP Oxford 2008–), available at http://www.mpepil.com/ (1 April 2019).
89    P.G. Carozza, 'Human Dignity in Constitutional Adjudication' in T. Ginsburg and R. Dixon (eds), *Comparative Constitutional Law* (Elgar 2011) 459.

similar approach granting some leeway to States as long as they respect certain core tenets.[90] This analysis is, in the end, a reflection of broader discussions in human rights law as to universality and multiculturalism; and how both can converge if common concepts like dignity are permitted some limited specification in certain contexts.[91]

---

90   N. Carrillo, 'La legitimidad como elemento crucial de la efectividad de pronunciamientos de la Corte Interamericana de Derechos Humanos ante casos complejos y desafíos regionales' (2015) 18 Revista general de derecho público comparado 1.

91   P.G. Carozza, 'Human Dignity and Judicial Interpretation of Human Rights: A Reply' (2008) 19 EJIL 931.

CHAPTER 13

# Disaster Militarism? Military Humanitarian Assistance and Disaster Relief

*Gabrielle Simm*

### Abstract

Military assets, which include personnel, make an important contribution to disaster relief. However, military deployments can be politically sensitive, and the relevant international law is contested and not binding. This article compares two sets of UN Office for the Coordination of Humanitarian Affairs (UN OCHA) Guidelines on this issue. The 2007 Oslo Guidelines[1] state that military assets should be used in disaster relief only as a last resort, while the 2014 Asia-Pacific Regional Guidelines[2] acknowledge that military assets are often the first to respond to disasters in the region. Drawing on examples primarily from Asia, this article explores the apparent conflict between these two UN Guidelines and asks two questions about the deployment of foreign military assets in disaster relief. First, to what extent does international law authorize or limit the deployment of foreign military assets in disaster relief? Second, what are the politics of deploying military assets in disaster relief? This article argues that, rather than representing a global standard, the Oslo Guidelines better reflect European practice within Europe, while the Asia-Pacific Regional Guidelines are more representative of practice worldwide. It concludes that the type of military aid provided is key to its compliance with international law and its political acceptance.

### Keywords

Disaster Relief – Military – Humanitarian Aid – UN OCHA Guidelines – Civil-Military – Asia Pacific

---

1 UN OCHA 'Guidelines on the Use of Foreign Military and Civil Defence Assets in Disaster Relief' (1994, rev. 2007) (Oslo Guidelines).
2 UN OCHA 'Asia-Pacific Regional Guidelines for the Use of Foreign Military Assets in Natural Disaster Response Operations' (2014) (Asia-Pacific Regional Guidelines) (APC MADRO).

1    **Introduction**

Military assets, which include personnel, make an important contribution to disaster relief.[3] Deployment of military assets in disaster relief is of growing importance as a response to the increased severity and intensity of climate-related disasters.[4] The United States (US) has unique capabilities and capacity to provide military assets in humanitarian assistance and disaster relief worldwide.[5] While there is a range of practice within Europe, the European States that deploy military assets in disaster relief tend to do so only outside Europe.[6] Japan has become an important Assisting State, particularly in Asia and the Pacific.[7] The Canadian Armed Forces' Disaster Assistance Response Team has deployed seven times since its establishment in 1994, including four times to Asia. The militaries of China, Taiwan and the Republic of Korea engage in disaster relief, as do those of Singapore, Australia, Indonesia, Thailand, Malaysia and Bangladesh.[8] Since 1992, France, Australia and New Zealand have co-ordinated the disaster relief they provide in the Pacific under the FRANZ Arrangement,

---

3  According to the Oslo Guidelines, military and civil defence assets (MCDA) comprise relief personnel, equipment, supplies and services provided by the foreign military and civil defence organizations for international disaster relief assistance (IDRA). Civil defence organizations are defined by reference to government organizations performing the functions in Art. 61 Protocol Additional to the Geneva Conventions of 12 August 1949, and relating to the Protection of Victims of International Armed Conflicts (Additional Protocol I).

4  Disaster means 'a calamitous event or series of events resulting in widespread loss of life, great human suffering and distress, mass displacement, or large-scale material or environmental damage, thereby, seriously disrupting the functioning of society': Art. 3 (a) UN ILC 'Report on the Work of the Sixty-eighth Session' (2 May–10 June and 4 July–12 August 2016) GAOR 71st Session Supp 10, Chapter IV 'Protection of Persons in the Event of Disasters' (ILC Draft Articles). IPCC 'Summary for Policymakers' in C.B. Field et al. (eds), *Managing the Risks of Extreme Events and Disaster to Advance Climate Change Adaptation: Special Report of the Intergovernmental Panel on Climate Change* (CUP 2012), at 5.

5  'The Use of Military Assets in the Humanitarian Response to Natural Disasters' Wilton Park Conference 994 (2009), available at www.wiltonpark.org.uk/wp-content/uploads/wp994-report.pdf (accessed 18 February 2019).

6  S. Wiharta et al., *The Effectiveness of Foreign Military Assets in Natural Disaster Response in Natural Disaster Response* (Stockholm International Peace Research Institute 2008), at 13.

7  T. Yoshizaki 'The Military's Role in Disaster Relief Operations: A Japanese Perspective' (2011) NIDS International Symposium on Security Affairs.

8  J. Engstrom, 'Taking Disaster Seriously: East Asian Military Involvement in International Disaster Relief Operations and the Implications for Force Projection' (2013) 29 Asian Security 38; Wiharta et al., *The Effectiveness of Foreign Military Assets in Natural Disaster Response* 14; J.D.P. Moroney et al., *Lessons from Department of Defense Disaster Relief Efforts in the Asia Pacific Region* (Rand Corporation 2013).

including deploying military assets.[9] Some States, such as China, Pakistan, and India, have demonstrated varying degrees of reluctance to accept foreign military deployments in disaster relief but rely on their own military to play a key role in disaster response at home. The military assets most often deployed, in order of frequency, are air transport, medical support and expert personnel.[10]

The Asia Pacific is the world's most disaster-prone region.[11] It includes two of the most seismically active fault lines and three major ocean basins. These geographic features, combined with large populations, increasingly concentrated in nine of the world's top 13 megacities,[12] mean that the region experiences deaths and economic losses from disasters disproportionately to its share of the population worldwide.[13] However, the region is very diverse in terms of economic development, political systems, and legal preparedness for disaster. It ranges from wealthy States such as Japan, which is very risk prone but expert in disaster risk reduction, through middle income disaster-prone States such as Indonesia and the Philippines, whose disaster law and practice has been hailed as world leading, to States such as Myanmar, whose vulnerability to seismic and weather hazards is exacerbated by economic and political factors and a lack of legal preparedness.[14] The Asia Pacific is also a region of the world where military involvement in disaster relief is common practice, both on the part of regional States assisting their neighbours in disaster and States outside the region providing disaster relief within it.

Drawing on examples primarily from Asia, this article examines two questions about the deployment of foreign military assets in disaster relief. The first asks: to what extent does *international law* authorize or limit the deployment of foreign military assets in disaster relief?[15] The legal situation in complex

---

9 New Zealand Ministry of Foreign Affairs 'The FRANZ Arrangement' (14 October 2014).
10 Wiharta et al., *The Effectiveness of Foreign Military Assets in Natural Disaster Response*, at 15.
11 UN ESCAP 'Overview of Natural Disasters and their Impacts in Asia and the Pacific 1970–2014' (March 2015), at 7.
12 Megacities are defined as those with more than 15 million inhabitants i.e., Tokyo, Osaka, Beijing, Shanghai, Mumbai, New Delhi, Dhaka, Kolkata, Karachi: UN University and Bündnis Entwicklung Hilft, 'World Risk Report 2014', at 8.
13 V. Thomas, J.R.G. Albert and R.T. Perez 'Climate-related Disasters in Asia and the Pacific' (July 2013) ADB Economics Working Paper Series No. 358.
14 UN University and Bündnis Entwicklung Hilft, 'World Risk Report 2014', at 64–65; on Indonesia and the Philippines see D. Petz, 'Strengthening Regional and National Capacity for Disaster Risk Management: the Case of ASEAN' (Brookings Institution 2014), at 25.
15 On domestic military assets in disaster relief and their interaction with international humanitarian agencies, see A. Madiwale and K. Virk, 'Civil–Military Relations in Natural Disasters: A Case Study of the 2010 Pakistan Floods' (2011) 93 IRRC 884.

emergencies, for example, where a disaster occurs in a conflict zone, is discussed only in comparison to the rules governing military relief in disasters.[16] The second question asks: what are the *politics* of deploying military assets in disaster relief? The article concludes that international law does authorize foreign military assets to provide disaster relief while imposing conditions that aim to address the concerns of some civilian humanitarian organizations to maintain a distinction between military and civilian disaster relief. But the article argues that Asian practices of military deployment as a *first* response may be more widespread than the global standard of military assets only *as a last resort* established by the Oslo Guidelines.

## II   International Law on Foreign Military Disaster Relief

This part aims to identify when international law authorizes the deployment of military assets in disaster relief and the limits placed on such deployment. As far as traditional sources of international law are concerned, there is no comprehensive international disaster treaty, but some bilateral and regional treaties address this issue. Customary international law establishes humanitarian principles but does not address the question of military assets in disaster relief directly. Due to the lack of 'hard law', the bulk of the discussion centres on soft law instruments, notably the Oslo and Asia-Pacific Regional Guidelines.[17]

Treaties provide limited guidance on the extent to which foreign military assets may be lawfully deployed in disaster relief.[18] Sub-regional disaster treaties, such as the Southeast Asian and South Asian disaster agreements, do not address this issue except in passing.[19] Many treaties are not public, particularly

---

16   See OCHA 'Guidelines on the Use of Military and Civil Defence Assets to Support United Nations Humanitarian Activities in Complex Emergencies Rev. 1' (January 2006) (Complex Emergency Guidelines). On the Mohonk Criteria developed by UN agencies, NGOs and USAID in 1993, see J.M. Ebersole, 'The Mohonk Criteria for Humanitarian Assistance in Complex Emergencies—Task Force on Ethical and Legal Issues in Humanitarian Assistance' (1995) 17 Human Rights Quarterly 192.

17   See also the International Federation of Red Cross Red Crescent societies (IFRC) 'Guidelines for the Domestic Facilitation and Regulation of International Disaster Relief and Initial Recovery Assistance' (2007) IFRC Doc 30IC/07/R4 Annex (IDRL Guidelines).

18   S. Sivakumaran, 'Techniques in International Law-Making: Extrapolation, Analogy, Form and the Emergence of an International Law of Disaster Relief' (2018) 28 EJIL 1097.

19   ASEAN Agreement on Disaster Management and Emergency Response (signed 26 July 2005, entered into force 24 December 2009); SAARC Agreement on Rapid Response to Natural Disasters (signed 11 November 2011, entered into force 9 September 2016). See further A. de Guttry, 'Surveying the Law' in A. de Guttry, M. Gestri and G. Venturini (eds),

in Asia, so it is difficult to judge to what extent they govern foreign military deployments in disaster relief.[20] Some Status of Forces Agreements (SOFAs) relating primarily to the privileges and immunities of visiting military forces may extend to disaster situations.[21] However, many disaster agreements do not grant immunity to disaster relief personnel.[22]

The customary international law rules on humanitarian action applying to situations of disaster are often borrowed from, or used by analogy with, the international humanitarian law applying to situations of armed conflict. For example, Sandesh Sivuakumaran argues that international law prohibits Affected States from arbitrarily withholding consent to humanitarian aid in disasters.[23] I draw on Sivakumaran's approach of arguing by analogy with international humanitarian law in order to apply humanitarian principles adopted or codified in relation to armed conflict to situations of disaster. However, I deal with the specific issue of foreign *military* deployments in disaster relief, the 'pointy end' of humanitarian aid about which the Affected States are most sensitive.

This part is organized in three sections that correspond to the three positions identified in relation to the legality or otherwise of the deployment of military assets in disaster relief. First, the broadest claim is that military assistance can never be humanitarian because military assistance can never be neutral, even in disasters. Second, the 2007 Oslo Guidelines state that military assets should only be used in disaster relief as a last resort. Third, and most permissive of military involvement in disaster, the 2014 Asia-Pacific Regional Guidelines refer to the Oslo principle of the military as a last resort but also recognize that military assets are often the first to respond to disasters in the region. After outlining and comparing the Oslo and Asia-Pacific Regional Guidelines, this

---

*International Disaster Response Law* (Springer 2012), at 22–26. For an overview of subregional mechanisms in Asia and the Pacific see D. Petz and E. Ferris, *In the Neighborhood: The Growing Role of Regional Organizations in Disaster Risk Management* (Brookings Institution–London School of Economics Project on Internal Displacement 2013).

20   Cf ASEAN Regional Forum 'Strategic Guidance on HADR', cited in US Department of Defense CFE-DMHA, *ASEAN Disaster Management Reference Handbook* (2015); J. Voetelink, *Status of Forces: Criminal Jurisdiction over Military Personnel Abroad* (Springer/TMC Asser Press 2015).

21   NATO 'Standard Operating Procedures, Annex 4: Model Agreement Covering the Status of National Elements of the EADRU on Mission in the Territory of a Stricken Nation' (2007).

22   G. Bartolini, 'Attribution of Conduct and Liability Issues Arising from International Disaster Relief Missions: Theoretical and Pragmatic Approaches to Guaranteeing Accountability' (2015) 48 Vanderbilt Journal of Transnational Law 1057.

23   S. Sivakumaran, 'Arbitrary Withholding of Consent to Humanitarian Assistance in Situations of Disaster' (2015) 64 ICLQ 501.

part concludes that two examples of the Guidelines in practice suggest that the principle of military first may have greater support than indicated by the regional limits on the Asia-Pacific Regional Guidelines.

1    Can Foreign Military Assistance Ever be Neutral?

To qualify as humanitarian, foreign military aid must be neutral. Although international humanitarian law recognizes neutral States, military forces are rarely perceived as neutral even when they are not engaged in combat, as is the case in disaster relief. For one thing, they are identified as an organ of a State, not as disinterested experts or individuals which, at the very least, invites curiosity as to why a State, and in particular that State, is involved. Despite international law's repeated invocation of neutrality as indispensable to humanitarianism, this section argues that this is not always the case for two reasons. First, the relationship between humanitarian aid and the military has changed over time, and second, humanitarianism is capable of different interpretations. This will be demonstrated through contrasting the philosophies and practices of two key international humanitarian aid agencies, the International Committee of the Red Cross (ICRC) and Médecins Sans Frontières (MSF).

Today, neutrality is often seen as indispensable to humanitarian action, but this was not always the case. Nevertheless, humanitarian agencies such as the ICRC have historically been embedded within the military.[24] During World War I, workers from the Red Cross, Young Men's Christian Association (YMCA), the Salvation Army and Quakers were under military command and wore uniforms.[25] During the Cold War and in wars of national liberation, humanitarian aid was used in an attempt 'to win hearts and minds' by the French in Algeria, the British in Malaya, and the US in Vietnam.[26] Hence, the relationship between humanitarian aid and the military changes over time and with political context.[27]

Many international lawyers understand humanitarianism by reference to the ICRC's philosophy that was adopted by the International Court of Justice in the case of *Nicaragua*.[28] As is well known, the International Court of Justice

---

[24]  J.F. Hutchinson, *Champions of Charity: War and the Rise of the Red Cross* (Westview Press 1996).

[25]  M.-A.P. de Montclos 'The (de)Militarization of Humanitarian Aid: A Historical Perspective' (2014) 3 Humanities 232.

[26]  Ibid., at 234–235.

[27]  D. Fassin and M. Pandolfi (eds), *Contemporary States of Emergency: The Politics of Military and Humanitarian Interventions* (MIT Press 2010).

[28]  *Military and Paramilitary Activities in and against Nicaragua (Nicaragua v United States)* (*Merits*) [1986] ICJ Rep 14.

found that the US had breached rules of customary international law prohibiting the use of force and the rule on non-intervention by funding, arming and training the *Contra* militias in their attempts to overthrow the government of Nicaragua. The Court examined whether part of the US assistance to the *Contras* could be considered humanitarian assistance, which did not constitute unlawful intervention. The Court referred to the fundamental principles of the Red Cross in defining humanitarian assistance, which aims

> to bring assistance without discrimination [...] to prevent and alleviate human suffering wherever it may be found. [...] It makes no discrimination as to nationality, race, religious beliefs, class or political opinions. It endeavours only to relieve suffering, giving priority to the most urgent cases of distress.[29]

For the final year of the period in question, the US House of Representatives had restricted the aid provided to the *Contras* to 'the provision of food, clothing, medicine and other humanitarian assistance' which did not include 'weapons, weapons systems, ammunition, or other equipment, vehicles or material which [could] be used to inflict serious bodily harm or death'.[30] Nevertheless, the Court found that as the aid was provided only to one side in the conflict, namely the *Contras* and their dependents, it did not qualify as humanitarian assistance, which had to be 'given without distinction to all in need'.[31] Dug Cubie points out that, following the Court's reasoning, consent would have been required from the government of Nicaragua for aid to both sides. The US government would not have given aid to the Nicaraguan government and the Nicaraguan government was unlikely to have permitted aid to the *Contras*. This highlights the importance of 'impartial humanitarian actors who can operate in a non-discriminatory manner'.[32]

While the ICRC's brand of humanitarianism is often considered the classic model, multiple interpretations of humanitarianism are possible.[33] More recent legal definitions of humanitarian aid adopt the humanitarian principles

---

[29] Ibid., at para. 242.
[30] Ibid., at para. 97.
[31] Ibid., at para. 243.
[32] D. Cubie, *The International Legal Protection of Persons in Humanitarian Crises: Exploring the acquis humanitaire* (Hart 2017), at 123.
[33] On the 'split' within the ICRC over Biafra's attempt to secede from Nigeria which led to the formation of MSF, see R. Brauman, 'Médecins Sans Frontières and the ICRC: Matters of Principle' (2012) 94 IRRC 1523; M.-L. Desgrandchamps, 'Organizing the Unpredictable: the Nigeria-Biafra War and its Impact on the ICRC' (2012) 94 IRRC 1409.

as if they were uncontroversial but their interpretation in practice varies. UN General Assembly Resolution 46/182 (1991) states that humanitarian aid must be provided in accordance with the principles of humanity, neutrality and impartiality.[34] These 'core principles' are reiterated in the Oslo Guidelines as follows:

> *Humanity:* Human suffering must be addressed wherever it is found, with particular attention to the most vulnerable in the population, such as children, women and the elderly. The dignity and rights of all victims must be respected and protected.
> *Neutrality:* Humanitarian assistance must be provided without engaging in hostilities or taking sides in controversies of a political, religious or ideological nature.
> *Impartiality:* Humanitarian assistance must be provided without discriminating as to ethnic origin, gender, nationality, political opinions, race or religion. Relief of the suffering must be guided solely by needs and priority must be given to the most urgent cases of distress.[35]

The International Law Commission (ILC), which is charged with the progressive development and codification of international law, has identified the humanitarian principles of humanity, neutrality, impartiality and non-discrimination as key to humanitarian assistance in its Draft Articles on the Protection of Persons in the Event Of Disasters (hereinafter 'ILC Draft Articles').[36] Following articles on dignity and human rights, draft Art. 6 states: 'Response to disasters shall take place in accordance with the principles of humanity, neutrality and impartiality, and on the basis of non-discrimination while taking into account the needs of the particularly vulnerable'.[37] The ILC Draft Articles do not address issues raised by the use of military assets in disaster relief directly, although the commentary recognizes 'the important role played by military personnel, as a category of relief personnel, in the provision of disaster relief assistance'.[38] The General Assembly has requested comments from States on

---

34   UNGA Res 46/182 'Strengthening of the Coordination of Humanitarian Emergency Assistance of the United Nations' (19 December 1991).
35   UN OCHA 'Oslo Guidelines', at para. 20.
36   ILC Draft Articles, commentary on Art. 6 (2).
37   Arts 4–6 ILC Draft Articles.
38   Draft Art. 3 (f) defines relief personnel to mean 'relief personnel sent by an assisting State or other assisting actor for the purpose of providing disaster relief assistance': ILC Draft Articles, commentary on Art. 3 (f).

this proposal and it remains to be seen whether the Articles will be adopted as a Convention or in another format.[39]

Humanitarians claim neutrality, yet neutrality means different things to different humanitarian organizations. The ICRC interprets neutrality as encompassing a duty to respect State sovereignty and to remain silent in many cases.[40] By contrast, MSF claims a right to intervene across borders without State permission and a duty to bear witness about the causes of suffering.[41] MSF has been the agency most vocal in advocating a distinction between (civilian) humanitarian actors on the one hand and military actors on the other.[42] According to Oxfam, 'to maintain their impartiality and independence, humanitarian agencies should not participate in military-led teams; accept funding from forces or defence departments; or accept money from any fund dedicated to military objectives, or that allows a donor to claim an agency's support for military or counter-terrorism objectives'.[43] The OECD Development Assistance Committee secretariat argues 'use of the military can at times politicize the delivery of humanitarian aid and threaten the neutrality, impartiality and independence of that aid'.[44] Oxfam and the OECD refer to the Oslo Guidelines in support of their arguments about the appropriate involvement of military assets in disaster relief; however, the Oslo Guidelines are interpreted differently by different parties.

## 2   The Oslo Guidelines: Military as a Last Resort

The Guidelines on the Use of Foreign Military and Civil Defence Assets in Disaster Relief, known as the Oslo Guidelines, represent a non-binding global standard that aims to 'establish the basic framework'.[45] Beginning in 1992, the

---

39   UNGA Res 71/141 (19 December 2016), at para. 2.
40   ICRC, 'The ICRC's Privilege of Non-Disclosure of Confidential Information' (2016) 97 IRRC 433.
41   F. Boucher-Saulnier, 'Consent to Humanitarian Access: An Obligation Triggered by Territorial Control, Not States' Rights' (2014) 96 IRRC 207.
42   M. Krause, *The Good Project: Humanitarian Relief NGOs and the Fragmentation of Reason* (University of Chicago Press 2012), at 106.
43   Oxfam International 'Policy Compendium Note on the Provision of Aid by Foreign Military Forces' (April 2012).
44   OECD 'Civilian and Military Means of Providing and Supporting Humanitarian Assistance during Conflict: Comparative Advantages and Costs' (1997) OECD Doc DCD/DAC(97), at 19.
45   'Civil defence', also known as 'emergency management', is 'the performance of […] humanitarian tasks intended to protect the civilian population against the dangers, and to help it recover from the immediate effects, of hostilities or disasters and also to provide the conditions necessary for survival'. Humanitarian tasks are 'warning, evacuation, management of shelters, management of blackout measures, rescue, medical services, including

predecessor of the UN Office for the Coordination of Humanitarian Affairs (UN OCHA) led a consultation process involving States, international organizations, universities, the International Federation of Red Cross and Red Crescent Societies (IFRC) and the ICRC. The Guidelines were adopted in 1994 and updated in 2007 following unprecedented military deployments in disasters in 2005. UN OCHA also has country-specific and operational level event-specific guidelines on humanitarian civil-military coordination.[46] The Oslo Guidelines are primarily intended for use by UN humanitarian agencies, their implementing and operational partners, UN coordinators, commanders of UN military and civil defence assets (MCDA) and other deployed forces supporting UN humanitarian agencies and UN humanitarian and foreign military liaison officers.[47] While they can also be used by decision-makers at the national level and in regional organizations, they are not binding on States.[48]

The Oslo Guidelines aim to safeguard against the misuse of military assets in disaster in three ways. First, and most importantly, the central principle of the Oslo Guidelines is that foreign military and civil defence assets should be used only as a last resort. Such assets

> should be requested only where there is no comparable civilian alternative and only the use of military or civil defence assets can meet a critical humanitarian need. The military or civil defence asset must therefore be unique in capability and availability.[49]

Second, the Oslo Guidelines encourage respect for the coordinating role of the UN through the OHCA. In practice, States consult with UN OCHA about military assistance in disaster and, in the examples discussed here, defer to

---

first aid, and religious assistance, fire-fighting, detection and marking of danger areas, decontamination and similar protective measures, provision of emergency accommodation and supplies, emergency assistance in the restoration and maintenance of order in distressed areas, emergency repair of indispensable public utilities, emergency disposal of the dead, assistance in the preservation of objects essential for survival, complementary activities necessary to carry out any of the tasks mentioned above, including, but not limited to, planning and organization': Art. 61 Additional Protocol I.

46   UN OCHA 'Draft Guidelines for Civil–Military Coordination in Pakistan' (March 2010); UN OCHA 'Guidelines for the Interaction and Coordination of Humanitarian Actors and Military Actors in Afghanistan' (20 May 2008); UN OCHA 'Guidance on the Use of Foreign Military and Civil Defence Assets (MCDA) to Support Humanitarian Operations in the Context of Typhoon Haiyan (Yolanda) in the Philippines' (12 November 2013).
47   UN OCHA 'Oslo Guidelines', at paras 13–14.
48   Ibid., at paras 14, 16.
49   Ibid., at para. 5.

its judgment. Third, the Oslo Guidelines define humanitarian assistance then divide it into three categories used to delimit the conditions under which the military can appropriately support humanitarian activities. This distinction appears directed at concerns about blurring the line between military and civilian assistance in disaster relief. Humanitarian assistance is defined as

> aid to an affected population that seeks, as its primary purpose, to save lives and alleviate suffering of a crisis-affected population. Humanitarian assistance must be provided in accordance with the basic humanitarian principles of humanity, impartiality and neutrality.[50]

*Direct Assistance* is defined as 'the face to face distribution of goods and services'.[51] Examples include the distribution of food aid, water, medicine, non-food items such as shelter materials, the provision of health services and search and rescue. *Indirect Assistance* is 'at least one step removed from the population and involves such activities as transporting relief goods or relief personnel'.[52] Military aircraft, particularly transport planes and helicopters, are often regarded as capabilities for which there is no comparable civilian alternative, such as delivering relief personnel to the remote villages in mountainous Nepal when roads were damaged by the 2015 earthquakes. *Infrastructure support* 'involves providing general services, such as road repair, airspace management and power generation that facilitate relief, but are not necessarily visible to or solely for the benefit of the affected population'.[53] The delivery by NATO of 103 prefabricated bridges donated by foreign governments to Pakistan in the wake of the 2010 floods and the operation of water purification plants by the Australian Defence Force following the 2009 earthquake in Indonesia provide examples here.[54]

The Model Agreement covering the Status of Military and Civil Defence Assets contained in Annex I of the Oslo Guidelines is a partial answer to critics of the Guidelines who argue that they are too general to be useful in an emergency. While the Guidelines list the minimum facilities to be offered by the Affected States, such as legal status, customs, visas, overflight and security,[55] the

---

50  Ibid., at para. 1.
51  Ibid.
52  Ibid.
53  Ibid.
54  Moroney et al., *Lessons from Department of Defense Disaster Relief Efforts in the Asia-Pacific Region*, at 64.
55  D. Fisher, 'The Law of International Disaster Response: Overview and Ramifications for Military Actors' in M.D. Carsten (ed.), *International Law Studies* vol. 83 *Global Legal*

Model Agreement serves as a basis for governing relations between Affected and Assisting States or between the UN and States. Issues covered in those agreements resemble those addressed in SOFAS negotiated between States in relation to visiting forces and the model MOU between troop contributing States and the UN in peacekeeping operations.[56] These include privileges and immunities from criminal prosecution or civil suit,[57] the exercise of jurisdiction,[58] passport and visa regulations,[59] and policing the operation.[60] Each of these has the potential to give rise to disputes, but the Model Agreement provides for dispute settlement through the establishment of a Claims Commission reminiscent of the UN model SOFA between the UN and host States for peacekeeping.[61] Lack of a binding agreement can delay or prevent the deployment of military assets as Assisting States usually want legal certainty and treaties are best concluded before a disaster strikes.[62] The confidentiality accorded to such agreements makes it difficult to judge to what extent the model has been adopted or varied in practice.

The Oslo Guidelines have been interpreted differently by different States;[63] in some situations, the Oslo Guidelines are sometimes even 'quietly ignored'.[64] Even when a national approach to the issues has been formalized, its

---

*Challenges: Command of the Commons, Strategic Communications and Natural Disasters* (Naval War College 2007), at 293.

56   UNGA 'Letter Dated 13 July 2017 from the Secretary-General to the President of the General Assembly: Manual on Policies and Procedures concerning the Reimbursement and Control of Contingent-Owned Equipment of Troop/Police Contributors Participating in Peacekeeping Missions' (COE Manual) (4 August 2017) UN Doc. A/72/288 Chapter 9, Art. 13.

57   UN OCHA 'Oslo Guidelines' Annex I, at paras 12–13 and 20–27.

58   Ibid., at paras 41–44.

59   Ibid., at paras 28–30.

60   Ibid., at paras 36–40.

61   Ibid., at paras 45–48; UNGA 'Report of the Secretary-General: Comprehensive Review of the Whole Question of Peacekeeping Operations in All their Aspects: Model Status-of-Forces-Agreement for Peace-keeping Operations' (9 October 1990) UN Doc. A/45/594, Art. 51.

62   For example, UK military doctrine is to include relevant issues in 'MOU, military/implementing arrangements and/or exchanges of letters between governments' where there is insufficient time to negotiate a SOFA: UK Ministry of Defence, 'Joint Doctrine Publication 3-52: Disaster Relief Operations Overseas: the Military Contribution' (November 2016).

63   For example, Canada and the UK have national guidelines based on the Oslo Guidelines, while the Singapore armed forces incorporate elements in Standard Operating Procedures: Wiharta et al., *The Effectiveness of Foreign Military Assets in Natural Disaster and Response*, at 20 and 97.

64   Moroney et al., *Lessons from Department of Defense Disaster Relief Efforts in the Asia-Pacific Region*, at 150.

implementation may be uneven at different levels or areas and by different types of personnel. The Oslo Guidelines are better known to policy-makers than to military commanders or responders working at the operational level outside capitals.[65] In Europe, the approach to deployment of military assets in a disaster may be conceived of as a spectrum. According to 2008 research, Finland and Norway are at one end, only considering military deployments if there is no other way to meet a crucial humanitarian need, while Belgium, Germany and France are more likely to deploy military assets in a disaster.[66] At the other end of the spectrum are the Netherlands and the UK, with the UK considering that 'last resort does not necessarily mean last. We can and will use military assets first if it considered the best way to save lives [and/or] alleviate suffering'.[67] Some decision-makers put the ability to save lives, feasibility and availability of military assets ahead of using civilian alternatives.[68] Thus, despite the Oslo Guidelines standing for military as a last resort, variations in interpretation mean that the practice of military first may be more widespread than the regional characterization of the Asia-Pacific Regional Guidelines suggests.

## 3  The Asia-Pacific Regional Guidelines: Military First to Respond

The 2004 Indian Ocean tsunami is acknowledged as the impetus for the development of the Asia-Pacific Regional Guidelines.[69] Military assets from 35 States including 30,000 personnel were deployed in response to the 2004 tsunami.[70] In 2005 the Indian Armed Forces hosted a regional meeting to discuss the problems in coordination and communication exposed in the military relief efforts. This became an annual event jointly hosted by UN OCHA and regional States to develop guidelines that were adopted in 2014.[71] The Asia-Pacific Regional Guidelines are 'a reference guide for Member States who plan and execute foreign military support for international disaster response'.[72] The Guidelines are 'voluntary', 'not binding' and 'will not affect the rights, obligations or responsibilities of States and individuals under international law'.[73]

---

65   Ibid., at 24, 49.
66   Wiharta et al., *The Effectiveness of Foreign Military Assets in Natural Disaster Response*, at 13, 20.
67   Ibid., at 20.
68   This is the approach taken by Belgium, the Netherlands and the US, ibid., at 20.
69   UN OCHA 'Asia-Pacific Regional Guidelines', at para. 2.
70   Wiharta et al., *The Effectiveness of Foreign Military Assets in Natural Disaster Response*, at 87.
71   UN OCHA 'Asia-Pacific Regional Guidelines', at para. 2.
72   at para. 4.
73   Ibid., at para. 4.

A critical difference between the Asia-Pacific Regional Guidelines and the Oslo Guidelines is that the former recognize that 'military capacities in Asia Pacific countries are often the first capabilities offered'.[74] This is the opposite of the Oslo standard of using military assets only as a last resort, although as discussed, there is a range of interpretations of this principle. Further, the Asia-Pacific Regional Guidelines state that military capacities 'make a valuable contribution in responding to regional natural disaster emergencies'.[75] As with the Oslo Guidelines, foreign military assets should be seen 'as a tool complementing existing relief mechanisms in order to provide specific support'.[76] The Asia-Pacific Regional Guidelines go on to incorporate the same standard as the Oslo Guidelines on using military assets where no comparable civilian alternative is available and when 'only the use of military or civil defence assets can meet a critical humanitarian need. In addition, any use of foreign military assets should be clearly limited in time and scale and present an exit strategy'.[77]

The titles of the two sets of guidelines also differ. The Oslo Guidelines refer to 'foreign military and civil defence assets' whereas the Asia-Pacific Regional Guidelines refer to 'foreign military assets'. Assisting States from outside the region will probably be using military, rather than civil defence, assets in relief due to the distance from Affected States. The reference to 'natural disaster' in the title of the Asia-Pacific Regional Guidelines compared with 'disaster' in the Oslo Guidelines might indicate a desire to narrow the scope for foreign military deployments in the region. In fact, most Pacific States and some Asian States are more open to international disaster relief, including military assistance, than many States outside the region.[78]

The Asia-Pacific Regional Guidelines adopt the same three categories as the Oslo Guidelines for disaster relief, that is, direct assistance, indirect assistance and infrastructure support, but with an important distinction. In line with the Oslo Guidelines, foreign militaries will normally not be used in the direct delivery of assistance, and their involvement in this way should be carefully weighed on a case-by-case basis. However, 'in the Asia-Pacific region, military actors are often required to provide direct assistance'.[79] The Asia-Pacific Regional Guidelines do not address the status of foreign military assets in an

---

74 Ibid., at para. 3.
75 Ibid.
76 Ibid., at para. 8.
77 Ibid.
78 On the Philippines' openness to foreign aid in the wake of 2013 Typhoon Haiyan, see L. Fan and H.B. Krebs, 'Regional Organizations and Humanitarian Action: The Case of ASEAN' HPG Working Paper (2014).
79 UN OCHA 'Asia-Pacific Regional Guidelines', at para. 17.2.

Affected State; instead, they refer to the Model Agreement in Annex I to the Oslo Guidelines and several other potential models being developed by the US and at an Asian regional and sub-regional level.[80]

## 4   The Guidelines in Practice

The Oslo and Asia-Pacific Regional Guidelines may, in fact, represent European and global standards respectively, rather than the global and Asia Pacific standards on military disaster relief that their titles suggest. European disaster relief practice is generally to deploy civil defence assets within Europe and military assets outside Europe. By contrast, in the Asia Pacific, military assets are deployed primarily within the region and rarely outside it.[81] In 2008, researchers at the Stockholm International Peace Research Institute argued that military-civilian tensions are 'a largely European construction [...] in most of Africa, Asia and Latin America and in the United States, the military is the primary domestic instrument of disaster response that is available to the government'.[82] On this view, the Oslo Guidelines are an anomaly, an example of developing European regional custom, while in the rest of the world, foreign military actors are integral and primary to disaster relief. A detailed study of State practice and accompanying *opinio iuris* is needed to provide evidence for this view as a matter of customary international law. However, due to the scarcity of reported practice under the Oslo and Asia-Pacific Regional Guidelines, just two examples will be considered here. In the first, the Oslo Guidelines were interpreted to prevent the use of military assets in the 2010 Pakistan floods (before the adoption of the Asia-Pacific Regional Guidelines); whereas in the second, a military response to the 2014 Ebola pandemic in West Africa was considered essential.

In the wake of the 2010 floods in Pakistan, the government of Pakistan requested NATO to deliver humanitarian goods via a proposed 'air bridge'. In a context where NATO convoys to Afghanistan were under frequent attack and Pakistanis were dying in US drone strikes,[83] the UN rejected NATO's offer as inconsistent with humanitarian principles on the basis that civilian alternatives existed and that military assets should only be used as a last resort.[84] (In the

---

80   Ibid., at para. 58.
81   Wiharta et al. *The Effectiveness of Foreign Military Assets in Natural Disaster Response*, at 13.
82   Ibid.
83   Oxfam International 'Policy Compendium Note on the Provision of Aid by Foreign Military Forces'.
84   Moroney et al. *Lessons from Department of Defense Disaster Relief Efforts in the Asia-Pacific Region*, at 78.

same response, US military rotary lift capacity was used as neither the UN Humanitarian Air Service, Pakistan military nor other donor governments could provide cargo helicopters.)[85] This example demonstrates that UN OCHA's views overrode those of States (the US and Pakistan) and international organizations (NATO), which considered that NATO military involvement in disaster relief did not violate the Oslo Guidelines. Country-specific guidance on civil-military coordination in Afghanistan (2008) and draft Guidelines on Pakistan (2010) were relevant in this case,[86] but the issue added impetus for the development of Asia-Pacific Regional Guidelines on the use of foreign military assets in disaster relief.

By contrast, in the 2014 Ebola pandemic affecting the West African countries of Liberia, Sierra Leone and Guinea, the Oslo Guidelines were not interpreted as posing a barrier to a military response to a public health emergency.[87] Following months of calls for urgent action from MSF, on 8 August 2014 the World Health Organization (WHO) declared the Ebola pandemic a 'Public Health Emergency of International Concern'.[88] On 2 September, MSF's President called for civilian and military medical capacity to be deployed to respond to the Ebola pandemic as MSF considered the military to be 'the only body that can be deployed in the numbers needed now' capable of the necessary swift response.[89] MSF also assumed that 'with the massive investment and knowing how much they are afraid of bioterrorism, [militaries] have some knowhow about highly contagious diseases'.[90] UN OCHA issued a Guideline on Civil-Military Coordination in the Response to Ebola, which stated that

> the civil-military relationship has to be managed carefully and on a case by case basis to avoid association and maintain a clear distinction between military and health and humanitarian aid workers. The perception

---

85   Ibid., at 62.
86   UN OCHA 'Oslo Guidelines'.
87   On the UN Security Council in relation to Ebola: UNSC Res 2177 (18 September 2014); J.B. Heath, 'Global Emergency Power in the Age of Ebola' (2016) 57 Harvard Journal of International Law 1; A. Hood, 'Ebola: A Threat to the Parameters or a Threat to the Peace?' (2015) 16 Melbourne Journal of International Law 29.
88   WHO 'Statement on the 1st Meeting of the IHR Emergency Committee on the 2014 Ebola Outbreak in West Africa' (8 August 2014), available at www.who.int/mediacentre/news/statements/2014/ebola-20140808/en/ (accessed 19 February 2019).
89   J. Liu, cited in S. Arie, 'Only the Military Can Get the Ebola Epidemic under Control: MSF Head' (2014) 349 British Medical Journal g6151.
90   Ibid.

by local actors and populations of foreign military and peacekeeping troops is also a factor to be taken into account.[91]

The Guideline goes on to provide examples of health-specific indirect and direct assistance.[92] The fact that the call for a military response came from MSF, the humanitarian agency known for its consistent stance against military involvement in disaster relief, is surprising. MSF's call may have meant that others were less likely to probe the effectiveness of the military response, believing it to be more timely and competent than that of the WHO, whose delay in acting on MSF's warnings was blamed for the pandemic getting out of control.[93] It might have meant that critics neglected to ask questions about the implications and value for money of a military response to a public health emergency.[94] Instead, a 2017 Chatham House meeting of experts considered that the Oslo Guidelines could be reviewed, with a focus on appropriate contexts for direct military engagement in disease outbreak response.[95] Committing civilian health resources to a health emergency before it reaches pandemic levels is important for future planning.

While these are just two examples, they challenge the principle of military as a last resort as a global standard summed up in the Oslo Guidelines. In the Pakistan floods, the Affected State (Pakistan) and the NATO Assisting States (from North America and Europe) all considered the military an appropriate response to the disaster at that point, but UN OCHA (an international organization) vetoed this course of action. Four years later, a humanitarian non-government organization (MSF) and UN agency (the WHO), together with the Affected and Assisting States, decided on the military as 'the only' option, a decision ratified by UN OCHA which issued a Guideline on that specific situation. Military response to the Ebola outbreak could be considered an exception that strengthens the rule of military as a last resort rather than undermining it. However, the military response to Ebola suggests that the Asia Pacific standard of 'military first' is not confined to that region but is global.

---

91   UN OCHA 'Civil–Military Interaction and Use of Foreign Military and Civil Defence Assets (MCDA) in the Context of the Current Ebola Crisis in West Africa' (20 October 2014), at para.13.
92   Ibid., at paras 18–19.
93   Adam Kamradt-Scott, 'WHO's to blame? The World Health Organization and the 2014 Ebola Outbreak in West Africa' (2016) 37 Third World Quarterly 401.
94   K.B. Sandvik, 'Evaluating Ebola: the Politics of the Military Response Narrative' Norwegian Centre for Humanitarian Studies blog (16 March 2015), available at www.humanitarianstudies.no/tag/military/ (accessed 19 February 2019).
95   Centre on Global Health Security 'Roundtable Summary: The Next Ebola: Considering the Role of the Military in Future Epidemic Response' (31 March 2017), at 2.

## III  The Politics of Foreign Military Assistance in Disaster

Using military assets in disaster response has costs and benefits for the military, Affected States, Assisting States and, not least, disaster affected people. Most of the analysis on this issue is undertaken from the perspective of Assisting State militaries. While there may be turf battles at a domestic level between the aid or foreign policy arms of government and its defence forces, Assisting States appear to evaluate the desirability of military disaster relief on a case by case basis. Civilian humanitarian agencies adopt a range of positions. Some decide whether to work with the military in the context of particular disasters, some refuse to be associated with the military on principle, and other agencies appear oblivious to the controversy and potential risks. This section will assess the advantages and disadvantages, and evaluate some of the critiques, of military involvement in disaster response.

Sometimes the distinction between the military and civilians is overstated. For instance, many aid agencies employ former military personnel in logistics, water, sanitation and hygiene, engineering and security assessment roles. It may be precisely their military training and experience that equips them for 'boots on the ground' humanitarian work.[96] Further, many of the problems of disaster response are common to all responders in humanitarian action. Examples can be found of a range of both military and civilian actors burdening Affected States with unwanted and inappropriate aid items and associated delivery, storage, processing and distribution costs and waste of time.[97] Cultural sensitivity to local circumstances has been found lacking in both types of actors. There may be little difference between militaries competing for strategic and political influence post-disaster and humanitarians competing for visibility and funding through display of logos in a rush to respond to televised disasters. The following discussion will, therefore, focus on issues that are more closely associated with military deployments.

### 1  *From an Assisting State Military Perspective*

From a military perspective, involvement in disaster response may offer opportunities. These include improving its reputation whether at home or abroad. Approval ratings for both Japanese and US military forces increased markedly according to surveys conducted with Japanese people on the response to the

---

[96]  In 1993, Irish army volunteers deployed to Somalia embedded in Irish NGO GOAL which sought their military expertise: OECD, 'Civil and Military Means', at 26.

[97]  D. Fisher, 'The Law of International Disaster Response: Overview and Ramifications for Military Actors'.

2011 East Japan earthquake, tsunami and Fukushima nuclear meltdown.[98] This may be due in part to the fact that US Operation *Tomodachi* (friend) was demilitarized from the start: 'no weapons, only smiles'.[99] Another example is how Indonesians' views of the US improved as a result of US involvement in disaster relief. In 2003, following the US invasion of Iraq, 85% of Indonesians held negative views of the US, but by 2005, when it contributed to Indian Ocean tsunami relief efforts, 65% of Indonesians held more positive views of the US.[100]

The opportunity may arise to build on and improve existing relationships or to heal past rifts between countries through cooperation in the wake of a disaster. For example, as an Assisting State, Japan uses 'disaster relief diplomacy' to strengthen its strategic relations with military forces in South-east Asia and to counter-balance China's influence in the region.[101] As an Affected State, Japan also welcomed US assistance following the Fukushima triple disaster as a demonstration that it had powerful friends who were willing to help in times of need.[102] Following the 2015 Nepal earthquake, India and China worked together. Despite their 1962 border war and continuing incursions, the two countries agreed to continue cooperative post-earthquake reconstruction through signing an MOU on earthquake science and engineering.[103]

Humanitarian assistance in disaster relief can be perceived as less political than such assistance in the context of conflict or counter-terrorism, for example, but this is not always the case. The Myanmar government's suspicion of foreign efforts in the 2008 Cyclone Nargis response is a case in point.[104] Offers of military assistance may be made for political reasons rather than in response to an identified need. Affected countries that accept foreign military assistance in times of disaster are extremely conscious of the political impact

---

[98]  Moroney et al., *Lessons from Department of Defense Disaster Relief Efforts in the Asia-Pacific Region*, at 86.

[99]  Ibid., at 94; R. Oriki, 'The Role of Self-Defense Forces (SDF) in Responding to the Great East Japan Earthquake' National Institute for Defense Studies (Japan) (9 November 2011).

[100]  D. Capie, 'The United States and Humanitarian Assistance and Disaster Relief (HADR) in East Asia: Connecting Coercive and Non-Coercive Uses of Military Powers' (2015) 38 Journal of Strategic Studies 317.

[101]  H. Futori, 'Japan's Disaster Relief Diplomacy: Fostering Military Cooperation in Asia' (13 May 2013) Asia Pacific Bulletin No. 213.

[102]  Moroney et al., *Lessons from Department of Defense Disaster Relief Efforts in the Asia-Pacific Region*, at 100.

[103]  Council on Foreign Relations / A. Anderson and A. Ayres, 'Expert Brief: Disaster Relief: China and India Come Together' (30 October 2015).

[104]  R. Barber, 'The Responsibility to Protect the Survivors of Natural Disaster: Cyclone Nargis, a Case Study' (2009) 14 Journal of Conflict and Security Law 3.

of a perceived failure on the part of government in the eyes of its constituents, as well as potentially appearing weak or incapable to outsiders.[105]

Disaster relief may provide valuable training opportunities and international experience for military personnel in an environment that is safer than conflict.[106] Demonstrating their usefulness in disasters, whether at home or abroad, can help military forces make a case to maintain or increase funding in the face of budgetary pressures. Finally, deployment in disasters may provide the opportunity for intelligence collection, although the Oslo Guidelines specifically prohibit 'intelligence collection, propaganda, or psychological operations'.[107]

From a military perspective, there are also costs to deployment in disaster relief. Both the Oslo and Asia-Pacific Regional Guidelines state that foreign military aid should be at no cost to the Affected State.[108] The Oslo Guidelines also specify that Assisting States should

> bear in mind the cost/benefit ratio of such operations as compared to other alternatives, if available. In principle, the costs involved in using MCDA on disaster relief missions abroad should be covered by funds other than those available for international development activities.[109]

One of the main reasons why military response to disaster may be seen as undesirable is that it usually costs more than a civilian response.[110] A related concern among civil society responders in Assisting States is that paying for a military response takes up too much of foreign aid budgets that could be better spent elsewhere.[111] Due to the lack of transparency in military budgets, it is difficult to know whether the Assisting States comply with the standard set in

---

105 Moroney et al., *Lessons from Department of Defense Disaster Relief Efforts in the Asia-Pacific Region*, at xxi.
106 Spanish pilots needed time to adjust to new helicopters used in delivering relief supplies in the Mozambique floods in 2000, see Wiharta et al., *The Effectiveness of Foreign Military Assets in Natural Disaster Response*, at 59, 61.
107 UN OCHA 'Oslo Guidelines', at para. 98.
108 Ibid., at para. 27; UN OCHA 'Asia-Pacific Regional Guidelines', at para. 6.
109 UN OCHA 'Oslo Guidelines', at para. 28.
110 Oxfam International 'Policy Compendium Note on the Provision of Aid by Foreign Military Forces'. Concerns about the disproportionate costs of military assets are prominent in the Mohonk Criteria, an initiative that advocated the use of as a last resort in complex emergencies; see Ebersole, 'The Mohonk Criteria', at 204.
111 L. Poole, 'Briefing: Counting the Cost of Humanitarian Aid Delivered through the Military' (2013) Global Humanitarian Assistance.

both the Oslo and Asia-Pacific Regional Guidelines, but if they do comply, it is likely that the cost comes out of military budgets.

Further, when time is critical, military personnel may find it frustrating to deal with civilian organizations that lack a command structure. Involvement in disaster relief can be time-consuming and may represent a distraction from their main focus, with troops literally being diverted from their missions to assist in disaster relief.[112] The view that humanitarian assistance and disaster relief is not a 'core mission' for defence organizations and best left to civilians is articulated by US, Australian and Indonesian defence sources.[113] Indeed, one of the critiques of military involvement in disaster relief is that military forces are being deployed outside their sphere of expertise, usually understood to be combat.

### 2   *From a Civilian Humanitarian Perspective*

Many of the features considered as advantages from a military perspective can be seen as disadvantages from the perspective of civilian humanitarian responders. For example, humanitarian workers caution against governments and the humanitarian community becoming dependent on military assets in disaster response. This is reflected in the Oslo Guidelines principle that military assets should only be used as a last resort. In addition, there is a consensus among military and civilian responders that military deployment in disaster relief should be of short duration: exactly how long will depend on the type of emergency and the military capability offered. There are concerns that involvement in disaster relief can legitimize military presence.[114] Where the military is better funded and has more extensive geographic reach than civil defence organizations, rather than being seen as an advantage, this gives humanitarians cause for concern.[115] Locating national disaster agencies under military command can be a source of tension between civil society disaster responders and the military at a domestic level. While a military chain of command may enable a faster response in an emergency, it also has the potential to narrow

---

112   Moroney et al., *Lessons from Department of Defense Disaster Relief Efforts in the Asia-Pacific Region*, at 46.

113   'Interview with US Marine Corps Brig. Gen. Paul J. Kennedy, Commanding General of Joint Task Force 505 Forward during Operation Sahayogi Haat in Nepal' (2016) VIII Liaison Magazine 28.

114   A.I. Fukushima et al., 'Disaster Militarism: Rethinking US Relief in the Asia Pacific' (11 March 2014) Foreign Policy in Focus.

115   Civil society groups pointed out that leading the response to the Pakistan floods in 2010 gave the Pakistani military a chance to consolidate its power, see Moroney et al., *Lessons from Department of Defense Disaster Relief Efforts in the Asia-Pacific Region*, at 57.

participation in key decisions regarding disaster relief by civilian and civil society actors who may have a longer-term perspective.[116] There is an accompanying risk that the military relief will be inappropriate or not inclusive.

The main concern motivating international guidelines is that military response to disaster encroaches on the domain of civilian humanitarians. Different NGOs take different approaches to this issue. For example, US NGO CARE decides on a case by case whether to work with the US military on transportation or logistics, as in some countries the US military is perceived as 'neutral or positive', in other contexts, being associated with the US military poses a security risk.[117] MSF has a policy of distancing itself from military forces: rather than become associated with the military, in some cases, MSF leaves the country, as it did in Afghanistan in 2004.[118] Its 2014 call for a military response to Ebola in West Africa is a stark contrast to this position. As Oxfam pointed out in the Indian Ocean tsunami relief effort, some NGOs appeared unaware that by providing lifts to Indonesian armed forces personnel, they were potentially exposing themselves to attack by separatist Gerakin Aceh Merdeka (GAM) (Free Aceh Movement) forces in the province of Aceh, hardest hit by the tsunami.[119] Hence, the implications of being associated with military forces are not uniform but rather depend on context. Likewise, different civilian humanitarian agencies have a range of policies on this issue.

The risk of blurring the line between military and civilian relief in complex emergencies haunts the interpretation of the principle of the military only as a last resort, even where disasters occur outside conflict. The use of military troops and assets as a tool for development or so-called stabilization and reconstruction activities, and as a key component of counter-insurgency (COIN) strategies, compromises the humanitarian notion of 'last resort'. Similarly, the use of military troops and assets to deliver aid for the purpose of winning the sympathy of the population ('winning hearts and minds') might compromise humanitarian access and the safety of humanitarian workers, and otherwise hamper humanitarian operations.[120] Former US Secretary of Defense Colin

---

116   P.C. Parisetti, 'The Use of Civil and Military Defense Assets in Emergency Situations' in de Guttry, Gestri and Venturini (eds), *International Disaster Response Law*, at 585.
117   Moroney et al., *Lessons from Department of Defense Disaster Relief Efforts in the Asia-Pacific Region*, at 79.
118   MSF 'Afghanistan: MSF Leaves Country Following Staff Killings and Threats' (16 December 2004). Note that MSF returned to Afghanistan in 2009: https://www.msf.org/afghanistan (accessed 29 March 2019).
119   Wiharta et al., *The Effectiveness of Foreign Military Assets in Natural Disaster Response*, at 38.
120   UN OCHA 'Foreign Military and Civil Defence Assets in Support of Humanitarian Emergency Operations: What Is Last Resort?' (2012), at 6.

Powell's statement that aid workers were 'force multipliers [...] an important part of our combat team' was angrily denied by humanitarian workers.[121] MSF referred to the Provincial Reconstruction Teams in Afghanistan, comprising armed military personnel deployed in civilian clothing, as 'the death of humanitarianism'.[122] The fake CIA vaccination program used as a cover to locate Osama bin Laden in Pakistan in 2010–11 was linked to the deaths of nine genuine health workers engaged in a polio vaccination program.[123]

Moreover, confusion about the military's role as spies, soldiers or relief providers can lead to suspicion and fear, and some people may not access relief as a result.[124] These risks are most apparent where a disaster occurs in an area where there is an ongoing conflict with government soldiers on one side and disaster-affected people, whether combatants or civilians, on the other. However, humanitarian agencies are conscious of the risk that humanitarian relief operations elsewhere, or in the same State in the future, may be perceived as linked to military forces where they provide direct assistance to disaster-affected people.

### 3  *From the Perspective of Disaster Affected States and Affected People*

Although the interests of disaster-affected people do not always coincide with those of Affected States, international law recognizes Affected States as their representatives. For Affected States, the acceptability of military assets in disaster relief often depends on the extent to which they have control over the process. Some States may welcome or decline all military assistance whatever its source, whereas for others the presence of certain foreign military actors is unacceptable. In 2008 following Cyclone Nargis, the Myanmar government forced military supply ships from France, the UK and the US to turn around without unloading after waiting offshore for ten days.[125] The Myanmar government nevertheless accepted relief materials delivered from two Indian warships and bilateral military support from Thailand and Singapore.[126] Some

---

121  Secretary C.L. Powell 'September 11, 2001: Attack on America, Remarks to the National Foreign Policy Conference for Leaders of Nongovernmental Organizations' (26 October 2011); C. Fournier, 'NATO Speech, Médecins Sans Frontières' (9 December 2009); H. Moslih, 'Why Are Humanitarian Workers Targeted?' (16 February 2015) Global Policy Blog.

122  P.C. Parisetti, 'The Use of Civil and Military Defense Assets in Emergency Situations', at 597.

123  'How the CIA's Fake Vaccination Campaign Endangers Us All' (1 May 2013) Scientific American.

124  A.I. Fukushima et al., 'Disaster Militarism'.

125  C. Allan and T. O'Donnell, 'An Offer You Cannot Refuse? Natural Disasters, the Politics of Aid Refusal and Potential Legal Implications' (2013) 5 Amsterdam Law Forum 36.

126  A. Collins, *Building a People-Oriented Security Community the ASEAN Way* (Routledge 2013), at 138.

States may feel unable to refuse aid; while in others there may be no domestic disaster response capacity or only very fragile governmental authority to decide, such as in the 2010 Haiti earthquake.[127]

Affected States have a soft law duty to consult affected people, but very little is known about what affected people think about humanitarian aid in general.[128] Both in disaster risk reduction and in relief operations, States are urged to consult 'relevant stakeholders'. Different instruments name particular groups as relevant stakeholders. For example, people with disabilities and women are listed in the Sendai Framework for Disaster Risk Reduction as leaders of disaster risk reduction while at the same time potentially particularly vulnerable.[129] By contrast, draft Art. 6 refers to 'the needs of the particularly vulnerable', while the commentary explains that a list of vulnerable groups was deliberately eschewed on the basis that who is particularly vulnerable may vary by disaster.[130]

It is difficult to know what disaster-affected people think about the use of military assets in disaster relief but their views are likely to differ according to disaster, Affected State, Assisting State, and type of aid. People's views may also change over time, from the immediate aftermath of a disaster to several years later. In at least one instance, disaster affected people did not distinguish between military and civilian relief provided, and this may well be the case elsewhere.[131] In States with ongoing or recent conflict, the use of military and civil defence assets is governed by the Guidelines on Complex Emergencies, which incorporate the Oslo principle of the military as a last resort. In these situations, affected people may be reluctant to access aid provided by military personnel, depending on which military actor is involved.[132] The gender of affected people and of military personnel may also be an important factor. The UK Ministry of Defence notes that where there has been forced conscription, men and boys may be reluctant to approach the military for help, while 'reputations of local and international soldiers' can inhibit women and girls from seeking disaster relief.[133] In short, empirical research is required into what

---

127  N. Rencoret et al., 'Haiti Earthquake Response: Context Analysis' (ALNAP 2010), at 19.
128  Cf M.B Anderson, D. Brown and I. Jean, *Time to Listen: Hearing People on the Receiving End of International Aid* (CDA Collaborative Learning Projects 2012).
129  Priority 4 refers to 'empowering women and persons with disabilities to lead' cf 'women, children and people in vulnerable situations [who are] disproportionately affected'. UNGA Res 69/283 'Sendai Framework for Disaster Risk Reduction 2015–2030' (23 June 2015), at paras 4 and 32.
130  ILC Draft Articles, commentary on Art. 6 (7).
131  Wiharta et al., *The Effectiveness of Foreign Military Assets in Natural Disaster Response*, at 36.
132  UN OCHA 'Complex Emergency Guidelines', at para. 7.
133  UK Ministry of Defence 'Disaster Relief Operations Overseas', at 17.

affected people want and how they perceive disaster relief delivered by foreign militaries.

## 4   Evaluating Foreign Military Disaster Relief

Several conclusions can be drawn about the circumstances in which the use of foreign military assets in disaster relief is appropriate and politically acceptable. These assessments rely on the rules regarding direct and indirect assistance and infrastructure support in the Oslo and Asia-Pacific Regional Guidelines. First, there is widespread support for military assets in infrastructure support, especially air and sea transport, and in many cases, military assets are the only capability available. Further, these assets are, at least theoretically, 'on permanent standby, available in large numbers, ready to deploy at a moment's notice'.[134] The military often leads the logistics cluster in countries that have adopted the UN Cluster System.[135] This is the case in Bangladesh and Nepal, but not in the Philippines, where the logistics cluster is led by the Office of Civil Defence but the Armed Forces lead search and rescue.[136] In different types of disasters, ranging from earthquakes in rugged mountainous terrain such as in Nepal or Pakistan to the low-lying coastal regions and islands of Indonesia and Sri Lanka devastated by the 2004 tsunami, certain specific military capabilities are essential, particularly cargo aircraft and long range heavy lift helicopters. In the 2009 West Sumatran earthquake response, Indonesian, Australian and US military aircraft and ships were used to transport aid from the island of Java to Sumatra for local and international NGOs.[137] Amphibious vehicles have proven 'ideal' for providing humanitarian aid following disasters.[138] Such military assets are usually unique with no equivalent civilian alternative capacity.

---

134   Wiharta et al., *The Effectiveness of Foreign Military Assets in Natural Disaster* Response, at 32.
135   Introduced in 2005 as part of the Humanitarian Reform Agenda, the Cluster Approach or Cluster System groups UN and non-UN humanitarian agencies in the main sectors of humanitarian action (eg, food, health, shelter, etc.) to enhance co-ordination: Humanitarian Response 'What is the Cluster Approach?' (no date), available at www.humanitarianresponse.info/en/about-clusters/what-is-the-cluster-approach (accessed 19 February 2019); S.F. Ali, 'Crowd-Sourced Governance in a Post-Disaster Context' (2015) 64 ICLQ 217; J.B. Heath, 'Managing the 'Republic of NGOs': Accountability and Legitimation Problems Facing the UN Cluster System' (2014) 47 Vanderbilt Journal of Transnational Law 239.
136   Regional Consultative Group 'Humanitarian Civil–Military Coordination in Emergencies: Towards a Predictable Model' (2017), at 6.
137   Ibid., at 62.
138   D. Capie, 'The United States and Humanitarian Assistance and Disaster Relief (HADR) in East Asia: Connecting Coercive and Non-Coercive Uses of Military Powers', at 314.

Different considerations apply to medical and engineering assets whose provision by the military is much more controversial. With military medical teams and field hospitals, there is often a mismatch between military capacity for trauma treatment of healthy, fit, adult, predominantly male populations and the need of disaster survivors, particularly the elderly and children, for primary health care and of affected women and teenaged girls for emergency obstetric and post-sexual assault care. Humanitarian civilian alternatives are designed to meet these needs. The 2014 Ebola pandemic may represent an exception to this general rule, where even MSF called for a military response to address the health emergency. It is difficult to know whether, had the crisis been addressed more swiftly, civilian resources would have been sufficient to contain it.

In regard to engineering, military standards are frequently too high to be sustainable and again there are civilian alternatives. In 2005 NATO engineers providing water supply in Pakistan could not find local materials that met EU standards so could not finish their task.[139] Civilian humanitarian engineering standards, such as those specified in the Sphere guidelines and The Good Enough Guide, are more likely to be able to be maintained in the future. Such standards provide adequate quality water for large numbers of people, by contrast with military engineering standards designed to provide high quality water for smaller numbers.[140]

A second conclusion to be drawn is that there is support for military personnel in the early stages of a disaster. Such personnel are capable of operating in harsh environments lacking in basic resources, such as food, water, sanitation, communications, and infrastructure, and are trained to establish such facilities and services from scratch. Some types of military assets, such as hospital ships and offshore bases, promote self-sufficiency and reduce strain on land resources destroyed by the disaster or under pressure from the relief effort. For example, in 2013 after typhoon Haiyan, the Philippines Navy established a temporary 'floating government'.[141] Many of these examples can be classified

---

139  Wiharta et al., *The Effectiveness of Foreign Military Assets in Natural Disaster Response*, at 117.
140  Emergency Capacity Building Project, 'The Good Enough Guide: Impact Measurement and Accountability in Emergencies' (Oxfam 2007); Sphere Association, *The Sphere Handbook: Humanitarian Charter and Minimum Standards in Humanitarian Response* (Sphere 2018).
141  Center for Excellence in Disaster Management and Humanitarian Response 'Advances in Civil–Military Coordination in Catastrophes, How the Philippines Turned Lessons Learned from Super Typhoon Haiyan (Yolanda) into Best Practices for Disaster Preparedness and Response' (2015), at 14.

as infrastructure support and hence do not infringe the Oslo principle of military disaster relief as a last resort.

A third conclusion is that, in some countries, the military may be the best funded and most powerful part of the State, with more extensive geographic reach within a country than other government agencies. In the 2005 earthquake, the Pakistan army was the 'only domestic institution capable of managing a response'.[142] In addition to these reasons, 'developing nations can ill-afford separate disaster response organizations'.[143] Domestic armed forces may have a legally mandated role in disaster response, such as in Indonesia and Bangladesh, while in Nepal and Myanmar, the role of military forces in disaster response is entrenched in the Constitution.[144] The Armed Forces of the Philippines play a role not just in disaster response but in reducing disaster risk and in building community capacity.[145] These arguments are put forward by military sources to justify continued funding. By contrast, civilian humanitarians argue that a policy of funding the military to respond to disasters, rather than investing in disaster risk reduction, may raise questions about the responsibility of States for continuing to maintain the vulnerability of their population.

Finally, military chains of command aim to enable orders to be carried out swiftly and this may enable a faster response in emergency situations such as disasters. The fact that military assets are provided only by governments means that they are present in smaller numbers, making coordination easier.[146] For example, the 2004 tsunami relief effort in Aceh, Indonesia, included 14 UN agencies, 16 foreign militaries, and 195 foreign civilian humanitarian groups.[147] Exchange of military liaison officers, development of standard operating procedures and participation in joint training exercises, especially if they focus on disaster relief, may enable smoother coordination between different military organizations. Military personnel may have more opportunities for joint

---

142   Wiharta et al., *The Effectiveness of Foreign Military Assets in Natural Disaster Response*, at 107.
143   Ret. Nepali Col. R. Khatri, 'Civil–Military Coordination after the Nepal Earthquake: Role of the HuMOCC' (2016) VIII Liaison Magazine 23, available at https://www.cfe-dmha.org/Portals/0/liaison/liaison-2016-VIII-1.pdf (accessed 17 April 2019).
144   Act No. 34 (2004) (Indonesia); Art. 267 (4) Constitution of Nepal (2015); Art. 341 Constitution of Myanmar (2008); Regional Consultative Group, 'Humanitarian Civil–Military Coordination', at 42; Khatri, 'Civil Military Coordination', at 9, 101; Standing Orders on Disaster (2010) (Bangladesh).
145   Regional Consultative Group; 'Humanitarian Civil–Military Coordination', at 128.
146   The involvement of the private sector, including private military contractors, in disaster response, requires further attention.
147   Wiharta et al., *The Effectiveness of Foreign Military Assets in Natural Disaster Response*, at 60.

training than civilian responders, although it is difficult to generalize as opportunities likely vary according to the size of the organization and funding available, whether military or civilian. Military deployments are not always fast, nor does the military always follow orders.[148] Nonetheless, in general, military organizations, especially those from within the region, can be faster and easier to coordinate than a more significant number of smaller, civilian agencies deploying in disaster relief. As in peace operations, participation in disaster relief raises issues for militaries about taking orders from other military command structures and consultation with national (Affected State) authorities and civilian responders.

## IV Conclusion

This article addressed two questions: first, the legal limits on the deployment of foreign military assets in disaster relief, and second, the politics of such deployment, described by critics as 'disaster militarism'. On the first question, international law does not prevent the military provision of disaster relief due to a lack of neutrality. Regional and bilateral disaster treaties and SOFAs may authorize military deployment in disaster relief, although it is difficult to generalize about international law on this issue due to the confidentiality of many of these bilateral agreements. The real issue is not whether, but how, the military should be involved in disaster relief.[149] Where should the line be drawn between the use of military assets as a last resort (the Oslo Guidelines) or potentially as a first response (the Asia-Pacific Regional Guidelines)? The Oslo and Asia-Pacific Regional Guidelines are not diametrically opposed, with both incorporating the central principle of the use of military assets as a last resort. However, the Asia-Pacific Regional Guidelines are more specific about the appropriate conditions for deployment and the requirement for an exit strategy. In practice, the Oslo Guidelines are interpreted differently by different countries. Despite their designation as regional guidelines, the Asia-Pacific Regional Guidelines are more representative of State practice worldwide.

On the second question, examining the politics of military assistance in disaster relief requires attention to the interests and concerns of a range of actors and the ways in which some are amplified and others are silenced in

---

148  Ibid., at 33.
149  M. Thapa, 'Ideas for Peace out of Barracks: Civil–Military Relations in Disaster Management: A Case Study of Nepalese Army's Humanitarian Response during 2015 Earthquake in Nepal' (UN University for Peace 2016), at 5.

international law. International law on disasters privileges the perspectives of States but also reflects the concerns of assisting entities such as humanitarian agencies. On the question of the legality of military deployments in disaster relief, the views of Assisting States through their militaries are particularly prominent. Some States have also been insistent about their right to refuse foreign disaster relief, in particular, the use of foreign military assets. Whether as actual or potential Affected States, they are keen to influence the development of international law through treaties and custom. Assisting entities, such as humanitarian NGOs and international organizations like UN OCHA, have questioned the legitimacy and highlighted the potential risks of military deployment in disaster relief. While humanitarian agencies claim to represent disaster affected people by emphasising the potential reluctance of the latter to access relief provided by the military, the views of affected people and how they might vary in different times and places are largely unknown.

## Acknowledgments

This research was funded by a UTS Chancellor's Postdoctoral Fellowship and conducted while I was a Visiting Fellow at the European University Institute, Florence. Thanks to Nehal Bhuta, Giulio Bartolini, Andrea de Guttry, Emanuele Sommario, Sarah Williams, Chris Michaelsen, Lucas Lixinski and Terry Carney for their feedback on presentations and earlier versions.

CHAPTER 14

# Social Movements and the Legal Field: Becoming-Constituent

*Xenia Chiaramonte*

### Abstract

The relationship between social movements and the legal field is controversial and complex. This paper begins by recognizing that the concept of social movement does not belong to legal doctrine and then synthetically reconstruct the relevance of it for a legal understanding. In fact, even if this concept is not formally taken into account by constitutions or by legal codes, a socio-legal approach underscores the need for the comprehension and inclusion of collective phenomena into legal theory. First, the paper explores the way in which 'social movement' has been taken up and translated in the legal field through the concept of social change and constitutional change. Second, this research goes through various cases in which social movements use law strategically, from the phenomenon of cause lawyering to the litigation strategy. Finally, it stands for a theoretical understanding of the role of social movements in legal theory as a lively expression of 'becoming-constituent'.

### Keywords

Social Movements – Litigation Strategy – Cause Lawyering – Legal Change – Social Change – Social Actor – Constitutional Actor – Becoming-Constituent

## 1    Social Movements as Social and Constitutional Actors

The social movements of the 1960s and 1970s were so different from previous mobilizations that it was necessary to find new analytical tools to understand them.[1] The *new* movements, which we know today, differ from the *historical* movements by scale—qualified as mass—but also by composition, given that the actors are no longer referring to schemes for differentiating systems

---

[1]    D. Della Porta and M. Diani, *I movimenti sociali* (La Nuova Italia Scientifica 1997), at 4.

in industrial societies.[2] Rather, today's movements are interclass, changeable groups, characterized by a 'fluid and open organization' and by an 'inclusive and non-ideological participation, an attention focused more on cultural transformations than on economic ones'.[3] The old categories interpreted the emergence of a movement as nothing more than the product of a historical conjuncture of a period of crisis[4] and tended to provide a homogeneous image of the collective phenomenon.

The impasse lies in the fact that the new features and claims were not attributable to any of the two great theoretical models of reference: the Marxist and the functionalist ones. Both the transversality of the involved actors' social class and the subject of their demands were difficult to fit into the category of class struggle. The Marxist tradition remained linked to the conception that social conflicts are inextricably connected to the development of productive forces and class relations. As a consequence, the focus was on the system rather than on the formative process of movements. Moreover, Marxists assumed the presence of a certain degree of homogeneity within movements, contrary to the new social movements which are heterogeneous and fragmented.[5]

Using the structural-functional conceptual schemes, it was possible to look at the psychology of the crowd and to interpret the actions of the subjects with regard to the system and its equilibrium. It was as if the movements constituted the 'fever' of the social 'body'; according to the functionalist tradition, collective action was a dysfunction of the system. While in Marxism we find no analysis of the movements as such, in the case of functionalism we find it under the concept of 'collective behaviour'. In this approach, research is often focused on the actors' beliefs, driven by the underlying idea that every society is 'a set of interacting elements, each of them cooperating, in a relatively orderly way through the functions it performs, to the achievement of well-being or the best state of the overall system'.[6] In historical moments of crisis, the social body would attempt to react by elaborating shared beliefs in order to reestablish collective solidarity.[7]

---

2   J.H. Cohen et al. (eds), *Problemi del Socialismo* vol. 12 *I Nuovi Movimenti Sociali* (Franco Angeli 1987).
3   D. Della Porta and M. Diani, *I movimenti sociali* (La Nuova Italia Scientifica 1997), at 26. My translation.
4   A. Melucci, *L'invenzione del presente: movimenti, identità, bisogni individuali* (Il Mulino 1982), at 11.
5   A. Melucci, *L'invenzione del presente: movimenti, identità, bisogni individuali* (Il Mulino 1982), at 13.
6   V. Ferrari, *Diritto e società. Elementi di sociologia del diritto* (Laterza 2006), at 10. My translation.
7   D. Della Porta and M. Diani, *I movimenti sociali* (La Nuova Italia Scientifica 1997), at 17.

However, since the Sixties, the issue of collective phenomena has grown so large that society was called *movement society*.[8] How to deal with mass mobilization? What then is a new social movement? The legal field could not help, since it is not equipped with this concept.

Among the different definitions now provided by social movement studies, one definition of a social movement is collective action manifesting a conflict and involving the breach of the limits of compatibility of the system to which the action refers.[9] A more recent definition considers it as a network of mostly informal interactions, based on shared beliefs and solidarity, which is mobilized on conflicting issues, through frequent use of various forms of protest.[10] The action of movements with respect to institutional politics is a contentious politics.[11]

Naturally, social movements embody and liberate an irrepressible conflictual element. Protestors know that they can face confrontation with the police, for instance, which geographically delimits the scope of their protest, the pre-ordered path that they are allowed to follow, and the rules of the field. Similar issues concern the juridical field, which offers to a collective formation some expectations while reducing others, being both a beneficial and harmful, even repressive, resource.

In light of this, the criminalization of social movements has gained increasing attention as a subject and matter for debate.[12] However, the usual way to approach the topic is curiously blinded by the presupposition that the agent of the criminalization is only the police, hence any 'encounter' with the penal apparatus is not taken into account, as if an effective criminalization could occur without courts. At any rate, empirical studies on police and protest are essential for capturing the conflictual elements of the field interaction.

---

8   F. Neidhardt and D. Rucht, 'The Analysis of Social Movements: the State of the Art and Some Perspectives for Further Research' in D. Rucht, *Research in Social Movements: the State of the Art* (Campus Verlag / Westview Press 1991) 421; D. Meyer and S.G. Tarrow, *The Social Movement Society: Contentious Politics for a New Century* (Rowman & Littlefield 1998).
9   A. Melucci, *L'invenzione del presente: movimenti, identità, bisogni individuali* (Il Mulino 1982), at 19.
10  D. Della Porta and M. Diani, *I movimenti sociali* (La Nuova Italia Scientifica 1997), at 30.
11  C. Tilly and S.G. Tarrow, *Contentious Politics* (OUP 2006).
12  See e.g. C. Davenport, H. Johnston and C. Mueller (eds), *Repression and Mobilization* (University of Minnesota Press 2005); J. Lovell, *Crimes of Dissent: Civil Disobedience, Criminal Justice, and the Politics of Conscience* (NYU Press 2009); '"Take back the Streets": Repression and Criminalization of Protest around the Worlds (October 2013), available at https://www.aclu.org/files/assets/global_protest_suppression_report_inclo.pdf (accessed 7 April 2019).

In fact, it is undeniable that the central aspect of a social movement, which distinguishes it from a political party or a pressure group, is the conflictual element. As Laurence Cox points out:

> What makes something a movement rather than something else is above all *conflict*: movements develop (and argue over) a sense of 'we' which is opposed to a 'they' (the State, corporations, a powerful social group, a form of behaviour) in a conflict which is about the shape and direction of society, on a large or small scale in terms of geography but also in terms of the scope of the issue.[13]

A social movement might act on a national level, could be connected to a network of transnational mobilizations or can be built as a global form of activism. In any case, social movements are able to display and strengthen the nexus between the local and the global, and a capacity to turn the one into the other.[14]

Due to their potential for change directed in several ways, through more or less explicit or shared claims, progressive or reactionary, social movements can be considered as social and constitutional actors who, through a varied repertoire of actions collectively claimed, are capable of generating a 'constitutional moment'.[15] 'By shifting the boundaries of the reasonable, and the plausible, they open up space for new forms of constitutional imagination and new forms of constitutional utopianism, both for good and for ill'.[16]

## II  The Concept of Social Change as the Translation of Social Movement into Legal Theory

It should be recognized that the concept of 'social movement' comes from the social sciences and not from the juridical field. Even if this concept is not formally taken into account by constitutions or by legal codes, a socio-legal approach underscores the need for the comprehension and inclusion of collective phenomena into legal theory. The way in which 'social movement' has

---

13  L. Cox, *Why Social Movements Matter: an Introduction* (Rowman & Littlefield 2018), at xii.
14  D. Della Porta and S.G. Tarrow (eds), *Transnational Protest and Global Activism* (Rowman & Littlefield 2005).
15  B. Ackerman, *We the People* vol. 1 *Foundations* (Belknap Press 1991).
16  J.M. Balkin, *Constitutional Redemption* (Harvard University Press 2011), at 11.

been taken up and translated in the legal field is that of 'social change' and more recently 'constitutional change'.

According to Friedman, change brought about by a social movement is one that arises outside of the legal system, that is, in the social world and that can either act in the legal system only or pass through the legal system while also reproducing itself as social change. In fact, legal change in its most important features follows social change and indeed depends on it.[17] Social movements play an indispensable role and their social claims determine a legal change, which in turn produces significant change in society.[18] Perhaps too schematically, the approach of the legal historian risks placing the social matter and the juridical form as separate elements, among which will prevail one or the other according to ideological positions.

A change is such not only when it implies adding a content to a constitutional charter, but also when it means activating a norm or a certain interpretation of it—as shown, for instance, by the case of the Italian movement for common goods, which proposed to value the social function of property envisaged by the Italian Constitution through the occupation of disused spaces that have 'opened up' to the population.[19] In general, 'many laws are made operative when people inside the affected social field are in a position to threaten to press for enforcement. They must be aware of their rights and sufficiently organized and independent to reach and mobilize the coercive force of government in order to have this effect'.[20]

A social movement is one of the engines of social change, although it cannot be the only actor of legal change. To achieve its objectives, it is generally advantaged by the possibility of relying on some fundamental resources: the

---

17    L.M. Friedman, *The Legal System: A Social Science Perspective* (Russell Sage Foundation 1975), at 439–440.
18    Ibid., at 450.
19    S. Bailey and U. Mattei, 'Social Movements as Constituent Power: The Italian Struggle for the Commons' (2013) 20.2 Indiana Journal of Global Legal Studies 965. As Veronica Pecile writes, 'the Italian movement for the commons has revealed the ambition of acting as a constituent power. In fact, it has acted as a collective actor able of trigger a bottom-up constitutional process in which a crucial strategy has been the recourse to legal tools at local, national and supranational level, in the realm of both private law and public law' (V. Pecile, *How the Commons Became Government* (Ph.D. dissertation, EHESS/Università di Perugia (2019)), at 89.
20    S. Falk Moore, 'Law and Social Change: The Semi-Autonomous Social Field as an Appropriate Subject of Study' (1973) 7.4 Law and Society Review 719, at 744.

tactical use of legal mobilization above all[21] through lawyers who are invested in their cause.

## III How to Make a Constitutional Change

An important historical case is that of Latin America and the struggle for the respect of the principle of self-determination of peoples.[22] In particular, in recent decades, indigenous populations traditionally not recognized by the constitutions have been able to establish a real constituent process. As a matter of fact, they have succeeded in obtaining a role that had classically rested only with the elites:

> Elites, not citizens, dictated constitutional change, and as a consequence, constitutions became as easy to change as ordinary legislation [but] a constitution that is politically constructed by an elite pact without the support of the citizens cannot stand the test of time whereas one that is constructed with adequate social moorings may do so.[23]

An emblematic case in undoubtedly the Ecuadorian one. Here the aboriginal cultures have undertaken through a successful organization the struggle for their rights both in terms of equality before the law and of difference regarding the cultural aspects:

> The indigenous movement of Ecuador has been a shining example of the battle of original peoples and ancestral cultures on a global scale. The most relevant of their achievements was the definition of Ecuador as an intercultural and plurinational State, incorporated in the 2008 Constitution. This definition entails the recognition of indigenous peoples as new social subjects.[24]

---

21 P. Burstein, 'Legal Mobilization as a Social Movement Tactic: The Struggle for Equal Employment Opportunity' (1991) 96.5 American Journal of Sociology 1201.
22 G.M. Sandoval Trigo, 'La libre autodeterminación de los pueblos en el siglo XXI: una mirada del Derecho Internacional por una apropiación de la historia del colonialismo y el neo-colonialismo desde los pueblos del Tercer Mundo' (2018) 15.1 Brazilian Journal of International Law.
23 M. Schor, 'Constitutionalism through the Looking Glass of Latin America' (2006) 41.1 Texas International Law Journal 1, at 36–37.
24 E. Martín Díaz, 'Entre el proceso constituyente y la revolución ciudadana: el movimiento indígena ecuatoriano en la encrucijada' (2015) 38.3 Historia Actual Online 23, at 23.

The case of Brazil is equally important: here the social mobilization employed the law as a weapon in social conflict[25] and the strategic direction has been to use local institutions and the regional human rights system to promote activists' purposes. A new constitutional moment pushed the Congress to elaborate a series of human rights legislation to address fundamental issues such as children and adolescents' rights (1989), racism (1989), health system (1990), social security (1991), free access to HIV drugs (1996), and torture (1997). 'This new and vast framework of constitutional, international and statutory rights was a direct consequence of civil society movements and progressive politics, which grew in strength during the transition process and through the first years of the new democratic regime'.[26] In addition, the American Convention on Human Rights was ratified by Brazil in 1992 which attributed jurisdiction to the Inter-American Court of Human Rights (IACtHR). Taking advantage of this new human rights framework, the non-governmental organization Justiça Global was created to guarantee justice to those abused by the military regime.

At an international level, the interaction between the processes of constitutional change and of state-building should also be taken into consideration. In fact, 'the impact of transitional justice initiatives on constitutional processes in countries that have made the transition from dictatorship to democracy is both "backward-looking and forward-looking, retrospective and prospective, continuous and discontinuous."' Such is the case for South Africa, where 'the effort was [...] self-consciously transformative, because it was meant not only to redress past wrongs but also as "an enterprise of inducing large-scale social change through non-violent political processes grounded in law."'[27]

Demands for reform in Brazil,[28] India[29] and Taiwan[30] are cases that demonstrate how a process of democratization may generate an increasing number of claims for litigation:

> In countries with strong democracies and a commitment to judicial independence, law is more likely to be seen by advocates as a viable tool to

---

25  A.T. Turk, 'Law as a Weapon in Social Conflict' (1975–76) 23 Social Problems 276.
26  O. Vieira, 'Public Interest Law: A Brazilian Perspective' (2008) 13 UCLA Journal of International Law and Foreign Affairs 219, at 235.
27  J.E. Méndez, 'Constitutionalism and Transitional Justice' in M. Rosenfeld and A. Sajó (eds), *The Oxford Handbook of Comparative Constitutional Law* (OUP 2012) 1270, at 1283.
28  O. Vieira, 'Public Interest Law: A Brazilian Perspective' (2008) 13 UCLA Journal of International Law and Foreign Affairs 219.
29  M. Galanter and J.K. Krishnan, '"Bread for the Poor": Access to Justice and the Rights of the Needy in India' (2004) 55 Hastings Law Journal 789.
30  W. Chang, 'Public Interest Litigation in Taiwan: Strategy for Law and Policy Changes in the Course of Democratization' in P. Yap and H. Lau (eds), *Public Interest Litigation in Asia* (Routledge 2011) 136.

advance reform. In authoritarian countries with weak legal institutions and fear of reprisal for dissident activity, lawyers adopt less adversarial strategies on day-to-day matters—working within the system to promote incremental change—although there are moments when they rise up and take significant risks to advance the democratic project.[31]

One of the most recent innovative legal thought was guided by the transnational movements against globalization of the 2000s, which contributed to rethinking social change at a global level, as a 'societal constitutionalism'.[32] The declining role of nation States has given way to the hypothesis of developing a radical, bottom-up democratic redesign, hence the idea of an innovative and grassroots constitutional construction. At its core there is 'a larger project to rethink international law through social movements rather than through States or individuals'[33] due to the weakening role of nation States in the most relevant political and economic decision-making processes.

This approach is best illuminated by the experience of the World Social Forum, which has been thoroughly analysed by scholars. The World Social Forum (o Fórum Social Mundial) is an annual meeting composed of several organizations representing global civil society, first held in Porto Alegre (Brazil) in 2001 and still active today. It is an open meeting place for resisting and actively opposing neoliberal policies and building a planetary society, and aims at developing an alternative future through counter-hegemonic practices. Hence, we might consider that even if this experience of democracy from below is a mobilization 'for the welfare of marginalized populations [...] at the national level against the State or the dominant national civil society', it has always implied a global scope. This is demonstrated by the recognition which emerged at the WSF that 'the State is now transnationalized and thus is no longer the privileged centre of political decision-making. This decentring of the State also brought about the decentring of the civil society, which is subjected today to many processes of cultural and social globalization'.[34]

---

31  S.L. Cummings, 'Law and Social Movements: An Interdisciplinary Analysis' in C. Roggeband and B. Klandermans (eds), *Handbook of Social Movements Across Disciplines* (Springer 2017) 233, at 258.

32  G. Teubner, 'Societal Constitutionalism: Alternatives to State-Centred Constitutional Theory' Storrs Lectures 2003/04, Yale Law School.

33  B. Rajagopal, 'International Law and Social Movements: Challenges of Theorizing Resistance' (2003) 41 Colum. J. Transnat'l L. 397, at 397.

34  B. De Sousa Santos, 'Beyond Neoliberal Governance: The World Social Forum as Subaltern Cosmopolitan Politics and Legality' in B. De Sousa Santos and C.A. Rodríguez-Garavito (eds), *Law and Globalization from below: Towards a Cosmopolitan Legality* (CUP 2005) 29, at 53.

Particularly in the case of Latin America, human rights have worked as a generative and operational frame for several types of struggles:

> [S]ocial movements, defined simply as sustained collective mobilizations for social change by civil society actors who use extrainstitutional routes (see, e.g., Snow and Soule 2010), are the key to understanding the puzzles of international human rights law—its widespread diffusion despite the potential to undermine State sovereignty and its remarkable successes despite weak enforcement mechanisms.[35]

A recent example of a beneficial intersection between civil society and international institutions is the 2018 session of the UN Commission on the Status of Women where female representatives from all over the world came to together for the struggle over inequality and discrimination (but also equal education, health and development). According to the UN Women Annual Report 2017–18, there were 'over 4,500 civil society advocates from 130 countries who attended the Commission. They represented over 600 organizations, from grass-roots groups to international coalitions'.[36]

In general, at a global level civil society mobilizations valued

> the small openings created for them in the UN system to push for stronger human rights norms, increasing the number of international human rights treaties and other instruments with help from sympathetic States while locally the elevated standards of international human rights laws have provided activists with political opportunities.[37]

On the other hand, there are also cases of non-progressive mobilizations, such as the growing anti-abortion movement. Worldwide, religious conservatives (pro-life) and feminists (pro-choice) have increasingly directed their efforts toward obtaining positive judicial decisions from courts. In fact, this is not the case of a domestic judgement: the reference is to *Artavia Murillo et al. v. Costa*

---

[35] K. Tsutsui, C. Whitlinger and A. Lim, 'International Human Rights Law and Social Movements: States' Resistance and Civil Society's Insistence' (2012) 8.1 Annual Review of Law and Social Science 367, at 368.
[36] UN Women Annual Report 2017–18.
[37] K. Tsutsui, C. Whitlinger and A. Lim, 'International Human Rights Law and Social Movements: States' Resistance and Civil Society's Insistence' (2012) 8.1 Annual Review of Law and Social Science 367, at 386.

*Rica*,[38] decided by the IACtHR in 2012. The IACtHR ordered Costa Rica to abolish the ban against in vitro fertilization (IVF), rejecting Costa Rica's argument that embryos could be considered as having personhood and thus enjoying human rights under Art. 4 (1) of the American Convention on Human Rights.[39]

However, Art. 4 (1) remains ambiguous and can offer room for a different interpretation. The case began in 2001, when

> 12 Costa Rican couples brought a case before the Inter-American Commission on Human Rights (IACmHR), claiming that the ban violated their rights to family, equality, and non-discrimination. The case was not brought as part of a focused litigation campaign but rather filed by former patients of the Instituto Costarricense de Fertilidad—married, heterosexual couples denied access to IVF following the 2000 ruling. In 2004, the IACmHR admitted the case.[40]

While formally accepting the decision, Costa Rica never followed the recommendations, pushing the IACmHR to eventually take the case to the IACtHR. Here the litigation made *Artavia Murillo* a major case for both conservative social movements and feminists alike. A total of 39 amicus briefs were filed: many of those from the feminist camp came from the US and Canada but the Latin-American feminist network on sexual and reproductive rights was also active. Eventually the pro-choice litigants won as the IACtHR adopted their interpretation and denied rights for embryos.

In the interpretation of the mentioned scholars, this trial presents a questionable result. According to them, the litigation resulted in undermining the potential of both feminists and conservatives. In general:

> By pursuing elite support through constitutional claims and court-based tactics, a movement may narrow its agenda [...]. [E]lites quiet social unrest by absorbing movement actors into established institutional arrangements. [...] In more nuanced iterations, elites are more likely to

---

38   *Artavia Murillo et al. ('In Vitro Fertilization') v. Costa Rica (Judgment)* IACtHR Series C No. 257 (28 November 2012).

39   American Convention on Human Rights (signed 22 November 1969, entered into force 18 July 1978) 1144 UNTS 123 (Pact of San José).

40   J. Lemaitre and R. Sieder, 'The Moderating Influence of International Courts on Social Movements: Evidence from the IVF Case against Costa Rica' (2017) 19.1 Health and Human Rights 149, at 152.

support goals and tactics that they recognize as part of the established system in which they operate.[41]

Using the words of Lemaitre and Sieder,

> the conservative side limited its references to faith and its close relation to the Catholic Church hierarchy and dogma, insisting instead on originalist and textual interpretations of the American Convention, as well as on scientific evidence of the beginning of life and of harms allegedly derived from IVF. On the feminist side, activists limited their emphasis on women's autonomy and reproductive choice, instead insisting on balancing rights and proportionality and recruiting liberal scientists to disprove the scientific evidence brought forth by conservatives. At the end of the day, feminist arguments won the case, but it was the more moderate frame, not the original claims for autonomy and abortion rights, that prevailed within the inter-American human rights system.[42]

## IV  Cause Lawyering as a Social Movement Tactic

Cause lawyering refers to a series of legal practices employed as a means of advancing social movement aims and achieving social change. Typically, legal institutions favour the 'haves' in a context where 'repeat players' are both those who make the rules and own the resources to enforce those rules.[43] Yet, people consider the law as a means to resist injustice in such a way as to pose the question on whether the law can be used as a counter-hegemonic tool.[44] This bottom-up viewpoint employs law as a resource and litigation, specifically, as 'a source of institutional and symbolic leverage against opponents' that may show abuses and help to ensure media coverage.[45]

---

41  D. NeJaime, 'Constitutional Change, Courts, and Social Movements' (2013) 111.6 Michigan Law Review 877, at 897–898.
42  J. Lemaitre and R. Sieder, 'The Moderating Influence of International Courts on Social Movements: Evidence from the IVF Case against Costa Rica' (2017) 19.1 Health and Human Rights 149, at 158.
43  M. Galanter, 'Why the "Haves" Come out Ahead: Speculations on the Limits of Legal Change' (1974) 9.1 Law and Society Review 95.
44  B. De Sousa Santos, 'The Counter-Hegemonic Use of Law in the Struggle for a Globalization from below' (2005) 39 Anales de la Cátedra Francisco Suárez 421.
45  M. McCann, 'Law and Social Movements: Contemporary Perspectives' (2006) 2 Annual Review of Law and Social Science 29, 29–31.

An example of this kind is provided by the LGBTQ rights movement, which has achieved great success at the international level thanks to a compact progressive action of cause lawyering. In addition, another resource that facilitates the success of a social movement in order to obtain constitutional change is certainly a favourable political moment, that is, a political opportunity.[46] The experience of the US revealed that 'given the nature of the lesbian and gay rights movement, litigation pursued by cause lawyers and individuals became one way to develop input into the direction and goals of the larger movement'.[47] In general, social movements learn from the context the best tactics to be used to achieve their goals. Their ability to select those social and legal spaces that are able to offer the greatest support to their cause, or at least the greatest potential benefits, should not be underestimated:

> It is no accident that LGBT rights advocates first asserted claims to marriage equality in state courts. Viewing the federal judiciary as largely hostile and seeing the Supreme Court as an especially dangerous venue, they sought more hospitable locations. [...] They selected venues with not only potentially supportive judges and doctrine, but also favourable conditions outside the courts. Advocates chose states where elite support existed for LGBT rights, legislative progress undermined arguments against marriage equality, public opinion was becoming increasingly favourable to relationship recognition, and the State constitution was difficult to amend. In other words, they viewed courts in a way that maps onto the political opportunity structure.[48]

Besides cause lawyering, it is often fundamental—as the Italian case of LGBTQ rights also demonstrates—to count on agreeable juries, which have gradually been able to operate a 'disruption through court',[49] that is, a change caused by a set of decision-making without changing the Constitution, but enhancing an evolutionary interpretation of the latter. In fact, the Italian Constitution has never provided for an explicit prohibition of marriage between persons of the same sex. In particular, the Italian case has demonstrated that a series of

---

46  D. McAdam, *Political Process and the Development of Black Insurgency, 1930–1970* (University of Chicago Press 1982).

47  A. Sarat and A.S. Scheingold (eds), *Cause Lawyers and Social Movements* (Stanford University Press 2018), at 96.

48  D. NeJaime, 'Constitutional Change, Courts, and Social Movements' (2013) 111.6 Michigan Law Review 877, at 901.

49  L.M. Friedman, *The Legal System: A Social Science Perspective* (Russell Sage Foundation 1975).

judicial decisions favourable to the recognition of the right to marry between persons of the same sex (in 2016, when no LGBTQ rights were included in the legislation) was reached through a precise strategy implemented by a group of activist lawyers. *Affermazione civile* ('civil affirmation') is an Italian campaign for recognizing same-sex marriage. Its method consists in finding couples willing to request the publication of their marriage. According to Art. 98 of the Italian Civil Code, if the registrar does not consider the proceedings as valid, (s)he will deny their publication. But, in so doing, (s)he has to provide the parties with a certificate including the motivations for refusal. It is a right for parties to challenge the decision and resort to the tribunal. This is the strategy followed by the legal team through a network of lawyers called Rete Lenford which generally takes charge of the appeal. The path of service begins before the legal phase, with support and attention in the explanation of the strategy.[50] In Italy, civil unions have been provided for by law (2016) but not same-sex marriage.

The recent Irish mobilization to 'Repeal the 8th' was a campaign aimed at the elimination of an article of the Irish Constitution prohibiting abortion. Here a social movement has been able to obtain a real and important change in the law through a campaign that succeeded in obtaining, first, a change in public opinion. Beyond being prohibited, abortion was a criminal offence and a woman could only obtain a lawful abortion when her life was at risk. The amendment equated the life of the pregnant woman with that of the foetus, effectively criminalizing the interruption of pregnancy and any other medical intervention that could put the life of the foetus at risk, also to save the mother. In 1981, in response to the legalization of abortion in several European countries during the Seventies, a movement of opinion became strong in Ireland, calling for the introduction of a Constitution clause that would block national legislation from the possibility of liberalizing abortion in the future. Two years later, this clause became part of the Constitution through a national referendum. However, over the years an anti-abortion movement was also forming, which has increasingly grown since 2013, bringing together different repertoires of protest, from marches to street art, diaspora movements such as the London-Irish Abortion Rights Campaign and in general a huge range of progressive population fighting for 'the choice', as in the case of the so-called Lawyers for Choice and other institutional figures that joined together to create the Coalition to Repeal the 8th:

---

[50] X. Chiaramonte, 'Un caso di disgregazione creativa. La corte di cassazione sul matrimonio omosessuale' (2012) 2 Sociologia del diritto 151.

The Irish Constitution might not have a formal process for the popular initiation of a referendum, but what the 2018 referendum shows—as did the referendum on the 34th amendment (marriage equality) and, indeed, on the 8th amendment itself—is that Irish constitutional change can be, and sometimes is, popularly driven.[51]

## V  Becoming-Constituent

The new theories of societal constitutionalism promote the rethinking of the role of social movements in the constitutional process at large. Starting from the new forms of government and global politics, the new constitutionalists invite us to change the perspective through which we typically look at the constitution, whether it is understood in a formal way or in a 'material way'.[52] The idea is that the law does not exhaust itself in the complex of the norms in force subordinated to a formally established constitution. According to this theory, above the formal constitution, there would be an original material constitution to be considered legal par excellence, because from it one derives the criterion for imprinting juridical nature on the whole system. In other words, the new constitutional thinking seems to be attached to the idea of a 'living instrument',[53] a law that cannot be considered only in its formal aspects, but which changes with the changing of society. We should 'see constitutionalism, not just as a formal State structure, but also as a dynamic process'.[54] It is a complex and broad constituent process, which does not only imply the modification of one or more legal norms.

According to the contemporary constitutional thought, it consists in the formation from below of a new constituent moment in which social movements are protagonists as organized forms of both the so-called civil society—in its version of 'disorganized civil society, genuinely plural, resistant to dominant representations that call it into line and thus undercut its radical potential'[55]—and of what Partha Chatterjee (2006) has called 'political society', namely that

---

51   F. De Londras, 'Repeal the 8th: Activism, Social Movement, and Constitutional Change in Ireland' (2 March 2018), available at https://constitutional-change.com/tag/ireland/ (accessed 7 April 2019).
52   C. Mortati, *La Costituzione in senso materiale* (Giuffrè 1940).
53   E. Ehrlich, *Fundamental Principles of the Sociology of Law* (Harvard University Press 1936).
54   D. Greenberg et al., *Constitutionalism and Democracy: Transitions in the Contemporary World* (OUP 1993), at xvi.
55   E. Christodoulidis, 'Constitutional Irresolution: Law and the Framing of Civil Society' (2003) 9.4 European Law Journal 401, at 401.

part of the population usually excluded but which instead can demonstrate negotiation skills using governmental techniques.[56] In other words, the challenge is to draw attention on those 'popular forms of politics which are of most relevance to the bulk of the planet'.[57] The potential of a new constituent process could lie precisely not in remaining theoretically stuck on the role of civil society—such is the research subject for social movements studies—but rather considering the broader social structure, *the governed*, as agents for change. 'Constituent power is the product of an internal and immanent social dynamic, the product of the life of the multitude constituting its fabric of expression'.[58]

Although it would be useful to offer concrete cases which demonstrate what a constitutional moment may be, one should recognize that the very notion of a 'constitutional moment' is more an ideal than an empirically verifiable phenomenon. In addition to the cases described in the previous paragraphs, it is useful to mention the role of the Permanent Peoples' Tribunal (PPT).[59] As its decisions are not binding, this institution plays an unofficial role, but the PPT has managed to support bottom-up charges against an entire system and against States that, by promoting market logic, end up legitimizing the system. The PPT is a non-State court which manages to cross national borders and therefore impeach States themselves. Furthermore, it is a court of opinion, hence it operates in a way which is fundamentally different than the criminal law which seeks to impose responsibility for wrongdoing through solely individual liability.

An important decision from the PPT is the case of *Fundamental Rights, Participation of Local Communities and Mega Projects: From the Lyon–Turin High-Speed Rail to the Global Reality*. In this case, the strongest and longest-standing

---

[56] P. Chatterjee, *The Politics of the Governed. Reflections on Popular Politics in Most of the World* (Columbia University Press 2006).

[57] G.W. Anderson, 'Societal Constitutionalism, Social Movements, and Constitutionalism from below' (2013) 20.2 Indiana Journal of Global Legal Studies 881, at 901.

[58] E. Christodoulidis, 'Constitutional Irresolution: Law and the Framing of Civil Society' (2003) 9.4 European Law Journal 401, at 431–432.

[59] As described in the decision of the case presented: 'The Peoples' Permanent Tribunal (PPT) is an international organization founded in 1979 with the aim of rendering the process that began with the Russell Tribunal on Vietnam (1966–67) and on Latin American dictators (1974–76) permanent: guaranteeing space for visibility, for voices to be heard, for judgments on systemic violations of human, individual and collective rights, as well as the rights of peoples who do not find an institutional response in single countries or in communities of States' (*Fundamental Rights, Participation of Local Communities and Mega Projects: From the Lyon–Turin High-Speed Rail to the Global Reality* (Judgment of the Permanent Peoples' Tribunal, Turin-Almese Session, 5–8 November 2015).

Italian social movement presented its case to the PPT: the motivations for their 'No' to the TAV mega-project are based on the established futility of the project, since it is neither at the level of saturation of the existing railway nor even in the face of an increase in freight traffic by road or rail. Their motivations for saying 'No' are also based on the high and unjustified cost of the project, which from being a passenger train has become a train for the transport of goods at quadrupled costs, on the release of harmful substances contained in the mountains to be excavated, mainly uranium, radon and asbestos.[60] This grassroots struggle was opposed not only to the substance of the project but also to the method under which the megaproject was negotiated in secret. After 25 years of seeking legal protection while being targeted by prosecution, the movement eventually appealed to the PPT. According to the tribunal, planned megaprojects 'do not respond to the outcomes of general interest proclaimed by the sponsors' but are rather based on illegitimate constitutional aim.

In particular, the Tribunal invokes

> the International Charter of Human Rights which is the basis for all national constitutions. It was later reinforced by other international instruments. More recently, it has explicitly stipulated social groups and ethnic minorities, after they had demanded recognition and self-determination for which a more general wording is provided by Art. 16 of the Universal Declaration of Human Rights proclaimed in Algiers in 1976. It is considered as the specific frame of reference (on the doctrinal and operational level) for all activities, working criteria and rulings of the PPT: 'Every people has the right to conserve, protect and improve its environment'.

The No Tav case is also mentioned in the 2018 World Report on the Situation of Human Rights Defenders of the UN Special Rapporteur on the Situation of Human Rights Defenders where it is noted that 'defenders associated with environmental rights group No-Tav have faced criminal charges of terrorism'.[61]

To conclude, thinking around social movements and constitutions together remains problematic because the classical constitutional theory does not take the former into consideration. And, as underlined by Anderson,

> the absence of social movements from the constitutional literature is not coincidental, but can be attributed to the potential difficulties they pose

---

60  L. Giunti et al., 'Economic, Environmental and Energy Assessment of the Turin–Lyon High-Speed Rail' (2012) 2.4 International Journal of Ecosystems and Ecology Sciences 361.

61  UN Special Rapporteur on the Situation of Human Rights Defenders Michael Forst, 'World Report on the Situation of Human Rights Defenders' (December 2018), at 477.

to some core elements of constitutional thought. In particular, bringing social movements into proximity with constitutional theory calls into question assumptions that constitutionalism is inherently institutional, Western in origin, and normatively positive.[62]

The issue at stake is a timeless one: people embody the constituent power but under the condition of a constitutional form. The paradox consists in the impossibility for the (symbolic?) holder of a power to effectively exercise this very power. Perhaps, one could hear the echo of Marx's famous argument in *The Eighteenth Brumaire of Louis Bonaparte* (1852): men make history but under circumstances existing already. We face the ancient and crucial problem concerning the intertwining of objectivism and subjectivism. In other words, there are 'two fundamental though antagonistic imperatives: that governmental power ultimately is generated from the "consent of the people" and that, to be sustained and effective, such power must be divided, constrained, and exercised through distinctive institutional forms'.[63] Subjects encounter objective forms and have to deal with those unavoidable and required conditions.

This topic should not be misunderstood. The forms can also be considered as disadvantageous, and eventually this would remind us that institutions, as such, have nothing natural about them, and for this very reason, should be changed if they are outdated. At the same time, institutions are necessary as long as we satisfy our instincts through them (in a common and shared way).[64]

Returning to the legal aspect of the matter, it seems that to overcome this dimension of constitutional scholarship, it is necessary to build a real 'theory of resistance' that aspires to lay the basis for a 'political' International law enabling legal scholarship to take the empirical reality seriously: namely, 'the praxes of social movements' that 'challenge the very foundations of international law, and provide a more realistic and promising means of imagining' a post-national and post-colonial societal constitutionalism.[65] 'Constitutionalism from below not only stands for a different approach to framing the exercise of political power, but also rests on a different understanding of the nature of that power'. In other words, not only are social movements 'often catalysts for

---

62   G.W. Anderson, 'Societal Constitutionalism, Social Movements, and Constitutionalism from below' (2013) 20.2 Indiana Journal of Global Legal Studies 881, at 884.
63   M. Loughlin and N. Walker (eds), *The Paradox of Constitutionalism: Constituent Power and Constitutional Form* (OUP 2007), at 1.
64   G. Deleuze, *Istinti e istituzioni* (Mimesis 2000).
65   B. Rajagopal, 'International Law and Social Movements: Challenges of Theorizing Resistance' (2003) 41 Colum. J. Transnat'l L. 397, at 418.

social transformation against apparently over determining structures, but to the extent their endeavours are directed to changing these structures, they can be seen to generate more than simply discrete acts of resistance'.[66] As Deleuze would say, we need a practice of becoming-constituent.

66  G.W. Anderson, 'Societal Constitutionalism, Social Movements, and Constitutionalism from below' (2013) 20.2 Indiana Journal of Global Legal Studies 881, at 902–906.

CHAPTER 15

# The International Regulation and Governance of Time

*Andreas Witte**

### Abstract

The paper examines the system for the regulation and governance of time, both with respect to the time of day (i.e., clock readings), and calendar dates. Sub-topics of the two areas include the definition of Universal Time Coordinated (UTC), time zones, daylight saving time, and the International Date Line (IDL). The analysis begins, for both areas, by briefly sketching out the scientific background—without which the subsequent legal and institutional discussion would not be meaningful—and the historical development. It then goes on to describe the present-day mechanism for the regulation of both areas. This examination will reveal noteworthy differences: whereas the regulation of clock readings is based on a complex interplay between national statutes and government laboratories, international organizations, and non-governmental organizations, hardly any formal legal or institutional framework is in place for the regulation of calendars. An explanation for this discrepancy is suggested. The paper then proceeds to address questions of interpretation where international legal instruments make reference to time without specifying the relevant time reckoning system; a solution is proposed which builds on 19th-century domestic litigation, adapted to the context of public international law. A final paragraph draws more general conclusions and undertakes a brief outlook into the future.

### Keywords

Time – Calendar – Time Zones – International Date Line – Metrology – Greenwich – International Telecommunication Union – International Bureau of Weights and Measures

---

* The paper is based on a personal interest of the author and not connected to the activities of the ECB or reflective of its positions.

## I  Introduction

*What time is it?* In today's world, people ask this question countless times each day and obtain the answer by consulting their wristwatch, a wall clock, or an indicator in the corner of their computer or smartphone screens. We take it for granted that there is an unequivocal answer to this question, and this answer may become of crucial importance in a legal dispute, for instance when the expiry of a deadline or an issue of chronological priority is at stake; events take place in time; and innumerable provisions in national as well as international law attach legal consequences to the points in time when events occur or to the period that elapses between the two events. An accurate measurement which attaches an unambiguous label to any given point in time for record-keeping or scheduling is essential to the functioning of modern society.

However, who defined what the clock and calendar should read? Who decided that one should turn back one's wristwatch by five hours when boarding a flight from London to New York? It turns out that there is both an extensive history and a surprisingly complex institutional mechanism behind this, which most people are not aware of even though it governs the rhythm with which they live their professional and private lives. No wonder the American Society of International Law put the 'globally recognized system for telling time' first on its list of a hundred ways international law shapes our lives.[1]

The present paper will examine this system—which has frequently been described from a scientific or historical angle—through the lawyer's eyes. Section II will focus on the time of the day, as expressed in clock readings; it will commence with a sketch of the scientific background and continue with a historical overview before examining in detail how the present governance for the regulation of time works, both institutionally and legally. Section III will discuss the calendar, again with short subsections on the scientific background and the historical development before describing the institutional framework for the definition of today's calendar system. It will also address the history and legal background of the International Date Line. Section IV is dedicated to interpretative problems when international legal instruments make references to time without describing the timekeeping system to be taken as authoritative. Section V draws summarizing conclusions on a more abstract level.

---

[1]  ASIL, *International Law: 100 Ways it Shapes Our Lives* (ASIL 2018), at 2.

## II Clock Readings

### 1 *Scientific Background*

The most intuitively obvious unit of time is the *apparent solar day*, whose duration[2] is astronomically defined as the interval between two noons, with noon being, for a given point on the Earth's surface, the moment when the Sun stands on the same meridian of longitude as the observer[3]—in other words, when, for an observer on the Northern Hemisphere, the Sun is due south. This is also the moment when it reaches its highest point above the horizon (*culmination* or *meridian transit*). This diurnal motion of the Sun around the Earth is, of course, only apparent. It is the perceived result of two actual motions of the Earth, one around its own axis (the *rotation* of the Earth) and one around the Sun (the *revolution* of the Earth). The velocity of the former is very constant (though not quite as constant as was thought for a long time; cf below), while that of the latter is not and varies throughout one revolution around the Sun, i.e., one year, owing to the elliptic shape of the Earth's trajectory and the angle at which its axis is tilted towards the plane of revolution.

Consequently, the duration of the apparent solar day varies within a range of fifty seconds. These fluctuations balance out throughout a year at an average of 24 hours, leading to the astronomical concept of the *mean solar day* which is based on the average durations of solar days over the course of the year rather than the actual duration of any given apparent solar day. It can, in other words, be said to be based on the notion of a hypothetical Sun apparently revolving around the Earth at constant, rather than varying, velocity.[4] Note that a definition of the length of the day based on sunrise or sunset would result in much more strongly fluctuating lengths of a day, since the times of these events vary considerably depending on the season.

This mean solar[5] day is the basis for *mean solar time*, whereby, conventionally, a clock reading of 12:00 is assigned to the mean noon moment, and the

---

2   The moment of noon defines the *duration* of the day but not necessarily its *beginning*. Throughout human history, social conventions differed as to the moment that marked the end of one day and the beginning of the next. Modern convention takes midnight (lying halfway between the two noons) as the point of reference, but astronomers and sailors preferred for a long time the noon moment. For Roman law, see Paulus, Digest 2.12.8.
3   E. Danson, *Weighing the World: The Quest to Measure the Earth* (OUP 2006), at 255.
4   J.C. Adams, 'The Definition of Mean Solar Time' (1884) 3 Science 323.
5   A concept different from the solar day is the *sidereal* day, defined as one full rotation of the Earth around its own axis. Since the Earth does not only rotate around its own axis but also revolves around the Sun, this rotation does not ensure the return of the Sun to the same point in the sky as one rotation before. The Earth has to rotate 'a little extra' to make up for the distance which the Earth has meanwhile revolved around the Sun. The sidereal day has a

day extends from there by twelve equal hours forwards and backwards. Astronomers have understood this for centuries and been able to calculate with great precision the difference between apparent and mean solar time, which is traditionally called the *equation of time* and which can amount to up to about 16 minutes depending on the season.[6] Since both apparent and mean solar time are defined on the basis of the diurnal motion of the Sun across the observer's meridian, they are dependent on the observer's location on the Earth. All points along the same meridian will share the same solar time, but points that lie on different meridians will experience differences in solar time relative to each other. This amounts to one hour of difference in time per 15 degrees of difference in longitude,[7] or one minute of difference in time per 15 minutes of difference in longitude,[8] and the mean noon position of the Sun travels at this pace across the surface of the Earth in an east-west direction.

For a long time, it was thought that the velocity with which the Earth rotates around its axis was constant. Since the variations in the length of an apparent solar day resulting from the revolution of the Earth around the Sun average out over the course of a year, this would mean that the length of the mean solar day, which averages out these variations, would remain unchanged over the years. This supposed constancy was the reason why the mean solar day was in the past chosen as the basis for the definition of the other units of time by subdividing it into 24 hours, with each hour consisting of 60 minutes and each minute of 60 seconds.[9] Consequently, the second would constitute the 86,400th part of a mean solar day, and indeed this was, for a long time, used as the formal definition of the second for both civil and scientific purposes, effectively regarding the rotating Earth as a timekeeping device of great accuracy. It is, however, now known that the rotation is steadily slowing down as a consequence of the tidal friction of the oceans created by the gravitational forces of the Moon. The length of a mean solar day thus increases by between one and two milliseconds per century and is already slightly longer than 86,400

---

duration of only about 23:56 hours. It is not easily observable and is thus historically of lesser importance as a basis for timekeeping than the solar day.

6  J.D. Betts, 'Solar Time' in *Encyclopaedia Britannica* (2007).
7  360° (full circle) divided by 24. One degree of angular measurement is subdivided into 60 minutes, of 60 seconds each.
8  For the sake of comparison: on the latitude of London, this corresponds to about 17 kilometres in straight east-west direction—roughly the longitudinal difference between Charing Cross and Hounslow.
9  The use of twelve and sixty as numerical bases for the sub-division of units of time is a consequence of very old mathematical traditions rooted in ancient Babylonia: F.R. Stephenson, *Historical Eclipses and Earth's Rotation* (CUP 1997), at 2–3.

seconds. In addition, other rotational irregularities exist which cause further, less steady and predictable, variations in the duration of the mean solar day.[10] The accumulation of such seemingly minuscule effects over longer periods is sufficient not only to be measured but to cause a practical need for adjustment, analogous to the periodical re-setting of a clock which has become desynchronized from the time which it is supposed to track. For this purpose, leap seconds are used, the mechanism for which will be explained below. This gradual deceleration of the Earth is also the reason why, since 1967, the formal scientific definition of the second has made reference not to the rotation of the Earth but rather to the frequency of a particular electromagnetic radiation which can be artificially generated in caesium atomic clocks and which is, in fact, constant. This re-definition has been calibrated so that this 'atomic second' corresponds in length to the 86,400th part of the mean solar day in the year 1820.[11] In this sense, the solar day can still be said to form the foundation of time measurement, even though for scientific purposes, not the day but the second derived from it is to be used as the standard unit.

## 2  Historical Development
### a  Prior to 1884

The ancient Babylonians, Egyptians, Greeks, and Romans measured time by subdividing daytime (from sunrise to sunset) and night-time (from sunset to sunrise) into twelve *temporal hours* each.[12] This meant that the duration of the hours varied depending on the season, and furthermore that on any given day (except for the two equinoxes) a day hour and a night hour were of unequal length. This was known to the Ancients but not perceived to pose a problem in practical use.[13]

---

10  R.A. Nelson et al., 'The Leap Second: Its History and Possible Future' (2001) 38 Metrologia 509, at 511–512.

11  M. Mobberley, *Total Solar Eclipses and How to Observe Them* (Springer 2007), at 18. The year 1820 was not chosen deliberately. It is a consequence of the fact that the 1967 definition of the second was based on astronomical observations made between 1750 and 1892, and the duration of the solar day in 1820 was the average during this period: D.D. McCarthy, C. Hackman and R.A. Nelson, 'The Physical Basis of the Leap Second' (2008) 136 Astronomical Journal 1906, at 1907.

12  G. Dohrn-van Rossum, *Die Geschichte der Stunde. Uhren und moderne Zeitordnungen* (Hanser 1992), at 26.

13  Ancient engineering was capable of building water-driven clocks (*clepsydrae*) which could measure hours of equal length (though with poor accuracy, by modern standards). They were, however, less widespread than sundials. In a system of varying temporal hours, such a water clock required either varying scales or constant re-adjustment:

After mechanical clocks became widely available in the late Middle Ages, this system was replaced with the now-familiar subdivision of the entire day, comprising both bright daylight and the night, into 24 hours of equal length. The usual practice for the subsequent centuries was for each town or city to have its own local apparent time, and from the 18th century onwards its local mean time[14] displayed on public clocks. This meant that no common standard for a greater region was available and that even cities in close proximity could be subject to a slight time shift relative to each other.[15] Again, these discrepancies were not perceived as posing practical problems because travel between places of different times was slow. For centuries, 'official' time was therefore for the city dweller whatever was indicated by the clock on the local church belfry or city hall, which differed from the time indicated on the clock of the closest neighbouring city; the peasant population, meanwhile, did not have a need for precise timekeeping and maintained its daily rhythm by direct observation of the Sun.

There were two developments which subsequently created a need for harmonization. The first was the realization that it was possible to determine the geographic longitude of a ship—which had long been a major problem in navigation—by observing the noon moment at the ship's location and calculating the difference of it against the local time of a defined meridian of reference.[16] The time difference between the two places can be directly converted into the difference in longitude. As soon as sufficiently accurate marine chronometers became available in the 18th century, it became common practice for ships to be equipped with them and set them, upon departure, to the precise time of a fixed meridian against which they would measure longitude during their voyage.[17] For Britain, this role was performed by the meridian of the Royal Observatory at Greenwich, where astronomical observations were made to determine its exact local time on a daily basis and display it visibly via the dropping of the famous time ball. This allowed passing ships to set their clocks to 'Greenwich Mean Time' (GMT, the mean solar time at Greenwich).

---

J.E. Armstrong and J.M. Camp, 'Notes on a Water Clock in the Athenian Agora' (1977) 46 *Hesperia* 147.

14  D. Howse, *Greenwich Time and the Longitude* (Philip Wilson 1997), at 88.

15  Sometimes, this was complemented by other irregularities, such as an odd local peculiarity existing for centuries in Basel: H. Stohler, 'Die Sonnenuhren am Basler Münster und die alte Basler Stundenzählung: Eine historische und technische Untersuchung' (1942) 41 Basler Zeitschrift für Geschichte und Altertumskunde 253.

16  Unlike latitude, where the equator constitutes a self-suggesting point of reference, no such natural zero exists for longitude. It requires definition by human convention.

17  For a bestselling account of this story, see D. Sobel, *Longitude* (Penguin 1995).

Other countries operated their own observatories, and consequently other prime meridians were also in use, e.g. that of Paris or of El Hierro in the Canary Islands. Nonetheless, Greenwich became the dominant standard internationally, since many seafarers of other nations also used the nautical almanacks published by the Royal Observatory for navigation.

The second development was the rise of faster means of communication and transport in the 19th century. This made time differences between cities perceptible in practice. Railway companies, in particular, faced difficulties in operating a regular service, scheduled to a precision of minutes, if the stations along the route were using different local times. The response consisted, first, in the use of conversion tables which permitted the translation of local mean times at different cities into each other, and subsequently in the definition of 'railway time' which was to be used throughout the entire network. The first country to do so was Great Britain, in which the various railway companies gradually adopted, in the 1840s, GMT as unified railway time.[18] The choice of Greenwich was the result of its already dominant position in shipping. Initially, this use of a de-localized standard was meant for railway purposes only and thus alongside local time, rather than superseding it. For a while, stations would thus feature separate clocks indicating both.[19] In practice, however, many local authorities in Britain soon decided to set all public clocks in their towns and cities to GMT rather than local time, a development which sometimes provoked resistance from contemporaries who perceived this 'railway-time aggression'[20] as a deviation from the divinely ordained local solar time. It also caused litigation to clarify the legal ambiguity between GMT and local time. The confusion finally came to an end when, by statute adopted in 1880, it was stipulated that all references to time in legal instruments were to be understood as references to GMT unless stated otherwise, effectively establishing it as the official time for all of Great Britain.[21]

The development in many other industrialized countries followed very similar lines. Railway companies in the United States, in particular, also standardized times across their networks, but owing to a large number of independently operating enterprises, there were many 'railway times' in use. An overall norm for the entire country was not practically feasible since its enormous east-west expanse meant that this would create differences between local solar times and

---

18   Howse, *Greenwich Time and the Longitude*, at 91–94.
19   E. Zerubavel, 'The Standardization of Time: A Sociohistorical Perspective' (1982) 88 American Journal of Sociology 1, at 9.
20   (Anonymous) 'Railway-Time Aggression' (1851) 15 Chambers's Edinburgh Journal 392.
21   Statutes (Definition of Time) Act 1880 (43 & 44 Vict. C. 9). It survives in s. 9 of the Interpretation Act 1978.

the nationwide standard of several hours. Building on proposals developed by the American college professor Charles Dowd and the Canadian railway engineer Sandford Fleming, a solution was agreed in 1881 by a conference of railway companies whereby the United States was divided into four stripes running in a north-south direction, each of them 15 degrees of longitude wide. All stations within one of these time zones would use the same standard time, and these standard times were offset by whole hours against each other as well as GMT. This was practical because the centre meridians of each zone were multiples of 15 degrees west of Greenwich, and 15 degrees of longitude corresponds to exactly one hour; the standardized time of each zone was thus identical to the local solar mean time of this central meridian. The preceding discussion had at times favoured the Washington meridian as the reference against which the full-hour offsets would be calculated,[22] but the scheme as finally adopted relied on the Greenwich meridian, which was already widely used in international navigation.[23] On 18 November 1883, the plan entered into force, and the four new time zones replaced 53 different company-specific railway times.[24] In effect, this meant that for most places—all those which were not located on the central meridian of their time zone—, the new standardized time would deviate from local mean solar time, but in no case by more than half an hour, which was considered a small price to pay for overcoming the problems which the previous state of affairs had created. As in Britain, it was, initially, a private law effort of cooperating privately owned commercial enterprises; it was not given official status under federal law until 1918,[25] and in the meantime, only few States had enacted State legislation to this effect.[26]

b    The International Meridian Conference of 1884

Despite this private character of the standardization in America, it soon served as a role model for public sector action. In 1883, an invitation was extended by the U.S. Government to all countries then in diplomatic relations with it to

---

22   The desire for Washington can partially be explained by patriotic sentiments, but also has a rational consideration in its support. The US Naval Observatory located there would have been able to provide high-quality data on the basis of its local meridian. This mirrors the importance which the site of the Royal Observatory had for the choice in favour of Greenwich.
23   I.R. Bartky, 'The Adoption of Standard Time' (1989) 30 Technology and Culture 25.
24   I.R. Bartky, 'The Invention of Railroad Time' (1983) 148 Railroad History 13. Contemporaneously (Anonymous) 'Railway Time Belts' (10 October 1883) New York Times 4.
25   Standard Time Act of 1918 (now 15 USC 260–267, as amended).
26   J. Parrish, 'Litigating Time in America at the Turn of the Twentieth Century' (2002) 36 Akron LR 1, at fn 26.

attend a conference in Washington in order to remedy what the invitational note called 'embarrassments' to commerce arising from 'the absence of a common and accepted standard for the computation of time'. Previous gatherings of scientific societies had discussed the matter, but this conference was supposed to bring together participants as representatives of their governments, rather than in an individual capacity. Two dozen countries accepted the invitation and sent delegates to Washington in 1884, with most major seafaring powers represented.

Contrary to what is sometimes stated, this International Meridian Conference did not define the present global system of time zones. Such an idea—effectively an extension of the American railway scheme globally—was an obvious suggestion, and it was presented to the Conference.[27] Alternatively, a counter-proposal of a more granular system was suggested, with narrower time zones two-and-a-half degrees of longitude, or ten minutes, wide.[28] The delegates, however, considered themselves not authorized to determine rules for the reckoning of local time. The final act[29] in which the outcome of the debates and votes was summarized thus limited itself to more modest resolutions: The definition of the Greenwich meridian as the prime meridian of the world from which 180 degrees of longitude would be counted eastwards and westwards; the definition of a 'universal day for all purposes for which it may be found convenient' which would be based on the mean solar day on this prime meridian; the extension of midnight as the definition of the beginning of the day also for astronomical and nautical purposes (where different beginnings of the day had for a long time been in use); and an expression of hope that the decimal system would also be introduced for angular measurements.

Even though the 1884 Conference did, thus, not formally establish the present time zone system, it did define the Greenwich meridian as the worldwide point of reference for the measurement of longitude—to which terrestrial time is directly linked. State practice in the subsequent decades strongly converged towards legislation which standardized time based on that meridian and offset against it by a round time shift—preferably an integral number of hours, following the American model. Even France, which had long opposed the Greenwich meridian and which, in 1891, defined the mean solar time at

---

27  International Conference Held at Washington for the Purpose of Fixing a Prime Meridian and a Universal Day (ed.), *Protocols of the Proceedings* (Gibson Bros. 1884), at 136–142.
28  International Conference Held at Washington for the Purpose of Fixing a Prime Meridian and a Universal Day (ed.), *Protocols of the Proceedings*, at 190.
29  International Conference Held at Washington for the Purpose of Fixing a Prime Meridian and a Universal Day (ed.), *Protocols of the Proceedings*, at 199–204.

Paris as its nationwide standard time,[30] subsequently succumbed and, in 1911, switched to the Greenwich standard.[31] All these measures were introduced by means of unilateral national legislation, not defined by a treaty or another international instrument. Nonetheless, by World War I, the system was so established on land that two smaller international conferences in 1917 and 1920 explicitly extended it to the high seas, recommending that ships should obey one-hour time zones 15 degrees of longitude wide, instead of continuing the old nautical tradition of resetting, every day at noon, the clocks that govern life on board to the local solar time of their position at that moment.[32]

c    Developments after 1884

Following the International Meridian Conference, the Greenwich-based system was continuously refined. Two major themes dominated this development: The construction of ever more precise timekeepers, culminating in today's atomic clocks whose drift amounts to fractions of a second in millions of years, and an ongoing internationalization of the institutional mechanism, which can only briefly be summarized here.

Initially, the astronomical observations and clocks necessary to express the abstractly defined concept of GMT—or Universal Time (UT), as it came to be called—in the numerical form of days, hours, minutes, and seconds, in other words, to produce 'realizations' of GMT/UT, remained purely national. Many countries operated their own observatories, which disseminated time signals for use by the public, first via telegraph lines, soon via radio. Discrepancies between these national signals motivated the *Bureau des longitudes*, a French scientific government commission set up in 1795 to address problems of navigation and timekeeping, to invite other countries to attend an international conference in Paris in 1912. This initiative resulted in the establishment of an executive body, the *Bureau international de l'heure* (BIH). The intention was to establish it as a genuinely international organization, based on a founding convention which would be a treaty under international law. Owing to World War I, this convention was never ratified, and so BIH continued to operate on a provisional and legally informal basis.[33] It remained operative until 1987, effectively as a department (without distinct legal personality) of the Paris

---

30    Law of 14 March 1891, Journal officiel, No. 73/1891, at 1233.
31    Law of 9 March 1911, Journal officiel, No. 68/1911, 1882. Patriotically, the wording of the statute avoided direct reference to Greenwich. It stipulated that the legal time for France was to be Paris mean solar time delayed by 9:21 minutes (which results in GMT).
32    V. Ogle, *The Global Transformation of Time* (HUP 2015), at 88; A.C.D. Crommelin, 'Time at Sea and the Astro-Nomical Day' (1918) 101 Nature 146.
33    Howse, *Greenwich Time and the Longitude*, at 155–156.

Observatory, which provided the necessary logistical and administrative resources as well as management.[34]

The main activity of the BIH was to collect high-precision time data from a large number of observatories worldwide, average it into an international standard (*heure définitive*), and to publish this standard in the form of the measured numerical deviation between it and each national signal—a concept which, as will be seen below, continues in refined form to this day. First, the national data came from high-precision pendulum clocks, subsequently from quartz clocks. In 1961, BIH then took over the administration of an international system of atomic clock signals which had begun as a bilateral British-American cooperation and which ultimately grew into the present TAI (see below). In 1965, it began to calculate UT on the basis of this atomic timescale with the addition of a fixed offset, a mechanism which persists to this day (see infra).[35] At the end of 1987, the BIH was dissolved, and its responsibilities were taken over by two successor institutions which will also be discussed in detail below.

### 3    The Present-Day International Mechanism for the Regulation of Clock Readings

a    Determination of UTC

The present mechanism for the harmonized time of the world is based upon the aim of reconciling two principles. The first principle is to have a time standard which is based on as accurate as possible a count of the seconds (as the basic unit of time) as they elapse. The second principle is to generate a time standard which stays close to the mean solar time on the Greenwich meridian and therefore to the astronomically observed rotation of the Earth. The two principles are not easily reconciled since the rotation of the Earth is not perfectly constant.

The first of these principles is realized by means of a time standard known as International Atomic Time (*temps atomique international*, TAI). TAI is simply a count of the number of seconds which have elapsed since its initiation in 1958 (when it was identical to GMT), even though it is, by convention, expressed not as a running tally of seconds but in the form of hours, minutes and seconds. There is no single international master TAI clock. Instead, a large number (currently about 70) of metrological institutes and laboratories maintained by national governments around the world each operate their own atomic

---

34   S. Dick et al. (eds), *Polar Motion: Historical and Scientific Problems* (Astronomical Society of the Pacific 2000), at 175–176.

35   Nelson et al., 'The Leap Second: Its History and Possible Future', at 511–515; Dick et al. (eds), *Polar Motion: Historical and Scientific Problems*, at 182.

clocks—several hundred in total—and communicate their data electronically to the International Bureau of Weights and Measures (*Bureau international des poids et mesures*, BIPM; its legal nature will be discussed below). The BIPM's Time Department collects this information and calculates a weighted average, which produces TAI. This method improves both accuracy—because the computation of the average smoothens imprecisions of individual clocks—and neutrality of TAI as an international standard—because no single national clock is authoritative for other countries. The use of TAI is thus closely linked to the scientific re-definition of the second in terms of caesium radiation, which is used in the oscillators of atomic clocks.

If TAI were used as a time standard, it would, gradually, fall out of synchronicity with the rotation of the Earth. This would produce problems for astronomy and classical (i.e., not based on satellites) navigation, which rely on observations of the skies. In order to avoid this, and thereby pay tribute to the second principle, TAI is continuously compared against a time scale called Universal Time 1, or UT1. Conceptually, UT1 is defined as the mean solar time at Greenwich, in other words, GMT.[36] For maximum accuracy, though, UT1 is determined not by observing the Sun but rather on data describing the Earth's rotation angle provided by the GPS satellite navigation system and by the observation of very distant celestial bodies by means of radio astronomy. These observations are conducted by public astronomy and geodesy institutions worldwide and coordinated and collected by a scientific body called the International Earth Rotation and Reference Systems Service (previously called the International Earth Rotation Service and still abbreviated to IERS; its legal nature will be described below).

UT1 provides, thus, the benchmark against which the TAI time scale is adjusted. The mechanism for this adjustment is simple: TAI is converted into the global standard, Universal Time Coordinated (UTC[37]), by means of subtraction. When the UTC system was established in 1972, it was defined as TAI minus ten seconds; these *leap seconds* were inserted to compensate for the discrepancy between TAI and UT1/GMT which had accumulated since the start of the TAI timescale in 1958. UTC is never allowed to deviate by more than

---

36  More precisely, it is defined as mean solar time at the prime meridian corrected for polar variation, a small movement in the Earth's axis of rotation. The aim of this very slight correction is to ensure direct correspondence of UT1 with the angular position of the Earth around its axis of diurnal rotation. See Recommendation ITU-R TF.460–6, Section A.

37  It is claimed that the oddly sounding term is a linguistic compromise between what one would expect in English (universal coordinated time, UCT) and French (*temps universel coordonné*, TUC): C. Lorenz and B. Bevernage (eds), *Breaking up Time* (Vandenhoeck 2013), at 206.

0.9 seconds from UT1. If the irregularities in the rotation of the Earth, as observed and expressed in UT1, accumulate to such an extent that the difference between UT1 and UTC were to exceed this limit, an additional leap second will be introduced, reducing the difference between UTC and UT1, and thus the actual rotation of the Earth, to below 0.9 seconds. Since 1972, 27 leap seconds, in addition to the initial ten seconds at the inception of the system, have been inserted, so that presently[38] UTC is defined as TAI minus 37 seconds.

This need for leap seconds is irregular and cannot be predicted over longer periods. The last leap second so far was introduced on 31 December 2016, when 23:59:59 UTC was followed one second later by 23:59:60 UTC, which was, in turn, followed one second later by 00:00:00 UTC, 1 January 2017. In other words, the last minute of 2016 contained 61 rather than the usual 60 seconds. The practice of the IERS is to introduce leap seconds either at the end of June or the end of December and to announce them about six months in advance.[39] The IERS also maintains the option of negative leap seconds (i.e., shortening the last minute of December or June to 59 seconds), to compensate for an accelerating rotation of the Earth, but so far none has occurred.

The UTC time scale thus generated is the closest approximation to an 'official time of the world' in existence, and has, for these purposes, replaced GMT, to which it corresponds almost exactly (with a maximum deviation of 0.9 seconds). It forms the backbone of the world's time zone system in the sense that time zones are defined by reference to UTC, with an offset added to (for locations east of Greenwich) or subtracted from (for locations west of Greenwich) UTC. UTC in its international variant is, however, not directly disseminated to private users: The time signals which are distributed via the internet and broadcast by TV and radio stations and to which radio-controlled clocks synchronize automatically are not maintained by the BIPM but rather by the national laboratories which contribute to UTC. These signals are based on their respective national atomic clocks and therefore referred to as national 'realizations' of UTC, labelled 'UTC(k)', with 'k' representing the national institute maintaining them (e.g. UTC(PTB) for the German *Physikalisch-Technische Bundesanstalt*, UTC(NIST) for the American National Institute of Standards and Technology, etc.). These differences between the various UTC(k) and the averaged international UTC are very slight—in the range of nanoseconds, i.e., billionths of a second, far below the inaccuracies created by the dissemination technology,

---

[38] Until at least June 2020. It was announced in July 2019 that no leap second will occur on 31 December 2019.

[39] In IERS Bulletin C, available at https://www.iers.org/IERS/EN/Publications/Bulletins/bulletins.html (accessed 4 July 2019).

which are in the range of hundredths of a second.[40] Therefore, these differences do not constitute a practical problem except for very special applications, where appropriate corrections need to be made.[41] For this purpose, the BIPM continuously publishes the measured discrepancies between UTC and each UTC(k).[42]

b    The International Legal Character of the Bodies and Instruments Involved

Subsection 'a' has illustrated that a number of different actors are involved in the realization of UTC: National metrological institutes and government laboratories which maintain high-precision atomic clocks and disseminate time signals; the BIPM which collects data from national clocks and, on this basis, determines TAI and UTC as well as the deviations between UTC and each UTC(k); national geodesy and astronomy institutes which monitor the rotation of the Earth; and the IERS, which, on the basis of this data, determines the discrepancy between UTC and UT1 (solar mean time at Greenwich) and takes the decision to introduce a leap second when this discrepancy is about to exceed the accepted tolerance of 0.9 seconds.

The international legal basis for the competence of the BIPM and the IERS in the standardization of time is a recommendation of the International Telecommunication Union (ITU), an international organization and specialized agency of the United Nations (under Arts 57 and 63 of the UN Charter) dedicated to matters of telecommunication.[43] The reason why the ITU took it upon itself to regulate the matter was the use of radio time signals to disseminate standardized time. It is the practice of the ITU to issue a large number of

40   P.B. Whibberly et al., 'Local Representations of UTC in National Laboratories' (2011) 48 Metrologia 154, at 155–156.
41   An example for a non-scientific application where great precision is required is the electronic trading of securities at short intervals by automatic algorithms. For such trading venues, legislation often requires accuracy of recording, as measured against UTC, within a range of micro- or milliseconds (see e.g., Commission Delegated Regulation (EU) 2017/574 of 7 June 2016 Supplementing Directive 2014/65/EU of the European Parliament and of the Council with regard to Regulatory Technical Standards for the Level of Accuracy of Business Clocks (31 March 2017) OJ L 87/148).
42   In its monthly Circular T, available at https://www.bipm.org/en/bipm-services/time scales/time-ftp/Circular-T.html (accessed 5 March 2019).
43   The ITU far precedes the United Nations. It was founded as the International Telegraph Union in 1865 and lays claim to being one of the oldest international organizations. See, N.A. Graham and R.S. Jordan (eds), *The International Civil Service* (Pergamon 1980), at 105. It was thus part of the first wave of establishing international organizations, which first emerged to facilitate cooperation in technical areas: D.J. Bederman, 'The Souls of International Organizations' (1996) 36 VaJIL 275.

recommendations establishing technical standards for telecommunication. One of these recommendations, ITU-R TF.460-6, governs the UTC system described above, including the allocation of roles to the BIPM and the IERS,[44] and is the formal defining document of the world's timekeeping standard. It was last re-confirmed for continued application by an ITU standard-setting organ, the World Radiocommunication Conference, in its Resolution 655 (WRC-15) of 2015, subject to the proviso that ITU-R (the radiocommunication sector of the ITU) should 'study in cooperation with the relevant international organizations, concerned industries and user groups, through the participation of the membership, the various aspects of current and potential future reference time scales, including their impacts and applications' and to report back on the results of this dialogue to the Conference in 2023.[45] There is, thus, the possibility that the UTC system could be revised by the ITU in the near future. The leap second, in particular, is controversial because some writers doubt that in today's world where navigation relies on satellites rather than celestial observations, the advantages of keeping UTC close to UT1 outweigh the operational costs of the occasional insertion of leap seconds.[46] In case a reform is undertaken, it will most likely take the form of a new recommendation of the ITU, adopted after consultation of the other organizations involved.

Technically, recommendation TF.460-6 only concerns wireless time signals emitted by ITU Member States, and legally, it is non-binding. Nonetheless, there are references to UTC in other documents which the ITU is empowered to enact, on the basis of Art. 4 of its Constitution[47]—a treaty under international law—in a manner binding upon its Member States. This is, in particular, true for the Radio Regulations, the international provisions governing wireless communication, which require (in Art. 2.6) that whenever a specified time is used in international radio communication activities, UTC shall be applied, unless otherwise indicated. Most ITU Member States have made

---

44  The International Radio Consultative Committee, the ITU body which develops recommendations for radio communication, had already adopted Recommendation 374 in 1963 which is the forerunner of today's TF.460-6. This system was less sophisticated than today's UTC system, into which it evolved. In particular, the BIH was only mandated 'to keep the time pulses in close agreement' with GMT by means of appropriate offsets between the time signals (now UTC) and the atomic scale (now TAI), without the clearer quantitative guidance given by today's leap second rule.

45  The reference to 'relevant international organizations' includes international organizations *stricto sensu* (some of them UN Specialized Agencies), e.g., the International Maritime Organization (IMO) and the International Civil Aviation Organization (ICAO), as well as non-governmental standard and scientific bodies such as the International Organization for Standardization (ISO) and the International Astronomical Union (IAU).

46  Nelson et al., 'The Leap Second: Its History and Possible Future'.

47  Constitution and Convention of the International Telecommunication Union (concluded 22 December 1992, entered into force 1 July 1994) 1825 UNTS 143.

compliance with the Radio Regulations mandatory for ship operators under their jurisdiction.

Similarly to the ITU, the BIPM as the main actor in the determination of UTC is an international organization. It was established by the Metre Convention of 20 May 1875, an international law treaty which entrusted it with safeguarding the prototype metre and prototype kilogram, two physical platinum objects which defined the fundamental units of length and mass in the scientific system of measurements.[48] This metrological role of the BIPM made it a suitable choice to take over the BIH's role in the determination of UTC, even though timekeeping was not originally part of the BIPM's activities.

Under the mere wording of the Metre Convention, it is not entirely unambiguous whether the BIPM—which is headquartered in Saint-Cloud near Paris—is supposed to be an international organization in the modern sense, with separate personality under international law. This ambiguity is a consequence of the fact that the BIPM was set up at a time when international law terminology with respect to non-State actors was less uniform than it is now; hence also the use of the word 'bureau'.[49] The BIPM itself now claims full international organization status,[50] and this is confirmed by a headquarters agreement concluded with its host nation which grants it the comprehensive privileges and immunities usually accorded to international organizations. Its highest decision-making body, the General Conference on Weights and Measures (*Conférence générale des poids et mesures*, CGPM), is also the body which adopted in 1960 the International System of Units (*Système international d'unités*, abbreviated correctly as SI; sometimes still informally referred to as the *metric system*, under which name its predecessor systems were known). It is the system of seven base units (the second among them, as the base unit for time) which form the foundation of all units of measurement used in modern science.[51]

---

48  In the beginning, both metre and kilogram were defined by reference to the physical prototypes held by the BIPM. This is no longer the case. Since 1983, the metre has been defined as the distance which light travels within a certain fraction of a second. And since 2018, the kilogram has been defined by reference to certain fundamental physical constants. The prototypes still exist but have lost their status as the authoritative definiens of these two units.

49  On this use, see J. Salmon, *Dictionnaire de droit international public* (Bruylant 2001), entry 'bureau'.

50  BIPM (ed.), 'Note on the Legal Status of the International Bureau of Weights and Measures (BIPM)', available at https://www.bipm.org/utils/common/documents/official/legal-status-BIPM.pdf (accessed 5 March 2019).

51  On its history and future development (anticipating the 2018 re-definition of the kilogram) see D.B. Newell, 'A More Fundamental International System of Units' (2014) 67 Physics Today 35.

By comparison, the legal status of the IERS is much less formal. It was set up in 1987 jointly by the International Astronomical Union (IAU) and the International Union of Geodesy and Geophysics (IUGG), both of which are not international organizations but rather private law bodies bringing together scientists active in the respective fields. The IERS itself operates under a constitutive document styled 'Terms of Reference',[52] and even though this document provides for the election of officers it does not grant the IERS the status of an international organization or even of a corporation under any national private law. It operates as an unincorporated network of scientists and scientific institutions,[53] and its officers are scientists attached to, and remunerated by, such participating national institutions, one of which (the German Federal Agency for Cartography and Geodesy in Frankfurt) also provides, under the heading of 'central office', resources for administrative and coordinating work.

c    Definition of Time Zones

It would be perfectly possible to use UTC directly as a worldwide time scale, applied globally without alteration. This is common in many inherently international fields, e.g., aviation. It would, however, have the consequence that many places would experience daylight or night darkness at clock readings not commonly associated with them, and this is not preferred for everyday life. UTC is therefore converted into local civil time by fixed offsets, set for each time zone, which are added to or subtracted from UTC.

There is no treaty or other international legal instrument defining time zones.[54] In line with the general rule of public international law that States have comprehensive freedom to act unless a rule of international law restricting that freedom can be demonstrated,[55] it is within the prerogative of States to define

---

52   IERS Terms of Reference, available at https://www.iers.org/IERS/EN/Organization/About/ToR/ToR.html (accessed 5 March 2019).

53   It may nonetheless be seen as a non-governmental organization, since that term (which certainly implies a lack of legal personality under international law) does not seem to strictly require legal personality under a national private law: S. Hobe, 'Non-Governmental Organizations' in R. Wolfrum (ed.), *Max Planck Encyclopedia of Public International Law* (OUP 2008–), available at http://www.mpepil.com (accessed 26 March 2019), at para 5.

54   The closest thing to an internationally harmonized definition of time zones is the recommendation adopted at the end of a 1917 conference (mentioned above) which suggested one-hour time zones for nautical use. This recommendation did define the boundaries of its time zones: Anonymous, 'Standard Time at Sea' (1918) 51 The Geographical Journal 97. This scheme applies only to ships on the high seas. Its 'nautical time zones' follow exactly the natural meridians and do not coincide with the civil time zones on land, which are often heavily crooked due to the reasons described in the main text.

55   The classical citation for this is *The 'Lotus' (France v Turkey)* (Judgment of 7 September 1927) PCIJ Series A No. 10. This postulate of a comprehensive freedom of states to act has

their own civil time by means of domestic legislation. The time zone maps that can be commonly found are unofficial compilations of these individual and unilateral national laws, and do not derive from an international instrument defining zones across jurisdictions.[56] States are therefore free to define their time unilaterally by setting an offset against UTC (which is commonplace in more recently adopted statutes) or against GMT (which can still be found in many national statutes adopted before the introduction of the present UTC system in 1972). Since the leap second mechanism keeps UTC within 0.9 seconds of UT1, and thus GMT, the only practical consequences arising from the discrepancy between UTC and GMT occur in technical or scientific applications where an accuracy below one second is key. For legal purposes, it appears safe to argue that references in older statutes to GMT can now be read as references to UTC, which has taken over GMT's role as the world's time standard.[57] From a legislative point of view, however, it is good practice to avoid mentioning GMT in the adoption of new statutes and to use the term UTC instead.

In some older statutes, the relation of local civil time to UTC/GMT is defined not in terms of an offset but by setting mean solar time at a given meridian. In such cases, it is common practice to use, as point of reference, a meridian which lies east or west of Greenwich by a multiple of 15 degrees of longitude. Since 15 degrees of longitude correspond precisely to one hour of the time difference between the two meridians, this has the same practical result as an offset defined in terms of hours.

This freedom of States to define their own civil time is, under the *lex lata*, unrestricted. The common practices noted in the present paper may be seen as *consuetudo* from the perspective of international law. Yet, there is no evidence of them being a consequence of *opinio iuris*, i.e., a belief by States that they are applying this practice because they are bound by it.[58] This means that no

---

come under attack, with debates around the question whether it fits modern needs as well as whether it is an accurate interpretation of the historical *Lotus* judgment; see, in this regard, A. Hertogen, 'Letting Lotus Bloom' (2016) 26 EJIL 901. In spite of this debate, the principle has proven to be robust and—with the possible exception of extraterritorial jurisdiction, which the *Lotus* principle appears to allow too liberally—is still widely seen to be part of the customary international law.

56   Another consequence of the fact that time zones are defined decentrally rather than centrally is the fact that the same time zone may be called differently in different jurisdictions. For instance, CET, Romance Standard Time, and West Africa Time are all the same time (UTC plus one hour).

57   See the debate of 27 November 1996, House of Lords Hansard vol. 576 column 257. UTC and GMT are also equated by the European Court of Human Rights in Application 29750/09 *Hassan v. United Kingdom* (Judgment of 16 September 2014), at para. 22.

58   In support of this claim, the case of Kiribati may be cited as precedent. This Pacific island nation adjusted its legislation in 1993 so as to apply UTC plus 14 hours (rather than UTC

customary international law can be concluded to exist which would be binding upon States in the definition of their civil time.[59] States are thus also free to set an offset against UTC which is not an integral number of hours. A prominent example is India, whose time (UTC plus 5:30 hours) is a halfway solution to avoid splitting the country between two time zones. Even more unusually, Nepal follows UTC plus 5:45 hours, which is a compromise between the desire to follow local mean time at Kathmandu (UTC plus 5:41:16 hours) and the aim of maintaining a reasonably round offset towards the rest of the world.

The definition of time zones by national legislation has the consequence that political or commercial considerations frequently come into play which can supersede longitudinal location as the basis for a state's choice of its time zone. Many countries prefer to avoid splitting their territory into different zones or to maintain the same time as neighbouring countries. Notable examples are Spain and France, both of which are roughly on the same longitude as the United Kingdom and for which UTC would, therefore, be self-suggesting geographically. They follow, however, Central European Time (CET; UTC plus one hour), which is historically a consequence of World War II[60] but nowadays supported by the membership of both countries in the EU. This has the

---

minus ten hours) to part of its territory, thereby redrawing, in effect, the International Date Line. This move met with opposition from neighbouring countries because it meant that the easternmost islands of Kiribati would experience the beginning of the new millennium, attracting tourists. In spite of these protests, the change was widely accepted by the international community. State practice therefore supports and recognizes a unilateral right of states to define their own time: N.D. Kristof, 'In Pacific Race to Usher In Millennium, a Date-Line Jog' (23 March 1997) New York Times; Q. Letts, 'Pacific Braces for Millennium Storm over Matter of Degrees' (25 January 1996) The Times. The latter article mentions that the UN were 'involved', but the present author was unable to locate correspondence in this regard on the UN's official document system.

59 In the words of H. Kelsen, *Principles of International Law* (3rd edn Rinehart 1959), at 440, a mere 'usage' is created by this *consuetudo* without *opinio iuris*. This is consistent with what has been said of ITU standards (which are, as will be shown below, part of the basis for the BIPM's authority in timekeeping). Even though they are widely followed out of technical necessity, they can normally not be taken to establish new international law. See, D. Westphal, 'International Telecommunication Union (ITU)' in R. Wolfrum (ed.), *Max Planck Encyclopedia of Public International Law* (OUP 2008–), available at http://www.mpepil.com (accessed 26 March 2019), at para. 27.

60 Both countries transitioned from GMT to CET in 1940. In the case of France, the measure was imposed by the German occupants to facilitate military administration: Y. Poulle, 'La France à l'heure allemande' (1999) 157 Bibliothèque de l'École des chartes 493. In the case of Spain, the reason for the transition lies in sympathies of the Franco regime with Nazi Germany and Fascist Italy: F. Valle Zubicaray, *Un cabeza volada* (Editorial Verbum 2014), at 150.

consequence that the natural diurnal motion of the Sun is, in these countries, unusually late by the clock.[61]

In federal systems, the question arises whether the competence to define civil time is assigned to the national or the subnational level. A comparative survey shows that in federal systems which are sufficiently small (in terms of east-west expanse) to have one single civil time for the entire country, this is usually defined federally, which is plausible considering that this definition transcends the scopes of the subnational entities. Constitutionally, this is often based on the competence of the central government to define units of measurement,[62] which, in turn, is usually justified by the consideration that such units have an impact on nationwide (i.e., transcending the boundaries of the subnational entities) commerce.[63] In federal systems which are so large that a division into more one than one time zone appears preferable, the allocation of competences is heterogeneous: In the United States, Brazil, and Russia, time zones are defined by federal statute;[64] in Canada and Australia, this matter lies within the competence of the individual provinces/states. The European Union—not a federal State, but a federated system of governance with a delineation of legislative competences between the central and the decentralized levels—has currently no Union legislation in place which defines time zones, meaning that the Member States remain free to do so by national legislation. Nonetheless, the fact that daylight saving time has been

---

61  As an example, the westernmost point of continental Spain, Cape Touriñán, lies 24 degrees and 18 minutes of longitude west of the 15th eastern meridian whose local time would correspond to CET. Therefore, mean solar noon at Cape Touriñán takes place roughly 97 minutes (and, in summer, 157 minutes, as a consequence of DST) after the clock reads noon. The example demonstrates that the counter-arguments which were articulated in the 19th century against the standardization of time were unfounded. People do not object to significant deviations of clock readings from the natural course of the Sun at their location.

62  E.g. in Switzerland the Federal Law on Metrology, based on Arts 95 (1) and 125 of the Federal Constitution, or in Germany the *Einheiten- und Zeitgesetz*, based on Art. 73 (1) (4) of the Basic Law.

63  Again, the United States provides an illustrative example. The first federal legislation codifying the time zone system, the Standard Time Act of 1918, made repeated reference to considerations of commerce as a justification for the measure, and delegated power to define the precise boundaries of the time zones to the Interstate Commerce Commission (now the Secretary of Transportation). Evidently, Congress saw the interstate commerce clause (Art. I, Section 8, Clause 3 of the Constitution) as the legal basis for taking federal (as opposed to state) action. The commercial aspects are also emphasized by L. Cuocolo, *Tempo e potere nel diritto costituzionale* (Giuffrè 2009), at 19–20.

64  For the US, 15 USC 261; for Brazil, Decree 2784 of 18 June 1913; for Russia, Federal Law N 107-FZ of 3 June 2011.

harmonized in the EU[65] on the basis of the general competence for harmonization of the internal market (now Art. 114 TFEU) can be interpreted as implying that, in the view of the Union institutions, a (concurrent[66]) Union competence exists which has, so far, been lying dormant. There is no reason to treat, from the perspective of Art. 114 TFEU, legislative competences relating to daylight saving time differently from those relating to the definition of time zones, since the internal market effect of both measures is the same.

In theory, States would also be free to define their civil time entirely autonomously and without any reliance on Greenwich, e.g. by reference to the mean solar time on a meridian which is not ahead of or behind Greenwich by a round number, or by reference to a time standard that is not mean solar time. This would not be incompatible with international law.[67] There are currently no jurisdictions which do so,[68] which illustrates that the use of Greenwich as the benchmark for the setting of the world's clocks is now firmly engrained.[69] However, in some niches, vestiges of the ancient adherence to local standards remain, e.g. for non-secular purposes: Judaism and Islam, for instance, regard sunset—a moment determined by local apparent solar time—as the beginning of the religious day, which defines duties such as resting on Sabbath or fasting during Ramadan. Another example is the tradition at Oxford University to begin lectures five minutes past the scheduled hour. This is not an analogy to the continental 'academic quarter' but a reflection of the fact that Oxford lies one degree and 15 minutes of longitude west of Greenwich. A delay of five

---

65  More on this in subsection 'd'.
66  On this terminology, see A. von Bogdandy and J. Bast (eds), *Principles of European Constitutional Law* (2nd edn Hart/Beck 2009), at 290–291.
67  In particular, the wording of the final act of the 1884 Conference as well as the verbal statements made by delegates during the discussions do not support the contention that in voting on the resolutions recorded in the final act, the countries participating in the Conference had the intention to create binding obligations under international law to base their time systems on Greenwich. The delegates did not carry full powers authorizing them to enter into such obligations on behalf of their states either. See, for example, R. Sabel, 'Conferences and Congresses, International' in R. Wolfrum (ed.), *Max Planck Encyclopedia of Public International Law* (OUP 2008–), available at http://www.mpepil.com (accessed 26 March 2019), at para. 9.
68  The last State to transition to a standard time based on Greenwich was Liberia, in 1972. See, C.W.J. Withers, *Zero Degrees: Geographies of the Prime Meridian* (Harvard University Press 2017), at 255.
69  This includes also seemingly innovative private initiatives like that of a Swiss watch manufacturer which, for marketing purposes, purported to have come up with an entirely new time scale. Its 'Internet Time' is nothing but UTC-based CET, expressed in a decimal format. See, H. Lee and J. Liebenau, 'Time and the Internet at the Turn of the Millennium' (2000) 9 Time & Society 43.

minutes compared to the civil time—defined on the basis of the Greenwich meridian—therefore ensures a start of the lecture on the hour according to Oxford mean time.

d    Daylight Saving Time

Daylight saving time (DST), also known as summer time, is the practice of advancing clocks by a certain amount (usually one hour) in spring and to revert to the non-advanced time in autumn.[70] It does not shift the jurisdiction to which it applies into a different time zone but rather mandates a change in legal time which operates independently of time zones. The rationale is to make the longer daylight hours in summer available for human use. DST effectively 'makes the sun set' an hour later than it would otherwise, and thus extends daylight in the evening. Of course, it does so at the price of also 'making the sun rise' later, and thus shortens daylight in the morning. But since in summer, sunrise takes place before most people rise from bed, DST has the advantage of increasing the number of effectively usable daylight hours by shifting them from the morning into the evening.

Even though similar ideas had been proposed since at least the 18th century,[71] DST in the modern sense was first introduced in 1916 by various nations as a wartime measure to save energy and increase production. In the subsequent decades, the international practice became erratic, with periodic abolitions in peacetime and re-introductions during the war. The oil shocks during the 1970s renewed interest in DST, and many national statutes still in place date back to this period. Like the definition of time zones, adherence or non-adherence to DST falls within the legislative prerogatives of States, which are not bound by international legal obligations in this regard. The EU has harmonized it by

---

70   Some countries have introduced a kind of 'permanent DST' whereby clocks would be advanced once but not reversed. The Soviet Union followed such a system for much of its existence ('decree time'). Conceptually, such measures should be regarded as placing the jurisdiction in a time zone which lies further east than the geographical location would suggest, rather than DST in the sense presently discussed. This may explain the globally observable trend of countries adhering to a time zone that is further east than geography would suggest, effectively skewing time zone boundaries to the west: It shifts daylight from the morning into the evening. Such considerations were present when the federally mandated time zone boundaries were drawn in the United States in 1918. See, Interstate Commerce Commission (ICC) Decision 10122 'Standard Time Zone Investigation' 51 ICC Reports 273, at 283.

71   A comprehensive account of the history of DST is given by D. Prereau, *Seize the Daylight* (Thunder's Mouth 2005).

means of Union legislation binding on its Member States.[72] UTC itself does not apply it, but civil time in the UK does.

DST has been controversial since its beginning, with the debate revolving primarily around whether the energy savings are sufficiently large to justify the expenses and inconveniences of two transitions per year which affect entire societies. International practice is heterogeneous,[73] and even among jurisdictions which agree in the use of DST, the dates of transition need not be synchronized. This effect can complicate the calculation of the time zone difference between the two places. Contemporaneously, there appears to be a trend against DST, as exemplified by an anti-DST referendum in California,[74] and by the intention announced by the European Commission to abolish DST in the EU following a poll among the Union population[75] (both in 2018).

## III  Calendar

### 1  *Scientific Background*

There are two natural[76] cyclical motions which suggest themselves as the basis for the counting of longer periods and which have been observed by humans since prehistoric times: The *(synodic) month*, defined as the period between two subsequent occurrences of the same lunar phase during the orbit of the Moon around the Earth; and the *(tropical) year*, defined as the duration of a full revolution of the Earth around the Sun. Both consist of a non-integer number of solar days (about 29.53 and 365.24217, respectively), and there is also a non-integer number of synodic months in a tropical year. All calendar systems,

---

72   Beginning in 1980 (Directive 80/737/EEC), the EU (then EEC) had issued annual directives harmonizing DST for any given calendar year. These have since been replaced with Directive 2000/84/EC, which applies generally and without limitation to any given year.

73   They differ even within the United States, since federal law mandates DST but leaves individual states the possibility to opt out (15 USC 260a). It does, at least, standardize the transition dates for those states that do apply DST.

74   The adopted proposal is legislatively complex. See 'Vote Yes on Proposition 7 to Force Another Look at Daylight Saving Time' (29 September 2018) Los Angeles Times.

75   European Commission Press Release IP/18/5709 (12 September 2018). The proposal would leave Member States the option to retain DST on a permanent basis but explicitly bar them from making seasonal changes to their time. This is consistent with the present suggestion that legal time is a concurrent Union competence under Art. 114 TFEU. It is also consistent with the situation in the United States, where case law suggests that if federal DST legislation were abolished, states would remain free to re-introduce it. See, *Massachusetts State Grange v. Benton* 272 US 525 (1926).

76   The week, on the other hand, is artificial: E. Zerubavel, *The Seven Day Circle: The History and the Meaning of the Week* (University of Chicago Press 1985), at 4.

therefore, need to make a fundamental decision whether they should be based primarily on the month (lunar calendar) or the year (solar calendar).

In particular, the non-integer number of days in a year poses challenges. If the calendar year were to comprise exactly 365 days, it would be significantly too short, and astronomical moments such as equinox and solstice, which cause the meteorological seasons of the year and thus have a perceptible impact on human life, would drift relative to the calendar by about one day per four years, or 25 days per century. To compensate for this, various leap day arrangements—to be discussed below—have been devised.

## 2    *Historical Development*

Purely lunar schemes exist, most notably the Islamic calendar.[77] It comprises twelve months defined on the basis of the orbit of the Moon around the Earth, of 29 or 30 days (depending on the actual visibility of the new Moon) each, with a total of 354 or 355 days in a year. It is thus not aligned with the tropical year. This means the equinoxes and solstices—and, by consequence, the meteorological seasons—shift, relative to the Western calendar, by about eleven days per year. It is therefore not surprising that it originated, historically, on the Arab peninsula, where the differences between the seasons are not pronounced.

In moderate climates, however, the desire to keep the calendar dates of the seasons constant led to a preference for solar schemes. The Roman republic counted twelve synodic months which were, every two or three years, complemented by a shorter thirteenth intercalary (leap) month to maintain rough alignment with the tropical year;[78] the mechanism for intercalation was, however, based on the discretion of priests and thus subject to manipulation. This led to fundamental reform by Julius Caesar in 46 BC, who introduced the now-familiar system of twelve months of 30 or 31 days each (except for February) and a total duration of 365 days. Therefore, the lunar phases do not occur during the same days within each month; the calendar sacrifices alignment with the Moon for the sake of maintaining alignment with the Sun. To compensate for a fraction of a day by which the tropical year is longer than 365 days, Caesar's Julian calendar also introduced the familiar leap year rule, according to which every fourth year would be extended to 366 days by means of inserting an additional day in February.

---

77    M. Ilyas, 'Lunar Crescent Visibility Criterion and Islamic Calendar' (1994) 35 Quarterly Journal of the Royal Astronomical Society 425.

78    On Roman calendar history, see J. Rüpke, *The Roman Calendar from Numa to Constantine: Time, History and the Fasti* (John Wiley 2011).

This system was to govern the Western world for more than one and a half millennia, even though the ancient terminology of denoting the days within a month by reference to certain fixed points (*Kalends, Nones, Ides*[79]) was replaced with a simple numbering. The era, i.e. the starting point from which the years were counted, varied throughout history, but throughout the centuries, Western practice converged towards the *anno Domini* count based on the—supposed—date of Jesus' birth.[80]

In the subsequent centuries, it became progressively apparent that the leap year rule introduced by Caesar was imprecise. Inserting one leap day every four years results in an average duration of the calendar year of exactly 365.25 days. This is slightly too long, and by the 16th century, the discrepancy had accumulated to a difference of ten days between calendar dates and the actual revolution of the Earth around the Sun. This was theologically unsatisfactory since the date of Easter is defined by reference to the spring equinox.[81] In 1582, this led Pope Gregory XIII to mandate a—thoroughly prepared and scientifically well-designed[82]—reform, establishing the calendar since named after him. Gregory modified Caesar's leap year rule: Every fourth year is a leap year featuring a 29 February, unless it is evenly divisible by 100 (such as 1900), in which case the leap day is omitted; with the counter-exception that in years evenly divisible by 400 (such as 2000), the leap day takes place. In order to compensate for the discrepancy already accumulated, ten days were, in a one-time offset, omitted from the calendar, and 4 October 1582 was followed immediately by 15 October.[83]

---

79   A. Philip, *The Calendar: Its History, Structure and Improvement* (CUP 1921), at 1617.

80   G. Jaritz and G. Moreno-Riaño (eds), *Time and Eternity: The Medieval Discourse* (Turnhout 2003), at 31. Since the calculation of Jesus's birth date occurred before the number zero was introduced into Western mathematics, there was never a 'year zero'; 1 BC was followed immediately by 1 AD. Historians now agree that the calculation was flawed, and that the historical Jesus was born several years 'before Christ'. The use of the Christian era for events which occurred 'before Christ' did not become common until the 18th century: 'Zeitrechnung' in C. Andresen et al. (eds), *Lexikon der Alten Welt* (Weltbild 1994), at para. 4f.

81   J. Dutka, 'On the Gregorian Revision of the Julian Calendar' (1988) 10 Mathematical Intelligencer 56.

82   On these preparations, see G. Moyer, 'The Gregorian Calendar' (1982) 246.5 Scientific American 144.

83   This did not interrupt the cycle of the weekdays; 4 October 1582 was a Thursday, 15 October a Friday. The motivation to preserve this regularity was most likely the biblical background of the seven-day week. See, P.K. Seidelmann (ed.), *Explanatory Supplement to the Astronomical Almanac* (University Science Books 1992), at 578.

As the Gregorian calendar was introduced by means of a papal bull,[84] it was initially obeyed only by the Catholic countries. For a long time, Catholic and Protestant Europe would, therefore, follow different dates.[85] Over the subsequent centuries, however, non-Catholic countries one by one transitioned from the Julian to the Gregorian calendar, some of them only relatively recently.

3    *The Present-Day International Mechanism for The Regulation of the Calendar*

a    Lack of an Institutional Set-Up

Unlike the time of the day, where an extensive institutional apparatus comprising the BIPM, the IERS and the national laboratories and observatories is necessary to determine UTC, no such apparatus exists for the Gregorian calendar. This is because the leap seconds in UTC compensate for variabilities in the rotation of the Earth which are irregular and unpredictable and therefore require constant monitoring to make *ad hoc* decisions whether a leap second needs to be introduced. The leap year rule in the Gregorian calendar, on the other hand, is defined in the abstract and sufficient to maintain accuracy over very long periods: It reduced the difference between the natural solar year and the calendar to such a small amount that it will take more than 2,000 years for it to accumulate to one day.[86] The Gregorian calendar thus still follows the straightforward non-discretionary rules predetermined in the bull of 1582 and will not require *ad hoc* intervention for millennia to come.

Interestingly, many jurisdictions do not provide for an explicit statutory basis for the use of the Gregorian calendar, or its definition. Exceptions are countries which transitioned only recently while their present-day political regime was already in place.[87] Among those jurisdictions which have a formal legal basis for the Gregorian calendar even though the transition occurred a considerable time ago is the United Kingdom, where the statute which provided for its adoption in 1752—and which also stipulates in detail its leap year rule—is still in force.[88] By extension, those former British colonies which follow the

---

84    *Inter gravissimas* (24 February 1582).
85    This lies behind the historical oddity that Shakespeare and Cervantes died on the same date, 23 April 1616, yet ten days apart: Spain was following the Gregorian calendar, and England the Julian calendar. It also explains why the anniversary of the Russian October Revolution is commemorated in November.
86    G. Moyer, 'The Gregorian Calendar', at 151.
87    E.g., Turkey, which transitioned in 1926, four years after the establishment of its present republican regime. On calendars in Turkey, see F. Georgeon, 'Changes of Time: An Aspect of Ottoman Modernization' (2011) 44 New Perspectives on Turkey 181.
88    The Calendar (New Style) Act 1750 (24 Geo. 2 c. 23).

doctrine of reception—whereby, upon reaching independence, the entire body of English common law and British statutory law in existence at the time of independence remains part of their law of the land, until and unless subsequently repealed[89]—can be said to have incorporated this provision into their laws. In other jurisdictions, on the other hand, no such provision can be found. This is typically the case where the adoption of the Gregorian calendar far precedes the presently applicable legal framework and is thus considered to be assumed by it, requiring no explicit statutory enactment.[90] Methodologically, one may regard this as either the formation of national customary law or an interpretation of existing national statutes making reference to time as including an implicit reference to the Gregorian calendar. Internationally, it deserves to be mentioned that Art. 2.3 of the ITU's Radio Regulations makes use of the Gregorian calendar mandatory whenever dates are used in radio communication, but without defining the meaning of the term 'Gregorian calendar'.

b       The International Date Line (IDL)

The IDL determines the day of the calendar rather than the hour of the clock, but it is closely linked to the time zone system—and a logical necessity: An observer travelling westwards would continuously set his watch back at the pace of one hour per 15 degrees of longitude. After completing a full circumnavigation, he would have set back his watch by a total of 24 hours. His watch and calendar would now deviate by one day from the time as counted by stationery observers on the starting point—a discrepancy which was understood but noted as sensational when the first voyage around the world was completed in 1522,[91] and which provides the dramatic dénouement in Jules Verne's adventure classic *Around the World in 80 Days*. In order to define a unique time and date for each place, it is, therefore, necessary to insert, at some stage during the journey, one day, and this insertion takes place at the IDL: Crossing it westwards requires the addition of a day, eastwards a subtraction.

Any meridian could, in principle, serve as IDL, but there is a long history—longer than the existence of the time zone system—of placing it in the Pacific Ocean. This is a consequence of the Age of Exploration, when European naval powers conquered their overseas empires. In territories which the European

---

89    The doctrine is more widely acknowledged for the common law, but is often extended also to statutes. See e.g., B. Kercher, 'Alex Castles on the Reception of English Law' (2003) 7 Australian Journal of Legal History 37.

90    E.g. for Germany: R. Herzog et al. (eds), *Maunz/Dürig/Herzog Grundgesetz-Kommentar* (83rd supplement Beck 2018), Art. 140 of the Basic Law and Art. 139 of the Weimar Constitution, at para. 45.

91    A. Pigafetta, *Magellan's Voyage around the World* (ca. 1524, J.A. Robertson (tr.), Arthur Clark 1906) vol. II, at 185.

conquerors typically reached sailing westwards, crossing the Atlantic, they would keep the same calendar as at home but clocks—following local apparent solar time—would be delayed against European clocks at a rate of one hour of time per 15 degrees of difference in longitude ('American date'). Conversely, territories which the Europeans typically reached on an eastward route, across the Indian Ocean, would also keep the European calendar but with clocks running ahead of European clocks at the same rate ('Asiatic date'). The areas of the two dating systems met in the Pacific Ocean, and so this became the region of the world where the leap between the dates would take place.[92] As in the case of the time zones, there is no authoritative international instrument, since the matter remains left to unilateral legislation by individual States.

Nonetheless, in the 19th century—still before the American time zone system of 1883 and the International Meridian Conference of 1884—it became common to visualize these national legislations in the form of a map drawing a distinctive line in the ocean, with one date on its Western side and another date, one day earlier, on the Eastern side.[93]

From a legal perspective, this state of affairs still applies: Even though the IDL follows roughly the 180th meridian, i.e. the anti-meridian directly opposite that of Greenwich, it deviates in many segments from it, occasionally creating significant bulges.[94] In all instances, the IDL as drawn on a map is only a non-authoritative cartographical representation of whether the adjacent States chose, by statute, to place themselves in a time zone ahead or behind UTC, rather than the result of a harmonizing international instrument.

IV   Questions of Interpretation

Problems of interpretation can arise where an international legal instrument makes reference to a certain date or point in time and it has to be determined which calendar system or time reckoning is decisive. The issue originates, most

---

92   This historical background explains irregularities, such as in the case of the Philippines, a Spanish dependency which until 1844 kept the 'American date' owing to its trade routes to Mexico, whereas other islands in the immediate vicinity of the Philippines kept 'Asiatic date' and were thus ahead by a day. See, A. Ariel and N. Ariel Berger, *Plotting the Globe* (Praeger 2006), at 143. Many 19th century publications perpetuated mistakes in this regard, e.g., I.R. Bartky, 'One Time Fits All' (Stanford University Press 2007), at 21.

93   E.g. (Anonymous), 'The International Date-Line' (1876) 3 New-England Journal of Education 39; J. Schedler, *An Illustrated Manual for the Use of the Terrestrial and Celestial Globes* (Steiger 1878), at 25–28.

94   An example is, again provided by Kiribati, whose easternmost islands follow the unusual time zone (the world's earliest) of UTC plus 14 hours, rather than UTC minus ten hours, as nearby French Polynesia does.

prominently, as a consequence of differences between time zones, but it may arise also for different reasons. For instance, within the Islamic calendar, it is controversial whether it is acceptable to calculate the beginnings of the months in advance on the basis of astronomical algorithms, or whether it is necessary to await an actual visual observation of the new Moon. Consequently, different Muslim countries may deviate from each other by several days in their expression of a given date in the Islamic calendar.[95] In the absence of an explicit reference to a specific calendar or time reckoning system, it is, therefore, necessary to determine which of these systems the author (in the case of unilateral instruments) or authors (in the case of bilateral or multilateral instruments, most notably treaties) intended to be authoritative. This analysis should be done in accordance with the established canon of interpretative rules in international law methodology.

The problem has parallels to a series of court cases in Britain and the United States when standardized time (GMT in Britain, railway time on the basis of the 1883 time zones in America) was already in widespread actual use but not yet defined by positive law as authoritative (which occurred in Britain in 1880 and in the United States in 1918). There were numerous cases in these jurisdictions—sometimes under whimsical factual circumstances—in which the outcome of the litigation depended, crucially, on whether a certain point in time mentioned in a contract or statute had to be taken to refer to standardized time, or non-standardized local solar mean time. Without delving into the details of this line of jurisprudence,[96] it can be summarized by stating that in the early years of the widespread use of standardized time, courts showed a tendency to accord precedence to local (i.e., mean solar) time. On the other hand in subsequent decades, with standardized time becoming more entrenched in everyday use, there was more willingness to lean towards standardized time, even in the absence of an explicit statutory enactment to this effect and even though it bears no direct relation to the local time at the place of the event in question.

Transposing this logic, which arose in two national jurisdictions, to the sphere of international law, it would—in the absence of international case law to the contrary—appear to be preferable to argue as follows: Since international law does not contain an authoritative definition of calendars or timekeeping

---

95   H.J. Birx (ed.), *Encyclopedia of Time* (Sage 2009) vol. I, at 132.
96   It has been analysed extensively by Parrish, 'Litigating Time in America at the Turn of the Twentieth Century'. In contradiction to footnote 50 of Parrish's paper, the present author considers himself as writing seriously about time even without citing an overused quotation from St Augustine.

in positive law (treaty or custom), and since there is—outside technical applications such as astronomy, aviation, or navigation—no widespread habit of using a given time scale (e.g. UTC) globally, references to times and dates in an international instrument should be read as references to the time scale and calendar in use at the place where the instrument was issued. In the case of unilateral instruments, this can be taken to be the place whose time the author of the instrument had in mind; in the case of bilateral or multilateral instruments, the place of issuance (most importantly, in the case of treaties, the place of signature) is the only place which all parties have in common to such an extent that it can be taken to reflect what they, collectively, intended as the meaning of their words.[97] Reference to the timekeeping system in use at that place is thus in line with the established principle in international law that interpretation aims to ascertain the common understanding of the parties to the instrument, rather than a special meaning understood unilaterally only by one of the parties.[98] This is also in line with the *lex loci contractus* rule widely used in private international law.[99]

In the present age in which all countries have, by means of national legislation, standardized time for their jurisdiction, this reference to the 'local' time at the place of issuance of the instrument should be understood as a reference to the time thus standardized in the jurisdiction in question, rather than the

---

[97] The same logic is underlying the conclusions of G. Wegen and S. Wilske, 'Applicable Time Zones for Deadlines in International Arbitration Proceedings' (2004) 21 Journal of International Arbitration 205.

[98] One could hold the alternative view that in case of 'localized' treaties, i.e., those relating specifically to some geographical place, the time reckoning at that place is conclusive. This view is, however, not supported by an important precedent, the cession of Alaska from Russia to the United States. The treaty of cession was signed in Washington on 30 March 1867 (Gregorian calendar). The English treaty text records this date. The equally authentic French version and the Russian version published in the Complete Collection of Laws of the Russian Empire, record both these dates and the Julian date (18 March). No document records only the Julian date, which was in use in the territory of Alaska, the subject matter of the treaty. In addition, dating in Alaska was complicated by the fact that under Russian rule, it used the Asiatic date (i.e., lied west of the IDL), even though it is located in North America.

[99] For similar reasons, the present author disagrees with the conclusion of the European Court of Justice in Case C–190/10 *Génesis* (Judgment of 22 March 2012) that for the purposes of establishing priority among conflicting trademarks, only the date, not the hour and minute of a filing, are to be taken into account. This leads to the absurd consequence (addressed and accepted in the opinion of Advocate-General Jääskinen but not discussed by the Court) that an applicant filing electronically shortly before midnight takes priority over another applicant filing shortly after midnight from another time zone further east, even though that second applicant's filing occurred earlier in real time.

actual solar time (mean or apparent) in the city in which the instrument was issued; non-standardized solar time has now fallen into disuse so universally that a reference to it cannot be understood to be in line with the 'ordinary meaning' of the words of the instrument, and it is this 'ordinary meaning' which guides the process of interpretation.[100] The reference to the legally standardized law at the place of issuance of the instrument should, however, be understood as static rather than dynamic, i.e., as referring to the calendar and timekeeping in force at the time of the issuance of the instrument. Otherwise the parties to an international treaty would effectively delegate power to one of the parties (the party in whose jurisdiction the treaty was signed) to unilaterally amend the substance of the treaty by reforming its national time legislation.[101] There is more room for flexibility where unilateral instruments issued by subjects of international law make reference to time; in such cases, customary law appears to accept, within the limits of *bona fides*, a right of the issuer to withdraw or amend the act.[102]

## v  Conclusions

Time is a fundamental physical property capable of being measured. Events take place within time, and timekeeping governs how and when we conduct our activities. Despite this importance, which undergirds all of our private, professional, and political lives, public international law does not treat the harmonization of time as a high-visibility matter. International regulation exists, but not in the form of multilateral treaties in which the international community solemnly agrees on a global standard. Even though the UTC system has been defined by a specialised agency of the UN, that agency did so by issuing a document on legal par with others which set, for instance, sound and data standards for broadcasting satellites in the 12 GHz range.[103] The day-to-day management of the system has been delegated to two bodies which most people will never

---

100   R. Gardiner, *Treaty Interpretation* (OUP 2008), at 165–166.
101   This approach is in line with the fundamental principle of intertemporal law, according to which the legal concepts at the time of an event, and not subsequent changes in meaning, are determinative for the legal assessment of that event. The classic citation is the *Island of Palmas* arbitration, (1928) II RIAA 829.
102   V. Rodríguez Cedeño and M.I. Torres Cazorla, 'Unilateral Acts of States in International Law' in R. Wolfrum (ed.), *Max Planck Encyclopedia of Public International Law* (OUP 2008–), available at http://www.mpepil.com (accessed 26 March 2019), at paras 30–33.
103   Recommendation ITU–R BO.712–1: High-quality sound/data standards for the broadcasting-satellite service in the 12 GHz band.

have heard of, a highly technical international organization and a network of national geodetic laboratories without legal personality. For calendars, as opposed to clock readings, the system is even more informal: The defining document of the world's predominant calendar is still a papal bull from the 16th century, and no institutional mechanism exists for its implementation.

This set-up was not designed from scratch. It emerged over centuries from actual practice. Subsequently, these practices were codified into an ever more precise system, but its fundamental principles—using the solar mean time of the Greenwich meridian as the global benchmark for clock readings, defining local standardized time as a round offset to it, and counting longer units of time on the basis of the tropical year whose subdivisions only very loosely correspond to lunar months—pre-existed formal definition. Even though States would, under international law, be free to stay out of this system, few do so for calendars, and none does for clock readings. From the economist's point of view, this may be seen as an instance of network externalities: The fact that the entire international community adheres to the Greenwich-based system makes it beneficial for each individual State to do the same. From the point of view of the international relations scholar, it can be seen as a set of principles around which actors' expectations converge, and thus an international regime.[104] From the lawyer's point of view, it may be seen as an instance of soft law: Codified standards which, though not legally binding, are still followed as a matter of practice. It might be seen as remarkable that a matter of such fundamental importance which pervades all of the law is governed at such an inconspicuous level. This is, however, not unique: In many areas, particularly highly technical ones, law—both national and international—makes reference to standardization arrived at through channels other than law-making and defines its own stipulations on this basis.[105]

For the international lawyer, the global system for the governance of time is therefore of interest from two angles: First, it provides the input for countless legal provisions which attach consequences to the timing of events or the period which elapsed between two events. Second, it constitutes an example for

---

104  A. Bradford, 'Regime Theory' in R. Wolfrum (ed.), *Max Planck Encyclopedia of Public International Law* (OUP 2008–), available at http://www.mpepil.com (accessed 26 March 2019), at para 2. The term, as used in the study of international relations, is deliberately broad and comprises both treaties and unwritten and unbinding norms with which States comply nonetheless. This width has provoked criticism. See, for example, M.A. Levy et al., 'The Study of International Regimes' (1995) 1 EJIR 267.

105  For examples, see J. Friedrich, 'Environment, Private Standard-Setting' in R. Wolfrum (ed.), *Max Planck Encyclopedia of Public International Law* (OUP 2008–), available at http://www.mpepil.com (accessed 26 March 2019), at paras 23–27.

informal and non-binding, yet nonetheless universally obeyed, rulemaking in an area which is perceived as technical and non-controversial.

From a forward-looking perspective, the Gregorian calendar is—despite all its deficiencies, such as irregular lengths of the months and an inability to keep the calendar dates on constant weekdays—most likely here to stay for the indefinite future; attempts to replace it with an entirely different system, such as the French revolutionary calendar,[106] have been short-lived.[107] This is at least partially a consequence of the lack of a global institution claiming authority over calendar matters as the Holy See did in 1582.

The same persistency is to be expected for the system of time zones set off (mostly) by whole hours against each other. It is, however, not certain that UTC in its present form will remain in place. It was designed to maintain—within an accepted fault tolerance—alignment with the rotation of the Earth. The irregularities of the latter are thereby imported into the UTC scale, even though more precise timekeepers would be available in the form of atomic clocks. The ITU has committed to undertake a review of the system in collaboration with some other international bodies, which may provide, in the coming years, a fruitful topic for scholars researching international institutional law, in particular, cross-sectoral cooperation among different players.

---

106   M. Shaw, *Time and the French Revolution* (Boydell 2011). In historiography, it remains in use to name events of the French Revolution, e.g., the Coup of 18 Brumaire VIII.
107   There are, however, private initiatives campaigning for calendar reform. See, C.M. Morin, 'The Perpetual World Calendar that We Need' (1949) 43 Journal of the Royal Astronomical Society of Canada 181.

# Book Review

∴

Andrea Bianchi, Daniel Peat and Matthew Windsor (eds), *Interpretation in International Law* (OUP 2015), 432 pages, ISBN 9780198725749

## I  Introduction

In this book, the editors set out to study, explain and question why international lawyers, by and large, restrict themselves to interpretative rules found in Arts 31–33 of the Vienna Convention on the Law of Treaties (or 'till a bounded field'[1] to use their expression) rather than drawing from the large(r) reservoir of insights from other disciplines.

Highlighting the implicit overvaluation of jurisprudence and the undervaluation of scholarly work, the book's introductory chapter laments that most of the scholarship on treaty interpretation is descriptive and practical, rather than theoretical.[2] Accordingly, it states that 'the book aims to provide readers with materials to enhance their awareness of the nature of interpretation, and the diverse reasons for engaging in it in international law'.[3] In this regard, the editors—as well as other contributors—of this well-researched book seek to provide a theoretical, and occasionally inter-disciplinary, perspective on interpretation to readers. Simply put, this book is about interpretation *in* international law and not the interpretation *of* international law

As such, this book is part of a growing trend in international law which focuses on the study of interpretation. The trend is evident in manifold ways, from the International Law Commission's ongoing work on 'Subsequent Agreements and Subsequent Practice In Relation To Interpretation Of Treaties',[4] to the International Law Association's study group on the 'Content and Evolution

---

[1] D. Peat and M. Windsor, 'Playing the Game of Interpretation: On Meaning and Metaphor in International Law' in A. Bianchi, D. Peat and M. Windsor (eds), *Interpretation in International Law* (OUP 2015) 3, at 8.
[2] Ibid., at 6–7.
[3] Ibid., at 4.
[4] See most recently UN ILC 'Report of the International Law Commission on the Work of Its Seventieth Session (30 April–1 June and 2 July–10 August 2018)' UN Doc. A/73/10, Chapter IV:

of the Rules of Interpretation' which is scheduled to deliver its final report at the 79th ILA Conference in Kyoto in 2020.[5] The trend is also evidenced in academic works such as the 2015 *Static and Evolutive Treaty Interpretation: A Functional Reconstruction* by Christian Djeffal; the 2012 *How Interpretation Makes International Law: On Semantic Change and Normative Twists* by Ingo Venzke; and the 2008 *The Interpretation of Acts and Rules in Public International Law* by Alexander Orakhelashvili. These books deal with—in addition to considerations of certain special regimes and topics of study—the relationship between interpretation and international law. Accordingly, while *Interpretation in International Law* acts as another milepost in this trend, it differs from the previous projects and works in that it aims to flush out theoretical perspectives on the phenomenon of interpretation in international law. That is to say, whilst the above undertakings primarily deal with ascertainment of international law's content through interpretation, this book calls for considering—and sometimes incorporating—theories from other disciplines in the study and practice of interpretation itself. Herein, it calls for a rethink on the aversion to applying interpretative rules from, *inter alia*, international relations theory and literary theory.[6] Similarly, it also highlights other interpretative techniques such as jurisgenerative[7] and jurispathic[8] interpretations, morphological approaches,[9] hermeneutics,[10] semantics[11] and semiotics.

The book—which consists of diverse contributions from several prominent scholars and practitioners—can be read in many ways. For instance, it can be read as (i) a guide to the interpretational practices that exist; (ii) a critique of the existing monotonous practi(s)e of interpretation; (iii) a clarion call re-evaluating the practice of interpretation in international law; and/or (iv) a scholarly study of the international legal theories of interpretation—*lex lata*, *lex ferenda*, and even *lex contenda*.[12]

---

'Subsequent Agreements and Subsequent Practice in Relation to the Interpretation Of Treaties'.

5    See generally ILA 'Report of the Working Session of the Study Group on the Content and Evolution of the Rules of Interpretation' (22 August 2018).

6    See generally Bianchi, Peat and Windsor (eds), *Interpretation in International Law*, at 4, 13, 15, 296, 298 and 305.

7    Ibid., at 102, 181–183.

8    Ibid., at 102.

9    Ibid., at 328–329.

10   Ibid., at 4, 13, 14, 15, 16, 183, 307, 311–30, 374, 383, and 390–391.

11   Ibid., at 10, 11, 374, 115, 168, 183, and 332.

12   Here, the *lex lata* refers to existing rules of legal interpretation; *lex ferenda* refers to the rules of legal interpretation which ought to be progressively *developed*; and *lex contenda*

Another feature of the book worth noting is the refreshing, and indeed helpful, metaphor of the game which is introduced by the editors Bianchi, Peats and Windsor. The editors liken the act, process and practice of interpretation in international law to the playing of a game. This metaphor is dutifully followed and developed in later chapters by contributors who delve into the 'object' of the game, its 'players', its 'rules of play' etc. The metaphor is used to assert that interpretation is a social, and not just juristic, practice.

For my part, I would view interpretation not as a game involving cards[13] or of chess,[14] but as a game of cricket. It may be played in many different formats ranging from a gruelling five-day affair to one which lasts a mere three hours; it involves many players who—despite being part of larger teams—have certain unique roles and objectives for which they attempt to interpret the rules of the game in their favour;[15] it involves umpires to apply the rules of play, as well decide on the permissibility of a team's interpretation of the rules; and, of course, there are certain rules—including traditions—governing the game and its play. Cricket is perhaps better suited to this book's metaphor since the game does not merely have rules, it has 'Laws'[16] (note the capital L).

## II    Summary

This section of the review summarizes the book's chapters with the intent of helping future readers navigate the richly varied, and sometimes overlapping, contributions. The book, through the course of 18 chapters divided into seven parts, delves into various aspects of the 'game of interpretation'. The introductory chapters of the book are summarized in greater detail since they set the scene for the consideration of later chapters and serve as a sort of vignette to the supposed malady plaguing the extant practice of interpretation in international law.

---

refers to those rules of legal interpretation which ought to be *created* even though there is no existing practice to that effect.

13    As has been suggested in Bianchi's chapter at 43.
14    As is suggested by the book's cover.
15    The infamous 'underarm bowling incident of 1981' comes to mind in this regard, which led to the Laws of Cricket being amended. For the uninitiated, a helpful summary of the incident may be found on ESPN's website, available at http://www.espncricinfo.com/magazine/content/story/498574.html (accessed 15 April 2019).
16    The 'Laws of Cricket' are in the custodianship of the Marylebone Cricket Club and may be accessed on their website, available at https://www.lords.org/mcc/all-laws (accessed 15 April 2019).

## 1     Part I: 'Introduction'

The introductory section of the book, comprising of Chapters 1 and 2 penned by the editors themselves, explains that the aim of the book is to look beyond the confines of Vienna Convention on the Law Treaties (VCLT) when the requirement of interpretation in international law arises. Chapter 1, while laying out the game metaphor followed throughout the book, calls for a reconceptualization of the manner in which the interpretative process in international law is practiced. At the outset, Daniel Peat and Michael Windsor lay out the 'state of play' extant in the game of interpretation post the adoption of the Vienna Convention. Overviewing the excessive, bordering exclusive, reliance of legal scholarship on Arts 31–33 of the Vienna Convention, they challenge the status of the VCLT as a 'one stop shop' for interpretative methods adopted by international lawyers.[17] In opposing what they view as unquestioning, almost blind, application of VCLT rules, Peat and Daniel analyse certain alternatives—such as Hans-Georg Gadamer's theory of hermeneutical play—in this chapter.[18] The chapter also delves into the approaches to interpretation followed in other fields beyond international law; urging international law practitioners and theoreticians to consider strategies adopted in other fields, such as constitutional and statutory interpretation.[19]

Andrea Bianchi's chapter overviews the setting of the game of interpretation as well as 'how to do interpretation'. The chapter explains the object of interpretation; the players in the interpretation game, focusing primarily on the international judiciary and judges; and the cards (tools) of interpretation. In discussing the cards, he provides an excellent, albeit brief, account of the early debates on textualism versus purposive interpretation which took place in relation to the adoption of the VCLT rules.[20] The sub-chapter dealing with strategies delves into the various tactics and moves (bold and conservative) used by players to enhance their credibility and power. Herein, it highlights how language is tailored to advance a player's moves (towards establishing interpretative supremacy) in different institutions such as the International Criminal Tribunal for the Former Yugoslavia and the World Trade Organization.[21] The chapter also considers the question 'why the game is worth the candle', but settles on the notion that international lawyers are socialized, intrinsically, to play the game without questioning it metaphysically.[22]

---

17     Bianchi, Peat and Windsor (eds), *Interpretation in International Law*, at 5.
18     Ibid., at 14–16.
19     Ibid., at 8.
20     Ibid., at 46–47.
21     Ibid., at 49–50.
22     Ibid., at 54–56.

Part I also seeks to examine fundamental questions regarding the nature of interpretation: addressing the debate of whether interpretation is meant to serve as a key to the mind of the drafters—serving as the proverbial 'treasure hunt' to ascertain the meaning intended by the original parties, or whether creativity could be employed in order to construct a meaning for the subject-matter of interpretation.[23] Later contributions in Part II, particularly by Duncan Hollis and Jean d'Aspremont, delve deeper into the law-ascertainment and content-determination aspects of interpretation in international law.

## 2   Part II: 'The Object'

At the outset, Iain Scobbie's chapter titled 'Rhetoric, Persuasion, and Interpretation in International Law', delves into how interpreters utilize persuasive rhetoric to convince audiences that their chosen interpretation is correct. In this exercise, Scobbie relies on the rhetorical theory of Polish legal philosopher Chaïm Perelman.[24] Thereafter, Duncan B. Hollis' chapter 'The Existential Function of Interpretation in International Law' explains how every act of interpretation contains, *ipso facto*, an existential element. Accordingly, the mere act of interpretation either creates, validates or rejects the existence of the object of interpretation.[25] In this regard, Hollis takes the example of a currently contested (emerging) legal norm—the 'responsibility to protect', in order to illustrate his argument.[26] Finally, Jean d'Aspremont's 'The Multidimensional Process of Interpretation' argues that interpretation in international law should be viewed as a multidimensional process, which leads not only to content-determination but also to law-ascertainment.

## 3   Part III: 'The Players'

Part III focuses on the different players (actors) in the game of interpretation. Andraž Zidar's 'Interpretation and the Legal Profession' analyses the role of the five most common international legal professionals—legal advisers, NGO lawyers, judges, academics and litigators before international courts—in the complex and dynamic interpretative process in international law.[27] Zidar also invokes Fuller's 'inner morality of law', to assert that the aforementioned

---

23   Ibid., at 9.
24   See generally, Bianchi, Peat and Windsor (eds), *Interpretation in International Law*, at 63–77.
25   Ibid., at 79.
26   See generally, Bianchi, Peat and Windsor (eds), *Interpretation in International Law*, at 78–108.
27   See generally, Bianchi, Peat and Windsor (eds), *Interpretation in International Law*, at 135–144.

professionals are guided by ethical, and not just professional, considerations.[28] Michael Waibel thereafter reflects on the 'Role of Interpretative Communities in Interpretation', arguing that the 'central insight is that the various actors that populate a regime exert an important influence on its operation, including through interpretation'.[29] Finally, Gleider Hernández's chapter focuses on the special role played by one the players in the interpretation game—the international judges and the judiciary. In 'Interpretative Authority and the International Judiciary', he asserts that judges have an inherent authority in the legal system.[30]

## 4   Part IV: 'The Rules'

Since the book's major premise (read: grouse) is that VCLT rules are ubiquitously applied without thought or deviation, it makes sense that this section of the book delves extensively into studying—and reinterpreting—the origin and scope of Arts 31–33 of the Vienna Convention on the Law of Treaties. Eirik Bjorge's chapter 'The Vienna Rules, Evolutionary Interpretation, and the Intentions of the Parties' argues that '[t]here is, in the context of treaty interpretation, a grammar that structures which arguments are legitimate and which are not. [T]his grammar is spelled out, where treaty interpretation is concerned, in the Vienna Rules'.[31]

In 'Accounting for Difference in Treaty Interpretation over Time', Julian Arato looks into the practice of affording some treaties—such as human rights treaties—special status when it comes to interpretation. Arato inquires what justification allows weighing some rules of interpretation more strongly than others (i.e., emphasizing object and purpose over text, or *vice versa*)?[32] And argues that differential treatment must be based on the nature of obligations under the treaty, and not merely on the basis of its object and purpose.[33] The chapter 'Interpreting Transplanted Treaty Rules' by Anne-Marie Carstens evaluates the best means of interpreting transplanted treaty rules. It also argues that transplanted treaty rules are to be interpreted differently from other—general—treaty rules and searches for avenues under the VCLT whereunder interpreters can consider the *travaux préparatoires* of the source rules in their interpretation of transplanted rules.[34]

---

28   Ibid., at 145.
29   Ibid., at 149.
30   Ibid., at 167.
31   Ibid., at 204.
32   Ibid., at 206.
33   Ibid., at 222.
34   Ibid., at 243–247.

## 5  Part V: 'The Strategies'

In examining the two most common interpretational approaches extant in international law: textualism and the intentionalist approach, Fuad Zarbiyev investigates how textualism came to be the dominant interpretative paradigm in modern international law in his chapter titled 'A Genealogy of Textualism in Treaty Interpretation'.[35] Harlan Grant Cohen's 'Theorizing Precedent in International Law' takes up the mantle of answering why a system of precedent has emerged in international law.[36] In this regard, Cohen also develops a framework to explain the emergence of precedent in international law. In 'Interpretation in International Law as a Transcultural Project', René Provost reflects on how a narrative of legality can be created around an act—in this case cannibalism. Using this particular act as springboard, he explains that international law runs the danger of being perceived as illegitimate, by the actors it wishes to regulate, if it does not take into account 'cultural differences' in its interpretative process.[37]

## 6  Part VI: 'Playing the Game of Game Playing'

In 'Towards a Politics of Hermeneutics', Jens Olesen expounds on the relationship between interpretation and politics, or the 'politics of interpretation' as he describes it.[38] The chapter argues that textual interpretations are influenced by ideology and power,[39] and relies heavily on the philosophy of Nietzsche in this exercise.[40] Martin Wählisch assesses how cognitive frames shape the interpretation of international law in his chapter 'Cognitive Frames of Interpretation in International Law'. It does so using three case studies on how linguistic choices reflect mindsets and values: the use of 'separation wall' versus 'security fence' in the ICJ's *Israeli Wall Advisory Opinion*;[41] the use of 'enhanced interrogation technique' versus 'torture';[42] and the use of 'terrorism' versus 'liberation'.[43] Subsequently, Ingo Venzke's chapter 'Is Interpretation in International Law a Game?' explores the metaphor of international law as a language of international relations, and studies it in combination with the

---

35   See generally, Bianchi, Peat and Windsor (eds), *Interpretation in International Law*, at 257–266.
36   Ibid., at 270.
37   Ibid., at 305 and 308.
38   Ibid., at 311.
39   Ibid., at 329.
40   Ibid., at 315.
41   Ibid., at 340.
42   Ibid., at 342.
43   Ibid., at 345.

game metaphor of this book.[44] He also discusses the three common ways of using the metaphor of the language of international law.[45]

## 7 Part VII: 'Conclusion'

The last chapter of the book, by Philip Allott, challenges many extant presumptions on interpretation and meaning. He raises the question of whether an interpreter's freedom is limitless and argues that social experience has evolved certain conventional constraints on the process of interpretation in general. In covering some 'notorious examples' in international legal interpretation,[46] Allott calls the VCLT rules 'worthless as a general rule of interpretation'.[47]

## III Discussion

At this juncture, I wish to make a few comments on the book in general, and certain chapters in particular. While some of my comments may have been raised in earlier reviews of the book,[48] I attempt to further develop these critiques with deeper analysis and elucidating examples.

### 1 Thoughts on the Scope of Study

While the book pushes for a critical relook at the extant rule-based approaches to interpretation in international law, it does so with a heavy—almost exclusive—focus on a particular type of international law: treaties. The study of interpretation in relation to customary international law rules does not receive any appreciable consideration. For instance, while Duncan Hollis' chapter covers the existential function of interpretation in (customary) international law,[49] it does not delve into the post-formation interpretation of those customary rules. Moreover, the rules of interpretation of customary rules do not receive any attention in this book. This might have been a worthwhile area of study because, though the initial 'existential' and 'content-determining' interpretations occur simultaneously through the same process (of referencing State practice and *opinio iuris*), the later content-determining interpretations would require different approaches. As Panos Merkouris has argued elsewhere,

---

44  Ibid., at 352.
45  Ibid.
46  Ibid., at 377–380.
47  Ibid., at 377.
48  This is particularly true when it comes to Christian Djeffal's review of this book in (2017) 28 EJIL 28 (2017) 649, at 653–658.
49  Bianchi, Peat and Windsor (eds), *Interpretation in International Law*, at 84–101.

the repetition of the existential interpretation process for each determination of a customary rule fails to take into account the continued existence, development and manifestation of that rule.[50] Furthermore, Jean d'Aspremont in his chapter asserts that we should not conflate rule-ascertainment with content determination, and while his chapter helpfully distinguishes between the deliberative processes of content-determination and law-ascertainment, it refrains from studying the former in any appreciable manner. Similarly, Hollis' chapter which provides an excellent analysis of the differing interpretative possibilities in the binary determination of a customary international law norm (i.e., whether a customary rule 'exists' or 'does not exist') stops shy of actually considering the interpretation of such norms. Such a consideration would form a separate interpretative process unto itself because further clarification regarding the content of a norm which has come into existence will not be amenable to the same method used to determine its existence (i.e., using State practice and *opinio iuris*), but rather will be achieved through an interpretative process *stricto sensu*.[52] One of the approaches to this interpretative process was suggested by Judge Tanaka in the *North Sea Continental Shelf* cases, where he said:

> Customary law, being vague and containing gaps compared with written law, requires precision and completion about its content. This task, in its nature being interpretative, would be incumbent upon the Court. The method of logical and teleological interpretation can be applied in the case of customary law as in the case of written law.[53]

Another dimension in the study of interpretation in relation to customary international law is the study of interpretation of the customary rules of interpretation, which Merkouris says 'is a process that should be completely distinguished from that of formation/identification of customary international

---

50  See generally P. Merkouris, 'Interpreting the Customary Rules on Interpretation' (2017) 19 International Community Law Review 126.
51  Bianchi, Peat and Windsor (eds), *Interpretation in International Law*, at 117.
52  S. Talmon, 'Determining Customary International Law: ICJ's Methodology between Induction, Deduction and Assertion' (2015) 26.2 EJIL 417; A. Roberts, 'Traditional and Modern Approaches to Customary International Law: A Reconciliation' (2001) 95 AJIL 757; A. Alvarez-Jiménez, 'Methods for the Identification of Customary International Law in the International Court of Justice's New Millennium Jurisprudence' (2011) 60 ICLQ 681, at 686–689.
53  *North Sea Continental Shelf Cases (Federal Republic of Germany/Denmark; Federal Republic of Germany/Netherlands) (Dissenting Opinion of Judge Tanaka)* [1969] ICJ Rep 3, at 181.

law'.[54] Such a study in the book might have also opened the avenue to discussing the ILC as a player or institutional interpreter of (customary) international law.

## 2   Thoughts on the ILC as an Important Player in the Interpretation Game

Here, while Andraž Zidar's chapter 'Interpretation and the International Legal Profession: Between Duty and Aspiration' covers a wide range of players in the interpretation game,[55] including scholars and legal advisers who very often constitute members of the ILC, there is an overall omission of the interpretational role of the Commission *per se*. A discussion or study on the phenomenon of the ILC acting as an interpreter of customary international law would have been timely considering the marked shift in the Commission's work from preparing draft treaties to creating non-binding instruments such as conclusions, draft articles and guidelines. Herein, while chapters by Hollis and d'Aspremont touch upon the interpretation of customary international law—including aspects of content-determination and law-ascertainment—there is still ambiguity as to what rules that the ILC applies in interpreting customary rules. As Danai Azaria pointed out in a recent lecture at the University College of London,[56] the Commission in its work on the 'Draft Conclusions on Identification of Customary International Law'[57] implicitly recognized interpretation as part of customary identification,[58] but did not go into the issue of interpretation of the rules of interpretation.

Azaria has also argued that the ILC actually *interprets* international law and that interpretation is, in fact, part of the existing function of the Commission and its mandate. She further asserted that

---

54   See generally Merkouris, 'Interpreting the Customary Rules on Interpretation, International Community Law Review'; J. d'Aspremont, 'The Idea of "Rules" in the Sources of International Law' (2014) 84 BYIL 103.

55   Bianchi, Peat and Windsor (eds), *Interpretation in International Law*, at 135–144.

56   Oxford University Public International Law Discussion Group (Part II), 'The International Law Commission as an Interpreter of International Law' (6 February 2018), podcast available at https://podcasts.ox.ac.uk/international-law-commission-interpreter-international-law (accessed 15 April 2019).

57   UN ILC 'Report of the International Law Commission on the Work of Its Seventieth Session (30 April–1 June and 2 July–10 August 2018)' UN Doc. A/73/10, Chapter V (E) 'Text of the Draft Conclusions on Identification of Customary International Law'.

58   Ibid. See generally Commentaries to Draft Conclusion 3 at 127–130 and Draft Conclusion 10 at 140–143.

[the] Commission's interpretative activity serves its long-lasting vision to reinforce international law by providing clarity and predictability as to its content thus convincing states to continue to use international law as a medium by which they regulate their affairs.[59]

Furthermore, in a recent case where a State may have adopted the Commission's interpretative finding of a customary rule, Marko Milanovic 'flagged a possible evolution in the UK's legal views on the diplomatic protection of dual nationals by one State of nationality against the other State of nationality'.[60] Herein, the UK has apparently shifted from its original position that diplomatic protection could not be exercised in such circumstances, to the more flexible position adopted by the ILC in its 2006 Draft Articles on Diplomatic Protection. In the Draft Articles, the ILC adopted an exception to the perceived interdiction against exercise of jurisdiction in cases of multiple nationality of an individual where the diplomatic protection is being exercised by the State of predominant nationality.[61]

## 3 Comments on the Characterization of the Vienna Rules

Lastly, I would like to comment on the first chapter by editors Daniel Peat and Matthew Windsor which lays out the fundamental premise of the book, that international lawyers reify the Vienna Convention on the Law of Treaties' interpretative provisions and follow a straightjacketed approach to interpretation in international law which relies almost exclusively on Arts 31–33 VCLT.[62] In challenging this status of the Vienna Convention as the 'one stop shop' for all things related to interpretation, the two editors call for a 'reappraisal', and indeed, reconceptualization, of interpretation in international law beyond the VCLT.[63]

---

59   Oxford University Public International Law Discussion Group (Part II), 'The International Law Commission as an Interpreter of International Law' (6 February 2018), podcast available at https://podcasts.ox.ac.uk/international-law-commission-interpreter-international-law (accessed 15 April 2019) (quote transcribed).
60   M. Milanovic, 'UK's Position on the Diplomatic Protection of Dual Nationals' (8 March 2019) EJILTalk, available at https://www.ejiltalk.org/uks-position-on-the-diplomatic-protection-of-dual-nationals/ (accessed 15 April 2019).
61   Art. 7 of the ILC's Draft Articles on Diplomatic Protection with Commentaries in UN ILC 'Report of the International Law Commission on the Work of Its Fifty-Eighth Session (1 May–9 June and 3 July–11 August 2006) UN Doc. A/61/10, at 16.
62   Bianchi, Peat and Windsor (eds), *Interpretation in International Law*, at 8.
63   Ibid., at 4–5.

Though Peat and Windsor call for a challenge to the VCLT rules' stranglehold in international dispute settlement,[64] one may doubt the ubiquity of VCLT adherence they claim in the premise of their chapter. For instance, the authors' assertion that formalism created by VCLT rules straight-jackets all interpretation[65] paints a picture wherein the VCLT rules are so omnipresent that all actors apply it in a drone-like manner regardless of how (un)desirable such an application may be. It is helpful to remember that actors (States in particular) are not always obstinately committed to the 'text, context, meaning' rule enshrined in the VCLT. Take for instance, the approach of States in the aftermath of the dissolution of the Union of Soviet Socialist Republics (USSR) where the Russian Federation took over the former's seat at the UN Security Council. The action was deemed acceptable despite the Russian Federation being substantially different—in terms of territory, population and political structure—than the USSR which is specifically referenced in Art. 23 (1) UN Charter. This stands to reason that when it comes to the operation of a treaty, actors *do* take into consideration outcomes that are politically desirable. In this regard, the first chapter's claims might have been buttressed if the editors had included specific examples where the reliance on VCLT rules was unhelpful or undesirable.

In addition to the above, the book's premise that VCLT rules 'totally determines the encounter of the interpreter and interpreted'[66] may appear ostensibly correct, in part because of the demonstrable deference that practitioners seem to provide for the rules. However, the rules cannot be attributed the absoluteness the authors wish upon it, and the same has been highlighted by scholars elsewhere. Take for instance, Nolte's observation that the VCLT does not prescribe a fixed canon or hierarchy for the purpose of interpretation, and merely indicates a few basic means of interpretation.[67] Accordingly, he adds that 'treaty interpreters thus possess some latitude' in interpretation under the VCLT.[68] The view is buttressed by other scholars who assert that 'the so-called canon [i.e., principles] of treaty interpretation [are] no more than logical devices for ascertaining the real area of treaty operation'.[69] Furthermore, the characterization that VCLT rules 'totally determine' the interaction implies a lack of choice available to the interpreter. This, however, is an extreme position when considering that Art. 31 (3) VCLT only requires that certain factors are to be 'taken into account' by the interpreter. As James Crawford has noted,

---

[64] Ibid., at 6.
[65] Ibid., at 9.
[66] Bianchi, Peat and Windsor (eds), *Interpretation in International Law*, at 15.
[67] Nolte, 'Introduction' in G. Nolte (ed.), *Treaties and Subsequent Practice* (OUP 2013) 2.
[68] Ibid.
[69] D. O'Connell, *International Law* (2nd edn Stevens 1970), at 253.

lawyers can take things into account in a variety of ways. They can take things into account by giving them effect [...]. Alternatively, things might be taken into account in the sense of 'we do not give it much attention'.[70]

This inbuilt discretion afforded to the interpreter appears incongruous with the narrative that VCLT rules aim to determine a process totally.

## IV   Conclusion

While the aforementioned comments fall squarely within the provenance of the reviewer's opinion, the book is a valuable contribution to the field and will surely help researchers by, perhaps, ameliorating what T.S. Eliot called the 'intolerable wrestle with words and meanings'.[71] In this regard, the book is thought-provoking and informative, while simultaneously serving as an exposition—and indeed introduction—to various international legal theories in the field of interpretation. It contains a well-researched, and diverse, collection of essays on the topic of interpretation in international law. Furthermore, it is timely as it has been published in the middle of an evident trend of legal scholarship focusing on interpretative issues and is likely to remain relevant in the study of the interpretative process for quite some time to come.

Finally, and at the risk of pettifogging, I would like to make a suggestion which the editors may wish to take on board for future reprints: readers (myself included) may be well served by the inclusion of a table of treaties/instruments as part of the book's front matter.

*Yateesh Begoore*

---

[70] See generally J. Crawford, 'A Consensualist Interpretation of Article 31 (3) of the Vienna Convention on the Law of Treaties' in G. Nolte (ed.), *Treaties and Subsequent Practice* (OUP 2013) 29.

[71] T.S. Eliot, 'East Coker' in *The Complete Poems and Plays: 1909–1950* (Harcourt Brace Jovanovich 1971), at 179.